Higher Education and Social Change

edited by
Kenneth W. Thompson
Barbara R. Fogel
Helen E. Danner

Published in cooperation with
the International Council for
Educational Development

The Praeger Special Studies program—
utilizing the most modern and efficient book
production techniques and a selective
worldwide distribution network—makes
available to the academic, government, and
business communities significant, timely
research in U.S. and international economic, social, and political development.

Higher Education and Social Change

Promising Experiments in Developing Countries

Volume 2: Case Studies

Praeger Publishers   New York   Washington   London

PRAEGER SPECIAL STUDIES IN INTERNATIONAL ECONOMICS AND DEVELOPMENT

Library of Congress Cataloging in Publication Data

Thompson, Kenneth W   1921–
    Higher education and social change.

    (Praeger special studies in international economics
and development)
    Vol. 2 edited by K. W. Thompson, B. R. Fogel,
H. E. Danner.
    Includes bibliographical references and indexes.
    CONTENTS: v. 1. Reports.—v. 2. Case studies.
    1. Underdeveloped areas—Education. I. Fogel,
Barbara R., joint author. II. Title.
LC2605. T45   378'.009172'4   76–14474
ISBN 0–275–23390–1

PRAEGER PUBLISHERS
111 Fourth Avenue, New York, N.Y. 10003, U.S.A.

Published in the United States of America in 1977
by Praeger Publishers, Inc.

Printed in the United States of America

This volume of case studies represents the combined efforts of 40 developing country educators and the three members of the New York staff who coordinated the project. Readers should know that while the New York staff took responsibility for the preparation of a 50-page study plan and numerous research guides, the main burden of investigation fell on experienced educators in Africa, Asia, and Latin America.

This pattern represents a new phase in cooperation in international education. By the mid-1970s, after almost three decades of partnership between educators and donor agencies in the United States and Europe, on the one hand, and the leaders responsible for educational advances in the developing countries on the other, it seemed appropriate that the responsibility for local studies should shift to national educators. The time has passed when hurried, short-term inquiries by Western educators suffice. Those who are permanently a part of the educational landscape in the developing countries, having the greatest stake in their own future, are now unmistakably in charge. The time has come for developed country leaders to listen to their judgments and assessments.

The nationals of the developing countries, who have made up this project's Regional Teams, have strengths that outsiders are unable to match. They enjoy the best access to and are most intimately in touch with educational developments in their own regions. At the same time, they are experienced and tested leaders, known to other nationals in their regions and to the worldwide community of educators. Their estimates and evaluations on institutional developments and educational innovations carry weight, both within the Third World and outside it.

The case studies represent a broad cross-section of higher education's approaches to problems of development. The choice of case study institutions was the responsibility of Regional Directors, appointed by the International Council for Educational Development, and their own Regional Team members. The case studies include studies of higher education's response to problems of rural development, especially as it affects the small farmer; of the university's role in designing and implementing health care delivery systems; of the efforts of higher education to improve learning in the primary and secondary schools; of manpower training; of the special problems (staffing, bilingualism, regionalism) of establishing a university in a developing country; of higher education systems as a whole; and of research and extension for industrial development. Whatever the problems and impediments, these case studies demonstrate that post-secondary institutions are taking significant steps to cope with urgent community needs through impressive institutional innovations.

The full accounts of these developments are found in the following case studies[*] prepared by the respective regional teams. While edited by the New York staff for purposes of uniformity and clarity, their content accurately and faithfully reflects the thinking and concerns of developing country educators.

The Director also requested outstanding educators to prepare special studies on subjects not covered in the institutional studies. R. Cranford Pratt served for five years as Principal, University College, Dar es Salaam in Tanzania and is singularly qualified to discuss values in relation to developing country educational systems. W. Arthur Lewis, who is intimately acquainted with problems of higher education in Africa and the West Indies, has firsthand knowledge of the importance of the university in preserving and transmitting cultural traditions. David Court brings to bear modern social science theory and analysis on problems of higher education in East Africa. The late Frank Bowles, adviser to this project, was concerned with stages of educational development and prepared a valuable paper on the subject. A. Babs Fafunwa, perhaps Africa's leading authority on the relation of higher education to primary and secondary education in Africa, was commissioned to do a special study on these questions. China was not included in the HED study, but President Howard Swearer of Carleton College graciously consented to the inclusion of his paper written following his trip to China in the fall of 1975. Soedjatmoko, the distinguished Indonesian philosopher and former ambassador to the United States, brings his considerable wisdom and experience to the heart of the project.

Taken together, the case studies and special studies provide a reservoir of unique materials on higher education for development prepared by educators close to the problems. They are made available at a time when there are questions and debate over the fundamentals of education for development. Those who made the studies would not claim for them the quality of definitive research papers nor assert that all the tools of social science and educational theory had been called into play; their wide educational experience, however, qualifies them to size up the problems. The case studies in particular are team efforts by broadly representative groups of African, Asian,

---

[*] A final report on the project and the three overall reports of the Regional Teams appear in Volume 1.

or Latin American educators. They are addressed to vital problems on which the future of nations depend.

At the same time, the educators who made the studies have claimed only that they were "opening up" the question. Their goal is to provoke others to carry the discussion further. Their aim is the widest possible dissemination of the studies to experienced educators and policy makers. They call for more in-depth case studies. Education for development is at an early stage both in theory and practice. The case studies and special studies, therefore, are a resource on which others can build. They are a beginning.

CONTENTS

ix

PART III: LATIN AMERICAN CASE STUDIES

PART IV: SPECIAL REPORTS

xi

LIST OF TABLES AND FIGURE

Figure

LIST OF ABBREVIATIONS

ACE — Accelerated Curriculum Experiment, University of Liberia

ACUAVALLE — Water and sewerage agency, Valle, Colombia

ADB — Asian Development Bank

AIM — Asian Institute of Management, Philippines

AMP — Advanced Management Program, Philippines

ASCOFAME — Colombian Association of Medical Faculties

ASEAN — Association of Southeast Asian Nations

BRASCAN — Bank of Brazil and Canada

CECISA — Center of Social Sciences and Administration

CECIMA — Center for Marine and Environmental Sciences

CEDED — Educational Documentation Center, Antioquia University, Colombia

CEDER — Center for Rural Development

CEDES — Education for Development Center

CEDUR — Center for Urban Development, Brazil

CEPID — Center for Investment and Development Projects and Studies, National Agrarian University, Peru

CERENA — Center for Natural Resources, University of Valle, Colombia

CIAS — Centro de Investigacion y Accion Social

CIAT — International Centre for Tropical Agriculture

CID — Center of Research for Development, Colombia

CIDA — Canadian International Development Agency

CIED	Educational Research Center of the University of Antioquia, Colombia
COLCIENCIAS	Colombian Fund for Scientific Research and Special Projects
COLIMPAS	Program of Research and Health Planning, University of Valle, Colombia
CONDER	agency responsible for urban planning in the metropolitan area of Salvador, Brazil
CPU	Corporación de Promoción Universitaria
CRC	Center for Research and Communication, Philippines
CREE	Center of Resources for Training, University of Valle, Colombia
CUPRED	University Center for Development Projects, University of Valle, Colombia
CUSS	Centre Universitaire des Sciences de la Santé, Cameroon
DANE	National Statistics Office, Colombia
DAP	Development Academy of the Philippines
DASP zones	Zones des demonstrations d'action en Santé Publique
DEF	Basic Studies Diploma
DUSO	Dar es Salaam University Students Organization
EASE	East African Societies and Environment course, Faculty of Arts and Social Sciences, University of Dar es Salaam, Tanzania
ECICA	Ecole Centrale de l'Industrie, du Commerce, et de l'Administration, Mali
ELT	English Language Teaching, Cameroon
ENI	Ecole Nationale d'Ingénieurs, Mali

ENS	Ecole Normale Supérieure, Mali
EPU	Economic Planning Unit
ERB	Economic Research Bureau, Tanzania
ETIOP	Executive Training Institute of the Philippines
EUS	Ethiopian University Service
FAC	Fonds Aide Coopération (foreign aid branch of the French government)
FAO	Food and Agricultural Organization
GCE	General Certificate of Education
GDP	gross domestic product
GNP	gross national product
HED	Higher Education for Development
HSIU	Haile Selassie I University
IBRD	International Bank for Reconstruction and Development (World Bank)
ICA	Colombian Agriculture and Livestock Institute
ICED	International Council for Educational Development
ICFES	Colombian Institute for the Development of Higher Education
ICOLPE	Colombian Pedagogical Institute
ICONTEC	Colombian Institute of Technical Systems
ICSS	Colombian Institute of Social Security
IDB	Inter-American Development Bank
IDELAC	Institute for Construction, Division of Architecture, University of Valle, Colombia

IDRC	Canadian International Development Research Centre
IEP	Industrial Economics Program, Philippines
IFES	see ICFES
IIR	Institute for Industrial Research, Mexico
IMPES	Instituto Nacional para Programas Especiales de Salud
INTRA	National Institute of Transport, Colombia
IPGP	Institut de Production et de Gestion Prévisionelle, Mali
IPR	Institut Polytechnique Rural, Mali
IRIC	Institut des Relations Internationales de Cameroun
ITESM	Monterrey Institute of Technology and Advanced Studies, Mexico
LDC	less developed country
MARA	Majlis Amanah Rakyat, Malaysia
MBM	Master of Business Management degree, Philippines
MDP	Management Development Program, Philippines
MEN	National Ministry of Education, Colombia
MIRD	Maeklong Integrated Rural Development Project
MIT	MARA Institute of Technology, Malaysia
MM	Master of Management degree, Philippines
MOD	Management and Organizational Development (a DAP program)
NATC	Ngee Ann Technical College
NAU	National Agrarian University, Peru

NCE	Nigerian Certificate of Education
NPSP	Nigeria Primary Science Programme
NUEUS	National Union of Ethiopian University Students
OAS	Organization of American States
OCEAC	Organization for Coordination in Control of Endemic Diseases in Central Africa
PEA	Philippine Executive Academy
PIA	Program Implementation Agency, Philippines
PINA	National Nutrition Program
PLANSAN	research program on health planning in Antioquia, Colombia
PRIMOPS	Program for Systems of Health Services Delivery, Colombia
PROPED	Program of Research and Education for Development, Brazil
PSC	Introduction to Sciences Project
PSI	Personalized System of Instruction in ITESM, Mexico
REPID	Research and Extension Program for Industrial Development of ITESM, Mexico
SEDA	Secretariat of Education of Antioquia, Colombia
SENA	National Apprenticeship Service, Colombia
SEPA	Science Education Programme for Africa, Nigeria
SMS	Municipal Health Service, Colombia
TANU	Tanganyika African National Union (national political party of Tanzania)
UBBS	University of Botswana, Basutoland and Swaziland

UBLS	University of Botswana, Lesotho and Swaziland
UCHS	University Centre for Health Sciences
UFBa	Federal University of Bahia, Brazil
UIS	Industrial University of Santander, Colombia
UNDP	United Nations Development Programme
Unesco	United Nations Educational, Scientific and Cultural Organization
UNET	Unit of Technological Economics of ITESM, Mexico
UNICEF	United Nations Children's Fund
USAID	United States Agency for International Development
UST	University of Science and Technology, Ghana
WHO	World Health Organization

GLOSSARY

B.A. (Lond) or B.Sc. (Lond)
: B.A. or B.Sc. degree granted by the University of London. All British degrees carry the abbreviation of the university following the degree symbol

Baccalauréat
: French exam, given at end of secondary school certifying successful completion and eligibility for admission to university

Bilingual
: capable of speaking, understanding, reading, writing a second language

Bursary
: scholarship

Certificate
: document recognizing completion of short course in some specific field

College (U.K. usage)
: institutions unconnected with a university for instruction of a more advanced or professional kind than given at a school; also used to refer to a society of scholars incorporated within, or in connection with, a university

Degree
: academic rank or distinction conferred by a university following completion of recognized course of study

Diploma
: document conferred by a college or other subuniversity institution, usually certifying completion of a recognized course of study leading to competence in some professional field

Employment exchange
: state employment office

Estate
: a large commercial farm or plantation, usually growing one crop (such as cocoa or tea) for sale

GCE	General Certificate of Education— British exam, given at end of secondary school, certifying successful completion and eligibility for admission to university
Long vacation	three-month vacation between end of one and beginning of next school year
"O" level "A" level	ordinary level advanced level levels for final exams under British education system. Usually A level requires an additional year of study in that subject
School leaving examinations	exam given to all students in a nation at a specific level. A pass in such an exam is equivalent to an elementary or high school diploma in U.S. practice
Secondment	temporary removal from regular position for employment with another organization
Sixth form	usually the highest class in a school

PART

I

AFRICAN CASE STUDIES

INTRODUCTION

The economic development of any nation depends on the effective and proper utilization of all her resources, both human and material. Material resources are useless without men and women able to employ them, and, therefore, the first priority should be the adequate development of human resources. Education is said to be the keystone to development, as it provides the knowledge and training in various skills that development requires. This education is given at various levels: primary, secondary, and tertiary or higher education.

The production of high-level manpower through higher education should ensure trained and responsible leadership for the development effort. Higher education, therefore, can be said to provide the main thrust in development. The assumption here is, of course, that the higher education will be of good quality and will, in content, be relevant to local circumstances and that it will be applied in the service of the nation.

During the colonial era, the colonized were "hewers of wood" and "drawers of water." Education and training in national development were both relatively neglected. What education was given had the primary aim of helping to facilitate the colonial administrative machinery. In certain African countries, no African was educated or trained to the subprofessional level, and higher education was unknown. In those countries fortunate enough to have benevolent administrators with courage and vision, a foundation was laid for future higher education. In general, as the move toward independence gathered momentum, plans for developing high-level manpower to succeed and replace that provided by the colonial masters were put in operation. Before then only a lucky few, whose parents could afford it, could go overseas to European and North American universities to become professionals: doctors, lawyers, and a few engineers. As secondary education developed and more people qualified for higher education, scholarships for study in universities abroad were awarded in various fields. On the eve of independence, and during the transitional period between self-government and independence, some higher educational institutions were established locally, but most of these institutions in Africa were founded after independence.

It is not surprising if Africans trained in a university abroad adopt European styles and outlook and are generally sympathetic to the higher educational system of which they are a product. It is perhaps fortunate that this "cultural enslavement" did not prevent some of them from agitating strongly for independence and from becoming national leaders at the time of independence.

With independence, the need for high-level manpower to take over the administration of the country became both urgent and vital. Institutions already in existence were rapidly developed and new ones established. The university in Africa was, however, a foreign transplant, established by expatriate staff, and some were indeed faithful replicas of their metropolitan counterparts. Even when local staff replaced expatriates it was inevitable that the first generation of African staff were themselves educated abroad and therefore in need of cultural reorientation. The university, not being conversant with local conditions, was largely insensitive to the problems of the immediate environment. Its curriculum was not much different from that in European and American universities. In short, teaching and research were considered to be largely irrelevant to local needs.

If the picture painted was true of the 1960s, it is still true in the 1970s. Now, however, there is an awareness of the need to create an African university that, without sacrificing its international academic standards, will be responsive to the needs of contemporary African society and so be deeply involved in national development on all fronts: economic, social, and cultural.

Besides being criticized for ivory-tower aloofness, the universities have been accused to taking more than their share of the national budget, particularly of the budget for education as a whole. This criticism is only partly justified, because the African university, usually situated on a campus miles from the nearest town or city, is obliged to develop and maintain expensive municipal services. The fact remains that huge sums of money are spent on the universities, for which the government and the public expect much in return. Indeed it is the duty and the responsibility of the university to be closely involved in the process of national development, for higher education in Africa is meaningless unless it is linked with the total development of the country.

The Unesco Conference on "The Role of Higher Education in the Development of Africa" in Tananarive (1963) came to the following conclusions: "That in addition to its traditional functions and obligations to teach and to advance knowledge through research, the role of higher education in the social, cultural and economic development of Africa must be:

1. To maintain adherence and loyalty to world academic standards;
2. To ensure the unification of Africa;
3. To encourage education of and appreciation for African culture and heritage and to dispel misconceptions of Africa, through research and teaching of African studies;

4. To develop completely the human resources for meeting manpower needs;
5. To train the 'whole man' for nation building;
6. To evolve over the years a truly African pattern of higher learning dedicated to Africa and its people yet promoting a bond of kinship to the larger human society."

The studies that follow examine the extent to which higher education in Africa is contributing to the economic development of our continent.

University of Botswana, Lesotho and Swaziland	Mulageta Wodajo
University of Yaoundé, Cameroon	F. Mbassi-Manga
University Centre for Health Sciences, Yaoundé	G. L. Monekosso
Addis Ababa University, Ethiopia	Aklilu Habte
University of Science and Technology, Ghana	E. Evans-Anfom
Mali System Study	Tidiane Sy
University of Mauritius	Mulageta Wodajo
Ahmadu Bello University, Nigeria	I. Audu
University of Khartoum, Sudan	Mohamed Omer Beshir
Sudan System Study	Frank Bowles
University of Dar es Salaam, Tanzania	G. Mmari

In Asia and Latin America, the case studies were prepared by several team members in consultation with their teams. The African Team, unlike the other two teams, assigned to each study individual team members, who, after team review, incorporated team suggestions into final versions of their studies. Only the African case studies, therefore, have individual authors listed.

AFRICAN TEAM MEMBERS

Director	Aklilu Habte, Addis Ababa, Ethiopia (formerly President, Haile Selassie I University)
Codirector	Tidiane Sy (Senegal) Division of Higher Education, Unesco, Paris, France
Other Team Members	I. Audu, Vice-Chancellor, Ahmadu Bello University, Zaria, Nigeria
	G. L. Monekosso, Director, University Centre for Health Sciences, University of Yaoundé, Yaoundé, Cameroon
	Pius Msekwa, Vice-Chancellor, University of Dar es Salaam, Dar es Salaam, Tanzania Later replaced by: G. Mmari, Head, Department of Education, Faculty of Social Sciences, University of Dar es Salaam
Other Active Participants	E. Evans-Anfom, Chairman, National Council for Higher Education, Accra, Ghana
	L. K. H. Goma, Vice-Chancellor, University of Zambia, Lusaka, Zambia
	J. Ki-Zerbo, Secretary-General, African and Malagasy Council for Higher Education, Ouagadougou, Upper Volta

F. Mbassi-Manga, Dean, Faculty
of Letters and Social Sciences,
University of Yaoundé, Yaoundé,
Cameroon

Mohamed Omer Beshir, Professor,
Institute of African and Asian
Studies, University of Khartoum,
Khartoum, Sudan

*Frank Bowles, former University
Planning Officer, Haile Selassie I
University, Addis Ababa, Ethiopia

Mulageta Wodajo (Ethiopia)
Education Department, World Bank,
Washington, D.C.

Ngu, Vice-Chancellor, University
of Yaoundé, Cameroon

Consultants   David Court, Institute for Development Studies, University of Nairobi,
Kenya

A. Babs Fafunwa, Dean of the
Faculty of Education, University of
Ife, Nigeria

---

*Died May 1975.

1

UNIVERSITY OF BOTSWANA, LESOTHO AND SWAZILAND

Problems for Regional Universities in Africa

From 1964 to 1975 the University of Botswana, Lesotho and Swaziland (UBLS) was administered as a single institution serving three countries with a combined population of just under 2.5 million. All three countries are poor and have a common need for trained manpower, but national rivalries eventually brought the joint venture to an end in 1975. A study of UBLS is nevertheless instructive and should be preceded by a brief account of the social and economic conditions in the three territories.

COUNTRY BACKGROUND

Lesotho

Lesotho is a small kingdom, landlocked and completely sur-rounded by the Republic of South Africa. This last point is worth noting, as it has shaped, and continues to shape, the geopolitics of the nation and the social and political attitudes of its people. Although politically, as in everything else, Lesotho looks toward the distant north, the independent nations of Africa, rather than toward its giant neighbor, it does not take a visitor long to realize how overwhelming is the influence of South Africa.

Lesotho has a population of only 1.2 million, of which 200,000— or 60 percent of the adult male labor force—live and work in the Republic of South Africa. While this employment elsewhere may mean a reduction in the size of the population for which the economy would otherwise have to provide social services and employment, it also means that there is a scarcity of adult male labor. As a result, women play a significant role in the economic (farming, marketing, and so on) as well as political affairs of the nation.

Economically, Lesotho is a poor country, with few known mineral or other resources. The economy is based mainly on sub-sistence agriculture, but, even in agriculture, the prospect for a

substantial increase in productivity is not bright, as unscientific cultivation and overgrazing has led to widespread erosion of the land.
There is, in fact, serious concern that unless erosion is checked, a
large segment of the country may become unsuitable for cultivation in
the not too distant future.

The government is making a concerted effort to improve the
economic condition of the nation. Its development plans give priority
to improvement in agricultural productivity, increase in rural employment, exploitation of natural resources, and improved access to
social services, particularly education and health.

Education

Western education in Lesotho was started almost 150 years ago
by missionaries. As a result, the missions have had a firm grip over
the educational system, operating over 90 percent of the primary and
secondary schools. Since independence (1966), the government has
been steadily increasing its financial contribution to education, thereby
gaining effective academic and administrative participation in and control of the school system.

The missionary legacy in the field of education is impressive.
Lesotho's literacy rate in 1973 was approximately 40 percent; 65 percent of the primary school-age and 8 percent of the secondary school-
age children are attending school. The participation rate for primary
enrollment is high by African standards; for secondary school enrollment it is about average.* The language of instruction in grades one
to four is Sesotho (the national language), but English is used as the
medium of instruction in the upper primary (grades five to seven) and
secondary schools.

A notable deficiency of the school system is the lack of adequate
schools or facilities for technical and vocational training. This lack
has resulted in a considerable shortage of skilled and high-level manpower, confirmed by recent manpower studies.

Swaziland

Swaziland is also small and landlocked, surrounded by the
Republic of South Africa and Mozambique, about 200 miles southwest
of Lesotho. It has a population of only half a million, of whom roughly

*Average figures for Africa were about 48 percent of primary
school-age and 8 percent of secondary school-age children enrolled
(World Bank, Comparative Education Indicators).

25,000 live and work in the Republic of South Africa. Agriculture is
the main source of livelihood, and traditional subsistence-level agriculture, in which a large segment of the Swazi people are engaged,
exists side by side with modern farms, plantations, and ranches
owned largely by foreigners. Indeed, according to a World Bank
source, foreigners own half of the land, and the rapid increase in
recent years in agricultural output on these foreign-owned farms and
plantations accounts for the comparatively high level of agricultural
development and productivity of the country as a whole. In addition,
Swaziland has a relatively diversified economy and export structure,
based on light manufacturing, forest products, and mining.

Education

Swaziland has a comparatively well-developed educational system, dating back to the advent of the first group of missionaries about
130 years ago. At the primary level, almost 70 percent of the children
of the relevant age group attend school; the participation rate at the
secondary level is close to 20 percent. Approximately 30 percent of
the adult population is literate. As in Lesotho, the school system in
Swaziland was largely in the hands of foreign missionaries with little
or no government control. However, since independence (1968), the
government has taken a number of steps to bring school administration,
curriculum, and academic standards under its supervision and control.

A major weakness of the school system is the lack of adequate
facilities for vocational and skill training. The schools are far too
academically oriented, with examinations exerting a disproportionate
influence on curriculum and teaching methods. After independence,
the government, with assistance from a number of external agencies,
including the International Bank for Reconstruction and Development
(IBRD), began diversifying the curriculum in the secondary schools
and also opening vocational and trade schools.

The government spends approximately 20 percent of its
recurrent budget on education. The schools also charge a small
tuition fee, as well as fees for textbooks, uniforms, and other school
materials.

Botswana

Botswana, with an area of 231,000 square miles, is by far the
largest of the three countries and is located north and west of the
other two. Since a large portion of the country, however, is covered
by the Kalahari Desert, Botswana's population is only 650,000. Until
the recent discovery of valuable minerals, including copper, nickel,

coal, and, most important, diamonds, Botswana's economic prospects were bleak. But with the exploitation of its mineral resources, the economy started to grow rapidly. For instance, GNP per capita grew from U.S. $100 in 1968 to U.S. $300 in 1973.

The great bottleneck to the further development of the economy is an inadequate supply of skilled manpower. This lack caused the government to put pressure on the University and the vocational schools to expand. Since UBLS was jointly operated by the three nations, however, Botswana's rapidly growing needs became a source of friction among the three governments.

Education
_____

Botswana's educational system is the least developed of the three. As late as 1973, only 9.5 percent of the government's total current expenditure was allocated to education, as compared to 22 percent in Lesotho and 20 percent in Swaziland. The adult literacy rate is 20 percent, low even by African standards, particularly when one takes into account the small size of the population. Participation rates at the primary and secondary levels are 49 percent and 5 percent, respectively. Inadequate facilities and shortage of qualified teachers constitute the most glaring deficiencies in the system.

UNIVERSITY OF BOTSWANA, LESOTHO AND SWAZILAND

Origins

The idea of starting a university for blacks in Southern Africa dates back to the late 1930s. In January 1938 the Synod of Catholic Bishops formally endorsed a proposal to establish a postsecondary institution for Catholic secondary school graduates. At that time, black secondary school graduates had little opportunity for postsecondary education. There was only one institution of higher education open to them—the South African Native College (since 1960 the University of Fort Hare)—and its enrollment was very limited. The only other possibility for these students was to enroll as external students of the University of South Africa and undertake their studies by correspondence.

Subsequent to the 1938 meeting of the Synod of Catholic Bishops, various proposals were discussed by Church authorities. These proposals differed in scope and ambition. Some were bold enough to propose the opening of a full-fledged university at the outset. Others were more modest and proposed merely to start hostels for Catholic students at an already existing institution such as the South African Native College. Subsequently, a compromise proposal put forward by one of the local bishops gained wide support. The proposal called for the establishment of an institution of higher education that would gradually develop into a full-fledged university. Unfortunately, these efforts were put to an end by the outbreak of the war in 1939 and were not resumed seriously until late in 1944.

At the end of the war, the situation changed rapidly, and an institution of higher education, later known as Pius XII Catholic College, was established in 1945 in Roma, a small community about 22 miles from Maseru, the capital of Lesotho (then known as Basutoland).

The College started in a very modest and humble way; initially it had only four priests (as lecturers), five students, and an abandoned primary school as its physical plant. In 1950, the Paramount Chief of Basutoland donated a site for the College, and temporary buildings were hastily erected.

Pius XII College was not authorized to grant its own degrees. Originally the College prepared students for the external degree of the University of South Africa, being thus limited to fields of study offered at that university. The College soon broadened its scope and responsibilities, however, and started to prepare students for other degrees, including the degrees of bachelor of commerce and bachelor of science, and a postgraduate diploma in education. In 1955, ten years after its opening, the College entered into a "special relationship" with the University of South Africa (much in the same way as other African colleges elsewhere on the continent would enter into a "special relationship" with London University), thereby gaining a good deal of autonomy over such vital areas as students' admissions, curriculum, and examinations.

The decade of the 1950s was a crucial period for the young institution. Beset by perpetual financial difficulties and staff shortages, the administration was looking for various ways to share the financial burden and the responsibility for running the College. Advisers from the United Kingdom, who visited as consultants, however, were practically unanimous in discouraging the College from becoming an independent university or from seeking association with an overseas university such as London University.

During the same period, the governments of the three High Commission Territories (Basutoland, Swaziland, and Bechuanaland) were studying the possibility of starting some kind of government-financed institution of higher education. It was thus more by coincidence than by deliberate plan that this small Catholic college became the nucleus of a trinational university. The Deed of Cession and

Indemnity, as the agreement for the transfer of the College from the Catholic Church to the government was called, was signed in June 1963, and UBLS was officially inaugurated in October 1964. The funds required for the transfer of the buildings and assets of Pius XII College to UBLS were provided in part by the British government and the Ford Foundation. At that time, the institution had only 32 academic staff members and 188 students.

Unifying Factors

Since it was in Lesotho that UBLS was first started, there was a tendency over the years for the University to be closely identified with that country. And yet, as a trinational university, UBLS had scrupulously to avoid any such image. In the 1970s the other two governments—Swaziland and especially Botswana—exerted pressure to increase their respective shares of student places, and, more importantly, to establish a larger University "presence" in their respective countries. Indeed, the pressure to develop the campuses in Botswana and Swaziland gave rise to persistent concern that UBLS might well break up into three separate universities in much the same way as the University of East Africa split into its three constituent units—Nairobi, Dar es Salaam, and Makerere. Until recently, however, UBLS managed to stay a single academic and administrative institution. A number of factors helped it to retain its organic unity, of which the following were perhaps the most significant.

Costs

First and foremost, all three countries recognized that they were poor countries and could not afford separate universities of their own. Even when the budget of the University was shared among the three governments, each government spent 20-30 percent of its total education budget on UBLS, which, with a per student cost of 2,900 Rands (or about U.S. $4,260) was one of the most expensive universities in Africa. Two of the three countries—Lesotho and Botswana—are included in the United Nations' list of 25 least developed countries and can ill afford costly universities. Economic considerations were among the important factors that kept the University intact for 11 years.

Size

Another restraining factor was the small size of the University. With a total student population of only 1,222 (1974-75 enrollment) and a staff of 135, there could not be many feasible options for launching viable academic programs on three campuses. In 1970, in response to pressure from Botswana and Swaziland, the University decided to offer the first two years (Part I) of the four-year degree course on all three campuses. In 1974-75, therefore, UBLS had 535 students on the main campus in Roma (Lesotho), 387 in Swaziland, and 300 in Botswana. The perennial and most controversial issue at the university was how further to apportion the University's resources fairly and equitably so each country would have its due share of the University's "presence," but the University was far too small to provide meaningful options for this exercise.

Existing Program

Any attempt to redistribute and reapportion University resources and facilities had to take into account those programs that could not be moved about for one reason or another. For instance, the College of Agriculture, which existed as a postsecondary institution before it was incorporated into the University, was so well entrenched in Swaziland that University authorities unanimously agreed to keep it in Swaziland. The Faculty of Education was involved in in-service teacher training in Lesotho and Botswana. This and similar localized functions could not be met centrally. The Extramural Services (extension) of the University also catered to specific target groups and therefore extension had to be decentralized. These considerations further limited the options available in efforts to redistribute University resources on the three campuses.

Political Factors

With the coming of independence, the three territories, which had been linked together politically (they were known collectively as the High Commission Territories) had practically no political or economic institutions to pull them together. Instead, each had to create its own political and economic linkages with the outside world (membership in the Organization of African Unity, and the United Nations, for example). Together with the Customs Union, the University linked the three countries horizontally, and they seemed keenly interested in preserving the link.

The three governments were strongly represented on the University council and on its important standing committees, and the University undertook regular consultation with the three governments on major policy matters, especially those involving University resources. Likewise, the three governments drew increasingly on the resources of the University for expert advice and assistance. The

Department of Government and Administration, for example, initiated
a study on local government in the hope that it would serve as a basis
for the formulation of government policy on local government, and on
the manner in which local institutions could participate in national
affairs. The University thus played an important role as a link among
the three governments, and, with the growth of the University's staff
and expertise, this role was expected to become increasingly significant.

The Question of Devolution

Some of the forces that helped preserve the basic unity of the
University for 11 years have been discussed briefly in the foregoing
paragraphs. Despite these restraining factors, the University was
under constant pressure to decentralize further. Indeed, the question
of decentralization (it is referred to locally as "devolution") was perhaps the issue most widely and heatedly discussed within the University
by students, staff, and administration. It was brought up in practically
every discussion and conversation, even with a visitor to the campus.
Devolution was also a subject on which a number of commissions,
set up by the University to study various aspects of its functions and
operations, have commented extensively. One of the earliest of these
commissions was established in 1966, just before Lesotho and Botswana attained independence, under the chairmanship of Sir Roger
Stevens, the vice-chancellor of Leeds University. The commission
had members from the United Kingdom, the United States, and the
governments of the three countries. After a survey of the manpower
needs of the three countries, the commission made the following
recommendation:

> It is clear to us that if UBBS* is to establish itself
> firmly as the University serving all three countries and
> is to meet their needs equally, it must take itself phys-
> ically to them. This remark relates not only to staff
> but also to buildings. . . . Our recommendation is:
> that UBBS consider generally ways in which it could
> devote more of its resources to activities in Botswana
> and Lesotho.[1]

------

*Before independence, Lesotho was called Basutoland; hence
the reference to the University as UBBS, instead of UBLS.

Two other important reports were published in 1968-69. The first, "Report of the Academic Planner to the Council of UBLS" (May 1969), was written by Sir Norman Alexander, formerly vice-chancellor of Ahmadu Bello University, whose services as planning officer had been secured by UBLS. The second was the so-called Pickard report, "Further Education in Botswana, Lesotho and Swaziland" (June 1969). Both reports recommended quite firmly the establishment of University centers or University complexes in Swaziland and Botswana.

The Alexander Commission Report (1970)

The recommendations of the Alexander and Pickard reports of 1969, favoring the establishment of University centers in Botswana and Swaziland, had important policy implications for the University. The reports were discussed and approved in principle by representatives of the University and the three governments in July 1969. Subsequently, in 1970, the University and the three governments set up yet another commission to study in detail the policy, administrative, and cost implications of the recommendations. This commission, also headed by Sir Norman Alexander, had an international membership (United Kingdom, United States, Canada, West Indies) and rather broad terms of reference. It reviewed thoroughly the progress so far made by the University and the manpower needs of the three countries as assessed by their respective governments, and then made the following recommendation:

> There should be established in Botswana and in Swaziland, partly in new and partly in existing buildings, and again partly by the establishment of new and partly by the incorporation of and association with existing institutions, "university complexes" which should provide courses for the PART I of the UBLS degree (i.e., the first two years of the four-year course), which also provides admission either to PART II of the UBLS degree or to outside universities.[2]

The commission's report contained detailed recommendations on which aspects of University structure and governance should be centralized and which should be decentralized. For instance, it was the commission's view that the University should have a single council and a single senate to assure the University's unitary character. Similarly, it recommended common registrar's and bursar's offices to assure unified administrative policies and procedures. A vice-chancellor—the commission preferred to call him "president"—would preside over the academic and administrative affairs of the University.

Each campus, however, would have its own pro-vice-chancellor (or vice-president). Likewise, each campus would have an academic board whose function would be roughly analogous to that of the University-wide senate. The board's membership would consist of the University president, the local vice-president (as chairman), members of the University-wide senate from that campus, the campus librarian, and three nonprofessional staff from the campus elected by the academic staff. The board would have almost complete authority on academic matters affecting that campus only, but would have to refer its recommendations to the University senate if they had implications (financial, academic, or administrative) for the University as a whole.

In addition, those schools that offered courses on more than one campus would have a head (chairman) on each campus, but the school as a whole would have a common board of studies consisting of the heads of schools on each campus and one member of that school from each campus, elected by the whole academic staff. The board of studies would report to the senate on matters affecting the University as a whole, but to the campus academic board on matters affecting that campus only. The structure and membership of the board of studies thus would constitute a rather well-thought-out blend that would give a good measure of local autonomy to the branch schools, while preserving the integrity and common objectives of the school as a whole.

Report of the Development Team: Devolution

In accordance with the recommendations of the various commissions referred to above, UBLS offered Part I courses on its three campuses for about four years. But, judging from interviews held with University staff and administrators in 1974, the devolution issue was far from resolved. The issue was again the subject of heated and sometimes even acrimonious discussions in the University's senate when the report of a joint University-government commission, set up by the senate in November 1973, came up for discussion. The commission, chaired by the dean of the Faculty of Education, included representatives from the three governments. Judging from its terms of reference and interviews held with its chairman, it was given an almost impossible task. It was asked, on one hand, to produce detailed plans for establishing "a balanced University presence on the three campuses" through the devolution of Part II teaching and any associated arrangement in Botswana and Swaziland. At the same time, it was repeatedly warned to "bear in mind the need to minimize the duplication of staff and facilities and the capital and recurrent costs of the University."

Under the circumstances, it is no surprise that the Commission's recommendations did not satisfy all parties to the controversy.

Lesotho, which, by and large, was content with existing arrangements, was reluctant from the beginning to adopt any plans that
would call for more devolution. On the other hand, the two other
governments repeatedly exerted increasing pressure for more
devolution, Botswana perhaps even more so than Swaziland.

The commission recommended a vertical devolution instead
of the horizontal arrangement then in effect; that is, instead of having
Part I courses (first two years) on three campuses, and then all
students having to come to the Lesotho campus for Part II (last two
years), students would be provided the opportunity to do all four years
on one campus. Specifically, the commission recommended that

1. The triplication of Part I studies should cease;

2. Botswana should have engineering and earth sciences,
and, in addition, half the number of students enrolled in B.A. and
B.Sc. courses (general as well as education);

3. Lesotho should have the other half of B.Sc. students
(general and education) and law;

4. Swaziland should have agriculture and the other half of
B.A. students (general and education);

5. Students in the Faculty of Economics and Social Sciences
would be distributed between Lesotho and Swaziland, depending on
their field of studies, as follows: government, administration,
sociology, statistics in Lesotho; and commerce and accounting in
Swaziland. Half the economics students would go to Lesotho and
the other half to Swaziland.

The commission claimed that it adopted this vertical plan after
studying in detail 12 alternative strategies of student and resource
allocation. On the whole, the commission claimed, "vertical" plans
were less costly than "horizontal" plans, and, while this particular
strategy was not the least costly of the 12 options it had considered,
"it was towards the lower end of the spectrum in terms of costs—
particularly recurrent costs," and, in the commission's view, it had
other strengths, such as a greater degree of academic diversity. The
commission also asserted that this strategy would be "significantly
cheaper than the cheapest of the horizontal approaches to devolution."[3]

The report of the commission was subsequently approved by
the senate and the council of the University. Two of the three governments also approved it in principle. The chairman of the commission,
however, readily admits that the report became so "controversial"
(as he put it) that its chances for resolving the devolution controversy
—an issue that sapped the University's resources and the morale of its

staff for such a long time—were very small indeed. While the report
may have had a therapeutic value in providing the staff a forum to air
their views openly, it probably raised far more issues than it resolved.
Indeed, it brought about so much controversy on the campus precisely
because it raised such basic, but extremely sensitive departmental
issues as staff load, and per capita costs. Perhaps the commission
had no choice but to face those issues squarely, but for a campus already riddled with long-standing controversies, adding further issues
was not quite what was needed.

In November 1975, the bitter dissension was brought to a head
by a dispute between the government of Lesotho and the vice-chancellor
of the University. The Lesotho government withdrew from the trinational university and unilaterally declared the Roma campus in
Lesotho the new National University of Lesotho, claiming that the
vice-chancellor, among other things, gave too many advantages to the
other two countries.

CONCLUSION

The question of university structure and governance—the decision-making machinery—is clearly of paramount importance if a
university is to play its proper role in national development. Even
under the most ideal conditions, universities are usually too cumbersome and unwieldy to be potent forces for social change. It takes many
weeks or even many months for a creative idea born in the mind of an
imaginative staff member or administrator to journey through the maze
of faculty and senate committees and gain faculty consensus and subsequently university endorsement. If and when the proposal has some-
how passed along this tortuous path in the search for consensus, it is
likely to have been amended, modified, and mutilated beyond recognition at every stage of its journey through the committee labyrinth.
Worse still, after all these frustrating efforts, the proposal may never
see the light of day; instead it may well be shelved by a hapless administrator allegedly for "lack of funds."

In the case of UBLS, in addition to all the cumbersome
machinery of the modern "democratic" university, there was the almost
impossible task of trying to satisfy three governments, when in fact it
is practically impossible to satisfy even one government. Is there then
a future for regional universities, even when the "economics" of the
situation is manifestly against setting up national universities? That

is, will economic common sense triumph over "academic nationalism"?

As early as the 1940s, when the minority report of the Elliot commission recommended the establishment of the University of Ibadan to serve the whole of British West Africa, the recommendation was immediately opposed by the leaders of the Gold Coast (now Ghana). The experience of the University College in Salisbury, Southern Rhodesia, designed to serve the federated territories of Northern and Southern Rhodesia and Nyasaland; the history of the University of East Africa, serving Uganda, Kenya, and Tanganyika; more recently, the attempt to establish one university—the University of Benin—to serve both Togo and Dahomey: and the dissolution of UBLS in 1975, all serve to show that regional universities either do not materialize, or, if they do, do not last long.

Because of political and ideological differences, for reasons of national pride and prestige, and despite economic considerations, there is strong pressure for the establishment of separate institutions of higher learning by and for each sovereign state. The idea of two or more sovereign states establishing one university under their joint control does not, therefore, seem likely to gain much popularity, at least at this stage of African economic and political development. What should be considered, perhaps, is how some form of cooperation could be established among the various universities in Africa so they may open their doors to students from neighboring African countries as a part of the international and universal mission of all universities.

Further, UBLS forces us to examine the entire question of university structure and governance in the context not just of southern Africa but of the entire continent. Practically all African universities have adopted, without any significant modification, the mode of structure and governance prevalent in the metropolitan countries. In Europe and North America, these were evolved over a long period of time in response to social and historical forces. Institutions such as the University "senate," "council," and "court," evolved over the years in response to the needs of the time. At times, these institutions helped to guard the university from the encroachment of the state or the church. At other times, they acted as a liaison between "town" and "gown."

The extensive and elaborate committee structure provided the checks and balances needed to protect the university from being unduly swayed by the fads and fashions of the day. Universities were expected to keep a detached (some would say "ivory tower") position. From their Olympian heights, undisturbed by the events of everyday life, they were meant to pursue quietly and profess vigorously the truth in its universality. (Hence the words "professor" and "university.") The committee structure, which by its very nature entails a slow and ponderous search for a consensus, served to guard the university from reaching hasty and ill-considered decisions at the prodding of an articulate but vocal minority on a purely ephemeral issue.

If the African universities are to adopt a faster tempo, and if they are to be intimately concerned with developmental issues, can these new functions be achieved through the old university mechanism?

It is not at all surprising that the university structure was imported wholesale at the time universities were started in Africa. Indeed, it is unlikely that major departures from the metropolitan university model, in curriculum as in structure and governance, would have been accepted by the African nationalist leaders and Western-educated elites of the time. No doubt, any deviation would have been considered inferior education, and the motives of those who would advocate deviation, or even innovation, would have been suspect. Nor were the metropolitan educators of the time capable of offering alternative models. They simply did not know of other models but theirs.

A good deal of effort has already been made to Africanize the staff and the course content of African universities. Efforts are also now underway to orient African universities toward development. These efforts should now be buttressed by new structures and modes of governance so the decision-making machinery at African universities will be more in tune with their mission and objective.

Obviously, the question of university structure and governance was not a problem peculiar to UBLS. However, it does assume a good deal of gravity and urgency in view of the fate of that university. The study of UBLS underscores the paramount importance of studying this hitherto neglected aspect of universities.

NOTES

1. Stevens Commission, Report (UBLS, 1969), p. 14 (original emphasis).

2. Sir Norman Alexander was brought back to UBLS to head the commission. Alexander Commission, Report (UBLS, 1970), p. 8.

3. Further Devolution: Report of the Development Team (Devolution), (UBLS, 1974), p. 33.

2

UNIVERSITY OF YAOUNDÉ, CAMEROON

Bilingualism

Language has been one of the serious unsolved problems in African higher education, cutting off large population groups not only from the rest of Africa but also from the rest of the world. Even within one country, scientific information within one language group has often been unavailable to groups speaking other languages. Efforts by external assistance agencies—public and private—to help solve the problem have not been notably successful. The Cameroon experiment with bilingualism, therefore, is especially significant for almost all aspects of life in West Africa.

The United Republic of Cameroon has tried to break the linguistic "divide" suggested by the labels "English-speaking" and "French-speaking" in Africa. The University of Yaoundé is an example of efforts to close the gulf and develop good communication between the two groups—Anglophones and Francophones—in the African university.

CAMEROON'S LANGUAGE HISTORY

There are today at least ten indigenous language groups in Cameroon, which break up into at least 285 language or dialect variants. There is also one contact language, Cameroon pidgin English, with regional and social varieties, and two received languages, French and English.

This situation is a product of historical contacts between Africans and Europeans that have succeeded one another in Cameroon for 500 years. Cameroon came into modern history in 1472 when the Portuguese arrived: in 1961 it became the Federal Republic of Cameroon and in 1972, the United Republic of Cameroon. During this time Cameroon has had seven linguistic periods superimposed on its indigenous languages. They are as follows:

1. Portuguese (1472-1600): Oral communication only through pidgin Portuguese.

2. Portuguese + Spanish + Dutch + French + English (1600-1700): Oral communication through a pidgin language that contained elements of these five languages.

3. English (1700-1884): Arrival of missionaries and introduction of formal education and a written language.

4. English + German (1884-1916): While German was the official language during the German administration, English was still used.

5. French (in French Cameroon) + English (in British Cameroon) (1916-61).

6. French + English official languages in a federal state (1961-72): In practice French was used in the East Cameroon state, and English in the West Cameroon state. French and English were taught and used in the secondary schools and in the university.

7. French + English official languages in a unitary state (since May 1972): French and English were introduced officially in the elementary school system. French and English are official languages throughout the whole educational system.

As a consequence of this frequent change of languages, the people of Cameroon developed varying types and degrees of bilingualism, and each language type took on a different function. Before independence and reunification (in 1960-61), most Cameroonians could use three languages: a home language (one of the 285 language variants), a received language (one of the two foreign languages, French and English), and a pidgin language (a hybrid language). After Cameroon's independence, its leaders institutionalized French-English bilingualism. The University of the Federal Republic of Cameroon, founded in 1961-62, thus became a French-English bilingual university.

HOW THE BILINGUAL MEDIUM HAS BEEN DEVELOPED AND MAINTAINED

The Federal University of Cameroon was started with the assistance of the French government. Since most of its responsible administrative staff were French nationals, the language of administration was exclusively French until 1974, when two English-speaking administrators, the vice-chancellor and a deputy head of cultural affairs, were appointed to work in the office of the chancellor. For 12 years, therefore, the language of day-to-day administration in the University was and, in 1975 still is, French. Although the Anglophone administrator can, if he so desires, use English, he has to put up with the inconveniences arising from eventual translation or interpretation, and English-speaking administrators thus find themselves pushed to do their work in French. Even if the head of the University were

English-speaking, it is likely that English-speaking administrators would be under pressure to learn French and not the converse.

Since the founding of the University, the majority of the teaching staff has also been French-speaking and/or French nationals. Table 2.1 gives the relative strength of Anglophone and Francophone academic staff in 1970-71 and in 1973-74.

Until recently, even a degree in English language and literature required French. Academic courses in English language and literature were designed and taught by French-speaking teaching staff who had lectured in English in France. The courses started with a preparatory year in Yaoundé (the French propédeutique), after which students continued in France for their first degree (la licence d'enseignement). English-language students, therefore, who wanted a degree in English language and literature, had to take their first year in French, succeed at the propédeutique in Yaoundé, and then continue in France for the rest of their degree work. This English degree in French tended to discourage English-speaking students, and as a result they preferred to read law. Lectures in law, however, were also given in French and demanded a preparatory language requirement period in Cameroon and France. In science, the situation was so bad that Anglophones were afraid to enter the science faculty. Because there were so few Anglophone students in the University, they had little influence, and their only alternative was to go to English-speaking universities. Table 2.2 gives the number of Anglophone and Francophone students in the university in 1970-71 and 1973-74.

Loyalty to the French language and the sheer weight of numbers of Francophones put such pressure on the Anglophones of the University that for some time the coexistence of English with French in the University became a matter of great concern to the authorities. There was no statutory provision in the University requiring teachers or students to be bilingual in French and English before being recruited for or admitted to the University, and consequently there was a great linguistic imbalance in the institution. Anglophone students considered themselves, sometimes very loudly, the victims of an unfair language policy, and the overemphasis on one language threatened to have profound psychological effects on the students, and far-reaching political and social effects on the country as a whole, if something was not done.

Fortunately, the political and government authorities were sincere in their commitment to French-English official bilingualism and firm in their demand for the implementation of their language policy. There was therefore overriding political support for any initiative, individual or collective, in the development of widespread

TABLE 2.1

Anglophone and Francophone Academic Staff
in the University of Yaoundé

	Anglophones		Francophones	
Year/Faculty	Cameroonians	Foreigners	Cameroonians	Foreigners
1970-71[a]				
Law	2	2	8	17
Arts	2	9	18	14
Science	2	—	18	32
Education	3	1	21	13
Agriculture	0	0	7	15
Medicine	3	—	3	8
Journalism	0	0	1	4
Total	12	12	76	103
1973-74[b]				
Law	5	1	11	20
Diplomacy[c]	1	2	—	1
Arts	11	5	26	22
Science	6	1	28	37
Education	8	3	22	25
Agriculture	0	5	13	19
Medicine[d]	8	0	15	27
Journalism	—	—	2	5
Polytechnic	1	—	2	16
Total	40	17	119	172

[a]Percentage of Anglophone academic staff to the total (203) equals 12 percent. Ratio of Anglophone to Francophone academic staff is approximately 1:7.

[b]Percentage of Anglophone academic staff to the total (348) equals 16.4 percent. Ratio of Anglophone to Francophone academic staff is approximately 1:5.

[c]IRIC.

[d]CUSS.

Source: Statistics handbook compiled by the University of Yaoundé.

TABLE 2.2

Anglophone and Francophone Students in the University of Yaounde´

Year/Faculty	Anglophones	Francophones
1970-71		
Law	33	1,445
Arts	138	432
Science	42	493
Education	49	338
Agriculture	48	—
CUSS	25	103
Journalism	4	26
Polytechnic	1	26
Business	2	122
Total	342	2,985
1973-74		
Law	54	1,251
Arts	249	983
Science	64	1,184
Education	64	499
Agriculture	—	56
CUSS	41	218
Journalism	10	77
Polytechnic	3	77
Business	5	83
Diplomacy	3	27
Total	493	4,455

Source: Statistics handbook compiled by the University of Yaounde´.

functional bilingualism in the University. The most convinced advocate and defender of Cameroon official bilingualism was the head of state himself. He has spoken about it on several occasions, and on each occasion his analysis has been forceful and supportive. On November 1, 1966, four years after the University had started, while on a tour of West Cameroon state (former British Cameroon), President Ahmadou Ahidjo said,

We are so busy that we cannot afford to waste time. We have got to forge our unity, we have inherited bilingualism and we want to preserve it because it is in our own interest.... some African countries, whether they be anglophone of francophone, do French or English as

compulsory subjects although they are not a federation.
We have been lucky to inherit these two languages. We
must maintain our bilingualism. It is bad to listen to
those within or without who with intent to divide us call
it a problem. . . . I am very proud to be at the head of a
state where French and English are spoken and I think
many African States would have liked to be in our place.
     We must keep this privileged position. I am proud
that bilingual reviews like Abbia, for which I am compli-
mented by many African heads of state, are published in
Cameroon. All these contribute to the reputation of our
country. I, therefore, appeal to you once more: let us
stop making this a cause of division. I am personally so
committed to bilingualism that I am firmly decided to
create a special indemnity for all those civil servants
who will make special efforts to be bilingual.
     This issue interests me, so much so that, I am
determined to demand that all ministers, all secretaries
of states, all parliamentarians from the three houses
learn English/French. Yes, fellow countrymen, let
us stop being sectarian. We've founded a nation and we
must avoid anything that will threaten its unity. One
such thing is quarrelling on languages.

Six years after this challenging address, on May 7, 1972,
President Ahidjo announced to the National Assembly and to the nation
the change from a federal republic to a united republic. The
following extract on bilingualism is from this important policy
statement:

It is really at the federal levels, namely, the central
authority governing the nation as a whole, that
bilingualism and pluriculturalism have been promoted.
At the level of federated states no special effort has
been made to introduce them either in public life or
in primary education.
     I do not pretend that there are no questions to be
asked about the eventual place of bilingualism and pluriculturalism within the state. But I solemnly declare
that both must be maintained and developed . . . because
they are now integral facts of our historical heritage and
constitute the original traits of our national personality.

WHAT HELPED TO PROMOTE, DEVELOP,
AND MAINTAIN BILINGUALISM

Before 1972, bilingualism developed mainly through the individual initiative of academic staff members. In addition, the fact
that Anglophone students, who had little or no French before coming
to the University, had developed such proficiency, led some Francophone students (who had had seven years of English in secondary
school but little incentive to use it) to emulate their English-speaking
friends.

In 1964, the British government, which in 1960 had accepted the
responsibility of a Chair of English in the University, sent English-
Language Teaching (ELT) staff to the Federal University of
Cameroon to develop English-language courses for Francophones
similar to the French-language courses for Anglophones started in
the University in 1962. These courses in service English and service
French were by 1964 well incorporated into the academic work in all
disciplines in the University and were subsequently included in the
statutory provisions. Every student (arts, law, science, medical)
had to fulfill this statutory requirement by having a pass in his or
her other official language. The student could receive a maximum
grade of 40. In some disciplines a mark of 10/40 in bilingual
training required the student to retake the whole of his examination.
Bilingual training covered at least two weekly hours on the student's
timetable.

Since 1964 this training in official bilingualism in French and
English has been the exclusive responsibility of the Department of
English. This department, which normally offers only courses in
English and teaches in English, had to accept the responsibility of
teaching French to the Anglophones. This curious situation developed
because in French academic tradition lecturers have statutory
teaching loads. According to his rank, a teacher has four, five, six,
or eight weekly hours of teaching and no more; extra hours must be
paid as overtime service. In addition, there is a marked distinction
between ex-cathedra lectures (cours magistraux), seminars
(enseignements dirigés), and practical work (travaux pratiques). A
professor does not do travaux pratiques, and an assistant lecturer
gives cours magistraux only under supervision. Bilingual training
did not fit into these categories. It was considered secondary-school
teaching and so beneath the academic dignity of a university teaching
staff. Individual initiative had to come in here, and the English
Department consequently took over the teaching of bilingual training
courses. Since 1964, therefore, this department has included on its
academic staff some French nationals and some Cameroonian
teachers of practical French.

For some time, every student came to the teaching premises of the Department of English, but teaching facilities there were inadequate for the number of students involved, and the head of the department asked the Council to open an Institute of Bilingual Training. Though approved by the Council, this idea ran into difficulties at its implementation. That is why the department decided in 1971 to carry bilingual training to the various other departments and faculties by posting some teachers permanently to a given faculty. A bilingual teacher posted to the medical school, for example, is required to help the student acquire both general competence in the language and also the special vocabulary of his field. Bilingual teachers have thus tended to specialize in specific fields, creating a division of labor within bilingual training. Some faculties, such as the University Centre for Health Sciences, have also included a language requirement in their conditions of entry. Every entering medical student at the Centre must have at least a pass in the General Certificate of Education (GCE) French and a pass in English at the baccalauréat examination. Other faculties, such as law, teach in both languages. French law is taught in French and British law in English. Cameroon law is taught in English or French according to the language of the teacher.

The importance of course structure and its content in providing needed motivation for bilingualism is probably best illustrated at the Faculty of Arts, where a bilingual degree course was designed in 1964. Faculty members must be bilingual, since students do 50 percent of the degree course in English in the English Department and the other 50 percent of the course in French in the French Department. French-speaking and English-speaking students who pass their first-year examination in June are sent to Britain and to France, respectively, for a special intensive course. This foreign training has proved an effective incentive to learn the second language, especially among the Francophones. Table 2.3 shows the number of students who have succeeded in doing this one-year intensive language course in France and in Britain since the 1970-71 academic year.

While every student who has left the University since 1968 can be considered more productive because he is able to communicate efficiently in both English and French at work and in his daily social interactions, the student who has completed his bilingual degree course renders special services to the nation. First, though not a professional translator and interpreter, he in fact translates and interprets in both the public and the private sector on a wide variety of occasions. Second, in keeping with labor legislation, his salary as a national is lower than that of an expatriate. He therefore contributes to national saving while giving the same services as an expatriate.

TABLE 2.3

University of Yaoundé Bilingual Students in
Britain and France since 1970-71

Year	Britain Bilingual Francophone	France Bilingual Anglophone
1970-71	14	11
1971-72	11	12
1972-73	31	11
1973-74	56	13

Source: Statistics handbook compiled by the University of Yaoundé.

The bilingualism program has also proved of immense help in placing students in English-speaking and French-speaking universities the world over for degree work not yet offered by the University of Yaoundé. Students have successfully completed research degree work in the United Kingdom, the United States, Canada, France, China, the USSR, and in many African universities. It would be revealing to know the number of Anglophones who have studied in French-speaking universities and the number of Francophones who have studied in English-speaking universities.

In little more than a decade, bilingualism in the University of Yaoundé has gone a long way toward increasing contacts between Anglophone and Francophone Cameroon students. With increased contacts have come knowledge of one another and increased mutual understanding. Anglophones now teach Francophones, and vice versa, without conflict. The situation is far from perfect, but it is at least a source of encouragement.

CONCLUSIONS

The case of the University of Yaoundé shows that bilingualism in French and English has continental significance in Africa, especially with reference to higher education for development. First, functional bilingualism in French and English helps to speed up communication between French-speaking and English-speaking academic staff and their students. It thus facilitates exchange programs between students and between teachers. It helps in the interchange of African specialists and in the subsequent circulation of knowledge. A competent Zambian entomologist should be able to explain ways to fight insect pests to both students and the people of Upper Volta. Language must not be a barrier. Advantages such as these should lead African university authorities and African governments to examine ways and means whereby functional bilingualism in French and English can rapidly be promoted, developed, and maintained in the African university.

Cameroon's language difficulties arise mainly in countries that have two official languages. In monolingual countries, conflict between minority and majority language groups is less likely. Loyalties to language, if any, will be between home language and the official language, but, since there are often several home languages to choose from, the received language will tend to exercise a uniting force for the nation.

Bilingualism needs a firm policy backed by political support. If French or English, now taught in the majority of secondary schools in Africa, is continued in the university, the African university student will certainly be at least functionally bilingual on leaving his institution. But such a program can succeed only if it can rely on African expertise and national staff fluent in two languages. Programs of staff development must include, at least for the younger staff, bilingual training courses, and senior administrators must be required to be functionally bilingual.

In establishing bilingualism, national pride may prove a problem, if it considers French and English to be unfit carriers of national culture. But if the African university is to provide more service without having to call for foreign assistance in academic personnel, it seems obvious that it should promote and develop bilingualism in French and English.

3

UNIVERSITY OF YAOUNDÉ, CAMEROON

The University Centre for Health Sciences

HISTORY

In Cameroon, the greatest obstacle to providing better health services is the chronic shortage of all categories of health personnel. For health action to be effective, there must be a variety of health personnel, in terms of level and nature of training, capable of adapting themselves for work in either rural or urban areas.

The University Centre for Health Sciences (UCHS),* an institution of higher learning within the University of Yaoundé,† was founded in 1969 to assist the Cameroon government to make the best use of manpower and facilities for national health care. It has the following objectives: to develop and implement a pattern of training of professional and auxiliary health personnel, sufficiently diversified to permit the creation of effective health teams; to provide comprehensive health care to the population of a selected area to be used as a model for the country as a whole; and to undertake operational research, which includes continuous evaluation of the country's health situation and utilization of health manpower, and to cooperate with responsible planning bodies in developing health plans.

Of these three interrelated objectives, the training of qualified and suitably oriented health personnel has a high priority. The design of the Centre developed out of this need.

The University Centre for Health Sciences in Yaoundé was not a fortuitous development but a significant step with historical precedents in Cameroon, Africa, and the world.

Cameroon has a long history of paramedical education, beginning with the famous training center in Ayos where medical

_____

*The French acronym is CUSS.

†See Appendix to this case study.

assistants, nursing aides, technicians, and other field assistants
were trained. Some of the graduates of Ayos eventually qualified
medically as Médecins Africains in Dakar, and, at independence,
holders of this degree were allowed to continue their medical studies
at university level in France.

In 1963, a World Health Organization (WHO) mission (including
three distinguished medical educators) visited Cameroon at the
request of the government to study the possibility of creating a medical faculty in Yaoundé. These experts recommended the creation
of a school of medicine instead. This report was discussed in some
depth, and in the following year (1964) two Cameroonian university
professors, resident in Nigeria at the time, submitted a paper to the
Minister of Health (Mr. Nzo Ekah Ngakhy) suggesting that a multi-
professional university medical center be created.

In 1965, the Cameroon government set up a special national
commission, under the chairmanship of Dr. Simon Pierre Tchoungui,
consisting of representatives from the University and external
academic advisers (including Professor G. L. Monekosso, then at
the University of Lagos). The work of this planning commission was
further strengthened by a medical educator assigned by WHO for
three years (1966-69) and given further impetus by a Workshop on
Medical Education organized by WHO in Yaoundé in March 1966, the
first conference on African medical education to include teachers and
health service administrators. As a result of all these discussions,
the National Planning Commission decided to create a University
Centre for Health Sciences, rather than a traditional faculty of
medicine.

The climate of opinion in Cameroon, in black Africa, and in
the world at large was favorable to this development. In North
America, South America, and the Middle East there was a strong
trend toward the creation of centers or faculties of health sciences.
Cameroonian physicians and educators visited the Faculty of Health
Sciences in the University of Brasilia in 1968-69. In Africa, the
Association of Medical Schools in Africa, begun in 1961 as an informal
meeting of five deans at the University College Hospital, Ibadan, had
become an influential body. In that meeting, and at subsequent annual
conferences held at various sites across the continent, teachers of
medicine from all over Africa discussed the adaptation of teaching
programs to African realities.

Over a decade one could see increased emphasis on the teaching
of preventive medicine, maternal and child care, tropical diseases,
teaching and research in nutrition, and the development of health
demonstration zones for the practical application of the new medical
technology. In addition, a new medical pedagogy was gradually being

adopted, and medical educators were defining objectives and using newer methods of evaluation. In Cameroon itself, discussions proceeded between the government, WHO, and the United Nations Development Programme (UNDP). The result was the successful application by Cameroon for UNDP funds to initiate the University Centre for Health Sciences, which incorporates many recent advances in the teachings of medicine and the health sciences.

BASIC PHILOSOPHY OF UCHS

Teaching

The guiding principles of UCHS, like those of most institutions of higher education, are teaching, service, and research. The UCHS teaching programs, however, unlike a traditional faculty of medicine, seek to train a wide range of health personnel at all levels, all in the context of the health team. Student physicians, nurses, and technicians, each group with different basic academic qualifications, pursue different programs but share common or core courses with all other students. The emphasis, however, is not on shared courses or lectures, but on participation in the same practical team-training exercises in the field. That is, medical, nursing, and technical students have a basic training in their respective disciplines at the appropriate academic level, sharing teaching staff and the same University buildings, but all levels (physicians, nurses, and technicians) eventually meet in practical clinical and rural community health assignments. A student team is assigned a health center and, from this base, helps run the health services for a village or group of villages, including curative and preventive medicine as well as community health education. Students thus get a chance to practice their future role and to appreciate the roles of other team members.

Teaching is also integrated by themes. Clinical, laboratory, and epidemiological aspects of medicine, for example, are taught together instead of by isolated subjects or disciplines such as anatomy, pathology, surgery, or public health. Theme teaching in the common courses (or core programs) helps to bring together students of different health professions, with different academic backgrounds.

Community Health Service

Fundamental to the philosophy of UCHS is the creation of a model community health care delivery system that can be reproduced in different parts of the country. Before UCHS was established, six health demonstration zones had been created (or proposed) in six ecologically different provinces of Cameroon. In these DASP zones (Zones des demonstrations d'action en Santé Publique) government health authorities, with the assistance of WHO and UNICEF, are attempting to integrate preventive and curative medicine, experiment with new methods of health care delivery, and give practical field training and refresher training to nurses and other health personnel. Students and staff of UCHS were faced with the initial dilemma of how to add their support to the work of the health demonstration zones, none of which were within easy reach of the Yaoundé campus.

To help link UCHS and the demonstration zones, a Community Hospital on the University campus has been planned as the focal point of a network of health centers, dispensaries, and health posts in the adjacent rural Mefou district (population 200,000). It will be used by all staff as a base for integrated health care—curative, preventive, and health education—in the Mefou district and elsewhere. A two-way flow of patients is envisaged between the Community Hospital and the network of health centers, dispensaries, and health posts of the district.

The ministry will first hand over to the director of UCHS responsibility for the Mefou district, where staff will practice and students will learn professional attitudes, skills, and the basic elements of their field. Students and staff will then undergo field training and application exercises in the health demonstration zones, beginning with one zone and, over the years, extending their activities into the others. These DASP zones are the intermediate or relay stations from which qualified students will carry the message to other parts of the country. Over a period of ten years or more, the pattern of integrated health care developed by UCHS in the Mefou district will be transmitted first to the health demonstration zones where receptivity is expected to be high and eventually to other districts in the seven provinces into which the country is divided.

UCHS teaching staff will also participate in the delivery of health care at provincial and central levels. Internal medicine, general surgery, pediatrics, and obstetrics are the major clinical disciplines that contribute to care at the community hospital or district level. Other laboratory, clinical, and public health specialties will find their place at the provincial hospital, the provincial preventive medicine unit, and the provincial medical laboratories. Some University professors are expected to run specialized services from the University Centre itself at what might be called a National Reference Centre.

Research

The principal research activity of UCHS is a continuous evaluation of the health situation of the country as a whole. In addition to

this major commitment, UCHS will also make studies of utilization
of health manpower and participation in the development of health
plans at the district, provincial, and national levels. The research
program requires not only clinical and laboratory techniques to
measure health and deviations from the normal but also epidemiological and statistical techniques to plan research and to evaluate results.
There is thus a need for clinical, laboratory, and public health
specialists to provide sound clinical observation, apply modern
laboratory techniques, and employ sophisticated data-processing
techniques. Researchers will seek to develop the simplest possible
methodology to interpret the most common health indices as a basis
for planning health care strategy.

Public health specialists at UCHS will be especially concerned
with the best way to use health manpower, beginning in the Mefou
district and proceeding via the DASP zones to the rest of the country.
Integrated efforts of the major health disciplines—clinical, laboratory,
and epidemiological—will also begin in the Mefou district and develop
in the same way through the DASP zones and eventually to the country
at large.

Other research relevant to national needs will undoubtedly be
stimulated by these institutional research obligations. For example,
pharmacologists, chemists, and botanists may develop research programs on the traditional herbal remedies; cardiologists may study
endomyocardial fibrosis; and hematologists may investigate sickle
cell disease. These activities may be carried out in University
laboratories under the auspices of the National Research Council.

ADMINISTRATION

Technical Units

The essential and most indispensable feature of UCHS's organization is the assignment of the academic, professional, and technical
staff into three technical units: Biomedical Sciences, Community
Hospital (or Clinical Sciences), and Public Health (or Epidemiological
Sciences). These units represent the principal groups of attitudes,
skills, and knowledge UCHS seeks to impart to students of the health
professions. A medical student must have a grounding in all three
major areas, although toward the end of his training he spends more
than half his time on clinical studies. A nurse requires rather less
biomedical science than the medical student but also requires public
health and clinical practice. A laboratory technician needs little
clinical training, rather less public health than a nurse or sanitarian,
but must have a sound foundation of biomedical laboratory technology.

The technical units are subdivided into sections or departments, each of which includes teachers from a number of related disciplines, who use the same or similar methodology and equipment. The principal disciplines included in the Biomedical Sciences unit are anatomy, histology, embryology, genetics, physiology, biochemistry, pharmacology, pathology, microbiology, and immunology. Those of the Clinical Sciences, Community Hospital, or Clinical Practice unit are internal medicine and its major specialties, psychiatry, obstetrics and gynecology, pediatrics, and radiology. The Public Health, Epidemiological Sciences, or Medicosocial unit includes human ecology and population studies, sociology, psychology, community medicine, health services organization, and various specialties such as occupational therapy, school health, applied parasitology, and entomology.

Each technical unit is headed by a coordinator whose duties are to ensure that appropriate staff are available, that there is suitable and adequate equipment, and that there is adequate physical space. It is his responsibility to see that the institutional objective of teaching, service, and research can be carried out effectively. The coordinator of the unit is not himself administratively responsible for any of these three functions: His job is to facilitate them. He thus differs fundamentally from a head of a traditional university department, who not only controls manpower, use of space, and equipment but also decides what should be taught, what services should be rendered, and what research can be done.

Divisions

At UCHS teaching, service, and research are the responsibilities of divisions, which must plan and evaluate these functions in an integrated and coordinated manner on behalf of the institution as a whole. The three technical units are themselves coordinated by the head of the Division of Technical Coordination. The complete organizational framework therefore includes at least four divisions: (1) the Division for Administrative and Financial Matters, (2) the Division for Academic Planning and Evaluation, (3) the Division for Health Service Delivery, and (4) the Division of Technical Coordination, which includes the three technical units. To these four, a Division of Medical and Pharmaceutical Research may eventually be added.

The overall responsibility for administrative and technical leadership lies with the director of UCHS, who is assisted by the deputy director. The latter is also head of the Division of Technical Coordination and is therefore immediately responsible for dealing with problems coming from the technical units, whereas the heads of the other divisions report directly to the director. Under this arrangement UCHS can harness all its resources to achieve the teaching, service, and research objectives, while at the same time coordinating these three major functions.

The Administrative and Financial Division is headed by a secretary general. A professional administrator, he is chairman of the main standing committees, which deal with administrative and financial questions; staff and students are represented on these committees whenever possible. The secretary general also coordinates the activities of the mail office, which also handles English/French translation; the personnel office, which, in addition to routine personnel work handles all disciplinary matters concerning junior staff and students; the purchasing and accounts office; and transport, maintenance, and general services. A standing committee reviews the policies, planning, and execution of major administrative and financial matters at the beginning of each trimester. Chaired by the secretary general, the committee's membership includes the director and deputy director, the coordinators of the three technical units, the heads of the other divisions, and the subchiefs of the Administrative and Financial Division.

The Academic Planning and Evaluation Division is headed by an academic adviser qualified in educational psychology and in medical and health sciences education. He is chairman of all committees responsible for the creation, planning, and phasing of teaching programs and for the evaluation of programs and students. He also supervises the Academic Office, which plans integrated teaching programs and keeps students' academic records; the medical sublibrary; the medical illustration unit; the audiovisual unit; the medical museum: and other teaching facilities. He is charged especially with following the day-to-day progress of teaching activities and presides over a committee that coordinates teaching programs. It includes among its members the director, deputy director, secretary general, other heads of divisions, the coordinators of the three technical units, and the subchiefs of the Academic Division (sublibrarian, assistant academic registrar, and others) and representatives of staff and students.

The main bulk of academic planning and evaluation, however, is done in committees set up by the Faculty Board. A main committee for medical studies has ad hoc subcommittees that group together teachers or disciplines included in the teaching themes. Every subcommittee is headed by a convenor. He must be a dynamic person interested in and convinced of the importance of integrated teaching, someone prepared to devote a great deal of time to consulting coordinators of technical units and their staffs in order to obtain consensus. A similar mechanism is utilized in planning programs for postbasic nursing and the various categories of health technicians—medical, laboratory, pharmacy, sanitary, radiography, physiotherapy, and dental hygiene. The Academic and Evaluation Division also plans and organizes refresher courses for health service staff.

The Division of Technical Coordination includes the three technical units and provides the infrastructure—teachers, physical space, and equipment—for the training of physicians, postbasic nurses, and technicians. Departmentalization for its own sake is avoided, and heads of sections or departments help the unit coordinator develop the physical facilities, staff, and equipment required for teaching, service, and research. The subdivisions are (1) Biomedical Sciences, including morphological, physiological, and pathological sciences, and possibly medical technology; (2) Clinical Sciences, including clinical medicine and specialties, general surgery and specialties, mother and child care, and nursing science; and (3) Epidemiological Sciences, including human ecology, preventive medicine, and health services administration.

Committees and Boards

UCHS has a number of statutory committees and boards. There are three internal committees presided over by the director: the School Assembly, the Council of Professors, and the Technical Committee.

The School Assembly includes teachers of all ranks, senior professional and technical staff, and student representatives. It meets at least twice a year and may express opinions on any matter that concerns the life of the school as a whole. (All members of the staff also belong to and can attend internal meetings of their technical units between meetings of the assembly.) The School Assembly has no power of decision, but its opinions cannot be ignored.

Membership of the Council of Professors is limited to full university professors. It meets once a month and may make recommendations to the University Council on appointments, promotions, examination results, teaching programs and syllabi, general administrative and financial questions, and research and service matters.

The Technical Committee includes the director, deputy director, heads of divisions, and coordinators of technical units. Team leaders of the various technical assistance groups are ex-officio members. *

*Donor agencies (December 1974) are the United Nations Development Programme and World Health Organization team (UNDP/WHO), French technical assistance, Fonds Aide Coopération (FAC), Canadian International Development Agency (CIDA), and the United States Agency for International Development (USAID).

as are heads of special projects attached to UCHS. The Technical
Committee constantly reviews the objectives of the project and
coordinates recommendations and opinions from the Cameroon
government on the one hand and the various technical assistance
agencies on the other.

There are three other boards or committees that link UCHS
to the health ministry, the University, and the government and its
collaborating sponsoring agencies. These are the Inter-Ministerial
Commission, the University Council, and the Board of Governors,
respectively.

The Inter-Ministerial Commission, presided over by the
chancellor, includes among its members the vice-chancellor, the
director and deputy director of UCHS, the director, deputy directors,
and technical advisers from the Ministry of Health—the principal
employer of health manpower in Cameroon—and the planning officer in
the Ministry of Education. This commission deals with any problems
that may arise between UCHS and the Ministry of Health.

The University Council, the supreme academic and administrative body in the University, is presided over by the chancellor and
includes among its members all the deans and directors of faculties
and schools of the University, representatives of students and staff,
and representatives of government ministries. It deals with, and has
a final say on, all questions of budget appointments and promotions
of academic staff, examination regulations for degrees and diplomas,
discipline of students and staff, and any other questions relevant to
the life of the University that its members may raise.

The Board of Governors of UCHS is chaired by the chancellor
of the University. It includes representatives from UNDP, WHO,
CIDA, USAID, and FAC, from the ministries of health, education,
finance, and economic development, from the faculties of arts and
science, and the UCHS director, deputy director, divisional heads,
and coordinators of the technical units. This board reviews the
progress of the project every six months and plans for future
developments.

STAFF DEVELOPMENT

The teaching staff of UCHS includes both full-time and part-
time teachers. The number of full-time staff has increased from
only five in 1969 to 55 in 1974. Cameroonian staff members, a
small minority in 1970, made up about 60 percent of all full-time
staff in 1974.

This rapid growth of full-time and Cameroonian staff was the
result of a staff development program launched about four years
before UCHS received its first students in September 1969. With the

help of WHO and other sources of finance, a number of Cameroonian physicians obtained fellowships to undertake postgraduate studies abroad. In 1968, a year before the Centre was created, the National Planning Commission reviewed available Cameroonian manpower and identified not only the "fellows" completing their advanced studies but also two Cameroonian professors and two associate professors qualified to teach in and organize the Health Sciences Centre. To this local talent were added medical, nursing, and technical staff recruited and paid for by various technical assistance agencies, which also bore the costs of visiting teachers and administrators in a wide variety of disciplines.

In the four years 1970 to 1974, recruitment of local staff has proceeded steadily, although shortage of medical manpower in government hospitals has resulted in a slowing down of the scholarship/fellowship programs. Fellowships are available, but candidates cannot be immediately released to take them up. In the early days, moreover, some physicians were not released for teaching duties by the government, despite their special training, because of this same shortage of manpower. By the time international assistance ends in 1977, however, it is expected that nearly all major posts will be occupied by Cameroonians and the institution will be self-supporting.

The majority of UCHS Cameroonian staff are graduates of medical schools in Britain or France, or of African medical schools, especially Ibadan in Nigeria and Dakar in Senegal. Others, however, have either trained or obtained postgraduate qualifications in India, Russia, East Germany, West Germany, Switzerland, Sweden, the United States, Canada, and Brazil. The two dominant groups are English-speaking teachers trained in Nigeria and/or Britain, and French-speaking teachers trained in Senegal and/or France. (Students are required to be bilingual and able to follow courses in either language; each teacher uses the language in which he is most competent. Official communications appear in both English and French.)

There are (as of December 1974) four professeurs agregés on the staff—one had already held the qualification when the Centre was founded and the other three qualified shortly thereafter. *

Part-time staff cover a wide range of disciplines. Qualified specialist staff—clinicians, public health, and biomedical scientists in various parts of the country—are recruited as part-time lecturers and demonstrators for student field assignments. They are given an academic rank and remunerated correspondingly. There is also a

---

*Professeur agregé—one who has passed the agregation—a competitive examination for admission to the teaching staff of, in this case, a Faculty of Medicine. Somewhat equivalent to "University Professor" in the British tradition.

category of associate staff, consisting of physicians in charge of
district and provincial hospitals where sixth-year medical students
have their internships.

BUILDINGS AND EQUIPMENT

Buildings and equipment are being developed in conformity
with a master plan drawn up just before the Centre was established.
(Before 1971, UCHS was housed in temporary huts on the old
University site.) New buildings on the University of Yaoundé campus,
built near each other, will eventually house the Biomedical Sciences,
Public Health, and Community Hospital units. The first two were
completed and occupied in October 1971 and October 1973 respectively—about 12 months behind schedule in both cases. The Community Hospital building was started in June 1974 (about two years
behind schedule) and is expected to be fully operational by December
1976. An administrative building with a library, cafeteria, meeting
rooms, and amphitheater is annexed to the Biomedical Sciences unit.

The Biomedical Sciences building contains 8 multidiscipline or
multipurpose laboratories (16 students per laboratory, 128 student
places) and the supporting interlaboratories, preparation rooms,
storerooms, dissecting room, photographic darkroom, and 12
office laboratory units for the teaching staff.

The Public Health building is a base for field activities,
teaching, and research. It has staff offices, two seminar/reading
rooms holding 40 to 60 students each, a large general teaching
laboratory with space for 42 students, a smaller research/demon-
stration laboratory for student research projects, map rooms, and
a data processing room. It also has a field office that will be linked
with the ambulatory section of the hospital so that field workers can
follow up patients in their homes or villages.

The Community Hospital will be used by all staff as a base for
integrated health care in the Mefou district and elsewhere. It is
modeled on the district hospital usual in developing countries so
that students can receive their basic training in an institution similar
to the one they will probably manage early in their professional
lives. Both staff and students are expected to work also in provincial or central hospitals that have developed an intermediate
degree of specialization, as well as in more highly specialized units.

The Community Hospital has three parts, all in one building:

1. A large ambulatory care unit, including space for unre-
ferred patients, consulting and clinical investigation rooms for adult
male and female medical and surgical patients, a section for ambulatory care of mothers, pregnant women, and babies, and an

emergency room with a few "holding" beds. There is also a
medical records office and an outpatient laboratory.

    2. A technomedical unit, including clinical laboratories,
diagnostic X-ray laboratories, surgical operating theaters, intensive
care and recovery rooms, and an obstetric delivery theater.

    3. Hospital ward blocks, two of which will be completed in
the first phase to give a total of 150 beds. One ward block serves
children and mothers. The other block contains beds for adult male
and female medical and surgical patients. Teaching space and
student laboratories have been provided so that all UCHS students
can benefit from contact with inpatients.

    Other buildings have been planned to include living quarters
for interns and other staff, more science laboratories, a museum,
audio-visual aids, more teaching and seminar rooms, offices for
teachers, and rooms for committee meetings. It is hoped that
hostels will be built adjacent to some of the health centers in DASP
zones to house student health team members.

    While awaiting construction of the buildings, the staff have
developed a number of temporary facilities with funds obtained by
the Ministry of Education. The Central Hospital in Yaoundé has been
used for teaching purposes since the establishment of UCHS and has
been extensively remodeled and extended. It is expected that even
after the UCHS hospital is completed the Central Hospital will be
used for special training for senior medical students, interns, and
postgraduate students.

FINANCIAL RESOURCES

    The principal source of finance for the UCHS project is the
government of the United Republic of Cameroon, assisted by the
UNDP, WHO, UNICEF, FAC, CIDA, USAID, and the United Kingdom
Ministry of Overseas Development.

    The government of the United Republic of Cameroon has donated
the land on the University campus on which UCHS is being built, and
the health ministry has put at the service of UCHS facilities of major
hospitals and health centers. The first building projects, the Biomedical Sciences and Administration buildings, were financed
entirely by local funds and cost about 200 million CFA francs. A
pavilion and an emergency reception block, both at the Yaoundé
Central Hospital, were also built with local funds at the cost of 27
million and 30 million francs respectively, as was a block of apart-
ments for 30 million francs.

    UCHS was created by an agreement signed by the UNDP and
the Cameroon government; WHO is executing agency for the UNDP.

In the first four years of the project (1969-73) the UNDP spent over U. S. $1 million. This fund included salaries of "experts" (teaching staff) assigned to UCHS ($700,000), scholarships for advanced training of Cameroonian staff ($180,000), and materials and equipment (over $180,000).

UCHS has sole responsibility for its recurrent budget (138 million francs in 1974-75), out of which it pays the salaries of Cameroonian academic, administrative, and technical staff and covers running expenses—water, electricity, and perishable laboratory and other equipment. The Cameroon government is paying half the total cost of building the Community Hospital, the most expensive capital investment of the project, and the remaining half is being shared between France and the United States.

French technical aid to date totals over 1 billion francs CFA. It includes 88 million for the salaries of French teaching staff, 665 million toward building and equipping the hospital and a students' hostel, and over 50 million for visiting professors, laboratory and clinical equipment, and for scholarships to all first-, second-, and third-year medical students. It also covers the cost of building and equipping a new X-ray block at the Central Hospital in Yaoundé.

Canadian technical aid includes $1,230,000 (Canadian) for the construction and equipment of the public health unit, salaries of eight public health teachers, and scholarships for advanced training of Cameroonian staff. U. S. technical aid is helping construct the community hospital (450 million francs CFA) and provides four teachers (170 million CFA) and scholarships for advanced training of both Cameroonians and non-Cameroonians in UCHS (about 72 million CFA). Other donors include WHO, which supports the School of Postbasic Nursing attached to UCHS, and the United Kingdom Ministry of Overseas Development, which supports the medical sub-library and museum.

TEACHING PROGRAMS

Teaching began in the 1969-70 academic year with the first class of medical students. By 1976-77, courses for nursing aides are expected to fill out the following range of teaching programs:

Medical studies: Degree of doctor of medicine. Entry— baccalauréat or GCE advanced ("A") level science. Six-year program. First class entered 1969; first graduates 1975.

Postbasic nursing: Postbasic nursing diploma. Entry—state registration plus four years' experience. Two-year program. First class entered October 1972; first graduates 1974.

Health technicians: State diploma in health sciences, with stated option. Engry—GCE ordinary ("O") level or equivalent.

Three-year program, of which the first year is common to all the options. First class—with options in medical laboratory technology, sanitary science, pharmacy assistants—entered in October 1973; first graduates in 1976.

Health education: Degrees of bachelor of health sciences and master of health sciences. Entry for bachelor's degree—baccalauréat or GCE "A" level with specialization in the humanities plus adequate scientific "O" level preparation. First class admitted for bachelor's degree in 1975. Entry for the master's degree—a bachelor's degree in arts, science, or medicine, and an appropriate "background." First class expected in 1976.

Basic nursing: State diploma, in collaboration with the Yaoundé and Bamenda schools of nursing. Entry—GCE "O" level or equivalent. First-year common program with UCHS health technicians. Second- and third-year programs at UCHS Community Hospital and in the DASP zones. First class in 1975.

Health auxiliaries: State certificate in health sciences. Entry-level nursing aides certificate. Further training for six to 12 months as dental, surgical X-ray, or surgical theater assistants, or field survey itinerants. First class in 1976.

This program will make it possible to train a wide variety of personnel in the health team concept, the main objective of the UCHS program. The team leader, the medical doctor, is trained to take responsibility for a district hospital and its satellite health centers at the start of his or her professional life. The four-month assignment in "integrated medicine" in the sixth year tests the student's readiness to take on such responsibility, and, as an intern, he or she is posted to work in a district hospital whenever possible. Acting as an assistant to the medical officer in charge, the intern participates in the administration of the hospital, in supervisory visits to satellite dispensaries and health centers, in public health education, and in the health science teaching of nursing aides. Interns take full responsibility for the care of hospitalized patients and supervise nursing staff in the management of out-patients. They practice surgery and anesthesia in appropriate cases and help supervise difficult midwifery cases. These duties are assigned on a roster so that each student carries out ward activities daily, surgery about twice weekly, and emergency weekend duties at least fortnightly.

The integrated program of medical studies, which enables the student to develop these skills, is as follows:

First Year: Introduction to Health Sciences: Basic principles, environmental studies (physical, biological, and social aspects); basic principles of human biology (molecular, cell and tissue biology, structure in relation to function, and population studies); and interaction between man and the environment. Structure, functions, and organization of health services—local, national, international. Practical assignments in the neighboring community.

Second Year: Human Biological Studies: Integrated study of the human being by organic systems—structure and function of the normal organ (embryological development, histology, biochemistry, biophysics, physiology, and pharmacology) and the common morbid anatomical processes, pathological physiology, and the relevant epidemiological aspects. Practical assignments in the neighboring community.

Third Year: Pathological and Therapeutic Studies: Integrated study, based on patients, of the major medical, surgical, and psychopathological syndromes, including clinical examination, pathological laboratory, and radiological diagnostic methods, and methods of treatment and prevention, including medicosocial and medicolegal aspects. Practical assignments in the neighboring community.

Fourth Year: Integrated Health Studies: Introduction to integrated health care: the individual (basic techniques of medical and surgical management in hospital practice); the family (the practice of family health, obstetric care, mother and child health protection); the community (organization of basic health-team activities in rural communities). Preparation of dissertation.

Fifth Year: The Basis of General Practice: Internal medicine, general surgery, pediatrics, obstetrics, psychiatry, and health center practice. Rotating senior clerkships in appropriate teaching centers. Preparation of dissertation.

Sixth Year: Internship: Full internship responsibility in the University's community hospital unit and in a district hospital with its satellite dispensaries. Presentation of dissertation.

HEALTH CARE AND OPERATIONAL RESEARCH

Until the UCHS Community Hospital is completed and in operation, health care functions will be (and have been) carried out in two main centers: a pilot health care project at Mvolye, in the Mefou district, about 2.5 miles from the UCHS campus units, and Yaoundé Central Hospital. In addition to the above, staff and students have organized health care team exercises in the Mezam DASP zone in the Northwest province.

The Mvolye Community Health Pilot Project has helped to prepare UCHS staff for its role in total health care delivery in the Mefou district. It was designed in 1971 to provide total health care for the community and to enable staff and students to both observe and provide care.

A five-year project, it was planned in three phases: (1) a preliminary 12-month phase to make contacts with the population of the district and the dispensary staff, collect basic information on the population, and obtain a suitable teaching site; (2) a three-year implementation phase to establish basic activities; and (3) an operational and evaluation phase.

A pilot survey of the Mvolye-Efoulam area was made to provide background information on the area's geography, population, administration, history, ethnic composition, economic activity, home structure, religion, and social and political institutions. The survey also provided a detailed description of the physical facilities, equipment, staff, and budget of the health center and health and disease figures for the year 1970-71.

To secure the cooperation of the community, senior UCHS teaching and administrative staff met with village chiefs, one of whom put at UCHS's disposal a building belonging to him. The building is used for consultations and health education talks and houses a doctor's office, small laboratory, pharmacy, and store.

In January 1972, a full-time physician, trained in pediatrics and public health, was appointed to head the UCHS activities at Mvolye. The Ministry of Health assigned a nurse-midwife to Mvolye, and other supporting staff were provided by UCHS. Equipment was obtained with UCHS funds and supplemented with UNICEF gifts.

During the present phase of implementation, the project is carrying out the following activities: prenatal and postnatal care; under-fives clinics; school health (in the local primary school); health care of workers (in the neighboring industrial complex); general medical/surgical clinics; family records for selected Mvolye-Efoulam families; vaccination campaigns (measles, triple vaccine, smallpox, etc.); a survey of the community that includes numbering houses and mapping the district; home visits and reports on sanitation; and health education talks and films in the UCHS annex.

The above activities complement routine health center programs, and it is hoped they may be merged into the main Mefou district total health care project when the UCHS Community Hospital is completed. Meanwhile, in 1973, UCHS clinical and public health staff began surveying the health center facilities of the Mefou district as a whole so that there is now available reliable information on the number, and accessibility at different seasons, of health centers and dispensaries, the quality of their buildings, the number and quality of staff who run them, equipment and drugs available, and the volume of work and its nature (how many patients and what they come for).

Much of this investigative work is ongoing. Medical and postbasic nursing students are studying administration and gathering information in several areas, and the surveys are expected to link up with similar activities being undertaken elsewhere in the Mefou district by OCEAC, an international organization of central African countries coordinating their fight against endemic disease.

The Yaoundé Central Hospital, previously staffed by Ministry of Health specialists and general doctors, has now been largely taken over by UCHS staff. Because of pressing needs elsewhere, the ministry has tended to withdraw its staff as more University staff become available. The latter thus have to cope with a heavy load of clinical duties in addition to their teaching. University teachers now head the departments of medicine (including cardiology), radiology, obstetrics and gynecology, pediatrics, hematology, pathology, and surgery (including orthopedics, urological, and neurological surgery).

It is likely that when the UCHS hospital is completed, at least 50 percent of the UCHS clinical staff will be withdrawn from the Central Hospital. Nevertheless, those qualified in the most highly specialized branches of medicine will undoubtedly work in the Central Hospital as they will in appropriate units to be created in the future National Reference Centre. The latter will develop facilities suitable for a postgraduate medical center.

Although clinical work can give useful glimpses into the distribution of disease in a country, fieldwork backed with laboratory observations is necessary to complete the picture. In 1972/73 and 1973/74, fourth-year medical students carried out health team exercises in the Mezam DASP zone, in association with postbasic nursing students and student nurses of the Bamenda Nursing School. The method of work was described in the section "Basic Philosophy of UCHS," above. These exercises will be continued in the 1975/76 academic year, when logistic and supervision problems have been resolved. Meanwhile, in the current year (1974/75), similar exercises are being organized in the Mefou district near Yaoundé, and this will be the future pattern for fourth-year medical students. Fifth-year students will in future head enlarged health teams, including technician and health education students, in the DASP zones (Mezam and elsewhere). Some of the new medical graduates posted to the DASP zone will be available to help in supervision.

ANALYSIS AND EVALUATION

UCHS is above all designed to change fundamental attitudes to health practice and medical education. After only five years, it is too early to draw final conclusions, but it is clear that its program has made an impact on students, teaching staff, the University, government ministries, national politics, the lay public, and other African countries. Most students accept the new philosophy of integrated learning and health care, and most are willing to begin their professional lives at the district hospital level in either the French-speaking or the English-speaking provinces of Cameroon. A new generation of bilingual physicians will clearly have an influence on the international African scene, and possibly beyond.

The project has brought together medical teachers from a large number of countries and disciplines. The two major groups—English- and French-speaking—are learning mutual respect for differences in training and outlook. Few of these teachers had experience with integrated teaching and modern pedagogy. The majority have accepted and implemented the new techniques and will probably take their teaching skill to future posts. All teachers have had to learn to train physicians rather than teach isolated subjects and to take responsibility also for training other health personnel. These achievements have not been easy.

The spirit of integration has been extended to technical assistance. Members of the technical committee have often been able to pool the resources of the different agencies, in spite of their varying regulations. The pooling of Cameroonian and other funds to build the Community Hospital is a fine example of international cooperation.

The decision of the Cameroon government to integrate the UCHS into the University has proved extremely wise. UCHS, which started in 1969, has helped transform the traditional parent university, founded in 1963, in the following ways. First, the new administrative organization of UCHS, adapted to curricula change and innovation, is now being actively studied by the University and by other faculties.

Second, as a result of accepting this health team concept, the University has had to open its gates a little wider to admit students with "lower" academic qualifications into technical courses previously considered outside its terms of reference. At least one other professional school now plans to admit intermediate-level technicians in addition to professionals.

Third, University colleagues now speak in terms of profiles of people to be trained, definition of educational objectives, and more rational methods of student evaluation. The idea of setting just "one long essay question" as an examination paper is being seriously challenged.

Fourth, the government has recognized the fact that medical teachers perform community service and has agreed to pay them an allowance, encouraging professionals in other faculties and schools to participate in community development and serve the nation in their respective spheres.

Fifth, although the University is officially bilingual, UCHS is the only part of the University that requires its entering students to be fluent in both French and English. The presence of many teachers speaking either French only or English only has compelled all Cameroon students to take both languages seriously.

Sixth, UCHS staff are recruited from a wide range of countries; consequently regulations drawn up to take account of only two traditions— the British and French—have had to be constantly reviewed. Despite their highly publicized difficulties, Anglophone and Francophone Cameroonians in the UCHS are working out a modus vivendi. It is interesting to note, in passing, that the first two African vice-chancellors of the University have been selected by the Cameroon government from among the medical professors in UCHS.

It is too early to know what effect UCHS will have on governmental ministries and national politics. Suffice it to say that new institution arrangements (interministerial commissions) have been set up to facilitate collaboration among ministries for the benefit of UCHS.

UCHS is a subject of much public discussion in Cameroon; its failures are widely publicized by its detractors, including some of its staff who are fundamentally opposed to its philosophy. But most people are enthusiastic about it, and a motion of support was recently passed by the supreme political body.

A number of other African countries have decided to create similar university centers, faculties, or schools. Team training has been generally acclaimed, and some schools of medicine or public health have adopted "thematic" teaching even where the overall structure of the faculty has not been changed.

The philosophy and programs of UCHS were the subject of discussions at the Conference of African Medical Schools held in Yaoundé in April 1972 and at the journées medicales in December 1973. UCHS was also represented in international meetings of WHO and has been visited by representatives from national and international organizations and from university centers for health sciences in other continents. In addition, senior UCHS university teachers have been invited to act as consultants to a number of African governments interested in creating similar institutions. The Faculty of Health Sciences of the University of Ife (Nigeria) and the Faculty of Medicine of the University of Dar es Salaam (Tanzania) are, like UCHS, organized by divisions rather than departments—of biomedical sciences, hospital care, and community health. They have included integrated teaching and field activities (in Bagamoyo in Tanzania and in Western Nigeria state hospitals) for staff and students and are beginning team training activities. More recently, schools or centers of health sciences have been created in Niamey (Niger) and Libreville (Gabon), and institutions with similar philosophies in Cotonou (Benin) and Lomé (Togo). Similar trends can be observed in Ghana, Nairobi, Lusaka, and Dakar.

PROBLEMS AND PITFALLS

Difficulties, problems, and pitfalls are inevitable in any such project as UCHS. They fall into four main groups: technical difficulties; problems of attitudinal change; organization and management; and leadership and orientation.

Technical Difficulties

Before the UCHS Community Hospital could be designed, a difference of opinion between donor agencies had to be settled. One donor group would only participate in financing a 50-bed hospital/health center complex; another donor group preferred at least 250 beds, with complex technomedical equipment. There were also other differences of opinion among individual Cameroonians trained in different academic traditions. These varying opinions were harmonized by discussions—open, frank, and sometimes diplomatic. Eventually, it was agreed to build a 150-bed community hospital, with large ambulatory services. It was also agreed that funds from the different donor agencies be pooled with Cameroonian funds, instead of each building separate parts of the hospital.

Some Cameroonian teachers and chiefs of technical assistance agencies also held divergent views on how field training should be organized, where it should be done, and at what stage medical students should be involved. The relative importance of formal teaching and field work also had to be faced. Some teachers and students preferred lectures to field work, in spite of previously defined educational objectives. There was a clear correlation between the attitudes of staff and their previous professional training and experience. Channeling and harmonizing these various views demanded much patience and considerable leadership.

Attitudinal Change

How does one change a whole system within a relatively short period? First, students have problems accepting and adapting to a new system, and, until the first graduates are fully integrated into the public service and accepted by the public, students may well fear being used as human guinea pigs. It is important, therefore, that students should see tangible advantages in the new system, and their scholastic problems should be given maximum priority. Planners of integrated teaching must remember that students need the challenge of integrating knowledge themselves; teachers should provide the conceptual framework of integration, but the rest should be left to the students. Problem-solving exercises in which knowledge and skills are applied to real-life situations and early exposure to patient care are very important. Large student numbers are difficult to manage when one uses integrated teaching unless there is adequate laboratory space and use is made of the newer educational techniques. Students should be encouraged to study in small groups rather than in isolation. They should also be encouraged to have within their "working parties" students of other health professions so that the caste system be replaced by the team spirit.

New staff may be disoriented, unable to grasp the new system, however well it may be described on paper. There are varying interpretations of integration and of the administrative organizational chart, and these differences result in conflicts between well-meaning and equally highly motivated colleagues. Furthermore, the system calls for a degree of perfection that is not easily achieved among human beings—excellent relations among all staff members. In the traditional departmental system the fact that two heads of departments do not speak to each other may have no effect on the teaching program. If integrated teaching is to succeed, a careful selection of staff is imperative. The creation of teaching and administrative committees, however, largely overcomes the "human difficulty" since decisions can be taken collectively. Orientation of new staff and students by public and private discussions is very important.

The UCHS threatens traditional approaches to the teaching of medicine and the established methods of health care delivery. Even those who question the existing systems are not necessarily prepared for a change; change to them means insecurity and risk. Should medical education take place entirely within the rigid ivory tower of a university and a university hospital? Should health care be limited to inhabitants of large urban centers where doctors prefer to live? Should health care tasks be delegated? Decentralization of medical education and practice is vigorously resisted, or dubbed as unrealistic.

The first five years after leaving medical school should be planned as carefully as the five to seven years spent in the school. In the present Cameroonian context, young graduates will begin their professional careers at the district level so that by the time they are married and have children of school age they will be posted to towns that have adequate educational facilities. The maldistribution of physicians cannot be solved except in the context of total community development. Integrated health care fits naturally into integrated community development; but it will only become possible when physicians and other health workers have been trained (as in the UCHS) to be equally competent in biomedical science, clinical medicine, and public health. Those who wish to preserve them as separate specialties vigorously oppose the UCHS project.

Organization and Management

Traditional methods of administration simply will not work. There are so many facets, so many interrelationships in the organizational setup, and so many telephone calls and confrontations that discipline is vital. Those responsible for running the project must be specially trained, and refresher courses in management techniques should be organized. Needed are flexible, highly competent, and highly motivated professional administrators who are good at problem solving. Failure to appreciate this need has caused many of the difficulties of UCHS. If managers are incompetent, professional staff are frustrated; they may be able to teach and carry out service commitments, but they will have little peace of mind in which to do significant research.

Leadership and Orientation

All members of the health team should feel they belong; there should be no complexes of superiority or inferiority. Teaching programs and professional services should be organized by appropriate health professionals. A physician should not run the nurses or laboratory technicians programs. The posts of director and of coordinators of units should not be monopolized by physicians. Leaders should be highly experienced professionals, open-minded, fair, strong, adaptable, and capable of wide vision; and if they plan to accomplish a revolution in health sciences, education, and health care delivery, they must be prepared for shocks and surprises. They should be firm on matters of principle and flexible on matters of detail.

One of the major difficulties of the UCHS project has been too much enthusiasm and too strong a desire to succeed. Integrated teaching is not an end in itself. Sponsors of the project, especially the representatives of international and bilateral assistance agencies, have had an almost pathological fear of failure. All participants have tried to do too much and to proceed too quickly. The leadership of UCHS must steer the program in such a manner that it achieves the desired attitudinal changes without a head-on collision between protagonists of the new and defenders of the old.

UCHS is a higher educational system geared to community development and the socioeconomic growth of Cameroon. A UNDP/WHO evaluation in 1974 reported that most of the objectives for phase 2 (1970-73) had been attained. The main lessons learned from its history so far are that higher educational institutions should adapt themselves to local realities; that manpower production and manpower utilization are inseparable; that attitudes can be changed, but that such change cannot be hurried. The program should be supported and expanded. Multidonor participation, with leadership in the hands of nationals, can be a very effective way of achieving developmental goals to the mutual satisfaction of both "donors" and "receivers." The UCHS experience can be recommended to other countries—whether "developed" or "developing."

APPENDIX: GENERAL UNIVERSITY BACKGROUND

The University of Yaoundé was created in 1962 as the Federal
University of Cameroon. The name "Federal" corresponded to the
Federal Republic of Cameroon, created in 1961 by the fusion of the
former English- and French-administered U.N. mandated territories,
which brought about the reunification of the Cameroonian nation. In
1972, the nation progressed from a federal administration to a unitary
state, and the name of the country was changed to the United Republic
of Cameroon. Shortly afterwards, in September 1972, the university
was renamed the University of Yaoundé, a change that symbolizes the
fact that other universities may be created elsewhere in the country.

From very humble beginnings—a law faculty, and a handful of
staff and students, working in temporary premises, in 1962—the
University of Yaoundé now has ten faculties, schools, and institutes,
with a total of over 500 full-time staff and about 8,000 students. These
schools and faculties are as follows: Faculty of Law and Economic
Sciences, Faculty of Arts and Social Sciences, Faculty of Sciences,
Higher National School of Agriculture, College of Education, University
Centre for Health Sciences, Higher National Polytechnic School,
Institute of International Relations, Instititute of Public Administration,
and International Higher School of Journalism. Apart from the three
faculties, all the sections of the University are professional schools
whose students are trained for a specific job. These professional
schools have been created over the past ten years, in response to
national high-level manpower needs.

Entry to the faculties is open, without examination, to all
students who possess the full baccalauréat, or the GCE at the advanced
level, or an equivalent qualification. There is no selection, and, with
the yearly increase in the number of school leavers, there has been a
veritable demographic explosion in the University. In the early days,
all students had full scholarships, but this became such a financial
burden that there are now only certain categories of scholarships open
to students according to well-defined criteria.

Entry to the professional schools is competitive and selective.
All Cameroonian students admitted to these schools have full scholarships. Students may enter directly from school, or after a year or
two in a faculty.

The style of administration and recruitment is based on a
combination of French and British traditions, the former being
predominant, especially in the early years. It is probable that
administration, staff selection, and student evaluation will in the
future be "Cameroonized"; they are being developed from first
principles.

4

ADDIS ABABA UNIVERSITY, ETHIOPIA

The Public Service Role of the University

GENERAL BACKGROUND

With a total area of over 1.2 million square kilomenters and an estimated population of 26 million, Ethiopia is one of the largest and most populous countries in Africa. Over 90 percent of the population lives in rural areas and is engaged mainly in subsistence agriculture. The country's mountainous terrain, cut by deep ravines and gorges, has made communication and transportation difficult and sometimes impossible, especially during the rainy seasons. Thus, the nation as a whole has been cut off from the rest of the world, and provinces and subprovinces remained largely isolated from each other.

Ethiopia is also one of the world's most ancient countries. It has rich and varied national characteristics, language, religion, and culture constituting both advantages and difficulties in the country's modernization. For a large part of the country and for a long period of its history, the monarchical form of government, the Ethiopian Orthodox Church, and the Muslim religion have left indelible marks on the thinking, living, and cultural behavior of the people.

Modern education in Ethiopia was preceded by the highly elaborate, largely status-quo-oriented system of education of the Ethiopian Orthodox Church and the Koranic school system. Several aspects of present-day formal education, however, had existed for many centuries, especially in the northern provinces—the notion of prescribed school curricula varying from one level of schooling to another, examinations to test the completion of prescribed curricula,

This case study was written by the former president of Haile Selassie I University before the 1974 change in Ethiopia's government. The formal programs of the University (now called Addis Ababa University) have been suspended and staff and students have been deployed in the campaign for rural development. Programs are expected to recommence in 1976.

56

ceremonial exercises marking graduation, and the awarding of a diploma with a seal affixed to it. These church schools used the Geez language (now used only for religious ceremonies), written in a script dating from early in Ethiopia's history.

Modern education as we now know it was not introduced until the twentieth century, the first school being opened in 1906. By the end of 1972, total school enrollment* was only 800, 000, of which 82. 3 percent was in the primary schools, 17 percent in the secondary schools, and 0. 7 percent at the third level. (The Italian invasion and occupation nullified the results achieved prior to 1935, so the figures should be evaluated in terms of the 30-year postliberation period only.) Over the past 15 years or so, government elementary school education has been growing at an average rate of 11 percent per year, while education at second and third levels has been expanding at 19 percent and 20 percent per annum, respectively.

The Ethiopian educational system has had a number of serious problems. Schools are unevenly distributed among regions and between urban and rural centers; boys and girls have unequal opportunity; an inadequate proportion of the national budget is allotted to education; the only selective mechanism for university admission has been the entrance examination, which has thus had an unreasonable influence on secondary-level curricula and methodology. In addition, there are clearly inadequate rates of participation at all levels of education. The enrollment figures above represent a 16. 3 percent participation rate for first-level education (the 7-12 age group); 4. 1 percent for second level (13-18 age group); and only 0. 2 percent for third level (19-24 age group). These inadequacies constitute a serious challenge, inviting a boldly different educational strategy. The question may be asked, What has all this to do with higher education in general and Haile Selassie I University in particular?

The answer seems to be: Nearly everything. First, higher education is part and parcel of the educational system of the country, and, as such, any imbalance has a profound influence on higher education. Second, the response, or lack of response, of higher education to these and other factors determines its relevance and responsiveness to the society in which it operates.

This essay reviews the background of the University, together with some of its activities in the decade or so of its existence, with particular reference to its efforts to relate to the development needs of Ethiopia. It considers in some detail the University's innovative program, Ethiopian University Service (EUS), as a way to provide students with educational enrichment through practical experiences,

---

* These statistics do not include those church, mission, private, and Koranic schools that do not follow the govermnent's prescribed school curricula.

and, at the same time, to render valuable assistance to the country's development effort. Three areas of activity have been selected as examples of the direct public service contribution of the university: the evening extension program, the summer school in-service training for teachers and other educational personnel, and the participation of members of the University staff in the major and comprehensive Education Sector Review undertaken by the country in 1971-72.

BEGINNING OF MODERN HIGHER EDUCATION: LEGACIES OF HAILE SELASSIE I UNIVERSITY

Although the University was established in 1961, its antecedents included a number of colleges instituted a decade earlier by the government. The University College of Addis Ababa was founded in 1950 to train personnel in education and administration and to provide basic preparation in medicine, public health, and engineering. The University College provided the foundations for the present faculties of arts, science, education, business administration, and, to a large extent, the Extension Department and was led and staffed mainly by Canadians recruited and paid by the Ethiopian government.

The College of Engineering was created in 1952 by the Ministry of Education and Fine Arts and was staffed and administered by a team of educators from Europe and North America. It is interesting to note in passing that the first director of the school proposed that half-time class work and half-time practical training in factories should be a regular feature of the College's program.

The College of Agriculture and Mechanical Arts was established in 1952 in the eastern part of the country at Alemaya. It was supported by USAID and planned and administered through a contract with Oklahoma State University, a land-grant institution. The College was run under the supervision of the Ministry of Agriculture.

The Building College, which is now part of the faculty of technology, was started in 1954 as the Ethio-Swedish Institute of Building Technology to train middle-level building technicians and to undertake research on the use of local materials in low-cost housing construction. The Institute was supported by the Swedish International Development Agency and staffed with Swedish personnel supplied through the agency.

The Public Health College was established in 1954 at Gondar, in the historic north central part of the country, in cooperation with WHO and USAID. Since its inception, the College has trained rural public health personnel, producing teams consisting of health officers, sanitarians, and community nurses. Practical work in rural health centers and stations has always been an important and integral component of the College curriculum.

Finally, the college division of the Theological College of the Holy Trinity was inaugurated in 1960 to train high-level personnel for church administration and for the mission of the Ethiopian Orthodox Church. In 1973, the church established a development commission, participated in the Education Sector Review, and started in-service training for the rural clergy, using graduates of the College.

In 1961, a university charter brought these colleges together as the nucleus of the University, each with its own history, its own purpose, its own form and style of organization and administration. Haile Selassie I University thus inherited these institutions with both their weaknesses and their strengths. In retrospect, it is the author's opinion that, for the state of the country's development and its preparedness, this diversity was a blessing in disguise. It is true that coordinating, harmonizing, and gradually fashioning these institutions into a coherent, purposeful, and integrated university required much time and energy that might not have been necessary if the University had begun from scratch. In many respects, however, the University was enriched by the diverse nature of its inheritance. The new university could not take anything for granted, nor could it rely on any one educational system. It had to argue and compromise. Usually, in the end, the test of acceptance or rejection of an idea was not its origin but its use to Ethiopia.

Another advantage to the University was its sponsorship. Both the colleges and the University were started and created by the Ethiopian government. As a result, degrees and diplomas did not, like those in many universities in Africa, have to await a sponsor from outside the country. Early attempts to encourage affiliation with European institutions and subsequent recognition of degrees were resisted and avoided.

The variegated nature of the programs in the incorporated colleges—ranging from degree-level to high school remedial courses for adults—gave the University, from the beginning, a complex and multipurpose character. Indeed, the incorporated colleges provided seeds for many attitudes and activities of the University. For example, the early concern for meeting national manpower needs, characteristic of the Public Health College and the Ethio-Swedish Institute of Building Technology, remained a strong feature of the new University. Concern for rural development and the exposure of students to practical training in the field was also exemplified by the Public Health College. University research oriented toward problems facing the development of the country was a feature of the building material and low-cost housing research of the Ethio-Swedish Institute and of the Debre Zeit Experiment Station of the College of Agriculture. The newly established faculty of education, moreover, retained and expanded several features of the University College of Addis Ababa: its admission of experienced schoolteachers without the usual requirement of the Ethiopian School Leaving Certificate Examination and the summer in-service training. The University College's extension program, the ad hoc courses given by the Engineering College, and the agricultural extension services of the College of Agriculture were also the precursors of the expanded University extension activity. *

Before the government decided to incorporate these colleges into a university, it appointed a commission on higher education. [1] In addition to several other recommendations, the commission strongly advised the government to establish a "service type" institution with a mission and orientation similar to the land-grant and other state universities of America.

A DECADE OF THE UNIVERSITY'S EXISTENCE

When Haile Selassie I University was established in 1961 as a national institution of higher education, its staff and administration spent considerable time developing and promulgating the rules and regulations[2] governing its activities. These regulations dealt with the membership of standing committees and their terms of reference, staff affairs, major educational policies of admission, graduation requirements, the grading system, the curricula, the organization of faculties, colleges and schools, research institutes, the library, student affairs, the Ethiopian University Service, and other matters of special concern to the newly established University. The formerly autonomous colleges, with different academic traditions, now had to pull together to support each other and to fit into a centrally coordinated, coherent system serving the needs of the society.

In the course of its development, the University added the faculties of education, medicine, and law, the College of Business Administration, and the School of Social Work to the older colleges, schools, and faculties of engineering, agriculture, public health, theology, building technology, arts, and science. The small extension unit within the faculty of arts was expanded into a separate administrative unit to coordinate all extension activities within the University.

University Growth

The University started with fewer than 900 students, a staff of 100, of whom only a handful of the professionals were Ethiopian, and an annual recurrent budget of U.S. $3.5 million. Ten years later, it had over 5,500 regular day students, a sixfold increase, while its extension enrollment had increased nearly threefold and its summer

*The extension activities of the Agriculture College were later transferred to the Ministry of Agriculture.

in-service teacher's program almost tenfold. The total student
enrollment, including part-time students, had grown from 2,166 in
1961-62 to over 10,700 students at the beginning of 1973-74. By this
date also the academic staff had increased to over 545, and the
proportion of Ethiopians, including academic administrators, had
increased to over 70 percent. The cumulative number of graduates
in the same period had increased from 221 to 9,507, of whom 3,695
received degrees, 4,779 diplomas, and 1,033 certificates.

During the same decade, the recurrent cost per student per
year decreased from U.S. $1,970 to U.S. $1,240* (without taking into
account foreign assistance). Although a decrease in cost was judged
to reflect to some degree the level of efficiency reached, it was
beginning to affect the quality of education, and the University community showed anxiety and discontent on this score. [3]

Review of Educational Developments

In the midst of accommodating increasing student enrollment and
resulting practical problems, universities sometimes spend too little
time reflecting upon their mission. To be sure, theoretical guidelines
might be found in their acts or charters, in the curricula of the colleges
and faculties, and in the actual university teaching. At the time the
writer assumed the office of University president, an effort was made,
in close cooperation with the then academic vice-president, to make
an explicit statement of the educational philosophy of the University.
The statement is reproduced below.

> As the university has grown, we have asked ourselves:
> What is its character to be? There is now clearly a
> need to begin to identify particularly some basic goals
> and articulate values underlying planning and our hopes
> for the future.
> That need is particularly forced upon us as our
> permanent staff will soon become over 50% of our
> total staff, and because this group, composed of many
> new staff-members, will most influence educational
> development; because new foreign staff must also
> catch the spirit of the University and work within the
> framework of its philosophy, because one cause of
> student unrest is—as younger citizens say—our failure,
> sometimes, to be relevant, to be concerned.

*The corresponding figures in Ethiopian dollars are Eth. $4,925
and Eth. $3,100.

Over the recent years,... I think a number of
elements in our basic philosophy have been developed.
Some of these are noted below.

We must recognize that the burden on the tax-
payer of higher education in Ethiopia, is, in relative
terms, exceedingly heavy. The University must be
seen as an investment in their behalf for the future.
Viewed as such, it must continously develop and
adapt and reform its training programs at all
levels. It must attempt to fill gaps, where called upon,
to provide training at post-secondary levels through
extension and part-time programs of various sorts.
It must relate in all sorts of ways to its "consumers,"
for example, the Ministries of Health, Agriculture
and Education, as it plans, evaluates itself and
develops its philosophy.

We must continuously make clear the University's
commitment to the values of sacrifice, service, work,
and greater social justice. This is a commitment of
individuals, of teachers and students alike. We must
avoid the danger of fostering the wrong kind of
essentially selfish, individualist, "elite" attitudes
which may have begun to characterize some other
universities in the developing world. It is simply
wrong, in my view, for staff and students to be pre-
occupied with white-collar, status-oriented, high-
salary jobs. Development means hard work—labor on
the farms, in health stations, in construction, in
factories, and in schools; higher education must more
strongly emphasize the dignity of labor, the value
of achievement through manual work as well as other
work.

We must make our curriculum more relevant
to the urgent problems of development and the hard,
inevitable choices at hand when development is
planned. Slogans about land reform, tax reform,
social reform, and other reforms may serve a
catalytic purpose, but slogans too often conceal
rather than expose the hard underlying problems
to be solved. The University must present these
problems and the resulting issues objectively and
realistically ... to all students to some degree.

Our educational philosophy must be <u>innovative</u>,
<u>not imitative.</u> We must learn—though it is sometimes
hard to teach the lesson to some University teachers—
that valid education is not simply a process of amassing
course credits according to some pre-ordained curriculum;
nor is education always fostered by listening to didactic
lectures and acquiring information. The experience
which constitutes a "higher education," in Ethiopia at
least, should include extensive work in the field, notably
in the country's less-developed rural areas, but also in
government offices, businesses, hospitals—wherever the
hard problems are. The experience must aim at
developing more self-reliance and initiative, and in
particular, capacities to work out problems in disciplined,
practical ways.

We must recognize the danger that the University
can too easily become "soft"; it may become a community
lacking tough intellectual discipline, a place where people
do not engage in enough sacrifice nor in very hard work,
a place where flabby generalizations and opinions are
substituted for careful research and objective reasoning.
We must never equate ideals of "academic freedom
and tenure" with a false philosophy which assumes that
increments and promotion automatically occur . . . .
Teachers should be ruthless in imposing both the
highest standards and the toughest work-demands on
themselves.

The University community must live under law,
for no university which becomes a lawless place, a
society where polemics and propaganda replace reason
and scholarship, will long preserve the spirit of a
university. . . . feeling and passion can hardly be recognized or condoned by adults as substitutes for intellectual discipline. [4]

Although this philosophy may not have been manifested in all aspects
of University work, it has permeated the University's major
undertakings.

Admission Policies

One of the tragedies of university educational systems is the
inflexible use of examinations as the only way to promote students from
one level of education to the next. In Ethiopia's highly competitive

system of education, where only about 20 percent of those who sit for the secondary school leaving examination pass, the psychological tension, social frustrations, and financial waste are immense. Though a large number of students were admitted to the University by examination, the University also introduced a number of other effective admission methods, some of which more accurately predicted students' college performance.

Among those admitted on a different basis were experienced teachers who were graduates of teacher training colleges, students from the special grade 12 preparatory course in the University's laboratory school, and a limited number of well-qualified graduates from technical schools, the Polytechnic Institute, agricultural high schools, the Community Development Training Program, and grade 12 health service training courses. These students were admitted into the various colleges and faculties of the University without an examination, in accordance with their previous preparation and work experience.[5]

Meeting Manpower Needs

At the time the University was established, Ethiopia did not have a specific manpower study or policy to use as a guideline. The University, therefore, developed a pragmatic approach, providing needed manpower not only at the degree level but also at the middle and certificate levels. Higher priority was given to such faculties as education, agriculture, public health, and engineering than to those of arts, social sciences, law, and related areas. The University's freshman program, into which all new students were channeled, admitted over 60 percent of its students into the science streams and less than 40 percent into the arts and social sciences stream. The University was also responsive to requests coming from ministries to organize new programs to meet demonstrated critical needs, such as the diploma program for land surveyors and the accelerated course for secondary school science teachers started at Alemaya.

In order to fix priorities and relate University development to national plans, a permanent University Planning Office was created. The office linked University staff, from department and faculty up to senate and council, in the University planning process. [6]

Curriculum Development and Research

The adaptation of curricula to Ethiopian needs and problems was a continuing concern of the University staff. It was to meet this concern that the Unesco Tananarive Conference on African Higher Education in the early 1960s, as well as the Association of African Universities' Accra Workshop a decade later emphasized this aspect of African university development. At Haile Selassie I University, curriculum was continually discussed, and improvements were suggested by the various departments and faculties.

The University was from the outset involved with the rural conditions of Ethiopia through its public health training, its building program, and its summer in-service training for elementary school teachers. The Faculty of Medicine had also organized a rural health training center in which all its students participated.

The Ethiopian University Service program, in which all students served for one academic year in rural areas, was established to expose students to·rural Ethiopia as well as to add practical experience to their education. More will be said about this program later. It is sufficient to note here that the EUS was an educational and curricular innovation practiced across the faculties of the University.

Research in the University was severely limited by heavy teaching loads, inadequate financial resources, a rapid turnover of teaching staff, and the absence of procedures to evaluate staff performance. Nevertheless, research activities, though limited, were in a number of cases geared to developing and publishing teaching materials and to investigating and solving rural problems. Thus, for example, the staff of the Law Faculty developed and published several books, monographs, and supplementary materials based on the Ethiopian codes to be used as teaching aids; the Institute of Development Research[7] was established to promote research in the social and behavioral sciences, with its main focus on rural development; and the Institute for Scientific and Technological Research and Development was set up to "promote and foster the application of science and technology in the development of commerce and industry, the discovery and development of methods for the utilization of natural resources, the industrialization of the country..."[8] These examples have been cited not because of any extraordinary research output, but because they indicate the orientation of the university.

Staff Development

One of the most serious and critical problems faced by most universities in Africa is the development of local staff. Haile Selassie I University was no exception. When the University was inaugurated, only a handful of Ethiopians, graduates of the various colleges who had been sent abroad for advanced training, were available for employment. Thus in 1961-62, nationals constituted about 30 percent of the teaching staff, and this proportion included instructors and advanced technicians. In 1972-73, the Ethiopian staff, including senior academic administrators, was over 70 percent.

The University achieved this increase in little more than a decade in several ways. It first established a large number of positions for "graduate assistants"[9] in the various departments and colleges. The best graduates of the University were selected by the departments, approved by the deans, and further appraised by the academic vice-president. They were then employed on probation for one year, renewable for another year. A faculty committee awarded scholarships for further training abroad* on the basis of their performance and on recommendation of the deans. In this way, the University sent 40 to 50 individuals to foreign universities every year and got back about the same number. For example, during the 1972-73 academic year, 45 staff members returned while 119 staff members were receiving further advanced training abroad.[10] A small permanent office under the academic vice-president was set up to supervise this program, to keep staff abroad informed of University developments, to maintain liaison with the scholarship committee and the donors, and to provide necessary administration.

At the beginning of the 1970s, the University realized that it was not enough to select the university where the candidate would do advance work. He or she must come back to do field work on a real problem of the country. Ways had to be found to expose him to experiences outside the University, to give him courses in teaching methods, and to arrange for regular refresher courses. These approaches, however, had not yet been fully implemented when the formal programs of the University were suspended. They constitute some aspects of the future direction staff development and promotion policies should follow.

THE ETHIOPIAN UNIVERSITY SERVICE

University education in Ethiopia, as in many other countries of Africa, is a privilege of a tiny minority. How to educate this minority so that its expertise and know-how benefit and serve the many becomes a challenge to university educators. Both historically and currently, education has tended to be too theoretical, too abstract, hardly touching on the real and fundamental problems of rural transformation. In several cases, education has resulted in alienation of the educated from their socioeconomic and political milieu and has uprooted them from their own history and culture. The excessive, if understandable, use of foreign teachers, texts and other books, and all other forms of teaching materials in schools and universities further accentuates and exacerbates the situation. Out of concern for these and other

*Valuable scholarships and fellowships supplied by the various donor agencies are gratefully acknowledged.

questions, the staff, students, and administration of the University inaugurated, in April 1964, the EUS program, which required students to serve for one academic year, mainly in the rural areas of Ethiopia.

Historical Background

It has been mentioned that some of the earlier colleges that made up the University had shown signs of concern about the nature of the education their students were receiving and early involved them in practical welfare activities. Thus, the Public Health College from the beginning prescribed a good dose of practical training in rural areas. The Ethio-Swedish Institute of Building Technology involved students in identifying and improving the use of local building materials. Some staff and students of the University College of Addis Ababa organized a group to teach shepherds literacy, using mobile teams. A student organized a literacy program for Addis Ababa's shoeshine boys. In the early years of the University, much interest was expressed in the poems and debates of the students and in the concerns of the organized student unions, such as the National Union of Ethiopian University Students (NUEUS), which in its annual meeting in 1961 selected the theme "What can we, as students, do for our country?" A few Ethiopian staff members also showed interest in service activities and advocated designing a more meaningful education adapted to Ethiopia's needs. One staff member wrote to the then president of the University:

> After spending one year's service in the rural areas, the students will become more conscious of their home problems and thus their education will be more meaningful to them. Mastering a book written either by an American or a European will have no real meaning unless we can determine the points which will be applicable to our own country... It [education] also becomes a highway to service and does not merely remain a ladder for personal promotion and accumulation of wealth... [11]

As the idea of rural service as part of the University program gained momentum, two committees were established to consider the practicability of the project and to present a draft statute to the executive committee of the Faculty Council. Ultimately, a full session of the council approved the program and ratified the statute in April 1964, decreeing that the first group of students should start in September 1964. The program was subsequently approved by the University's board of governors and welcomed by the government.

Under the statute,[12] students were required to spend one academic year while the University was in session working in the field to serve rural communities or aid national welfare. They could receive their degrees or diplomas only after their service obligation was completed. The program of service was to be carried out in collaboration with government ministries and other appropriate agencies, and students were to be expected to meet the requirements and standards of these agencies while engaged in service. But the administration of the program—planning, orientation, assignment, liaison, and logistical arrangements—would rest with the University in accordance with the basic premise that the EUS is a part of the University's education program. Providing services to local communities in this way was held to be not only beneficial to the nation but also educationally valuable to the students, helping them to understand the problems and needs of their country, particularly in its less developed areas.

The Program in Action

Although the intention of the program was to assign students to work using their field of study, placements were often unrelated to academic interests. Owing to the pressing need for teachers, especially in the rapidly expanding junior high schools of the nation, a large number of students (110 out of 129) of the first group were assigned to teach. The Ministry of Education was ready and willing to place the students in local schools, and it was easier for the University administration in the beginning to deal with only one agency. Nineteen students, however, were placed in nonteaching positions in the first year. Between 1964-65 and 1973-74, 3,759 students participated in the scheme (see Table 4.1). Of these, 2,771 were assigned to teaching and 988 to nonteaching jobs (see Table 4.2). Over a third of the students placed in teaching jobs were in the Faculty of Education.

Students worked in all parts of the nation. In nonteaching areas, students of the Building College served as building supervisors in the elementary school building program; law students were assigned to the Ministry of Justice and other governmental or semigovernmental institutions; students of social work participated in urban and rural community development activities of the Ministry of National Community Development or worked in the hospitals of the Ministry of Health; pharmacy students were placed with the provincial hospital services; and a number of agriculture students worked with the Ministry of Agriculture and related organizations.

The EUS administration had its own limited budget and a core of full-time supervisory staff. It oversaw the smooth running of the program, including student orientation, assignment, visiting assigned

TABLE 4. 1

Ethiopian University Service: Student Participation

Academic Year	Number of Participants
1964–65	129
1965–66	189
1966–67	261
1967–68	349
1968–69	394
1969–70	558
1970–71	472
1971–72	561
1972–73	303*
1973–74	543
Total	3,759

*Decrease due to 1971–72 student disturbance.
Source: EUS figures.

TABLE 4. 2

EUS Participants 1964–74 by Faculty and Type of Assignment

Faculty*	Teaching	Nonteaching	Total
Agriculture	317	149	466
Arts (including Social Sciences)	394	61	455
Business Administration	456	85	541
Education	1,134	17	1,151
Law	12	169	181
Pharmacy	1	82	83
Science	195	62	257
Social Work	14	72	86
Technology	186	291	477
Theology	62	—	62
Total	2,771	988	3,759

*The following units of the university do not participate in EUS: Directors' and supervisors' course, Faculty of Education; Summer school teachers' in-service course; University extension; Public health college; Faculty of Medicine.

Source: EUS figures.

students, liaison with employing agencies, planning future placements, and evaluating the program. The administrative unit was in direct touch with the students. It provided each student with a basic living kit, including first aid kit, folding bed, chair, and table, and in some cases, a water filter and kerosene lamp. Although the administrative unit was largely autonomous, it was earlier attached to the extension division of the University and lately moved to the School of Social Work, which has special expertise in community and rural development.

At one time, the orientation program (which was not especially successful) was given a few weeks before students went to their field placements, but more recently it was given during the second semester of the third year and included lectures and discussion on carefully selected major problems of Ethiopian society in general and rural communities in particular. Orientation included the administrative problems of education, methods of teaching, community development, health practices, problems of change, and the relation to development of agriculture, education, and law enforcement. The course carried one credit hour.

Major Difficulties Encountered

It would be naive to imagine that a program of this nature could operate without difficulties. The program indeed faced several. The very novelty of the idea was a problem to some staff and some nonuniversity people who tend to equate university education with classroom instruction. Although many of the teaching staff strongly supported the program, others gave it low priority. When asked to spare a few days or more for EUS evaluation trips, some staff members concocted excuses to avoid the trip, and others took advantage of the evaluation trip for other studies. Thus, the first group of difficulties came from the University itself.

Success in assigning students in fields related to their training depended on the cooperation of the various governmental and nongovernmental agencies, who seldom could be persuaded to use undergraduates. The usual excuse was budgetary limitation. Yet these very agencies complained of the theoretical nature of university education. The University tried to get ministerial sanction, but assignment was largely dependent upon the whim of the official at the top of the particular agency.

The third major problem was the lack of funds to employ more staff to counsel and supervise students more regularly and systematically, to provide teaching aid kits, to purchase essential vehicles for transportation, to employ staff to evaluate the program, and to provide post-service or in-service workshops and conferences. As a result, students complained that once assigned to a distant region little communication existed and that they felt neglected and cut off from what was going on in the University. Students also complained that their allowance was inadequate and irregularly remitted, and there were often conflicts with colleagues, administrators, or people in the community because of the students' lack of experience.

Lastly, and especially in the early 1970s, the politicization of the students in general, and some of the activities at the local level in particular, brought them into direct conflict with governmental and police authorities, who consequently developed a feeling of antagonism toward the University.

Achievements of the Program

Despite these and several other constraints, the EUS existed for a decade. When it began, it was a lone pioneer in African higher education circles: now there are similar programs throughout the continent. It may be too early to be sure of its major contributions, but some positive conclusions may be drawn from the answers to questionnaires (administered to students and employers), from staff and student evaluation reports, and from general observations.

The Schooled Become Educated

In the circumstances in which it was created and subsequently, the major contribution of the program was to the University students themselves. Their education was made richer by practical experience. Living and working with the rural population gave them "the experience of performing a full-time job, with all the attendant responsibilities and restrictions, satisfactions and frustrations... the experiences of feeding, housing and clothing themselves and budgeting their money, and the chance to see the relevance or otherwise of their education. "[13] It was generally agreed among the faculty that the students came back more mature and more practical and more "realistic in their approach. "

The students themselves said they returned with more insight into the problems of their country. The majority felt that the experience was rewarding and thus worth continuing, with improvements. [14] All the students with whom the writer spoke, without exception, attested to the value of the program for their education and to its contribution to the nation. It seems thus that the major purpose for which it was created was fulfilled satisfactorily.

Contribution to Ethiopian Education

There seems no doubt that University students contributed to the expansion of school enrollment and to the enlargement of the teaching force. They also improved the local schools to which they were assigned by organizing such activities as night sessions to help weak students and by their frequent willingness to carry an excessively heavy teaching load. We have seen that some 2,771 of them taught classes, and, if we assume the average class to have between 40 and 45 pupils, it is clear that over 120,000 schoolchildren received schooling from the University students. Furthermore, if one compares the average salary for teachers at this level of education (Eth. $350 per month, according to the Ethiopian Civil Service Personnel Salary Scale) and the $175 per month allowance given to the EUS student, even when the budgeted overhead cost of the University for the ten years is subtracted, the Ministry of Education has saved over $3.8 million by employing EUS students instead of regular Ethiopian teachers. * The amount saved would double or triple if calculated on the basis of salaries for teachers imported from abroad; the foreign exchange saving is also no small contribution to the country.

Contribution to the Overall Development of Ethiopia

It has been shown that 988 students were placed in nonteaching assignments: in rural hospitals, in community development centers, in the courts, in construction work, in geological explorations, in agricultural research stations, and in several other activities. Although it may be difficult to put a money value on their services, it is clear that had it not been for these students, several of the activities either would not have been performed or would have meant a large financial burden to the nation. In addition, student contributions ranged from assisting researchers to demonstrating how to grow better vegetables, from literacy night sessions to weekend voluntary coaching to students needing help, from classroom sports activities to drives to establish or improve school and public libraries.

Contribution to the Image of the Educated

In a country where the few educated end up living and working in urban areas with little or no desire to serve in rural areas, the presence of thousands of university students living and working amidst the rural population, even for a brief period, had a positive effect. The students took the University to the people in all directions. Their presence challenged the oft-repeated complaint that the educated are not willing to serve the rural people.

-----

*2,771 x $350 x 10 months - [(2,771 x $175 x 10 months) + ($100,000 x 10)] = $3,849,250.

An Example to Others

Andrew and Diana Quarmby, of the International Secretariat for Volunteer Service, were right when they wrote, "[A] major achievement [of the EUS] and perhaps in the long run its most significant and far-reaching one, is to prove to the rest of the world that such a student service program is both feasible and potentially very valuable. The EUS's pioneering experience will prove invaluable to other countries contemplating such a program."[15] Recent discussions in several other African countries and universities seem to confirm the above contention.

The Future of EUS

The idea of requiring practical training as a component of formal education has a long history in several countries of the world. The medical profession and to a lesser degree the legal profession have insisted on practical performance. Countries outside Africa such as China, Russia, and the United States and, more recently, Cuba, have experimented with it. Within Africa, the governments of Zambia, Tanzania, and Zaire have already prescribed national service requirements for their students. Ghana and Nigeria require a one-year national service from all university graduates outside of the university operation. Kenya is actively considering the requirement of national service from its students before too long. These, however, are all governmental requirements: Ethiopia's was a pregraduation university requirement. The eight-month practical experience required of its students by the Institut Polytechnic Rural at Koulikoro, Mali, is an educational requirement similar to that of Ethiopia.

Despite the differences, the importance of practical education seems to have gained momentum in Africa[16] to such an extent that a number of countries have called for major overhaul of the educational system at all levels. Two education sector reviews—one in Ethiopia[17] in 1972 and one in Sierra Leone in 1973—were undertaken to look at educational needs. The Ethiopian review recommended the creation of an Ethiopian National Service, which, in the initial phase, would invite secondary school leavers to volunteer and gradually, over two or three years, convert to a compulsory universal service. The review suggested that secondary school leavers be required to serve before being considered as candidates for institutions of higher learning. In some circles in Ghana too, the writer was told, thought is being given to the possibility of requiring national service of secondary school leavers. Tanzania recently announced the abolition of direct entry from secondary schools into the university; secondary school leavers must first work in rural areas to prepare them "for

work in national development. "[18] These moves will necessitate further
thought on how, in what manner, and for how long to require practical
experience in the university curriculum. It is hoped, however, that
university people will take this opportunity to introduce a more
creative and flexible program rather than to do away with university
work-study programs altogether.

The EUS program was visited and commented upon by several
teams from inside and outside Africa. It was described by the
University of Zambia team as a "most impressive venture... an
attempt to find the true identity of interest that should link academic
work with the real situations of people's lives," and by Lord Ashby,
quoting an American educator, as "an inspiration of genius." It
would be a pity if such a program should give way to a new one which
did not incorporate its considerable strengths.

THE PUBLIC SERVICE ROLE OF THE UNIVERSITY

The normally accepted functions of the university—teaching,
research, and the dissemination of knowledge—are public services in
the true sense of the words. In this section, the extension, or continuing education, involvement of Haile Selassie I University will be
briefly presented. Three aspects of the University's activities have
been selected—namely, extension, or part-time teaching; summer
in-service training; and the involvement of members of the University
staff in the comprehensive Education Sector Review undertaken by
Ethiopia in 1972.

The Extension Activities

As mentioned earlier, some of the colleges incorporated into
the University had already been involved in organizing part-time
evening and Saturday classes for adults, largely for civil servants,
employees of quasi-governmental agencies, and the business community. The importance of public service through extension was
emphasized in the report of the international team appointed by the
government to study higher education in Ethiopia. Thus, shortly
after the creation of the University, the extension division of Haile
Selassie I University was set up as an independent administrative
unit, with rules and regulations laid down by the Faculty Council. [19]
The extension division was made the coordinator of and responsible
for all continuing education activities in the University.

Although it started by merely continuing the activities of the
various colleges, the extension division gradually consolidated and
created new courses and expanded the number of extension students,
not only within the several units of the main campus, but also in the

branches subsequently established at Asmara (northern Ethiopia), Harrar (eastern Ethiopia), and at Debre Zeit (40 kilometers southeast of Addis Ababa). A legal training course was also given for two years at Jimma (in the southwestern part of the country) and at Dire Dawa for three years. According (mainly) to first-semester enrollment figures, the number of extension students increased from 1,026 in 1961-62 to 2,784 in 1971-72 and 3,448 in 1973-74 (Table 4.3). Of the 3,448 extension students in 1973-74, a total of 1,279 were following degree-level courses, while 2,169 were enrolled in nondegree-level courses.

TABLE 4.3

Enrollment in the Extension Division

Academic Year	Number of Students
1961-62	1,026
1962-63	1,457
1963-64	1,458
1964-65	1,523
1965-66	1,535
1966-67	1,750
1967-68	1,800
1968-69	2,562
1969-70	2,261
1970-71	2,221
1971-72	2,784
1972-73	3,292
1973-74	3,448

Source: Compiled by the author.

Program of Studies

The level and nature of the courses offered varied with the interest of the students as well as the availability and capabilities of the University staff. Thus, at the beginning, some remedial secondary-level courses in languages, mathematics, and other subjects were given. These were later dropped when a number of second-level institutions began to offer them. The extension courses were then organized at certificate, diploma, and degree levels, the level depending on the needed skill and the educational level of participants. Most courses were offered in English, with a small number in Amharic, the national language. The University legislation stipulated that the respective faculties were responsible for the academic supervision of the degree-level courses, and the extension division for the

academic supervision of diploma and certificate level courses and
for the administrative backup of all levels of training.

The extension program covered such areas as business and
public administration, accountancy, the social sciences, law, and
education at degree level; public administration, accounting,
economics, social work, law, secretarial sciences, political science
and government, education, highway technology, civil, electrical
and mechanical engineering, statistics, and library science at diploma
level: and certificate courses in law and statistics.

A total of 135 courses[20] were given during the first semester
of 1972-73: 92 courses at the central campus, 23 at the technology
campus, 14 in Asmara, 12 in Harrar, and six in Debre Zeit. During
1973-74, there were 140 courses given, of which 51 were degree
level and 99 diploma and certificate level. Of these courses, 113
were in education, management, law, and related fields, while only
27 were in scientific and technological subjects.

A large proportion of the faculty members came from the regular
staff of the University, while others were recruited from government,
industry, and business, screened and approved by the respective
department heads of the various faculties.

The number of students graduating from the extension division
has also increased from year to year (Table 4.4). From 1963 to 1974,

TABLE 4.4

Number of Graduates by Year and Type of Diploma

| Year | Type of Diploma | | | Total |
	Degree	Diploma	Certificate	
1962-63	12	—	10	22
1963-64	22	—	26	48
1964-65	6	34	21	61
1965-66	13	72	55	140
1966-67	9	99	—	108
1967-68	24	226	—	250
1968-69	40	286	111	437
1969-70	28	181	230	439
1970-71	23	192	148	363
1971-72	34	105	6	145
1972-73	26	470	6	502
1973-74	15	297	4	316
Total	252	1,962	617	2,831

Source: Compiled by the author.

the extension division graduated a total of 2,831 students, 252 with
degrees, 1,962 with diplomas, and 617 with certificates. As all

these graduates were taking these courses while working, it is greatly hoped that their training has enabled them to improve their services, thus directly benefiting themselves, their employers, and their country.

Major Difficulties Encountered

The development of extension activities faced several major difficulties. The greatest obstacle, and the one with the broadest consequences, was the limited and narrow view the staff had of the nature, philosophy, and mission of university extension, especially in a society like Ethiopia's, which is largely composed of illiterate, subsistence-level farmers. The staff tended to transpose the admission requirements, kinds of courses, and methods of teaching used in teaching a young, inexperienced, unpaying population to an experienced, paying, and highly motivated adult population. Staff members at times gave the impression that they felt the only difference between the two was that day courses started with sunrise and the evening courses with sunset. In addition, some of the staff did not consider that their duty to extension work had high priority. This feeling that extension was second best was demonstrated in the kind of legislation suggested, in the failure of academic administrators to oversee the work of the extension teaching staff, and in other ways. The whole University had not yet accepted the commitment to take the expertise of the University to the people and to involve itself in solving their problems rather than wait for them to come to the University campus. As a result, University extension did not spread beyond the three or four major urban centers of the country.

The extension division clearly suffered also from financial and budgetary limitations. Manifestations of this situation were the lack of much needed permanent core teaching, supervisory, and research staff, the failure to improve extension libraries, and the very inadequate physical facilities at the disposal of the extension service.

Another important weakness of the program was, as implied above, the limitation of extension activities to the urbanized, already educated, modern sector, a tiny fraction of the population. Most extension students were teachers, bankers, lawyers, judges, parliamentarians, businessmen, civil servants, members of the police and armed forces, and technicians. With few exceptions, they are the products of modern education, relatively young (below 30), and well-to-do. A survey conducted by the extension division showed that more than 60 percent were earning Eth. $300-$400 per month—in a country where the per capita income is less than Eth. $200. Extension has touched only a small fraction of the population.

Summer School In-Service Activity

A major contribution of the University was the refresher course it gave to elementary-school teachers. The course was started in 1958 by the department of education of the University College of Addis Ababa, at the instigation of the Ministry of Education. Its original purpose was to select promising candidates for further training as secondary-school teachers, but it gradually became the major means for upgrading the teachers of the country's elementary schools in both subject matter and methods of teaching. A few of the students were later admitted to degree-level programs in the Faculty of Education. Graduates of this course are now to be found in almost every elementary school in the country. The course was, in addition, an excellent way for the ministry to communicate new policies and ideas, and to get feedback from the teachers. The Ethiopian Teachers' Association, now one of the most powerful professional associations in the country, was able to publicize its activities and to recruit members.

The in-service program steadily increased—it grew almost tenfold in a period of 13 years (Table 4. 5). Following consultations with Ministry of Education officials and in accordance with the interests of students, the program was also diversified to include

TABLE 4. 5

Summer School In-Service Enrollment

Summer of Academic Year	Number of Teachers
1961-62	192
1962-63	233
1963-64	351
1964-65	527
1965-66	512
1966-67	887
1967-68	833
1968-69	948
1969-70	1, 073
1970-71	1, 100
1971-72	1, 220
1972-73	1, 908
1973-74	1, 819*

*No new students were taken in two of the four programs owing to the phasing in of the newly revised program.

Source: Compiled by the author.

special training for elementary school principals, supervisors, and district education officers. In the early 1970s, the faculty added in-service training for junior secondary-school teachers, and in November 1973, organized a consultative workshop on the in-service program for senior secondary-school teachers. Thus, the program expanded to include training affecting the whole educational system. There is hardly a government primary school in the country that has not profited from this program, and two out of three school principals and almost all the supervisors of the country are graduates of the summer in-service training course. Ministry of Education officials, impressed with results, usually worked very closely with the faculty in evaluating, criticizing, and improving the course. The government also released ministry officials to conduct the courses with University staff so that courses could become more practical and more realistic. Table 4. 6 shows the program's enrollment in 1972 and 1973.

TABLE 4. 6

Summer School Programs and Enrollment

Nature of Program	Enrollment 1972	Total 1973*
Elementary-school teachers	1, 153	1, 096
School administrators and supervisors	497	450
Junior secondary school Amharic	211	175
Junior secondary school mathematics	139	98

*The general enrollment decrease was due to the phasing out of old programs and phasing in of new ones.

Source: Compiled by the author.

The program was also becoming financially self-sufficient. Originally, when the program began, the Ministry of Education paid for the trasport of students from their school to Addis Ababa and back, and provided living allowances. Later, students paid their own transportation and maintenance and also a large portion of their education with a U. S. $50 tuition fee per summer. In a country where education is free at all levels, where the government provides maintenance scholarships for all University students, this example might well be followed by others in the future. Indeed, the Education Sector Review recommended shifting the maintenance charge to students at the higher education levels and instituting a loan scheme for deserving, needy students.

University Involvement in the Education Sector Review

In 1972, Ethiopia undertook a comprehensive and fundamental review of its educational system. Over the past 30 years, there were several efforts to improve and reorient the system. A long-term planning committee, established in 1955, submitted a report entitled "A Ten-Year Plan for the Controlled Expansion of Ethiopian Education." Early in the 1960s, again in 1966, and several times thereafter, committees and commissions were established by the government to study and report on various aspects of the educational system. The continued discontent of the university and secondary-school students, at times violently expressed, gave birth to the National Commission for Education. But all these studies were limited. The Education Sector Review, which began in October 1971 and was completed in August 1972, was different from all the others in scope, method, overall approach, and organization. In fact, its approach was novel and experimental.

The tasks of the Education Sector Review were:

1. To analyze the education and training system of Ethiopia, and its capability for promoting economic, social and cultural development;
2. To suggest, wherever necessary, ways to improve and expand the education and training system in order that it might achieve aims relevant both to the society and the overall development of the country;
3. To suggest ways in which education could best be utilized to promote national integration; and
4. To identify priority studies and investments in education and training. [21]

Although the study was made with the active participation and financial contribution of the World Bank, the direction, conception, organization, and execution was largely in the hands of nationals. The study grouped together various representatives of ministries, agencies, professions, international organizations, and bilateral agencies.

The secretary general of the Ethiopian National Commission for Unesco, a graduate of the University, was appointed director of the review. Fourteen task forces and an additional five working groups were established. The membership of the task forces and working groups, excluding the professional members of the secretariat, numbered close to 90, of whom over 50 came from ministries, chartered agencies, and professions. The rest came from long-time foreign residents of Ethiopia and from international organizations. In addition, the review used an international panel of consultants, half of whom were Ethiopians, and a consultative committee consisting of the key personnel from the development and social services ministries. International consultants noted for their specific expertise were also employed. Members of the task force visited and consulted with the personnel of over 100 projects, institutions, and agencies in rural areas and urban centers. A questionnaire was supplemented by carefully selected interviews. The review organized two seminars and conferences, the first to pinpoint the problems and questions to be tackled by each task force and working group and to assess the methods and procedures suggested by them, and the second to evaluate the reports of the task forces and to agree on ultimate recommendations and proposals.

Each task force and working group presented its report to the second conference. All in all, there were some 65 documents prepared during the period of the review. [22] A summary of the discussion, major recommendations, together with the alternative strategies agreed upon, were presented in a report entitled Education: Challenge to the Nation.

University staff played a major part in the review. For several years, staff members had, without much fanfare, been used as consultants and as members of committees and commissions set up by various government ministries. Nothing, however, compared to the University's involvement, its top administrators as well as its staff, in the Education Sector Review (Table 4.7). Thirty-three out of 87 participants, ten out of the 14 task force chairmen, and four of the five chairmen of the working groups were University staff. If one includes the other members from the ministries and agencies who were graduates of the University—another 33—the impact of the University is seen to be even more pronounced. The University even made available its stationery and its publication machinery and staff to the sector review. It is not an exaggeration to assert that the single most powerful contribution to the review came from the staff of Haile Selassie I University.

The Future of Extension

The University was not fully satisfied, however, that it was preparing itself sufficiently for the challenge it would be facing in the near future. However valuable the extension, summer course, and other consultant service contributions of the University were to Ethiopia, the magnitude of unfinished business, especially in relation to the rural, provincial population, was formidable. In 1972, the University, aware of the task, was preparing to initiate a correspondence school as a unit of extension, and its library had instituted a successful innovative system of serving the rural audience through

TABLE 4. 7

Sector Review Manpower Deployment Table

Assignment	Total Participants	Of Whom			HSIU Staff Participation	
		HSIU Staff	HSIU Grads	Others	Chairmen	Members
Professional secretariat	4	1	2	1	—	1
International panel of consultants	4	1	—	3	—	1
Consultative Committee	4	1	2	1	—	1
14 task forces	68	26	29	13	10	16
5 working groups	7	4	—	3	4	—
Total	87	33	33	21	14	19

Source: Compiled by the author.

a "books-by-mail" system. The correspondence school was actively preparing teaching materials, and the books-by-mail project was demonstrating its usefulness beyond doubt. Meanwhile, the Education Sector Review had charted avenues for the University to follow in the immediate future. It thus seemed time to invite a team from outside, partly to assess the extension division but mostly to propose a forward-looking extension role for the University in cooperation with other institutions and agencies.

In 1972, therefore, the University invited a Unesco team to evaluate the performance of the extension division and to suggest new approaches. The team arrived in Ethiopia on July 23, 1972 and stayed until August 15. Its report, available in January 1973,[23] after critically examining the past and current activities of the extension division, its legislation, organization, administrative setup, program, and output, stated:

> In sum, it could fairly be said that what has been done,
> has been well done. Despite a clumsy, frustrating admin-
> istrative and decision making framework; a lack of human
> and material resources; and a lack of opportunities for the
> University authorities to concretise their insight regarding
> the realistic potential of a vigorous Extension to the devel-
> oping Ethiopian society; despite these restrictive elements,
> the growth, impact and significance of Extension has been
> substantial in the areas in which it has programmed.[24]

The team presented a new concept of university extension based on Ethiopian life styles—the already enunciated concept, mission, and objectives of the University. [25]

> Under this comprehensive concept of Extension, the
> university thus fulfills its role as a major animator
> of Ethiopian life and aspiration. Extension is means,
> mechanism, channel, medium between the university
> and society. But, as Marshall McLuhan has suggested,
> "the medium is the message"; so while Extension
> expresses the university's concern, knowledge,
> expertise and presence, Extension itself has its own
> character and quality that shapes the university's mes-
> sage to fit the life styles and learning needs of the
> university's varied publics away from the campus,
> throughout the Empire. [26]

To accommodate its comprehensive, perhaps idealistic concept of extension, the report suggested a structure and organization that related extension to the University administration and faculties on one side and the "target populations of Ethiopia" on the other.

Following the sector review and this evaluation, the University began to review its position and to consider whether or not to accept the several recommendations. But it seems clear that, with its past experience and commitment, and in view of the confident expec- tations of the participants of the sector review, whose report looked "forward to Haile Selassie I University and other higher educational institutions in the country being the inspiring fountainhead for... the educational regeneration of the country,..."[27] the University, its leadership, its staff, and its students will have to face the challenge confronting them.

NOTES

1. Higher education in Ethiopia: Survey Reports and Recom- mendations (Salt Lake City: University of Utah, 1959-60), pp. 21, 25-28.

2. Consolidated Legislation of the Faculty Council, Haile Selassie I University (HSIU) (with revisions up to 17 September 1973).

3. For more details, see Aklilu Habte, "Higher Education in Ethiopia in the 1970s and Beyond: A Survey of Some Issues and Res- ponses," in Education and Development Reconsidered, ed. F. Champion Ward (New York: Praeger Publishers, 1974), pp. 214-40; Aklilu Habte, A Forward Look: A Special Report from the President

(Addis Ababa: HSIU, 1969); John Summerskill, Blueprint for Development (Addis Ababa: HSIU, 1970); and several of the president's annual
reports to the board of governors.

4. Aklilu Habte, A Forward Look, pp. II-12 to II-16.

5. See Haile Selassie I University, Consolidated Legislation of
President's Annual Report 1972-1973, pp. xiv-xxiii.

6. For a detailed description of the planning process, see
President's Annual Report 1972-1973, pp. xiv-xxiii.

7. See Haile Selassie I University, "Statute of Institute of
Development Research", Consolidated Legislation of the Faculty
Council, pp. 96-99, and Institute of Development Research, Research
Activities (Addis Ababa: HSIU, 1973).

8. Aklilu Habte, "Higher Education in Ethiopia in the 1970s and
Beyond," p. 238.

9. For a detailed description of their status, see Haile Selassie
I University, Consolidated Legislation of the Faculty Council, pp. 43-44.

10. See Haile Selassie I University, President's Annual Reports
for details.

11. Quoted in HSIU Public Relations Office, The Ethiopian
University Service: An Inspiration of Genius (Addis Ababa: Haile
Selassie I University, March 1973), p. 9.

12. For details see Haile Sellassie I University, Consolidated
Legislation, pp. 56-64.

13. Andrew and Diana Quarmby, The Ethiopian University
Service, Report no. 76 (Geneva: International Secretariat for Volunteer Service, 1969), p. 26.

14. For further detail, see Kebebew Daka, "A Survey on the
Attitudes of EUS Participants Towards the Program and Related
Problems" (1973, mimeo.); HSIU Public Relations Office, The
Ethiopian University Service: An Inspiration of Genius; Andrew and
Diana Quarmby, The Ethiopian University Service; and D. C. and
F. F. Korten, "Ethiopia's Use of National University Students in a
Year of Rural Service," Comparative Education Review, 1966, 1969.

15. Andrew and Diana Quarmby, The Ethiopian University
Service, p. 28.

16. T.M. Yesufu (ed.), Creating the African University:
Emerging Issues of the 1970s (Ibadan: Oxford University Press,
1973), p. 48.

17. Education: Challenge to the Nation, Report of the Education
Sector Review (Addis Ababa, August 1972), pp. IV 20-21.

18. Tanzania Daily News, January 8, 1975. See also case
study on University of Dar es Salaam and special study by David
Court, in this volume.

19.   See Haile Selassie I University, <u>Consolidated Legislation</u> <u>of the Faculty Council,</u> pp. 84-86.

20.   1972-1973 Annual Report, Extension Division HSIU. This number does not include the multiple sections of several courses.

21.   <u>Education: Challenge to the Nation,</u> p. I-3.

22.   Listed in Annex VII of ibid.

23.   C.A. Wedemeyer et al. , <u>Evaluation of Extension at the</u> <u>Haile Selassie I University, Addis Ababa, July-August 1972</u> (Paris: Unesco, 1973), Serial No. 2838/RMO.RD/EHT.

24.   Ibid. , p. 30.

25.   Ibid. , pp. 38-41.

26.   Ibid. , p. 41.

27.   <u>Education: Challenge to the Nation,</u> Annex V, p. 8.

5

UNIVERSITY OF SCIENCE AND TECHNOLOGY,
KUMASI, GHANA

Technology at the Service of Rural and
Industrial Development

This study examines the extent to which higher education in
Africa is contributing to the economic development of the continent.
It confines itself to the role of technology in national development,
using as a case study the University of Science and Technology (UST),
Kumasi, and examining the way in which that institution places its
technological expertise at the service of rural and industrial development in Ghana.

HIGHER EDUCATION IN GHANA

The move for independence in Ghana started in the 1920s, a
decade that coincided with the governorship of the late Sir Gordon
Guggisberg, a man of deep foresight, enormous courage, and clear
vision: founder of Achimota College (now School), Korle Bu Hospital,
Accra (now Korle Bu Teaching Hospital), and builder of Takoradi
Harbor and of a strategic network of roads in the Gold Coast. In
founding Achimota College, Sir Gordon envisioned the College developing into an institution that would train the high-level manpower needed
for the country's development and for its administration after independence. His vision began to materialize in the 1930s when Achimota
College began offering courses up to intermediate B. Sc. (Lond) level
and up to the B. Sc. Eng. (Lond). Many students who took this course
completed their degrees overseas. The first engineering student
graduated in 1935. By the end of World War II, the demand for higher
education had become so great that the Elliot commission, set up by
the colonial secretary in London, recommended the establishment of
a university college in Ibadan, Nigeria, to serve all British West
Africa. The Gold Coast government of the day rejected this recommendation and decided to start its own institution. This institution was
eventually established in 1948 as the University College of the Gold
Coast, affiliated to London University. It was concerned mainly with

the humanities and social sciences and was geared to the training
of administrators for the civil service.

In 1952 the Kumasi College of Arts, Science, and Technology
was established. Both the University College and Kumasi College
became independent universities in 1961, on the recommendation of a
commission appointed by the government to examine the future of
university education in Ghana. At the same time, a third institution,
the University College of Cape Coast, affiliated to the University of
Ghana, Legon, was founded and charged with the responsibility of
training teachers of science in the secondary schools.

All three institutions have made, and are making, significant
contributions to the development of Ghana. The University of Ghana,
successor to the University College of the Gold Coast, trains administrators for the civil service, lawyers, doctors, agriculturists, and
scientists. Through its Institute of Adult Education, it is performing
valuable extension services, reaching the rural areas and offering
education at all levels to those who care to take advantage of the service. Its Institute of African Studies is conducting research into
African history and culture, and focusing attention on and educating
the public generally in Ghana's rich heritage.

Since it was founded, the University of Cape Coast has trained
hundreds of teachers of both arts and sciences for Ghana's secondary
schools and the impact on education of the country has been tremendous.

This study is concerned, however, with the role of technology
in national development, and it is therefore on the University of
Science and Technology, Kumasi, that we must focus our attention.

THE UNIVERSITY OF SCIENCE AND TECHNOLOGY, KUMASI

The University of Science and Technology, Kumasi, was
established in 1961 to succeed the former Kumasi College of Arts,
Science, and Technology. The College had been charged with training
middle-level subprofessional manpower for the technical and scientific
services. The courses were therefore short, leading to the award
of diplomas and certificates, although in later years courses leading
to the London University B. Sc. degree in engineering were offered.
The fields covered were teacher training, commerce, engineering,
pharmacy, agriculture, architecture, town planning and building, and
general studies. The University is situated on a campus seven square
miles in area south of Kumasi in the forest region. It is surrounded
by 16 small villages, a fact that gives it an unrivaled opportunity for
extension work.

As at most British-heritage universities, governance is handled
by a number of boards and committees, including the University

Council (the supreme governing body), the Academic Board (responsible for all academic matters), and the Welfare Services Board (responsible for all matters affecting the campus and welfare of personnel). The vice-chancellor is the administrative head of the University.

In its first five years the University expanded rapidly. A number of student residence halls and new academic buildings were constructed to replace the inadequate prefabricated structures used by the University's precursor, the Kumasi College of Technology. No new academic disciplines, however, were added during this period; the departments of teacher training, commerce, and general studies were transferred to other institutions, and academic development was thus marked by a certain instability.

The beginning of the second five years coincided with the military takeover in 1966, a time when the finances of the country were in dire straits, and little money was available for physical expansion. Steps were taken, however, to consolidate what had already been achieved to formulate clear-cut academic regulations, previously either nonexistent or woolly. Important plans were also laid for the future, culminating in the establishment of a Faculty of Social Science in 1970 and the Technology Consultancy Centre in 1972. More will be said later of this center, as its establishment marks an important milestone in the University's development.

At the close of the first decade of the University's existence, the University council appointed a committee to evaluate the University's role in national development. In his letter announcing the appointment of the committee, the chairman of the council stated:

> This university not only owes it as a duty, because it is financed 100% out of public funds, to integrate itself with the community on which it feeds but is also the most suited by its nature to make significant contributions to the economic, industrial and social development and advancement of this country and its people.... The study should and ought to reveal areas in which the university can make significant contributions to the future.

In what ways can a technological institution play a role in national development? The answer to this question requires a close examination of the three principal functions of the university—namely teaching, research, and service—and a determination of the extent to which these functions are being properly carried out. The following questions therefore need to be answered:

1. What is the scope of the teaching and training being carried out in the institution and how can it be improved?

2. Is the content of the curriculum relevant to the needs of the country?

3. What is the nature of research being done by the university? Is it relevant? What are its problems, and how can they be overcome?

4. What, if any, service does the university render to the community? What are its objectives? What are its problems and how can they be overcome? Is it effective?

5. Are the graduates of the institution equipped to carry out specified roles in the development process?

We shall now try to examine these questions as they relate to the UST.

The University offers courses leading to degrees in all faculties, and diplomas and certificates where appropriate. The University appreciates the pressing need for middle-level manpower and feels a responsibility to help in the training of personnel at this level. Its diploma and certificate courses are therefore designed to achieve this purpose until other institutions, such as the polytechnics, become sufficiently developed to take over this responsibility.

TRAINING

The seven University faculties are agriculture, architecture, art, engineering, pharmacy, science, and social studies. The teaching program is designed to produce both high- and middle-level manpower for the economy. The areas covered and the types of personnel produced are as follows:

Agriculture: horticulturists, plant producers and experts in plant protection, livestock farmers, farm managers, and agricultural engineers.

Architecture: architects (designers), building technologists, urban planners, physical planners, and regional planners.

Art: painters, sculptors, and industrial artists, such as ceramists, textile designers, graphic designers, and metal product designers.

Engineering: civil, geodetic (land surveying), electrical, mechanical, sanitary, highway, and mining engineers.

Pharmacy: general pharmacists, pharmaceutical chemists, pharmacologists, and microbiologists.

Science: biologists, biochemists, chemical technologists, and physicists.

Social Sciences: industrial managers, land economists, estate managers, administrators, and teachers.

The main courses are the four-year degree courses. In addition, at the postgraduate level, two-year master's and one- to two-year postgraduate diploma courses are offered. In certain faculties—agriculture, architecture, and engineering, for example—subdegree and certificate courses are given.

Practical Training

Whatever the course, practical training is an essential element and much time is spent in laboratories and workshops. During the long vacations all students are expected to spend a minimum of eight weeks acquiring practical training in industry or in an organization appropriate to the course being offered. During term time, students undertake field work in different parts of the country. All four-year courses require project work in the final year, which provides an opportunity for students to coordinate the practical and theoretical aspects of the training.

There have been problems with vacation training. Properly organized, it should help the student acquire practical industrial and professional experience during this training. At the initial stages, however, some students felt that the establishments to which they were sent provided too little opportunity for learning because facilities were inadequate or employers uncooperative. It must also be admitted that, in some cases, the students' own indifference and lack of interest in the training contribute little to their learning. By far the most important factors in the success of the plan, however, are proper coordination and cooperation between the department or faculty in the University and industry. Under the present plan a vacation training organizer arranges for students to be placed in various industrial organizations and members of the University staff visit the students to make sure that they are properly deployed. This process has not always been carried out effectively.

One major problem relating to the practical training of students is the lack of industrial experience of some lecturers. The University has sought to remedy this in two ways: (1) by arranging for some lecturers to spend varying periods in industry to acquire practical experience and (2) by engaging professionals as part-time lecturers to enable them to give the students the benefit of their practical knowledge. In addition, the University appoints professionals from industry as external examiners, especially in the practical examinations.

Training for Management

The importance of the Faculty of Social Sciences, established in 1970, cannot be overemphasized; students of science and technology must have some aspects of the social sciences incorporated in their training. In Ghana, as in other developing countries, young graduates often find themselves in positions of responsibility early in their career. Sometimes they have difficulties with personnel working under them, particularly at building or construction sites, and, especially in designing roads, houses, or other buildings, they do not always understand costs or the socioeconomic implications of their designs. In recent years, therefore, the University has provided, through its Faculty of Social Sciences, courses in management, human relations, and applied economics for all students pursuing professional courses.

Since its inception, the University has produced 3,083 graduates, subdegree diplomates, and certificate holders. All these products of the University occupy important positions in both the public and private sectors of the economy in Ghana and in other African countries; an increasing number are now going into the private sector and a few are starting their own businesses. Engineering graduates of UST constitute over 80 percent of engineers employed by the Volta River Authority, the Ghana Water and Sewerage Corporation, the Public Works Department, and the State Construction Corporation. Many former students of the University who were interviewed by the council Committee on the Role of the University in National Development felt that, on the whole, the training they obtained at UST was adequate and relevant to the work in which they are employed, subject to the practical-training content being improved.

Problems

Problems related to the training of professional technologists, particularly engineers, in a developing country, include the following:

Difficulty in Attracting Qualified Staff

As the teaching staff for professional courses in universities (and other higher educational institutions) must have both high academic and professional qualifications, the universities constantly compete with industry for their services. A professional is generally better paid in industry than in an educational institution. The relatively experienced professional engineer or architect, for example, can earn far more money in professional practice than he would if he taught full-time at a university. Highly qualified and brilliant university staff, therefore, see their compatriots with lesser academic

qualifications engage in successful professional practice, with its
concomitant material rewards, while they have to depend on relatively
low salaries (though with reasonable fringe benefits) in the university.
As a result, it is difficult to attract teachers to the university staff
and frequent resignations cause instability. In 1970, for example,
there was a mass exodus of staff from the Engineering Faculty of the
UST when 24 Ghanaian teachers resigned simultaneously over what
they considered to be low salaries. Many went into industry or set up
private professional practices, where the pecuniary rewards were
greater, and by all accounts they have done well. The University,
however, has not yet recovered fully from the blow dealt to the
teaching program by this episode.

Inadequate Professional Experience of Teaching Staff

In spite of what has been said above, the teaching staff of the
faculties of engineering in Africa, with few exceptions, have little
or no professional experience, though they are highly qualified academically, many having done postgraduate work up to Ph. D. level.
Teaching thus tends to be theoretical, and it is important that measures
should be taken to remedy this deficiency. Some of these have already
been mentioned and may be listed briefly as (1) vacation training for
all students, (2) arrangement for the teaching staff to spend short
periods in industry, (3) the employment of professionals from industry
for part-time teaching, and (4) consultancy work by staff (discussed
below).

Embryonic State of Industry

Most developing countries in Africa are primarily agricultural
countries, and it is natural that priority should be placed on the
development of agriculture. Whatever industry exists is usually small
scale, the stage of development varying from country to country.
Opportunities for the industrial training of students are therefore
limited. In developed countries, students of engineering, for example,
have many opportunities for visiting factories and working to gain
practical experience during their training. The sandwich courses
organized in certain institutions are possible only because industry
itself is highly developed, the planned assignments for specified
periods usually guaranteeing excellent industrial training for the
students.

Meager Facilities in the Universities

The training of technologists usually involves a wide variety of equipment, all of which has to be imported from abroad. This means that the foreign exchange component in the budget of an engineering faculty each year is quite high. Because financial resources in a developing country are severely limited, funds available for the university itself are usually inadequate. Practical training is thus hampered by limited accommodation in laboratories and workshops and by inadequate equipment. If the graduate engineer of the African university is accused of not having enough practical experience, it is because of this combination of factors. It can be said in his favor, however, that the sound theoretical training he receives makes it easy for him to adapt himself quickly to the peculiar demands of the sector of his profession or industry in which he may find himself.

RESEARCH

Perhaps one of the important differences between a technological university and a polytechnic, which also trains both high-level and middle-level personnel, is that whereas the latter confines itself to teaching and training, the university in addition concerns itself with research, with investigations that should lead to new knowledge.

Research can be regarded as being complementary to teaching in a university. It helps to keep the curriculum up to date and to make the teaching more forward looking and lively. From the point of view of the staff, it should help to develop and sharpen their intellect, and, provided the research is conducted in an atmosphere of absolute freedom, it helps to broaden their outlook and to make them open-minded. In universities in developing countries, however, scarcity of funds limits what can be done. Because of this relative lack of means, it is essential that the resources available should be spent on research efforts that are relevant to local circumstances and can be seen to contribute to national development.

It can be argued that in these circumstances there is little room for "fundamental" or "pure" research and that the emphasis should be on applied research, the former being considered irrelevant and the latter relevant. It must be pointed out, however, that no research can be looked upon as totally irrelevant, for, in the long term, even negative results are bound to indicate what should not be done or how to do better what should be done.

The vice-chancellor of the University, in introducing an appeal for funds to expand the University's activities, stated:

> The University of Science and Technology, Kumasi, has reached a stage in its development at which, whilst consolidating its gains, there is urgent need to lay plans for expansion in areas important to Ghana's economy. So far it has established itself as a first-rate teaching institution but, whereas a certain amount of research goes on, a serious restriction is placed on this most important activity owing to lack of funds.... If the University is to rank with the best in the world it is most important that research activity should be intensified. When the research undertaken is related directly to the country's development, the results properly applied, should be of immense benefit to the country.

Very little fundamental or pure research goes on in the University at present. Briefly the research objectives are (1) the development of import substitution products through investigation into natural resources, and, by so doing, the conservation of foreign exchange; (2) the promotion of small-scale industries that are labor intensive; and (3) the development of products that are cheap and so help reduce the cost of living.

Important Research Projects

Some of the important research projects, either completed or in progress, are as follows:

Faculty of Agriculture

Kenaf production: Kenaf is a plant that produces fiber of commercial importance. Since Ghana imports large quantities of fiber for the manufacture of bags for cocoa and other products, it is believed that this study, if it leads to improved yields and harvesting methods, will be of great economic importance to the country, as it can lead to cultivation of kenaf on a large scale with consequent improvement of and expansion in the fiber industry, a saving of foreign exchange, and an increase in employment. The Department of Biological Sciences is also doing work on the retting of kenaf.

Hybridization of pigs: An attempt is being made, by crossing imported and local varieties, to produce a strain with high meat content yet resistant to local environmental hazards.

Faculty of Architecture

The most important research work in progress is that into low-cost housing. The program is testing local materials, including soil and wood, and attempting to improve methods of design and construction for both the rural and urban low-income population. Low-cost demonstration houses have been built in all regions to demonstrate the applicability of these design and construction methods to rural and semirural areas.

College of Art

The textiles section of the Department of Industrial Art undertakes research into local dye materials. Over the years it has also developed a broad loom for use by village craftsmen, aimed at improving technology and increasing output. Research work is also in progress in the Pottery and Ceramics section into local clays for industrial use. This research is expected to lead to improvement in the manufacture of bricks, tiles, china, sanitary wares, polythene, and glass.

Faculty of Engineering

Research currently in progress in the Faculty of Engineering includes the following:

1. The development of a national standard for testing cement.

2. Investigation of the properties of Ghanaian clays to find out if they have suitable electrical and other properties for the manufacture of electrical insulators for power distribution and telecommunications.

3. The designing of a bore hole pump, which, when produced commercially, will provide a cheap means of pumping abundant clean water from wells and bore holes in the rural areas.

4. The designing of a hand-operated soil block press. This machine, designed for making stronger soil or adobe blocks for rural areas, will not only speed up the block-making process and thereby help to reduce labor and production costs, but also improve the actual construction of rural houses.

Faculty of Pharmacy

Investigation of local herbs and other natural products for their medicinal properties has led to notable results. Some local herbs have been found to contain well-known therapeutical substances, which can now be developed on a large scale by the pharmaceutical industry. Research in this field is a never ending process, as there are thousands of natural products awaiting investigation. There are also plans to establish a small pharmaceutical production unit.

Faculty of Science

The faculty collaborates in many of the research projects enumerated above. It has also instituted research into possibilities for the development of new industries, using natural resources, wastes, and byproducts of existing industries. A recent example is the manufacture of caustic soda from quicklime, a waste product of the Air Liquide factory at Tema. The faculty's Department of Chemical Technology has also surveyed local industries with a view to rationalizing or modernizing medium- or small-scale industries.

Problems

Inadequate finance and lack of essential equipment are two well-known obstacles to research. Some years ago, the University launched an appeal for funds, setting a target of ¢6 million* to be attained over a five-year period. This figure included provision for capital development, which accounted for about 70 percent of the estimates. The response to this appeal was disappointing. While in light of the economic conditions prevailing in the country, this target figure is now considered unrealistic, only about ¢300,000 (U.S. $261,000) has been received since the appeal was launched in 1968. Considering that almost half of this amount was contributed by the Bank of Ghana to support research into livestock development and that the response from the industrial community was very slight, it can only be concluded that the Ghanaian public in general and Ghanaian industry in particular do not fully appreciate the enormous potential that the University has for contributing to the country's industrial development.

Along with inadequate facilities, there is the problem of heavy teaching loads; the staff have little time for research. Within the limits of budgetary constraints, every effort has been made over the years to recruit more staff and to train promising young Ghanaians so that teaching hours can be better distributed and individual schedules lightened. For some time research work tended to be on an individual and departmental basis. Efforts are now being made to adopt a more interdisciplinary approach to research problems, thus bringing the

*U.S. $5,220,000 (July 1976 rate of exchange: ¢=U.S. $.87).

departments and faculties closer together. The University is also
cooperating more with research institutes both on and off campus.

SERVICE

Within the University there is a wealth of technical expertise and
facilities that have the capacity for contributing significantly to the
economic development of Ghana, if properly used. The University
could help solve economic problems such as expansion of nonfarming
employment in rural areas and the introduction of important economic
import substitutes. It can be said that university teaching and
research are meaningless unless they are linked with the economic
development of the country. The university, and especially the UST,
must provide service to the community if it is to justify its existence.
At a time when Ghana's economic policy is based on the principle of
self-reliance, an institution such as the UST should as a matter of
course associate itself with the government's economic policy and
assist in the achievement of its economic goals.

Individual and Faculty Service

There are many ways in which the UST is endeavoring to fulfill
its third principal function, that of service to the community.
Members of the staff serve on management or advisory boards of
national and international organizations. Some faculties and departments as well as individual members of staff participate in national
projects. The Faculty of Architecture, in particular, is closely
involved in problems relating to housing, physical planning, and the
building industry. The Faculty of Agriculture gives advice to farmers
on a number of problems and arranges short demonstration courses
for their benefit.

The University encourages staff members to undertake consultancy work under controlled conditions, in the belief that teaching
is enhanced by professional practice. Provided the extent of such
consultancy work does not interfere with normal teaching and research,
there is no problem in obtaining permission from the vice-chancellor
to undertake it. Any fees accruing are shared among the individual,
the department, and the faculty on what is considered an equitable
basis.

THE TECHNOLOGY CONSULTANCY CENTRE

In 1972, in order to increase the scope and effectiveness of its
service to industry and the community, the University established the
Technology Consultancy Centre, charged with the following:

Consultancy. The provision of a consultancy service to both private and public sectors, utilizing the technical resources of the University as well as associated organizations outside.

Research and development. The initiation and coordination of research and development programs carried out at the University on behalf of outside organizations.

Coordination of production units within the University. The setting up of production units, in collaboration with faculties and departments or by the Centre itself, where no industry or entrepreneur in Ghana is prepared to take up the manufacture of products developed at the University.

Documentation. The documentation of industries and of technologies which are appropriate to the country.

The forerunner of the Centre was a voluntary association of University staff, formed in 1968, known as the "Kumasi Technology Group," which sought to solve specific technical problems referred to it by Ghanaian small businessmen, manufacturers, farmers, and others. There were about 20 people in the group, which charged only for expenses incurred. The technical information given and services provided by the Technology Group for its six years of operation were most impressive and aroused the interest of the University. Its success led to the formation of the Centre, which placed the University's consultancy work on a more formal and better organized footing. The Centre's activities since its establishment, as will be seen from the ensuing pages, more than justify its existence, and because of it the UST stands out as a pioneer institution in applying appropriate technology to rural industrialization.

Organization

The Centre is an autonomous unit within the University, headed by a director who has complete freedom in the management of its day-to-day activities. Its accounts are also managed independently.

The director is responsible to the academic board and the University council through a management committee chaired by the vice-chancellor and composed of deans of faculties, the directors of the Building and Road Research Institute and the Forest Products Research Institute, the director of the Centre, the chief accountant of the University, and two members appointed by the University council.

There is a consultative board that meets approximately once a year to advise on general policy. Also chaired by the vice-chancellor, its members are deans of faculties; the directors of the Building and Road Research Institute, the Forest Products Research Institute, the

Soil Research Institute, and the Crop Research Institute; the chief
physical planning officer; representatives of the University Convocation, the Capital Investment Board, the Chamber of Mines, the
Ministry of Finance and Economic Planning, the Institute of Planners
and Industrial Research, the Ghana Manufacturers' Association, the
Management and Productivity Institute, the Ministry of Industries, the
Ghana Institute of Management and Public Administration, and the
National Investment Bank. Additional members are coopted as and
when the need arises.

Operation

The Centre is the clearinghouse through which the University
makes available its expertise and resources to promote industrial
development in Ghana. It negotiates consultancy contracts with outside bodies and is responsible for maintaining close contact with
outside organizations and for submitting research and consultancy
proposals to the government. The director, through the deans of the
faculties, recruits consultants from the University staff and, when
necessary, from outside bodies. He coordinates multidisciplinary
projects and is in a unique position to assess the contribution that
members of the various departments and faculties can make to
prospective projects.

In his annual review of the Centre's activities for the year
1972/73, the director wrote:

> Increasingly the Centre is becoming an agency for the
> stimulation of grass roots development through the means
> of intermediate or appropriate technology. It is seeking
> to upgrade existing craft industries such as textiles,
> pottery and woodwork by the introduction of new products
> in the important manufacturing techniques and it is
> endeavoring to generate new small-scale industries based
> on products developed in the Faculties of the University
> and utilizing as far as possible locally produced raw
> materials. The aim is to assist the craftsman to take a
> forward step in technology, but a step of which he himself
> has appreciated the need and has anticipated the reward.
> The aim is to assist the would-be entrepreneur to achieve
> the ambition with which he has identified and in which he
> has in some measure prepared himself.

Important Projects

Since its inception, the Centre has undertaken numerous projects.
For example, in 1972 a small manufacturer of cassava starch

approached the Centre and requested to be taught how to make a good paper glue from the starch. The Department of Chemical Technology perfected a formula for a rewettable glue. In conjunction with the Management and Productivity Institute, the Centre then helped the manufacturer put his requirements down on paper and to determine a cash flow for the business. With the Centre's help, he obtained overdraft facilities from Barclay's Bank and now has his glue on sale throughout the country, with an estimated turnover per month of ₵20,000 (U.S. $17,400). He is currently exploring export market possibilities overseas.

In another instance, a Physics Department staff member designed simple scientific instruments for use in secondary schools in Ghana. A businessman in Kumasi started producing these instruments and has since diversified into other products. The range includes potentiometers, resistance boxes, electrophoresis units, primary school teaching aids, wooden drawing boards, T-squares, and meter rulers. This company is also exploring the export market.

Finance

The Centre derives its funds from the following:

1. An annual grant given by government through the University. The grant is modest and is spent on the salaries of office staff and on office and administrative expenses.

2. Contributions from outside organizations. To date the following organizations have given generous support: Barclay's International Development Fund, London; Rockefeller Brothers Fund, New York; Oxfam, Oxford; World Council of Churches, Geneva; and Scottish War on Want.

3. The Centre's share of fees accruing to members of staff, departments, and faculties for consultancy services.

The Centre needs financial support as it sets its present priority on helping the small businessman, who cannot afford high fees, and on contributing to the development of small-scale rural industry. Eventually the Centre expects to be self-supporting, when it does its major work for industry and its income thus rises. There will, of course, always be the need to perform free or low-cost service to help in establishing rural industries.

Staff

The director is assisted by a deputy director. There are also technicians, a foreman in charge of the Centre's own production units,

and junior technical staff, as well as a few technical assistants, who
are young graduates, and accounting, administrative, and secretarial
staff. Currently the staff is small, but it will grow in relation to the
growth of the work of the Centre itself.

Production Units on the University Campus

When it is felt that a new product is needed but local industry
is reluctant or unprepared to manufacture it, the University establishes
small-scale production units. These units seek to train craftsmen
and managers for the new industry; complete product development
under production conditions; test the market for the new product; and
demonstrate to entrepreneurs the viable operation of a new industrial
activity.

The idea is that, when the University has shown what can be done,
the production units will be taken over and operated, off the campus,
by entrepreneurs or craftsmen's cooperatives. Meanwhile, some units
are run by the Centre, some by individual faculties, and some jointly
by the Centre and a faculty. The Centre is usually closely associated
even with those operated independently by a faculty.

Steel Bolt Production Unit

The Centre started this unit in collaboration with the Faculty of
Engineering because of the poor quality of bolts manufactured by local
craftsmen and high cost of imported bolts. Through a grant from
Barclay's Overseas Development, two lathes and a milling machine
were purchased in the United Kingdom for the unit, which currently
produces about 2,000 nuts and bolts a month using metal scrap steel
from Tema. Besides deriving income, the unit trains craftsmen and
encourages local businessmen to establish their own production units,
by showing them what can be done, how it can be done, and that it can
be done.

Plant Construction Unit

This unit, on a commission from the Ministry of Industries, is
currently concerned with the construction of a prototype soap plant
at Kwamo, a village near the University campus. The factory was
designed by the Faculty of Architecture. Another plant is being built
by the Centre to be used for production of caustic soda and other
small-scale chemical processes. It was designed by a member of the
staff of the Department of Technical Technology. These units are
expected to have a multiplier effect through the training of other craftsmen in the building of small industrial plants.

Weaving Production Unit

In collaboration with Department of Industrial Art at the College
of Art, this unit has set out to (1) gain experience of a University-
designed loom under realistic production conditions; (2) assess the
various economic factors which determine the viability of the hand-
weaving industry; and (3) offer training facilities for the local weavers
in a commercial environment. The Centre is using the experience
gained from this production unit to help a businessman from an
Ashanti kente-weaving village who has established a broad-loom
weaving enterprise. Needless to say, there will be employment
openings for many young people from his village.

Metal Products Design Unit

This new unit, set up in collaboration with the College of Art,
seeks to develop a wide range of fittings for domestic use, produced
from local materials. It emphasizes products of low-cost but good-
quality design, for which an interested entrepreneur may some day
take up production.

Production Units in the Faculties

The College of Art has established a unit in the ceramics section
that produces a wide range of tableware for coffee and tea service.
The sales from this unit so far indicate that there is a good market;
in fact, a former student of the College of Art has set up his own
successful ceramics production unit in Accra. The unit, like the
others, seeks to train local craftsmen.

The Faculty of Architecture has an important production unit
in the Department of Housing and Planning Research. It manufactures
low-cost concrete, sanitary ware, and land concrete blocks, which
have been adopted by the National Housing Corporation for use in
all its low-cost housing projects.

The Building Technology Workshop is developing wood products,
including school furniture, for local manufacture.

The Faculty of Engineering runs a traffic light production unit,
a metal plating unit, and a well pump unit, in addition to collaborating
with the Centre on the steel bolt unit.

The Faculty of Science is currently planning a unit for making
scientific instruments for educational institutions and research
establishments.

Consultancy Services

The air-conditioning and refreigeration unit of the Department of Mechanical Engineering undertook, in 1972, to repair the central air-conditioning plants at Korle Bu Teaching Hospital, Accra, and the Okomfo Anokye Hospital, Kumasi. Both plants had been out of order for years. In spite of difficulties encountered, work has progressed satisfactorily and a number of units have been restored to working order.

The Department of Geodetic Engineering undertook a survey and design of feeder roads totaling more than 50 miles, on a commission from the Ashanti Regional Administration.

Research into methods of extraction and crystallization of sugar from local sources is being done by the Department of Chemical Technology, to show how sugar can be manufactured on a small scale for rural areas.

In response to a request from the Regional Commissioner of the Central Region, the Centre will survey opportunities for rural blacksmiths and will establish workshops to train them in new techniques and the handling of new tools. Blacksmiths in rural areas, though highly skilled, are handicapped by a lack of working tools and up-to-date technical knowledge. Simple agricultural tools made by them are already of great importance in rural agriculture, and when their skills and tools have been updated, blacksmiths can make an immense contribution to the development of rural agriculture.

CONCLUSION

This study has been necessarily sketchy and does not include references to the contribution of other institutions of higher education in Africa in the field of technology in relation to rural and industrial development. It has attempted to indicate the way in which the University of Science and Technology, Kumasi, has responded to the challenges of economic development in Ghana by

1. Producing high technical manpower for vital sectors of the economy;
2. Realizing the pressing need for manpower at the subprofessional and middle levels and training personnel at this level;
3. Gearing its research efforts toward the country's economic development, particularly the development of small-scale industries in the rural areas, with the aim of bringing about a transformation

of these areas and thereby stemming the tide of migration to the towns; and

4. Organizing the expertise available on the University campus through the establishment of the Technology Consultancy Centre, which provides a clearinghouse for problems relating to industry and agriculture and a point of contact between the University and the community, offering the University a unique opportunity for involvement in the process of industrialization in Ghana.

6

HIGHER EDUCATION IN MALI

A New Model for Developing a University

In 1962, two years after gaining its independence, Mali reorganized its former educational system under an educational reform law. The new law was designed to increase literacy, to establish more primary schools in rural areas with a program "rooted in the environment," and to train, on the secondary and postsecondary levels, the technicians, specialists, and professionals the country needed.

In 1970, of the school-age population 23 percent were in schools, a growth of 250 percent in 11 years, but students were leaving rural areas for the cities, where most secondary schools were located. To halt urban immigration, the Malian government, with help from Unesco and UNICEF, tried to link basic education more firmly to rural life through work programs in industry and crafts. Teachers, however, were unwilling to change their methods, and basic education is still seen as an "escape route from the bush." The 70 percent who do not pass the entrance examination to the seventh year in the basic schools have no vocational or educational alternatives, and many do not return to the land.

The 11 public secondary schools contain about 2 percent of the total number of Malians in school. Most secondary school graduates receive arts diplomas, but authorities hope that eventually 70 percent of secondary students will receive scientific and technical education.

HIGHER EDUCATION

Higher education has developed as a series of specialized schools and institutes, not yet organized into a university, although a university appears to be an official goal. Despite what is often stated, official texts have never dismissed the concept of the University of Mali. Rather, they define higher education as being constituted by the University, the major schools, and the various institutes. Although higher education is not only the university as commonly understood, Mali remains attached to the "university model" for the shaping of higher education. Reference to the university is constant,

105

even if it is set aside in practice. The Malian system has not formally set up a university _body_, but its approach remains essentially identical to the university model. This approach is, nevertheless, a break with the French model, as it has been reproduced elsewhere in French Africa. Mali seeks to integrate teaching and development by adapting training to the needs of the country.

The country has many practical problems to resolve. The Senegal/Sudan war, only recently ended, brought about the dissolution of the Mali Federation. The University of Dakar, which until recently was supposed to meet the needs of higher education in Mali, was nonetheless a French university in Senegal. At the moment, the Malian system includes only specialized institutions, which are responsible for training upper-level personnel. It has been in operation since 1962, when the Reform of Education Law went into effect.

Organized around certain sectors of the economy, the system has followed a pragmatic rather than a planned course of development. It sought effective direction, adequate student enrollment, and a structure to meet professional manpower needs. These general considerations gave the system of higher education its particular aspect.

As is the case in all countries that have adopted this formula of a functional or planned higher education, teacher training is always among the tasks assigned to higher education. [1] The Malian system does not seem to have escaped the rule, for it was begun by the Higher Teacher Training School at Bamako.

Although the promoters of the Reform declared themselves influenced by the Russian and Vietnamese experiments, among others, and declared their desire to link the school to life and higher education to the national economy, there has been no sign of careful planning of training as a function of the needs of the nation. There is, as we shall see later in the detailed analysis of each institution, a gulf between rhetoric and reality. The institutions are not linked to the nationalized enterprises (which themselves suffer from the lack of far-sighted management) although these enterprises hire three quarters of the labor force outside those in government.

One can note, however, a certain degree of articulation between individual training institutes and the relevant sector of the nation's economy. This is the case with the Rural Polytechnic Institute, which prepares cadres for agriculture and livestock raising. It is generally believed that the urgent needs of the national economy, a desire for efficiency, and a certain sense of social justice inspire the Malian model. We question whether these needs indeed determine educational decisions. Even if they do, the "model" presently suffers from the effects of rapid expansion, from the way the programs of the different institutes have been equalized, and from its extremely limited resources.

Enrollment in higher education has not ceased to grow since the establishment of the system. In 1963, 70 percent of the Malian B. A. 's were trained abroad. In 1966, 43 percent were trained locally in the new institutes. This figure reached 62 percent in 1970, and nearly 80 percent in 1972. This growth is explained in part by the turmoil and upheaval in the universities in Dakar and Abidjan, which have forced Malian students to return home to be trained locally. Another and even more important factor is a political decision by the Malian authorities to train their personnel locally. This option of local training is not in itself debatable, since we know the problems that training abroad can bring. Local training, however, should not become inward looking or feed on itself or become provincial, especially in a world where science knows no boundaries. A degree of isolation may be necessary in the beginning, but training must be dynamic and expanding. In other words, isolation can emphasize the special needs of the system and encourage it to nourish itself on its own environment, but it must also be creative and outward looking if the system is to be efficient.

Although the choice of local training permits national direction of this training, localization is not an end in itself. In many areas the Malian system remains dependent on the outside world. There are risks with so large a number of foreign professors in the system that the new system will become simply another form of "overseas" training.

THE HIGHER TEACHER TRAINING SCHOOL

As mentioned above, the training of teachers is the keystone of the Mali system. Teaching always depends on the quality and value of those who teach. Mali should therefore concentrate on the task of training the following three groups of teachers at the three levels of reform.

1. One group, called first-level teachers, are trained to handle the basic education classes. These teachers are recruited from among students completing the nine years of the basic cycle. They receive one year of further teacher training in Regional Teaching Centers.

2. A second group, called second-level teachers, are trained at the Secondary Teacher Training School for the second cycle of the primary schools. They are recruited from among those receiving the DEF (Basic Studies Diploma), and their training extends over 23 months.

3. A third group, teachers of general secondary education, are trained at the Higher Normal School or ENS (Ecole Normale Supérieure). Recruited after having passed the baccalauréat, these student-teachers spend three years at the ENS.

The first development plan (1961-65) clearly showed that there were not enough teachers. The role of ENS was thus to provide the country with the teaching corps it lacked. It was inevitable that ENS undertook activities normally handled by a faculty of letters or of science. It must be noted that the content of teacher training has not always had its proper place in pedagogy. The various departments of ENS (literature, philosophy, psychology of teaching, Russian, history, geography, mathematics, English, German, physics, chemistry, biology, geology) and the department of teaching and research have functioned as faculties, suffering from the same divisions.

The professional character of ENS, which is found also in other schools, reflects the efforts of the system to turn out "finished products." Those who have left ENS, up to the present, know that they are to teach. Thus, all through their training they are aware of the demands of the teaching profession. But—and it is clearly here where ENS is weakest—it trains for clearly defined work: teaching. However, its pedagogic resources are rudimentary. At a university, the faculties offer the intellectual means whereby a student learns about the problems in his own discipline, but ENS lacks these resources. Nonetheless, ENS has become a faculty of letters and inherited all the resultant contradictions. Its base has grown considerably, and it suffers from the quality of its teaching.

The study program at ENS certainly tries to guarantee a link between the theoretical training by the faculties and the training usually known as "pedagogic." It was hoped that the six months of practice teaching that complete the four years would establish this link. However, the senior students with whom we have spoken themselves admit that they do not learn enough in these six months.

Moreover, the weakness of the Department of Psychology of Teaching is such that it has made itself felt in the training of student-teachers. Thus a Unesco report states, "... it will be necessary to provide a great strengthening of the department of psychology of teaching which ought to provide courses in the specialized methodology for the material of the other departments."[2]

ENS has given valuable service in training teachers for the secondary schools. Graduates have increased from 17 in 1964 to 50 in 1972, about 20 of those in the sciences. Eighty percent of the teachers at the secondary level are Malian graduates of ENS. From this point of view, one can say that the ENS is doing a satisfactory job.

In the coming years, however, one can foresee an explosion of arts graduates. Of 550 students admitted to ENS last October, 400 are in arts fields, owing to the imbalance that now exists in general secondary education between the scientific and arts divisions.

The development and the evolution of the institution reflect the problems of its environment. Almost the entire teaching staff of ENS are technical assistance personnel. This high ratio of expatriate staff members is common in higher education in Africa, and Mali is no exception. The system is attempting to improve this situation by establishing a Center for Advanced Teacher Training or CPS (Centre Pedagogique Supérieur) whose principle aim is to train professors for higher education, but above all for ENS.

Responsible for organizing graduate scientific research and the postgraduate training needed for teaching at ENS, the Center began in September 1970 with students in mathematics, biology, and physics. Eleven students successfully defended their theses before an international panel in 1973. This system of an international panel is also important, and it is one of the changes mentioned. In effect, at a traditional university, the doctorate, received after years of research, is approved by a small group of "notables." Now, with an international panel, the hold of this small group is broken while at the same time a diploma of international standard is given.

The idea of the Center for Advanced Teacher Training is interesting in itself, but the formula has its limits. Recruiting Ph. D's from among the graduates of ENS means bringing visiting professors into a system with limited local facilities and an absence of relevant and high level research. CPS grants doctorates but not from a strong context of advanced training and research. CPS could and should be a dynamic factor for higher education in Mali, but it has not yet proved so.

RURAL POLYTECHNIC INSTITUTE

Located in the former quarters of the Federal Agriculture School at Katibougou, the Rural Polytechnic Institute or IPR (Institut Polytechnique Rural) has, since 1965, undertaken the training of middle and upper-level agricultural personnel. At this Institute, Mali hoped to break away from the traditional methods of agricultural training, which, while providing agricultural extension agents and foremen, did not provide the necessary integration between the two levels of training.

One of the dominant characteristics of the IPR is that it trains, under one roof, personnel who are expected to contribute to agricultural development and who are expected to work together. The Institute, which is the only school giving this double-level training, has two courses, A and B. The A course is aimed at future applied science engineers, recruited from those who have received the baccalauréat or are already in the profession. The B course is for middle-level technicians. Entrants must have received the DEF, the Basic Studies Diploma (Diplome d'etudes fondamentales).

The training programs for the two levels are carried out in the various departments: science and technology of agriculture, of livestock breeding, of forestry, and of rural economics. For each course, the first year aims at evening out the students' levels (since some enter direct from secondary school and others have been working in the field for some time), and giving them certain basic knowledge of the field—for example, biology oriented toward agriculture. This common course permits students to acquire, from the beginning, the sense of working together and to recognize that the two levels are complementary. It is also clear that this system reduces the cost of the training.

In the second year, students begin work in their specialty, selected on the basis of needs expressed in the Development Plan and of the desires and abilities of the students. Practical work begins to take more time, but it is very specialized, concentrated on seedlings or on use of fertilizers. This practical work gives the teaching its professional character.

The third year is notable for its six months' residency and for more practical work. Still more specialized, this practical work is done jointly by students of both courses from the same specialty. It is here that the theme of agricultural cooperation finds its place in the programs of all specialties. Cooperatives, education of members of cooperatives, problems linked to commercialization, and supply in the rural areas are discussed and studied.

During the fourth and last year, classroom work is reinforced, for eight months, by field work. Students are sent to organizations that will give them specific jobs to do and thus expose them to the activities of their future profession. This period, during which practical training and theoretical training are integrated, ends with the writing of a report that records the theoretical knowledge and the practical experience gained in the past years. This report is decisive at IPR, and is another original feature of the school.

Especially important is the part played by technical services that employ the students in the training period. The participation of employers is certainly a guarantee of liaison between training and employment. The Production Ministry also participates in the design of programs and student training at IPR, and the minister is a member of the board of directors.

In the annual report of the director general of agriculture, one notes reservations expressed by employers on the training given the first class. The report observes that this class suffered from too academic a training and that it has not had enough introduction to agricultural practice and the rural environment. Employers now sit on the examining boards that evaluate student work, providing a link

between teachers and employers. Such a link should improve the
training at the Institute.

The linkage of the two courses has not been without problems.
First, the instructors, mostly specialists themselves, are not
always capable of giving this sort of instruction. There is also the
psychological problem for the students, especially those in course B,
of accepting the fact that some will eventually work as foremen even
though they have been trained alongside extension agents.

Despite these problems, the IPR experiment is of great interest.
The concept is valuable even if material constraints retard the development of the Institute. (Located about 50 miles from Bamako, the
IPR does not have all the facilities that it needs to fulfill its role, but
it is hoped that financial aid foreseen under the Five-Year Plan will
ease this problem.)

NATIONAL ENGINEERING SCHOOL

Even during the colonial era the question of training Africans
for public works jobs arose. The Higher Technical School was thus
established in 1939 in Bamako to train assistant technicians, overseers,
and workers for the Public Works Department and for the railroad
company. This training took four years after primary school.

In 1950, this school became the Public Works School, responsible for training public works technicians and surveyors. The four-
year course was retained, but entrance was restricted to those holding
the brevet elémentaire (which was formerly granted at the end of
secondary school). For ten years this school trained all intermediate-
level technicians in public works for the countries of the former
French Overseas Africa.

After independence, and in view of the principles of the Education Reform, it was decided to establish a single form of technical
and professional instruction, preparing for a specific profession.
The reform distinguished three stages in technical and professional
education.

1. Trained workers. This stage covers students recruited after
the fifth year of primary education. At the end of two or three years
(depending on the field) they receive a Certificate of Aptitude in their
field (masonry, electricity, and so on).

2. Technicians. These are the middle-level personnel. They
are recruited after the ninth year of school and are trained at a
technical high school. They receive a Technician's Certificate.

3. Engineers. The higher-level personnel, principally from
the National Engineering School, are an elite group. Unitl 1969, they

were recruited from students receiving the DEF, for the emphasis was placed on the need to train so-called "manufacturing" engineers to staff and direct nationalized enterprises. (At that time two types of engineers were trained, "manufacturing" and "creative. ")

The three-year plan (1970-73) predicated a growth rate in the industrial sector of about 64 percent, not including new industries. At the same time, the planners predicted that 170 positions for engineers would be established. If the growth rate (64 percent) was correct, Mali would need over the three-year period an additional 110 engineers. At this time, Mali had 50 engineers in training abroad, 20 of whom were to return in 1973. *

It was obvious that the deficit was huge—at least 90 positions would need to be filled, without taking into account the teachers needed for technical training schools. To make up this deficit in higher technical personnel, the government decided to strengthen the National Engineering School (ENI, Ecole Nationale d'Ingénieurs). At a national seminar on problems of training technical personnel the concept of "manufacturing" and "creative" engineers was discarded. Henceforth, ENI would train one type of engineer (ingénieur des sciences) who should know how to conceive as well as execute a project.

Because of the emphasis that is placed on the problems of Malian industry, ENI is, with the Rural Polytechnic Institute, one of the pivots of the education system. It is expected to train, eventually, enough engineers to handle all business development in Mali.

Recruitment is from students receiving the baccalauréat, and the course lasts four years. The programs and lessons are developed along lines set up by the employers. But contrary to the situation at the Rural Polytechnic Institute, the amount of theoretical training necessary at ENI makes the time available for practical work very limited. From this point of view, ENI remains more or less a model of the traditional engineering faculty. Nonetheless, efforts are being made to open ENI to businesses (special seminars on current problems, consultations, or participation of the Department of Education and Research in research activities relating to industries).

NATIONAL SCHOOL OF PUBLIC ADMINISTRATION

Created in 1963, the National School of Public Administration or ENA (Ecole Nationale d'Administration) was intended to train both upper and middle-level personnel for Mali's civil service. Since

*We attempted to locate these 20 engineers, but, in fact only five returned and are presently at work.

1969, ENA has been restricted to higher-level training, and middle-level personnel are trained at another institute, the Central School of Industry, Commerce, and Administration, ECICA (Ecole Centrale de l'Industrie, du Commerce et de l'Administration). Entrants must hold the baccalauréat, but officials already in service may take a professional course.

The School of Public Administration, like the other schools in the system, has been inspired by the philosophy of the reform of 1962. It also seeks to train in four years personnel linked to the development of the country.

The School has three sections, each of which takes on some of the attributes of a faculty of law or of economics. These sections (Public Administration, Economics and Management, and Law) suffer, however, at the methods level from the influence of the traditional faculties at a French university. The lecture method has been maintained, and, although discussion sessions and directed work are provided for, the time allowed for them (1.5 hours as an elective) is so little that the program remains largely theoretical. In the fourth year, the student is assigned a job for three months in the department in which he will serve after graduation. He completes his work period by writing a report on this department.

As in the other schools, teaching at ENA is organized in departments of teaching and research. There are three departments at ENA, corresponding to the three sections. The organization of teaching at ENA seems rather flexible, to permit adaptation to the needs of the Civil Service. Since its founding, ENA has graduated 318 students (12 in 1966; 20 in 1967; 47 in 1970; 42 in 1971; 56 in 1972; 69 in 1973; and 72 in 1974).

An offshoot of ENA is the Institute of Production and Management Forecasting, or IPGP (Institut de Production et de Gestion Prévision-nelle). Acting as an organizing and counseling office, it trains management personnel in 15 months. IPGP also provides retraining for personnel already working in businesses. With 15 professors (of whom 10 are expatriates) and 26 students, the IPGP is for the moment a very expensive institute.

Teaching at IPGP is organized in two sections. The first period takes in four months of courses and two of internship. The second has five months of courses and four months of internship. There is an effort to reinforce teaching through these internships. Interns perform research and identify problems that the management of Malian businesses present.

MEDICAL SCHOOL

At the beginning, the idea was to train medical assistants or intermediate personnel who would be recruited from students receiving the baccalauréat. Very soon, this idea was abandoned in favor of the School of Medicine, whose students would be trained as physicians. The School became, in fact, a model that, while different from the traditional faculty of medicine, remains somewhere between a health school and a traditional faculty.

Opened in October 1969, the School intended to train physicians in 5.5 years, contrary to the custom in other countries in the region where medical studies take seven years. The teaching is based primarily on public health and tropical medicine, and clinical training is begun in the first year (unlike the faculty of medicine at Dakar, where students do not begin hospital work until the third year).

In the fourth and fifth years, the students act as interns without taking exams, again a change from the traditional (French) faculty. This early internship permits the future physician to familiarize himself with medical administration and problems of preventive medicine. Another innovation that should be noted is that students may not specialize until after at least two years of professional practice.

There are major research efforts in each of the four departments of the School. The proximity of a 1,500-bed hospital and access to all other hospitals and dispensaries in Bamako permit them to carry out this research. All hospitals are open to the School.

The Medical School has 155 students, including 15 women in the first year. These students, as in all the other schools, are on full scholarships from the State. The personnel and equipment are mostly furnished by French foreign aid.

CONCLUSIONS

At the end of this study, five principle conclusions seem evident:

1. In selecting a system of schools and institutes rather than a classic university, Mali supported its wish for education that was socially and economically useful. It was the ideology of the era that determined the choice of model.

The grounds for the system are not that the "model" responds better than a university to the training needs of personnel, but rather that Mali desires to liberate education from a colonial past and is willing to adopt a certain pragmatism in the face of immediate needs. These factors have shaped the Malian system and its professional orientation.

2. The system admits those who, it feels, ought to train for a profession. It is thus a training that has been adapted to the explicit needs of the job market. Such training raises the question, in the end, of the subjugation of higher education to the power structure and the supposedly known objectives of the Malian economy.

Rather than being an innovation, the system is thus based on professional training understood in the narrow sense of the term. Mali is a country where the problem of unemployed graduates does not exist. Numerous development projects and the limited number of people available remove the possibility of unemployment.

3. One might expect that in such a system training would be rigorously planned and interrelated. The several institutions in the system, however, have no link among themselves. Each seems to act according to its own logic. The specialized character of the training prevents multiple use, but liaison should be established to permit them to plan together the overall aims of the system. Indeed, the structure of the schools is similar from the standpoint of organization (the departments of teaching and research), administration, and the length of the course (four years except for medicine).

The absence of educational directives, moreover, whether at the heart of the system or in planning, on one type of training or another, makes almost impossible any integration of teaching. Each institution is a closed system unaware of what is being done elsewhere, and this lack of integration sends into the job market personnel suffering the effects of such cloistered training.

4. It is regrettable that, in such a system, research, an essential element of higher education, should be absent. CPS, which is the only part of the system that claims to do research, is neither materially nor scientifically equipped to carry on research activities. We are, thus, far from agreeing that CPS can, under present conditions necessary for a true postuniversity training. This lack, however, takes nothing away from the originality of the model.

5. Once all the elements of the system have been established and have attained their objectives, the idea of a national university—which has never been abandoned—will probably come up again. In any case, since, on the one hand, the system of higher education is under the direction of a ministry of higher education, and, on the other, the pressure on higher education continues to grow, it is probable that the institutions will multiply and that in the end Mali will have a university structure, shaped of course to the needs of the country, but responding better to the criteria of higher education.

APPENDIX

Mali is a vast country of about 1,204,000 square kilometers, twice the size of France. More than half of this territory is desert, so that arable and pasture land is at a premium (50 million hectares in the entire country).

The population, estimated at about 5 million in 1970, is expected to double by the year 2000 and is distributed unevenly throughout the various regions of the country. About 90 percent live in rural areas, of whom more than 80 percent are illiterate. Per capita income in 1970 was estimated to be $100. The population is young: 60 percent are under 20 years of age. Persons of working age (15-64) comprise about 53 percent, while those of school age (6-13) comprise about 20 percent of the population.

Thus, one can say that the demography of the country is favorable to development, the more so since there are few urban slum dwellers or "marignal men" constraining the development process.

The economy of Mali, despite over ten years of effort, is basically agricultural and is particularly susceptible to weather. In the last ten years, the agricultural sector, badly damaged by three years of drought, has grown very little. The average yield of basic food crops has dropped markedly, creating a severe nutritional imbalance. The production of millet, for example, has dropped from 750 kilograms per hectare in 1960 to 700 kilograms per hectare in 1972, and millet and rice production showed a shortfall in 1972-73 of 400,000 tons from predicted figures. While the country required about 900,000 tons for survival, only about 600,000 tons were available. All foodstuffs have been affected in the same way during this period although cash or export crops such as cotton have shown sharp improvement. [3]

Livestock production has also suffered in the drought—it is estimated that the country has lost at least 30 percent of its stock. In the region of Gao, almost all the cattle died. It is easy to see the problems this situation creates and the importance of help to the affected people.

The industrial sector, on the other hand, has grown rapidly in the past ten years. Despite this growth, however, (from 4 percent in 1960 to 7 percent in 1970) industrial progress has been impeded by a series of constraints, in particular the location of the country and the limited and irregular market. [4]

Aims of the Five-Year Plan (1974-78)

The brief exposition above explains why among the priority aims of the current Five-Year Plan the accent is on (1) satisfying the fundamental needs of the country, principally in food grains; at the same time, it must solve the problem of water for both urban and rural populations (the government is planning the construction of a dam on the Sallengui River); (2) building cadres that can work in agriculture and livestock production, the concern of the Rural Poly- technic Institute at Katibougou; and (3) training cadres for development (on both higher and middle levels) so that in five years there will be no need for expatriate personnel, especially in the field of scientific research.

In the field of education and training, the expected investment for the five years 1974-78 is about 27.4 billion FM (U.S. $60,280,000). * Higher education has been allotted about 4 billion FM (U.S. $8,800,000) for the same period. These funds are allocated principally for the Rural Polytechnic Institute at Katibougou, the Medical School, and the National Engineering School.

Reform of Education

Since gaining independence in 1960, Mali has been faced with all the problems of building a modern state. One of the principle concerns of the government in this period has been establishing a broad-based policy of decolonialization, aimed at changing ways of thinking and acting influenced by a long period of colonialism.

The Report on the Reform of Education declared in 1962 that education must bring about this change, necessary to development. Malians are aware of the need to link the school to life and to provide mass education of high quality. The need to educate the human being, to prepare him as fully as possible for life, has led them to seek out new ways of teaching and strategies for speeding the training of much needed manpower. They hope educational reform will achieve democratization and efficiency and that it will be guided by the values of the black African.

Basic Education

It was hoped that basic education, covering nine years and divided into two sections (first and second) would be possible in a local school, open to all. The reform spirit envisaged essentially a mass education, perhaps unique in Africa, which would permit young Malians from the "bush" to receive an education while remaining rooted in their environment.

Reform was intended also to develop a taste for agriculture among Malian youth. This attempt to ruralize education has not succeeded, despite help from Unesco and UNICEF in establishing programs of practical work in industry or crafts. These programs foundered on the traditionalism and conservatism of teachers, unwilling to change their methods.

This unwillingness to change has also meant that reform has not had the success hoped for. After the sixth year, the system begins to be selective—so that, to enter the seventh year, students must pass

*This figure includes training and cultural activities.

an exam. Many, therefore, find themselves back on the street, as
reform efforts have not provided any alternatives. In 1974, 70 percent
of the students could not pass the exam for entry into the seventh year.

Classes may be repeated at each stage following the seventh up
to the level of the DEF. Beginning in the seventh year, students now
have alternatives for professional training, such as the National
School of Post and Telecommunications and the School of Veterinary
Nursing.

As we have noted, basic education, instead of keeping the young
Malian in the rural areas, has in fact had the same effect as the old
schools. Since basic education is seen as an "escape route from the
bush," it contributes to the disintegration of rural communities and
to a feeling of insecurity among parents—a phenomenon that we see
all across Africa.

General Secondary Education

Secondary education covers three years and is open to all
students holding the DEF. Priority is given to the younger students.
At the end of the second year, students must pass the first part of
the baccalauréat in one of four fields: classics, modern letters,
physical sciences, or biological sciences. Those who succeed continue
through the final year to the second half of the baccalauréat.

At present, there are 11 public high schools (one of which is a
technical school), which accept the 5,000 students in general secondary
education. Six are located in Bamako and take 78 percent of the
students. All students are boarders, with costs covered by the state.
There are also three private general secondary schools in Bamako.

In 1964, there were 3,307 general secondary students in the
country. By 1973/74, this had grown to 4,800, and at present about
5,000 are registered. The number of graduates, only 500 in 1970/71
(200 in arts and 300 in sciences), reached 920 in 1974, almost doubling
in three years. Of these, more than two thirds received arts diplomas.

This heavy proportion of arts graduates in 1974 is explained by
overly academic teaching and by a natural tendency of students toward
"easy" studies and has led to a uniformity of secondary education
starting in the tenth year. Since 1970, students have been required
to study the same subjects, and scientific training has been intensified.
Through this greater emphasis on science and a system of course
requirements, the authorities hope to correct the top-heavy enrollment
in arts, and it is intended that eventually 70 percent of the secondary
students will be in scientific and technical education.

Problems of Reform

Reform poses many problems. First, at the level of basic education there is always the risk of a return to illiteracy. In effect, at the sixth-year level, when a first division is made, parallel routes to the basic cycle rarely exist and, when they do, seldom return the youths to the land. The experiment with functional literacy stumbled on this contradiction, and this problem has not been solved. Because when one enlarges the base, quality suffers, certain criteria of selection and "rites of passage" were reintroduced in 1968. There is also the fact that the system does not cope with its own failures. The dropout rate is very high and leads to questions about internal efficiency.

Finally, reform has not had the results that were expected, socially or economically. It has not succeeded in giving Malian youth a taste for manual labor, nor has it succeeded in adapting the school to the cultural environment of the child, even if it has succeeded in removing French lesson plans from the schools. For obvious financial reasons, the system has maintained the concept of selection, which reformers had hoped to remove.

TABLE 6.1

Position of Education Costs in Total Public Budget

	Exact figures at Current Prices (in millions of Mali Francs)				Growth Between 1967/68 and 1971 After Inflation[b]	
	1967/68	1969	1970	1971	index	annual growth
a. Gross National Product	130,500	135,500	148,900	—	—	—
Administration:						
b. National budget[a]	21,858	21,191	21,195	22,331	90.4	-2.8
c. Amount allocated for education[c]	3,651	4,841	5,433	5,991	145.2	11.2
Capital:						
d. National budget	946	375	956	1,128	—	—
e. Amount allocated for education	87	—	55	30	—	—
Administration and Capital:						
f. National budget	22,804	21,566	22,151	23,459	91.0	-2.6
g. Amount allocated for education	3,738	4,841	5,488	6,021	142.5	10.6
Total budget as percent of GNP	17.5	15.9	14.9	—		
Total education costs as percent of GNP	2.9	3.6	3.7	—		
Total education costs as percent of total budget	16.4	22.4	24.7	25.7		
Capital budget costs as percent of total budget	4.1	1.7	4.3	4.8		
Capital education costs as percent of total education costs	0.2	—	0.1	0.05		
Capital education costs as percent of capital budget	9.2	—	5.8	2.6		
Education administration costs as percent of administrative budget	16.7	22.8	25.6	26.8		

[a]The national budget, since 1963, has included both the central government budget and the regional budgets.

[b]The indices and annual growth rates in real terms were calculated according to figures provided by the Administration of the Plan (132.2 for 1967/68; 149.4 for 1971).

[c]Lacking sufficient information for the years in question, the expenditures do not include those created by foreign technical assistance or the expenditures on educational programs of the Ministries of Production and of Health.

Source: "Enfance Jeunesse et Plan de Developpement," Mali Planning Board, December 1971—for figures on administrative costs for overall budget and education sector. Capital budget figures were obtained from the Planning Board. Calculations made by author.

TABLE 6.2

Number of Degrees Between 1963 and 1974

Year	Number of Degrees	Precent Trained Locally	Precent Trained Abroad
1963	89	30	70
1964	99	30	70
1965	146	31	69
1966	180	43	57
1967	196	70	30
1968	258	51	49
1969	283	53	47
1970	382	62	38
1971	536	70	30
1972	693	79	21
1973	800	87	13
1974	1,095	90	10

Source: Ministry of National Education.

121

FIGURE 6.1

Education in Mali

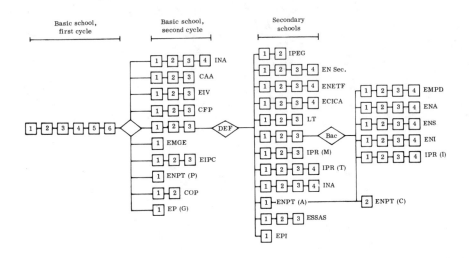

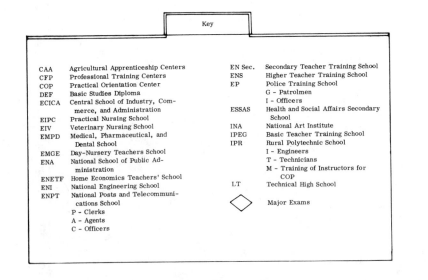

Source: Ministry of National Education.

TABLE 6.3
Growth of Enrollment

School	1962–1963	1963–1964	1964–1965	1965–1966	1966–1967	1967–1968	1968–1969	1969–1970	1970–1971	1971–1972	1972–1973	1973–1974	1974–1975
ENS	17	88	47	84	117	141	209	236	232	313	466	627	1,083
ENA	—	12	31	55	89	128	132	234	295	353	447	462	488
ENI	—	—	—	—	—	50	44	61	85	135	217	254	322
IPR	—	—	—	—	27	76	79	98	93	157	227	289	320[a]
ENM[b]	—	—	—	—	—	—	—	14	26	21	25	40	155
Total	17	100	78	139	233	395	464	643	731	979	1,382	1,672	2,368

[a] The 630 students in the advanced technicians course (middle level) are not included in this figure.
[b] Ecole National de Medicine.
Source: Ministry of National Education.

TABLE 6.4
Enrollment at ENS: 1974–75
(total students = 1,083)

Year	Literature	Philosophy	Psychology of Teaching	English	Russian	German	History/Geography	Physics/Chemistry	Biology	Classics	Math
First Year	279 {			44	43	33	45	33	66	15	26
Second Year	43		33	31	24	19	29	24	11	11	11
Third Year	12	44	10	18	16	12	22	15	13	—	12
Fourth Year	12	5	21	—	—	—	24	10	11	—	6
Total	67	49	64 } 459	93	83	64	120	82	101	26	55

Source: Ministry of National Education.

123

TABLE 6.5

Degrees Awarded by IPR

Course	Specialization	Malians			Others		
		1970	1971	1973[a]	1970	1971	1973[a]
Engineers	Agriculture	10	2	16	5	—	—
	Stock-raising	7	2	6	—	—	—
	Water and forests	—	—	8	—	—	—
	Subtotal	17	4[b]	30	5	—	4
Technicians	Agriculture	6	30	17	5	17	—
	Stock-raising	12	15	7	12	9	—
	Water and forests	6	5	6	—	1	—
	Cooperatives	6	3	—	—	—	—
	Rural life	—	5	3	—	—	—
	Subtotal	30	58[b]	33	17	27	26
	Total	47	62	63	22	27	30

[a]Owing to the change in the program of studies, no diplomas were awarded in 1972. Those awarded for 1973 are those of ISA and TS.

[b]This figure includes those finishing the former training program (first-level engineers and middle-level technicians).

Source: Ministry of National Education.

124

TABLE 6.6

Enrollment at ENI

Year	1971–72	1972–73	1973–74	1974–75
First year	65	65	65	65
Second year	53	58	58	59
Third year	23	50	56	56
Fourth year	—	22	48	53
Total	141	195	227	233

Source: Ministry of National Education.

TABLE 6.7

Number of Diplomas by Division

Division	1971–72	1972–73	1973–74	1974–75
Electromechanics	—	6	16	17
Public Works	—	10	19	22
Topography	—	4	6	6
Geology	—	2	5	5
Total	—	22	46	50

Source: Ministry of National Education.

NOTES

1. See the case of the USSR: "Higher Education in the USSR" in Studies and Documents on Education no. 39, (Paris: Unesco, 1962).

2. Unesco Report, August 1973 MLI/62/501 p. 29. Emphasis added.

3. Plan de Développement, p. 4.

4. Ibid.

7

UNIVERSITY OF MAURITIUS

Developing a University in a Small Country

The most notable feature of the University of Mauritius is that it is almost entirely a "service" institution devoted to the training of middle-level manpower. Practically all its programs are nondegree programs at the certificate and diploma levels, with only about 10 percent of the students pursuing degree-level courses. The University has only three faculties or schools: agriculture, administration, and industrial technology. There are no faculties of science or arts.

The University has an enrollment of slightly over 1,000 "award" students—that is, students who are working for a particular diploma or certificate. In addition, there are a number of "nonaward" students who follow short, intensive courses in a variety of fields. Usually, these courses run for two or three weeks and are designed to upgrade the skills and capabilities of lower-echelon government employees or those from commerce, industry, and the private sector in general.

University officials point out that theirs is a "development-oriented" university, and, in terms of the institution's massive commitment to relate its training programs to the immediate needs of the country, this designation is altogether apt. At this stage, it would be useful to examine the factors that helped to shape this mission and focus of the University.

HISTORY OF THE UNIVERSITY

The path of the University was charted as much by an accident of history as by deliberate design. While the University of Mauritius was created in 1965 (teaching started even later, in 1968), one of its constituent units, the School of Agriculture, dates back to 1924. The College of Agriculture (as it was called before its incorporation into the University), which for a long time was the only postsecondary institution in the country, had had a long and distinguished tradition

of organizing its training programs around the island's major industry,
sugar. The College had been producing middle-level manpower
(including technicians, managers, and extension workers) for the sugar
industry for 40 years prior to its incorporation into the University.
When the University was launched in 1965, it was only natural that
it should build on this rich experience and tradition.

There were also other factors that helped shape the focus and
character of the institution. For example, in the early period of its
history (1965-68) there was a rapid turnover of staff and administration, and an acute shortage of funds. These major constraints forced
the School of Administration, the first unit created, to cancel its very
first course, a degree program in economics, and to send the students
to U.S. colleges on scholarship schemes provided by the U.S. government. The School did not recover sufficiently from this traumatic
experience to launch other degree courses for a number of years.
Instead, it felt it had no choice but to pursue a path analogous to the
one followed by the College of Agriculture in offering subdegree
courses in such areas as cooperatives, accounting, and banking for
government employees and others released for this purpose by their
employers.

Once the University leadership stabilized, these tendencies were
further reinforced by an astute and pragmatic viewpoint that visualized
the role of a small university on a poor and tiny island in extremely
practical terms, as the following statement by Dr. P. O. Wiehe, the
former vice-chancellor of the University, testifies, "The objective
of the University is to identify itself with the immediate needs of the
country and to undertake in Mauritius training and education which
can best be done in Mauritius."

If the University's mission is, as the vice-chancellor claims,
to serve the immediate needs of the island, the University would
obviously have to have a clear conception of the social and economic
issues that the island faces. These are summarized briefly in the
next section.

SOCIAL AND ECONOMIC SETTING

Mauritius is a small island in the Indian Ocean, about 500 miles
east of Madagascar. It has a population of about 850,000 (1972 census),
which breaks down as follows: Hindus of Indian origin (51 percent),
Franco-Mauritians and Creoles (30 percent), Muslims of Indo-
Pakistani origin (16 percent), and Mauritians of Chinese descent
(3 percent). Population is expected to increase by 25 percent in the
next decade.

The island's economy is—and is likely to remain during the
1970s—heavily dependent on a single crop, sugar, which accounts

for over 90 percent of its export earnings. In view of the population increase and an unemployment rate of about 20 percent (1972), the government considers the diversification of the economy and an increase in employment opportunities objectives of the highest priority.

The government is accordingly promoting the cultivation of other crops, notably tea; has initiated a program of rapid industrialization; and has made a vigorous effort to attract foreign industrial partners. For instance, under the Export Processing Scheme established in 1971, over 30 industries, already created in the government "industrial sites," are expected to provide more than 90,000 new industrial jobs during the 1970s. The government's industrial policy is heavily influenced by the experiences of Singapore, Taiwan, and Hong Kong. It seeks to attract, in particular, labor-intensive export industries, and, in return, provides generous tax incentives and concessions. With crop diversification, it plans also to create an additional 30,000 agricultural jobs.

On the whole, the economy, which had been rather stagnant in the 1960s, is now showing "impressive progress." This was the conclusion reached by an economic mission from the World Bank that visited the island in August 1973. The Bank mission ascribed this success to two major factors: (1) the vigorous economic and trade policies pursued by the government and (2) the island's "human resources." Elaborating on the latter point, the IBRD report states:

> The unique Mauritian blend of races which had to cohabit within a small area resulted in a population that is open to the external world, is receptive to outside ideas and can easily adapt to imported techniques. Developments in the last few years have enhanced the confidence of Mauritians in themselves and brought about a new spirit of enterprise which probably was less evident before Independence. *

Despite the positive developments discussed above, the Mauritian economy remains a single-crop economy with all the risks and constraints usually associated with such an economy. In addition, two major issues dominate the economic situation—the extreme discrepancy in income distribution, which in fact follows and subtly reinforces the ethnic groupings of the population, and persistent unemployment.

EDUCATION AND TRAINING

The education system comprises six years of primary education, and five or seven years of second-level education leading, respectively,

*Memorandum on Recent Economic Development and Prospects of Mauritius (Washington, D. C.: International Bank for Reconstruction and Development, February 1974), p. 1.

to a Cambridge School Certificate, and Cambridge Higher School
Certificate. (The recently established National Institute of Education
is charged with the responsibility of developing local examinations in
place of those from Cambridge.)

The education and training sector in Mauritius is comparatively
well developed: at the primary level, 86 percent of the children of the
relevant age group are attending school; at the secondary level, the
corresponding ratio is 31 percent. By African standards, these are
high ratios. Other strengths of the education system include low
repetition and dropout rates and high progression (promotion) rates.

Despite these positive features, the system suffers from a
number of qualitative weaknesses commonly found in other African
countries. The syllabus, particularly at the secondary level, is too
theoretical and examination-centered. Facilities for the teaching of
science and technical subjects are inadequate, as are those for
agriculture and training for rural workers.

The government has almost no control over the quality of second-
level education. In fact, close to 95 percent of secondary school
enrollment is in private schools. Most of these private schools are
poorly equipped and housed, often in run-down, rented facilities
scattered throughout the island, and are scarcely more than profit-
making institutions. Aware of these deficiencies, the government
is seeking assistance, including International Development Association
loans, for school facilities, equipment, and the diversification of the
syllabus. It is endeavoring to have a much larger control over the
secondary schools than it has at present.

Language teaching constitutes another bottleneck in the school
system. Although English is compulsory at school, the children speak
Creole, French, or Oriental languages at home. Consequently,
students have difficulties in following their studies, and often language
difficulties account for the high failure rates in the Cambridge School
Leaving Examinations. As noted earlier, the new Institute of Education is giving high priority to the introduction of a local school-leaving
examination, which will give adequate recognition to the language
problem.

Primary education in the public schools is free. The secondary
schools, both public and private, charge fees. The government spends
roughly 15 percent of its recurrent budget on education. This is
allocated approximately as follows: 73 percent for primary education,
14 percent for secondary schools, and 0.2 percent for the University
of Mauritius. The rest goes for teacher training, vocational schools,
and adult education. The small ratio allocated to secondary education
is explained by the fact that those schools are for the most part
privately owned and operated.

UNIVERSITY STRUCTURE AND GOVERNANCE

The University structure follows the British pattern. The University of Mauritius Act, 1971, set forth in considerable detail the functions and responsibilities of the various organs of the University. The act and the accompanying statutes contain much of the substance and spirit of similar documents of other British-style universities of the Commonwealth and Africa.

The act designates the chancellor as head of the University, but as in other British-style universities, his duties are largely honorific. He is appointed by the governor general "on the advice" of the prime minister. His main responsibilities are to confer degrees and diplomas (awarded by the University council or senate), including honorary degrees, and to preside at "any ceremony of the University."*

The principal academic and administrative officer of the University, as in other British-style universities, is the vice-chancellor. He is appointed, usually for life or until his retirement, by the council after "consideration of a report" of a joint council-senate committee (of equal membership), with the chairman of the council serving ex-officio as chairman of the committee. As the chief executive officer of the University, he is vested with the general responsibility "for maintaining and promoting the good order and efficiency of the University." His main duties and responsibilities are simialr to those of vice-chancellors in other universities. There is one feature that may be worth noting: Article 6(b) of the act seems to give the vice-chancellor almost unlimited power over student admissions. The article, in enumerating the main functions of the vice-chancellor, states that he is entitled "to refuse, without being required to explain his decision, to allow any person to be registered as a student" (emphasis added). In a developing country such as Mauritius, where universities are young, and where authority and responsibility have not as yet been fully institutionalized, it might have been wiser and more prudent to confer authority on such instituted organs as the senate rather than on individual officers. In any event, the University may not always find it possible to reconcile the apparently unlimited authority conferred on the vice-chancellor with the far more liberal provisions of Article 6:

> No discrimination on account of nationality, race, caste, religion, place of origin, political opinions, color, creed or sex shall be shown against any person in determining whether he or she is to be appointed to the academic or other staff of the University, to be registered as a

---

*Article 3 of the statutes.

student of the University, to graduate thereat or to hold any
advantage or privilege thereof.

The act also contains provisions for the appointment of a pro-
vice-chancellor and a registrar. The duties and responsibilities of
those officers are similar to their counterparts in other British-style
universities. Also, the heads of schools mentioned in Article 11 of
the statutes have duties similar to deans in other universities.

The committee structure, too, reproduces on African soil the
British pattern. The University Act provides for the formation of a
convocation, court, council, senate, and boards of schools. In
addition, it provides for the setting up of statutory committees and
subcommittees that report to either the senate or the council. Every
attempt has been made to have as wide a group as possible represented
on the 29-member council, including representatives of the students'
union as well as the University's academic staff association. The
intricate system of checks and balances and power sharing between the
council and the senate is in line with British tradition. The question
that arises is whether this intricate balance of power and responsibility,
which depends so much on unwritten custom and tradition, will in
fact work effectively in Mauritius or for that matter in other developing
countries where the university is a new and novel institution.

THE SCHOOL OF AGRICULTURE

As already noted, the School of Agriculture is the oldest constituent unit in the University. Established in 1924 by the Ministry of
Agriculture, the College of Agriculture (as it was called at that time)
concentrated its efforts from the very beginning on the training of
technicians for the island's major industry, sugar, and extension
workers for its main crop, sugar cane. Under the Ministry of
Agriculture, the College had a tradition of being intimately involved
in all phases of cane cultivation and sugar production. A significant
number of its staff consisted of personnel seconded from the Ministry
of Agriculture and other agencies to teach part-time at the College.
Upon completion of their training, the students were readily employed
in the various sugar estates. A good many of them were in part already
employed in the industry and released to attend various courses at the
College. In short, the College and the sugar industry worked very
closely together.

When the University was formed in 1965, the College was
renamed the School of Agriculture and incorporated into the University.
However, it retained a good many of its staff, administrators, and
more importantly, its character and ethos. It continued to be responsive to the needs of agriculture and industry.

Since its inception, the core program at the School of Agriculture has been the joint diploma course, Agriculture and Sugar Technology. As the name implies, the course seeks to train versatile workers who can work either in agriculture or industry.

Students must have obtained five "O" levels to enter the three-year program. The first year consists of general courses in basic science, which attempt to remedy the gross deficiency in science teaching at the secondary schools. For all practical purposes, the program starts during the second year. The courses include the following:

Crop Science and Production, which puts heavy stress on crops commonly grown in Mauritius—sugar cane, tea, potatoes, and tobacco. It emphasizes practical issues such as common diseases and pests that afflict those crops, and methods of treatment and prevention.

Animal Science and Production, which concentrates on a study of those animals of economic potential for the island, including poultry, goats, and cattle. The emphasis is on their production and care, prevention of disease, and milk and beef processing.

Agricultural Economics, which elaborates on the economic aspects of crop and animal production.

During the third and final year, the program deals with Sugar Technology. Courses in this area include Sugar Manufacture and Processing and Sugar Crystallization. The courses offered in the final year, like those in the previous year, are taught with Mauritian conditions in mind. Students visit sugar plantations and refineries, and every effort is made to acquaint them with local conditions and problems.

Those who complete the program are readily absorbed by the sugar industry. There is a constant dialogue and feedback between the School staff and employers, and, indeed, as already noted, a number of the professional staff of the Ministry of Agriculture and the sugar estates teach part-time at the School, helping to maintain the practical and utilitarian nature of the program. The student intake, 20 to 30 a year, has been carefully regulated to reflect the manpower needs of the industry and the employment market in the island as a whole.

The School launched its first degree program in 1970; the first group of nine graduates was awarded the B. Sc. degree in Agriculture in 1972-73. As practically all the students admitted to the first degree course had had previous work experience and were in fact graduates of the diploma program, even the degree course was not as theoretical as it might otherwise have been. Intake to the degree course is not expected to exceed ten students per year.

The course takes one year after the completion of the diploma program.

The School of Agriculture runs other diploma and certificate courses, principally (1) a diploma course in Medical Laboratory Technology with an annual intake of 15 students, a course started in 1973-74; and (2) three certificate courses in Tea Agronomy and Production, Sugar Analysis, and Sugar Manufacture, which are certificate courses of short duration (20 to 30 weeks) and are offered to part-time students in cooperation with the School of Industrial Technology.

THE SCHOOL OF ADMINISTRATION

The School of Administration is another of the three constituent schools of the University. It started with the opening of the University in 1965-66. Its early attempt to launch a degree course having been abandoned, the School has concentrated its offerings in subdegree programs. There are four "centers": the Center for Public Administration and Local Studies, the Center for Professional Studies, the Center for Economic Studies, and the Centre d'Administration des Entreprises, a unit set up in 1969 with the assistance of the French government and the University of Aiz-Marseille. During the 1974-75 year, the School had a total of 900 students, of whom roughly 50 percent were full-time students. Only one degree course is offered, a general degree in administration, the rest being all subdegree. The bulk of the course offerings are geared to persons already employed in the civil service and private firms.

THE SCHOOL OF INDUSTRIAL TECHNOLOGY

The School of Industrial Technology, like the other two schools, concentrates its offerings on diploma programs of various durations. The programs cover practically the whole spectrum of the physical and health sciences and include courses leading to diplomas in mechanical and electrical engineering, building and electrical engineering, and sanitary science. The School also offers part-time courses at the certificate level in a variety of fields including refrigeration and air-conditioning technology, and road construction. In addition, one degree course with a limited student enrollment, an honors degree in sugar technology, is offered.

THE FUTURE

Over the years, the University of Mauritius has earned a well-deserved reputation as a small but "development-oriented" University whose thrust is clearly and decidedly on middle-level manpower training. There is no question that a number of universities in the developing regions of the world could learn from the Mauritian experience and model. The inevitable question is, What does the future hold for the University? Obviously, this question cannot be answered in isolation. Much will depend on what the future holds for the island as a whole. The University will have to reassess its mission continually and renew its efforts in light of the changing needs and conditions on the island.

The University must also be continuously alert and sensitive to subtle social and political pressures and counterpressures in Mauritian society. In doing so, it will have to address itself to some of the most awkward issues facing Mauritius today. For instance, in a society where the social stratification appears to follow ethnic lines rather closely—with the whites on top, the Chinese next, the Indo-Pakistanis in the middle, and the "blacks" more or less at the bottom—is the University, by putting its thrust on middle-level training, unwittingly catering to the middle layer (the Indo-Pakistani group), thereby reinforcing, indirectly, the ethnic stratification of Mauritian society? How is the University coping with the inevitable alienation of the black population? What corrective measures (such as special admission avenues) are being taken by the University to redress inequity and to respond to the aspirations of the blacks? These issues become even more pressing when one realizes that since over 90 percent of secondary school enrollment is in private hands, the maldistribution of educational opportunity will have to be rectified below University level.

The trend in higher education in a number of African countries is toward "umbrella" (comprehensive) universities—that is, universities that integrate professional with technical programs. This trend is confirmed by the study on Higher Education and Development of which this case study is a part. The universities of Ahmadu Bello (Nigeria), Yaoundé (Cameroon), Zaïre, Ethiopia, and others illustrate the trend. These universities offer training programs at various levels (certificate, diploma, and degree) as well as in a variety of fields (health, agriculture, engineering, teacher training).

In many ways, the Mauritius case is quite different. The University's strength, and its distinctive feature, has been its pragmatic and realistic approach; it has put its thrust where it would have the most impact, namely, middle-level training. The larger universities may find the "umbrella" setup more appropriate because they cater to a much larger population, with a potentially much broader economic base. Since the area and population of Mauritius make it one of the smallest nations in Africa, the University has

been prudent in concentrating its efforts in only three faculties
(schools) and at the intermediate level.

Will the University be able to continue to adhere to this strategy?
The writer is not in a position to provide a definitive answer. However, it is worth noting two factors that are already discernible.
First, it appears that the labor market for middle-level manpower is
gradually drying up. This change will obviously have tremendous
implications for the University. Indeed, the writer was told during
his visit to the University that some courses had to be postponed or
even discontinued because of insufficient student enrollment. (And
student enrollment is one of the best gauges of the labor market!)
Second, as already noted, the ethnic and social stratification of
Mauritius being what it is, it will be very difficult for the University
not to respond to the aspirations of the black segment of the population.
Further, as families in the upper layer (whites and Chinese) are
probably wealthy enough to send their children abroad for university
degrees, even the middle layer (Indo-Pakistani) may not remain content
for long with subdegree qualifications.

These two factors—the small size of the labor market and the
inevitable aspirations for degree qualifications—will surely affect the
University's future course and direction. It has been successful so
far, as the example par excellence of a development-oriented university, precisely because for over 40 years it defined its role for
maximum impact with enviable precision. No doubt it will have to
redefine its objectives and its mission continually, a task the Mauritians themselves are best able to undertake.

8

AHMADU BELLO UNIVERSITY, NIGERIA

The Agricultural and Educational Role
of the University

HISTORY OF UNIVERSITY EDUCATION

When Nigeria became politically independent on October 1,
1960, there was only one institution of university status in the
country—University College, Ibadan, founded in 1948 by the government of Nigeria. This college had been set up at the recommendation of the British Elliot Commission on Higher Education
in West Africa. It was in a position to award its own certificates
and diplomas, but degrees were awarded by the University of
London with which the college enjoyed a special relationship. In
1962 the college achieved full university status and awarded its
first degrees in June 1963. By 1971 four additional universities
were in operation.

In the intervening period, however, the country suffered a
bitter and protracted civil war (1967-70), and money was diverted
from education to the war effort. With the cessation of hostilities,
a vast program of reconstruction and rehabilitation was undertaken.
High-level manpower needs have since become even more pressing,
and the universities, backed by the federal and state governments,
are doing all in their power to meet this challenge.

The history of the development of university education in
Nigeria is dramatic and rapid. By 1954 the pressure on the University College of Ibadan was great; preparations for Nigeria's political
independence were underway and already a large increase in manpower
needs was anticipated. That year, a federal constitution was adopted
dividing the country into three regions. Higher education was placed
on the concurrent legislation list, and both federal and regional governments had the power to create universities. The University College
of Ibadan was designated a federal responsibility, but by the end of
the year, it became increasingly clear that a single university institution would be inadequate for the manpower needs of an independent
Nigeria.

By 1958 the date for Nigerian independence was fixed, and a series of commissions began work, investigating the needs of the country with regard to higher education over the first 20 years of independence. The most important of these commissions was set up in 1959 and chaired by Sir Eric Ashby (later Lord Ashby of Brandon), of Clare College, Cambridge. The Ashby Commission report was published not long after independence and recommended the establishment of more universities so that Nigeria's university student population could reach a target of 7,500 by 1970 and over 10,000 during the 1970-80 decade. The commission pointed out that the existing British academic system was, in many ways, too inflexible to meet the needs of an African country, while American universities were more flexible and still managed to maintain very high academic standards.

THE AGRICULTURAL AND EDUCATIONAL ROLE OF THE UNIVERSITY: AHMADU BELLO

Three universities emerged in 1962 as a result of the Ashby report—Ile-Ife, Lagos, and Ahmadu Bello—each with its own charter to award its own degrees. * Ahmadu Bello University was specifically founded to serve the needs of the northern two thirds of Nigeria. This area covers approximately 250,000 square miles and has a population of about 50 million people, according to the November 1973 national census. The University made an impressive beginning in 1962 with 519 students, and by the 1973-74 session enrollments had risen to a total of 9,750 students in both degree and nondegree programs.

An accident of history, which on the one hand has posed enormous problems to the young institution, particularly in the area of administration, physical development, and harmonious integration, has on the other hand proved to be a cause of strength to the University in pursuing its mission to the peoples and area it was established to serve. The historic accident was the incorporation of four existing institutions of higher learning to form the broadly based University as follows:

1. The headquarters branch of the Nigerian College of Arts Science and Technology in Zaria became the main campus of the University and accommodates the disciplines existing before, now as degree programs. As a result, the University found itself with the following faculties on this campus: the Faculty of Arts, including the School of Fine Art, to which social sciences were added later; the Faculty of Science; the Faculty of Architecture—subsequently renamed the Faculty of Environmental Design to include urban and regional

*The other universities, and university governance, are described in Appendix 8.1.

planning and building technology as well as architecture; the Faculty
of Education; and the Faculty of Engineering.

Two faculties were added on the main campus—the Faculties of
Human Medicine and Veterinary Medicine.

2. The Institute of Administration, Zaria. The Institute was
started in the early 1950s by the government of the then northern
region of Nigeria to train all grades of public, local, and legal administration personnel in anticipation of independence and self-government.
With incorporation into the University, three of the University's
programs became based there: the Faculty of Administration, which
provides degree courses in public administration, business administration, accounting, and international relations; the Faculty of Law,
which provides degree and diploma courses in law; and the Institute
of Administration itself, which directly provides both undergraduate
and postgraduate diplomas in public administration, largely as in-
service training programs, as well as undergraduate diplomas in
accounting, banking, insurance, local government, and law. The
Institute also runs a conference center open to all sectors of the
national community.

3. The Research Division of the Northern Nigeria Ministry of
Agriculture, together with the Extension Research Liaison Service,
headquartered at Samaru, 13 kilometers from Zaria, was incorporated
into the University as the Institute for Agricultural Research and
Special Services. A faculty of agriculture was developed parallel to,
and in close association with, the Institute. Subsequently, the Division
for Colleges of Agriculture and Animal Science was added to the
University's agricultural complex. This division is composed of four
colleges for the training of middle-level extension workers in general
agriculture, home economics, horticulture, agricultural mechanization,
and irrigation agronomy and engineering.

4. The Higher Muslim Studies Section of the School for Arabic
Studies at Kano, some 110 miles north of Zaria, was also incorporated
into the University. It was first known as Ahmadu Bello College but
almost immediately became the Abdullahi Bayero College. The College
has only the one Faculty of Arabic and Islamic Studies, later renamed
the Faculty of Arts and Islamic Studies.

This brief historical background is important for an understanding of the subsequent development of the University. While acceding
to the University the academic capacity to train administrators and
management personnel at all levels for government, law, local
administration, and the private sector, the government was anxious
that the University courses and research not become ivory towers.
The Institute of Administration therefore was incorporated as a
semiautonomous entity, with an advisory (later changed to governing)

board, its membership drawn on an approximately 50-50 basis from government and University, but with the vice-chancellor of the University as chairman, thus giving the University veto power (which happily has never been needed). The Institute for Agricultural Research and Special Services set up a similar advisory (later governing) board in response to the government's anxiety to keep research practical and oriented to problem solving. The advisory board arrangement was novel both to the government and to the University, and despite initial difficulties in its operation, it soon became obvious that the University and government working together at the policy-making level offered an enormous opportunity for the University to make a meaningful impact on development. The model was quickly adopted for other areas of the University's activities, notably health, education, social and economic research, cultural studies, and adult education. Even what could be regarded as "pure" academic (though professional) faculties, such as education and veterinary medicine, have experimented with inviting the chief professional officers of the respective government ministries to serve as full members of their academic faculty boards, an experience that has proved rewarding for both sides. The opportunity for government officials to provide University academic staff with information on the practical problems of professional services in the field has galvanized the latter into a reorientation of their teaching and research: teaching to produce University graduates capable of adapting themselves to the practical realities in the field, and research to tackle the pressing developmental problems of the country. Over the 12 years of its existence, an attitude of mind has gradually evolved in which even the teacher of the most esoteric engineering science refuses to be left behind in the attempt to bring his knowledge and skills to bear on the developmental problems of the remotest and most backward village.

Against this background, the University's involvement in Nigerian education and agriculture will be described in more detail.

EDUCATION

Experience with the first two institutes* was so encouraging that barely three years after their inception, on the initiative of both the University and government, an Institute of Education was established with the following functions:

1. To act in an advisory and consultative capacity to the ministries charged with responsibility for education in the northern region of Nigeria (subsequently the six states created out of the

*See Appendix 8.2.

northern region) on any matters pertaining to education, and to collaborate with the said ministries both in the planning and extension of educational facilities in the six states and in the provision, either by itself or in conjunction with other bodies, of suitable courses of study and instruction;

2. To conduct and promote research, and to act as a coordinating agency for research in all matters pertaining to education and development of education in the states;

3. To promote the training of teachers and other persons engaged in or intending to engage in educational work;

4. To provide or coordinate courses, conferences, and lectures for persons concerned with, or interested in, education;

5. To provide educational centers for persons concerned with or interested in education; and

6. To advise on the establishment and maintenance of professional library services in the states.

The Institute of Education has clearly a tall order, but a challenging and exciting one. It has two governing bodies, a board of governors, under the chairmanship of the University vice-chancellor, composed of University representatives from the professional, art, and adult education fields and the six top policy makers of the education ministries of the states, and a professional and academic board under the chairmanship of the Institute director, with University members and the six professional officers of the education ministries. At first, the dean of the University's Faculty of Education (for training graduate teachers) served also as the director of the Institute. Quite early on, however, it became clear that the operations in the field are so vast and so vital that they cannot be carried out effectively by a part-time director. They were separated, and a full-time directorship for the Institute was created.

The Institute is divided, for operational purposes, into a number of divisions that do not, however, operate in watertight compartments.

The Division of Primary Education is the largest of the professional divisions. It is concerned with the following:

(1) The development of primary school curricula in all subjects, both in vernacular languages and in English. This is undertaken through 10-to-14-day workshops. Participants consist largely of outstanding primary-school teachers in the particular subject areas. The Institute's primary education specialists merely provide professional guidance.

(2) The production of primary teaching materials in all subject areas—science, mathematics, social science, and others. Familiar local materials and concepts are used as much as possible.

(3) The testing of new curricula and new teaching materials, and training teachers in the use of them are among the most important functions of the Division. The Institute operates through 30 model primary schools strategically located throughout the six states. Under a technical assistance agreement with Unesco/UNICEF, primary science equipment and materials have been prepared, provided, and are being tested in these primary schools. Unesco provides a primary science specialist who serves as a supervisor and inspector of operations under the direction of the head of the Division of Primary Education.

Division of Teacher Education: The Institute concerns itself primarily with the training of primary-school teachers. All the 80 or so Grade II teacher training colleges throughout the states are encouraged to become Affiliate Members of the Institute. This membership confers prestige. The Institute lays down basic minimum standards for affiliation, and new colleges strive to surpass this minimum as soon as possible in order to qualify. In return, the Institute organizes, among the teachers of the affiliated colleges, subject area boards of studies for curriculum development and improvement, provides professional leadership through its subject area specialists, coordinates syllabi, moderates examinations, and generally serves in a variety of advisory and consultancy capacities for the colleges. In order to ensure uniform standards, the Institute has even been requested to consider a takeover of the common college entrance examination as well as major involvement in the final qualifying examinations. It has however been making haste slowly because of the limitations of its own capacity.

In addition to regular institutional courses, seminars, workshops, and boards of study organized and run under the professional leadership of this Division, there is a Mobile Teacher Training group that moves from one teacher training college to another, to advise, assist, or train as may be required. The Division also provides vacation refresher courses for the teachers of the colleges and provides them with a platform for exchange of ideas on various topics suggested by the Institute or the colleges.

This Division provides one-year certificate training in educational administration for personnel wishing to qualify for service in the local education authorities, who run all the primary schools throughout the six states. Shorter refresher courses are also provided.

In addition the Institute runs two three-year Advanced Teachers Colleges that between them graduate 1,000 Nigerian Certificate of Education (NCE) holders each year, qualified to teach their subjects at lower levels of secondary schools and Grade II teachers' colleges, or to serve as primary school principals. Experienced teachers holding the NCE are also given one year at academic and professional training in their main subject area—for example, science, mathematics, social science, or vocational education. This training enhances their professional status and financial rewards and makes them more contented and more committed teachers.

Three years ago the Institute took over from the Faculty of Education the running of the one-year postgraduate Diploma (Certificate) of Education. Under a "sandwich" program, graduate students seeking formal teaching qualifications need not spend a whole year away from the classroom. They now come to the Institute for an intensive ten-week summer school, then go back to teach in their normal places of work for the nine months of the school year. Professional supervision and guidance of their teaching is organized by the Institute. During a second summer school session they complete their theoretical training, write up research dissertations on materials collected during the nine-month period of teaching, and take their final examinations. This program has become so popular with the graduate students involved, and in the country at large, that while initially the Institute was requested to reserve places for students from other universities, these universities are now instituting similar programs of their own.

The Division of Languages, the Division of Physical and Health Education, the Division of Vocational Education, and the Division of Art and Materials Development are complementary to the Division of Primary Education and the Division of Teacher Education, but in view of the intrinsic importance of these four subject areas and the tendency to allow them to become swamped in a total educational effort, it was considered desirable to separate them to enhance their special contributions to the whole. Materials Development is a service for the whole Institute. In view of the importance of illustrations in written materials for primary education, this service is being associated with art education for the present.

The Division of Research and Evaluation has essentially two functions: (1) coordination of all research work of the Institute itself, either initiated by the Institute or requested by the states and (2) assistance to the states in the collection of educational statistics, and advice on educational planning; the unit also monitors and evaluates all Institute and state programs in which the Institute is involved.

Library Services: In addition to its own model headquarters library, the Institute is required to establish and maintain model libraries for the teacher training colleges at strategic centers and assist them with acquisition of books and journals. A lack of professional library staff has hampered this development thus far. With the increased output of degree and diploma library graduates

expected from the University in the next few years, this service
should become operational.

The above statement on the Institute is by no means exhaustive.
A picture of university and government working harmoniously together
is envisioned that will have great impact on educational development
throughout the country. The average level of primary education
enrollment for eligible children in the northern states of Nigeria is at
best around 15 percent. With the recent decision of the Nigerian
government to achieve universal free primary education by 1980, the
role of the Institute as a think tank as well as a source of professional
leadership connot be overstressed.

AGRICULTURE

The agricultural complex of Ahmadu Bello University includes
the following organizations: (1) the Institute for Agricultural Research
and Special Services; the Rural Economic Research Unit at the
University is closely associated with this Institute; (2) the Faculty of
Agriculture; (3) the Faculty of Veterinary Medicine; (4) the Division
of Agriculture and Livestock Services Training (or the Division of
Colleges of Agriculture and Animal Science); and (5) the Extension
Research Liaison Service. Although these are administered separately
as semiautonomous units, their activities are coordinated at the top
by a provost for Agriculture and Veterinary Medicine who reports
directly to the University vice-chancellor.

The Institute for Agricultural Research and Special Services
was established to serve the following functions: to conduct research
into matters pertaining to agriculture, with special reference to
agriculture in the six northern states, and to administer matters
relating thereto; to cooperate with other bodies in the dissemination
of knowledge throughout the states of agricultural matters and of the
results of research conducted by the Institute; to provide (special)
agricultural extension services to the states; and to arrange for such
conferences, courses, and lectures for government officers and other
persons as may be considered to further the above functions.
The Institute is governed by a policy-making board of governors
under the chairmanship of the vice-chancellor. Members include the
chief agricultural and veterinary officers of the six states and representatives of the University. A professional and academic board
under the chairmanship of the director of the Institute is responsible
for the day-to-day running of the research programs. With its over
250-member research staff and five research substations, the
Institute conducts all the crops research for the six state governments

covering cash and food crops, rainfed and irrigated agriculture in all the ecologic zones covered by the 250,000 square miles of these states. In addition, the Institute undertakes contract research for the Federal Ministry of Agriculture and for the International Institute of Tropical Agriculture located in Ibadan. It is perhaps the largest agricultural research organization in central Africa.

Although it is also charged with responsibility for research on livestock, the Institute has not achieved much in this direction apart from extension work on animal feeds. It has, however, conclusively established that the local varieties of cattle cannot be suitable as dairy cattle; exotic breeds need to be imported and full modern animal husbandry and veterinary services provided for successful urban dairy schemes. For beef production, the local breed has been shown to be quite adequate with good feeding and adequate disease control. Selection and cross-breeding experiments to improve beef production are well underway, and an artificial insemination center is under construction, to be developed as a central service for the states. After the drought in the early 1970s devastated the cattle herds in Nigeria and the neighboring territories, the need for greater emphasis on livestock research became even more pressing. While such research is being carried out under the aegis of the Institute for Agricultural Research at present, a separate Institute for Research in Animal Production is planned within the University's agricultural complex. Work on sheep, goats, and poultry improvement is also being carried out in the Institute and will be greatly increased in the projected research institute.

The extension services being provided by the Institute are confined strictly to plant pathology diagnostic services in the field, surveillance and organization of control of locust invasion or grass-hopper and other pest damage, partial quarantine of imported plants and plant products, initial stages of production of improved seed, fertilizer, and pesticide recommendations, and monitoring and control of aflatoxin levels in groundnuts to internationally acceptable levels.

The Institute plays a dominant role in the Nigerian National Agricultural Research Council, and when that body was charged with the preparation of a 15-year plan for agricultural development in Nigeria, the draft provided by the Institute formed the basis of the program accepted by the federal government. The Institute has also provided the scientific and technological information required for the federal government's contemplated accelerated food production (Green Revolution) program in the areas of food grains—such as maize, millet, rice, and wheat.

The Rural Economic Research Unit, though not classified as a separate entity within the agricultural complex, works closely with the Institute for Agricultural Research and deserves special mention here. When the Research Division of the former government of Northern Nigeria became the Institute for Agricultural Research of the University, the University was disappointed to see that, despite its existence for approximately 38 years, and despite extension work by the Agricultural Ministry based on the research results, this research organization appeared to have brought about no change whatsoever in farming methods and practice. It became obvious that there was a serious communications gap between researchers and the local farmer; the big question was, Where?

The answer is a general one. "Experts" from outside Africa took the attitude that the African's methods are primitive and therefore must be totally swept aside and replaced by the scientific methods of these foreign experts. No one had ever bothered to find out why the local farmer did what he did and how he did it. As a result, the local farmer, who is not a fool, refused to accept changes that had no relevance to his circumstances and that he knew quite well would only lead to disaster.

The University decided, therefore, to introduce social science research, in particular agricultural economics and rural sociology, into the research program. It hoped that needed changes could be brought about in cooperation with the local farmer rather than forced down his throat willy-nilly. This cooperative approach seemed revolutionary. The Nigerian governmental elite, which had earlier tacitly accepted "white boss" superiority, was not likely to swallow the new idea immediately and provide funds for the necessary social science research. An approach was therefore made to the Ford Foundation, which responded generously and provided all that was required for the exercise. The Rural Economic Research Unit was born and has now been working in the field for about eight years.

Basically, it proceeded to ask the following questions: What does the local farmer do? Why does the local farmer do what he does? Can change for the better be brought about? How can this change be introduced? Most of the answers to the first three questions have been obtained and are indeed most fascinating. One interesting finding has been that agricultural research had been conducted on a European/American-style monocropping basis. Largely for insurance reasons, Nigerian farmers had evolved multicropping or intercropping patterns so that, where one crop failed, another was bound to succeed. It was not surprising, therefore, that extension advice based on monocropping failed totally. As a result of this discovery, agricultural research is now being conducted increasingly on a multicropping basis, and it is fascinating to find that yields under these circumstances have improved over the last few years, proving that the Nigerian farmer is not a fool after all. Not only does multicropping provide insurance against failure of a single crop, but the intercropping also augments total yield for a given acreage. It is when these fundamental questions are answered that the fourth—how to bring about change—can be approached in a rational, scientific manner.

The next stage of the work of the Unit is referred to as "guided introduction to change. " It consists basically of working with the farmers, introducing appropriate simple technology like fertilizers and pesticides, as well as providing credit through various arrangements. It is the writer's view that if a breakthrough is to come in the improvement of peasant agriculture in Nigeria, this work of "guided introduction to change" offers the best hope. The Nigerian government has since appreciated the importance of this work and is now fully funding the Unit.

The Faculty of Agriculture was established in 1962 in order to produce general agricultural scientists at the bachelor's degree level, with a view especially to manning the professional posts in government agricultural ministries. After the first ten years, this particular need has been largely satisfied, and training is now structured to provide specialization in major areas such as plant science, crop protection, soil science, and agricultural engineering. This training seeks to provide research workers urgently needed for the existing and projected agricultural research institutes throughout the country. As this area of need in turn becomes satisfied, the faculty proposes to put more emphasis on producing graduates trained in actual farming operations who will on their own take up farming on a scientific basis as a career. Specialist research workers of the Institute for Agricultural Research assist with the teaching programs of the faculty in their respective areas. Staff members of the faculty contribute to the research program of the Institute as well as carry on their own research in agricultural science.

The Faculty of Veterinary Medicine was established in 1964 with primary responsibility for training veterinarians and undertaking research in major disease problems of the country's livestock. The faculty has provided a good 80 percent of the veterinarians serving in both the public and private sectors in the country. The faculty emphasizes veterinary public health and preventive medicine and a positive approach to animal health.

A significant achievement has been the cooperation between this faculty and the Faculty of Agriculture. The Department of Animal Science in the Faculty of Agriculture is also a full constituent department within the Faculty of Veterinary Medicine. The two faculties have cooperated in developing a bachelor's degree program for specialists in animal husbandry and health, animal nutrition, and animal production. The decimation of the livestock populations during the recent severe drought of the Sahelian zone has created a special demand for these cadres of scientists. They will serve both as research scientists in institutions for animal production research and as animal production specialists on government-run cattle ranches.

The faculty has also undertaken outstanding research work in major diseases of cattle and poultry that will be standard reference works for generations to come.

Division of Agriculture and Livestock Services Training: The University inherited the three schools that constitute this Division— a school of general agriculture and home economics, a school of horticulture, and a livestock services training school. The schools provide one, two, or three years' middle-level certificates and diploma training for extension workers for the northern states. At the time the University took over in 1969, the total enrollment in the three schools was 300, but by 1974 it exceeded 1,000. The goal is to produce up to 1,000 extension workers each year for the governments of the northern states. Without this number of workers, it is difficult to make a meaningful impact on agricultural development in the country. With their availability through the University, pious hopes are being translated into practical reality.

In 1972, the University decided to open a fourth school for irrigation agronomists and mechanics. Up to about a decade ago, the country depended largely on rainfed agriculture; the severe drought made it clear that irrigation agriculture could no longer be considered a luxury but had to be developed in a big way. In response to this need, the Institute for Agricultural Research has established a research station in the drought-affected area for the development of relatively drought-resistant crops, as well as for the study of problems of irrigated crop production. As governments will be expanding their irrigation agriculture activities, it is essential to have suitably trained extension workers; this fourth school within the Division was established by the University to provide them.

Extension Research Liaison Service: No matter how excellent or how proper agricultural research may be or how well-trained extension workers are, results cannot be achieved without adequate extension research liaison. This service unit of the University bridges the gap between the University and its resources on the one hand and the government agricultural ministries and farmers on the other. It acts as a channel whereby problems of agriculture in the field can be passed on to University-based research workers, and research results can be put in a form suitable for passing on to the agricultural ministries responsible for direct extension to the farmers. The Service employs extension specialists in various agricultural subject areas who are in constant touch with research workers on the one hand and with farmers and government agricultural ministries on the other. They continually interpret one to the other. In addition, the Service runs radio and television programs, the former in 14 local languages. It also has a team of its own extension workers that tour farming regions extensively, answering farmers' questions on the spot. This particular service has been so successful that the federal Nigerian government has directed that all other agricultural research stations in the country develop similar extension research liaison services.

With the establishment of the Institute for Research in Animal Production, the Service will also supervise the extension research liaison for the new Institute. It hopes to develop a unified extension service for both crops and livestock. Up to the present, extension services for livestock farmers have not only lagged sharply behind those for crop farmers but have also often fallen between different government ministries. It is hoped that the University Service will set a pattern that will further encourage a mixed farming approach rather than separate advice from different government ministries. Too often at present, one set of extension workers advises on crop production and another set advises on animal production, each operating in watertight compartments.

Special Services: The Institute for Agricultural Research provides special services for all units of the agricultural complex. The services include surveillance—with respect to locust invasion, to impending adverse climatic factors, and to sudden appearance of plant or animal epidemic diseases—and prompt diagnosis of the situation. Special Services also implements corrective measures where the University has adequate resources; where it does not, Special Services provides prompt information to federal and state governments so that they may mobilize their own resources to control or cope with the situation.

Evaluation by ICED - HED Staff

Ahmadu Bello has emerged as one of the strongest development-oriented universities in Africa. The institutes reviewed above have all provided direct contributions and approaches to urgent community problems with a considerable measure of success. From a University standpoint, the coordination and unification of these several efforts have been made difficult by their autonomous status and relationships to different departments and ministries of government. They are spread over a wide geographical area and serve non-University clients as much as the University itself. They are subject to the play of national and tribal politics to a greater degree than more traditional university departments. They run the risk of becoming primarily service units, but this risk is balanced by contributions they are making in service to the nation and the region.

APPENDIX 8.1

Nigerian Universities

In the recent past, University College, Ibadan, which became the University of Ibadan in 1962, came in for a lot of criticism, partly because of limited student enrollment and partly because many observers felt the courses were too academic and narrow in concept and should be broader based. Greek and Latin, for example, were taught from the very beginning of the life of the College, and it was some time before courses more relevant to the political and cultural circumstances of the country, such as economics, politics, and African studies, were offered. To create a university whose mission was closely related to the social, economic, and political needs of the day-to-day life of the Nigerian people, Dr. Azikiwe's eastern region government sent an educational mission to Europe and North America to study the feasibility of setting up such a university.

The outcome was the formal opening of the University of Nigeria, Nsukka in 1960, as a climax to the independence celebrations. Nsukka is unique in many ways among African universities south of the Sahara and north of the Limpopo. It is the first university in modern times to be started wholly as a result of African initiative. It started with its own charter to award degrees and has a broad curriculum, including such subjects as music and physical education. A branch campus was opened in Calabar in 1974. (Nsukka was badly affected during the Nigerian civil war, but has been resuscitated, and efforts are being made by the federal government, with the assistance of other Nigerian universities, to put it back on its feet. It has been taken over by the federal government.)

Even before the Ashby report was published, the premier of the western region announced that his government intended to set up a university, and Ile-Ife was chosen as the location. This University began its first full year in October 1962, at a temporary site in the buildings of the former Nigerian College of Arts, Science and Technology (Ibadan Branch). In January 1967 the University began to move to its new permanent site at Ife and at present plans to expand to over 10,000 students.

The University of Lagos also opened in October 1962, with 130 students. Arts, education, engineering, and science faculties were added by October 1964, and since then, student enrollment figures have risen steadily. This university has worked hard to assist in the promotion of professional in-service courses, such as mass communications and business administration, through its continuing education centers. These courses have been of immense value in

providing well-trained, high-level manpower particularly for
the running of many commercial firms in the federal capital of
Lagos.

Future Developments

It is to be expected that the progress and expansion of the
universities will continue. Already the student enrollment figure
recommended by the Ashby commission, some 10,000 to be attained
during the 1970-80 decade, has been surpassed. In addition, the
Mid-West Institute of Technology became the University of Benin in
1972. Four new federal universities are to be established between
1975 and 1980.

The University of Ibadan has opened a branch at Jos offering
preliminary courses in the arts. One hundred students have been
enrolled, and courses started in January 1972. Degree courses in
the humanities and basic sciences are to commence soon.

Constitution

The Nigerian universities all have similar constitutions. Provision is usually made for a chancellor, the official head of the
university (the University of Nigeria in Nsukka differed: there, prior
to the civil war, the chancellor was also the chairman of the governing
council of the university). The supreme governing body of the university is the council, presided over the pro-chancellor or chairman,
who is appointed by the chancellor. In some cases, membership
includes lay people and overseas members. The senate is chaired by
the vice-chancellor; its members are professors and senior officials
of the university, such as the librarian, and also more junior academic staff selected by their colleagues. As an academic body, it
generally manages and often advises the council on academic affairs.
Faculty or school boards deal with courses of study and matters, such
as examinations, relating to the faculty and report to the senate
through their deans. A congregation, consisting of all members of
the academic staff and graduate members of the administration, can
make representations to council and senate on any matter affecting
the university. Provision is also made for the office of "visitor."
This office is usually held by the head of state in the case of federally
sponsored universities and by the governors of the states in the case
of universities founded by regional governments. The visitor is able
to order an inspection of the university, though such an inspection
is usually made only at the university's request.

Relationship to Government

All Nigerian universities are autonomous statutory bodies established by either the federal government or regional governments. At first, universities obtained their funds from the appropriate government, whether federal or regional, and thus naturally had strong financial links with the government concerned. The National Universities Committee, set up in 1962, now acts as a channel for government financial support to the universities.

Finance

Nigerian universities obtain the greater part of their funds from the federal and state governments. Fees and money from other sources, foreign aid, grants, gifts, and benefactions, account for approximately 20 percent of the univeristies' incomes.

External Aid

External aid constitutes only a small percentage of the universities' total income, yet does provide valuable assistance to the universities concerned. Some universities have entered into contracts with various external aid organizations, such as USAID and the Ford Foundation. Such agencies assist the universities by providing the services of experts in certain fields to help train Nigerians as counterparts. Reciprocal links have also been formed with certain overseas universities in the United Kingdom and the United States that also assist in providing the services of experts in fields where there is an acute shortage of local manpower. It is a notable fact that, as such contracts expire, having played their part in building up a strong body of nationals to take over, a considerable amount of good will and mutual cooperation continues to operate between the universities and the bodies concerned. External grants have also been made for equipment and buildings.

Preuniversity Education

Nigeria inherited a basic network of schools from the colonial era. The south of the country on the whole benefited from these schools far more than the north, which was rather neglected and even today faces massive problems in education and has a higher illiteracy rate than the rest of the country. Today, in the south primary education is more or less universal; in the north far fewer children of school age attend school. Since the creation of states in 1967 in place of the former regional divisions of the country, however, the

north of Nigeria has been tackling these problems energetically, and
great improvements have already taken place.

Throughout the country, the problems of developing secondary
education remain. Along with a number of grammar schools, there
are a few secondary modern schools and some commercial schools
of secondary education standard, although these latter schools are
mostly privately owned and financed. Generally children begin
secondary education at the age of 12 or 13. Throughout the country
students sit for the same school-leaving examination—the West
African School Certificate, which is organized by the West African
Examinations Council in collaboration with the University of Cambridge. A number of pupils continue with a sixth form education, if
available, and study for university entrance. After two years they
sit for the Higher School Certificate examination. A number of
students make their way into university by studying GCE "O" and "A"
levels through private study or correspondence courses. These
methods often result in a considerable gap in time between leaving
school and obtaining the minimum requirements necessary for a
university place.

Staff

The Nigerian universities are remarkable for the way in which
academics from all over the world work in harmony to promote the
well-being of their particular university. Most Nigerian universities
have staff members from at least ten different overseas countries as
well as a high percentage of nationals. As graduates from the Nigerian
universities return from postgraduate training (many having studied
in the United States or the United Kingdom), most of them are absorbed
back into their university of origin to begin their careers within that
university. No restrictions apply to any nationality with regard to
staff recruitment, and the results of this policy are clearly seen in
the universities today, which enjoy a truly cosmopolitan atmosphere.
The universities regard research as one of their basic functions, and
adequate time is available for individuals to pursue their research
projects in term time as well as during the long vacation. In most
universities, one or two terms of study leave may be taken every three
years. The universities usually try to provide all senior staff
members with accommodations on the campus, for which a rent of
7–8.75 percent of their salary is normally charged. If local circumstances dictate, staff members may be accommodated in off-campus
houses rented by the university.

Teaching is mainly done through lectures and laboratory
classes. Seminars and tutorials also form an important part of the
teaching.

Academic Year

The academic year runs from October to June, divided into
three terms: October-December, January-March, and April-June.
Each term is of 10-11 weeks' duration. The long vacation falls between
June and October. This calendar is in the process of being reviewed.

Interuniversity Organizations

A committee of vice-chancellors acts as a coordinating body
among the universities and forms a channel through which the joint
opinion of the universities on any matter affecting education can be
expressed. This body, however, has no legal status. It cooperates
with the National Universities Commission, the National Manpower
Board, and similar bodies.

All the universities have formed associations of university
teachers with varying forms of activity and have federated themselves
into a national association.

There is also a National Union of Nigerian Students, which is
a federation of the students' unions of the various universities. This
body is active in the organization of interuniversity activities such
as sports and conferences.

APPENDIX 8.2

There are three other institutes at Ahmadu Bello. The first,
the Institute of Administration, provides undergraduate and postgraduate diplomas in public administration, largely as in-service training
programs, and also offers diplomas in accounting, banking, insurance,
local government, and law. The second, the Institute of Health,
maintains facilities for training medical students and runs hospital
services for the community. It is trying to better rural health by
training teams made up of physicians, nurses, midwives, and
technicians. The third, the Center for Nigerian Cultural Studies
conducts research on the culture of Nigeria, particularly of the six
northern states, which Ahmadu Bello University serves. The Center
concentrates on archaeology, dance, drama, and musicology and
seeks, through popular theater and children's television, both to
preserve and present cultural traditions in these fields.

9

THE UNIVERSITY OF KHARTOUM, SUDAN

Staff Development in an African University

ORIGINS OF THE UNIVERSITY

In July 1956, six months after Sudan became independent, the University of Khartoum attained the full status of an independent university. Since 1948 it had been a university college, awarding University of London degrees under the Special Relationship Scheme. Before that, the college had awarded its own diplomas on behalf of several postsecondary institutes, known at that time as the Higher Schools. The first of these was the Kitchener School of Medicine, established in 1924. The Khartoum School of Law was established in 1934. These were professional schools, linked to their repsective government departments, and their teaching staff was appointed by the departments concerned.

It was only after World War II that the idea of establishing a true university was given serious consideration. As in other British colonies, the first step was the establishment of a university college linked with London University. At the time of independence, the academic and senior administrative staff of the university college were mainly recruited from Britain and from the other partner in the Condominium Administration, Egypt. Although the council of the University, the highest authority, consisted predominantly of Sudanese and had a Sudanese chairman, the senate, the highest academic authority, had a majority of expatriates, with only a few Sudanese academic staff. The vice-chancellor, the registrar, the librarian, the bursar, and all the deans were expatriates. Only the warden of students and a few junior administrative officers were Sudanese.

SUDANIZATION OF THE UNIVERSITY

Decision making regarding academic and administrative affairs was thus in the hands of expatriates. This preponderance of expatriates in the University, especially in the senior administrative

posts, was unusual in the country at the time. The Sudanization of
civil service posts had been completed at the time of independence,
and Sudanese were making the decisions at all levels of government.
Bringing more Sudanese into the University administration was
therefore looked upon as the starting point for staff development.

Administration: Senior Posts

The University of Khartoum focused on administrative rather
than academic staff positions for a number of practical reasons. In
the first place, few Sudanese were sufficiently qualified for the
academic staff. In the second place, the civil service had attracted
those who were eligible for university appointment, and the few
Sudanese graduates who might have been trained for academic positions
preferred to work in the civil service, attracted by the status such
jobs conferred. The civil service also provided better conditions of
service than the University, which, at that time, did not have clearly
established career patterns. While the University had trouble
recruiting academic staff, however, there were a number of Sudanese
qualified and available to take over the senior administrative posts.
Such posts carried with them the power and authority that was
indispensable if new policies were to be initiated and implemented
and if more attractive conditions for academic staff were to be
established.

Priority was thus given to the Sudanization of senior administrative posts as a step in making and implementing staff development
policy. By 1958, Sudanese had been appointed to the posts of vice-
chancellor, registrar, librarian, academic and administrative
secretaries, and financial controller. The appointees were chosen
from both inside and outside the University. The criteria for selection
were not based on academic qualifications alone; experience in institutions similar to the University was an important consideration.

By 1960 the University administration was completely Sudanized.
Today, all administrative posts, at both University and faculty levels,
continue to be filled by Sudanese. This would not have been possible
without a continuous flow of young graduates into the administration
and on-the-job training inside and outside the University. The training
included short-term visits to postsecondary institutions outside the
country and long-term courses for further degrees.

Financial affairs officers were the most difficult to recruit. A
shortage of qualified financial managers and accountants, and the
absence until recently of local training in this area, meant that the
University had to rely on outside resources—that is, outside the
University but inside the country—and to depend on retired government
employees rather than qualified graduates.

Another problem area was engineering and physical plant administration. Building, with its attendant problems in a developing residential university such as Khartoum, is inevitably a crucial matter, for which a special type of administrator is needed. Again, the shortage of engineers made recruitment for the post of administrator-engineer difficult.

Deficiencies in financial management—budget-making and control—and the management and administration of buildings can become real obstacles to the efficient running of a university. A plan for the development of administrative staff should include these two important areas of university administration. Financial and plant administrators need not only specialist qualifications but also well-developed managerial and administrative skills. No university administration can afford to underestimate their importance.

Administration: Academic Positions

The policy of bringing nationals into the University administration was not, however, confined to executive or nonacademic positions. The healthy development of the University requires that nationals should participate fully in academic decision making—as deans of faculties and heads of teaching and research units and departments. The effort to bring Sudanese into these positions, however, ran up against the inherited system of academic seniority. Since the majority of the academic staff were expatriates, following this tradition meant that Sudanese academic staff were exluded from such appointments.

To overcome this problem, a new system of promotion and appointments to the positions of dean and head was devised. Academic seniority ceased to be the only criterion for appointments to these posts, and appointments were made from among Sudanese with adequate experience whenever they were available. Successful implementation of this system was not easy. It required the cooperation of the senior academic expatriates. As expatriates continued to be much needed as teachers, it was important not to alienate them. In addition, competition arose among the Sudanese for the posts, which carried with them certain privileges. The solution chosen was to rotate the posts. Although this system did not promote the continuity that was so greatly needed at the time, it was less disadvantageous than a system that did not take into consideration the national aspects of the issue, and, by 1960, all University deans and many heads of departments were Sudanese.

Teaching Staff

The second stage in staff development was in the area of the academic or teaching staff. At the time of University independence

in 1956, the Sudanese academic staff of the level of lecturer and above
did not exceed 5 percent of the total in the whole University. In 1958,
when the first Sudanese vice-chancellor was appointed, they constituted
about 10 percent. By 1967-68, ten years later, the number of Sudanese
academic staff had risen to 50 percent.

Table 9.1 shows the distribution of academic staff, according
to nationality and status, during 1972-73.

In the next two years, the percentage of Sudanese increased to
about 80 percent of the total staff. The University of Khartoum is in
this respect unique; according to information available, no university
in sub-Saharan Africa has achieved this high a percentage of local
staff. Expatriates are dominant in most of these universities, the
Africanization, or localization, process having been rather slow or
having been offset by the sharply increased demand for additional
faculty generated by increased student enrollment.

Table 9.2 shows that there are 25 universities in Africa where
the language of instruction is English, 14 where it is French, eight
that use both Arabic and English, six Arabic and French, and one
French and English. Although no detailed information on the nationality
of staff is available, it can safely be said that the majority of staff
in these universities, except for those in Egypt and to a lesser extent
Sudan, are expatriates.

Senior Scholars and Research Fellowships Scheme

This increase in Sudanese staff was achieved in Sudan through
a special training scheme known as the Senior Scholars and Research
Fellowships Scheme. The scheme involved the following procedures:

1. University departments selected outstanding Sudanese
graduates each year. The University then would appoint them as
teaching and research assistants and send them to universities outside
the country to take postgraduate degrees (masters and doctorates)
with a view to their joining the academic staff upon successful completion of their course.

2. University departments selected outstanding Sudanese
undergraduates who had spent at least two years in the University
and sent them abroad to take first and postgraduate degrees in areas
of special shortage, for example, mathematics and physics.

3. The University departments nominated young Sudanese
members of the academic staff—assistant lecturers without doctorates—
and sent them abroad to obtain a doctorate.

A great deal of persuasion was needed before this policy could
be implemented. Some expatriates looked upon the scheme as

TABLE 9.1

Sudanese and Expatriate Staff by Status and Faculty, 1972–73

(total staff = 382)

	Status							
	Professor		Reader		Senior Lecturer		Lecturer	
	Sudanese	Expatriate	Sudanese	Expatriate	Sudanese	Expatriate	Sudanese	Expatriate
Agriculture	1	—	—	—	12	—	28	—
Arts	1	1	2	—	4	7	27	19
Economics and Social Sciences	—	1	—	—	1	3	19	12
Engineering and Architecture	1	3	—	—	4	6	31	6
Law	1	—	—	—	1	2	5	—
Medicine	6	2	4	1	12	2	40	5
Pharmacy	—	2	—	—	2	—	6	3
Science	—	2	4	—	8	11	32	6
Veterinary Science	2	3	1	1	7	—	21	1
Subtotal	12	14	11	2	51	31	209	52
Total	26		13		82		261	

Source: University Statistics Office.

TABLE 9.2

Staff Positions in African Universities, 1971-72

| University | Language | Academic Staff | | | Number of Students |
		Full-time	Part-time	Total	
Algeria					
University of Algeria	A/F	n.a.	n.a.	500	9,500
University of Constantine	A/F	n.a.	n.a.	300	8,600
University of Oran	A/F	n.a.	n.a.	370	4,600
Burundi					
University of Burundi	F	n.a.	n.a.	68	466
Cameroon					
University of Yaoundé	F/E	n.a.	n.a.	356	3,544
Central African Republic					
Bokassa University	F	n.a.	n.a.	54	550
Chad					
University of Chad	F	n.a.	n.a.	25	300
Congo					
University of Brazzaville	F	n.a.	n.a.	n.a.	2,000
Dahomey					
University of Dahomey	F	91	48	139	1,135

Egypt					
Ain Shams University	A/E	n.a.	n.a.	1,047	60,351
Al-Azhar University	A/E	n.a.	n.a.	705	16,500
University of Alexandria	n.a.	n.a.	n.a.	2,350	42,476
American University in Cairo	E	148	193	341	5,990
University of Assiut	A/E	471	137	608	22,715
University of Cairo	n.a.	n.a.	n.a.	2,892	64,606
University of Mansoura	A/E	152	20	172	15,024
University of Mid-Delta	A/E	n.a	n.a.	414	6,449
Ethiopia					
University of Asmara	E	43	32	75	774
Hailie Selassie I University	E	514	n.a.	514	4,978
Gabon					
National University of Gabon	F	75	60	135	947
Ghana					
University of Cape Coast	E	178	n.a.	178	1,100
University of Ghana	E	428	24	452	2,549
University of Science and Technology	E	256	4	260	1,885
Ivory Coast					
University of Abidjan	F	.287	139	426	5,202
Kenya					
University of Nairobi	E	n.a.	n.a.	340	3,857

(continued)

TABLE 9.2 (Continued)

| University | Language | Academic Staff | | | Number of Students |
		Full-time	Part-time	Total	
Lesotho					
University of Botswana, Lesotho and Swaziland	E	146	10	156	923
Liberia					
Cuttington College	E	32	1	33	313
University of Liberia	E	n.a.	n.a.	140	1,000
Libya					
University of Benghazi	A/E	225	n.a.	225	5,114
Malagasy					
University of Malagasy	F	n.a.	n.a.	260	7,000
Malawi					
University of Malawi	E	157	17	174	1,073
Mauritius					
University of Mauritius	E	33	57	90	2,000
Morocco					
University of Mohamed V	A/F	n.a.	n.a.	n.a.	15,803
University of Qarawiine	A/F	n.a.	n.a.	n.a.	866
Niger					
University of Niamey	F	42	11	53	224

Nigeria					
Ahmadu Bello University	E	925	n.a.	925	3,082
University of Benin	E	n.a.	n.a.	n.a.	417
University of Ibadan	E	566	n.a.	566	4,210
University of Ife	E	n.a.	n.a.	n.a.	3,455
University of Lagos	E	423	7	416	3,053
University of Nigeria	E	500	n.a.	500	3,909
Rwanda					
National University of Rwanda	F	60	n.a.	n.a.	525
Senegal					
University of Dakar	F	n.a.	n.a.	n.a.	5,319
Sierra Leone					
Fourah Bay College	E	165	41	124	936
Njala University College	E	114	n.a.	n.a.	700
Somalia					
National University of Somalia	E	99	20	79	1,617
Sudan					
University of Cairo, Khartoum Br.	A/E	80	n.a.	80	5,100
Islamic University of Omdurman	A/E	53	n.a.	n.a.	625
University of Khartoum	E	870	205	665	6,719
Tanzania					
University of Dar es Salaam	E	325	n.a.	n.a.	2,346
Togo					
University of Benin	F	131	n.a.	n.a.	1,400
Tunisia					
University of Tunis	A/F	628	n.a.	n.a.	10,849

(continued)

TABLE 9.2 (Continued)

| University | Language | Academic Staff | | | Number of Students |
		Full-time	Part-time	Total	
Uganda					
Makerere University	E	400	11	411	3,935
Upper Volta					
Center for Higher Studies	F	30	20	50	360
Zaïre					
National University of Zaïre	F	1,410	73	1,483	16,054
Zambia					
University of Zambia	E	320	34	354	2,248
Total	—	n.a.	n.a.	21,089	397,273

*A: Arabic; E: English; F: French.

n.a. = not available.

Source: Information from Association of African Universities.

calculated to replace them by Sudanese. Some argued that a university should be international in outlook and only concerned with the best, and therefore should not go out of its way to train Sudanese for university jobs. They argued that this would deprive the University of badly needed expatriates. Some expatriates, although on a different and better salary scale than their Sudanese colleagues, argued that the scheme, being exclusively for the Sudanese, was discriminatory against non-Sudanese graduates and non-Sudanese lecturers. Notwithstanding the open and hidden opposition, the scheme was approved as a matter of general policy.

After approval, further problems arose. These concerned selection, finances, and placement.

The problem of selection involved two questions: (1) Who should make the recommendations, and with whom should the final decision rest? and (2) What were the criteria for selection in terms of numbers and academic qualifications?

To leave the matter of selection wholly in the hands of departments where non-Sudanese were in charge was considered unsatisfactory. On the other hand, to bypass the department meant going against University tradition.

Concerning how many and who should be selected, it was decided that the numbers should be left open and the minimum qualification for selection would be an upper second-class honors degree. This was the minimum accepted in British universities for appointment to academic teaching posts. Two more problems then arose as to whether the department would have to include persons selected in its budget, and what would happen in cases where the standard was not up to the level of upper second-class honors but where the need was greater than the supply.

In order to overcome these problems, a special committee (the Senior Scholarships and Research Fellowships Committee) was created to receive recommendations and make final decisions. In addition, it was decided to create a special fund in the University budget to finance the scheme. The fund would be under the control of the scholarships committee, which consisted of faculty representatives and was chaired by the vice-chancellor, as the chief academic and administrative officer of the University.

In the early years, because only a small number of graduates had the required qualifications, the problem of finance was not serious. The funds needed were included in the annual estimates. As recruitment of expatriates became more difficult, because of competition from other universities and for other reasons, the need for training greater numbers of Sudanese was increasingly felt, and the University's own resources became insufficient to cope with the demand.

Two steps were taken to raise needed funds. First, the allocation in the University's own budget was increased, and second,
outside help was sought, especially from foundations, from other
governments, such as the United Kingdom, and from other institutions
inside and outside the country. In most of the "exchange and cooperation" schemes entered into with other universities, a provision for
training Sudanese staff was included. Thus a revolving fund, fed
from internal and external resources, was established. The fund was
enough to finance the planned training program. The total fund rose
from Ls. 100,000 in 1965 to Ls. 180,000 in 1967, and to Ls. 250,000
in 1974. In addition to this, external assistance permitted the training
of an average of 40 persons every three years on British government
scholarships and ten every three years on scholarships offered by
other governments and institutions.

During the period from 1960-61 to 1967-68, the numbers of
Sudanese graduates selected by the Univeristy under this scheme
(for training abroad with a view to joining the academic staff of the
University) were as follows:

60/61	61/62	62/63	63/64	64/65	65/66	66/67	67/68
50	61	101	140	148	177	196	226

The increase in numbers reflected the growth in demand for
qualified academic staff, the decrease in the number of qualified
graduates, the need for new specializations, and the realization that
expatriates were not readily available for appointment, especially in
shortage areas, such as mathematics, physics, and engineering.
Under the fellowships scheme, 300 Sudanese were prepared and trained
during the period 1960-74 to fill the academic and teaching posts of
the University. It took three to four years on the average to train one
graduate, at an average cost of $1,000 per year (excluding salaries
paid at home), depending on the country of training and the discipline.
It normally cost three times as much for a graduate to be trained in
the United States as in the United Kingdom.

The other problem, that of the academic standard to be accepted
when not enough candidates were available, was overcome by making
some exceptions. For example, when an upper second-class honors
candidate was not available, a good lower second-class candidate was
selected. A student with a good general degree in the first or second
division would be selected if it was found that no better candidate was
forthcoming. Later, as postgraduate studies were developed in the
University, candidates with a general degree plus a good master's
degree were eligible for selection. A less strict adherence to the
rules originally laid down was found to be the best answer to the
problem of widening the basis of selection and increasing the numbers

so as to meet the expected demand for staff resulting from expansion
in enrollments. Later, selection was extended, through advertisement,
to include Sudanese graduates from other universities. The scheme,
started exclusively for the graduates of the University of Khartoum,
eventually included Sudanese graduates in general, irrespective of the
university from which they had graduated.

Generally speaking, there was little wastage. Because the system
of selection gave priority to high academic standards and was based on
competition, very few of those selected failed to attain the required
level. Moreover, very few elected to stay behind and not return to
their country.

Placement of candidates in universities abroad did not usually
present a problem. The close relationship with British universities,
and the exchange programs, were useful in this respect. External
examiners and visiting professors were particularly helpful. As the
number of those to be trained grew, and as new relationships, both
official and personal, were created, the training was no longer confined
to a few universities. Graduates were sent to the United Kingdom,
the United States, the USSR, France, Egypt, Australia, and other
countries. This variety of countries in which candidates were placed
meant a diversification of training: The future University staff would
no longer have had their training solely in the British system.

Technicians

The University of Khartoum depended largely on expatriate
laboratory technicians. As the University expanded and its laboratories increased, the need for qualified laboratory technicians became
greater and greater. Here also, there was a shortage of supply from
inside and outside the country.

The answer was to establish a scheme of training similar to that
for the academic staff. The Senior Scholarships and Research Fellowships Scheme was thus later extended to include technicians, and
candidates were selected and sent abroad to qualify; later, a local
center was created in the University. The technicians' training
scheme, however, did not achieve the same success as the academic
staff scheme. In the first place, there were few candidates with a
suitable background; selection was from secondary school graduates
who had failed to get a place in a university. Second, there was a
language problem. Third, the salary structure for technicians did
not attract good candidates. A few of those selected for training
abroad, especially in the area of medical laboratory work, elected
to stay behind because of the high salaries paid to them compared to
what they would have received if they had returned to Sudan. A few
others joined other Sudanese institutions that paid better salaries.

It was only when a local training scheme was established to supplement the overseas training scheme that it became possible to increase the number of qualified technicians. In addition, it was found necessary to adjust the salaries of technicians so as to make them more attractive.

The experience of the University of Khartoum shows that it is necessary to combine internal and external training schemes. It may be necessary to create a special fund for this purpose. In addition, it may be valuable to appoint a qualified person to be in charge of this important area.

CONCLUSIONS

The training scheme, which began in a modest way, has become one of the most important aspects of University policy. It would have been impossible for the University to meet the need for expansion without the successful implementation of such a scheme, a scheme including all categories of staff—administrators, teachers, and technicians.

The making of detailed plans for staff development is usually difficult. There are a number of unknown factors: financial resources, availability of qualified candidates and of places for training outside the university. The most important factor, however, is the attitude of the trainees and whether on their return they continue to serve in the university. There is always the attraction of international organizations and other universities, particularly African universities, which continue to require, and attract, young academics to meet their growing need for staff. Because of national interests a university must sometimes allow someone whom it has trained to leave and join another university or an international organization.

On the other hand, it is always difficult to predict the development of university education in a developing country. Pressures are such that the numbers planned for may bear no relation to the numbers actually admitted. It would have been difficult for the University administration ten years ago to predict the present number of students in the University of Khartoum. Today there are 7,500 undergraduates as compared with the figure of 5,000 agreed on in 1965 as the maximum. It can thus be seen that it is important to train as many candidates as are available, in all fields and in different institutions, and continually to increase the funds for this purpose.

Successful staff development schemes, however, do not only mean the training of nationals to fill teaching posts. Since university functions are teaching, carrying out research, and contributing to national development, a university should ensure its staff continuous access to and links with their colleagues inside and outside the country.

Exchange programs with other universities and a system of sabbatical leaves are helpful in this respect.

Such schemes are valuable because of the opportunities they provide for young academics to bring themselves up to date and to rub shoulders with their colleagues in other insitutions. In addition, they provide periods away from teaching and an opportunity to do research. Thus, a successful staff development scheme should include training both before and after staff appointment.

A final word: Preparing and training staff to teach the increasing number of students enrolled in the universities of the developing countries is perhaps the most important task that a university can undertake, and it should be a constant preoccupation.

10

THE HIGHER EDUCATION SYSTEM IN SUDAN

A Critique of a National Education System

Sudan, which has the largest land area in Africa, * a high potential for agriculture, forestry, and animal husbandry, and some of the most fertile irrigated land in the world, has also one of the lowest per capita incomes and gives a complex picture of development. On the one hand, there has already been development over the last 50 years, which in any other country would have to be counted as enormous, in terms of the amount of land and the number of people affected, the cash returns, the institutional growth, and the potential for economic growth for the next 50 years. On the other hand, the land area so far developed is small in proportion to the potential; the increase in the employed labor force is small in the same terms; the cash returns have nearly all gone into infrastructure and the expansion of government with almost none left over for improved living standards; the institutional development is small in relation to the size of the country and its population (15 million); and development schemes implemented in recent years are hardly more than extensions of the basic schemes already in operation. The huge task of planning and establishing development on the scale that the potentials suggest has been underway for a relatively short time.

Still another view is of a country moving rapidly to a confrontation with a future of growth and action after a time of inaction on development problems. Today, international agencies, bankers, suppliers of heavy equipment, experts of every variety, and buyers and sellers of every kind of commodity pass through the airport and the hotels in an endless stream. Development is so near that it is almost real, but underneath the excitement there is the fact that it has not yet arrived.

---

* 2.5 million square kilometers.

DEVELOPMENT AND GOVERNMENT

Against the exciting view of the future there is the reality of the present. Just as the Sudanese per capita income is one of the lowest in the world, so the Sudanese government income for the support of its agencies is also one of the lowest in the world. As a result, the government bureaucracy lives in a harsh present while the political leadership, supported and encouraged by the international development agencies, and buoyed by the hopes of the people, sees the brightness of the future. In fact, young people from age 15 to 25, representing as much as a third of the population, take a brilliant future for granted and chastise the government for not moving faster to make use of it. So it follows that of all government activities, education, in the broadest sense of the term, is the one most affected in modernizing an inadequate and outdated system to prepare for a future already populated by ambitious and critical youth.

THE EDUCATIONAL SYSTEM

The educational system is based on a six-year elementary school with an enrollment of approximately 1,100,000. Forty percent of those who enter the first grade move on, after the primary school leaving examination, to the next three-year stage of general education. An additional small number who finish the sixth grade but fail the leaving examination go on to vocational training centers. In 1973-74, there were approximately 165,000 general secondary students, of whom slightly less than half can be expected to enter the higher secondary level. This next level includes a three-year academic course preparing for university entrance with a total 1973-74 enrollment of 53,000, a four-year secondary technical line with an enrollment of 4,000 students, and a four-year secondary program training primary-school teachers with an enrollment of about 5,000 pupils. Thus the number of students entering primary school is cut by almost two-thirds at the end of six years, by another half after three more years, and then by another half after the final three years of secondary school, yielding between six and seven secondary school leavers for every 100 primary school entrants.

Students who pass the higher secondary examination may go to three universities or 36 other postsecondary training institutes. Of the school leavers in 1973-74, about one out of four was admitted to the University of Khartoum (6,783 students), about one out of five goes to one of the higher technical schools (2,400 students), and about the same proportion goes either to the University of Cairo, Khartoum branch (9,500 students) or to an overseas university on a bilateral scholarship arrangement. (According to government figures,

there are 4,600 students outside Sudan.) Sudan has a total of some
21,500 university students, of whom approximately two thirds are
enrolled either in the University of Cairo—Khartoum or Cairo
campuses—or in foreign universities.

A first-grade student has, therefore, about one chance out of
24 to enter higher education, which in terms of developing country
norms is a relatively high percentage. Selection is, in effect,
controlled from the first grade on by the criterion of university
requirements as interpreted at successive grade levels, and the spur
of ambition for university entrance is the force behind student
persistence. The candidates for the universities are screened and
selected by grade point average, ensuring an intellectually homogeneous
student body. Ambition and persistence on the part of students in the
lower schools are further encouraged by the premium government
salaries paid to university graduates.

In most developing countries, the selections in the lower schools
are either economic, based on tuition charges that may seem nominal
but are not, or achieved de facto by location of secondary schools in
urban centers, which rules out most rural students. However, in
Sudan the schools are free and the secondary schools are well
distributed and offer free room and board, so that the products of the
schools represent a cross-section of the population, at least insofar
as the present school system actually reaches the country as a whole.

THE PROBLEMS OF HIGHER EDUCATION

Higher education in Sudan is characterized by three special
problems: a lack of technical training, inadequate provision for women,
and a situation in which the University of Khartoum is protected from
a clamor for expansion and relevance because a large proportion
of Sudanese students in postsecondary education study abroad or in
the Khartoum branch of the University of Cairo.

Lack of Technical Training

There are apparent surpluses annually of both secondary school
leavers and university graduates and, at the same time, a serious
shortage of technicians. If the technical programs were expanded to
the size required to meet the shortage, and fully enrolled, they would
take up the present surplus of school leavers. None of the Sudanese
universities, however, offers technical or teacher training programs,
and graduates of training programs in these areas are not ordinarily
eligible for university entrance, further contributing to the homogeneity
of the student body. Students directed into secondary-level teacher
training and technical education are those who stand lowest in the

ninth-grade leaving examinations but still pass. In theory these students can qualify for university entrance on finishing their four-year secondary training program, but in practice, few are admitted. (Students of the same age are directed into vocational training after failure on the ninth-grade leaving examination.)

The same discrimination between technical and teacher training institutions and university entrance exists at the postsecondary level. Only the ones who do not get into university apply, and there is almost no possibility of later movement to university for either undergraduate or postgraduate work.

Technical schools at every level are underenrolled in terms of their capacity. They also have a very high rate of student withdrawal, because graduates are not assured of jobs on graduation, a life career structure, opportunity for later return for advanced schooling, or a reasonable range of salary. There is a tremendous difference in prestige between universities and the technical schools. In other words, technical education presents an essentially unattractive alternative, whose unattractiveness is reinforced by university and government attitudes toward the quality of technical school entrants and graduates.

Despite the serious lack of technicians (it is estimated that at most there is no more than one technician for each professional in the same field), there does not appear to be any strong demand for expansion of technical training, nor have other steps, such as changes in career structures and salary levels, been taken to enlarge the numbers. Professionals must thus accept with equanimity the fact that they must do their own technical work, and much important but not imperative technical work is simply not done. In either case, the quality of professional work must suffer, while the demand for technicians is diminished.

There is indication of indecision on the part of government in the development of technical education. The only effective technical training operation in the Sudan, the Khartoum Polytechnic Institute, was broken up several years ago, and its parts were dispersed among several localities. The move proved disastrous and has since been largely reversed, but the institutional strength and unity that existed has not been recaptured, and no alternative organization has appeared. The Ministry of Education, which has about half of the technical institutions under its authority, has no specific organization for policy making in technical and vocational fields. The National Council for Higher Education (NCHE), which does have a Committee of Principals, has not convened that body for any significant purpose and does not appear to consider it as a policy group. The other ministries that control small technical institutes do not coordinate these activities with the Ministry of Education.

The total impression that remains after inquiry into technical education is that of a history of disinterest and pro-forma support on the part of the government. A very fresh and forward view at high levels in the Ministry of Education seems now to exist. This new attitude, it is hoped, will bring rapid improvement to the present situation.

Education and Women

The educational selection process not only discourages technical training, but it is also failing to make use of women, a very large potential labor force of individuals who can work effectively at professional, technical, and clerical levels. Aside from the need for an efficient labor force, however, concern is occasioned by the traditional sanctions still imposed on women in many areas and circumstances. In a nation whose rising generation will live most of its adult life in the twenty-first century, there is no place for customs that, however appropriate ten centuries or even one century ago, are no longer relevant.

Out of the 22 institutions of higher education under the NCHE, all except four enroll women. These institutions range from the Institute of Secretaries and the Khartoum Nursing College to the Khartoum Institute of Mechanical and Electrical Engineers. What is most striking is that out of 223 women students admitted to the University of Khartoum, the Higher Technical Teacher Training Institute, Islamic University, and the Higher Institute of Financial and Commercial Studies in 1973/74, only 81 (36 percent) were admitted in nonscientific disciplines. In 1973/74, a total of 489 women (about 20 percent) were enrolled in the 18 postsecondary higher institutes and colleges (except Khartoum Polytechnic, which is being liquidated, the universities, and two-year teacher training institutes) out of a total enrollment of 2,439.

Even then, total female participation is only 13 percent of total enrollment in all the institutions of higher education. Attempts should be made to expand such institutes as the Institute of Secretaries, Khartoum Nursing College, and the Ahfad University College for Women in which the programs offered are very necessary for the country at the moment.

Higher Education and Political Decisions

The Sudanese government has been perceptive and courageous in facing the fact that the function and structure of its system of higher education are not well adapted to the national requirements. What it has yet to face is the fact that Sudan cannot solve the problem of educational organization, control, and planning until it solves the political problem: Whether the educational system exists to support a protected, university-trained elite, or whether the system exists to advance the general standard of education and raise the standard of living. As a political dilemma, the problem has two parts.

The first part is internal and has to do with the extraordinary position and protection that the universities enjoy, particularly the University of Khartoum and the Islamic University. Coupled with the failure of government to support and advance technical education, this protection removes any possibility of competition between professionals and technicians in the same field of activity. Should the latter point seem far-fetched, it is worth pointing out that the downgrading of technical training has in the past been an almost inevitable concomitant of the establishment of professional training in developing nations, and the result is the elevation of professional status, but not necessarily of professional skill and achievement.

The second part of the problem is a matter of external politics and has to do with the policy of the Sudanese government in allowing approximately three fifths of its university students to be educated at foreign universities. The University of Cairo, with between 7,000 and 8,000 Sudanese students in Khartoum and at least another thousand in Cairo, is in a sense the largest Sudanese university. However, other thousands of Sudanese students are enrolled in universities of the socialist countries, and a considerable number are the the United Kingdom and Europe. Under this policy, the two government universities are relieved of pressure to take more students than they can comfortably accommodate, or to establish the programs and schools that would inevitably be demanded by an increased student body. As a consequence, university education is the raison d'être of the entire educational system, and the government universities are the protected and stable institutions within the present—and rather unusual—university structure. Given this situation, the political problem can be posed in the form of a question, "Does the present organization of the educational system effectively support the development of the Sudanese nation?"

THE DEVELOPMENT TASK

There are development plans, but not a unified development plan. Some development planning has included gross manpower estimates by levels of skills required, and it is from these estimates that estimates given below were derived. Official policy on either the magnitude and timing of development plans or on the training of development manpower could not be identified. From the size of the schemes under study, however, and from additional ideas being considered, it is reasonable to estimate that, over the next 20 years, a variety of schemes, including the Rahad and its extensions, the rechanneling of the White Nile, and the development of woodlands and agricultural lands in the south, will require the expenditure of at least U. S. $1 billion or approximately LS 400 million. This money would go primarily into agricultural development and supporting infrastructure. It would pay for irrigation, roads and railroads, supporting industrial development, engineering, construction, labor recruitment, and initial production.

The Development Labor Force

On the basis of information extracted from current studies, * it can be estimated that each expenditure of a million Sudanese pounds creates between 3,800 and 4,300 jobs for one year and for each 100 new jobs, training facilities will be needed for 1.5 individuals at university level and 11.5 at the technical level. The remaining jobs would be agricultural, mainly hand and unskilled labor, requiring minimum training only.

If the Sudan spends LS 200 million over a ten-year period at the rate of LS 20 million a year, each year's expenditure of development funds will support between 75,000 and 85,000 jobs for one year. Of these, between 10,000 and 12,000 will require secondary education or higher, and, of those, 1,000 will require university training. It must be emphasized that such jobs are purely a product of the development process. When a project is developed to the point of production, jobs on the project must be supported from the proceeds of production. No estimate of jobs resulting from postdevelopment productivity has been made.

The Sudanese postsecondary training institutions produce 600 graduates of science, applied science, or technical programs, annually, including those in universities and institutes. More than half of the graduates are from universities. Even if the institutions graduated twice this number and all technical graduates were channeled into development programs, the ten-year output of technical graduates would not meet the start-up requirements of the development programs envisioned.

The university output is more favorable. Counting all university graduates in pure and applied sciences and technology, the staffing needs for new development could be met in three years and thereafter maintained with a continuing input of 100 graduates a year to compensate for turnover. If the output of engineers and agriculturalists from overseas universities were included, the lead time could be

*Southern Regional Government Plans, 1972-73 to 1975-76.

reduced to two years. Note that foreign institutions produce no technicians. In fact, the rector of the Khartoum branch of the University of Cairo stated that his institution was not concerned with technical training.

In short, Sudanese secondary and higher education is not ready to support the large development programs that are seen as the Sudan's best hope. This hope has been building up over 50 years and will not be easy to change. There are ways, however, to bring Sudanese manpower more closely in line with anticipated development needs. These possibilities are discussed in the next section.

MANPOWER AND EMPLOYMENT PROBLEMS

Despite its great potential, especially in agriculture, Sudan has experienced little economic growth for the past several years. Some of the reasons for this poor performance have been political instability, lack of foreign aid, and transportation difficulties. A recession beginning in 1963, followed by hostilities in the South, caused considerable unemployment among the better educated and skilled workers, contributing to political unrest. Of the least developed countries, Sudan received the least foreign aid as a percentage of GNP during 1969-71 and, in addition, had to contend with a poor export market for cotton, which supplies over 60 percent of foreign exchange. Following the closing of the Suez Canal, increased costs of transporting exported and imported goods and the inadequacy of the overland transportation system also hindered economic growth. These failures, not surprisingly, have had adverse effects on capital investment, and hence upon growth projects depending on such investment. Development strategy up to now has involved heavy concentration of investment and effort on the most accessible income sources to provide the foreign exchange needed. A change in strategy will broaden the base of this development program, allow investment to increase, and reduce the problems of unemployment and underemployment. Many of the development projects in the Sudan, such as roads, dams, irrigation ditches, afforestation, and the development of plantations, can be profitable with labor-intensive methods. Sudan has not so far taken as much advantage of irrigated agriculture, which makes the agricultural economy less seasonal, as it might. However, extension of the land allocated to wheat in 1973 was one indication that diversification may be increased to make agriculture a year-round occupation.

The latest available statistics of the economically active population of Sudan are shown in Table 10.1.

According to these figures, over 70 percent of the labor force was employed in the primary sector (animal husbandry, agriculture,

TABLE 10.1

Percentage Distribution of Employment

Sector	Percentage			
	Urban	Semiurban	Rural	All Areas
Animal husbandry	0.38	0.97	4.77	3.96
Agriculture, forestry	6.03	30.19	79.98	67.45
Industry and Mining	3.89	2.09	0.33	0.89
Handicrafts	6.60	6.46	2.93	3.62
Building and construction	3.28	3.33	1.10	1.54
Transport and communication	6.91	4.33	0.80	1.78
Commerce and trade	11.83	12.41	1.63	3.66
Other government services	29.39	19.32	2.03	6.56
Other private services	24.12	15.02	5.30	8.24
Seeking work for first time	7.56	5.87	1.17	2.29

Source: Sudanese Government, 1967-68 Household Sample Survey.

and forestry). Industry and mining contributed about 8 percent of the gross domestic product (GDP), but employed less than 1 percent of the labor force. If the industrial sector is to be developed further (it appears to be capital intensive now) and if more people are to be employed, the country must adopt a different strategy for industrial development, in which industry changes size and structure and uses intermediate technology. As things are now, most people in the Sudan must continue to seek employment in the rural sector. This will create more underemployment in that sector and further stimulate the exodus of young people to urban areas.

HIGHER EDUCATION AND EMPLOYMENT

During the joint sovereignty of the Sudan by Egypt and Great Britain, educational policy was directed mainly toward training personnel in certain skills to serve as junior administrative officers so that the government could avoid relying on Egyptian employees. After 1930, there was a limited program of training local high-level manpower as teachers, agricultural officers, and medical, army, and police officers. There was no plan for spreading literacy nor any generalized high-level manpower training. Table 10.2 gives the production of all graduates in the Sudan to 1973.

Out of the 16,955 graduates trained in Sudan, 8,522 (about 50 percent) were arts graduates from the three universities. Technical higher education started only in the 1950s (Khartoum Polytechnic was founded in 1952). Although science education started earlier,

TABLE 10.2

Production of Graduates

Institution	Graduates
Higher institutes	887*
University of Khartoum	5,832
University of Cairo, Branch	4,226
Islamic University	1,342
Khartoum Tech. Institute	2,414
Shambat Institute of Agriculture	617
Higher Nursing College	203
Forest Rangers' College	241
School of Hygiene	366
Senior Trade College	827
Foreign universities and institutes	830

*Graduates of higher schools and Khartoum College to 1958.
Source: Sudan Department of Labour, Ministry of Public Service and Administrative Reform.

there were only about 400 engineering, medicine, and agriculture graduates produced within the whole country until 1958. The number of students who are expected to graduate during 1972–75 are estimated in Table 10.3.

TABLE 10.3

Number of Postsecondary and University Students Expected to Graduate

Institute	1972	1973	1974	1975	Total
University of Cairo	655	655	655	750	2,725
University of Khartoum	717	746	820	849	3,132
Ahfad Univ. College for Women	4	9	32	32	77
Shambat Agric. Institute	37	127	127	127	418
Islamic University	163	49	134	155	501
Khartoum Polytechnic (includes all the institutes before fragmentation)	37	67	145	145	394
Foreign institutes and universities	300	350	400	500	1,550
Senior Trade School (converted lately to HTTTI)	163	59	59	59	340
Total	2,076	2,062	2,372	2,617	9,127

Source: Sudanese Ministry of Public Services and Administrative Reform.

Employment of Graduates

The output of higher education graduates in Sudan has increased
at a much faster rate than the absorptive capacity of the economy.
Until 1972, the government budget included a special account called
the Employment Relief Fund for the employment of graduates who
could not find a job. The guarantee that all graduates of a university
with the same degree would be put on the same government scale
irrespective of the needs of the economy attracted too many students
to the universities, and in 1973-74, the practice of paying unemployed
graduates was stopped. Apart from the financial burden, the employment of graduates without real need for their services created serious
social and administrative problems.

The absorption of so many school and university graduates is
obviously a matter of concern unless economic development
accelerates. The number of unemployed 1973 graduates registered
at the Department of Labour until March 1974 is shown in Table 10.4.

TABLE 10.4

Unemployed Graduates Registered at Department of Labour to 1974

University of Khartoum, faculty of:	
Arts	49
Economics	66
Law	17
Science	29
Total	164
University of Cairo, faculty of:	
Arts	153
Commerce	222
Law	61
Total	436
Senior Trade School	21
Khartoum Polytechnic	13
College of Fine Arts	10
Islamic University	10
Foreign	93
Total	147
Grand total	747

Source: Sudanese Department of
Labour.

The interesting feature of the above information is the
unemployment of technicians. It is clear that Sudan is short of
this kind of manpower. It may be that these graduates were waiting

for civil service posts. The private sector does not have the same
job security and is not satisfied with locally trained technicians.
The Department of Establishment states that the private sector prefers
expatriates to nationals, even though expatriates receive higher
salaries.

The University of Cairo produces the largest number of unemployable graduates, although employment does not seem to be a
problem for graduates of the engineering, medicine, and agriculture
faculties. While Cairo students apparently cost the government
little (the entire financial burden being borne by the Arab Republic
of Egypt)', as graduates they compete for jobs with University of
Khartoum graduates whose education costs the Sudan an average of
ŁS 4,560 per student. * Although the number of posts in public
services (total classified, excluding police) increased from 14,151
in 1955/56 to 55,636 in 1972/73, the economy did not grow propor-
tionally, and productivity per head is bound to decrease.

The Salary Structure

It has been indicated before that salaries of civil servants are
rigidly tied to the certificate or degree level of the incumbent and the
normal duration of the course leading to that degree. This tie between
salaries and degree plays an important role in the choice of a specialization by secondary school leavers. Table 10.5 gives the starting
salary of different graduates.

TABLE 10.5

Starting Salary of Different Kinds of Graduates

Duration of Postsecondary Course	Starting Salary per Year (ŁSs)
2 years	280
3 years	320*
4 years	400
5 years—Honors in Arts	425
5 years—Scientific Fields	450-475
6 years—Engineering and Architecture	530
6 years—Medicine	560

*Shambat graduates are placed at ŁS340 per year.
Note: These salaries do not include cost of living allowances.
Source: Sudanese government.

---

*Mohammed Elmurtada Mustaga, "Manpower and Employment
Problems in Developing Countries: A Case Study of the Sudan,"
unpublished M.A. thesis, Northeastern University, 1973.

This table explains why there is pressure from the students at the three-year institutes to extend the course to four years. It does not give the details of promotion opportunities for different types of graduates. Doctors, engineers, and police officers are most preferred in this respect, while teachers advance very slowly.

SUMMARY OF OBSERVATIONS

So far as postsecondary and university graduates are concerned, the problem in the Sudan at present is not unemployment, but the method and nature of their employment. The government had a policy of employing every postsecondary and university graduate who was not able to find (or did not wish) a job, whether in the private sector or in government departments and public corporations. After nationalization of all large businesses in 1970, most graduates were employed by government, whether or not there were specific jobs for them. This problem was aggravated by overproduction of graduates in the nonscientific fields, for whom there was no real need, and underproduction of technicians, who were needed. The salary scales, value systems, rigidity of the educational system, and existence of opportunities to earn a cheap degree have contributed to this problem.

There is an urgent need for up-to-date and comprehensive data on the labor force—its composition, distribution, and characteristics—for economic and social policy purposes. Employment exchange data on registered unemployed persons can seldom provide a complete picture of the employment situation in a country unless both registration and placement through exchanges are compulsory, unless the exchanges exist in all parts of the country, and unless the law is efficiently administered. These requirements are seldom met. Some general, though limited, observations about the trend of unemployment and shortages in occupations can be made, however, if exchanges are efficiently organized and the procedures well defined. The organization of employment information leaves much to be desired, unfortunately, even at the institutional level, which is simpler and more manageable.

A LONG-TERM LOOK

Sudan has tremendous agricultural potential. If her cattle wealth, irrigable land, and forestry are properly developed, she can easily supply basic requirements of life to all the neighboring countries where there are shortages. The energy situation would make such interdependence welcome on both sides. The international organizations have also been aware of Sudan's potential. Most important, Sudan has a very good supply of qualified manpower, that, if properly

mobilized and utilized, can take the country a long way in development
in the near future.

Large-scale development programs appear to be in the offing,
but no development policy has yet been formulated. Without that
policy, it becomes difficult to foresee the role of the higher education
system in that development. Training and manpower needs can be
roughly estimated, however, by analyzing each of the development
projects. Most of these projects call for on-the-job training, in-service training, and crash programs. The institutions of higher education will have to adapt themselves to meet these needs, for they can
only be met by a highly flexible education system.

EDUCATIONAL REQUIREMENTS AND REMEDIES

Sudan presents a paradox in its higher education. Viewed as a
system, without regard to the political implications of foreign intervention, it has, among developing nations, a relatively high provision
for higher education. At the same time, however, it suffers a crucial
shortage of technicians, compounded by difficulties in recruiting
secondary leavers for technician training, even though there is a
large group of secondary leavers who are currently unemployed.
Shortages of certain other categories of university graduates are
combined with substantial unemployment and underemployment of
graduates in other areas.

It is obvious that a situation as complex as the one described
above is not created quickly, and equally obvious that it cannot be
cured quickly. However, there are lines of action that can be
followed that will improve matters. Briefly, they are, first, to
establish firm government regulation and control of all higher education; second, to establish a new Sudanese university, carefully
planned as to site and program, to support development plans; and,
third, to establish basic institutions for specialized postsecondary
training in the southern regions, planned so as to form the foundations
of a university of the South.

The problem of firm government regulation and control is
political rather than educational. It involves relationships with Egypt,
with the socialist countries of Eastern Europe, with Muslim leaders
in Sudan, and with the already militant secondary-school students.
These are all serious matters outside the province of this report.
Political settlement of these problems, however, is interlocked with
the provision of additional internal educational opportunity as outlined above and discussed in the next paragraphs.

The second line of action suggested was the establishment after
careful planning, of a new university. Suggested conditions necessary
for its effective establishment and function include the following:

1. A well-developed local school system that can contribute
a significant group of students to the new institution and receive the
children of the institution's staff;

2. A level of regional prosperity, including prospects for
economic growth, not below the national mean;

3. Agreement on a program of studies and educational needs
to be met;

4. Demonstrable manpower requirements for graduates of the
institution at the regional as well as the national level, assuring
regional employment prospects;

5. Availability of potential staff;

6. Assured funding for essential construction and operating
budget;

7. Communication and transport offering ready access to
other parts of the country; and

8. Established need for institutional contribution to regional
growth and development.

In Sudan, the area that most nearly fulfills the above conditions
is the Gezira—the large, fertile, industrial agriculture area between
the Blue and the White Niles, 200 kilometers to the south of Khartoum.
In addition, it has a potential for development of perhaps as much as
ten times the land area now under cultivation, and manpower requirements in proportion.

To meet manpower needs at technical and professional levels,
a new institutional structure might include the following components:

1. A medical center with a Faculty of Medicine, degree programs in nursing and laboratory technology, and diploma programs
for medical assistants, dressers, and related areas of training. A
Faculty of Pharmacy, a Faculty of Dentistry, a postgraduate medical
program, and a major research center would be development goals.
The orientation of the center would be toward preventive medicine.

2. An agricultural education center, developed, like the medical
center, around a teaching center and research activity (now in
operation), with supporting technical programs.

3. A Faculty of Engineering offering agricultural, irrigation,
and sanitary engineering, supported by appropriate technical programs
at diploma level, and by engineering research laboratories.

4. A community college offering basic science courses in
preparation for the above professional program and serving as the
vehicle for in-service, extension, and even nonformal programs.

5. The conventional university faculties of arts, law, commerce, and social science are not included in the basic plan.

The mixture of university-level and technical programs, and the omission of faculties usually considered central to a university, would make the proposed institution a most unusual one. The result, however, would be a university planned to meet specific needs, and radical only in the sense that unusual measures are required to meet unusual needs. It is, in fact, much in line with trends in university development that produced the Universities of Malawi, Mauritius, and Yaoundé as "umbrella" universities sheltering a range of offerings unknown and unimaginable in the classical university tradition.

The third item, the establishment in the South Sudan of foundation institutions that can develop toward university status, is difficult to achieve. The South has been the locus of hostilities for nearly ten years, many public buildings have been destroyed, nearly all commerce, industry, and transportation have come to a stop, many schools are occupied by military units, and many of the trained teachers have abandoned their schools. A sizeable proportion of elementary education is now in bush schools directed by untrained teachers.

The immediate need is not for conventional university programs but for practical, functional training at secondary and postsecondary levels in the subjects most needed for the economic regeneration of the region—animal husbandry, agriculture, fisheries, forestry, wildlife, and similar subjects. There is also need, of course, for an educational college to provide for the upgrading of hundreds of untrained teachers now presiding over self-help rural schools.

The challenge of providing basic, prevocational, vocational, technical, paraprofessional, and perhaps some professional education for a region without transportation, teachers, or buildings, and with only one functioning secondary school, requires a most flexible institution. Such an institution must include a variety of technical courses with strong emphasis on supervised work experience. Despite the political demands for an autonomous university, it would appear to be the best immediate solution for the South's educational problems, particularly if external assistance is available to supply experienced teachers.

THE FUTURE

Sudan is at a developmental takeoff point, and its educational system must be able to adjust. It cannot depend on formal structure alone; to meet the country's need for trained skills, it will also need a nonformal structure that includes crash programs, on-the-job training, and short-cycle higher education. This new type of education will have a different cost structure from that of the present higher

education system. The IACOD training programs of JUBA and the
Sudan Gezira Board training schemes, suitably modified, could provide some guidelines. An approximate investment of $LS\ 4,000$ in
training facilities will be needed for each 14 people in the kind of development that Sudan is awaiting.

It is also evident that the time has come to review the entire
area of training abroad. The present emphasis on undergraduate
studies outside of the Sudan produces many side effects, such as long
absence; adoption of foreign outlooks, modes of life, and work
patterns; and reliance on resources that may be unavailable in Sudan.
In fact, Sudan can now provide undergraduate training in most fields.
What it needs is postgraduate and higher professional training, along
with operational research. Higher training is available in most
nations that now provide undergraduate training for Sundanese students,
as well as, to a limited extent, at the University of Khartoum.
Research must be provided internally on site, preferably in the Gezira
for most of the pressing problems.

11

UNIVERSITY OF DAR ES SALAAM, TANZANIA

Responses to Manpower Needs

> In fact, a university in a developing society must put the
> emphasis of its work on subjects of immediate moment
> to the nation in which it exists, and it must be committed
> to the people of that nation and their humanistic goals.
>
> Julius K. Nyerere, on
> "The Role of Universities," June 1966, in
> <u>Freedom and Socialism</u> (London: Oxford University
> Press, 1968), p. 179.

Some of our best critics who also wish us well have spared no
efforts to point out some of the glaring contradictions between what
we are doing and what we ought to be doing. African nations have
been criticized for contenting themselves with the flag of independence
they won either through bloody struggles or through champagne parties.
These critics have pointed out the tendency to build prestigious buildings and status symbols: national airlines, national shipping lines,
national currencies, and an expensive diplomatic service, ad nauseam.
One institution that has been singled out for criticism as being more
of a status symbol than a necessity is the national university. These
institutions, say the critics, have tended to be carbon copies of those
found in Europe and America. Some have even more students from
Europe and America than from the countries in which they are built.
The curriculum has been imported in its entirety. In some cases, an
African university has even insisted on teaching courses already discarded in the university it was copied from.

Those interested in the economics and management of higher
education have argued that in many disciplines it is cheaper to send
African students to well-established European and American

See also David Court, "Higher Education in East Africa," p. 460
below, for another treatment of many of these issues.

universities than to set up an institution in Africa to teach those courses. To these critics, therefore, it is a waste of money to spend so much on what could be obtained more cheaply elsewhere. As an analogy, they might argue that it is useless to establish textile factories in Africa, because cloth can be manufactured more cheaply in well-established factories in Europe and America!

Because many African nations cannot provide universal and free education to all those who ought to go to school, some critics say university education is unjustified since it would be available only to a very small minority who will eventually become the elite of their societies. And since it is natural for members of privileged classes to safeguard their interests, those in the elite group will make sure that the universities are used to perpetuate their kind. Of course, the very cream of society will tend to send their sons and daughters to the best universities in the world, where status and prestige make a difference. Under these circumstances, is it proper to provide any financial aid to universities in Africa?

There is another category of critics of university education for Africans, comprised of those with racist attitudes. They argue that to members of an inferior race the higher realms of knowledge are incomprehensible, and even if they were comprehensible, the resulting benefits of higher education would be short-lived. Members of this category wish to see the establishment of "native" universities where special courses tailored to "African needs" will be offered. To these critics, it must be stated emphatically that there is no research evidence to indicate superiority of one race over another in abilities to handle abstract concepts. If African universities, like the early land-grant colleges in the United States,* choose to lay emphasis on the applied aspects of knowledge, this is a question of priorities during a given period of development of the society in which the university is situated.

Whether the university one is discussing is European or Indian, Western or African, one yardstick must be applied to all of them: whether the purpose of that university is the development of man. The question of values is of crucial importance.

African universities, like universities elsewhere, may be "factories" responsible for producing the high-level manpower of a given nation; they may be in the forefront in maintaining the status quo; they may be centers where pure learning is taking place; they

---

*In the United States, institutions were established in response to demands for places where American development problems—such as agriculture and the mechanical arts—could be studied.

may be tools for exploiting the lower class of society; or they may be
institutions that develop men's intellectual and practical skills for
efficient service to society. It is hoped that even our critics will
recognize that there are universities in Africa today that attempt to
justify their existence through serving society.

In the rest of this case study, an attempt will be made to show
how the University of Dar es Salaam is trying to serve the Tanzanian
society. More specifically, an attempt will be made to show that the
University has been and still is fulfilling its obligation to the nation by
relating its programs to the nation's socioeconomic needs.

HISTORICAL BEGINNINGS

Unlike West Africa, East Africa in general and Tanzania in
particular cannot boast any long tradition of higher education, such
as that of the University of Timbuktu, or early university studies by
students in Europe, such as Mr. Amu[1] of Ghana who was a scholar in
Germany two centuries ago. The oldest institution of university
standing in East Africa is the University of Dar es Salaam, founded
in 1961 and from 1963 to 1970 part of the then University of East
Africa. In its turn, the University of East Africa had its historical
origins in Makerere[2] (Uganda) where a college was established in
1922. The earliest college graduates in Tanzania are those who graduated from Makerere College in the late 1920s and early 1930s, while
the earliest university graduates (University of London degrees) came
out as late as the early 1950s. This latter group includes the president
of the United Republic of Tanzania, Mwalimu Julius K. Nyerere.

The impact of Makerere College in Tanzania must have been
minimal in terms of manpower going through the college, according
to Table 11.1. Even if one were to be generous with the colonial
government, and even if one were to assume regular outputs during
the years 1945-47, the figures in the table are very unimpressive.
It is rather ironic that the same colonial authorities argued in the
mid-1950s that Tanganyika (Tanzania mainland) could not hope to
become an independent nation for several decades because there were
no African graduates to man the civil service. It should also be noted
that no degree courses were offered at Makerere during this period
and the first B.A. (Lond) and B.Sc. (Lond) were graduated from
Makerere in 1953.

The purpose of higher education in East Africa cannot be
described as training highly skilled manpower. The type of graduates
turned out were expected to assist the colonial officers. That many
of them did better than just assist was accidental rather than by design.

TABLE 11.1

Tanzanian Graduates of Makerere College, Uganda

| | | | Course | | |
| | | | Veterinary | | Special |
Year	Medicine	Teaching	Science	Agriculture	Course
1940	1	0	0	0	0
1941	1	3	0	0	0
1942	2	6	1	0	0
1943	1	4	0	0	0
1944	0	7	0	4	0
1945	n.a.	n.a.	n.a.	n.a.	n.a.
1946	n.a.	n.a.	n.a.	n.a.	n.a.
1947	n.a.	n.a.	n.a.	n.a.	n.a.
1948	2	3	0	0	0
1949	1	3	0	2	1
1950	0	4	0	0	1
Total	8+	30+	1+	6+	2+

n.a.: not available.

Source: Tanganyika Government, Department of Education, Annual Reports, 1940–50 (Dar es Salaam: Government Printer, 1940–50.

Higher education reached a turning point when government decided to implement recommendations of the De la Warr Commission.[*] Special relationships were entered into with the University of London that enabled Makerere to prepare students for the external degrees of the University of London. With the best intentions in the world, London could not fail to leave its imprint on Makerere and its graduates. The London imprint lasted until the University of East Africa started to offer its own degrees.[†] One cannot point an accusing finger at London alone in this type of relationship. It is common the world over for

[*] De la Warr was the chairman of the 1937 commission appointed by the secretary of state for the colonies to study and make recommendations on higher education in East Africa.

[†] The University of East Africa was inaugurated in 1963. Degrees of the University of London were awarded after this date to those students who were already registered under the old regulations.

consultants, for donor agencies, for advisers, and others to make some demands on those they advise or give aid to. These demands vary in degree but normally not in kind. Research is required to find out the extent to which the London imprint has affected the attitudes of policy makers throughout East Africa and Central Africa.

According to the De la Warr Commission,[3] the main purposes of higher education in East Africa should be: (1) to provide postsecondary education to qualified students; (2) to train students for the professions, namely teaching, agriculture, medicine, veterinary science, and engineering; (3) to engage in research; and (4) to maintain close association with other research organizations in the world, especially British.

For political reasons, Tanzania's future was tied in with that of Kenya and Uganda even in matters of socioeconomic development. Tanzania got an institution of higher learning many years before it expected to get one. That a university-level institution was built at the time it was mainly due to the great foresight and demands of the political party in power, the Tanganyika African Political Union (TANU). Nyerere concedes this when he says,

> This college has been started in a rush. Recommendations
> for opening a University College in Tanganyika had all put
> a much later date as the operative one, but my Government
> felt that this was a matter of the highest educational priority.
> It has been said that this was a political decision. It was.[4]

TANU went to the extent of sacrificing its own brand-new headquarters building to the college in order that there would be no excuses for not starting it in 1961 on the eve of the political independence of Tanganyika.

Nyerere justified opening a college in 1961, preparing students for the external degrees of the University of London, on the grounds that with independence, educational programs at the preuniversity levels were going to expand so fast that it would be impossible for Makerere and Nairobi to absorb all those who qualified for university admission. At this stage it had not become apparent that political differences would later justify independent universities in the East African states. National interests in socioeconomic development as well as political ideology would override other considerations in justifying separate institutions.

The young college started with 13 students, all enrolled to study law. This decision was an educational one determined by priorities for university education development in East Africa. In the master plan for expansion of the University facilities, it was decided to avoid duplication of courses given at other campuses so as to make the best use of human and physical resources available in limited quantities and qualities. According to this plan, Dar es Salaam would take all East African students wishing to study law while Nairobi would take engineering students and Makerere medicine. This distribution of students did not last long since national needs for high-level manpower could not be met this way. The University College, Dar es Salaam, found itself establishing faculties of arts, science, and medicine as well as agriculture and engineering (in that order) to meet the demands of the nation.

Higher education came of age in East Africa in 1963 with the inauguration of the University of East Africa, which was both federal and international, consisting of the University Colleges of Makerere (Uganda), Nairobi (Kenya), and Dar es Salaam (Tanzania). The immediate implication of the birth of the University of East Africa was that students would cease receiving external degrees of the University of London and would instead receive the degrees of the home university. To maintain "standards," arrangements were made to continue links with the Inter-University Council in Britain, through which scholars, staff development, external examinations, and related matters could be negotiated.

The long-term implication of establishing the new University was that an opportunity had presented itself for the national leaders to examine more closely the purpose and function of a university. At the inauguration ceremony, Julius Nyerere, the first chancellor of the University of East Africa, took the opportunity to spell out what role the University was expected to play in East Africa. He said, "the university has not been established purely for prestige purposes. It has a very definite role to play in development in this area . . . ."[5] He challenged those at the university to take an active part in the social revolution the people of East Africa were engineering. And so, while conceding that the University was partially established for prestige purposes, he declared that the main purpose in investing millions of shillings from the sweat of the peasants and workers of these nations was to enable the University to help in fighting disease, ignorance, and poverty. Faculties of medicine were being challenged to produce the manpower to fight disease and also to engage in research that would lead to better public health. Academic departments and institutes were being challenged to find efficient and scientific ways of liberating man from ignorance about his environment and the forces operating there. All faculties, departments, and institutes were being challenged to address themselves to finding ways they could increase national productivity.

These challenges were far different from the thinking of "developing-country" universities about their roles. Some of these institutions have a distorted view of standards and academic freedom. Standards are considered high only when the subject matter is identical to that in the Western countries, and academic freedom is interpreted to mean freedom even to ignore problems of society in which the institutions are situated. This stand was being questioned and challenged.

Seven years after the inauguration of the University of East Africa, an historical decision was made to disestablish the federal university and to set up separate national universities. The new development ushered in the birth of the University of Dar es Salaam on July 1, 1970.

How well did the University of East Africa serve Tanzania? If quantity is a useful measure in making this assessment, Table 11.2 will help us reach a decision.

From Table 11.2, a number of observations can be made as regards the role of the University of East Africa and later the University of Dar es Salaam in meeting the manpower needs of Tanzania.

1. In the period 1961/62-1963/64 Tanzania relied entirely on other members of the University of East Africa in the training of students in all disciplines except law.

2. In the period 1965/66-1973/74 the University of Dar es Salaam embarked on a massive training program for teachers in arts and science subjects. This program coincided with the two national development plans, the 1964-69 First Five-Year Development Plan[6] and the 1969-74 Second Five-Year Development Plan,[7] which emphasized education as an investment for development. In other words, education at the secondary level was given an important place in the development equation as one of the key inputs. The plans also indicated the need to give priority to science- and math-based disciplines.

3. Courses introduced in the University of Dar es Salaam indicate the pattern adopted by the University in responding to the national needs and priorities.

1964/65	B.A. (General)
1965/66	B.A. (Education), B.Sc. (General)
1966/67	B.Sc. (Education)
1967/68	M.B., Ch.B. (Medicine)
1970/71	B.Sc. (Agriculture)
1971/72	B. Commerce
1973/74	B.Sc. (Engineering); B.Sc. (Forestry)

The pattern stressed general administration, education (teachers), medicine, agriculture, business and financial administration, engineering, and forestry, in that order. Every one of these subjects is crucial for national socioeconomic development.

As pointed out already, 1970 saw the disestablishment of the University of East Africa and the birth of national universities. A point had been reached in the growth of the University of East Africa

TABLE 11.2

Tanzanian Students Enrolled in University of East Africa

Period	Institution	B.A.	B.A. Education	B.Sc.	B.Sc. Education	B.Sc. Agriculture	B.A. Fine Art	B.A. Architecture	Law
1961/62	Dar es Salaam	—	—	—	—	—	—	—	7
	Makerere	41	—	5	—	9	9	—	—
	Nairobi	—	—	—	—	—	—	12	—
1962/63	Dar es Salaam	—	—	—	—	—	—	—	17
	Makerere	37	—	22	—	7	4	—	—
	Nairobi	2	—	—	—	—	—	—	—
1963/64	Dar es Salaam	—	—	—	—	—	—	—	34
	Makerere	89	—	27	—	8	—	—	—
	Nairobi	10	—	—	—	—	—	7	—
1964/65	Dar es Salaam	52	—	20	—	—	—	—	37
	Makerere	67	—	11	—	6	—	—	—
	Nairobi	22	—	11	—	—	—	11	—
1965/66	Dar es Salaam	95	94	21	—	—	—	—	61
	Makerere	41	—	16	—	18	—	—	—
	Nairobi	30	—	13	—	—	—	11	—
1966/67	Dar es Salaam	115	190	—	62	—	—	—	74
	Makerere	11	—	5	—	34	12	—	—
	Nairobi	23	—	13	—	—	—	5	—

Year	Institution							
1967/68	Dar es Salaam	153	318	37	105	–	–	–	98
	Makerere	17	–	3	–	51	–	–	–
	Nairobi	24	–	33	–	–	–	18	–
1968/69	Dar es Salaam	224	399	17	192	–	–	–	109
	Makerere	20	–	2	–	–	58	16	–
	Nairobi	21	–	20	–	–	–	–	–
1969/70	Dar es Salaam	309	419	23	269	–	–	–	108
	Makerere	15	–	2	–	62	6	16	–
	Nairobi	18	–	14	–	–	–	–	–
1970/71	Dar es Salaam	408	329	23	285	61	–	–	95
	Makerere	35	–	–	–	15	4	14	9
	Nairobi	1	–	5	–	–	–	–	–
1971/72	Dar es Salaam	477	299	69	259	114	–	–	101
	Makerere	37	–	–	–	15	–	16	9
	Nairobi	2	–	–	3	–	–	15	–
1972/73	Dar es Salaam	562	89	119	261	164	–	–	117
	Makerere	57	–	33	–	25	–	–	–
	Nairobi	2	–	–	–	–	–	–	–
1973/74	Dar es Salaam	592	258	159	295	189	–	–	115
	Makerere	35	–	36	1	25	–	–	–
	Nairobi	–	–	–	–	–	–	26	–

Note: During 1973/74, a total of 33 students were enrolled to study for B.Sc. (Hydrology).

Source: Kijitabu cha Takwimu 1961–1974, Wizara ya Elimu ya Taifa 5 April, 1974 (Statistical Handbook 1961–1974, Ministry of National Education), Dar es Salaam.

when it was considered most prudent to allow the constituent colleges to grow into full-fledged universities. This decision was reached for economic and administrative reasons, although it cannot be denied, of course, that political considerations contributed to it. The East African states are known to have different political ideologies, which permeated government policies at all levels and in all matters, higher education included. Whether this political factor was major or minor is difficult to determine from literature available on the subject.

PURPOSES OF UNIVERSITY EDUCATION
IN TANZANIA

The birth of the University of Dar es Salaam gave policy makers and national leaders an opportunity to redefine the place and purpose of a university in a socialist society such as Tanzania. It has also given economic planners an opportunity to justify the expenditure of such vast amounts of money on an institution built in a relatively poor country. Because events in Tanzania are so closely connected to and influenced by the thoughts of the president of the United Republic, it will be appropriate here to present his views on the purposes of education. Most if not all of his views are normally translated into official policy for action.

President Nyerere has defined the purpose of a university and university education at different public functions. When the University College, Dar es Salaam was inaugurated in 1961, he stressed two purposes. One was to respond to the nationalistic demands of an independent and sovereign state. He argued that "an independent country depending on charity for all its higher educational opportunities is in great psychological danger." This argument was directed at those who claimed that developing countries could rely on foreign experts and on foreign institutions to train their high-level manpower. The second purpose of a university in a developing African country, he said, was to fulfill the educational need for a place where an African-oriented education could be given. He qualified this purpose by defining such education as "an education not only given in Africa but also directed at meeting the present needs of Africa."[8] Some foreign universities have African Studies Centers, and departments of "tropical" this and that, but none of these can claim to duplicate the African environment or African problems. Nor can they claim any close interaction between those institutions and the peoples of Africa they claim to study.

At the inauguration of the University of East Africa two years later, President Nyerere went further in defining the purpose of a university in an African context. He stressed two purposes. The first

purpose was a universal one, namely to provide a center for higher
learning, where the most able minds of a society meet to pursue
knowledge for its own sake with the hope of expanding the frontiers of
knowledge. The second purpose, which is the most important for
a developing country, is to act as an instrument of development. The
development he had in mind here is both economic and human. As a
tool for economic development, a university is expected to act as a
service, research, and teaching institution. As an active participant
in human development, a university is expected to provide man with
intellectual skills that will enable him to realize in full his potential
and that of his fellow men. These skills include scientific skills, for
critical and objective analysis, and skills in data collection and dissemination. He calls upon a university to be the torchbearer of
society as well as its protector.

In 1964, the University College, Dar es Salaam, moved to its
present site, and the president was there to commemorate this
occasion. He took the opportunity to clarify his own, as well as the
government's, views on what the university ought to be doing for
Tanzania. He introduced a new element that, though implied in earlier
statements, had not been stated in such specific terms. He defined
the purpose of the university as being a tool for a revolution that was
already underway in Tanzania. This revolution had two sides to it,
economic and political. As long as people lived in abject poverty,
misery, and ignorance, the university could not be content with its
performance. As long as there was injustice, inequality, and servi-
tude in society, the university again must find it very difficult to
justify its existence. In short, the university had to consider itself
part and parcel of the overall development of the country. This need
to cooperate with government was reiterated in 1966 in an address to
the World University Service conference held in Dar es Salaam. He
emphasized the place of the university in the revolution through its
contribution of ideas, manpower, and service for the furtherance of
human equality, dignity, and development.

During a state visit to Liberia in 1968, the president addressed
the university community there. He stressed two principles that are
relevant to this discussion on the purposes of a university, especially
in developing countries. The first principle is that a university must
serve society by identifying with the society. He argues that, as a
tool for transformation of society, the university and its graduates
must consider themselves as servants and not masters of society,
the majority of whose members do not have any education. To serve
well, they must be part of and not apart from society. The second
principle he stresses is the need for universities to conserve human
and social values built up by African societies. This reminder is
timely since there has been some tendency to regard universities in

Africa as agents for Westernizing the local elite in all matters, including cultural heritage. This has led to a gulf between the society in which the university is built and the emerging black Englishmen, black Frenchmen, or black expatriates.

The breakup of the University of East Africa and the establishment of the University of Dar es Salaam marked the beginning of a new era in Tanzania's higher education. For the first time, Tanzania alone had the responsibility of defining the kind of university she wanted. The chancellor of the University defined its purpose as an institution of higher learning where people's minds are trained for clear thinking, for independent thinking, for analysis, and for problem solving at the highest level. He outlined three social functions of the university.

> 1. To transmit relevant knowledge from generation to generation. This knowledge would have to be of a type that would increase man's power over himself and his environment, i.e., development of man and mankind.
> 2. To advance the frontiers of knowledge, based on local society needs, the nation's political ideology, and the local environment. While advanced countries might be seeking ways of helping those who live too long, for example, we should be seeking ways of helping those who are not able to live long enough.
> 3. To provide for the high-level manpower needs of the society. [9]

The University of Dar es Salaam was therefore being asked to ensure that its teaching and research activities highlighted service to the needs of a developing socialist Tanzania. To this end, the subjects offered, content of the courses, methods of teaching, organization of the University, and relations with the community should all be determined by a central purpose, which is to serve a socialist Tanzania.

These views of the chancellor, who is also the president of the United Republic, are well entrenched in the Act of Parliament, which legally established the University. According to the Act, "the objects and functions of the university shall be":

> (a) to preserve, transmit and enhance knowledge for the benefit of the people of Tanzania in accordance with the principles of socialism accepted by the people of Tanzania;
> (b) to create a sense of public responsibility in the educated and to promote respect for learning and pursuit of truth;

    (c) to prepare students to work with the people of
          Tanzania for the benefit of the nation;

    (d) to assume responsibility for university education
          within the United Republic and to make provision
          for places and centres of learning, education,
          training and research;

    (e) to cooperate with the Government of the United
          Republic and the people of Tanzania in the planned
          and orderly development of education in the United
          Republic;

    (f) to stimulate and promote intellectual and cultural
          development of the United Republic for the benefit
          of the people of Tanzania;

    (g) to conduct examinations for, and to grant, degrees,
          diplomas, certificates and other awards of the
          university.[10]

Reading through this section of the Act, one can see the great
emphasis placed on service to a socialist Tanzania. The performance
of the University therefore must be judged by the extent to which it
has responded to these demands both quantitatively and qualitatively.
In this essay, the main emphasis is on the manpower production
aspect of the University performance.

PERFORMANCE

In Table 11.2, an attempt was made to show student enrollment
figures for Tanzanian students at the three universities in East Africa.
Table 11.3 shows enrollment of Tanzanian students at the University
of Dar es Salaam in a selected year.

The academic staff in the same period were deployed in different
faculties, institutes, and bureaus as shown in Table 11.4.

A number of observations can be made on these tables. It is
clear that the courses offered (if the name of a degree is any indication)
are relevant to Tanzania's socioeconomic development. The one disturbing feature of Table 11.3 is the very small proportion of women
students in the overall enrollment pattern of the University. This is
somewhat unsocialist, although it is perhaps beyond the powers of the
University to control. The University can take in as many as qualify
for admission up to a ceiling determined by the government. If few
women apply and qualify, their numbers in the University will be
limited. There were, until 1974, three methods of entry into the
University. These were (1) by direct entry from secondary schools,
(2) through the Mature-Age Entry Scheme, (3) by Special Entry.

TABLE 11.3

Tanzanian Students Enrolled in Different Degree Courses
During the Academic Year 1973/74
at University of Dar es Salaam

	Year				
	First	Second	Third	Fourth	Fifth
B.A.					
Male	180	183	142	—	—
Female	26	39	22	—	—
B.A. (education)					
Male	80	54	80	—	—
Female	14	15	15	—	—
B.Sc.					
Male	59	40	38	—	—
Female	10	8	4	—	—
B.Sc. (education)					
Male	106	83	72	—	—
Female	9	12	13	—	—
B.Sc. (hydrology)					
Male	15	18	—	—	—
Female	—	—	—	—	—
B.Sc. (agriculture)					
Male	54	55	48	—	—
Female	16	11	5	—	—
B.Sc. (forestry)					
Male	16	—	—	—	—
Female	—	—	—	—	—
B.Sc. (engineering)					
Male	61	—	—	—	—
Female	—	—	—	—	—
M.D.					
Male	49	45	26	20	27
Female	—	2	4	2	1
LLB					
Male	25	38	38	—	—
Female	6	5	3	—	—
Total					
Male	645	516	444	20	27
Female	81	92	66	2	1

Grand total: 1,894.
Source: University of Dar es Salaam.

TABLE 11.4

Academic Staff in University of Dar es Salaam
as of October 31, 1973

| | Expatriates | | Citizens | | | | Total |
| | | | Active | | In Training | | |
Faculty	Number	Percent	Permanent	Temporary	Permanent	Temporary	Staff
Agriculture	19	45	10	—	13	—	42
Arts and							
Social Sciences	88	51	47	3	30	3	171
Engineering	11	61	2	—	4	1	18
Law	11	55	7	—	3	—	21
Medicine	37	58	12	1	11	3	64
Science	34	49	17	—	13	5	69
Institute of							
Development							
Studies	5	63	2	1	—	—	8
Institute of							
Kiswahili							
Research	1	13	4	—	3	—	8
Total	206	52	101	5	77	12	401

Source: University of Dar es Salaam.

Those who entered direct from school were required to have fulfilled
certain admission requirements, while those who apply under the
Mature-Age Entry Scheme sit for aptitude tests and written achievement tests. This latter group comprises candidates who have improved
themselves through private study or courses since they left school.
The third category of students covers students who have good academic background preparation in institutions other than normal
schools. Most of these are older than the direct entrants. But even
with all these different methods of entry to the University, women fail
to increase their number to any appreciable extent. A policy decision
is called for to change this pattern if the nation is serious about human
development that includes men and women.

Another observation from the tables is in respect to the staffing
of the University. In Table 11.4, the proportion of expatriate staff is
still quite high in most faculties. The University appears to be responding to this problem by embarking on a training program for citi-
zen staff. As pointed out elsewhere, the national leadership does not
believe that it is a healthy situation to rely on expatriate personnel,
including its institutions of higher learning. It may be many years
before a nation is 100 percent self-sufficient in this respect, but, all
the same, it cannot and should not rely on that source to such an
extent.

THE UNIVERSITY AND THE NEEDS OF SOCIETY

In terms of manpower, the tables show that the University of Dar es Salaam has performed reasonably well for its age. There are today Tanzanian graduates of that University working in practically all ministries of government and its parastatal organizations. They are in the High Court, in the secondary schools and colleges of national education; they are cabinet ministers and junior ministers; they serve in the party, in the foreign service, and on state farms; they are in the administration of government at the district, regional, and national levels; in short, they are everywhere. Whether they are all doing a good job is difficult to say, and it is their failures as well as their successes that will determine public confidence in their institution.

The University takes students into courses as determined by the government planners. Through its different organs, the government decides on the national requirements of high-level manpower in the different professions, in the civil service, in the parastatal organizations, and in national institutions. Each year, the National High-Level Manpower Committee directs that a certain number of students will be allowed to study courses leading to specific jobs required by the nation. When the required quota has been filled, the remaining applicants are either allocated places in unfilled vacancies in the public sector or released for other types of training or direct employment. This means that the University cannot, at any given time, produce more of a certain type of professional than is required by the nation. The committee determines even such details as how many B.Sc. (Education) will be allowed to prepare to teach mathematics and physics or biology and chemistry and so on. In other words, not only is the University required to prepare science and arts teachers, but it is also required to prepare them in very specific subjects. It has happened, for example, that the University has been asked to produce no more teachers of economics because there were too many in the schools already.

This exercise in deciding who and how many will study which subjects at the University is controlled even at the school level. Government planners inform the Ministry of National Education on the national priorities in manpower. They next inform the Ministry of National Education on the required quantities of pupils preparing themselves in the different subject combinations during their two years prior to university entrance. These numbers are later reflected in the quantities admitted into the University. For example, it is decided beforehand how many school pupils will be allowed to study science subject combinations leading to medicine, engineering, veterinary science, agriculture, and science teaching. It is then the responsibility of the Ministry of National Education to make sure that the right numbers of pupils are taught these science subjects. When the University admits students into the related professional courses, it has this pool of school pupils to draw from. To relate enrollment as closely as possible to national needs, the admission process involves all interested parties: the University, the Ministry of National Education, the Central Establishment (for Civil Service Training), and the economic planners.

The University has also responded to the needs of society by creating its own service institutions whose responsibility is to serve the nation and its citizens. Under this category fall such institutions as the Economic Research Bureau (ERB), which undertakes research on behalf of the government in areas determined by a joint government/ University committee; the Bureau of Resource Assessment and Land Use Planning, which, like the ERB, undertakes research in relevant areas as determined by the government; the Institute of Adult Education, which attempts to reach the masses and raise their educational level through evening classes, correspondence courses, radio courses, and special lectures; the Institute of Education, which serves the nation through curriculum development at all levels of preuniversity education; and the Institute of Kiswahili Research, which does research on the national language and participates actively in the growth of the language. The usefulness of these services has been acknowledged, and the continued existence of these service institutions within the University is a proof of their need.

In this category of service, one could also note the great contribution made by staff and students to society in varied circumstances: computer service to the Ministry of National Education for examination purposes; consultancy and advisory services to government ministries and parastatal institutions; writing reports; writing school syllabuses; setting and marking examination papers; legal aid to those who cannot afford to hire defense lawyers; preelection and postelection research into political attitudes of the voters; and commission assignments by the Party or the governments.

The University has not contented itself with its performance to date and has continued to look for better ways and means to respond to the needs of society even more intimately. Examples of these attempts are many, but, to quote just a few, one could begin with the attempt to make sure that engineers produced by the University are trained in areas of relevance to Tanzania. To meet this need, the "Committee for Relations with Industry"[11] has been set up. It is expected to advise the Faculty of Engineering Board on all matters concerning the relations of the faculty with industry, particularly on

1. Adaptation of curricula to the needs of Tanzania;

2. Practical training of engineering students on sites or in factories during vacation time;

3. Faculty services offered to industry, such as laboratory facilities and applied research work;

4. Assistance in providing Tutorial Assistant Trainees to join the faculty staff after completion of postgraduate studies.

The committee is made up of representatives of industry, the Faculty of Engineering, the University, and engineering students. There is no doubt that if this kind of committee succeeds in functioning, and there is no reason why it should not, the University will have gone a long way toward making itself relevant to Tanzania rather than to Europe, North America, or the Soviet Union.

A second example of further attempts by the University to make itself of greater service to society is the recent decision to introduce a fourth academic term in the University year. In the past, students have studied for three academic terms, each term lasting ten weeks. At the end of the three terms, they had a long vacation of three months, during which they did what they pleased, including temporary employment for money. The new decision means that the long vacation will be shortened by almost a half, and during this extra term students will be posted in factories, offices, and ujamaa villages where they will not only work with the workers and peasants but will also learn from them. In this way, the students will be closer to the real needs of the masses of Tanzania and, it is hoped, interpret what they learn in terms of these needs.

RELATIONSHIP BETWEEN GOVERNMENT, PARTY, AND UNIVERSITY

The University of Dar es Salaam is a state university. Its budget is presented to Parliament by a government ministry; its plans for development are routed through relevant government ministries; more recently, some University staff have been posted to government ministries by the government; practically all the Tanzanian students hold government bursaries; in short, it operates like a parastatal organization of a government ministry.

The highest policy-making body of the University is the University council, where government is very well represented. According to the University of Dar es Salaam Act, 1970, [12] the council should be composed of:

(1) A chairman appointed by the chancellor;

(2) The vice-chancellor, who shall be an ex-officio member;

(3) Seven members appointed by the chancellor, two appointed after consultation with the vice-chancellor;

(4) Three members appointed by the minister for the time being responsible for Education;

(5) One member appointed by the minister for the time being responsible for Finance;

(6) One member appointed by the minister for the time being responsible for Economic Affairs and Development Planning;

(7) One member appointed by the Executive Council of the National Union of Tanganyika Workers established by the National Union of Tanganyika Workers (Establishment) Act, 1964;

(8) Two members appointed by the Halmashauri Kuu (the General Committee) of the Cooperative Union of Tanganyika Limited;

(9) Three members elected by the National Assembly from among the members of the National Assembly;

(10) Three members elected by the Senate;

(11) One member elected by the Convocation;

(12) Five members elected by the Students' Organization.

According to this act, at least 17 percent of the membership of the council is directly appointed by government ministries and 21 percent by affiliates of the political party. Since Tanzania is a one-party state and since the government of the day carries out the policies of the party, it will be seen that at least 38 percent of the council represents the party and government. It is significant to note also the student representation on the council (17 percent). Through this machinery, both government and the party have direct influence on the policies of the University. The council has a number of statutory committees[13] whose membership is drawn from the council. These committees cover such matters as appointments of both the academic and administrative staff, and appeals. In addition, the council has established committees to deal with student affairs, staff development, estimates and development, finance and development, and an executive committee. With this wide coverage, there is no doubt that the government and the party are intimately connected with day-to-day affairs of the institution.

The University Act has provisions for a senate and faculty board, but does not provide for government or party representations on them. All matters from boards and the senate that have policy implications eventually reach the council, and in this way the affairs of the University are known to council members.

It is important to note here that the vice-chancellor of the University is an appointee of the chancellor, while the latter is the president of the United Republic. It follows that a vice-chancellor of the University has the blessings and approval of the head of state. The first vice-chancellor was the National Executive Secretary of TANU, which had important and significant implications. The relationships between the University and the party are therefore not just a question of polemics; they are embodied in the persons of officials and administrators. The first chairman of the University council was the head of the National Bank of Commerce, the financial parastatal organization, and his successor is the person who has succeeded him at the bank in the same capacity. The first vice-chairman was a government servant and the current vice-chairman is another government servant—both of them principal secretaries of their respective ministries.

At other levels, there are several committees where University and government meet, so much so that the traditional separation between town and gown or between the "ivory tower" and the "bureaucrats" does not exist to the degree that it does in some other countries. The government has vested interests in the University and is inevitably very closely concerned with what is happening there.

THE QUESTION OF QUALITY

After all this has been said about the University, it is proper to look at the other side of the story—the question of quality. What programs does the University offer? How are the courses organized? What research programs are emphasized? These and related questions will be looked at below.

Programs Offered

The University runs undergraduate as well as postgraduate studies—that is, for the bachelor's, master's, and doctoral degrees. The length of the courses depends on the field of study, the undergraduate ranging between three and five years. Some courses also cover a greater proportion of time than others.

Table 11.5 indicates the length of programs. This list does not include courses already approved but not yet offered.

The University works on the unit system in most faculties. A unit is equivalent to three contact hours per week per academic year, and students are expected to take 12 units each academic year. In the Faculty of Arts and Social Science, the choice of units is tied in with the type of person to be produced at the end of the course—for example,

TABLE 11.5

Length of Courses at University of Dar es Salaam

Course	Duration	Other Remarks
Bachelor of Arts	3 years	12 weeks more for Education students
Bachelor of Science	3 years	12 weeks more for Education students
Bachelor of Law	3 years	
Doctor of Medicine	5 years	This replaces the M.B. and Ch.B. of the past
Bachelor of Science (agriculture)	3 years	
Bachelor of Science (forestry)	3 years	
Bachelor of Science (hydrology)	3 years	
Bachelor of Science (engineering)	4 years	
Master of Arts	1 year	Education, History, and Social Sciences
Master of Science	$1\frac{1}{2}$ years	
Master of Medicine	2 years	Post-M.D. course
Ph.D.	—	Minimum of 2 years after registration
Diploma in Adult Education	2 years	Nondegree course
Diploma in Law	2 years	Nondegree course
Certificate in Law	1-2 years	Nondegree course

Source: University of Dar es Salaam Calendar, 1973-74

planners and managers. These courses are specified under each major career, and students select their courses depending on the career they have in mind. For example, a student preparing for planning would take courses in economics, political science, management and administration, geography, and statistics. A student preparing for industrial development would, on the other hand, take courses in economics, sociology, management and administration, political science, and history.

Apart from essential courses relevant to one's discipline, students in the Faculty of Arts and Social Sciences are also required to take an interdisciplinary course called EASE (East African Society and Environment). The purpose of the course is to enable every student to study the problems of development and ways these can be tackled from different angles. Students outside the Faculty of Arts and Social Science and all education students take the Development Studies Course, which has the same emphasis as EASE but is more ideologically oriented. It is perhaps correct to say that, in terms of the theme of this case study, the two courses, EASE and Development Studies, help students to see how their own university education can be related to problems facing the developing countries in the Third World. They seek further to show how these problems can be tackled and solved in the interests of the masses and justice.

The University tries very hard to make its teaching program relevant to problems of Tanzania. Courses in economics, chemistry, education, and agriculture, for example, all try in one way or another to address themselves to the needs of today's Tanzania. Names given to courses can be misleading but a sample might illustrate this philosophy: Political Economy of Underdevelopment and Planning; Planning Experience under Socialism; Economic History of Tanzania; Problems of Rural-Urban Interaction; Land Use and Potential; Imperialism and Liberation; Traditional Forms of Theater in Africa; Swahili Phonetics and Phonology; Constitutions and Legal Systems in East Africa; Social and Community Health; Wildlife Ecology; and Administration and Natural Resources. It is possible that there are some centers in Europe and the United States that teach these and similar courses. In Tanzania, in view of the nature of the society the University is expected to serve, it would be inexcusable not to teach them.

The postgraduate program of the University has been growing steadily and it is on this program that the University expects to build its research activities, in addition to the work done by its research institutes. All Ph.D. students write theses, but the master's program is varied. Some departments have regular students do their masters degrees by course work, while others have their students present theses. A study of the topics selected for research indicates the advantages of having a local institution of university standing. Most of these students, if allowed to go overseas, would have selected less relevant topics for their research, with an obvious loss to Tanzania.

Research Programs

The University has supported research right from its founding. Most of its research activities have been of the applied kind, where the University has been requested to solve a practical problem for

the nation. One example here will suffice. The Ministry of Agriculture
and the Ministry of Economic and Development Planning were faced
with the problem of how best to help the cotton farmers of western and
northwestern Tanzania. There had been a perennial problem of how
to transport all the cotton picked during the cotton season from the
peasant farmers to the local gins and from the gins to the ports of
export and to the local textile mills. This transportation has to be
organized in such a way that there are no bottlenecks in the process.
The Economic Research Bureau was given this problem as a top-
priority research project by a University/government committee
responsible for identifying research topics and determining priorities
for research. The government made money available for research
while the University made its economists and students available. The
results were communicated to government for appropriate action.
Many other examples can be cited to illustrate how research done at
the University is linked with national priorities, both long and short
term. The broad policy guidelines for research are clearly indicated
in the University Act.

The University is also interested in pure research in areas that
might not be of immediate economic importance to the nation but that
might help to advance the frontiers of knowledge and the betterment
of human life. An example here is the decision to establish a Traditional Medicine Research Unit within the Faculty of Medicine. In its
estimates for 1974/75, financial provision was made for a small
staff, necessary equipment, and office backup to permit field research.

There is no doubt whatsoever that the results of research carried
out by this unit will be of both academic and practical importance.
The breakthrough that has taken place in the People's Republic of
China has been very encouraging, and there is every hope that the
decision by the University to set up this unit will help in finding alternative ways of solving national problems.

In addition to the type of research described above, there are
arrangements for foreign researchers to be affiliated with the University of Dar es Salaam for short periods while their research relevant to Tanzania is in progress. Research scientists have come
from Japan, for example, to study the behavior of special species of
chimpanzees; archaeologists are doing on-the-spot investigation of
the sites settled by certain communities known for their well-
organized irrigation systems; and political scientists have been interested in the structural changes in certain established patterns. Approved researchers of this type undertake to furnish the University
with reports of their findings. Throughout their stay in Tanzania,
they are attached to a member of staff in the University, who acts as
the local contact.

Mention has been made earlier of the role played by the research institutes and bureaus in their capacities as service wings of the University. Recent proposals from government indicate that the Institute of Education and the Institute of Adult Education will be disconnected from the University and set up as separate parastatal organizations under the Ministry of National Education. Without going into the pros and cons of this move, it can be argued that services rendered by these institutes have been so good that the government wishes to have a direct control over them. The government would not have been interested in failing ventures!

AN ASSESSMENT OF THE UNIVERSITY'S
ACHIEVEMENTS AND FAILURES

Given the financial constraints under which the University has had to operate, it has done very well in producing the quantity of (male) manpower requested by the government. If there have been any serious errors on this score, it has been in the misallocations of the graduates after they have left the University. Every graduate produced by the University is a planned statistic, and the government cannot complain about over- or underproduction of certain categories of graduates.

The main failure with respect to quantity lies in the failure to graduate equivalent numbers of women. Although the University is not responsible for the very few girls coming from the schools, it is certainly in a position to influence government to do something about the situation by either increasing the number of schools for girls or by being a little more concerned about providing a variety of programs for women at the University.

When it comes to quality, there are both successes and failures to be recorded. The University can take pride in maintaining very high standards, as testified to by many visiting scholars in their capacities as external examiners. However, in the process the University has failed to accommodate special cases of students who already have advanced standing at the time they are admitted. If these same students had gone to Canada or the United States, they would have been admitted with advanced standing and their studies shortened by a few terms or semesters. The University also needs to make its courses still more relevant to the country, particularly in relation to Tanzania's ideological revolution. Steps in this direction have been planned, and it is hoped that there will be a different story to tell in the future.

Given its short life and the period in which it has grown, the University can be considered to have played its role very well. It has built a base on which it can rely for greater future service to the people of Tanzania.

THE UNIVERSITY AND THE FUTURE

During November 1974, the political party's National Executive Committee met in Musoma and passed resolutions that will affect the future of the University in a very direct way.[14] One of the resolutions makes it mandatory for all students taking "A" level examinations and aspiring to enter the University to join Tanzania's work force for a period of not less than one year before they are admitted. There will thus be no direct entry into the University from secondary school. At their places of work, these students will be assigned tasks to perform alongside other workers. Skills for performing these tasks are supposed to have been acquired in the secondary schools, since, according to the party resolutions, secondary education should be complete education in the sense that secondary school graduates are expected to have learned sufficient practical skills to be productive workers.

When a student has finished his one or two or more years of work with other peasants and workers of Tanzania and wants to enter the University, he will be required to fulfill three conditions:

1. He must have done well at his school-leaving examinations—that is, he must have good academic records.

2. He must produce a satisfactory report from his place of work, indicating that his character and attitudes toward work and toward his fellow men are good. In addition, this report must indicate that the additional skills he will learn at the University will be of use to the kind of work he will do upon graduation.

3. He must produce a satisfactory report from the local branch of the political party showing that his attitudes toward the nation's political philosophy are good.

A student who fulfills these three conditions will then qualify for admission to the University. Those who wish to join the University during the academic year 1975/76 can only do so under two other schemes, these being the Mature Age Scheme and the Special Entry Scheme. Under the Mature Age Scheme, a student will be required to have satisfied three conditions: (1) he must have passed an aptitude test during the previous calendar year; (2) he must have done well in a written examination (after successfully going through the aptitude test); and (3) he must produce a satisfactory report showing that he has had work experience prior to joining the University.

A student who applies under the Special Entry Scheme is expected to satisfy three conditions: (1) he must have completed a diploma course with good grades in relevant subjects; (2) he must have work experience prior to joining the University, affirmed by a good report from his employers; and (3) he must have a satisfactory report from his party branch showing that he is sympathetic to and an active participant in the national development efforts.

Students admitted under the Mature Age and Special Entry Schemes will, of necessity, be fairly mature older students. The University will, therefore, need to look afresh at its own programs to take into account this new type of student. Committees are working on these adjustments and will pay particular attention to course content, methods of teaching, and degree structure. The Faculty of Agriculture will, for example, be dealing with students who have done both theoretical and practical studies. Instead of beginning from scratch, these students will need courses more challenging than the usual introductory courses. The University will also be required to introduce special theory courses to prepare for subsequent courses. For example, these students will require special courses in mathematics to enable them to cope with economics and statistics courses.

The methods of teaching will also require modifications to cope with the adult learners. Possibilities for seminars and tutorials rather than lectures will have to be explored. Seminars will enable students to exchange ideas based on their practical background. Methods developed for extramural or adult programs will be studied for use in the new situation.

According to provisional announcements, it is likely that students with backgrounds in such subjects as fisheries, domestic science, nursing, and horticulture will be admitted to the University in 1975/76. Since the present degree structure does not take into account this type of background, the University must either introduce new degree course combinations or new degrees. For example, it is possible to change the B.Sc. degree so that nursing or domestic science courses have the same footing as botany, physics, or mathematics. If such changes are made, students entering with these backgrounds can remain in their original professions; otherwise some might transfer to other professions and the country would thus lose the vast wealth of their practical experience.

Such changes will involve setting up domestic science laboratories, recruiting teaching staff in specialized areas, and mounting new courses in the shortest possible time. It will also mean that different types of accommodation will be needed for women students with children and men students with families. This might mean allowing more students to live off campus and/or putting up married students quarters on campus.

CONCLUSION

Tanzania is committed to building a socialist society. Examples from other socialist countries will be studied and adapted for Tanzania. One of these examples is the pattern of elementary to higher education. In many socialist countries, it is an accepted principle that a place of work is also a place of study and a place of study is a place of work. This principle is going to affect university education as we know it today. The University of Dar es Salaam is taking steps in this direction by responding to the people's wishes as expressed at the recent meeting of the party's National Executive Committee. Failure to respond to these wishes will mean certain death for the University, since its existence is justified only by its service to the society.

This short essay has attempted in a small way to show that the University of Dar es Salaam has tried to avoid pitfalls into which other universities have fallen, namely, attempts to be carbon copies of institutions in foreign countries. It is hoped that it will strive to excel in its role as an institution of higher learning for greater service to a socialist Tanzania.

NOTES

1. Alex Quaison-Sackey, Africa Unbound (New York: Praeger 1963), p. 14.

2. M. Macpherson, They Built for the Future (London: Cambridge University Press, 1964).

3. These purposes are as extracted by M. Macpherson from "Higher Education in East Africa: Report of the Commission Appointed by the Secretary of State for the Colonies," Colonial no. 142 (London: HMSO, September 1937).

4. J. K. Nyerere, "Education and Law" in Freedom and Unity (London: Oxford University Press, 1966), p. 130.

5. J. K. Nyerere, "Inauguration of the University in East Africa," in Freedom and Unity, p. 218.

6. The United Republic of Tanganyika and Zanzibar, Tanzania First Five-Year Plan for Economic and Social Development, 1st July 1964–30th June 1969 (Dar es Salaam: Government Printer, 1964).

7. The United Republic of Tanganyika and Zanzibar, Tanzania Second Five-Year Plan for Economic and Social Development, 1st July 1969–30th June 1974 (Dar es Salaam: Government Printer, 1969).

8. J. K. Nyerere, "Education and Law," in Freedom and Unity, p. 130.

9. J. K. Nyerere, "Relevance and Dar es Salaam University," in Freedom and Development (London: Oxford University Press, 1973), p. 193.

10. The University of Dar es Salaam Act, 1970, Act No. 12 of 1970 (Dar es Salaam: Government Printer, 1970), Part II, Section 4.

11. A. G. I. Shayo, "Committee for Relations with Industry: Its Role in the Training of Engineers," UHANDISI (Newsletter of the Faculty of Engineering, University of Dar es Salaam), Vol. 1, no. 1 (December 1974), p. 22.

12. University of Dar es Salaam Act, 1970, Part IV (b), Section 11(1).

13. Vice-Chancellor, University of Dar es Salaam, A Report on the Activities of the University of Dar es Salaam for the Year 1971-72. Report submitted to the Chancellor of the University, University of Dar es Salaam, p. 243.

14. Tanganyika African National Union, Resolutions of the National Executive Committee, Musoma, November 1974, Resolutions 7-7.9 (Swahili version).

PART

II

ASIAN CASE STUDIES

The university is the traditional seat of higher education, and, whether in the advanced or the developing countries, the classical role of the university—to preserve, transmit, and increase knowledge—cannot be neglected. In the developing countries of Asia, moreover, many of which did not have scholarly traditions, these functions must be pursued more assiduously than ever as part of the process of raising the level of the nation's intellectual and, therefore, economic, political, social, and cultural development. Because of pressures from government and society, university scholars may be forced to devote their research efforts to immediate problems, but, even in a developing country, basic, fundamental research, in the long run, may be more important to public needs. A university's commitment to intellectual excellence is its primary and most significant contribution to a developing nation.

Nevertheless, universities in today's circumstances are compelled to be more than ivory towers. The land-grant colleges in the United States more than a century ago showed the way for their counterparts today in the developing countries, through their efforts in public service and extension work. To the three earlier functions of the university must, therefore, be added that of attention to the needs of the community and the nation.

Crucial as universities are to national development, higher education also takes place in colleges below university status, technical schools, community colleges, academies, and special institutions of various sorts. Moreover, nonformal education such as extension courses, short-training programs, and radio and TV series, provide postsecondary education.

In our view, both traditional and nontraditional institutions of higher education must become instruments of national development. The objectives to which higher education must respond have both national and international dimensions, which may be briefly stated as follows:

———————

This introduction is taken from the Report of the Asian Regional Team, Higher Education and Social Change, vol. 1 (New York: Praeger Publishers, 1976).

National Objectives

 1. Focus informed attention on the most serious national problems;

 2. Strengthen the capacity to solve urgent local and community problems, such as food and nutrition, health and environment, employment and human resource development, housing, planning, urban in-migration, and equity;

 3. Broaden and strengthen the indigenous capacity to absorb and advance science and technology for development; promote accumulation and transfer of skills;

 4. Disseminate and apply more effectively existing knowledge as well as art and culture; and

 5. Promote national integration. The nations of Southeast Asia have moved ahead since the grant of independence in the 1940s and 1950s; on the whole, therefore, consolidation of independence has been superseded by the quest for national unity.

International Objectives

 1. Improve the country's position in international markets;

 2. Develop capabilities to deal with international problems such as the monetary system, scientific problems with worldwide sources of knowledge, and the environment; and

 3. Participate in international dialogues on issues of human well-being and make more effective contributions to the world community of nations through cooperation at the bilateral, regional, and international levels.

THE SOUTHEAST ASIAN REGION

 The Southeast Asian region, which is the locale of the case studies presented here, consists of 11 independent nations running from the Philippines in the East to Burma in the West. In this part of the world, 283 million people lived in 1970, with per capita GNP ranging from as high as $1,075 in Brunei and $844 in Singapore to $96 in Indonesia and $78 in Burma. This is neither the most populous of the regions of the world nor is it the most backward in terms of national development. The five nations of the Association of Southeast Asian Nations (ASEAN) are perhaps at this stage of time the most developed and the most homogeneous grouping in the region. Indonesia is the largest in area and population—1.9 million square kilometers on which 120,000,000 people live; it also has the lowest per capita GNP, $96. The leading island of Java is densely populated (70 million people), but the outer islands are sparsely populated. On the other hand, Singapore encompasses 2.2 million people in an area of 580 square kilometers and has the highest per capita GNP at $884. In between are Thailand: 40 million people in 514,000 square kilometers and earning a per capita GNP of $210; the Philippines: also 40 million people in 299,000 square kilometers and with a per capita GNP of $240; and Malaysia: 12 million people in 332,600 square kilometers and enjoying a per capita GNP of $400. It appears that in Southeast Asia the larger the area of the country and the population the lower the per capita GNP—although, of course, the relationship is more complex than that.

Except for Thailand, the Southeast Asian nations were ruled, up to the post-World War II period, by metropolitan powers from Europe and North America. Even Thailand, though nominally independent, was subject to external pressures during the colonial period, hemmed in as she was by territories ruled by outside powers. From the second half of the nineteenth century to World War II, Thailand was within the sphere of influence of the United Kingdom. Under colonial rule, cultural ties were built up in each country with the political suzerain, and, for good or ill, many aspects of the culture and institutions were implanted or absorbed. Education especially was influenced by such cultural ties, which explains the diversity in educational system, outlook, and experience of the different countries.

Director

Puey Ungphakorn, Rector
Thammasat University, Bangkok,
Thailand; Member of the National
Assembly of Thailand

Deputy Director

Sippanondha Ketudat, Acting Deputy
Secretary General, National
Education Commission of Thailand;
Member of the National Assembly
of Thailand

Other Team Members

Amado A. Castro, Professor of
Economics, University of the
Philippines, Quezon City, Philip-
pines

O.D. Corpuz, President, University
of the Philippines, Diliman; President, Development Academy of the
Philippines

Yip Yat Hoong, Deputy Vice-
Chancellor, University of Malaya,
Kuala Lumpur, Malaysia
Later replaced by:
V. Selvarotnam, Lecturer in Sociol-
ogy, Rural Development Division,
University of Malaya, Kuala
Lumpur, Malaysia

Amnuay Tapingkae, Director,
Regional Institute of Higher Educa-
tion and Development (RIHED),
Singapore

Consultants

Soedjatmoko, National Development
Planning Agency, Indonesia

12

AHMEDNAGAR COLLEGE, INDIA

Centre for Studies in Rural Development

In 1961, Ahmednagar College, situated in a rural area then considered the most backward in its district, started the Rural Life Development and Research Project to fulfill what it described as the "social mission" of the college. It hoped to harness student energies not to the usual "symbolic acts of participation in national development" but rather to studying the problems and goals of the society of which the College was a part. By such a study the College sought to create responsible citizens and able leaders and to act as a yeast for rural progress. It also hoped to "sensitize the academic community to the needs of society and to integrate the educational process with that of the economic, social and political processes of the country."

By 1969, students were not only observing but also taking part in the process of change. The region's farmers, with project help, had formed cooperatives for credit, growing, and processing, and were tackling many of their own problems. India's Ministry of Education was impressed enough to use Ahmednagar's project as a model for its 1969 National Service Scheme—designed to encourage Indian students to study firsthand rural and urban poverty conditions—and named Ahmednagar as overseer of the Scheme in about 100 colleges. Today, 14 years after the project was launched, farm production in the region has quadrupled and is expected to increase tenfold. Poona University, with which Ahmednagar is affiliated, has incorporated the program into its regional outreach, and 41 colleges have adopted some or all of its aspects.

———————

This case study, unlike the others, which were made at the institutions themselves, is based on written material obtained from S.K. Hulbe, the project's director, and from John Peters, president of World Neighbors. Project staff also interviewed Mr. Hulbe, Mr. Peters, and Telfer Mook of the United Church Board of World Ministries, which has helped fund Ahmednagar.

ORIGINS

Ahmednagar College was founded in 1947 by an Indian Christian, B. P. Hivale, a Ph. D. from Harvard, with church support. (Of the 4,000 students enrolled today, 90 percent are Hindu.) Hivale's purpose, he said, was to give rural young men an opportunity for an education so that they would provide leadership in the social uplift of their people. In fact, however, like most other rural educational institutions, the College attracted the brighter young men of the region, who were seeking education to escape the village. Hoping to provide leadership to the villages, the College was instead luring away their most promising leaders.

In 1959, the College's principal, Tom Barnabas, met John Peters, president of World Neighbors, a nonsectarian foundation interested in self-help and grassroots programs. As a result of their conversations, World Neighbors agreed to support a program combining research and service in which the village rather than the campus would be the focus and laboratory. S. K. Hulbe, who had a B. A. from Ahmednagar, an M. A. from Bombay University, and had just finished work on his Ph. D. in economics at the University of Texas, was chosen to be its director.

OBJECTIVES

The project had four aims: to meet the national demand for responsible citizenship and effective local leadership; to confront students with practical economic and social problems of rural society; to reach villagers and involve them in programs of improvement; and to bridge the gap between the College and its larger community.

PROBLEMS AND SOLUTIONS

The program ran into immediate opposition. College faculty disapproved of students and faculty working alongside villagers in the heat and dust of the villages and held further that the project detracted from the primary purpose of an educational institution. Such "social work," its critics said, might be morally worthy, but had no academic benefits. Giving credit for such work, moreover, would disrupt the entire examination system. Government officials were also unenthusiastic, and the villagers themselves, suspicious of social

workers who come out to preach, resisted what they considered a
collegiate invasion. (Because of the opposition, the project failed
initially to become part of the educational program of the College and
became instead a rural development arm of the social science faculty.
No credit was given for the course since it was outside the university
syllabus.)

In the face of antagonism, suspicion, and apathy, Hulbe and a
few interested students, with the support of the College and World
Neighbors, set out to design a pilot project and to win the confidence
of the various groups involved. They organized discussion groups,
seminars, and lectures and invited staff and students to attend; they
made personal contact with members of the administration and government officials; they surveyed village conditions to identify needs, attitudes, and leaders; they brought movies and plays to the villages and
organized programs for school children, to which they invited village
leaders, and they held discussions with village elders and established
personal friendships.

As understanding grew on both sides, the project selected an
area of work—a poverty-ridden tribal community near Chand Bibi,
six miles from the College. Students and faculty visited the village
daily to discuss problems and ways of solving them, to help villagers
decide on their own priorities, to help organize classes in literacy
and public health. They invited experts to demonstrate agricultural
methods and looked for new ways to encourage village initiative and
leadership.

SCOPE AND IMPACT

The results have been impressive. Over the past ten to 12
years, the Rural Project—now the Centre for Studies in Rural Development—has initiated a program of soil conservation in which it introduced new methods of cultivation and helped spread the use of improved seeds, fertilizers, and insecticides. It instituted health and
literacy programs, adult education, food projects, and family planning.
(Health clinics established by the program have become self-supporting.) Farmers exchanged views in four conferences that highlighted typical problems of the district and brought them to the notice
of government departments. Students in the project helped farmers
start cooperatives—for credit, farming, poultry raising, and processing. The cooperative processing society, organized to take total
responsibility for village development, raised money locally, despite
near famine conditions, to tide it over financial difficulties.

Originally the project confined its activities to two villages.
Now, 14 years later, the program has been extended to 29 villages
surrounding Ahmednagar, with an impact on more than 100 villages
and 15,000 people. Recently, ten villages formed their own association and, guided by the project, built an oil mill (to process peanuts),
a poultry center, and a medical facility. One of the 24 villages has
become an important seed production center, and the area was awarded
first prize in family planning.

When the project started, it took three years to get a village to
accept it and understand it; now a new village can be won over in six
months, and villagers take active roles. Three years ago, the Centre
wished to start an immunization program. Students were sent to the
villages overnight and within three days had persuaded parents and
had rounded up 5,000 children for inoculations. When the College
withdrew from a village public health program after three years,
villagers invited the participating doctors to continue, and the villages
took over the running of the weekly clinics. Thus there was no drop-
off in activity when the initiating agency left. One of the major advantages of the Centre is this ability to draw on urban doctors for their
health programs, or on agricultural experts for farming problems.
The Centre people do not themselves pretend to be technical experts,
but when there are problems, they know where to go and what experts
to call. The program has also won confidence and support from official and nonofficial members of the district administration and of the
local panchayats, who cooperate in running the program.

EDUCATIONAL PROGRAM

"To initiate change," says Mr. Hulbe, director of the project,
"requires skills in human organization and social engineering rare
in our country today." To develop these skills, the Centre for Studies
in Rural Development has an interdisciplinary program of study and
research combined with participation in community affairs. It offers
one- and two-year graduate diploma courses in rural studies (for
M.A.—the only master's degree in Rural Social Work given in India—
and Ph.D.), both granted by Poona University. Out of about 60 applicants for each graduate program, the Centre accepts 15-20, a number
based on Centre estimates of the market for its graduates.

Along with specialized courses, such as agronomy, animal
husbandry and public health, and philosophy, principles, and of community development in India, students have practical assignments in
rural work, guided by the Centre's staff. They learn research methodology by making surveys of the villages; they discover the nature

of prevailing leadership, channels of communication, and the processes of decision making. Teaching staff is drawn from the regular social science faculty of the college, and technical specialists from government and private agencies are invited to give lectures.

Undergraduates at Ahmednagar College (about 80 percent of them come from rural areas) may volunteer for field work in the villages too, under Centre auspices. They receive no credit for the work, but about half of each class of 200 students volunteers and spends as much as 60 days a year working in public health programs, learning community organization, and similar activities under faculty supervision. The Centre is trying to expand the volunteer program so that students and teachers can remain together in the villages for a week or so at a time. About 90 percent of the rural students go back to rural areas after graduation.

About half the applicants for the graduate programs come from this group of undergraduate student volunteers. Other applicants come from science and social studies faculties of other colleges, and some are sponsored by a private or government employer. (The Centre takes all those so sponsored.) Applicants are chosen for the graduate program on the basis of a written test as well as by estimates of attitudes and motives. Five women are at present in the graduate program. (Of the 52 students who completed the social work diploma course between 1968 and 1973, 13 are agricultural extension officers, five are in medical services, four are in the Social Welfare Department, three in banks, one in women's welfare, three in youth welfare, three in the rural ministry, and three have gone on for further education. Others are in educational institutions, in mass communication, or are self-employed. The Centre has lost track of a few students.)

In addition to its own graduate program, the Centre offers courses in agriculture, family planning, and general community development for professors in charge of the National Service Scheme and for the Scheme's more than 500 student leaders from other colleges. Since 1967, the Indian government has sponsored these training programs, at Ahmednagar's Centre, for professors in 140 colleges. These professors receive a two- to three-week orientation course designed to equip them to set up similar programs at their own colleges. To persuade both students and professors to take the training program, the Government Planning Commission granted 30 rupees per trainee. While some professors accept the government money for their training without showing any interest in the orientation, Mr. Hulbe says, most benefit from the training and about 60 percent have succeeded in setting up programs elsewhere.

The Centre also provides training for other groups. It was asked by the University of Bombay to train 35 students in problems

of rural development under the Land University Scheme. The Catholic
Seminary in Poona sends seminarians to the Centre for three to 12
weeks' orientation in rural village work. The Centre also cooperates
with the government of Maharashtra, the Zilla Parishad, and other
agencies in organizing one or two day programs for government
workers in family planning, public health, agriculture, and small-
scale industries. The research part of the program, "buttressed
with the authority of practical experience," has produced 19 major
papers in rural development, including one Ph.D. thesis.

Ahmednagar has the only program in India, Mr. Hulbe says,
that specializes in rural social work; most other social work courses
are oriented to urban problems. For the first time, the Indian government has said it would give preference to job applicants with social
work training. In fact, the Ministry of Education is eager to incorporate the National Service Scheme, which encourages field work like
Ahmednagar's, into as many as possible of the nation's colleges.
Most colleges have resisted, citing the difficulty of evaluating field
work. Ahmednagar is the only college that gives academic credit for
field work—200 out of 800 credits for the one-year graduate course
go to field work, evaluated by teachers in the course. (The graduate
programs are conducted by two full-time social work professors who
combine field work and academic courses; 12 other Ahmednagar professors volunteer their time outside of classes to field work.)

According to its director, the Centre has imparted "a unique-
ness to the educational program of the college." Teaching and learning, he said, have been improved by direct confrontation and involvement of both faculty and students in the problems of the surrounding
society. The college, said Mr. Hulbe,

> while endeavoring to serve the community will in the
> process be enriching its own academic life. Through
> the mutual influence of the college and the community
> on each other, the quality of living and learning . . .
> significantly improve. Ultimately the aim will be to
> make education more substantive and relevant to the
> demands of . . . changing society. There is an urgent
> need for educational institutions to include community
> development as an important area of study. *

---

*S.K. Hulbe, "A Case for the Adoption of College and Univer-
sity Extension Programmes for Development," mimeographed, 1969.

ROLE OF THE COLLEGE

Mr. Hulbe and Ahmednagar's principal, Mr. Barnabas, see the role of the college and of the Centre as a catalytic agent. Able to draw upon available resources and expertise in government and private sources in the district, they say, the college can help organize village people to make effective use of these resources. By helping to identify rural problems, the Centre brings these to the notice of the development administration.

Most Indian colleges, Mr. Hulbe feels, have not caught the spirit of the Centre's program, even though the program has had political support. He is especially disappointed in the agricultural universities, which, he says, do considerable research but fail to reach out to the surrounding villages. Their graduates, he says, on the occasions when he has worked with them, have not been able to communicate with rural people or persuade them to use new methods.

Nevertheless, says Mr. Hulbe, colleges and universities must take the lead in "collecting, describing, systematizing, and presenting in perspective the different goals, methods and results of community development programmes." Like a number of other Indian educators, he feels that the colleges can better fulfill such a role if the recommendation of the Kothary commission on autonomous colleges is adopted. Once freed from the necessity of gearing all course material to standard university examinations, innovative colleges can then change their educational programs to fulfill objects more in keeping with national needs.

COSTS AND FINANCE

During the 14 years of its association, World Neighbors has provided about $400,000 to the program (including a three-story building which contains offices, classrooms, and a library). Recently the Centre has also received funds from state and central government.

13

GADJAH MADA UNIVERSITY, INDONESIA

Rural Development

Gadjah Mada University, founded in 1946 and legally established in 1949, four years after independence, is the oldest state university in Indonesia. It is located in Jogjakarta in central Java, a city that for centuries has been the center of Javanese culture. Here the University and its staff are not as subject to pressures to provide services to the government as are the institutions in Jakarta, the capital of the republic, and Gadjah Mada has thus had a better chance to nurture its own intellectual life. It has, indeed, been animated from its birth by a revolutionary spirit of reform and national independence.

In 1972, under a comprehensive plan of the Ministry of Education to develop "centers of excellence," Gadjah Mada University was one of five institutions of higher learning chosen to assist less developed educational institutions in central Java. Although the "pembina" plan of the strong helping the weaker institutions has since been abandoned as inviting invidious comparisons (the universities have instead agreed among themselves to specialize), Gadjah Mada is still recognized as the leading institution of learning for its region. Not only is it looked to by other colleges for training and assistance but it also plays a large role in economic and social planning for the central Java region.

HISTORY OF HIGHER EDUCATION

Indonesia, which is today a nation of 120 million, was a Dutch colony until it gained independence in 1946. It is among the most populous nations of Southeast Asia but has one of the lowest per capita incomes. Before World War II, there were only a few institutions of higher learning of any description—two medical colleges (established in 1927), a civil engineering college (1924), a faculty of law (1925), a dental college, and a college of agricultural and veterinary science. All were located in Java and had been set up by the state (except for the engineering college, which was a private institution). The teaching staff were all Dutch with the exception of two Indonesian professors. Only 230 Indonesians and 107 from other Asian countries graduated from these institutions in Indonesia between 1923 and 1940. Most Indonesians seeking higher degrees went to the Netherlands. In 1939, the total number of Indonesian residents (Indonesians, other Asians, and Europeans) enrolled at institutions in Indonesia was 318, while 355 Indonesians and other Asians were enrolled in institutions in the Netherlands.

One of the central aims of the revolution after World War II, reflecting a national hunger for education, was an expansion of the educational system, especially higher education. Today, Indonesia has over 300 higher educational institutions enrolling over 100,000 students. Of these, about 29 are state universities; the rest include private universities and colleges of varying standards, from missionary and church schools to proprietary schools, teacher training institutes, and academies (both state and private). There is also a network of Muslim religious institutions (Pesantran) run by the Ministry of Religion; these are distinct from the secular schools. Started as training schools for religious purposes, the Pesantran have gradually added courses in such areas as agricultural methods and general education.

GADJAH MADA UNIVERSITY

Objectives

As the first and oldest university in the Indonesian Republic, Gadjah Mada illustrates both the problems and challenges of building up a university in a young republic that, despite its continental European cultural connections, had no university tradition either imposed by the colonizing power or developed indigenously. From the beginning, it was expected to serve the nation's development. Its objectives, according to its charter, were "to form self-reliant and educated people who can contribute to the development of science and knowledge and who can help in the improvement of the social welfare of the Indonesian community, and the world as a whole"; "to conduct a continuous quest for truth through research"; and to preserve and expand the culture of its society.

Structure

The University originally consisted of three groups of faculties, namely,

  1. The Faculties of Klaten (founded in 1946), consisting of the Faculty of Medicine, Dentistry and Pharmacy; the Faculty of Agriculture; and the Faculty of Veterinary Medicine;
  2. The Faculty of Engineering (founded in 1946);
  3. The Faculty of Law and Social and Political Sciences. This was a private hoogeschole, founded in 1946 under the sponsorship of a foundation for higher learning called "Gadjah Mada."

In 1950, the Faculty of Literature, Pedagogy, and Philosophy was added to the original three faculties. In 1952, a Division of Economics became part of the Faculty of Law and Social and Political Sciences, and a Division of Forestry was attached to the Faculty of Agriculture. Further additions and rearrangements of the faculties took place in 1955, 1959, 1960, 1963, and 1969. Today, the University has 18 faculties divided into two broad categories: pure science and social sciences. Under the pure science category are the following: engineering, medicine, agriculture, veterinary medicine, forestry, agricultural technology, dentistry, biology, science and mathematics, geography, pharmacy, and animal husbandry. In the social science category are psychology, philosophy, law, arts and literature, economics, and social and political sciences.

The University was established on the continental European, specifically Dutch, model. The members of the medical faculty who comprised the nucleus of the fledgling university were Dutch-trained, as were many of the scientists and scholars in other faculties. They were familiar with a university model having fixed specializations, highly independent faculties with few interrelationships among themselves, and little interest in public service. Lecture and study systems for students were loosely organized; course grades and academic credits were not in use. Added to this Dutch background was the Indonesian oral tradition of instruction with its emphasis on lectures rather than independent reading and study. The older members of the faculties, trained in a continental European higher education system, still dominate the senate of the University, and their conservative biases and work habits have clashed with the methods of younger, often American-trained, staff members.

Enrollment and Faculty

Students wishing to enter Gadjah Mada University register for the faculty (or department within a faculty) of their choice and take the entrance exam. The entrance age is 18 or 19, so that students graduate after five years of course work at 23 or 24. The number of students wishing to enter the University far exceeds the number of places available; in 1970, 12,918 candidates applied for admission, but only 2,286 were accepted. Students often register for more than one faculty, and, if rejected by one, may still have an opportunity to study if accepted by another. It is not impossible for a student to study simultaneously in more than one faculty because each faculty has an independent program of classes. All students are considered full-time, despite the fact that many students do not in fact spend all their time in study. Scholarship funds are meager; only about 5 percent of the student body receives financial aid from government or private sources.

In its first year of operations, Gadjah Mada University had only 483 students. In 1967, enrollment peaked at 17,035; in 1968, it was 16,780; and in 1974, following some tightening of entrance standards, it was nearly 15,000.

The teaching staff numbered 1,472 in 1967, of whom 945 were part-time and 527 full-time. In 1968 the number of full-time staff increased to 725, and in 1974 to 982.

Method of Instruction

At present most of the faculties base their curricula on the bachelor/master system (Sarjana Muda/Sarjana). A number of faculties do not confer a degree at the Sarjana Muda level (the end of the third year), but they do use the term Sarjana Muda to indicate a certain stage in a student's program.

In most faculties, students enter a preparatory year (first year), then proceed to Sarjana Muda I (second year), then to Sarjana Muda II (third year). Sarjana Muda holders are entitled to continue their study at the graduate level, entering Sarjana I (fourth year) and Sarjana II (fifth year). At the end of the fifth year, students take a comprehensive examination and defend their theses. Success in these examinations entitles the student to a Sarjana degree. In a number of faculties, a student must continue his study for one or two years beyond the Sarjana level (usually a program of supervised practice) in order to obtain the professionally recognized degree in these disciplines (medicine, dentistry, pharmacy, and veterinary science). He will thus have a total of seven years of postsecondary education.

While the three-year-plus-two-year system is still generally followed, the University plans to change this sequence to a four-year Sarjana Muda course, plus two years for the Sarjana degree. The faculties of economics and agriculture have already instituted the four-plus-two system, and other faculties will follow in coming years.

The Development of the University

Gadjah Mada University has chosen excellence and relevance as the two objectives of its development plans. Put in other terms, the University would like to strengthen its educational capacity and serve the community, the region, and the country better.

The University Development Board formulated a ten-year development plan in 1971. In the plan, the projected maximum student body is set at 20,000, which is slightly larger than the present enrollment, but considering the estimated manpower requirements of the economy as a whole, the composition of the student body is to be changed: The enrollment of social science students is to be reduced to 5,000 and that of pure science students increased by 500 to 600 students each year. It is expected that in 1975-76 the ratio of pure science students to social science students will be 2:1 and by 1984 3:1, a goal that the planners consider optimum for the University.

For a student population of 20,000, and with a 3:1 ratio, the capital budget per student will be Rp. 400,000 (about U.S. $965) for pure science students and Rp. 125,000 (U.S. $300) for social science students.

As a state university, Gadjah Mada University receives its main funding from the government under (1) recurrent or operating budget ($\pm$ Rp. 200 million) and (2) development or capital budget ($\pm$ Rp. 600 million). Other sources of funds are students' fees ($\pm$ Rp. 84 million); allocations from the Department of Education and Culture; donations from other institutions, both domestic and foreign; and gifts from University alumni.

Performance

Today, with a full-time faculty of over 950, the University staff includes only ten faculty members with Ph.D.s. Of these, five are in the Faculty of Economics, and one each in the faculties of medicine, psychology, history, law, and agriculture. Upgrading the

faculty is a matter of highest priority since most of the faculty either
have never been exposed to education and teaching abroad or have
been abroad only for short-term visits, which did not give time to
assimilate new methods and ideas. University leaders are concerned,
therefore, about the faculty inbreeding that results from little if any
exposure to other educational approaches and systems.

To counter this inbreeding, the University is trying open recruitment or the opening up of appointments and positions to qualified graduates of any university. Also, visiting professors are involved in
teaching and supervising local staff, developing new courses, and
serving as examples or models for the Indonesian faculty. By carrying
out their work as they would have done in their home universities (with
some adaptation, of course, to local conditions), the visiting professors are slowly helping to improve teaching methods, course content, and research.

Two major sources of outside help are the Rockefeller Foundation and the Midwest Universities Consortium for International Activities (MUCIA). The program of assistance of the Rockefeller Foundation has been limited to the social, medical, and agricultural sciences.
MUCIA has provided visiting professors and researchers in the Agricultural Complex, which includes agriculture, animal science, veterinary science, biology, agricultural technology, and forestry. In
concentrating their assistance, these donors hope to build up faculties
to serve as examples for all the rest. The three faculties in which
aid has been concentrated are by common agreement the most modernized in the University. Fellowships for the staff for advanced
training, usually abroad, are available from the U.S. Agency for
International Development, the Rockefeller Foundation, the Ford
Foundation, the Agricultural Development Council, and others.

Another set of problems concerns basic administrative complexities and inefficiencies such as the government budgetary system
or red tape in the procurement of library books. As in many academic
institutions, there is a need to restructure the University so as to
promote better communication and coordination among the faculties,
to centralize administration among related faculties, and to use
scarce resources more efficiently.

The structure of the University is a legacy of its early history,
patterned after the continental European structure with strong separate
colleges or faculties, traditional in structure and outlook, oriented
to teaching and with little commitment to public service. This was
the system most familiar to Gadjah Mada's founders but ill-suited to
the needs of a developing nation. This conservative legacy has hampered integration of the University; the faculties, especially the older
ones, resist all change.

The separation among faculties was accentuated during the difficult period of the early 1960s. Owing to financial pressures (caused in part by extremely high national inflation rates and low salaries), staff members demanded payment when they taught students from other faculties. In turn, each faculty insisted that since it was paying, the teachers should go physically to the faculty and teach the course there. There was much waste of faculty time, and faculties became increasingly possessive about their teaching staffs, their laboratories, and their courses.

At the same time, there are agents and instruments of change at work. External donor agencies, when they decide to assist a university, tend to choose faculties with forward-looking attitudes. These faculties serve as models for the more conservative ones in such areas as requiring academic credits and written rather than oral examinations. When donor agencies assist in the creation of institutes, they demand the participation of several faculties. The deans of the faculties meet every two weeks, and already there are moves to share facilities; for example, new laboratories for physics and chemistry are being built and will be used jointly by several faculties. In related faculties such as those in the Agriculture Complex, committees— such as a library committee—have been formed to coordinate matters of common concern.

Academic improvement is also taking place in such areas as the English competence of students and faculty. To upgrade their students' command of English, different faculties have organized English language programs on a noncredit basis. The British Council supervises a program for the faculty as well as a limited undergraduate program for upper division students in four of the faculties. These programs appear to be reasonably effective.

Another residual problem stems from the oral tradition in central Java. Lecturers do not assign readings to their students, and students themselves do not read or use the libraries. Certain faculties, such as economics, and visiting professors are taking the lead in revising teaching and learning methods.

Still another culture-linked problem arises from the fact that it is not the Indonesian pattern to fail or dismiss students. Many students who cannot finish their programs in the allotted five years continue for another two or three years. Such prolonging of programs is encouraged by the examination system inherited from the Dutch, whereby the candidate takes examinations whenever he feels prepared, and can take them as often as he wishes. The dropout rate of the student body is high, however—up to 85 percent in the arts faculty—the principal reasons being financial. Carrying on studies is expensive, and there are many well-paying jobs easily available as soon as the student learns English.

As one answer to the problem of academic dropouts, the University plans to offer nondegree certificate programs for bookkeepers, instrument makers, glass blowers, nurses, and others, with about 700 students involved at the beginning. By bringing them under the University umbrella, Gadjah Mada will be following a practice accepted in other developing country institutions, especially in Africa.

Research

The total research money available to the University from the Ministry of Education in 1974-75 was Rp. 45 million (about $108,500). This may seem adequate for the 80-90 research proposals supported out of the 174 submitted, at an average of Rp. 500,000 ($1,200) per project. In practice, however, the real effect of the research funding is dissipated, as the available money is parceled out equally among 17 faculties in the University. Such a method of apportionment, which does not distinguish between simple and more complex and costly research, leads in the end to inadequate funding. Fortunately for the others, there are some faculties, such as economics, that do not draw on University research funds, as their research projects are joint undertakings supported by government ministries or overseas sources.

Furthermore, research is generally not of high quality; it is often little more than compilations and the rearrangement of available data, with little original work. Much of the research is undertaken for government ministries and, being confidential is not publishable. The research climate has been improving, however; in the early 1970s, two institutions were set up that point the way to more effective research work in the future. They are the Population Institute and the Institute for Rural and Regional Studies.

The Population Institute, funded by international agencies and foundations, is specialized, perhaps too specialized, in its undertakings. Enjoying generous support from foreign donor agencies and led by a well-qualified and active director, it stands out in some ways from the rest of the University with a degree of independence greater than that of other University research programs.

The Institute of Rural and Regional Studies is broader in its scope and activities. In 1974 it was involved in three pilot research projects:

1. A survey of rural patterns, including communication and irrigation, marketing and credit systems, and systems of landholdings. The aim of the project is to help define the proper regional

units of development from the ground up rather than from the central government down.

2. An inventory and evaluation of ongoing development programs, governmental and nongovernmental.

3. Field projects defined and initiated by village leadership representing people who are willing to help push developmental programs.

In addition, data for development are being compiled.

Research staff is drawn from various faculties, and the director of the Institute acts as research manager and coordinator. He solicits the projects, prepares the research designs, looks for people to do the research, and organizes the projects. For some projects the director assists project officers. The Institute has its own independent budget. Researchers, affiliated with the Institute on an annual basis, are paid basic salaries by their own faculties, but an honorarium is provided by the Institute from the specific research project. At this point it is still too early to judge the value of the research undertaken.

Public Service

The separate faculties of the University, such as the Agricultural Complex, have been carrying out various extension or public service projects for some time. As for the University itself, Gadjah Mada University is central Java's leading institution of higher learning. Its concentration of expertise should bring demands for help from the provincial and local government but there have been few such demands, in part because of town-gown tensions and political difficulties. In the early 1970s, however, a Provincial Development Council was set up by the government, and the rector of the University was named its chairman. For its part, the University has established a Council of Social Development (formerly called the Bureau of Public Service).

The council has three leading projects and 12 proposed projects for 1975-76.

Project I. This project is at Girirejo Mangunan, located in the southern part of the Jogjakarta region, where more than 50 percent of the soil is very poor. It covers a land area of 150 hectares and aims to develop improved methods of increasing agricultural production. Since the soil is poor and eroded, the project began by improving soil fertility through reforestation and through seeking better methods for preventing erosion.

Project II. The Merapi Slope is a pioneering project located near the mountains, about 25 kilometers from the Jogjakarta region. The region is characterized by poor water supply; those natural springs or wells that exist are difficult for the people to reach. The members of the project are trying to improve the situation by laying water pipes from the wells to the villages.

Among the persons involved in this project, three are lecturers, ten are students from the faculties of engineering, agriculture, and animal husbandry, and the rest are people from the villages. Their work has benefited three villages with an estimated 12,000 people.

Project III. The Kulia Kerga Niata (KKN) Mahaseiswa Project is a public service endeavor by students in three subregions near Jogjarkarta under the KKN service-study plan proposed by the federal government. (Gadjah Mada was one of 15 universities to run pilot studies of this plan which is expected eventually to involve all university students during their third or fourth year.) Thirty students, who are paid Rp. 10,000 (about $24) per month, are involved in teaching or helping villagers to implement government programs, such as intensive planting of rice and secondary crops, raising poultry, reforestation, or assisting with local programs, for example, the construction of small dams or improvement of rural roads. Students receive academic credit for their work. The project plans to employ 100 students in 1974 and receives government financial support.

CONCLUSION

Gadjah Mada University illustrates the difficulties of developing a true university when the prerequisites are lacking. Indonesia had no university tradition; the Dutch during their period of stewardship did not set an example because they were loath to establish higher education institutions within the country and colonial officials tended to look down on the few degrees granted by the hoogescholen. When the independent republic began its drive to establish institutions of higher learning, it did not follow the typical pattern for an ex-colony by setting up a few elite universities on which it concentrated resources. Rather it chose, or was forced, to build institutions scattered throughout the sprawling nation, all at the same time. In view of the public clamor for higher education and the demands for trained manpower, there was probably little alternative.

In the years since its formal establishment, Gadjah Mada has not attained educational maturity, even when compared with universities in other developing countries in the region such as the University of the Philippines. Still, Gadjah Mada, even at this early stage, is following the pattern of the U.S. land-grant universities, as demonstrated in the research and public service activities launched in recent years.

Certain new directions in instruction are embodied in the Regional Development Planning course to be offered early in 1975, patterned after the Development Planning course set up in 1970 at the University of Indonesia in Jakarta and the Training Program in Development Economics at the University of the Philippines. Also, plans are now being made for an M.A. program in economics.

In the development efforts of the University, the generation gap between the older staff members and the younger ones is apparent. One arena of conflict is the University senate, composed of 75 senior professors, including those emeritus professors who are still teaching. Again, the leadership styles and policies of the rectors of the University have reflected their background. The first (then called the president) was a doctor of medicine who received his training in the Netherlands; he served for 13 years, the longest term so far. He was cautious and conservative, and the university he built up was in the Dutch model. The three succeeding rectors, who served from 1962 to 1968, carried on in more or less the same directions. In 1968 the beginnings of change came with a young political scientist, at that time only an associate professor, who had received his training in the United States. Four years of shaking up were perhaps too much for the University at that point, and so at the end of 1973, an economist, a little older in years and higher in rank, took over. This American-trained economist is continuing many of the programs of his predecessor and is adding a number of his own, such as efforts to use scarce resources more efficiently.

At this point, it is safe to predict rapid advancement toward the goal of a true university. The Faculty of Economics, which has consistently and for a long time received foreign aid, indicates the potential for development. The hope of the University is its younger faculty, those who are the beneficiaries of foreign training and assistance.

14

UNIVERSITY OF MALAYA, MALAYSIA

National Culture and University Development

Peninsular Malaysia* (formerly known as West Malaysia) is a multiracial society with three main population groups, divided by economics, culture, and religion. Malays comprise approximately 51 percent of its population, Chinese 36 percent, and Indians and others 13 percent.

The geographic and economic distribution of these groups has had a significant effect on the nation. The Malays are still predominantly (just over 70 percent) engaged in subsistence agriculture—in padi (rice), rubber, and coconut cultivation. The Indians work mainly as laborers in the public utility services and on plantations, most of which are owned and managed by Europeans and are oriented to export.

The Chinese work in both rural and urban areas. In the rural areas they are mainly involved in tin mining, rubber small holding, and vegetable gardening, while in urban areas they are in commerce, construction, and manufacturing and in skilled and semiskilled occupations. Because most of them live in cities, however, the Chinese as a community have higher incomes and are stronger economically than the two predominantly rural groups. They have better access to education and, therefore, have a head start.

Religion also divides the groups. The Malays are Muslims, and Islam is the state religion. The Chinese and Indians are predominantly Buddhists or Hindus, although a significant minority are Christians.

----

*The Malaysian Federation, consisting of the Federation of Malaya, Sabah, Sarawak, and Singapore, was formed in September 1963. Singapore left the Malaysian Federation in August 1965. Sabah and Sarawak were known as East Malaysia, while the Federation of Malaya was known as West Malaysia. However, there has recently been a change in nomenclature. West Malaysia is known as Peninsular Malaysia while the East Malaysian states are now known as Sabah and Sarawak.

The relative imbalance in economic and educational development among the racial groups has created serious problems in the competition for economic and political power within the country. Race riots in May 1969 pitted Chinese against Malays and polarized the groups still further. In this tense situation, the nation has looked to higher education to help change the balance of power among the groups and also to establish national unity.

HIGHER EDUCATION IN PENINSULAR MALAYSIA

Social and cultural pluralism during the period of British rule led to separate educational systems for different segments of the population and different communities. The government set up and supported elementary Malay-vernacular schools. Urban youth, predominantly from the upper-income groups of the Chinese and Indian communities, and the Malay aristocracy attended English-language schools run by the government or by Christian missionaries. The others attended their own vernacular schools, established and maintained by their own communities, by the government, or by plantations in the case of most Tamil (Indian) schools. In these early days of formal education, private initiative and enterprise were the main force.

In the years after World War II, rapid political changes affected education, and, with the nation's independence in 1957 and the transfer of power to the Malay elite, educational policy changed. The most important changes in education were formulated by the Razak report of 1956, which aimed at achieving a national identity and promoting national integration, as well as producing the educated manpower that the nation required. A number of Malaysians felt that both a common Malayan language and a unified educational system were needed to achieve a single Malaysian nation.

With the formation of a nation-state, public education, particularly higher education, has been geared to train civil servants and professionals for the public and private sector to meet the expanding demand and, wherever possible, to replace expatriates. The new nation-state also looked to education to create the national consciousness so vital for political survival, although the May 1969 race riots showed education's failure to reach this goal. Since 1969, therefore, the government has used education within the framework of the Rukunegara (the national ideology) and the Second Malaysian Plan, 1971–75, first, to restructure Malaysian society and, second, to redress the imbalances between the "haves" and the "have-nots" in order to create a masyarakat adil (just society). In the process, the government has gradually taken over the higher education system, so that it is now almost exclusively state supported.

At the present time, there are five universities in Malaysia: the University of Malaya, established in 1949 in Singapore and in 1959 in Kuala Lumpur; Universiti Sains Malaysia (the University of Science Malaysia) established in 1969 in Penang; Universiti Kebangsaan (the National University) established in 1970 in Kuala Lumpur (soon to move into a new campus in Bangi about 20 miles from Kuala Lumpur); Universiti Pertanian (the University of Agriculture), which was a spinoff from the University of Malaya, established in 1971 in Serdang; and Institut Teknoloji Kebangsaan (the National Institute of Technology) established in 1972 in Kuala Lumpur.

Three other institutions of higher learning deserve mention. These are Majlis Amanah Rakyat (MARA) Institute of Technology, or MIT (1965) in Shah Alam; Tengku Abdul Rahman College (1969) in Kuala Lumpur; and the Ungku Omar Polytechnic (1969) in Ipoh. These institutions give diplomas (not degrees) in commerce, sciences, engineering, and other technical specializations. However, MIT prepares its students for British external professional and degree courses.

The University of Malaya is the oldest, largest, and still the most prestigious of the five universities. It has been modeled, with some adaptations, on the British provincial universities and incorporates their value system. It has, however, a unique role to play, not only in national development but also in the development of national consciousness and cultural integration.

HISTORY OF THE UNIVERSITY OF MALAYA

The beginnings of the University of Malaya go back to the establishment of King Edward VII College of Medicine and Raffles College in Singapore, in 1905 and 1929, respectively. The former was set up to produce assistant surgeons to supplement the government medical service and general practitioners to improve the private medical sector. The latter was established as a tribute to Sir Stamford Raffles, Singapore's founder, with the twofold aim of improving the educational facilities of the country and of laying the foundation for a university in the future. In 1948 the Carr-Saunders Commission recommended the amalgamation of these two colleges into one university—the University of Malaya. That University was established in 1949, situated in Singapore, with arts, science, and medicine as its first three faculties. It served Singapore as well as the Federation of Malaya, now known as Peninsular Malaysia.

In the ensuing years the demand for higher education in the two territories grew so rapidly that it soon became evident that the one university in Singapore was inadequate to meet the need. Accordingly the Aitken Commission of Enquiry was set up in 1957 to study the possibility of establishing a separate and independent university at Kuala Lumpur. Such a possibility was given greater impetus when Peninsular Malaysia gained its independence in 1957. As a first step, a division of the University of Malaya was established in 1959 in Kuala Lumpur. Like its counterpart in Singapore, it had a principal, a divisional council, and a divisional senate. The University of Malaya was administered by the vice-chancellor and the central council. Initially subjects such as medicine, pharmacy, dentistry, and law were taught only at the Singapore division while engineering studies were available only at Kuala Lumpur. Arts and sciences were offered at both places, though philosophy, social studies, and Chinese language and literature were available only in Singapore, and Malayan and Indian studies and geography in Kuala Lumpur.

When Singapore and Peninsular Malaysia became separate states, political considerations and Malaysian educational policy and needs called for the establishment of a separate university in Peninsular Malaysia. Accordingly, in October 1961, the parliament in Kuala Lumpur and, in December 1961, the Legislative Assembly of Singapore each passed legislation to establish separate universities. Thus on January 1, 1962, the University of Malaya in Kuala Lumpur and the University of Singapore were established as separate and autonomous institutions. Today the University of Malaya has approximately 9,000 students and offers degree courses in various fields.

CONTRIBUTIONS OF THE UNIVERSITY TO
NATIONAL UNITY

The original purpose of the University was to produce enough high-caliber manpower for the public and private sectors and to develop the human and natural resource potential of the country. The importance attached to tertiary-level education by the government of Malaysia is shown in the large amount of resources devoted to it; the per student cost of higher education for the state was $1,257 in 1965, which was 5.4 times the per capita GNP of $232.[1] This cost increased to $4,356 in the 1974/75 academic session and is expected to increase to $4,928 in the 1975/76 session. The cost per student, however, varies considerably from faculty to faculty, the lowest being economics at $2,860, while the highest is medicine at $10,299. The University in 1973 had a budget allocation of $38,756,714, of which $34,464,389 was spent on operating expenses, while $4,292,325

was allocated for development. For the year 1974, a total of
$50,564,849 was allocated.[2]

This large investment must be productive. Moreover, since
government educational expenditure can affect income redistribution
by favoring certain social and economic groups, care must be exercised in the choice of those privileged to enter the universities. Although Malaysia is anxious to avoid the problem of educated unemployed, University expansion has not been carefully planned or
delimited in the fields of humanities and social sciences, including
economics. The total enrollment of students in these disciplines increased from 50.5 percent in 1959 to 65.2 percent in 1970. Demand
for graduates in these disciplines is unlikely to keep up with the supply,
and the discrepancy may have political repercussions similar to those
in Sri Lanka.

One of the objectives of the steady government takeover of higher
education was to promote national unity. The University of Malaya
has set out to implement this objective in three major areas: the
language of instruction; enrollment and the composition of the student
body (especially the Malay component); and the composition of the
University teaching staff.

Language of Instruction

For the universities, perhaps the most symbolic of the government decisions in the aftermath of the May 1969 racial conflicts was
that henceforth Bahasa Malaysia (Malay), to which relatively little
attention had been paid so far in the universities, would be used as
the instrument of unification throughout the entire university system.
Bahasa Malaysia is to replace other languages gradually until, in
1983, when students admitted to universities will have had their entire
primary and secondary education in Bahasa Malaysia, it will become
the sole medium of instruction.

At present, the media of instruction in the University of Malaya
are English and Bahasa Malaysia. (The Faculty of Arts offers courses
in English, Chinese, Tamil, and Bahasa Malaysia.) To conform to
the government policy of increasing the use of Bahasa Malaysia, the
University now requires students in all faculties to take a compulsory
language course in Bahasa Malaysia, and faculties have been directed
to draw up realistic implementation programs for the greater use of
Bahasa Malaysia in their teaching. In the Faculty of Economics and
Administration, for example, beginning with the entering freshmen
in 1973, all instruction was to be in Bahasa Malaysia. This change
meant that not only the students but also the staff had to acquire

competence in the language. In the Faculty of Arts, 117 courses were offered in Bahasa Malaysia during the school year 1971-72. Istilah (stylistic) Committees have been set up for each faculty; these work out technical terms in Bahasa Malaysia and have considerably eased the language implementation program.

As was to be expected, resistance to the Bahasa Malaysia program was encountered in the initial stages. Now the program has general acceptance and is gaining momentum, but it also has some handicaps. Bahasa Malaysia, for example, still does not have an adequate independent technical vocabulary and literature. This lack can considerably hamper new research, weaken links with the international scientific community, and prevent students from keeping abreast of new scientific and technological developments. These problems, in turn, can curtail the program of modernizing the country's economy through science and technology.

Enrollment

The expansion in enrollment has been promoted, not only to fill the present and future needs for trained manpower but also to increase the number of qualified Bumiputra (native Malay students), since this group, although the national majority, is viewed as having been educationally disadvantaged in the past. The racial composition of the student body has, in fact, changed and is now more in accord with the population characteristics of the nation as a whole.

There is another pressure to train more Malays. The government requires that jobs in the government service must be apportioned at the rate of three or four Malays (the proportion varies with the particular government department involved) to one non-Malay. In the private sector, 40 percent of new employees are to be Malay.

Admission to the University is governed by qualification examinations. If students were selected and admitted purely on the basis of examination scores, however, those educated in the predominantly rural Malay-language stream of the elementary- and secondary-level system would fare less well than the urban English-language graduates. Accordingly, admission to the University is now determined not only by examination scores but also by quotas based on the racial proportions of the national population. In a multiracial society such as Malaysia political considerations must take precedence over the maximizing of academic standards, research output, links with an international scientific community, manpower needs of the country, and cost-benefit implications.

This selection procedure is reinforced by a generous system of state scholarships given to Malay students. The scholarship awards carry the condition that the grantee will, upon graduation, serve the government for a period of five years.

As Table 14.1 shows, these policies have led to an expanded student body of almost 9,000 students in which Malays constitute 47.5 percent, Chinese 42.9 percent, and Indians and other 9.6 percent.

Once the student comes to the University, the University attempts to promote interracial harmony by integrating hostels or dormitories; students from different racial backgrounds live together. Academically, however, a student enrolled in the arts faculty, if he or she has the requisite qualifications, can opt for the Chinese, Malay, or Indian studies programs, which tend to polarize students according to their ethnic origins. The University has yet to make a concerted effort to develop an integrated course covering the various cultures and communities of the country, although respected individual scholars have urged that this be undertaken. If such a course were devised, it might give students a better perspective on other ethnic groups in the University and contribute to greater ethnic harmony.

Teaching Staff

Despite these efforts, racial balance has not yet been fully achieved. While the University as a whole is racially balanced, the faculties are not. For example, Chinese students, who come from urban areas where preuniversity instruction in mathematics and sciences is superior to that in the rural areas, dominate the medicine, science, and engineering faculties, constituting 80 percent of their students. In contrast, the student body of the Faculty of Arts (and especially the Malay studies program) is 80 percent Malay. Even in the Faculty of Economics and Administration, which is better balanced than other faculties, Chinese are more prominent in the statistics program, where mathematical knowledge is called for. In the academic years 1973/74 and 1974/75, it became apparent that the Indian community was underrepresented in the student body. This imbalance then became a source of agitation.

Formerly, the University was heavily dependent on expatriate staff and was criticized for not fostering the ideals of national unity with a definite Malayanization policy. Expatriate staff, with notable exceptions, considered it their main business to teach and do research, tasks they did well, but they did not feel obliged to identify the problems of the nation and help solve them. In recent years, however, more and more Malaysians have joined the academic staff,

TABLE 14.1

Annual Enrollment of Students
(with racial breakdowns)

Year	Chinese	Malays	Indians	Ceylonese	Eurasians	Others	Total
1959–60	195	62	41	16	4	4	322
1960–61	367	144	88	36	9	9	653
1961–62	585	217	120	62	14	12	1,010
1962–63	786	274	161	82	16	22	1,341
1963–64	1,042	358	211	75	26	24	1,736
1964–65	1,330	543	211	100	18	23	2,225
1965–66	1,669	721	292	103	24	26	2,835
1966–67	2,034	1,038	329	142	32	28	3,603
1967–68	2,559	1,401	377	159	32	32	4,560
1968–69	3,102	1,825	402	175	39	23	5,566
1969–70	3,532	2,373	516	177	35	39	6,672
1970–71	3,785	3,123	565	191	28	85	7,777
1971–72	3,892	3,737	620	176	26	93	8,545
1972–73	3,762	4,151	577	140	20	98	8,748

Sources: Mohamed Suffian bin Hashim, "Problems and Issues of Higher Education Development in Malaysia," Development of Higher Education in Southeast Asia: Problems and Issues, Yip Yat Hoong, ed. (Singapore: Regional Institute of Higher Education and Development, 1973), p. 64; and Annual Reports: University of Malaya (Malaysia: 1970–71 and 1972–73), pp. 115 and 147.

and at present there are only a few expatriates left. Replacing all
expatriates with Malaysian staff while maintaining the University as
an internationally recognized center of higher learning involves considerations to be weighed by the University. Although local staff are
concerned with the vital necessity of using the University as an instrument for welding the various races into a united nation, national integration is still a long way from being achieved. Conflict between the
different communal student groups has been minimized, however,
through a covert process of coercion and consensus. Dissensions
from minority groups are deferred to the wishes of the Malay majority,
considerably minimizing overt conflict.

CONCLUSION

The University of Malaya mirrors the race relations of the
country and the society; it may in fact reflect these more sharply
because it shelters what may be regarded as leading elements of the
society. Malaysia is still in the process of coming to grips with its
problems of racial integration and national unification. The 1974
elections, however, may have helped the country to take a large step
forward. The winning party campaigned on a platform of representation for all races in a multiracial government. Discussion of race
problems was prohibited during the campaign (perhaps sweeping the
dust under the carpet), and, as a result, the elections seemed the
least racially charged of the five that have taken place in the postwar
period. The elected government received a resounding mandate and
may now be in a more powerful position to promote a just multiracial
society. With guidance from the government, the University of Malaya
can in turn be expected to contribute to the effort.

But even without any change in government policy, simply by
waiting, the University will already have contributed to national
development. Well within a generation, the impact on the government and the society of Malay students from rural areas put through
the University and taken into the civil service is bound to be substantial.

It is disappointing, however, that political unity has not developed among the different racial groups. Instead, there appears to be
an attempt to unify the country within the politically dominant culture—
the Malay culture and the Bahasa Malaysia language—a strategy that
in itself is not sufficient for national unity. Attempts to integrate the
nation along the tenets of cultural nationalism can be a divisive rather
than an integrative force if basic economic problems are ignored.
Such attempts may strengthen the identity and cohesiveness of the

Malay community vis-à-vis the other communities in both the nation and the university but may ultimately prove to be counterproductive in nation building.[3]

Education, and higher education in particular, has played an important role in many countries in promoting national integration and development. Whatever integrative and developmental measures institutions of higher learning may pursue, they will have no effect if, in a multiracial society like Malaysia, the basic economic problems of poverty and underprivilege are not identified and solved across a broad front. What are fundamentally class problems have been ignored when development projects have been treated exclusively as communal projects. Recent events in Malaysia, however, have demonstrated that not even ethnocentric economic policies have brought adequate economic benefits to the Malay masses at large, especially in the rural sector. Instead, they have increased the wealth of a "closed circle" of upper-class Malays in both urban and rural areas and created a small class of new rich and privileged and powerful bureaucrats and technocrats, who are mainly products of the University. What has in effect happened and is happening is that the University has to some extent contributed to the creation and perpetuation of a clientele social class of local bourgeoisie, a bureaucratic and technocratic elite in association with local and foreign capitalist interest.

NOTES

1. F. H. Harbison, J. Maruhnic, and J. R. Resnick, Quantitative Analysis of Modernization and Development (Princeton: Princeton University Press, 1970), cited in ECAFE, Economic Survey of Asia and the Far East, pamphlet (UN: 1973), Part I, Ch. V.

2. Treasury of Malaysia, The Expenditure Budget (Kuala Lumpur: Government Printers, 1974), pp. 251-56.

3. Sinnappah Arasaratnam, "History, Nationalism and Nation Building: The Asian Dilemma," inaugural lecture delivered at the University of New England, Australia, April 1974.

15

THE PHILIPPINES: PROGRAMS IN MANPOWER TRAINING

Development Academy of the Philippines, Asian Institute
of Management, Center for Research and Communications

The Philippines falls in the middle of Southeast Asian nations
in respect to land area (299,000 square kilometers), population (40
million), and per capita income ($250 in 1973). But it is at or close
to the top in literacy rates (87 percent), in institutions for development, and in certain other social indicators. This situation has led
some observers to characterize the country not as an Asian but as a
Latin American underdeveloped economy.

In no country in Asia has tertiary education been as widespread
or as easily available as in the Philippines; with 1,737 per 100,000
of population enrolled in tertiary-level education, it has one of the
largest proportions in the world of its school-age population enrolled
in college-level courses. The Philippines spend 6.7 percent of its
GNP on education. Furthermore, the number (over 600) and variety
of tertiary education institutions is substantial, functioning in the
public and private sector. In fact, the bulk of tertiary-level education
is carried on by private institutions; 92 percent of the tertiary-level
students are enrolled in private institutions. The system is marked
by such a high degree of freedom and flexibility that education authorities in recent years have sought to introduce more order and system.

Mass education is a legacy of the colonial period under the
Americans. The result has been the largest pool of trained technical,
managerial, and entrepreneurial manpower of any country in Southeast Asia; with only 17 percent of the population of Southeast Asia in
1972, the Philippines had fully 40 percent of the managerial-level
personnel. Its manpower is its most vital resource for future development. In the past, largely because of political factors, this manpower pool could not be harnessed effectively for national development.
Now, however, a stronger government can mobilize and direct manpower resources to development ends.

In the Philippines the institutions and programs engaged in
manpower training at different levels are many and varied. The three
institutions examined here are involved in manpower training for
economic development for both the public and private sectors. They
are the Development Academy of the Philippines (DAP), the Asian

Institute of Management (AIM), and the Center for Research and Communication (CRC). The first is a semigovernmental institution, although it operates as flexibly as a private body; the latter two are endowed by the private sector and are mainly, though not exclusively, directed at the needs of the private sector.

These programs have been chosen to illustrate the innovation that is possible when a moderately high level in manpower skills and professional competencies in various fields is already available to a country and when private-sector initiative is permitted. They have been responses arising spontaneously to felt national needs and as logical and natural next steps in the training of manpower for development. All three programs are relatively new, having been established within the last eight years: CRC in 1967, AIM in 1968, and DAP in 1973. All three are located outside the universities and the traditional tertiary education system, and, unlike the other Asian case studies in this volume, they are unique in the region, as nothing like any one of them is found anywhere else in Asia.

DEVELOPMENT ACADEMY OF THE PHILIPPINES

The Antecedents: the Philippine Executive Academy

University training programs, especially for middle- and high-level management, have obvious advantages and disadvantages. There is still no substitute for the academic regimen as a basic foundation for the professions in general and for management in particular. In specific fields such as business administration, university-based or -inspired training programs are generally superior.

Universities, however, have not generally performed satisfactorily in responding to development management requirements, especially in the public sector. Perhaps this poor performance is due to the academic and theoretical orientation that is the university's strength but that may not suit development management needs. Perhaps it is due to a lack of dialogue between government and university. Or perhaps a nonuniversity but university-related arrangement is best.

In the Philippines, the Philippine Executive Academy (PEA) and the newer Development Academy of the Philippines (DAP) represent two different approaches to middle- and high-level management training. There are superficial similarities and differences between the two. Both have government affiliations. They were created at different stages in Philippine development, the PEA in 1962 and the

DAP in 1973. Course or curriculum contents are similar. The courses are "live-in" or residential, the PEA favoring a three-month course while the DAP courses run from one to ten weeks. Both institutions now have all-Filipino staffs; however, the PEA started with a considerable number of staff members from Australia, Norway, the United Kingdom, and the United States. The DAP, on the other hand, reflecting the growth of a cadre of trained national leaders in the 1960s, never included nonnational staff. Another difference is that while the PEA program was consciously patterned after that of the Administrative Staff College at Henley-on-Thames, England, the DAP programs were formulated as deliberate responses to local requirements and capabilities. Against these apparent similarities and minor differences, however, are certain fundamental differences.

The PEA was organized in 1962 as a unit of the University of the Philippines, a chartered government institution. The PEA itself was developed by officers and staff of the Institute of Public Administration, a unit established by the University in 1952. The Institute had been initially successful in inspiring and conducting personnel training courses for the lower echelons in the government civil service. The graduates of this training program, however, soon began to report that they could not effect adequate innovations in their offices because their top-level officials were not responsive. The PEA was a response to the need for an executive academy for higher management or administrator levels.

The PEA has conducted 14 sessions since its founding, with an average of 28 participants per session. Slightly less than half its total of 400 participants since 1962 come from the private sector; a mix of government and private-sector managers have been served by the program, with obvious advantages to the program itself, the participants, and better government-business relationships. In addition, up to six places per session are made available for participants from elsewhere in Asia and the Middle East.

The course of studies is modern in content and methodology. Sensitivity training, case studies, games, simulation, and lectures are worked into the areas of management and development studies. In addition, students in the PEA course work on a training-related problem while living in a barrio (Philippine rural village). The realities of rural life and rural problems add a significant experience to urban-bred administrators, and they gain new insights into a culture that often resists city-inspired formulations of development strategy.

Judged on its own merits, the PEA has been a successful response to the burgeoning problems of management in a development milieu. It provided an example of university flexibility to manpower needs. It produced graduates equipped with the newer skills and

afforded opportunities for private and government executives to compare notes and understand each other's perspectives.

Thus, it was natural that the PEA and its graduates (who had
developed affectionate loyalty to the PEA program) were somewhat
surprised when the DAP announced, late in 1973, that it was polishing
its training program for high-level government executives. Was not
the DAP a needless duplication? Was not the PEA program successful
enough? What about the high promotion rate of its graduates—was this
not proof of the high quality of the program? Why should the government spend additional resources for another institution?

Establishment of the DAP

The DAP was formally established in May 1973 by agreement
among five large government financing institutions, which agreed to
support it with annual contributions of ₱500,000 ($71,500) each for
five years, and by the National Economic and Development Authority.
It was chartered in June and became operational in July 1973.

The title of "Academy" is, in certain respects, a misnomer.
The DAP's initial programs involved not only training but also research policy studies, and a range of "special services," including
urban industry assistance and consultant services to government and
financial institutions. These programs were designed to utilize a
beautiful complex, costing up to ₱17-18 million ($2.5 million), with
hotel-quality accommodations (140 rooms) and conference, lecture,
and seminar room facilities located in the highlands at Tagaytay City
some 40 miles south of Manila. (An earlier plan had been to use the
facility as a training center for bank personnel, mainly of the Development Bank and the Central Bank.)

Work Programs

By October 1973, the DAP's programs had developed enough to
require some 600 staff members; in another year, the staff exceeded
1,000. By the end of 1974, the earlier activities had evolved into the
following programs: Management and Organizational Development
(MOD), Human Settlements, Industry Assistance, Rural Development,
Information Systems, and Special Projects. The DAP was by this
date occupying the Tagaytay facility and two four- and five-story
buildings and extensive rented floor space in three others in metropolitan Manila. The DAP's annual rental bill exceeds ₱2.5 million

($357,000); in contrast, the PEA still books hotel rooms for its
training sessions.

The DAP sees development as requiring complex and diverse
tasks along a wide-ranging front. It extends a continuing flow of technology, information, consultant services, training, and applied research assistance to some 135 corporations and factories. It developed a medium- and small-scale industry program and undertook and
financed (with ₱700,000, or $100,000, of its earnings) implementation
of the program during its first year. With assistance from the National
Electrification Administration and the National Irrigation Administration, it designed and put into operation a highly successful small-
irrigation systems program that will irrigate some 50,000 hectares
in 1.5 years (20,000 hectares are already completed). The DAP
Human Settlements staff, in cooperation with other government experts, produced the initial national physical framework plan for the
country into 2000 A.D., based on population projections, resource
and industry location, and growth center identification. The same
group (including about 400 engineers, architects, urban planners,
social scientists, and technical staff) prepares the national land use
plan, regional planning studies, and ecological management schemes.
The MOD staff designs and conducts training at various government
executive levels and offers consultant services to a variety of institutions. Its Information Systems staff designs systems (mostly com-
puter-based) for improved decision making, programing, resource
allocation, implementation, and monitoring. Its Special Projects include a "Scenarios for 2000 A.D." project and a social indicators
scheme for the Philippines.

It is hardly true, therefore, that the DAP is a duplication of
the PEA. While the latter receives an annual appropriation of
₱375,000 ($53,500) from the national government budget, the DAP
enjoys no such allocation from the government yet spends almost 80
times the amount. For its first five years, the DAP will receive a
total of ₱2.5 million annually from its five financial sponsors. In
the fiscal year 1974-75, however, its operations totaled some ₱29
million ($4.14 million), all of which it raised itself. The DAP earns
its funds by operating as a business and collecting for its services.
Its surpluses have been spent during the year they were earned to
defray costs of its nonrevenue projects—about ₱1.5 million ($214,000)
in its first 18 months of operations.

Training Programs

The DAP does some training in the Rural Development program—of farmer-irrigators, for example—and the other DAP

programs have similar modest training activities. Most of its training programs, however, are in its MOD department or program. Until October 1973, DAP training activities were limited largely to rural bankers (to date, some 900 rural bankers have been trained), who provide the vital source of credit for rural development. Because of the unprecedented magnitude and diversity of the new national development programs, however, the DAP realized the urgency of retooling the higher bureaucracy of the government. The existing PEA program, averaging 28 participants per session, would take a long time to "process" the approximately 650 government executives in the higher civil service posts exclusive of those who would be retiring in two or three years. The MOD officers and staffs thus developed their training program for middle- and higher-level government executives, despite possible PEA objections and resistance.

More important, although the Integrated Reorganization Plan, enacted into law in September 1972, had stipulated that the PEA design and prepare the appropriate executive development program for the new "Career Executive Service," more than a year later, the PEA had not discharged its legal duty. The DAP prepared the required plan, proposed the necessary amendments in the law, arranged for financing, and finally received the assignment to conduct the program.

The DAP seeks alternatives to the PEA and conventional training approaches. Conventional training schemes are based on a staff-prepared package of courses—a curriculum—embodying staff ideas of what participants should learn and do in order to become "efficient, innovative, and development-oriented" executives. Then the curriculum is sold in the market, and almost anybody who can pay the fee is accepted. The measure of success for these programs is the promotional advancement of the graduates. Furthermore, each training session is considered separately. One executive comes to the program from one agency, another from a different institution, and, when the optimum class size is reached, the course is offered.

The DAP training approach is very different. The DAP itself will not accept applications from individuals. It regards training as a component of a total development program. Before designing a training program, therefore, it identifies key agencies or crucial government programs, the resources available, the agency or program goals, the target outputs by time periods, the agency or program executives, their backgrounds and assignments, and future personnel plans involving their movements in the agency or program. The proposed training scheme is analyzed and discussed with the agency or key program officers, and necessary changes are considered. Then interviews are held with the prospective participants. A draft training curriculum is framed and is subject to further improvement. Ultimately, the DAP produces a training plan designed

exclusively to enable the agency or office where the participants work
to meet target outputs or program goals, or to facilitate achievement
of interagency program objectives.

In other words, DAP training courses are tailored to the needs
of specific agencies or programs. In each case, all the key executives of the agency or program must undergo the training. The DAP
seeks to ensure a critical mass of decision makers or managers in
the office or program, instead of training one executive from an institution of 10,000 to 50,000 employees and then devoutly hoping that
he will not be suspect when he returns or hoping that he will single-
handedly infuse everybody else in his agency with a development
orientation.

After the training course, the DAP conducts posttraining on-
the-job evaluation and assists in meeting individual graduates reentry
problems. Consultancy arrangements are worked out for agency programs after the graduates return. The DAP also helps its alumni
mobilize their expertise and resources to meet their own problems.

Although there is considerable formal similarity in the course
content of the PEA and DAP higher- and middle-level executive development programs, the differences are significant. The DAP deliberately blends academic course work, sports, social gatherings, and
informal faculty-participant interaction into a "total experience."
This broader experience fosters the sense of a "development team"
rather than of the solitary individual or loner. The stress on outputs
and program objectives also somewhat deemphasizes concern over
promotions—although DAP sees to it that promotions and/or job
security are virtually guaranteed its government graduates. The
team idea also yields dividends. Participants from the same agency
or program learn to work together on a development task, not as
individuals separated by an artificial hierarchy. Thus the DAP fosters
interagency or agencywide teamwork, vital in most contemporary
development programs.

Furthermore, the DAP faculty is drawn from various fields,
while the PEA faculty comes almost exclusively from public administration. The faculty for DAP's Executive Development Program includes engineers, economists, planners, political theorists, behav-
iorists, systems analysts, business management experts, sociologists,
psychologists, and ecologists. Whenever outside staff is required,
as for special lectures, the DAP engages the top expert in the country,
with no cost limits.

Again, the wide range of DAP programs, and the staff versa-
tility that this range requires, leads to the channeling of rich materials into the training courses. These courses are based on firsthand data and individual staff insights rather than on rehashed versions
of other agency reports.

There are two more advantages of the MOD training programs. In the first place, the MOD staff head was recruited by the DAP president from a private development bank assistant vice-presidency when he was in his late 30s. He had complete freedom to recruit his staff and drew them from the church, the government, the universities (both government and private), and private industry and business. All are on the young side. Second, because the DAP receives no direct appropriations from the government (except as payment from individual agencies for services), DAP salaries are not subject to government scales, and, in the case at least of the MOD faculty, their salaries are higher than those of almost any participant in DAP training programs. In brief, staff members are highly paid, enjoying considerable margins over their academic counterparts who struggle on university pay. Thus their age (young), their backgrounds and fields (diverse), their life and work styles (causal—participants in a course for presiding judges of the courts of first instance were stripped of their official titles and addressed by their nicknames, which, since it is a somewhat common practice in Philippine culture, they enjoyed), and their income (high) combine to give them a fresh, innovative, flexible, and un-self-conscious approach to the bureaucratic culture and to development problems.

In fact, staff members' zestful and what they call their "celebrative" attitude to their jobs can be a problem, especially with a year's schedule calling for four ten-week sessions with only two weeks intervening between sessions. To keep their freshness and energy, the DAP sometimes assigns them to other training programs involving other groups and often (especially in the case of the government Executive Development Program) recruits additional staff to constitute a 150 percent faculty. The 50 percent excess faculty is available for other tasks or for a follow-up, and can consult with graduates.

Conclusion

In the less than two years of its existence, the DAP has acquired considerable prestige. Many of its graduates, including those who have attended PEA, say that there should be a government prohibition on all executive development programs for government officers, except for the DAP training. Even the Philippine cabinet has held planning and development sessions at DAP's Tagaytay complex, with DAP staff guiding and/or assisting.

Not everything, of course, is rosy. Bigness and success pose the prospect of creating an unwieldy bureaucracy, which the staff dreads, and financing could be a problem if the DAP becomes

over extended. Moreover, additional success in an expanding range
of activities may generate anxiety and insecurity in other government
agencies.

On the other hand, the leadership and staff regard problems as
inevitable. They say that it is infinitely better to have problems
arising out of success than those arising out of inaction or failure.
They feel that the DAP has opened a large market for services that
had been largely neglected. Doubling the training and conferences
facility to accommodate the private sector is expected to generate
enough income to permit a surplus. Good projects always attract
funding. Indeed, the DAP in its initial years has deliberately shunned
external assistance, in both personnel and funding. Anxiety and suspicion from other government agencies are a fact of life. What the
DAP does is to meet the issue head on by offering service packages to
such agencies. In a confrontation the DAP always tries to demonstrate
that it is supporting a development project or program that was otherwise unserviced or floundering.

The DAP's apparent success as a "business" that serves government is that it seeks out and creates "markets" that other institutions,
universities, and others do not serve. It will, for example, analyze
government-formulated river basin development programs and suggest
improvements without charging a fee. It has put together a natural
resources perspective plan for the government, again on a "good-will"
basis. Its success as a training institution, similarly, is that it takes
the initiative in identifying the important, but sometimes overlooked,
training component of development projects. It designs a training
scheme to meet the goals of a given agency and tailors it to the
agency's own needs and circumstances.

A strong point in the DAP organization is that its founding board
is made up of development-oriented men, bankers, and financiers,
who see the DAP as one of their investments in development. They
combine a large view with a disinclination to meddle in internal operations. The influx of foreign capital into the Philippines stresses the
need for large-scale thinking, long-range planning, and meticulous
project systems and monitoring, which are characteristic of DAP.
The skills and attitudes required for this approach are encouraged in
DAP, where the officers and professional staff are engaged collegially
in designing not only projects but also the departmental structures of
the DAP as a whole.

Finally, it is useful to observe that the DAP is a "second-
generation" institution. Its officers and staff are products of an extensive higher education system, which it complements and without
which, in fact, it cannot exist. Its programs reflect the growing
awareness of development as a multifaceted effort, and it regards
training as interlinked with management, project monitoring, and

financing. The PEA effort was an innovation in its time, but it is now inadequate. Higher education institutions, with their much richer staff resources, can derive some lessons from the DAP model in organization and in responding to national requirements.

ASIAN INSTITUTE OF MANAGEMENT

AIM is a private, nonprofit educational organization established under the laws of the Republic of the Philippines. It is a graduate school of business administration based on the model of the Harvard Business School and is the only one of its kind in Asia; not even in Japan is there graduate business education like this. One of AIM's precursors was, in fact, a six-week Advanced Management Program (AMP) begun in the summer of 1956 by a group of professors from the Harvard Business School in collaboration with the Executive Training Institute of the Philippines (ETIOP). That program continued for a dozen years, at the beginning with official support from Harvard, but later as a joint enterprise between ETIOP and the individual professors from the Harvard Business School.

AIM was also preceded by a cooperative effort of three leading graduate schools of business—the colleges of Business Administration of the University of the Philippines (U.P.), De La Salle College, and the Ateneo de Manila. In 1963, the Ford Foundation made a grant of $250,000 to permit the three institutions to strengthen business education. The institutions were to decide among themselves on individual specializations (the University of the Philippines chose financial management, De La Salle production management, and Ateneo marketing) and to develop their faculties through the use of visiting professors and overseas fellowships for staff members. The grant was also expected to stimulate research leading to the writing of case studies for classroom use.

Although the effort was successful, the three institutions realized that each could not hope to develop a first-class graduate business school and that there was a need for one strong graduate school with full-time faculty and students. Hence a proposal was made for such a joint endeavor. As a state institution the University of the Philippines felt it should develop its own program, and thus U.P. College of Business Administration dropped out of the proposal. De La Salle and Ateneo were left to carry on.

There followed a period of intense effort to organize the new institution. The Rectors of Ateneo and De La Salle solicited financial and other support for the project. USAID was enlisted in the effort. The Ford Foundation, which had provided the original grant for the

upgrading of the business schools, was in a sense the catalyst. In
September 1968, AIM was incorporated as an affiliate of the Ateneo
de Manila University and De La Salle College for the purpose of
offering high-quality, full-time management education designed to
meet Asian needs. However, both Ateneo and De La Salle (as well as
the University of the Philippines) continued their respective, largely
part-time, graduate programs in business.

The package brought together to form AIM consisted of a donation by the Ayala Corporation of 13,000 square meters of prime real
estate, then worth about ₱6.5 million ($1.67 million), in the pres-
tigious Makati commercial district; a donation by the Eugenio Lopez
Foundation of ₱6,472,000 ($1.64 million) for the building; a grant by
the Ford Foundation of $244,000 for faculty development (including
visiting professors during the initial period); a grant by USAID of
₱1,331,341 ($341,000) for library facilities and equipment; and a loan
of ₱3 million ($769,000) from the Social Security System (a govern-
ment financial institution) to finance student loans. * In addition, 20
of the most prominent Philippine and foreign business firms and individual businessmen gave an average of ₱250,000 ($64,100) each to
endow faculty chairs. The AIM Scientific Research Foundation was
incorporated in November 1968, as a private nonprofit organization
to accept and manage funds from donations and endowment. Besides
the five leading "social investors" and the donors of the 20 faculty
chairs, there were 18 charter members of the foundation who contributed large, though varying, amounts. It was an unprecedented
mobilization of private funds for an educational project.

Structure

The official governing body of AIM is the eight-man board of
trustees made up of representatives of the two founding educational
institutions and the public. The majority of the trustees are Filipinos,
but all are residents of the Philippines.

During the school year 1970-71, a board of governors, composed
of distinguished government and business leaders from eight Asian
countries, was established to ensure AIM's relevance to the Asian
community. The board, which serves in an advisory capacity to the
board of trustees, meets formally once a year. Between meetings,

---

*The exchange rate at the time was ₱3.90 to U.S. $1.00. At
the present time, it is approximately ₱7.03 to $1.00.

the Institute keeps the board of governors informed of its activities. The members of the board assist representatives of AIM in their respective countries.

The faculty is not large, consisting of some 30 persons, most of whom serve full-time. As is characteristic of tertiary-level institutions in the Philippines, and in contrast with other high-quality efforts in Southeast Asia, AIM is staffed by Filipinos, not by expatriates. However, there have been and will be visiting foreign faculty members. Almost all the faculty have advanced degrees, largely earned in the United States; the majority have M.B.A.s, but a number have doctorates. At the present time, six faculty members are in the United States pursuing advanced studies. Although at the beginning the faculty tended to be young, today there is a balanced age spread. It is planned to raise the number of faculty members to 35 or 40 so that they can undertake more programs and more field work.

The faculty is a harmonious and well-knit group, and AIM is effectively a faculty-run organization. In this, the first two presidents, both Americans and professors at Harvard Business School, had made their impact. The first president was a professor of personnel management. He not only contributed to the development of the staff but also, because of his standing in the Philippine business community, built up during many years of association with the AMP, rallied the support of the business firms behind the Institute. The second president devoted himself somewhat more to the internal affairs of the institution and built up a system of faculty committees and faculty decision making in academic affairs, finance, personnel including faculty recruitment, development, and discipline.

Programs

The original degree offering of AIM was a two-year full-time master of business management (M.B.M.) program, but at present three other major programs are offered: the one-year master of management (M.M.) degree, the nondegree Management Development Program (MDP), and another nondegree Basic Management Program. In addition, AIM offers several short management programs, usually in cooperation with industry associations. In keeping with the Harvard connection, instruction is carried out using the case method.

Master of Business Management: The program aims to (1) give the students practical experience in the basic areas of business management, (2) help them understand clearly the relevant concepts and techniques involved, and (3) develop in them a competence and willingness to undertake the responsibility of solving problems arising in their future work situations.

The MBM program involves full-time study, consisting of two parts corresponding to the two years of the program. The entire first year is devoted to core courses required of all students. The second year builds on the knowledge and skills acquired during the first year. Elective courses provide the student with an opportunity to concentrate in one area. A thesis is required for graduation.

Unmarried students, male and female, in the first-year program are required to live on campus for the first three months of the program. Second-year male students may also be accommodated if space is available. Facilities consist of 39 fully air-conditioned suites of six beds each. There are no residence facilities on campus for families of married students; however, they are assisted in making arrangements for board and lodging in houses and living halls near the AIM.

The entire two-year program costs approximately ₱33,000 ($4,700). Tuition fees and other academic expenses come to about ₱6,300 ($900) per year. Lodging at the school dormitory is ₱4,200 and board at the cafeteria is ₱4,200 ($600) per year. In addition, personal expenses are estimated at a minimum of ₱150 ($21) per month.

Local and overseas scholarships are available for deserving candidates. For Filipino candidates, there is a loan fund of ₱3 million, made possible by the Social Security System, where students may borrow the necessary funds for the program at relatively low interest rates.

The M.B.M. program enrolled its first class of 143 students in July 1969. Enrollment figures for the first year program for the succeeding years are as follows:

	Filipinos	Non-Filipinos
1970-71	136	26
1971-72	136	29
1972-73	119	30
1973-74	92	41
1974-75	114	45

From 1970 to 1974, there were 436 graduates of the program, representing 84 percent of 519 entrants from 1969 to 1973, a high ratio.

Master in Management: The Master in Management program, which was offered for the first time in the school year 1974-75, is especially designed for junior and middle managers. Since firms cannot always release people for two years, the program was designed to take only one year and one semester. The objectives of the program are (1) to develop in the student a general management perspective that is Asian and developmental in outlook, and (2) to develop in the student a high degree of skill in analysis, decision making, and implementation both at the strategic and operating management levels.

The applicant for the M.M. program must be at least 28 years old and should have had six years' work experience, during three of which he served as supervisor or manager. He must hold a bachelor's degree in any field from a recognized college or university.

The M.M. program covers skills in analysis and decision making. The primary learning tool is the case method. The cases are commonly drawn from business, but a number come from government and nonprofit organizations.

The entire one-year program costs ₱9,076.50. The tuition is ₱3,000 per semester and ₱2,000 per summer.

Classes were formally opened on June 3, 1974, with 54 participants (33 Filipinos, 21 non-Filipinos).

Management Development Program: In May 1971, AIM inaugurated the Management Development Program for middle- and upper-level managers. The program is patterned after the Harvard Business School Program for Management Development. It is offered for eight weeks during the summer and requires the full time of its participants, who stay in the school's dormitory during the period.

The MDP has two primary objectives: (1) to equip the participants to handle their present assignment more effectively and (2) to prepare them for greater responsibility.

The candidate must be a manager at the middle or upper level of his company's organization. In larger companies, he would probably be a department manager; in smaller companies, a vice-president; in government, a bureau director or an assistant director. He must have a minimum of five years' experience in supervising the work of others and be sponsored by his firm. Since there are no formal qualifying tests for admission, the sponsorship of a candidate's company serves as an assurance that the candidate will be capable of contributing to and profiting from an exchange of ideas among experienced and successful managers from various Asian countries.

The primary learning tool in this program too is the case method. Lectures, readings, role-playing, simulation, and report writing are supplementary learning aids.

The program fee of ₱6,500 includes tuition, meals, dormitory room, bedroom linen, and reading and case materials.

Enrollment over the first four years in which the program was offered was 1971—83; 1972—102; 1973—112; and 1974—128.

Basic Management Program: The Basic Management Program is a new venture of AIM. It is designed for practicing first-line to middle-level managers and functional specialists. Its object is to provide grounding in basic management concepts, practices, and skills. It is an intensive, full-time, four-week, live-out program.

An applicant not in a management position will not be admitted to the program unless his sponsoring company agrees to promote him into management upon completing the course. Sponsoring companies are required to release a program participant from all his duties during the program period. Candidates must be proficient in both oral and written English.

The program seeks understanding of three basic business components—the enterprise, the manager, and the worker—and has three corresponding areas of study, each of which has learning units that vary in duration from one to six sessions. Each session normally takes one hour and 20 minutes, although departures from this norm are often necessary. There is extensive use of short cases or "incidents," of lectures, readings, exercises, and games. There is also strong insistence on participant feedback in the form of examinations, both written and oral.

The first program, which started on September 30, 1974, and ended on October 26, 1974, and 79 participants.

New Directions

In the years since it was founded, AIM has developed over a broad front, showing in the process not only its strong commitment to manpower training but also its special capacity to innovate and to adapt to changing circumstances. It has expanded course offerings from the original two-year M.B.M. degree to the shorter programs designed to fill the needs of student groups with different backgrounds, age brackets, and needs. It has instituted special programs and continuing education courses, such as a two-week course for airline executives given under the sponsorship of the Orient Airlines Research Board. The participants are executives from all over Asia. The program is seen to be highly useful to the airlines; therefore, AIM can charge full costs plus a small "profit" to subsidize its regular programs. The airlines are more than glad to pay for the training. In the process, the Institute becomes more relevant to the needs of the country and the region.

Another program of service is the Southeast Asian Faculty Development Fellowship, for which the Ford Foundation made a grant of $150,000. The program calls for putting 15 Fellows through the regular two-year M.B.M. course over a four-year period. The Fellows must be at least 25 years old, with some business experience, and from Southeast Asian countries. To encourage Fellows to join AIM faculty the fellowships have been made "forgivable" loans; that is, they are to be repaid in the form of teaching either at AIM or at an acceptable institution in the home country. Every year of teaching at AIM means that one-fourth of the loan is forgiven; thus the ratio is that four years of service at AIM pays for two years of study. If the teaching is done at a home institution, the ratio is six years of service for two years of study, so that for every year of teaching, one-sixth of the loan is forgiven. The loan may be repaid through varying combinations of service at AIM or at home.

In the years to come, AIM intends to maintain the M.B.M. program at its present capacity of 166 students. With regard to the MDP, however, the Institute intends to maintain its present capacity level of 112 students until 1975, and then increase it by approximately 40 percent. Much of the increase is expected to come from non-Filipino Asian students, as it is hoped that ultimately the proportions of Filipino and foreign students in the student body in all programs will be 50/50 (the delay is caused by the lagging English-language proficiency of the foreign students). Finally, an AMP for general managers and company presidents will be offered in 1976.

Problems

It may seem that with the solid financial support it has enjoyed, AIM should have no problems. Yet it does have problems, especially with inflation. Financial pressures, combined with its commitment to service, have spurred efforts to develop innovative activities.

At present, the endowment income of AIM totals between ₱500,000 to ₱700,000 ($71,400 to $100,000) a year, while total faculty salaries are ₱1.3 million ($185,700). The gap is filled in various ways: by raising tuition; by varying the program mix so as to offer more fee-producing short-duration training programs to meet specific needs of the business sector; and by pricing these programs higher so as to leave some surplus to be used for the basic academic programs. Increasingly, the Institute solicits grants—as for example, from USAID for the Asian scholarship program—and accepts research commitments, as from IBM Philippines for work on the development of information systems.

Not only do the board of trustees and the president involve themselves in efforts to raise funds, but the administrative officials and
faculty also pitch in. Local financial support was substantial at the
start of the AIM's existence, declined after that, but has been rising
again; of late, for example, two U.S. financial institutions have given
to the faculty endowment and one local ethnic Chinese businessman
has offered to donate a new wing for the Institute building. Seven contributors are now corporate members of the AIM Scientific Research
Foundation. Scholarships for students are maintained by 32 donors.
Six individuals and corporations have given general purpose funds.

A heartening development, which shows the acceptance that AIM
has gained, is that it is beginning to get Asian support. Sony Corporation of Japan has given a faculty chair; a group of Malaysian financial
institutions have contributed for a faculty chair to be filled by a Malaysian; and the same type of package has been framed by businessmen from Taiwan. Talks are starting for similar arrangements by
groups from Singapore and Japan.

Evaluation

One of the inevitable criticisms of AIM is that it is elitist in
orientation; another is that it is a copy of institutions in Western industrialized society and of training methods that are not suited to
Asian conditions. The Institute is keenly aware of these criticisms
and misgivings.

As to its being elitist, this is a charge faced by tertiary education as a whole, for it is well known that selection procedures, financial requirements for higher education, and many other factors combine to create the problem of elitism. The solution must be initiated
by the education system as a whole through modifying its curricula,
selection methods, and qualification requirements especially at the
secondary education level. AIM, in particular, cannot help being
elitist to some extent, as the gift of becoming a successful professional
manager is not given to everyone. But it is precisely AIM's objective
to widen the circle of such people, the better to serve the business and
economic development of Asian nations. The Institute is reaching out
to many areas in its search for students, and generous scholarships
and loan facilities are made available not only to Filipino students but
also to other Asians.

Another aspect of elitism is in the attitudes of the new graduates,
who are often criticized for arrogance. To some extent these attitudes
are normal manifestations of self-confidence and energy, but, at the
same time, the AIM tries to inculcate some sense of humility in the

students. For example, business executives are brought in to meet the students and show them the complexities of the business world, which will expose the gaps in the students' learning. The faculty talk to the students about the realities of the job market. In career planning exercises, graduates of AIM tell the students about the outside world and warn them against excessive self-esteem.

The results of intensive full-time training seem to be effective, as is seen in the distribution of AIM's graduates (Tables 15.1 and 15.2). They are not being sent primarily to the multinational corporations, but go mostly to domestic corporations (211 out of 316 graduates or 67 percent), not to the large corporations only, but also to medium-sized and small ones. A significant number are going into self-employment, to government and international organizations, education, and some to nonprofit organizations. Indeed, AIM's placement officers feel that graduates tend to shun multinational corporations and big domestic corporations, looking rather for smaller organizations or self-employment as the best career opportunities. Graduates show elements of idealism and patriotism, too, in the desire to serve their own countries. When graduates do go to multinational corporations, it is often because the students were sent by these firms and there are service contracts to be fulfilled.

TABLE 15.1

Placement of AIM MBM Graduates by Types of
Company or Organization, 1970-74

	Philippines		Overseas	
	Number	Percent Distribution	Number	Percent Distribution
Business				
Domestic	195	67.7	16	44.3
Multinational	55	19.1	10	27.8
Government				
National	30	10.4	1	2.8
International	2	0.7	2	5.6
Education	4	1.4	6	16.7
Other nonprofit				
organizations	2	0.7	1	2.8
Total	288	100.0	36	100.0

Source: Asian Institute of Management.

TABLE 15.2

Placement of AIM MBM Graduates in Business
Firms in Philippines, 1970-74

	Domestic Corporations		Multinational Corporations	
	Number	Percent Distribution	Number	Percent Distribution
Top 100 corporations*	36	18.5	19	34.5
Top 200 corporations*	72	36.9	25	45.5
Top 1,000 corporations*	113	57.9	25	45.5
All others	82	42.1	30	54.5
Total, top 1,000 corporations and others	195	100.0	55	100.0

*Corporations are ranked by annual sales.
Source: Asian Institute of Management.

Both elitism and a sense of irrelevance can be produced by the
nature of the case materials used in the training. AIM seeks to be
more than a copy of Western training methods for business. The case
material is continually reviewed, American cases are dropped, and
faculty members have been taken away from teaching, given research
funds, and occasionally sent abroad, to develop a bank of Asian as
well as Philippine case studies. Contacts among the alumni and others
assure a stream of Asian materials. Small community enterprises
as well as large or urban-based firms are studied, although cases
of small community businesses often do not completely lend themselves to effective teaching, and the use of such material is consequently limited.

To increase the relevance of the teaching materials, research
is being conducted in association with other bodies on the purchasing
patterns of the poor, such as the scavengers of Manila. A plan to
study entrepreneurship will be a regional Asian effort, perhaps to be
funded by an outside donor agency.

One other source of the criticism of AIM as elitist is its relationship to other business schools in the country and outside. As has
been seen, the Institute has a program for development of faculty in
other Southeast Asian institutions. Some of its graduates teach either
full-time or part-time in other schools in the Philippines, and individual faculty members serve as consultants to other schools.

Although AIM, as an organization, does not do industrial consulting and the faculty feels it neither can nor should do so under present circumstances, the Institute has from time to time lent faculty members for a year at a time to other organizations and institutions, such as the Fertilizer Industry Authority, the Department of Local Government and Community Development, and the new group for Management of Population Programs, which has headquarters in Bucharest. Individual faculty members, of course, do industrial consultancy work.

Since AIM is now run almost entirely under Philippine leadership, it may be helpful to assess the transition from expatriate (that is, American) to Philippine management. One of the features of the original Ford Foundation grant for the Institute was provision for training of a Philippine staff. From the evidence, the staff transfer does not seem to have had any adverse effects. Indeed, AIM under Filipinos is now running more programs than ever under tighter constraints, and the faculty turnover rate has been gratifyingly low. Innovation in such areas as curriculum design and redesign is continuous. The first two presidents, Americans, served full-time, whereas today the president is part-time, with the faculty running most of the institution. AIM is also beginning to receive more financial support, both from local and foreign sources. Perhaps, therefore, one of the wisest decisions made at AIM's inception was not to rely on an expatriate faculty.

Conclusion

There seem to be a number of striking features in the development of AIM from which lessons can be learned.

1. Since the organization was new, it was wise to set it up outside a traditional university and give it autonomy and freedom to develop. This independence, of course, was possible only because there were enough able persons to carry out the task of building up the new structure.

2. AIM attracted a good faculty in a number of ways—first of all by the mission of the institution itself and also by the appeal to status and prestige: the regional name, the Harvard connection, and judicious publicity. Naturally, the salary scales had to compare favorably with opportunities in the private business world.

3. Impressive facilities were important, but these had to be used well, for there are many grand monuments that become empty shells.

4. As already mentioned, it was a sound strategy not to rely on an expatriate staff for then the operation became less costly, more stable, and more relevant and flexible.

5. Overambition is a danger that should be guarded against. If AIM tries to be everything to everybody it can easily become over-extended and overproliferated. A delicate balance must be maintained between too many services to the community and too few.

6. Another danger is arrogance on the part of the faculty and the Institute and that students come only to benefit from AIM's name rather than to work hard and to learn.

As AIM has grown in age and in number of alumni, its standing both within and outside the Philippines has steadily risen. One index of this rise in status is the number of applications; five times more applications are submitted for its programs than can be accepted. Abroad, AIM's high reputation, especially in Singapore, Malaysia, and Taiwan, has accounted for an increasing stream of applicants, many of them company-sponsored. Its development, in summary, has been positive and generally successful.

THE CENTER FOR RESEARCH AND COMMUNICATION

CRC had the most modest beginnings of the three Philippine institutions studied, and it is still the smallest in staff, student body, and finance. Yet the work it is doing and its results are significant in their own way. As its activities expand, especially in the business world, and its studies are well publicized, summaries of the findings appear regularly in all the metropolitan newspapers and business publications, as well as on the desks of leading business executives.

As its name implies, CRC started out as a research group on business and economic problems. In 1965, a young economist, just returned from advanced studies in the United States and working at the Program Implementation Agency (PIA), perceived the need for more economic research on the problems of the Philippine economy as well as for the popularization and dissemination of this knowledge, especially to the private sector and through the mass media. In the course of his work at PIA, he saw that economic planning in the government sector was being developed to a high degree but that such planning could not be effective if private businessmen did not understand, cooperate with, contribute to, and implement the planning and did not, at the same time, protect their own legitimate interests. He felt it important for the total benefit of the nation that private business have the same access to good economic training and research as the government had.

He discussed his ideas with other economists, chiefly another young and newly returned economist who, as department chairman, was engaged in building up the economics program of De La Salle College, a high-prestige private religious school. The latter saw the challenge in the idea and joined in setting up a new institution: the Center for Research and Communication.

CRC was established on August 15, 1967, as a center for business and economic research devoted to the needs of the private sector. It is operated by the Southeast Asian Science Foundation, an organization of industrial, educational, and other professional leaders in the Philippines. The spiritual guidance of the Center has been entrusted to Opus Dei, an international Catholic association.

In the beginning, CRC engaged in economic research mainly on problems commissioned by private business. In the course of this work, it was found that the young staff research assistants and associates had to be trained, largely on the job. It was, therefore, decided to formalize the instruction: Staff members would go to the classroom in the morning and in the afternoon would study and do research. CRC applied to the Department of Education for authorization to award a graduate degree on the basis of this unique work-study program and was accordingly authorized in 1969 to run a master's program in Industrial Economics and, a year later, to give another master's program, this one in Economic Education. In 1974 authority was granted for a master's program in Business Economics.

Structure of CRC

CRC is divided into various centers specializing in different aspects of its research and communication work. These are the Regional Economics Center, the Business Economics Center, the International Economics Center, and the Education for Development Center. The Regional Economics Center works mainly with business enterprises in promoting projects that can have broad regional economic significance. The Business Economics Center does continuing research work on the economics of a firm, an industry, or an economic sector. It is charged with translating broad economic concepts into more manageable business guidelines. The International Economics Center promotes the ideals of internationalism within the context of long-term interest for all countries, particularly those within the Association of Southeast Asian Nations (ASEAN). The Education for Development Center is engaged in the task of upgrading the quality of economics education in the country.

Finance

The Center for Research and Communication is a private, nonprofit institution supported by foundations and friends—that is, business firms and individual donors. It derives income from foundation grants for specific projects, as well as from fees for research projects undertaken for private firms and, on occasion, for government agencies. In addition, there are over 400 "Friends of CRC" who contribute varying amounts and who, in turn, are entitled to the use of different CRC facilities and activities. The size of the list of friends, covering not only the largest and most prestigious private firms in the country but also smaller and less well-known ones, indicates the wide acceptance, in so short a time, of the work of the Center. It should also be mentioned that no single firm contributes any significant percentage of the total operating fund requirements of CRC. This practice guarantees the academic freedom of CRC and the independence of the research activities undertaken.

Faculty

At the present time, the full-time resident faculty of CRC consists of only eight persons, two with Ph.D.'s and the others with M.S. degrees in Industrial Economics from CRC itself. From time to time, the Center makes use of the services, full-time or part-time, of other economists with Ph.D.'s or with master's degrees from other institutions who may be free for a particular period. In addition, the research staff (who are also in large part CRC's students), take part in the Center's activities.

It is apparent that at this stage the faculty is somewhat inbred. Accordingly, in 1974, eight staff members were working for the Ph.D.'s in the United States, Australia, England, Italy, and Spain. These eight were in diverse doctoral programs in the fields of business economics, urban planning, development education, and the humanities.

Because of this small staff complement, the faculty carry heavy research and teaching loads demonstrating their commitment and dedication. The fact that CRC can draw on a larger research staff and also has a small but competent administrative group eases the burden somewhat.

272 HIGHER EDUCATION AND SOCIAL CHANGE

Educational Programs

CRC is a degree-granting institution, duly authorized by the Department of Education. At the present time, three graduate degrees are offered: the Program in Industrial Economics, the Program in Economics Education, and the Program in Business Economics. In an earlier period, CRC offered special courses in economics to selected undergraduates, chosen and seconded by affiliated colleges, most of them Catholic schools, which felt that they did not have the staff to offer high-quality, specialized courses in economics. The courses taken at CRC were given academic credit by the home institutions so that the work counted toward degrees. This activity, however, has since been dropped.

Master's Program in Industrial Economics: The Industrial Economics Program (IEP) grew out of the research activities of CRC when it was found that the research assistants had to be trained on the job. IEP is CRC's own staff development program; those enrolled are called staff members or graduate staff, not students. In accordance with CRC's open-door policy to the business community, however, companies may send one or two of their promising young professionals to participate in the program. The program seeks to develop a high level of technical competence and professional responsibility. It also seeks to inculcate the Christian spirit of service and, more specifically, the ideal of using one's professional skills and position in order to promote economic development and social justice. The program stresses communication and cooperation. Teamwork is integrated into the mechanics of the IEP in order to highlight the need for working together for common goals through individual initiatives, for sharing responsibility, and for giving and taking within a group.

IEP is a full-time, two-year combined work and study arrangement. Mornings are devoted to classroom instruction and afternoons are for study or research, often on concrete topics worked on by CRC or commissioned by business firms. On occasion, the staff are released for internship programs in business firms, after which they return to the classrooms. The course content is never exclusively theoretical; it relates to current issues, Philippine economic facts, and vital business questions. The research demands integration of theory, statistical techniques, and development perspective; and it necessarily leads to communication.

Each participant is expected to become competent in five special fields: economic forecasting, interindustry relations, specific industry analysis, economic planning, and specialized research activity. Basic courses include economic history, economic theory, mathematical and applied statistics, econometrics, economic policy, social ethics, and social economics. Study topics range from accounting for management, finance, marketing and production to industrial analysis, linear programing, and economic growth experience of various countries.

Applicants to the program must be of above–average intelligence with a respectable undergraduate record and an acceptable degree of extracurricular achievement. Preference is given to individuals with two to five years of actual work in business or government. While applicants newly graduated from college are not automatically rejected, they have to show a high degree of maturity to be considered. Some 50 percent of all acceptances are reserved for applicants with an engineering, mathematics, or natural science background; 25 percent for those with a business and economics background; and 25 percent for those whose undergraduate specialization was in humanities and other social sciences. Only 50 percent of all acceptances go to applicants from Luzon and metropolitan Manila; the remaining 50 percent go to applicants from the Visayas and Mindanao.

Scholarships covering tuition and living allowance of ₱400 per month are available for successful applicants. These scholarships come from foundations, schools, and companies. Companies that send their employees to the program contribute ₱24,000 per year for each employee.

From 1969 to 1974, there were 62 participants in the program. Eleven of these were sent by private firms, while 51 were granted scholarships from CRC. Of the 51, six are now with CRC's faculty, and eight are at present pursuing further studies abroad.

Master's Program in Economics Education: This program is a response to the need for competent economics teachers at the secondary and even tertiary levels. Originally, it was funded by the Ford Foundation, which had earlier sponsored a crash program for the master of arts in teaching economics in Mindanao, the second largest island in the Philippines, in response to the poor quality of economics education in high schools and tertiary-level institutions in areas outside Manila, specifically in Mindanao. As part of the assistance effort of the Ford Foundation, the Notre Dame Consortium of Catholic Schools in Mindanao was chosen for an experiment to upgrade the competencies of teachers of economics. The Ford resident representative asked the academic dean of CRC how the Center might help broaden the coverage of the program. The dean had felt that the needs of teachers in smaller and more remote areas of the country were being neglected, and CRC agreed to conduct the program for them. The Master's Program in Economic Education that resulted showed the creative relationship that can exist between a foundation officer and a local center and was an example of a local institution helping the rest of the educational system.

When the program was first offered in the school year 1970-71, it was spread over one school year and two summers. In addition to this full-time program, a program was started in the summer of 1971 that lasts for three school years and four summers. During the regular school year, the participants go back to teach economics and conduct research studies in their respective schools. An Off-Summer Training Program complements the academic work done during the summer with laboratory work, for which credits are earned, during the school year.

The program is open to any economics or social science teacher in high school or college who has taught for at least one school year. Men and women who have earned a bachelor's degree in any field and who are 35 years of age or under may apply.

The entire tuition costs ₱3,500. Upon admission, scholarships are available to cover 80 percent of tuition (excluding books, living allowances, materials, and travel). Scholarship terms, however, are subject to change, depending upon the academic performance of the participant during the preceding summer session.

At the beginning of school year 1972-73, CRC was forced to phase out temporarily the full-time program because the Ford Foundation, which at the time was restructuring its aid programs all over the world, withdrew its support. The resources available to CRC in undertaking its research and communication activities were so limited that without the help of the Ford Foundation, the conduct of the full-time program in economics education at the high level of quality that CRC is committed to maintain exerted an excessive burden on its finances.

During the school year 1973-74, in line with the government's efforts to mobilize the rural areas, a number of the economics educators being trained by the Center gave economic advice, under CRC guidance, to small-scale entrepreneurs in their respective regions. Another group specialized in market research activities—with their students as field workers—geared toward specifying the content and composition of the market baskets consumed by low-income households. These research activities have provided businessmen with information about consumption patterns in various regions, thus helping them to devise appropriate marketing strategies for "wage goods" as well as to develop more humane wage policies.

As of 1974, 117 educators had been admitted into the program, which now also involves study during the summer vacation, when the teachers are free. Sixteen have so far graduated, and 17 have finished the course requirements and are writing their theses.

Other Activities

While only young professionals can join CRC's executive training program, the Center tries to reach out to operating executives in business and in government through a number of other activities that make CRC a vigorous and active center. These activities include professional conferences, survey programs, study sessions, a corporate planning program, and a professional development program.

Professional Conferences: CRC has been running a series of professional conferences at the Makiling Conference Center, maintained by CRC in Batangas province, about 50 kilometers south of Manila. While the subjects of the conferences have been varied, the discussions on industry economics and on the economic prospects of the Philippines and of various subsectors of the economy have predominated.

Survey Programs: Also at Makiling Conference Center, CRC conducts a live-in program for company executives. The program lasts for three days, during which the participants are given a survey of economic ideas, Philippine economic data, and CRC research results.

Study Sessions on Economic Policy: This is a nine-month program during which executives, together with the graduate staff, read a compilation of economic ideas as applied to the Philippine scene, a set of essays written by economists from various parts of the world and addressed to present Philippine economic policy concerns, and a resume of research results derived from an analysis of facts behind some policy questions.

Those who have attended this program have generally been top executives responsible for long-range planning in their respective corporations. These businessmen have become so involved in analyzing and evaluating the research findings of CRC staff members that another degree program has evolved from the study sessions on economic policy. The participants in these sessions may now work for the degree of M.B.E.

Corporate Planning Program: This program is designed for managers and a few carefully selected staff assistants who fill corporate planning roles in their company. The program lasts for eight months. It covers all the basic functional areas of business, and the application of the basic concepts and selected techniques of analysis to business economic questions. At the end of the program, participants are expected to have a good operational grasp of the various requirements of corporate strategy making.

Professional Development Program: This program is designed to train research analysts. It takes the participants through the rudiments of basic economics, basic research techniques, and practical research exercises in economic forecasting and industry analysis. A follow-up program is designed to guarantee that participants are fully comfortable in applying concepts and techniques of research to practical questions regarding economic forecasts and specific industrial situations.

Research

CRC's research activity is voluminous and wide-ranging, especially considering the small size of the staff. It issues research papers, monthly bulletins, and monographs.

Plans and Problems

So far, CRC's activities, apart from those at the Makiling Conference Center, are carried on in rented quarters that are physically dispersed and that rapidly have become inadequate. A long step toward physical integration and alleviation of the space problem will be the construction of a building complex, to cost ₱10 million, on a donated lot in Greenhills, an attractive real estate development in the suburbs of Manila. CRC has put together a financing package, consisting of loans from banks and donations by private firms and individuals. The first building to be constructed under the plans is expected to meet CRC's needs for five years.

The expansion of CRC's activities and staff are interrelated, for activities are limited by the personnel available. Given the value and the acceptance of the Center's activities and, therefore, the desirability and even the need to expand, perhaps the main present constraint is the limited faculty. A faculty training program is in operation, with eight faculty members abroad for advanced training in 1974. Taking advanced work at various foreign institutions, it might be mentioned, is a solution to the problem of an inbred faculty.

The process of training faculty takes time, however. Meanwhile, one of CRC's weaknesses is that its moving spirits are really only the two founders, and much of the success of the institution depends on them. Unfortunately, until the fruits of the faculty training program are realized, the Center is likely to be somewhat unstable, perhaps inevitable during the growth period of a small pioneering institution.

Conclusion

The experience of CRC provides a number of lessons. The first of these is that from modest beginnings, an innovative institution can still have major impact. To be sure, much of the success has depended on the dedication of CRC's two founders. But their efforts have also attracted significant support from donors and clients, as is evidenced by the 400 friends of the CRC, the many persons who attend its conferences and read its publications, and the firms who eagerly snap up its graduates and call on it for special research efforts.

The response of its clientele and the concrete support that CRC has generated are in their own way guarantees of the stability and continued viability of the institution. Even if the two young men who are the Center's heart at present should for some unforeseen reason no longer be able to serve, the many friends of CRC will undoubtedly see to it that the institution carries on.

COMMENTS

The above review of selected manpower training and research programs for development in the Philippines has examined three of the more significant efforts, but by no means the only ones. Although the programs are diverse, they are united not merely by their focus on manpower training for development but also in some characteristics of the institutions themselves, as well as of the society, which have contributed to their success. These features may be listed as follows:

1. A hospitable society: Programs of the sort found here require an appropriate setting in the society. These are second-generation institutions, and for their launching and subsequent success there must already be a minimum supply and level of competence of manpower resources. In the Philippines, as a result of a mass higher education system that has been in operation for two-thirds of a century, that minimum level was surpassed some time ago.

2. Flexibility in attitudes toward education: The three institutions were established and now carry on outside the universities and the traditional tertiary-education system. They are not bound by governmental bureaucratic regulations. Innovation in education can best flourish in a setting that is congenial to it; where the society encourages it, where people value higher education, and where the government is flexible in regard to its attitudes toward educational innovation.

3. Private-sector initiative: In the Philippines, there is a long tradition of the private sector involving itself in educational initiative, and the government respects and encourages this. The three examples cited show vividly what can happen when initiative is allowed to flower, not only within the narrow confines of the government but also in the private sector.

4. The key role of innovating individuals: The several ideas for the programs seem to have started with one person or a small group of individuals who perceived a problem and sought ways to solve it. In the case of the Development Academy of the Philippines, it was the chairman of the Development Bank of the Philippines and the man he commissioned to design ways to utilize existing training facilities. With CRC, it was the young economists who saw a need for greater public appreciation of economic problems. At AIM, a large group of persons in the business community, the rectors of two universities, and the resident representative of a foreign foundation took the initiative. These were the modernizers in the society, and in all three institutions they had the benefit of study abroad as a modernizing influence. This is not to say that foreign training is an essential element of educational innovation, but if these experiences are any evidence, foreign exposure was a key element in equipping individuals for innovation.

5. Outside financial support: The ideas germinating in the minds of the innovators had to be sold to outside agencies—government, foundations, local as well as foreign donors—and the financial support allowed the programs to take off and also made them sustainable. In outstanding cases (such as AIM), a foreign philanthropic foundation served not only as the initial supporter but also as a catalyst, bringing in other donors.

6. Importance of physical facilities: The original homes of the DAP in Tagaytay and AIM in Makati as well as the CRC conference center at Batangas are impressive, even lavish, architectural monuments. Compared with similar structures in other countries, they were not excessively expensive to build, as building costs in the Philippines are low—one sixth to one tenth those in the United States. Nor do bricks and mortar necessarily make a university; Socrates taught in a park. But it is undeniable that adequate and comfortable quarters affect the spirit and allow it to move forward on its mission. The donors who made possible the physical complexes at Tagaytay, Makati, and Makiling appreciated the importance of physical facilities and, therefore, deserve a large measure of the credit for the success of the three institutions.

7. Variety of programs: Although the unifying theme is the same—that is, manpower training and research for development— the responses have been varied. The different institutions (DAP, AIM,

and CRC) have perceived that the needs can be different and have carved separate niches for themselves as they have catered to different clienteles; not one of the three duplicates the efforts of the others.

8. No proliferation of programs: Despite the multiplicity of manpower training institutions and programs in the Philippines, most Philippine observers doubt that there is danger of an oversupply of trained people. It is felt that the programs address themselves to different needs, and even when the programs might seem to be almost the same, the need for trained people is so great as to call for massive and sustained efforts. If this is true for a country that has a greater number and variety of training programs than other Southeast Asian countries, it should also be true for others that are not as advanced in this respect.

9. Local, not expatriate staff: The three Philippine institutions are managed and manned by Filipino staff, although one of them, AIM, had in the beginning foreign professors, both for their contribution and for the prestige attached to having professors from the world-renowned Harvard Business School. The present reliance on local, rather than expatriate staff, means that the operations are less costly, more stable and permanent, more relevant and flexible. Of course, an adequate base of trained manpower is required to carry on the work, and in the case of AIM, training of faculty was an essential component of the package when the institution was launched.

10. Contribution to manpower resources: Because of the contribution to the supply of trained manpower by the three institutions, as well as numerous others in the Philippines, economic and national development efforts become easier and more effective. In addition, production costs become lower, and this decrease lowers the cost of living for the mass of the people and adds to the comparative advantage of the nation in the international exchange of goods and services. For example, a typical AIM graduate expects starting pay of ₱1,500-2,000 per month ($214-286) on graduation. A Singaporean or a Malaysian commands three times as much ($700 per month) at home, whereas it cannot be said that his productivity is that much greater than that of his Filipino classmate.

11. Dedication of teachers: The individuals who serve in these training and research programs are dedicated educators with a mission. This sense of mission is essential to success and cannot but rub off on the trainees, to the benefit of the nation as a whole.

12. An appreciation of the value of education: It was inspiring to note that not only the faculty but also the clientele of the various institutions—that is, the trainees in the different programs—had deep convictions about the value of manpower training to themselves, to the agencies with which they were connected, and to the country.

One young man, still going through his training, pleaded earnestly with the team to convey to aid agencies his view that investment in manpower training is the most fruitful possible contribution to a country's national development.

16

NGEE ANN TECHNICAL COLLEGE, SINGAPORE

Training Technicians through Nondegree Programs

In a sense, Singapore aims to be the Switzerland of Southeast Asia. A small nation, Singapore has a limited land area and natural resources and depends, therefore, largely on its human resources. Industrial development has played a significant part in its recent economic growth, and the fast pace of industrialization has required greater technological know-how and brought an increasing demand for technical as well as professional and managerial personnel.

Continued national growth is dependent on highly trained and intellectually agile manpower. To meet this demand for suitably trained manpower and to encourage the growth of technology-intensive industries, the Singapore government has, as a long-term measure, reorganized the entire educational system in Singapore to focus on technical education. The functions of higher education institutions are clearly delineated, and their numbers and enrollment are strictly limited to avoid unnecessary duplication. Their curricula and the places available in these programs are determined largely by estimates of the high-level manpower required to achieve the nation's current and projected social and economic development goals. The overall philosophy guiding the planning for higher education aims at selective as opposed to mass access. The recent words of a leading educator and policy maker emphasize these concerns:

> The universities . . . should be regarded as expensive investments for manpower that will serve Singapore's society . . . It certainly does not make sense to appease the demand for more university education if the end result is to create social unrest through graduate unemployment, and ironically, in spending more millions of dollars on higher education, the University is not only reduced to a state of morass but also held responsible for adding to the economic and social problems of the country. It is not the quantity of higher education but the nature, type and quality of education

281

that we need to bring our minds to bear on. The
universities and colleges of many developing countries
are swollen with numbers but these countries continue
to remain at the bottom of the World Bank League.[1]

Six institutions of higher education serve the republic's 2.2
million people. The University of Singapore and Nanyang University
both offer four-year programs of study leading to a degree. Four
diploma-level institutions offer two- or three-year training programs:
Singapore Polytechnic, Singapore Technical Institute, the Institute
of Education, and Ngee Ann Technical College (NATC).

HISTORY OF NGEE ANN TECHNICAL COLLEGE

Ngee Ann College was established in 1963 by the Ngee Ann clan
as a technical training institution, catering primarily to the needs of
the Chinese-speaking young men and women seeking to enter the
labor force, just as Nanyang University had been established by the
Hokkien clan as the Chinese University in Singapore. These two privately established institutions were distinct from the two government
institutions, the University of Singapore and Singapore Polytechnic.
Although Ngee Ann, like Nanyang University, catered mainly to
Chinese-language students, conducting most of its courses in Mandarin, it also offered instruction in English, helping thereby to integrate graduates into the existing job market, where English-language
facility is a valuable qualification.

The College began as a private, four-year, independent institution, granting bachelor's degrees in arts, science, and commerce.
Ngee Ann graduates, however, found they were at a disadvantage compared with graduates of the other two universities. The government
did not recognize the degree awarded by Ngee Ann for civil service
and statutory board salary scales, and private employers paid lower
salaries to Ngee Ann graduates. This situation, along with the College's financial difficulties, led the Ngee Ann clan to appoint a committee of review to consider the organization and future development
of the college.

At the same time, the government of Singapore was reviewing
Ngee Ann's status in terms of overall manpower needs and seeking
recommendations from experts on what the institution's role should
be. As a result of these recommendations, and with the willing
participation of the Ngee Ann clan, the government enacted the Ngee
Ann Technical College Act in 1967, which changed the College's
status from a private to a public institution. The College began to

phase out its degree programs, and a year later an amendment to the act transformed the degree-granting institution into a technical college offering three-year diploma programs in engineering and commerce to meet the increased demand in Singapore for technical personnel. Singapore is perhaps the only country in the region that has demoted an institution from university to college status.

At first, there was resistance to the change in status from the students, expressed in several demonstrations on the campus, none serious in terms of injuries or substantial damage to property. The staff members too were unhappy, and by 1972 only one remained, the rest having obtained posts elsewhere.

The present staff and students, however, appear to accept fully and support the role of NATC as well as the change in the language of instruction from Mandarin to English in 1970. Many of the present staff have been recruited since that date, and so were not involved in the change. Some of the current staff have availed themselves of the language laboratory facilities and the formation of an English Language Unit in 1972 to improve their own command of oral English. Students who have been educated in Mandarin are well motivated to continue their English language studies, largely because of the adoption of a bilingual policy by the government, emphasis on the importance of bilingualism, and the demand for English as a job qualification. Present-day students have been satisfied with Ngee Ann's certificate status; they have not tried to upgrade the courses to degree level, and the present demand for admission is five times the number of places.

Outside bodies, including private employers, have welcomed the change in status of Ngee Ann, although some smaller employers still retain the old image and believe that the language of instruction is still Mandarin. This image is particularly a problem with commercial companies, which demand a high level of English, but through the Industrial Orientation Program progress is being made in demonstrating that Ngee Ann Business Studies graduates have achieved the necessary standard.

In 1968 Ngee Ann moved from its borrowed premises in the Ngee Ann clan buildings in Tank Road to its new and present campus in Clementi Road, about 7.5 miles from the center of the city, and enrolled its first students for the Technician Diploma in mechanical engineering. In March 1969, it established two more departments, in electrical and electronics engineering (previously known as the industrial electronics department), and in business studies. These three departments, plus an English language unit, now constitute NATC.

THE COLLEGE TODAY

Goals of the College

As stated in the Ngee Ann Technical College Act of September 1967, the objects and functions of the College are (1) to assist in the preservation, dissemination, communication, and increase of knowledge; (2) to provide regular courses of instruction in the sciences, the technologies, and commerce, and in such other branches of knowledge as the council may from time to time determine; and (3) to stimulate the intellectual, cultural, commercial, and industrial development of Singapore and thereby to assist in promoting its economic and social welfare.

Students and Staff

In 1974-75, NATC had a student body of 1,400 full-time students, not including about 200 preparatory class students—that is, candidates on provisional or probationary admission. (There are no part-time students.) Of these, 26.5 percent were women, the largest proportion being in business studies. Foreign students, including some from Indonesia, Malaysia, and Thailand, comprised 33.5 percent of the enrollment. In the same year, there were 78 academic staff members, 8 workshop instructors, and 16 workshop and laboratory assistants. The faculty-student ratio was thus about 1:14 overall. Of the academic staff, approximately half were expatriates.

The college now graduates about 160 engineering students and 60-70 business students a year. By 1978, Ngee Ann expects to have a student body of between 3,000 and 3,500, from which there would be 800 graduates yearly. These numbers are in line with projections of need and the policy of increasing enrollments at the middle level while limiting growth at the university level. In view of constraints, however, mainly of staff and facilities, Ngee Ann is planning for a student body of 2,000 in 1976.

Programs

The programs in electronic and electrical engineering, mechanical engineering, and business studies each take three years (six

semesters). The medium of instruction is English. In the summer
(August–October vacation), some students in the second year and all
students in the final year are placed by the Industrial and Business
Orientation Programme, a summer work program, in business firms
and government agencies. This program, actively supported by leading
industrial and commercial establishments in Singapore, gives the
prospective employer the opportunity to meet and assess future graduates of NATC. It also provides valuable feedback to NATC on the
requirements of commerce and industry.

Tuition in 1974–75 was S$150 each semester (or S$300 per
annum; U.S. $125).* In addition, workshop, laboratory, library,
sports, and other fees come to S$86 per semester for engineering
students and S$46 per semester for business students. All students
pay fees, but there are various scholarships: for students who qualify
under the "Free Education for Malay Students" Scheme; Singapore
government scholarships and bursaries through the Public Service
Commission; and private scholarships and bursaries. Loans are also
made available by the Rotary Club of Singapore.

Development of the College

NATC occupies a unique position in Singapore's manpower
training because it was established under private auspices in order
to supply a felt need. In attempting to fulfill this mission, NATC has
grown steadily in strength and has made constructive changes, especially since the government took over the main burden of support in
1967.

With a loan of S$9,300,000 (U.S. $3,875,700) from the Asian
Development Bank (ADB), Ngee Ann began in 1971 to expand its facilities to meet anticipated enrollment and an enlarged curriculum (to
include engineering and building services). The five-year Expansion
Project provides for the building of additional workshops and laboratories with a full complement of suitable equipment. A second language
laboratory has been installed and a small audiovisual aid unit established. Also to be built are a lecture block, consisting of lecture
theaters, lecture rooms, and tutorial rooms, as well as a student
union/canteen and additional administrative and academic staff offices.
The loan also provided for architectural consultants for campus

---

*At the present time, the exchange rate for the Singapore dollar
and the U.S. dollar is approximately S$2.40 = U.S.$1.

planning and building, office equipment, and other civil works, including a sports complex. The project, when completed, will cover a total area of 40 acres of land in Clementi Road with which the Ngee Ann clan has resolved to endow the Ngee Ann Technical College.

The entire project will cost a total of S$12.5 million. While the idea for the ADB loan came from the Ngee Ann clan, the Singapore government negotiated it and signed the loan agreement in the bank's headquarters in Manila on December 29, 1970. The rest of the financial support will come from the Singapore government.

Part of the loan package was technical assistance. Affiliation with the Polytechnic of Central London (Regent Street Poly) was arranged, and a consultant came over on a British government grant to assess the situation and advise on what the Polytechnic could provide. This consultant is now the deputy principal and in effect the chief operating official of the college. The affiliation with the Regent Street Poly means that an external examiner scheme links the two institutions academically. On graduation, diplomas are awarded jointly by NATC and the Polytechnic of Central London.

As a result of this affiliation, and the presence of a Polytechnic of Central London adviser in each department, a constant upgrading of staff, instruction, and student body has taken place. In the three years from April 1971 to April 1974, the staff more than doubled, from 30 to 64, or a 113 percent increase, while student enrollment in that period rose from 1,189 to 1,354, or only 33 percent; the staff-student ratio thus improved. Despite a smaller teaching load, however, staff is still in short supply, and the college must recruit regularly, seeking expartiates in addition to local staff. In the 2.5 years between July 1972 and December 1974, 3,109 applications for academic posts were received and processed. Short-listed candidates have been interviewed in seven different countries. Faced with competition from the private business sector, Ngee Ann has raised staff salaries and benefits in an attempt to hold qualified people. A development program for native staff has also been instituted.

The physical development program under the ADB loan is underway, and the bulk of the construction and installation of facilities should be completed in 1976. In addition, and not part of the ADB program, a staff residential bloc is being built on campus, initially for the purpose of housing expatriates.

A number of steps have been taken to improve instruction. For example, rules regarding examinations were changed so that fewer students receive provisional pass or repeat grades. These rules, while ostensibly more liberal, do allow more students to be moved on to succeeding courses; on the other hand, the staff are now able to be more strict in dismissing students. More counseling is given to students who are on referral (that is, who have received provisional passes); now every student referred is assigned to a staff member for supervision and guidance. Continuous efforts are being made to improve course syllabi and reduce the number of examinations.

The student body is now not only larger but also more carefully selected. The entrance requirement is three "O" (Ordinary) level subjects in the secondary school certificate, which means that the candidate is within the top third of his graduating school class. Typically, only 20 percent of applicants can be admitted. In fact, a number of "A" (Advanced) level graduates who are eligible for admission to the university are enrolling at Ngee Ann, partly because of the good job market for Ngee Ann graduates; usually a graduate finds employment within one month after final examinations. An electronics or mechanical engineering technician gets a starting salary higher than that of a university arts graduate.

MEETING NATIONAL NEEDS

Manpower planning in Singapore is initiated in the Economic Planning Unit (EPU) of the Ministry of Finance, which produces forecasts of manpower needs, based on a 15 percent growth in the GNP. (The present predictions foresee a smaller rate of increase in demand for university graduates but a big bulge in demand for middle-level managers and technicians.) The EPU forecasts are passed on to the three technical institutes (Singapore Polytechnic, Singapore Technical Institute, and Ngee Ann) for comment. The heads of the three institutes meet from time to time and then convey their reactions to the plans to the EPU. Then budget negotiations for the additional funds needed for the programs take place. Thus, review and coordination of the efforts of the three institutes are done through the budget process.

The hope is that by about 1978-80 there will be 2,000 graduates per year at the university level coming from the University of Singapore and Nanyang University and 3,000 at the middle or technical level from Singapore Polytechnic, Singapore Technical Institute, Ngee Ann, and the Institute of Education. The government feels that Ngee Ann's contribution will be greatest in the field of commercial education; the other institutions are concentrating more on engineering.

In taking on Chinese stream students and training them to be competent in English, in which most business around the world is conducted, Ngee Ann contributes very effectively to increasing the trained manpower pool of Singapore as well as upgrading the skills of individual students. With such efforts, it is anticipated that the deficit in technicians will be met by the end of this decade.

Though there is increasing public demand for university degrees, the government remains firm in its policy of selective higher education and in its efforts to meet middle- and high-level manpower requirements for national development through technical and professional education. To emphasize these considerations, a Ministry of Education official states:

> In developing nations, there is the more urgent need to have education meet specific national economic, political and social needs. In advanced countries, possibly a more liberal attitude can be adopted towards educational goals. Developing nations, with limited resources and time, have to be more practical in deciding the purpose of education. Tertiary education, particularly in developing countries, cannot be freely offered, and this is the stand the Singapore Government firmly adopts. We cannot afford the luxury of frustrated intellectuals unable to find a permanent place in society because the system did not take cognisance of requirements or needs on the outside.[2]

The deputy principal of Ngee Ann, Philip Limb, points out, however, that there is a limit to the accuracy of forecasts of outside needs and that there is, therefore, always some danger of graduate unemployment; for one thing, it takes at least five years to produce people trained to meet a need. The solutions to such a danger, he says, lie in "careful manpower planning by the government and speed and flexibility by the tertiary institutions in designing and approving new courses."[3]

An example of flexibility in course design is the business studies program at Ngee Ann, in which the first two years cover the basic disciplines (economics, accounting, statistics, law) and the final year offers a series of options—in accounting and finance, personnel management and industrial relations, or marketing and international trade. Mr. Limb hopes that this course structure will allow emerging needs to be met much more quickly than they were in the past.

PROBLEMS

Several of Ngee Ann's problems, however, arise out of this very emphasis on employment. Because of it, academic staff, says Mr. Limb, "begin to feel that they are no longer able to pursue their

legitimate interest in scholarship, research, and academic excellence. " Secondly, students tend to choose "only those courses which
have bright employment prospects shining at the end, " passing up
subjects such as art, cultural studies, and philosophy. [4]

Lack of appreciation of the arts seems to be part of a more
general problem of materialistic values among Ngee Ann graduates
and of Singapore as a whole. Both educators and government ministers
have commented on a situation in which students appear to have more
interest in salaries than in the nature of their jobs and more interest
in jobs than in public service or social values. In June 1974, the Ministry of Education organized a seminar on national values to "develop
a greater awareness and understanding of personal and social values
which the youth of Singapore find relevant and meaningful to our
society today. "

Ngee Ann and other Singapore institutions have another culturally based problem: Students find it difficult to apply what they
have learned to real-life problems. Philip Limb cites the electrical
engineering student who, when asked what he would do if an electric
motor, properly plugged in, did not start when the switch was turned
on, could not answer the question. He also cites two possible reasons
for this phenomenon. First, he says, "education and learning are
highly valued in their own right, and applying what has been learnt
is of secondary importance. Secondly . . . machines and equipment
in the educational institutions are in short supply and therefore difficulties arise in trying to obtain a proper balance between the theoretical and practical parts of a course. "[5]

To contribute most effectively to Singapore's national development, manpower-oriented institutions such as Ngee Ann must give
more emphasis to applying training. They must also develop values
of service as well as of personal gain and a broad rather than a
merely vocational awareness of social needs.

NOTES

1. August 1972, Convocation Address by Dr. Toh Chin Chye,
vice-chancellor of the University of Singapore and minister for
science and technology.
2. Speech by Singapore Parliamentary Secretary (Education),
Mr. Ahmad Mattar, reported in Straits Times, September 14, 1974.
3. Philip Limb, "Employment of Graduates of Tertiary Institutions in Singapore, " Workshop on Development Strategies and Manpower Needs: The Response of Southeast Asian Universities, Regional

Institute of Higher Education and Development, December 15-17,
1974, Vientiane, Laos, p. 4.

    4. Ibid. , p. 4.

    5. Ibid. , p. 6.

17

KASETSART, MAHIDOL, AND THAMMASAT
UNIVERSITIES, THAILAND

Maeklong Integrated Rural Development Project

The Maeklong Integrated Rural Development Project (MIRD)
which began in January 1974, is a pilot project in interuniversity
cooperation in Thailand for community service. It brings together
three of the leading Thai universities, each with its own professional
expertise, to promote development in an area of the country that deserves attention because of past neglect and future potential.

The three universities involved are Kasetsart, Mahidol, and
Thammasat, specializing in agriculture, medical sciences, and social
sciences respectively. Over the years, each of these universities
has developed its own programs designed to relate teaching and research activities to the solution of national problems. Recently,
these programs have been most directly concerned with the rural
people, who have benefited least from previous development efforts.
This common interest in rural development, plus the fact that
Kasetsart University was establishing a new campus in a rural area
near Bangkok (through a World Bank loan), led the three universities
to consider the possibility of joining together in a multidisciplinary
integrated rural development program. Concurrent with these discussions in Thailand, the Rockefeller Foundation reexamined its
University Development Program and decided to place increased
emphasis on the developmental aspects of higher education. This
concerted effort of the three universities, drawing on their respective sources of strength and expertise and a strategic seed money
grant of $125,000 over three years from the Rockefeller Foundation,
is the unique feature of the MIRD.

BACKGROUND

Thailand is a country of approximately 40 million people, of
whom about 70 percent are rural residents dependent upon agriculture for their survival. Although progress in raising GNP and per

capita income has been commendable, the benefits have tended to concentrate primarily in the urban sector. This is not to say that rural problems have been ignored. Large investments have been made in rural road networks, irrigation power dams and water distribution systems, and land development projects. While these efforts have brought certain benefits, the impact on the rural population has fallen short of expectations. In some cases, failure has been due to inadequate planning and implementation, in others to lack of funds, shortage of properly trained personnel, absence of proper understanding of traditional beliefs, or the lack of appropriate technology. Whatever the reasons for failure, it has become obvious that new approaches to rural development are needed.

Formal education as a governmental function is relatively new in Thailand, dating from the last part of the nineteenth century. Until then, the only education of a semipublic nature was that offered by the Buddhist monasteries and the royal court. During the reign of King Chulalongkorn (Rama V), the influence of Western education was strongly felt, and soon a number of centers of higher education were introduced. Initially, institutions for higher learning served as training centers for the administrative ministries of the government. The first such institution, the Royal Medical College at Siriraj Hospital, created in 1889, was followed by the establishment of the Law School in 1897. In 1902, the Royal Pages' School was opened to educate and train students for government positions, and, eight years later, was reorganized and expanded as the School of Civil Servants. In 1917, the School of Civil Servants, the Royal Medical College, and the Engineering School were merged into one institution, called Chulalongkorn University in honor of the king, with four faculties: arts and sciences, medicine, engineering, and political science.

In 1932, Thailand's first political revolution transformed the government from an absolute monarchy to a constitutional monarchy. One of the results of this political change was the creation of Thammasat University to teach law and social sciences.

Thammasat University was founded as the University of Legal and Political Sciences in June 1933. Law was the primary concern of the University, but other areas of study were added until, by 1949, enrollment had increased to the point where it was felt that the administration of the University would be better served by creating separate faculties. Consequently, the faculties of law, commerce and accountancy, political science, and economics were established. The Faculty of Liberal Arts was added in 1962.

In the decade of the 1940s several government agencies opened new universities to meet their manpower needs. The Ministry of Public Health established the Medical University, later named Mahidol University, in 1942. In 1943, the Ministry of Agriculture created an

agricultural university known as Kasetsart University, while the
Ministry of Education founded the Fine Arts University called Silpakorn
University. These universities were more like advanced colleges (or
American colleges) for they were involved with degree programs only
in specific fields.

Kasetsart University was established in 1943 by amalgamating
the College of Agriculture and the School of Forestry. Since then it
has acquired, by creation or transfer from other schools, faculties
of economics, business administration, fisheries, veterinary science,
engineering, and science and arts. (In 1967, the Faculty of Veterinary
Science was transferred to Chulalongkorn University.) In 1956 the
University began to offer graduate courses. Master's degree programs
are now offered in agricultural sciences, economics, forest sciences,
and biological sciences.

It is apparent that except for Chulalongkorn University, Thai
universities have been essentially professional schools, specializing
in different fields of higher learning. Each university has developed
expertise in special areas, rather than attempting to cover a broad
range of knowledge.

HISTORY OF THE MAEKLONG PROJECT

The possibility of a new approach to rural development in
Thailand arose when Kasetsart was considering the establishment
of a new agricultural campus and experiment station within an area
scheduled to have facilities for irrigation. Planners saw that, if the
farmers were to make effective use of the water as it became available, new land and water use technology would have to be developed.
Both the University and Rockefeller Foundation personnel also felt
strongly that the establishment of a major teaching and research institution designed to solve rural problems carried with it a responsibility to help the surrounding rural people to improve their status.
It soon became apparent that Kasetsart, as an agriculturally oriented
University, could not provide all of the expertise needed to mount a
large-scale development project. It was suggested that two other
universities might be willing to join in such an effort. These universities were Thammasat, primarily oriented to the social sciences,
and Mahidol, emphasizing the medical sciences. Both were invited
to join the project, and both responded favorably.

At that time, each of the universities already had its own public
service projects. Kasetsart, as befitting an agricultural university
attached to the Ministry of Agriculture, had numerous agricultural
extension projects. Mahidol University had a Community Service

Department alongside the traditional medical school departments, and conducted community health projects such as the Ramathibodi Community Health Program in Bang Pan-In, a district of 46,000 people about 55 kilometers north of Bangkok. At Thammasat, the Graduate Volunteer Certificate Program had been organized in May 1969. Under this program, open to graduates from any Thai university, although originally most were from Thammasat, young men and women were dispatched to the rural areas to serve as teachers and community improvement workers. The purposes of the program were, first, to train the graduates to sacrifice and work for the public good; second, to give the graduates the opportunity to involve themselves in field work in rural areas and to stimulate interest in this; and third, to encourage them to apply their initiative, knowledge, and human relations skills in the communities in which they lived and worked.

MIRD is thus a natural and logical extension of the public service interests of the three universities. It is unique in the Asian region, however, in that it involves interuniversity cooperation for rural development.

The three universities are responsible for fields of activities as follows:

Kasetsart: agricultural production, irrigation engineering, agricultural engineering, soils, agricultural economics, and education;

Mahidol: population, health, nutrition, and medical services;

Thammasat: administration (political science), social welfare, mass communication (media), sociology, anthropology, economics, and law.

LOCATION OF THE PROJECT

MIRD is being carried out in the Plains area of the Maeklong River basin west of Bangkok, chosen because of its proximity to Bangkok and to the universities. The favorable economic potential of the area, as is evidenced by present investments and development, government plans and other expenditures, and the varied topography, soil conditions, and climate make the region a good laboratory.

The Plains cover 1,466,700 hectares (5,600 square miles) and includes about 1,800 villages and a population estimated in 1972 at about 2,000,000 persons. Nearly 70 percent of the people depend on agriculture for their livelihood. In 1966, there were 138,065 individual holdings, it was estimated, averaging 3.3 hectares each and supporting 6.53 persons per holding. The Greater Maeklong Multi-

Purpose Project now under construction is planned to provide irrigation for 402,880 hectares classified as irrigable, and is expected to
cover 550,880 hectares in later phases.

The soil and topography of the Maeklong Plains vary sharply.
This variety, together with the area's proximity to cities, roads,
and rivers has influenced the types of crops produced, density of
population, and socioeconomic status of the people. Since the basin
is not homogeneous, it has been subdivided into five areas. Major
development efforts will not be initiated in all of these areas simultaneously. Decisions on priorities will be made as more information
on the present conditions within the basin becomes available.

OBJECTIVES

The objectives of MIRD are as follows:

1. To evaluate the present status of the population of the
Maeklong Plains with specific reference to the feasibility of initiating
a program designed to improve the well-being of a major portion of
its people;

2. To prepare suggestions and recommendations for a longer-
range program to improve the production, income, standard of living,
health, education, and livelihood of the population in the rural areas;

3. To outline an interdisciplinary and interuniversity approach
to the identification and solution of problems facing the rural population;

4. To use the experience and results in the planning and implementation of development programs in other areas.

ADMINISTRATIVE STRUCTURE AND FINANCE

MIRD is administered by a policy board of four persons representing Kasetsart, Mahidol, Thammasat, and the Rockefeller Foundation, with the Kasetsart representative serving as chairman. A
project director has been appointed by the board to be responsible
for the overall administration of the project, and has a small administrative and clerical staff. Each university assigns researchers to
work on the various aspects of the project, coordinated by the project
director.

At each of the three universities, the project director is assisted by an assistant project director who is directly responsible for

the parts of the project assigned to that particular university. Close supervision is exercised over the field workers by this supervisory staff.

Progress

During 1974, MIRD's first year, the main thrust of the work was to gain as much knowledge as possible about the area, as a guide to long-range planning. Cooperating university departments specified the data they needed, questionnaires were drafted, pretested, and revised, and investigators were trained. Transport, local accommodation, and food were also arranged for field workers who collected data and conducted surveys. Later in the year, follow-up surveys filled in the missing data.

By early September 1974, the first teams were located in six different locations throughout the region. Teams typically consist of four persons: a team leader who is a university teacher-researcher, plus students in agriculture, medicine, and/or social sciences. The teams consist of both male and female members. Their first jobs in situ were to make friends with the local people and enlist their support, especially that of the village chiefs, to determine the needs of the locality, and to collect firsthand information and data concerning the general livelihood of the village. The pay for the volunteers is modest, the living conditions are rudimentary, but, in keeping with the essentially missionary character of the enterprise, morale is high.

The project activities carried out during 1974 provided the necessary proof that a long-term integrated rural development project coordinated by three universities was feasible. Some of the main reasons for encouragement are as follows:

1. Faculty members and students are enthusiastic in their support of the project, and respond quickly and effectively when given an opportunity to work in rural areas.

2. Faculty and students from many disciplines and all three institutions demonstrate a willingness to work together effectively and are able to get along with both rural people and government officials.

3. The data on the Maeklong Plains collected through secondary official data and through firsthand sources by faculty-student teams reinforce each other and the original concept that it is a desirable area both for the study of development methodology and the improvement of the well-being of the rural people.

4. There are strong indications that the rural people will accept the change, especially when working hand in hand with university teams.

5. There is a strong indication from the National Economics and Social Development Board that one of the major policies for the Fourth National Development Plan (1977-84) will be redistribution of income to rural areas and rural development.

PLAN OF ACTION, 1975

The 1974 Appraisal Project thus confirmed the initial belief that effective, integrated, rural activities can be planned and carried out by faculty members and students of the three universities working in close cooperation with responsible government agencies. A long-term integrated rural development program, however, requires a mechanism for screening the many special concepts of development now existing, selecting projects that seem to offer real opportunities for improvement, and organizing them into integrated action programs.

The real differences in socioeconomic conditions existing in the various defined zones of the Maeklong Plains area make it necessary to develop and test several different development "packages." Activities in 1975 continue to be exploratory in the sense that development theories are being put to the acid test. Will they stimulate measurable beneficial changes in the areas under study? Even more important, can programs that benefit one group of villages be successfully extended to provide similar benefits to entire zones? Thus, if Phase I was the accumulation of necessary information, in Phase II this information will be used to formulate and implement practical integrated development programs. This should lead to Phase III, where successful programs, proven in pilot zones, will be implemented throughout the area.

Emphasis will be placed next on methods of identifying and solving problems that affect the welfare of the rural population in the Maeklong Plains. The procedure will be as follows:

1. Each research leader will be asked to prepare a list of problems in each zone of the area, using information available to him from survey and secondary data as well as from his own observations and the reports of live-in teams. He will be asked to rank these problems in order of difficulty, possibility of solution, and the probable impact on the people if solution is achieved.

2. The results of these analyses will be screened by the executive committee, which will select a group of problems and solutions that seem to offer the greatest possibility of both successful implementation and impact. Where the problems to be solved overlap several disciplinary fields, these will be coordinated into interdisciplinary efforts. Priorities will also be established, so that some activities may be scheduled to begin sooner than others. In this way, a proposed program for action in each of the zones will be outlined.

3. The proposals will then be presented to the research leaders and invited specialists for study and discussion in a series of seminars. Modifications will be made as necessary and work plans for implementation prepared.

4. A series of pilot projects will be established in which the plans will be implemented through direct action of university staff or through their intervention with government organizations or private agencies. Regardless of how the program is put into effect, the effort will be to coordinate various related activities to achieve the greatest impact.

5. The effectiveness of development efforts will be evaluated continuously by the individuals responsible for the development activities, by other program staff members, and by teams of staff and students living in the areas under development who are in a position to determine the reactions of the beneficiaries. Evaluation will be designed to provide a basis for modifying or even dropping existing programs and shifting to others that have a better chance of succeeding.

6. As effective development approaches are identified, efforts will be made to introduce them into adjacent areas. In cases where successful development requires major new government programs and/or major financing, arrangements will be made, in cooperation with the relevant government department, to introduce these programs into the next five-year national development plan.

Examples of problem-solving efforts that are being considered are the following:

1. Improvement of health and nutrition. Interested village residents will be given an opportunity to attend a training course conducted jointly by staff members of Mahidol University and Provincial Health Ministry personnel. Individuals who show aptitude will be appointed as village health leaders. They will be trained to handle first-aid problems, to recognize common problems requiring more expert attention, and to help the patient obtain the necessary assistance from district or provincial health personnel. They will also be trained to advise villagers on problems of sanitation and dietary improvement.

2. Adult education. According to the general survey as well as reports from live-in teams, there is a need for literacy training and vocational education for the whole area. Thus, MIRD and the Adult Education Division of the Ministry of Education will jointly institute a drive for functional literacy and vocational training, beginning in the pilot zones and spreading gradually to cover the whole Maeklong River basin. Live-in team members will recruit students and organize classes and, at first, will serve as teachers until they are replaced by selected villagers. The Adult Education Division, together with MIRD, will organize the curriculum, supply teaching materials, and train both the team members and villagers who will serve as teachers. Team members will identify local vocational training needs. When enough students have been recruited, the Adult Education Division will supply teachers for specific types of training from their mobile units.

Both general and vocational education will emphasize training selected villagers to continue the teaching after the teams have left the area and to organize classes in the surrounding areas. For general education, the emphasis will be on functional literacy where general ideas and necessary development information may be combined and used as teaching materials.

3. Improvement of crop and animal production. Experience in rural development elsewhere has shown that improvement in economic conditions is a prerequisite to general development. Activities planned and carried out in cooperation with government and private agencies will be expected to include, but not be limited to, the following: improvement in cultural practices and introduction of new varieties of existing crops when initial on-farm tests show this to be desirable; introduction of better pig, poultry, cattle, and water buffalo husbandry practices; improvement of methods of using both rainfall and available irrigation water as well as the development of improved farm drainage where necessary; more efficient use of agricultural chemicals including fertilizers and insecticides, and cooperative programs with medical personnel to reduce present health hazards, particularly in insecticide use; improvement of arrangements for production credit and marketing arrangements for crops and animals; assistance to government agencies in identifying needs and planning the development of area irrigation and drainage problems; introduction of more productive breeding stock for animal production; and introduction (after on-farm testing) of multiple cropping to maximize efficiency of land and water use.

Activities will require continued collection of data and analysis of information. In the case of sugar cane production, for example, there is a need for additional studies to provide necessary information. The area planted to this crop has expanded rapidly in recent years, and it is now the largest single source of cash income in the Plains area. Since production is controlled by representatives of the sugar mills and advances are made to cover such costs as land preparation, planting material, and fertilizer, the farmer goes into debt to the mill and is liable to exploitation. Many farmers who formerly produced their own rice and other foods have put all of their land into sugar cane and thus become dependent on purchased food for the first time. How has this situation affected the nutrition of the family? Graduate students, encouraged to do their thesis research in the study area, have been important sources of information on similar problems.

In order to encourage other staff of the three universities to become interested in the rural area and to help get the most out of the available data, a small grants program will be initiated. Staff members not regularly associated with the program will be encouraged to propose projects that use these data effectively. Support will be limited to the costs of computer time and related expenses of analysis.

EXPECTED RESULTS

MIRD proposes to develop a workable system of problem identification and solution in a series of "pilot" zones within each of the five regions of the Maeklong Plains area as now identified. This system will work with and through existing government and private agencies, but will bypass bottlenecks as necessary. The objective will be to accelerate development in these pilot zones and to use the lessons learned in the process to design and implement similar systems, in other locations, which require less intensive activities on the part of MIRD staff. Development programs will not "spread" to other areas unless they are proved effective, so demonstration of success must be given top priority during the next phase of the program. The need to carry out programs in partnership with existing agencies will be kept constantly in mind, however, since a failure to do so would make later transfer of responsibility much more difficult.

The universities themselves will benefit from the participation of their faculty members in effective development activities. Staff should introduce learning experiences into their teaching to give their students a better understanding of rural development. Students will be encouraged to involve themselves directly in field work so that they can learn by doing.

EVALUATION

The job of rural development is difficult, and no single group of persons can accomplish it. The pilot project for the Maeklong region, however, is an imaginative approach to rural problems, tailored to the circumstances and the needs of Thailand. It can serve as an example not only to the youth and the university administrators of Thailand but also to those in other parts of Southeast Asia. The efforts of the young men and women in the project are bound to have an impact not only on the people in the area but also, by focusing attention on the problem of rural development, on the entire society as well. There is another justification for the enterprise as well. If nothing else, the missionary effort carries its own rewards, spiritual and even perhaps material, for the individuals concerned. This is enough to give purpose to human endeavor.

INTRODUCTION

In this study, our concept of development, while not ignoring material development, is essentially related to the quality of life. We do not pretend to define development for each country, but seek only to describe the framework as we see it and have applied it to examples of higher education for development within the region.

In Latin America, social well-being as the aim of development includes the ideas of change, equality, and independence as well as individual development and dignity. While each country must set its own objectives and plan its own strategies for reaching them, each country and region can help others achieve common goals. In an interdependent and interrelated world, a problem in one country affects others, and all countries have a role to play in its solution.

To understand the programs, accomplishments, and goals of the institutions in the case studies, it is well to remember the historical, social, and political conditions they confront.

On the positive side, the circumstances of higher education in Latin America would seem favorable, at least as compared with many other areas of the world. If longevity could be equated with development, Latin American higher education would be highly advanced. As the region of the Western Hemisphere first colonized by Europeans, Latin America contains the oldest universities in the Americas, several dating from the early sixteenth century. The national capitals all boast major centers of learning, and almost all secondary cities have their own local institutions. State and private colleges are widely dispersed throughout the larger nations—Mexico, Columbia, Peru, Brazil, Argentina, Chile, and most other countries. Altogether, there are now an estimated 1,000 universities or affiliates in Latin America*—a higher ratio of institutions of higher education to population than Africa and Asia have.

---

*The figure may be exaggerated. Some institutions call themselves universities though most instruction is at the secondary level. (The University in Society: An International Dialogue [New York: Institute of International Education, 1974], p. xv.)

This introduction is taken from the Report of the Latin American Regional Team, Higher Education and Social Change, vol. 1 (New York: Praeger Publishers, 1976).

In addition, a greater proportion of youth of university age, 6.7 percent in 1970, attend academic courses in Latin America than in Asia and Africa, and the proportion more than doubled during the 1960s. Some modern and impressive university complexes—such as the national institutions in Mexico City, Rio de Janeiro, and Buenos Aires—throng with tens of thousands of students. As the numbers of students have increased, new academic institutions have appeared, especially in the private sector, where they have emphasized vocational and technical subjects. The number of such institutions more than doubled between 1960 and 1970, from 11 percent of the total to 23 percent.

Although Latin America has been hospitable to foreign scholars who occupy teaching positions in its institutions, the institutions do not depend on them; the region does not lack its own supply of professors, at least in the more traditional subjects. Taken as a whole, therefore, it can be said that Latin America's higher education has developed considerably in the sense of growth of physical plant, staff, and student body, placing it next to the so-called developed world in its quantitative aspects.

It must be confessed, however, that much of higher education in Latin America is inadequate. Many Latin American institutions are groping in a haze of speculation and ideological and theoretical discussions that evade reality and the search for specific data necessary to cope with immediate problems.

Latin American students have been activists for decades while their counterparts in other continents passed serenely through their schooling. This student activism, with its notable political ingredient, is a distinctive social phenomenon of Latin America that must be recognized in any consideration of higher education. The constant pressure from students to modernize and broaden the role of the university also bears directly on the importance of the turn toward higher education for development; the students' idealistic goals and realistic concerns need to be tended to and their energies need to be utilized constructively.

Educators seeking the pedagogic and institutional changes necessary to bring Latin American higher education into the development process confront a number of barriers: a feudal heritage, the traditional conservatism of Latin American institutions, the entrenchment of vested interests, the mixed effects of previous reforms, and the politics of student activism. Perhaps most difficult to conform to traditional ideas are the concepts underlying higher education for development, that society is a whole rather than a collection of parts, that the university has a responsibility to the whole rather than to a select segment, and that higher education should become an outgoing active participant in programs serving society as a whole.

In addressing themselves to higher education for development, therefore, the institutions surveyed in this study deserve recognition for their initiative not easily undertaken and for their direction not easily pursued. These five institutions suggest several routes that may be taken by higher education for development. Many other institutions in Latin America are looking and moving in the same direction.

LATIN AMERICAN TEAM MEMBERS

Director	Dr. Alfonso Ocampo Londoño, President, Fundación para el Desarollo Industrial, Cali, Colombia
Deputy Director	Rene Corradine, Universidad del Valle, Cali, Colombia
Other Team Members	Carlos Tunnermann Bernheim, former Rector, Universidad Nacional Autonoma de Nicaragua, Leon, Nicaragua
	Pablo Willstatter, Institute for Educational Development, Lima, Perú
	Alvaro Aranquibel Equí, former Chief of Planning Office, Universidad del Oriente, Cumana, Venezuela
	Gabriel Velazquez Palau, Rockefeller Foundation Representative, Universidade da Bahía, Salvador, Brazil
Consultants	Farzam Arbab, Rockefeller Foundation Representative, Cali, Colombia
	Frances Foland, Fellow, Institute of Current World Affairs, New York
	Carlos Medellin, ASCUN (Asociación Colombiana de Universidades), Bogotá,
	Henrique Tono Trucco, Regional Director, Centro Internacional de Investigaciones para el Desarrollo (CIDA), Bogotá, Colombia
	Ramon de Zubiria, ex-Rector, Universidad de los Andes, Bogotá, Colombia

Rafael Rivas, ex-Dean, Universidad del
Valle and Universidad de los Andes,
Bogotá, Colombia

Agustín Lombana, Academic Dean,
Faculty of Interdisciplinary Studies,
Universidad Pontificia Javeriana, Bogotá,
Colombia

Alberto Alvarado, Fondo Colombiano de
Investigaciones Científicas y Proyectos
Especiales "Francisco José de Caldas,"
Bogotá, Colombia

Beverly B. Cordry, Director of Research,
Phoenix College, Phoenix, Arizona

Carlos Vidalon, International Bank for
Reconstruction and Development, Washington, D.C.

Translators   Sadie de Paredes, Clara Serra, Elisa
Escobar

18

FEDERAL UNIVERSITY OF BAHÍA, BRAZIL

Center for Urban Development

In its regulations, the Federal University of Bahía (UFBa) states that its objective is to "participate in the region's development by carrying out a systematic study of its problems and establishing its needs through the use of scientific and technical charts." This objective and the University's present community orientation have their origins in efforts in the 1950s to identify community problems and plan appropriate solutions. Later, under the University Reform Law, the University established postgraduate courses that were intended to strengthen the University as a development agent.

The Post-Graduate Teaching and Research Unit, which coordinates these courses, gives priority to projects that (1) undertake multidisciplinary and interdepartmental research, (2) apply science and technology to find out what methods are most effective in solving national and regional problems, (3) attempt to solve regional problems, and (4) carry out systematic studies for the delivery of services.

Specific institutional guidelines established for such projects include provisions that (1) University personnel should participate in administering projects and in preparing and implementing their research, (2) University personnel should benefit from the projects, and (3) every six months, projects must send progress reports to the Post-Graduate Teaching and Research Unit, specifying the difficulties encountered and suggestions for overcoming them. Within these guidelines, approximately 437 projects have been completed or are underway for 1974.

BACKGROUND

Brazilian Development

These University projects are being carried on within a certain context of development, which in Brazil was launched in the first decades of this century with industrialization as its main support.

The past 50 years have been characterized by rapid and continuing economic growth, except for a brief decline between 1962 and 1967.* Recently, Brazil has attempted to combine an orthodox economic policy with a development policy. At a time of strong nationalism, it has simultaneously expanded the private and public sectors and stimulated foreign investments.

Most observers agree that in the last decades economic policy has been based more on growth than on distribution. The economic policy proclaimed by the Second Development Plan for the period 1975-79, however, shows a new concern for social affairs as well as for growth. The policy seeks to distribute national goods more equitably in order to benefit the low-income population and to reduce absolute poverty through education, public health, nutrition, and housing programs. It also puts special emphasis on industrial and agrarian development. The national economic policy also attempts not only to adapt itself to the new circumstances of the modern world but also to adopt a foreign policy that supports international actions for national social well-being.

Changes in Formal Education

The history of formal education in Brazil began with the European classical-humanistic tradition as conveyed through the activities of the Society of Jesus when Brazil was a Portuguese colony. At that time, only a minority—the elite and the clergy—had access to this education. Higher education leading to professional degrees was established at the beginning of the nineteenth century to meet the immediate needs of the monarchy. The universities consisted of isolated professional schools whose purpose was to train social and political leaders. Secondary schools fed directly into these professional schools and thus became primarily the channel to higher education.

The University Reform Law of 1968, which was finally implemented in 1971, sought to adapt the country's changing educational system to the concept that social development depends on the educational level of Brazilians. An educational policy was accordingly designed to provide effective opportunities for individual and professional advancement and to meet some of the manpower needs of a developing society. Universities receive government and social support to train administrators, economists, and managers, in addition to doctors, lawyers, and other professionals.

---

*Data supplied by the Getulio Vargas Foundation.

THE FEDERAL UNIVERSITY OF BAHÍA

Bahía was the first site of the Brazilian government, of Brazil's first primary school, and, in 1575, of the Jesuit Colegio Real da Bahía, which offered degrees in theology and sacred sciences. The first public higher education institutions were set up when the Portuguese court moved to Brazil in 1807. The oldest, the Medical Surgical College, founded by the Regent Dom João in Bahía in 1818, later became the Bahía Faculty (School) of Medicine. The Academy of Fine Arts, founded in 1877, became the Bahía School of Fine Arts with an annexed Faculty of Architecture. By the end of the century, the Faculty of Law (1891) and the Polytechnic Institute (1897) (later the Polytechnic School of Bahía) had been founded. The Commercial School of Bahía was founded in 1905 and renamed the Faculty of Economic Sciences in 1934. The Faculty of Philosophy, Sciences, and Letters was the last unit founded prior to the constitution of the University.

The University of Bahía came into being in 1946 and incorporated these six faculties (Medicine, Law, Polytechnic School, School of Fine Arts, Economic Sciences, and Philosophy). Over the following 20 years, the University underwent a number of changes. Courses in pharmacy and dentistry were separated from the Faculty of Medicine and became new teaching units, and the Faculty of Architecture was separated from the School of Fine Arts. The Schools of Nursing, Nutrition, Dance, Theater, and Geology were organized; the Institutes of Mathematics, Chemistry and Physical Sciences, as well as the French-Brazilian Institute, the Institute of Hispanic Culture, and the Institute of Portuguese Studies were established. Later the Institute for North American Studies, the Center for East African Studies, the Institute for Professional Orientation, the Museum of Sacred Arts, the Laboratory of Geomorphology and Regional Studies, and the School of Administration were also established, and the School of Library Sciences was gradually incorporated into the Federal University of Bahía.

In 1965 UFBa began to plan a ten-year expansion program, and funds were secured from the Inter-American Development Bank (IDB) and Unesco. Subsequently, the University took steps toward reorganizing its administration and improving the quality of teaching and research. The University signed joint program agreements with the Canadian International Development Research Centre (IDRC) and with Harvard and Cornell Universities in the United States in the fields of agronomy and health. During this period the Schools of Agronomy and of Veterinary Sciences were incorporated into the University.

TABLE 18.1

Enrollment at UFBa, 1974

Distribution of Professional Degree Students	Number
Mathematics, physics, technology	4,032
Biology and health sciences	3,337
Philosophy and human sciences	4,904
Letters	696
Arts	581

Source: Federal University of Bahía.

Enrollment

The population of Brazil—somewhat over 100 million people—is a conglomeration of different races and cultures and is increasing by approximately 3 percent a year. Half the population is under 18 years of age.

UFBa has 14,611 enrolled students. Of these, 13,550 students are pursuing courses leading to professional degrees (see Table 18.1); 237 are working for master's and Ph.D. degrees; 116 are in specialized courses; and 41 are in technical courses (for example, nurse's auxiliaries). The remaining students are enrolled in special courses offered by UFBa in arts, first and second grade teaching, and preparation of professors in other specialized subjects. Other programs have also been organized in metallurgical engineering, environmental sanitation, and tourism administration.

The increase in demand for admission has been spectacular— 795 percent over the past ten years. Enrollment has been increased 350 percent by expanding the entrance quota for some old programs and by creating new programs such as mechanical engineering, data processing, analytical and industrial chemistry, and a B.S. program in general sciences. For the next two years, enrollment is expected to stabilize at around 15,000 students. Because of shortages of space, equipment, and human resources, there are no plans for further expansion.

Finance

UFBa receives more than three quarters of its funds from the federal and state governments. Other institutions contribute through agreements that represent 20 percent of UFBa's total budget. The financial resources that were collected directly by UFBa represent only 4 percent of the total budget.

International agencies that contribute include the Ford Foundation, Population Council, World Health Organization, British Council, Rockefeller Foundation, Kellogg Foundation, Bank of Brazil and Canada (BRASCAN), and the Organization of American States (OAS). Funds received from international agencies or other sources are mainly used to expand graduate programs, research, and extension. University-level teaching is paid for by funds coming from the federal government or collected directly by UFBa.

THE CENTER FOR URBAN DEVELOPMENT (CEDUR)

History

In 1960, the Faculty of Medicine of UFBa established an internship on Preventive Medicine within its medical training program in order to teach and carry out research in the field of health. For six consecutive weeks, fifth-year medical students participated in the medical and preventive care of the families residing in the district of Federação. They sought to identify environmental, social, cultural, and economic factors directly or indirectly related to health problems. This internship became the initial framework for teaching preventive medicine in a community environment.

In 1968, Dr. Roberto Santos, rector of UFBa and Professor José Duarte, public health secretary of the state of Bahía and former head of the Preventive Medicine Service of UFBa, signed an agreement under which the University was enabled to utilize the state's health services for its preventive medicine program. This agreement was implemented by assigning fifth- and sixth-year medical students to the second and fifth health centers of the city of Salvador.

The same year, the rector appointed a faculty committee to develop a project covering the interrelationships between the University Hospital and a health center in the urban zone of Salvador. The proposed project was submitted to the Kellogg Foundation, approved and granted financial support.

This project established two types of programs. One sought to reorganize the University Hospital to provide a system of progressive medical care to patients. The other, a community health program, set out to develop a system for educating and training qualified personnel in research methods in preventive and community medicine. This second program was initiated in State Health Unit no. 2, the district of Northeastern Amaralina. In 1971, this unit became a training center for graduate students and, in 1974, for postgraduate students in community health. During 1971-74, the center provided training for 1,361 medical students, 378 nurses, 47 dentistry students, 13 nutrition students, and a number of government professionals and paraprofessionals. In the same unit, various UFBa professors carried out applied research in such areas as socioanthropology, maternal and child health care, and infectious-contagious diseases, as they affected the population of Northeastern Amaralina.

As they worked in the community, health personnel began to see how social organization influenced the problems of community health. To increase community participation in the program, local leaders were identified and a community council was created.

Nature of the Program

In July 1973, after an agreement was signed with the Rockefeller Foundation, UFBa created the Research and Education Program for Development (PROPED), a program to enable the University to participate in the socioeconomic development of the northeastern part of Brazil. The vice-rector and the Rockefeller Foundation representative submitted to a group of professors from different UFBa faculties and schools a proposal to create various interdisciplinary centers, one of which, CEDUR, was to be in charge of studying urban development problems. (The others were CEDER, focused on rural development; CECIMA, the Center for Marine and Environmental Sciences; and CEDES, the Education for Development Center. All were designed to revolve around and feed back into an academic nucleus, CECISA.) One of CEDUR's main functions was to be to advise government agencies concerned with the community's social and economic development.

At weekly meetings, the interdisciplinary faculty group discussed and exchanged information on present and former University projects, such as (1) the experience in community health that the Department of Preventive Medicine had in the district of Northeast Amaralina; and (2) the experience of the Urban Planning Department of the School of Architecture, acquired through an urban planning program in the town of Itapetinga, state of Bahía; (3) the experience of the Faculty of Education in a program carried out in conjunction with Peace Corps volunteers in the district of Engenho Velho de Brotas.

After the first meetings, the group recognized the need to establish common objectives, to define priority areas for research programs, and to develop an integrated outline or operational plan that would meet both the University's objectives and the needs of the community. The group spent six or eight sessions discussing a framework of operation for new projects in each area. Because, according to members of the group, there was not enough time to establish an integrated plan, each project was presented in accordance with each member's field of specialization.

The program plan was based on the following assumptions: Health, education, housing, and sanitation are interdependent, and their problems are closely interrelated. Because of the complexity of these problems, an interdisciplinary approach is essential. In addition, there is a need for support from government and private institutions, both because "solutions" require large investments of financial resources, not available to a university or a community, and because efforts to solve urban problems at different levels of responsibility must be coordinated.

Objectives

CEDUR, accordingly, was designed to (1) create, test, validate, and document interdisciplinary operational models to promote development (understood as a standard of living in relation to the population's well-being) by utilizing community resources; models were to be adaptable to other areas with similar problems; (2) carry out sectorial, interdisciplinary research on which the government could base better economic and social policies; (3) facilitate interdisciplinary work by University professors and students as well as by professionals and officials from different governmental agencies; (4) evaluate progress achieved through interdisciplinary research; (5) conduct periodic interdisciplinary and multiinstitutional seminars to establish guidelines for CEDUR's work; and (6) provide advisory services for public and private institutions interested in community development projects.

The Community

CEDUR's interdisciplinary work team looked for a low-income population district where the program could create replicable community development models. They wanted a district that had well-defined geographic boundaries, a densely populated area, uneven urban growth, inadequate education and housing, a low level of social organization, high mortality, morbidity, and birth rates, and inadequate sanitation.

The district of Northeastern Amaralina, located on the border of Salvador's metropolitan area, fulfilled these requirements. In addition, Amaralina had been the site, for three years, of the University community health program that grew out of the University-state of Bahía agreement described previously. The district has 10,000 families with an average of six persons per family. It appeared to be a good choice for CEDUR's program.

To obtain information on Amaralina's demographic, economic, and sociocultural characteristics, a preliminary study was designed and initiated in December 1973 (see Appendix 18.1). Twenty-five specially trained volunteer students from different areas of the University collected data, and three students from the Faculty of Architecture mapped the area.

From September to November 1973, ten psychology students, supervised by a professor, carried out an exploratory study of elementary schools. They sought to identify student behavioral problems and student-teacher relationships, and to correlate them with teaching methods used in the first grade, a common bottleneck in the public education system. Questionnaires were used to collect the reactions of elementary-school teachers to the changes being introduced into the elementary schools. Three different psychological tests were also given to 698 elementary-school students to obtain information on perceptual and motor development of low-income-group children.

At the end of 1973, the CEDUR interdisciplinary team, at the request of PROPED's director, prepared proposals for applied research to be carried out in Northeastern Amaralina during 1974. PROPED's Technical Committee approved these proposals—in education, health, nutrition, and architecture—and financial support was secured from the Rockefeller Foundation and subsequently from the Ford Foundation.

Organization

CEDUR is administered by PROPED. A general coordinator, who is an assistant professor in the Department of Preventive Medicine, provides CEDUR's academic direction, and special coordinators preside over architecture, education, economics, socioanthropology, nursing, and nutrition. The general coordinator meets once a week with the area coordinators and representatives of each project to determine priorities and discuss the projects and any difficulties they encounter.

A four-member Technical Committee consults with CEDUR's general coordinator on the current projects and supervises the curricula of students participating in the program. The general coordinator and the Technical Committee act under the plans and general policies established by PROPED's board of directors, who are responsible for CEDUR's finances and administration.

Financial Resources

CEDUR's financial and economic assistance comes from the UFBa, the secretary of public health, and the Rockefeller and Ford Foundations. The University contributes teaching staff as well as administrative expenses, despite the negative attitudes of some professors. The secretary of public health, in accordance with the agreement signed with the University, provides salaries for health professionals and paraprofessionals as well as money for materials and health service maintenance. The funds contributed by the Rockefeller Foundation are assigned to specific aspects of each project, such as salaries for research assistants, scholarships, purchase of equipment and supplies, and transportation.

Since its initiation, CEDUR has relied on the economic and financial support of the Rockefeller and Ford Foundations—a total of approximately Cr. 850,000 ($119,000)* distributed as follows:

Funds from the Rockefeller Foundation assigned to research and extension programs in the areas of

Community health	Cr. 500,000
Environment	100,000
Socioanthropology	70,000
Education	120,000
Total	Cr. 790,000
	($110,800)

Funds from the Ford Foundation assigned to research and extension programs in the areas of:

Nutrition	Cr. 60,000
Education	4,000
Total	Cr. 64,000
	($9,000)

Tables 18.2 and 18.3 indicate the origin of human resources and time dedicated to the CEDUR program.

---

*Cr. 7.13 = U.S. $1.

TABLE 18.2

UFBa–CEDUR–Human Resources, 1974

Academic Units	Full Time	24 Hours per Week	6 Hours per Week	Total
Faculty of Medicine	6	5*	–	11
School of Nursing	3	1	–	4
School of Dentistry	–	1	–	1
Economics	1	–	1	2
Faculty of Education	4	–	4	8
School of Architecture	2*	3*	–	5
Socio-Anthropology	1	–	1	2
Demography	2	–	2	4
Social Service	–	1	–	1
Total	19	11	8	38

*Fellowship recipients.
Source: Federal University of Bahía.

TABLE 18.3

Secretary of Public Health–
Human Resources, 1974

Area	40 Hours per Week	24 Hours per Week	Total
Pediatrics	–	1	1
Nutrition	1	–	1
Dentistry	–	2	2
Auxiliary personnel	4	25	29
Total	5	28	33

Source: Federal University of Bahía.

Favorable Conditions and Drawbacks

According to CEDUR's director, the program has had a number of assets. They are

1. The support given by PROPED's director, who, as vice-rector of the University, obtained the institution's approval of the CEDUR program.

2. The interest of professors connected with the program, especially those from the Department of Preventive Medicine, who have worked directly with the problems of the Northeastern Amaralina community.

3. The favorable acceptance given to the program by the community through the Community Council. The latter is composed of three religious leaders, two businessmen, two elementary-school directors, and a first lieutenant.

4. The financial support given by the Rockefeller and Ford Foundations.

5. The presence of distinguished visiting professors who contributed new ideas to the development of the project.

6. The relationships with governmental agencies and their approval of the program. The mayor's office of Salvador has signed an agreement for the development of CEDUR's activities.

7. The participation and support of students.

The program director says the program has had the following drawbacks:

1. At the beginning there was no well-defined overall strategy to determine the priorities of community needs. This difficulty was partially overcome after a basic study was made.

2. The program relies on volunteer participation by professors who, in some cases, dedicate a minimum of their time to the activities of the CEDUR program.

3. The participants in CEDUR do not know enough about one another's work and lack, therefore, a group identity within the University.

4. The academic units (faculties and schools) are not convinced of the importance of the program. Owing to a lack of communication, there is some ignorance about the program's activities.

CEDUR PROJECTS

In Education

The exploratory study of education in 1973 led to the present project, which began in March 1974 and seeks to find out why so many students repeat the first grade. (See Appendix 18.2.) Seven psychology students, two psychologists, and a supervising professor are studying the 650 first-grade elementary-school students in three out of the five primary schools belonging to the public, state, and

municipal educational system. Seventeen first-grade teachers in the
elementary schools were selected to participate.

The group is looking at the first graders' vocabulary development, writing skills, motor coordination, time and space perception,
and understanding of mathematics and social studies. Another
research project is concerned with how the use of performance
objectives affects the learning of eighth graders in science. (See
Appendix 18.3.) Although the secretaries of education for the state
of Bahía and the city of Salvador do not directly participate in either
project, they have given them indirect support.

In Socioanthropology

In October 1974, an exploratory study was made of social
awareness in children and preadolescents from low-income groups
of Northeastern Amaralina. The study, based on observation of 20
families, seeks to analyze certain variables, such as status, role,
and self-respect of each family member. (See Appendix 18.4.)

In Architecture

Two professors and 90 third- and fourth-year architecture
students made a survey of the environmental conditions of Northeastern Amaralina as part of the course on urban planning. This
study, which represented two semesters of work, analyzed in detail
the problems related to urban living—housing, extension of electrical
and water supply networks, and sanitary improvement. (See Appendix 18.5.) It was recently presented to the Division of Urban Planning
of the Mayor's Office and to CONDER, the agency responsible for
urban planning in the metropolitan area of Salvador. Although the
study was accepted by these authorities, its contribution to solving
the urban problems of Northeastern Amaralina will depend on the
financial resources that governmental agencies may assign.

In Health

At present, there are eight applied research projects in
health. Using the health group's previous experiences in Northeastern Amaralina, the projects will seek to develop systems of
health services delivery. In January 1975, the University's School
of Nursing initiated a project, designed by a doctor and two nurses,
to train 16 health promoters who will provide direct community

health services. (See Appendix 18.6.) The project was approved
by the secretary of health of the state of Bahía and by the Department
of Public Health. The team of architects who work with CEDUR
have been requested to identify possible sites for two health posts
that could serve the entire area of Northeastern Amaralina. A group
that includes four doctors, three nurses, a dentist, and a social
worker will study the restructuring of the present organization of
the State Health Unit in Northeastern Amaralina and will submit
a proposal for a health program for the district.

Another professor, with the collaboration of three students,
will measure the effect of two different types of diet on the nutrition
of children in the area. They will also attempt to analyze the relationships between diet and conditions such as diarrhea and respiratory
infections in children. (See Appendix 18.7.) Seven nurse's auxiliaries,
trained in interviewing and coding techniques, will cover both an
experimental and control group. Students doing postgraduate research
will also use the basic data from this investigation as material for
their dissertations.

ASSESSMENT

CEDUR seeks enough information and experience to design
operational models for community development, to evaluate them,
and to adapt them to similar communities elsewhere.

How the Program Affects Development

CEDUR also contributes to development in the following ways:

1. By defining social needs and problems. The basic study
constitutes a special inventory of the social needs and problems of
an urban area, probably representative of low-income districts in
Salvador's metropolitan area.

2. By preparing effective contributors to social development.
Students learn development skills through curricular activities
closely related to actual community situations and through postgraduate courses, such as the one on community health, which
emphasize practical learning and interdisciplinary applied research.

3. By strengthening education at other levels. CEDUR is
beginning to collect information and gain experience in the field of
primary school education.

The CEDUR program has been in operation for only 16 months,
and the problems of Northeastern Amaralina are complex. Although

there has not been time enough to assess development needs, the following are positive signs of future success:

1. CEDUR is an integral part of PROPED. Its top leadership has connections with governmental and private agencies and has thus obtained their support. Especially important is the advocacy of the governor of the state of Bahía, Roberto Santos, a former rector of UFBa. At present there is an attempt to integrate efforts being made by public and private agencies and institutions at the state as well as federal levels.

2. An important group of professors from UFBa's faculties and schools is now collaborating with and participating in CEDUR.

Lessons Learned from the Program

Community needs and government priorities: A program should identify community problems through systematic scientific studies and define the most urgent needs. The information obtained should be presented to and discussed with governmental agencies so that priorities can be set and approaches designed. Determining priorities in cooperation with government, however, is a slow process. Governmental agencies are influenced by political pressures and often have little interest in innovation.

University interest: Professors and students in all departments must be convinced of the program's importance and the advantages of participation. Adequate information about the program is likely to overcome any existing uneasiness. A wide demand for admission to the program provides a pool of applicants from which motivated and enthusiastic professors and students can be selected. How well the program is incorporated into academic course work depends on the professor participating in the program and, to a lesser degree, on the curriculum's flexibility. Both graduate students (health) and postgraduate students (architecture) now participate in the program.

University-government-community relationships: University and government agencies must be careful to establish good relations with the community. In the past, the community has been disappointed in the promises of government agencies and tends to regard the University as just another government agency. If it is to accept a program, the community must participate in establishing its own needs and planning action to meet them.

Multidisciplinary approach: Professors and specialists from different disciplines and sections must have special motivation and interest in order to work well as a team. There must also be time for exchanges of information and different points of view before the group is ready to act together.

Management of resources: Full-time professionals with decision-making powers are needed to coordinate the projects and the various activities of a multidisciplinary and multiinstitutional group such as CEDUR.

Distribution of information: In a program's initial stage, collecting information and observations on similar programs is very useful. Knowing more about other programs helps participants avoid errors, speed up procedures, and even plan joint actions. The director and his associates should plan observation visits.

Financing and implementation: Because of such a project's multiinstitutional nature, financial assistance for its various activities should come from several agencies. There is a special need, however, for flexible support at the early planning stages of the program, when government agencies do not always provide the necessary money.

Suggestions for Improving the Program

Since the program was established to provide a model that could be adapted to other urban environments, suggestions for improving the program have to do primarily with structure. The following are some aspects of the program that require additional study and analysis:

The program's role within PROPED: The organization of the program would benefit from a manual on policies and procedures, including its powers of direction and decision making.

The organization of multidisciplinary teams: To date, professors working in health form the most effective and coherent group. In other sectors, the few professors who participate in CEDUR are overloaded with other activities, and there is a need for stronger scientific and technical support. Two types of action might be useful: continue a systematic search for professors and students within the University, as well as professionals and officials from other Brazilian agencies, to reinforce the program's permanent personnel; or assign personnel to CEDUR's daily administrative activities, performed at present by professors, so that professors can spend more time on the program itself.

Relationships with governmental and private agencies at top levels: These relationships should be defined more clearly at the operational level of specific projects. Seminars might be organized to discuss ways in which officials and other professionals might best participate.

Ways to secure information about similar projects: Observation trips could be complemented with specific ad hoc training in short courses, seminars, or workshops where experiences and opinions could be exchanged and joint action planned.

Program planning: The CEDUR project has initiated programs that attempt to meet specific development needs of Northeastern Amaralina. Programs should continue to focus on one urban area, but might be designed to solve related problems, and all programs might be integrated under a more general development approach.

Recommendations Based on
CEDUR's Experience

1. Establish research projects that utilize an integrated approach to problem solving. Participants in the various CEDUR projects are fully aware that none of these projects will be very effective until they are related to an overall view.

2. Create programs or centers with enough autonomy to carry out innovative projects and use unorthodox academic criteria and methodologies. The acceptance of development programs within the curriculum and the present academic and legal regulations of UFBa requires a slow and difficult negotiating process. The best way to help the University fulfill its goals for speeding up economic and social development in the northeastern part of Brazil is to create effective organizational structures with sufficient autonomy to blaze new trails.

3. Establish communication among the different projects that make up a program and among some programs that are working with similar or complementary approaches. The experiences and knowledge gained from such projects as those carried out at the University of Valle (Colombia) or the Monterrey Institute of Technology and Advanced Studies (Mexico) could be of great use to the CEDUR program and to its institutional framework, PROPED. An attempt should be made to achieve close and effective cooperation among development programs, based on the exchange of information and personnel and on joint action.

4. Encourage scientific research in which community members, university professors, students, and officials from government and private agencies participate. The CEDUR programs have found that the people best qualified for the program work are scarce and therefore expensive. Programs could be improved, however, by using all available human resources. CEDUR should help community members seek solutions for their own problems, encourage students to act as agents or catalyzers in the search for a process of change, and use University professors and government officials as contributors of knowledge and resources.

APPENDIX 18.1

Area: Interdisciplinary Interests
Title of Project: Basic Study of Northeastern Amaralina
Researchers: S. Plank, L. Milanesi, C. Pugliese, S. Maia,
         H. Teixeira, A. Fuenzalida, L. Neves, J. C. Brasileiro,
         C. Matias

Objectives
    1. Obtain information on basic characteristics of the socio-
cultural, economic, environmental, and health aspects of the
Northeastern Amaralina community.
    2. Analyze the interrelationships of these characteristics in
relation to the present needs of the community.
    3. Utilize the results of this analysis to establish a master
plan for the development of Northeastern Amaralina.

Methodology
    A systematic survey of each family, covering the entire
population. A total of 10,000 families residing in the area were
interviewed by students from the Faculties of Medicine, Nursing,
Economics, Architecture, Sociology, and Psychology. The interviews were initiated in December 1973, completed in July 1974.

APPENDIX 18.2

Area: Education
Title of Project: Psychopedagogical Assistance in the First Years
               of Primary School
Researchers: Gizelda Morais, José Carlos Tourinho da Silva,
               Elizete de Jesus Ferreira

Objectives
    1. Development of an assistance model in the affective and
cognitive area for students repeating first grade (primary school)
to reduce the incidence of repeaters and dropouts.
    2. Develop a new role for the teacher in the classroom.

Methodology
    Introduction of special activities in the classroom for developing
vocabulary, writing, and reading skills. This approach includes
exercises for psychomotor development, activities for developing
self-expression and understanding of mathematics, grammar, and
social studies. The study is being carried out at five public elemen-

tary schools in Northeastern Amaralina. Three are an experimental group, and the remaining two are controls. Fourteen first-grade teachers and a total of 650 children ranging from seven to 13 years of age participate in this program. During 1974, two evaluations were carried out, the results of which are being tabulated for statistical analysis.

APPENDIX 18.3

Area: Education
Title of Project: The Effects of Utilizing Performance Objectives
on Learning in Eighth-Grade Science
Researcher: Hermes Teixeira de Melo

Objective

Determine how the utilization of performance objectives act upon the eighth-grade students' learning level in sciences.

Methodology

The sample will be made up of approximately 600 students, divided into two groups—an experimental and a control group. The students in the experimental group will use the material produced by the Introduction to Sciences Project (PSC) and the performance objectives prepared by the researcher. The program was carried out during the 1975 school year. During 1974 the researcher prepared the necessary materials.

APPENDIX 18.4

Area: Socioanthropology
Title of Project: Social Awareness of Children and Preadolescents
from Low-Income Population Groups in Northeastern
Amaralina
Researcher: José Pereira de Queiroz

Objective

Achieve a better understanding of the social awareness process by analyzing the normal daily activities of a group of families.

Methodology

The study will be carried out in two areas of Northeastern Amaralina. A group of families will be identified, and each one will be visited for one week. On the basis of these first interviews,

questionnaires will be prepared for obtaining information from other
family members, and a scale of attitudes will be drawn. This study
was initiated in October 1974. About 20 families are expected to be
interviewed before a complete program of activities for the project
is determined.

APPENDIX 18.5

Area: Architecture
Title of Project: Definition of Urban Planning Variables in North-
                  eastern Amaralina
Researchers: Laerte Neves and João C. Brasileiro

Objectives
       1. Determine the urban planning variables that contribute
to the development of the Northeastern Amaralina community.
       2. Define and quantify the location of basic community
facilities (schools, health centers, recreation areas, for instance)
in relation to the aspirations and needs of the Northeastern Amaralina
community.

Methodology
       The methodological approach includes field surveying, drawing
of maps, and the tabulation of data. The initial outline on urban
planning will serve to define and orient studies and research. The
study was initiated in March 1974, with the participation of 80 fourth-
year architecture students who carried out a mapping project in the
entire Northeastern Amaralina area. During the second semester,
55 students of the Urban Planning Course submitted proposals for
improving sanitation, water supply, sewage and garbage disposal,
as well as health services and education.

APPENDIX 18.6

Area: Health
Title of Project: Training of Health Promoters
Researchers: Ivone Moura, C. Pugliese

Objectives
       1. Prepare personnel for the health sector at a low cost.
       2. Increase the quantity and improve the quality of health
services being offered in Northeastern Amaralina, and make them
more efficient.

Methodology

A four-month course will be offered, which will include
concepts of socioanthropology; medical terminology; maternal and
child health care; research and control of contagious diseases; and
concepts of basic sanitary improvement.

Personnel Selection

Women residing in the community who have at least completed
elementary school will participate in the project. Sixteen candidates
will be selected on the basis of interviews and tests that attempt to
identify characteristics such as sense of responsibility, attitude
regarding their participation in community work, and knowledge of
Portuguese. The program has been approved by the public health
secretary of the state of Bahía, as well as by the Department of
Public Health of the School of Nursing.

APPENDIX 18.7

Area: Nutrition
Title of Project: Prospective Studies on Nutritional Habits and Their
                  Influence on Infant Morbidity and Mortality
Researchers: Lucila Milanesi Plank, Stephen Plank, and
             Celso Pugliese

Objectives

1. Become acquainted with the causes and consequences of
prevailing nutritional habits of children in order to define an educational program for the future.

2. Correlate duration and degree of breast feeding and time
when other nutrients were introduced with the duration of postpartum
amenorrhea.

Methodology

The starting point for the study will be the identification of
women in their sixth month of pregnancy. A minimum of 1,000
pregnant women will be selected and asked to answer a questionnaire
to determine, among other facts, age, marital status, level of
education, number of pregnancies, and nutritional habits. These
women will be periodically observed until childbirth. Subsequently,
the child will be visited every 15 days during the first three months.
Later on, monthly visits will be made during which special information relevant to the study will be obtained. The study was initiated
in October 1974, and the field work began during the latter part of
November 1974. In the first phase, nurse's auxiliaries were trained

in interviewing techniques and handling of questionnaires. Three persons residing in the Northeastern Amaralina community were selected to help identify the women to be included in the study. Three professors from the Faculty of Medicine are collaborating in the study.

APPENDIX 18.8

UFBa's estimated budget for 1974 amounts to Cr. 187,408,500 (U.S. $26,284,502.10), out of which 70.3 percent is utilized for current expenses—Cr. 131,658,500 (U.S. $18,465,427.77) and 29.7 percent for capital expenses, such as building construction and investments—Cr. 55,750,000 (U.S. $7,819,074.33).

APPENDIX 18.9

Sources of Finance of UFBa

	Cruzeiros	Dollars	Percent
Ordinary resources, coming from the Union (federal government)	104,303,600	14,628,836.00	55.7
Resources coming from federal agencies (agreements and special assistance)	39,104,900	5,484,558.20	20.9
Resources that are collected directly by UFBa	6,900,000	967,741.94	3.7
Resources coming from other institutions (international, national, private and public institutions, state and municipal institutions)	37,100,000	5,203,366.06	19.7
Total	187,408,500	26,284,502.10	100.0

Source: Federal University of Bahía.

19

UNIVERSITY OF ANTIOQUIA, MEDELLÍN, COLOMBIA

Education in Rural Areas

THE UNIVERSITY AND DEVELOPMENT

The University of Antioquia started as the Royal Franciscan College, established in 1803 under Spanish rule; became the College of Antioquia in 1822 shortly after Colombia's independence; and acquired university status in 1871. While the University has been the main educational institution in this region of Colombia since that time, most of its professional programs have been established only recently.

In 1974-75, the University had a total enrollment of 12,084 students: 399 in postgraduate programs (master's); 7,061 in professional programs; 941 in short-term programs; and 3,683 in technical or intermediate programs (nonprofessional). In the same year, there were 1,061 professors, of whom 497 had professional degrees, 414 master's degrees or the equivalent, and 13 Ph.D.s. There are no data on 137 professors, but it is believed that most of them have only a basic professional degree.*

Service and Research Programs

So far, there has been no coordinated plan for development-related activities. Individual professors or groups of professors, however, have started a number of service and research programs that the University has supported. Such programs include studies of employment levels, family savings, and rural health services; a financial analysis of the state of Antioquia; the operation of an adult literacy program; and technical assistance to small cattlemen.

---

*The Latin American professional degree is roughly equivalent to the U.S. bachelor's degree, representing three or four years of postsecondary education. U.S. professional programs, such as law or medicine, are postgraduate courses, usually requiring that applicants already hold a bachelor's degree.

Through these programs, the University attempts to (1) give future professionals an awareness of national problems; (2) offer training to in-service personnel; (3) transfer and adapt technological innovations; (4) provide consulting services; and (5) establish close relationships with the community, especially in health.

Most of the programs deal with concerns of the state of Antioquia, although a few extend to other states. Most also try to meet the needs of the poor, although other groups are included. The University provides, for example, engineering consultation to industry. There is some feeling that more University cooperation with both private interests and the National Planning Office would ensure better coordinated programs.

At present, service and research programs are being carried out in the following fields.

Health

There are 135 research projects in health fields (medicine, public health, and dentistry), many of which will influence areas of development such as nutrition, sanitation, water treatment, drug addiction, and hospital regionalization. They include

1. A research program on health planning in Antioquia (PLANSAN), conducted jointly by the University, the Ministry of Health, the Pan-American Health Organization, the Health Service of Antioquia, the Colombian Institute of Social Security (ICSS), and the National School of Public Health. The program studies health service delivery systems in the rural towns around Santo Domingo in order to improve decision-making processes at different health service levels.

2. Several joint programs in dentistry, in which the University and the Ministry of Health test different models of dental service delivery.

Education

1. An adult literacy program, carried out jointly with the Laubach Foundation, has been operating for three years. Relationships with this foundation have now been discontinued, and the program will proceed with the combined support of the Secretariat of Education in Antioquia (SEDA), the Colombian Agriculture and Livestock Institute (ICA), the National Learning Service, and the Archepiscopal Curia.

2. The One-Teacher School Program to reinforce rural learning, in which one teacher manages the five grades of primary

education, was carried out in conjunction with the Secretariat of
Education of Antioquia and with support from the National Ministry
of Education. This program is the subject of Case A, below.

3. A program in Individualized Instruction and Flexible
Schooling, carried out jointly with the Colombian Pedagogical
Institute (ICOLPE) and the Secretariat of Education of the state of
Sucre. It also seeks to improve primary schooling in rural areas.
This program is described in Case B.

4. The Open University Project, carried out in conjunction
with the Colombian Institute for the Development of Higher Education
(ICFES), is adapting the open university approach developed in
England to the Colombian university system.

The Faculty of Education also carries out five other research
projects, gives training courses, and helps business, government,
and educational institutions, mainly secondary schools, design and
administer psychological tests.

Veterinary Science

1. A technical assistance program, run jointly with the
Ministry of Agriculture, offers assistance to small cattlemen so
that they can utilize credit facilities that the national government
recently established for them.

2. A rabies prevention program, part of a national campaign,
is operated in conjunction with the National Health Service.

3. Consulting services are provided to the National Apprenticeship Service (SENA), and National Nutrition Program (PINA). The
University also collaborates with the Colombian Agriculture and
Livestock Institute (ICA) in placing students on regional farms and
has 22 research programs that study practical veterinary problems
of special interest for the country.

Law

The Faculty of Law has a legal bureau that serves the poor.

Library Science

The University has established, with the aid of the Rockefeller
Foundation, Unesco, and the OAS, a program that gives training
and assistance in library science to Colombian and other Latin
American students. The program publishes several bibliographical
indexes in science and the humanities.

Sanitation

This faculty, in cooperation with the Pan-American Health
Organization and Antioquia's Health Service, has for two years
measured levels of air pollution in the valley of Aburra.*

Economics

A research center in economics studies the economic problems
of coffee growing, inflation, and the recent financial emergency.

Communication Sciences

The Communication Sciences Department offers refresher
courses, does research on prison systems, publishes books for
children, and promotes rural communication. It is also in charge
of two important and widely known programs: the University of
Antioquia's magazine and its radio station.

Finances

The University is financed largely with funds from the
Colombian government. Its annual budget for 1974 was 221 million
pesos (about $13,812,000 in U.S. dollars), over 80 percent of which
is from the government.
Most of the research or community service programs rely
on financial support from outside the University, the major portion
coming from international agencies. The University seeks long-
term financing of these programs either with its own funds or with
national assistance. When foreign financing of large-scale programs
comes to an end, the University often has difficulties incorporating
the programs into the institution and, on some occasions, has not
been able to obtain continuing support.

RURAL EDUCATION

Three quarters of the rural schools in Colombia have only one
classroom; 80 percent have only one teacher. The teacher, usually

---

*This valley includes the metropolitan area and suburbs of
Medellín and has approximately 1.5 million inhabitants.

isolated from the community and its services, with little training
and few resources, is generally ill-equipped to teach five elementary-
school grades.

In addition, attendance is poor and the dropout rate high. A
third of all schools in rural areas have fewer than ten children
enrolled. More than half the rural school-age population does not
attend school at all, and only 20 out of each 100 students enrolled
in the first grade proceed to the second grade.

The Faculty of Education at the University of Antioquia is
attacking these problems through two projects. The first is the
One-Teacher School Program, in which teachers in small rural
schools receive special training and specially designed teaching
materials to improve the quality of rural elementary school education.
The other project focuses on the difficulty of keeping children in
school in these areas. Because children are needed at home and on
the farm, the Program on Individualized Instruction and Flexible
Schooling accepts limited attendance and helps teachers and parents
adopt flexible schedules whereby children study at home as well as
in school. The two projects are described below as Cases A and B.

Case A: The One-Teacher School

In 1967, the University of Antioquia's School of Education
and the State Secretariat of Education held a training course for
teachers in the town of Rionegro, consisting of lectures and seminars
on audiovisual aids, parent education, one-teacher schools, and
educational administration. A group of women students from the
Normal School of Rionegro was chosen to test approaches to the
one-teacher school, a rural elementary school in which one teacher
conducts all courses. Such a school requires not only special
training for the teacher but also considerable flexibility and a reliance
on teaching materials and techniques for using them.

The results of the course on one-teacher schools were promising,
and the Faculty of Education accordingly began to develop teaching
materials and to train more teachers for such schools. An agreement
was signed between the Secretariat of Education of Antioquia (SEDA)
and the University to establish a project with the following aims:
(1) direct special attention to primary education, a major problem
for both the region and the country; (2) define the organization and
functioning of the one-teacher school; (3) develop student materials
in all subjects; (4) experiment with teaching techniques which help
a teacher manage all five grades of elementary school in rural areas;
(5) structure a basic training program for primary school teachers
and administrators; (6) evaluate the functioning of the one-teacher
school; and (7) publicize the one-teacher school model.

The project began in 1968 with a pilot program in one school. In 1969, seven one-teacher schools, and in the next year 30 one-teacher schools in various parts of the state of Antioquia were using the project's materials and training facilities. In 1971, there were 70 elementary schools (not all one-teacher schools), out of a total of 343 schools in the rural areas of the state of Antioquia with less than 30 students per school, that used the program's instruction materials. At present 43 one-teacher schools in the state of Antioquia and 30 multiteacher schools in the state of Sucre are working with materials produced by the project.

So far, the project has published materials for the first four years of elementary school and hopes to complete others for the fifth grade by 1976. It has put special emphasis on language (Spanish, writing, and spelling) and mathematics, but it has also produced course work in social sciences (history, geography, civics, and culture) and natural sciences (health and sanitation). These teacher aids include both programed written material and suggestions for activities in which students do practical tasks and actively observe their environment rather than merely sit at their desks. The Ministry of Education determines curriculum content for all primary schools.

Although a full-scale teacher training program has not been developed, teachers have been trained in group dynamics, psychology of learning, and evaluation. The project helps them plan and organize their own schedules. They are also trained to work with teaching cards, and special emphasis is put on language and mathematics methodology. The one-teacher school model has been publicized through discussions at normal schools and at seminars and meetings with deans of education, the Ministry of Education, ICFES, and ICOLPE.

Organization

The project has been directed by the head of the Department of Extension of the University of Antioquia, with the assistance of a coordinator, nine programers, four part-time illustrators, and two secretaries. The coordinator meets frequently with the head of the One-Teacher School Section of SEDA to discuss selection of teachers and pilot schools, coordination of training programs, and supervisory reports. Major policy decisions are made by the dean of the Faculty of Education and the state secretary of education. Project administrators meet periodically with teachers to distribute materials and discuss their use.

Resources and Finance

In 1971, the Faculty of Education and SEDA were operating the project with 234,000 pesos (U.S. $9,360) in aid from the National Ministry of Education (MEN). In 1973, ICFES contributed 150,000 pesos (U.S. $6,000).

For its day-to-day operation, the project relies essentially on SEDA and the Faculty of Education. SEDA pays salaries for programers and teachers, provides library materials, and helps improve facilities in participating schools. Its total expenditures from 1968 to 1974 have been estimated at approximately 1,107,120 pesos (U.S. $44,284). The Faculty of Education pays the program coordinator's salary (he is a member of that faculty), other professors' salaries, and interest expenses.

The University of Antioquia estimates its expenditures for the project from 1968 to 1974 at 1,257,480 (U.S. $50,300). Since the University received contributions totaling U.S. $15,360 from MEN and ICFES, its net contribution has been U.S. $34,940.

The project has also been supported, although in small amounts, by the towns where the one-teacher schools are located, by parents, by the National Federation of Coffee Growers, and by National Community Action. Since it has received no foreign assistance and has few additional financial resources, the project has been unable to expand substantially. The possibility of selling the instruction materials it produces has been suggested, but the project does not yet have the organization necessary to carry out such a plan.

Favorable Conditions

The following conditions have contributed to the project's success:

1. The support given by SEDA and by SEDA's collaboration with the University. Although SEDA is in charge of personnel, for example, the Faculty of Education interviews potential teachers before they are seen by SEDA and advises SEDA on their hiring.

2. The interest and enthusiastic support given by the deans and professors of the Faculty of Education and by several members of other faculties. Professors of education, by and large, particularly those who received training abroad, have been sympathetic to the new methods and techniques used; professors of science, mathematics, sociology, and other disciplines have collaborated in reviewing the content of the courses and in supervising them.

3. The financial support given by the National Ministry of Education. The ministry has had a continuing interest in this experiment as a possible solution to the problems of primary education in rural areas.

Limitations

The program had to contend with the following difficulties:

1. An initial lack of trained people to structure and carry out the program. This situation has improved, but there is still a need for trained program directors and supervisors.

2. An absence of stable financial resources. Since the program for the following year is not established until the budget is approved at the end of the year, it has been impossible to plan more than a year in advance.

3. A lack of consistent leadership. When the director of the project resigned after the first year of operation, the program was suspended for ten months until another director could be found. There is a need for more stable direction, not subject to internal changes in the government or the university.

4. A need for more sophisticated techniques for designing and programing teaching materials and a need to experiment further with teaching methods.

5. Lack of an evaluation. Although the Faculty of Education's department of research has planned a broad evaluation of what has been done up to now, it has not yet had adequate financial resources to do so. If the ministry, SEDA, and a large number of towns in Antioquia are to decide to extend the program, they will need an objective assessment of the project's results. The project has mainly produced and distributed materials but has not tested their utilization or their relevance to rural concerns.

6. No clear definition of the roles to be played by the various participants (SEDA, Faculty of Education, ministry, towns, teachers, and parents). Good relationships and economic commitments have been worked out slowly.

7. Limited communication with the schools participating in the project, regarding the value of the project, the use of materials, problems, and the success of teaching methods.

8. An inadequate supply of specialists in primary education. University professors who approve the content of the instruction materials produced by the project are specialists in sciences, mathematics, Spanish, or social sciences. Although they know the teaching methodology of their respective specialty, they have no special knowledge of primary school learning.

9. The unwillingness of trained teachers to remain in rural
areas. To extend the network of one-teacher schools, the project
needs teachers with experience in one-teacher-school classes.
After working for two years with the project, however, teachers
are likely to move to the towns and cities. While efforts are made
to select teachers able to adjust easily to rural environments, and
although teachers receive financial incentives to remain in the
villages, neither selection methods nor incentives prevent the loss
of trained teachers and are unlikely to do so until the rural environment is modernized.

Results

The project is considered the Faculty of Education's main
contribution to the community. Not only has it produced instructional
materials for the first grades of primary schools and has trained
supervisors, teachers, and programers, but it has also cooperated
successfully with SEDA. Relationships between the faculty and SEDA
are harmonious and well defined. Decisions regarding personnel,
teacher retirement, improvement of the schools, supervisors, and
others are made jointly.

The national Ministry of Education has been interested in the
project for some time. It postponed plans to extend it when there
was a change in government, but the new government is expected
to give the project substantial assistance.

The faculty, however, believes the project should not be
extended on a large scale until it has been more carefully evaluated;
until students, teachers, and parents are better prepared; and until
costs have been more accurately determined by specialists in
organizational theory and cost analysis. In 1975, therefore, only
four schools with 30 students each were added to the 30 schools
already functioning under the project.

Case B: Individualized Instruction and
Flexible Schooling

The One-Teacher-School Program was one result of a search
for new methods and materials to increase effectiveness and decrease
costs in rural schools. The Program on Individualized Instruction
and Flexible Schooling was established and carried out by a professor
at the University of Antioquia as another experiment in programed
instruction for rural schools and a way of meeting the problem of
low attendance rates. The project was designed especially for
regions where class attendance is affected by rainy seasons, floods,

harvest, or transfer of livestock, the most common reasons given for children not attending school.

The new model, called WINNETKA, includes both instructional methods and materials and noninstructional elements such as motivation for teachers, children, and parents. The model requires children to attend class only three days a week. During the remaining two days, some schoolwork is done at home. The days on which children will attend school are chosen in consultation with their parents, according to when they will be needed at home or to help out on the farm.

The project starts with a meeting with parents to explain schooling arrangements. Parents are asked to have their children dedicate at least two hours daily to the self-instruction materials. (Most material has been completed within one third of the time expected, indicating a high level of motivation.)

Objectives

A goal of the project is to train teachers to use individualized instruction techniques and to apply motivation for achievement (McClellan-Atkinson) methodologies. They learn to be flexible with children in their classrooms, to create an atmosphere conducive to participation and creativity on the part of the children, and to help children experience feelings of success. Desks are arranged more informally, and library books are available in the classroom. Children are also encouraged to be independent. They evaluate their own work and observe their own progress. In addition, they are guided in choosing their own objectives and goals.

The project also seeks to prepare semiprogramed materials that allow the child to work on his own, consulting individually with the teacher. It tries also to reduce costs by modifying the One-Teacher-School materials, which Bernardo Restrepo, the program's originator, feels are too bulky and too costly. The Individualized Instruction Program has set up a system of teaching cards.

Organization

The project has been divided into two stages. The first stage was carried out by the Research Center of the Faculty of Education and included 24 schools within an 80 kilometer district around Medellín.* It was administered by a director, part-time coordinator,

_____

*Medellín is the capital of the state of Antioquia and has a population of 1,200,000.

and two research assistants, and used the programing and secretarial services of the One-Teacher-School Program.

In the second stage, the project covered 130 students from ten out of a total of 467 rural schools in the state of Sucre. It was run by a part-time coordinator, three professionals (including two half-time research assistants), five programers with the degree "Normalistas" (a special high school program for teachers who have had 11 years of formal education), and a secretary. Professors from the Faculty of Education and other faculties, such as sciences, mathematics, language, and social sciences, have reviewed subject content and methodology of the project. ICOLPE has given support and financial aid to this aspect of the program.

The project offers special training to its participants. The five programers, who are elementary-school teachers who have taken some courses at the University, have received training in two courses equivalent to a four-week full-time schedule. Nine programers of the One-Teacher-School Program have also received training through three short courses of the same intensity. These courses concentrate basically on Dick's model, utilized at Florida State University (Tallahassee), and include seminars, teamwork, and workshops. Participants are instructed in planning, development, and evaluation of the new model systems.

In addition, "Normalistas" receive one week of training, focused mainly on how to use programed materials. Fifteen teachers have received training in the first stage and ten in the second stage.

Evaluation

The program has been evaluated twice a year, and materials have been compared with those of the One-Teacher-School Project. A cost efficiency scheme has been used to test the effectiveness of the second stage in Antioquia. In a comparative test, individualized and flexible schooling rated higher than conventional methods, and success was found to be particularly high in poor, underdeveloped areas. The work in Sucre is now also being evaluated. While the government authorized this experimental program, no attempt has been made to adapt the pilot curriculum to other rural areas. On the other hand, a number of ideas and methods developed by the project are being applied to urban area schools.

Resources and Finance

The initial stage of the program was financed with funds from AID and the Ford Foundation. These agencies paid the project director's travel and general expenses. Seventy percent of the

experimental phase of this first stage was financed by ICOLPE
with funds from the Ford Foundation. The remaining 30 percent
was financed with contributions from SEDA and the Faculty of
Education of the University of Antioquia. The total cost of this first
stage was approximately 600,000 pesos (U.S. $24,000), which was
divided approximately as follows: ICOLPE (Ford Foundation) 300,000
pesos (U.S. $12,000); University of Antioquia 170,000 pesos (U.S.
$6,800), and SEDA 130,000 pesos (U.S. $5,200).*

The second stage is financed jointly by ICOLPE (with funds
from the Ford Foundation) and the University of Antioquia. For
the second stage the total amount contributed is approximately
500,000 pesos (U.S. $20,000), which has been divided as follows:
ICOLPE (Ford Foundation) 367,000 pesos (U.S. $14,680); and
University of Antioquia 70,000 pesos (U.S. $2,800). The secretary
of education of Sucre announced support for this stage in the amount
of 20,000 pesos (U.S. $800). Since this donation was not made,
however, ICOLPE added this sum to its budget. ICOLPE also
contributed 60,000 pesos (U.S. $2,400) to cover the revision of
the materials carried out by professors from the University of
Antioquia.

Favorable Conditions

The project has had the advantage of the following favorable
circumstances:

1. The opportunity the project's director had to receive
specific training in educational technology.
2. Support from the University and from the state secretaries
of education in Antioquia and in Sucre.
3. The support of ICOLPE, made possible through the Ford
Foundation. Ford assistance has thus given both supplementary
aid to the program and generated action by other agencies.
4. Acceptance of the project by students, teachers, supervisors, and parents.

Limitations

The project has experienced several difficulties:

1. Some members of ICOLPE's board of directors have
objected to limiting in-school time to three rather than five days

---

*Approximate rate of exchange in 1974: Col. 25 pesos =
U.S. $1.

a week. Because this time flexibility is considered vital to the project, however, no change has been made in this aspect of the program.

2. Production of instructional materials has been hindered by lack of funds.

3. Costs have not been adequately assessed, and, therefore, it has been difficult to project costs of an expanded model.

4. The project's methods and materials have not been sufficiently tested.

5. The link at the University between the project and curriculum needs to be strengthened and reinforced.

6. There have been too few professors qualified to conduct training courses on primary-school curriculum and method for teachers and specialists.

Results

These two education projects are circumscribed experiments under careful supervision. While they have been promising approaches to the problems of rural education, support and resources have been limited. Cities produce more political pressures for funds than do villages, and state officials are consequently less likely to approve rural spending. It is, moreover, difficult to introduce new methods into an established system supported by its own hierarchy; decision makers fear that any mistakes or increase in costs will doom the effort.

Nevertheless, the Individualized Instruction and Flexible Schooling Program has established and validated a model for the delivery of educational service in rural areas. Through a classical research approach within previously determined guidelines, it has focused on the effectiveness of rural education by dealing with its practical operating problems. It has succeeded as well as it has partly because its initial working group was small, because it had several years of experience with the One-Teacher School Project to build on, and because it had state government support.

Both its content and its administration lend themselves to expansion by the national government and could be related to national programs and plans such as Concentrations for Rural Development.* ICOLPE, as its main financing agency and as an agency of the Ministry of Education, could help the national government develop

---

*Concentrations for Rural Development is a government program partially financed by the World Bank. It attempts to integrate the services of various state agencies on behalf of rural education.

a policy which included the project's approaches. There are, however no definite proposals for using the results of this experiment
on the national level.

PROJECT SUGGESTIONS

For Planners

The One-Teacher-School and the Individualized Instruction
and Flexible Schooling programs have great potential value for
solving serious problems of rural schooling. The One-Teacher-
School Program has produced programed instructional material,
and the Individualized Instruction Program has set up a system of
teaching cards. This material should be evaluated, revised, and,
where proved effective, widely distributed to other regions.

Such extension requires three things: long-range financial
assistance, close cooperation between government and university,
and stable direction. These needs might be fulfilled by an autonomous national center for rural education with its own budget. It
should have the participation of State secretariats of education,
regional faculties of education, and ICOLPE, and it might preserve
the University of Antioquia's leadership. It would especially need
the support and cooperation of the Ministry of Education to facilitate
approval of projects, a difficult process when done independently.
The center should, however, have enough independence to assure
autonomous direction without political interference.

A center of this sort could be in charge of administration and
technical research. It should include an evaluation section that
could note and record the development of the project. It should
also publish tested and approved material for all regions and could
have regional groups working with state secretariats of education
in various areas. Such a center could also be established in other
nations, adapted to their special conditions.

For Donor Agencies

Improving rural primary education in Colombia requires
uniting the efforts of the government, which regulates teaching
programs, and the technical capacity of the faculties of education,
which until now have dealt only with secondary education. In
implementing such cooperative projects, however, a way must be
found to strengthen both curriculum and administration, not only
in the central unit but also at the regional level.

While such programs require substantial financial and technical assistance, local and national participation and initiative should be preserved. The valuable relationship between an official agency and a faculty of education should also be preserved. Central administration might be handled by the Ministry of Education or by the center already described. At the same time, both government and members of education faculties who have had experience with these programs should continue to be involved.

20

UNIVERSITY OF VALLE, CALI, COLOMBIA

Program for Systems of Health Services Delivery

THE UNIVERSITY

In 1945, industry in the Valle del Cauca was developing rapidly, and population growth at 5 percent had outstripped most of the rest of the country. The Assembly of the state of Valle founded the University of Valle principally to educate leaders who could take responsibility for the future development of the region. The University was to transmit and augment knowledge, but it was also to act as an agent of change in the community. Students who heretofore had had to go to Bogotá, Medellín, Popayan, and other cities for a college education could now be educated at home, at less cost, to serve both the management needs of a growing number of private companies and the professional needs of a growing population.

Although the needs of the region were of primary concern from the beginning, it was only in the 1960s that the University's role as an instrument of development for the region and country was defined explicitly. At the beginning of the decade, the University's rector maintained that universities should not only establish rigorous academic standards, but "should also be immersed in the life of their nations, in a reciprocal action of giving and receiving."[1] This concept of the university, deeply concerned with the problems of its own community, has characterized the University of Valle since that time and continues to be its goal.

Service, however, was seen as enriching teaching and research. The main objectives of the University, said a later rector, are "teaching, research, and community service, interrelated in such a manner that complete fulfillment of one is necessary to accomplish the others."[2] The University of Valle, he said,

> has become completely immersed in its community
> through various service programs, which are increasing
> continuously. . . . However, the function of service
> should have a different dimension from that of occasional
> assistance; it should be an unlimited source of teaching
> resources and one of the most formative activities of

346

future leaders. . . . I would like to emphasize the
importance of this service and present it as one of the
main foundation pillars for research and teaching,
. . . to be considered not a simple additional or
secondary function. . . .[3]

It is a mistake, said this same rector, to consider development
an exclusively economic problem. Man seeks not only to increase
his income but also to improve himself and his values.

The goal of development is not a simple concept, but
rather a combination of social, spiritual, economic,
cultural, and political improvement. In the world and
in Colombia there is a revolutionary movement taking
place which attempts to change the existing conditions of
poverty, ignorance, and illness [and] which can be
summarized in the word "development."[4]

History

The University's first 160 students were distributed among
four schools: agriculture, nursing, business, and a secondary
school for girls. After a few years, however, the secondary school
was discontinued, and technical programs were initiated in architecture and electromechanical engineering. The Faculty of Medicine,
established in 1950, soon became one of the leading medical schools
in Colombia and in Latin America. Based on a departmental system,
with full-time staff and full-time students, it blended, from the
beginning, teaching duties with research and service. Its prestige
stemmed largely from the superior level of training—often abroad—
of its professors and administrators. The University benefited
also from a change in its statutes, which gave it autonomous status;
the rector was no longer appointed by the state governor but was
now nominated by a board of directors composed of community and
University representatives.

Over the next few years the University of Valle entered on
a remarkable period of progress and growth that influenced the
university system throughout Colombia. Innovations in both organization and substance attracted widespread attention. It established
the Office of the Dean of Studies, the Office of the Dean of Students,
and the Planning Office. It initiated a general studies program;
established, in conjunction with the University of the Andes, a
premedical program; reorganized its central administration; and
established a fund-raising office that obtained, through the Foundation

for Higher Education (FES) substantial financial assistance from
industrial and private sources. The departmental system was
introduced at the University, the library was centralized and rebuilt,
and a Central Research Committee gave special stimulus to integrating
research, service, and teaching. Divisions of sciences, humanities,
and education were added to the already functioning divisions of
architecture and health sciences.

During this decade of development (1961-71) the Ford and
Rockefeller Foundations supplemented the initial financial assistance
given by the Kellogg Foundation. The Rockefeller Foundation's
assistance played an important role in the development of the Faculty
of Medicine, the Faculty of Social and Economic Sciences, and of
the University in general. Ford Foundation aid helped establish
the Divisions of Engineering and Sciences, the Planning and Promotion
Offices, and a new campus.

In 1971 a student crisis interrupted most of the University's
activities; a number of professors resigned, and relationships with
the community deteriorated. Within two years, however, the
University recovered its former good relations with the community
and, since then, has preserved and strengthened its role in development. Despite a decrease in financial support from private and
foreign agencies, it continues most of its community programs.

The University functions on two campuses: One at the old site
in the San Fernando area south of Cali; and the other—the new
campus—in Meléndez, a region farther south. On the San Fernando
campus are the Divisions of Health and Architecture, the Departments of Music and of Industrial Management (formerly part of
the Division of Social and Economic Sciences and now of the Division
of Engineering), and the University hospital. The campus at
Meléndez was opened in 1973 to meet the increasing requests for
admission. This campus can handle more than 10,000 students.

In 1973-74 the University had 5,163 students and 611 members
of the teaching staff. Table 20.1 shows the level of staff training
as of that year.

Development Projects

In 1974, continuing its policy of integrating teaching and
research with community service, the University established the
University Center for Development Projects (CUPRED) to identify
and coordinate education for development projects and to encourage
professors and students to participate in these projects. An attempt
is made to place the student in situations which involve complex
national problems, as often as possible including the needs of the

TABLE 20.1

Staff Training 1973-74

Divisions	Professors					
	Ph.D.	Master	Special-ization	Other Degrees	On Leave of Absence	Total
Sciences	11	18	7	32	18	86
Humanities	8	18	1	35	8	70
Social and Economic Sciences	4	6	1	7	1	19
Education	3	17	6	3	2	31
Architecture	–	4	5	23	–	32
Health	20	40	117	45	11	233
Engineering	9	40	12	63	16	140
Total	55	143	149	208	56	611

Source: University of Valle.

poor. Tackling such problems has three important educational advantages for students: They see the need for interdisciplinary efforts, they collaborate with others, and they learn to work within the limitations of the world outside the University.

From its inception, the Division of Health has led the way in designing activities directed not only to a search for knowledge and to the training of health workers, but also to solving the problems of the local community and of the larger society. The origins of most University development activities go back to a program on family health initiated in Siloé in 1955 by the Medical School and later expanded into health delivery systems in the town of Candelaria and in urban communities such as Luis H. Garcés, Villanueva, and El Guabal. Several of the University's rectors and other top administrators have come from the Faculty of Medicine and have taken the lead in promoting development programs.

Community health programs stimulated an interest within the faculties of architecture and economics in the housing and environmental problems in these same communities. In 1961, the Faculty of Architecture, with the Faculty of Sanitary Engineering and ACUAVALLE (a government agency responsible for water supply lines and sewerage systems in the state of Valle) successfully designed and implemented water supply and sewerage systems in Candelaria. Architectural graduate students designed an urban model in Siloé in 1961-63 and a rural model in San Joaquín, a district of Candelaria, in 1964. The Faculty of Economics conducted and published a census on agriculture and cattle of the Valle del Cauca in 1961 and made periodic surveys of employment in Cali. Most development programs continue to maintain close ties with the Division of Health. They are generally started by a professor or small group of professors, supported by University leaders, but some program proposals are submitted through government agencies.

Besides the community health programs (described in the second part of this study), the following development programs are presently underway on the University campus.

Center for Multidisciplinary Research on Rural Development (CIMDER)

Several regional agencies (the Cauca Valley Corporation, CVC, the Cauca Health Service, the Valle Committee of the National Federation of Coffee Growers, and the Foundation for Higher Education) are collaborating to improve the conditions of rural families. This interdisciplinary multiinstitutional program is based on the belief that economics, agriculture, and education play important roles in the health and well-being of the community. The experimental area covers four rural towns in the northern part of the state of Cauca.

Population Education Program

A School curriculum that combines social problems (such as drug abuse), sex education, and study of population and environmental problems has been developed at the University's Center for Population Studies and is being tested in 24 primary and secondary schools in Colombia, under the auspices of the Minister of Education, with technical assistance from Unesco and from the United Nations Fund for Population Activities. The Center for Population Studies at the University was established in 1963 with Ford Foundation assistance when several University social scientists, impressed with the results of the University's health program in Candelaria, organized a multidisciplinary group to study the interrelation of problems. The Population Education Program seeks to develop in primary- and secondary-school children an awareness of how the behavior of the individual has social and environmental consequences in relation to population growth. The supplementary materials include slides, films, books, magazines, and pamphlets.

Program for Research in Health Planning (COLIMPLAS)

The general objective of this program is to improve health services through better administration and planning. The program

is the result of a joint effort of the World Health Organization and,
in Colombia, the University of Valle, the Ministry of Public Health,
the Institute of Social Security, the Institute of Family Well-Being,
the National Institute of Special Health Programs, and the Association of Faculties of Medicine. There are four basic activities:
(1) description and evaluation of services; (2) design of new administrative and planning methods; (3) development of ways to introduce
innovations; and (4) introduction of selected innovations in the health
system.

To carry out these activities, an International and Multidisciplinary Group for Research was set up in Cali, composed of
professionals in health services administration, epidemiology,
sociology, systems analysis, and economic analysis for health
service. The concepts and methods developed in the program are
also being used in a similar study to be carried out at the Cauca
Valley Regional Office of the Colombian Institute of Social Security.

Foundation for Human Ecology Research

This project is investigating the physical and psychological
repercussions of poverty on preschool children; its specific objective
is to develop techniques for improving their educability and level of
health. Specialized child care centers will be established, using
the results of the research. The project is attempting to develop
several systems that can be applied to different socioeconomic
groups in Cali and can later be utilized on a national scale.

Community Experiments in Reducing Malnutrition in Colombia

This project seeks to develop a planners' guide for decreasing
malnutrition at the community level. Five small communities
(2,000 to 4,000 inhabitants) with high rates of malnutrition have
been carefully selected on the basis of their cultural and geographical differences, and the study will analyze the size of the gap between
individuals' nutritional requirements and the actual food they con-
sume. The possible causes of malnutrition will be identified, and
an effort will be made to determine solutions and costs.

Regional Nursing Program

This joint program for the development of nursing education
in southwest Colombia is being carried out at the state universities
of Caldas, Nariño, and Valle and in the district of Putumayo, with
the cooperation of the Colombian Institute of Health and the Kellogg
Foundation. It includes programs in continuing education and delivery

of health services in rural areas through health promoters and
University personnel. The number of nurses graduating from the
program increased from 30 in 1970 to 172 in 1974—100 in basic
programs and 72 in postbasic programs. The Regional Nursing
Program is in the process of being evaluated.

Nonformal Education in Northern Cauca

This experimental and exploratory program is attempting to
find new ways to develop skills needed for community development,
including reading, writing, first aid, and community organization.
The orientation and content of the program are determined by the
users' needs, and the program focuses on language arts, arithmetic,
and social sciences. Community members work closely with
specialists in education and other areas.

Division Projects

The Division of Engineering has a curriculum oriented toward
the community and planned to meet environmental needs in each of
its departments.

The Center for Natural Resources (CERENA), under the
direction of the dean's office, was organized to provide technical
assistance in the field of natural resources to private or public
agencies.

The Department of Civil Engineering runs research and consulting programs in cooperation with Delft University of Technology
(Netherlands) in hydraulics and fluid mechanics. (Delft University
also advises on academic programs and the establishment of a postgraduate program in hydraulic resources.) Among the programs
are (1) a study of the possibilities of establishing a lumber port in
Buenaventura Bay; (2) a study, in conjunction with the CVC, of
hydrographic basins in the Cauca Valley; and (3) construction of a
hydraulic model in Buenaventura Bay in collaboration with the
Colombian Ports Organization. Along with the Municipal Office
of Appraisal in Cali the department is also studying, at the Soils
Laboratory of the University of Valle, expansive clays in Cali and
their more effective use in construction.

The Department of Electrical Engineering has programs for
(1) maintaining the control and balance of the electrical system in
Cali, under an agreement with the Municipal Light, Water and
Telephone Company; (2) certifying electric conductors under agreement with the Ministry of Development, through the Colombian
Institute of Technical Systems (ICONTEC); and (3) providing technical
training for the affiliates of the Association of Electrical and Mechani-

cal Engineers. The division also has a contract with the Colombian Petroleum Company (ECOPETROL) to train its personnel. Faculty members go to company headquarters in Barrancabermeja to give these courses. This same procedure is being used in local companies.

The Department of Sanitary Engineering works closely in the field of air pollution control with the Ministry of Health, the Regional Health Service of Valle, and international agencies such as the World Health Organization. It collaborates with the Municipal Light, Water, and Telephone Company in controlling the water supply system of Cali and is studying the contamination by sewage of the Cauca River. The department also has had a number of interesting programs in rural development. As part of their classwork, students have successfully designed windmills with disposable storage containers, and well filters for use in rural areas. Aqueducts have been installed in several small rural communities.

The Department of Systems Engineering provides consulting services for public service agencies in small towns of the State; designs programs and data-processing systems to facilitate the use of small computers; investigates the use of computers in countries, such as Colombia, with very high rates of unemployment; and is trying to establish ways to use systems analysis methodology on problems of malnutrition.

The Department of Agricultural Engineering has made studies of the following: conservation of agricultural products (for example, drying yucca); packaging and storage of agricultural products (for example, humidity control of cold-storage rooms to prolong product freshness); semiprocessed products; quality control of foodstuffs; utilization of agricultural wastes; and adaptation of agricultural machinery to local conditions. The department also advises a private laboratory (Miles) regarding the production of texturized vegetable protein as well as quality control of foods.

The Department of Chemical Engineering's projects include production of alumina from bauxite found in the Cauca Valley; analysis of bauxite samples; selective hydrogenation of soybean and cottonseed oils; quality control of soybean cakes purchased by the Colombian Marketing Agriculture and Cattle Institute (IDEMA); and substitution of alcohol derivatives for petroleum derivatives and a mixture of alcohol-gasoline to be used as a fuel.

The Division of Education extends the opportunity of obtaining the degree "Licenciado" (licenciate) in Education to high school teachers and thus raises the level of teacher training in high schools in the state of Valle. This program began in 1973 and has been carried out in a number of cities of the State (including Buga, Tuluá, Cartago, and Zarzal). The University, through the Division of Education, has in the past offered numerous training courses for

high school teachers in different areas. It trained 575 teachers in
1965; 770 teachers in 1966; 1,028 teachers in 1967; 1,702 teachers
in 1968; 1,002 teachers in 1969; and 769 teachers in 1970. From
1971 on, a considerable decrease was apparent—during that year
only 77 teachers were trained and only 336 teachers in 1972. A
total of 136 courses have been offered to 6,370 students.

The Division of Architecture, through its Institute for Construction (IDELAC), studies, analyzes, investigates, evaluates, and
publicizes all matters relating to the field of construction. It also
has an Information and Documentation Center for compiling, classify-
ing, and processing construction information.

University Finances

The University of Valle, like the rest of the higher education
system, relies on the Ministry of Education for its financing and
orientation. Each academic division maintains independent links
with other state agencies or private institutions, and, in the Division
of Health especially, orienting training toward specific problems
strengthens its bonds with the Ministry of Health and other service
agencies. Recently, the Ministry of Health has been giving financial
aid to programs that show results in their first experimental stages.

Though the programs have been supported by the University
and government ministries, their design and implementation rely
heavily on foreign assistance, particularly from international
agencies. The use of foreign resources for these and other types
of programs occasionally causes two kinds of problems: one
involving external and the other internal politics. A few students
and teachers see imperialism and interference with the University's
autonomy in any foreign (national or international) assistance.
Since all foreign technical assistance must now be approved by the
central government, however, there has been less opposition from
these groups, although, under the new procedure, foreign aid may
now be more subject to national political fluctuations.

Financial aid can also create special institutional problems
and internal antagonisms. Some academic divisions have evolved
more rapidly than others and are therefore prepared to request and
absorb more aid, creating imbalances and jealousies among divisions.

Effect on Teaching and Research

Although long-term programs of education for development
are expected to improve teaching, there have been occasions in which

service activities have taken professors totally away from normal teaching duties. Few attempts to link teaching with such programs have been entirely successful, especially since the University does not give academic credits for most service activities. On the other hand, service programs encourage new teaching methods and have also affected the content of the curriculum.

Education for development programs have had a major impact on basic research. Theories can be tested in actual situations within the community, and the programs have brought at least part of the faculty into contact with problem solving and social reality. The Research Committee, made up of representatives from all units of the University, has stimulated interest in research and has provided research facilities and financial assistance for qualified research programs. The committee has been used as a model for other institutions and national agencies, and the quality and quantity of research at the University of Valle has given the University a reputation as a leading research institution in Colombia.

Institutional Relationships

Good programs need approval and participation from the following sectors:

The community: A program's success depends largely on how well it is received by the community it serves. Although program planners stress the need for community groups to assume partial responsibility for the programs, community participation is difficult to achieve. In the Division of Health, for example, experience has shown that the group that takes the initiative makes the final decisions.

The government: Authorities, while often initially skeptical about programs for development, are likely to support positive results, and financial contributions are significant indications of approval, especially in a country such as Colombia that lacks financial resources. The Ministry of Health, for example, is substantially increasing its economic assistance; its contribution to the Program for Systems of Health Services Delivery (PRIMOPS) has replaced foreign assistance, essential to the program up to now. University programs for development have been backed by the Minister of Health, the Regional Health Service, the CVC, the Colombian Agriculture and Livestock Institute (ICA), the Cali Public Works Department, and the Cali Municipal and District Authorities. Through COLIMPLAS, the University Division of Health has participated in national health planning. This program was conceived by the University and accepted and approved by the national government and the World Health Organization.

The private sector: The University has tried to maintain close ties with private business. A course for executives leading to a master's degree was designed to change the attitudes of business executives and make them more aware of their social and economic responsibilities to the region. The course did, in fact, develop a heightened sense of responsibility in organizations which provide most of the jobs in the country. Until now, private companies have not participated directly in education for development programs, but their inactivity may be due to the University's lack of assertiveness on behalf of the programs.

At present, there is no systematic means of evaluation or of dissemination of experience and results. Program participants, government agencies, and business firms lack information. To publicize the program experience and increase the number and variety of programs, two procedures, already tested in the Division of Health, are recommended: (1) designate government officials or business executives as part-time teachers, thus establishing and maintaining closer relationships with government agencies and private enterprise; and (2) offer scholarships in specially oriented programs for development so that qualified personnel can afford to participate in the programs.

PROGRAM FOR SYSTEMS OF HEALTH
SERVICES DELIVERY

In 1955, the Division of Health, then the Faculty of Medicine of the University of Valle, assigned to each second-year medical student responsibility for the health of a family in the district of Siloé* in the city of Cali. During his remaining years in medical school, the student was to write a paper on the socioeconomic, environmental, and health conditions of each family member. While this program was later discontinued (both students and families became too involved emotionally with each other), the experiment heralded the beginning of the Division's focus on preventive and family medicine, which evolved into community health care. The Faculty of Medicine was the first medical school in Colombia to concentrate not only on the training of professionals but also on the well-being of the individual and the community.

The aim of the original program was to carry out a teaching and research program that could contribute to knowledge about and

---

*Siloé was then a district inhabited mostly by immigrants from rural areas and lacking almost all community facilities.

solution of health problems in this urban district. Since Siloé was
considered atypical, however, and since the Faculty of Medicine
needed broader knowledge and experience, the program included
other city districts, particularly El Guabal and Villanueva, * which
had more stable populations and were of special concern to municipal
health authorities.

A number of conditions gave impetus to the new medical school
concept. Sixty percent of the country's population was living in rural
areas, and the need for better health services in these areas was
becoming urgent. At the same time, a new law made it compulsory
for recent medical school graduates to practice in a rural area for
a specified period. The Division of Health saw the importance both
of training future physicians, nurses, and other medical personnel
to meet the population's needs and of developing and testing new and
more comprehensive health delivery systems.

Building on its experience in Siloé, the Division of Health set
up in 1958 a health center in the urban community of Candelaria,†
which offered facilities for teaching and research in rural medicine.
For ten years, medical, sociological, economic, and demographic
studies analyzed Candelaria's population. The Division of Health
developed health teams composed of doctors, nurses, paramedical
personnel, students, and volunteers recruited from the community
and began to reassign their functions. Massive immunization
campaigns for endemic diseases were launched. Multidisciplinary
teams of University staff and students, with the cooperation of
community leaders and community organizations, sought to meet
such problems as housing, sanitation, nutrition, and education
encountered in the course of the health programs.

The success of the health program in Candelaria was confirmed
by the falling death rate, a decrease in malnutrition, increased
availability of medical services, and improved sanitation and water.
From 1970 to 1972, the death rate was cut in half from 14 per
thousand to 7 per thousand, and the infant death rate from 20 per
thousand to 8 per thousand. Malnutrition in preschool children went
down from 40 percent in 1964 to 22 percent in 1971. Ten years ago
only 40 percent of Candelaria's residents had a potable water supply
in their homes; in 1975, 95 percent had pure drinking water. (See
Appendix 20.1.)

---

*El Guabal and Villanueva are two low-income city districts in
Cali.

†Candelaria has a population of 15,000 and is located 30 kilometers from Cali. Its proximity to the University was a deciding
factor in the location of the project.

In view of the success of the Candelaria program, the University determined to extend the experiment to a low income group in the city of Cali. A new program, PRIMOPS, was designed by two physicians, a nurse, and a social worker, all of whom had worked in the health services delivery system in Candelaria. (Both physicians had graduated from the Division of Health; one was also assistant professor and had participated in several of the Division's previous programs.)

Health services were most needed in maternal and child health (mortality of children under five represents 50 percent of the country's total death rate). In the rapidly growing Cali community chosen for PRIMOPS, 40 percent of the population were low-income women of childbearing age and children under five, all lacking health services. There are approximately 90,000 inhabitants in the six districts covered by the program (Unión de Vivienda, Mariano Ramos, Antonio Nariño, República de Israel, Periquillo, and El Diamante). The area has good access to transportation—an asset for the university program—and is a high-priority target of the Cali Municipal Health Service.

Program Objectives

PRIMOPS had three objectives. The first was to design, implement, operate, and evaluate an efficient model of health service delivery—a system that could offer good health care, high coverage, and low operating costs and could meet the needs of low-income inhabitants of urban areas. Such a system, the program planners believed, should use community resources, coordinate health activities of other agencies in the area, and redefine the basic medical group (public health specialist, physician, nurse) for the delivery of health services.

The second objective was to deliver maternal and child health care—specifically to decrease maternal and infant mortality and the number of unwanted pregnancies; to provide prenatal supervision; to improve nutrition; and to prevent infections leading to diarrhea and dehydration (a major problem in the target population).

The program's third objective was to modify teaching and curriculum in order to prepare better-qualified health professionals and paraprofessionals. It was hoped that the program would lead to curricular changes in some of the study programs (at postgraduate, graduate, and undergraduate levels) in various professional areas of the Division of Health.

Although University staff members planned the program, and the year's planning was financed by the University and the Family

Health Foundation of Tulane University, the University needed government sponsorship and cooperation to put it into effect. The University
thus came to an agreement with the Municipal Health Service (SMS),
which was already providing health care in the Cali area, that the
University would design changes in the existing system of health
services delivery, that it would consult with SMS on its operation,
and that it would evaluate the new program. SMS, however, was
to have sole authority over the operation of the system incorporating
the PRIMOPS pilot program.

In 1972 and 1973, the University of Valle made three basic
studies of the community's health, demographic structure, and
socioeconomic and cultural conditions. The first, carried out by
ICMR (International Center for Medical Research, financed by
Tulane University and USAID) at the end of 1972, investigated the
use of existing health services. The second, carried out by PRIMOPS
at the beginning of 1973, investigated family planning attitudes,
knowledge, and practices. The third study, carried out by DANE
(National Administrative Department of Statistics and PRIMOPS)
in October 1973, collected information on basic demography and
housing.

The program got underway in October 1973 in Unión de Vivienda
Popular, an urban district with 15,000 inhabitants. It was financed
by the Municipal Health Service, the University, and the Ministry of
Health. In February 1973, PRIMOPS project participants set out
to present the program to the community and obtain its support.
They met with Unión de Vivienda's Community Action Board, made
up of district residents and teachers from the district's schools.
Over a period of three months they presented the project at public
meetings, attended by as many as 500 people. Posters and bulletins
were distributed, and health films were shown to audiences of
several hundreds. Meetings were followed up by home visits.

This procedure, with some variation, was carried out in each
of the six districts. In two districts, the community action boards
changed membership, and the work had to be repeated. One district
(Unión de Vivienda Popular) proposed the creation of a health
committee to support the program, but funding for such a committee
has so far been unavailable. PRIMOPS is currently planning ways
to inform people of program results.

Program Organization

Methods used in the PRIMOPS program are based on the
system tested in Candelaria, and on experience in other programs
carried out by the University, by the Colombian Ministry of Public

Health, and by the Municipal Health Service of Cali. Program
planners have also drawn from systems and methods developed by
Tulane University in its Family Health Foundation, which has provided
technical assistance for the program.

The program itself is based on the health delivery system used
by the Ministry of Health and incorporated into the health services
operating in Cali. Under this system medical care is organized by
levels, depending on area size, complexity of services offered,
level of administrative supervision, and teaching and research
responsibilities. In ascending order, these levels are health post,
health center, district hospital, and university hospital. In addition,
PRIMOPS for the first time includes systematic house calls as a
preliminary step or level.

Under the PRIMOPS program, therefore, health services
are delivered to the community on five levels:

Level 1. Home. Families are visited by the following people
(all employees who work at Level 1 live in the community):

1. A Health Promoter, who visits each family every three
months. She identifies women who suspect pregnancy, supervises
the nutrition of children in the family, informs couples about the
family planning program, administers immunizations, and reports
the results of her visits to the nurse's auxiliary. The Health
Promoter must have graduated from elementary school. She
receives six weeks training under the program and is expected
to serve 420 families, or about 2,500 people.

2. A Midwife, who has probably served in this position for
many years without training. The program registers and trains her
(for six weeks) and supervises her work. She reports deliveries
she attends so that the nurse's auxiliary can make the postpartum
visit in the home. She is responsible for 500 women. Midwives,
unlike other personnel in the system, are not paid by the Municipal
Health Service; they charge the women they attend.

3. A Nurse's Auxiliary, who trains promoters and supervises
promoters and midwives. She is responsible for prenatal and postpartum supervision, attends minimum risk deliveries at the Health
Center, gives instructions on recording clinical histories, advises
mothers on nutrition for themselves and their children, instructs
families in family planning, and refers cases that she cannot handle
to the Health Center's physician. She must have a seventh-year
(high school) certificate and two additional years of training, plus
six weeks of special training. She covers an area of 7,000 people.

Level 2. Health Post. Each urban political district (with
10,000 to 20,000 inhabitants) has a Health Post, built with government funds secured by members of the community. It is managed
by a nurse's auxiliary under the direction of a supervising nurse

headquartered at the Health Center. The Health Post processes
the statistical data of each urban district; gives first aid; treats the
child suffering from diarrhea and/or dehydration (first level), fever,
influenza, or parasites; attends to pregnant women with minor com-
plications; provides family planning education; and refers the sick
child or adult who requires a higher level of treatment.

Level 3. Health Center. The Antonio Nariño Center in Cali
is responsible for the entire 90,000 inhabitants covered by PRIMOPS.
Personnel at the Center include a head doctor, two other physicians,
a part-time dentist, a head nurse, six nurse's auxiliaries, and a
supervising nurse who coordinates activities of the Health Posts.
In addition, the Center has a pharmacy and clinical laboratory. The
Center supervises the 30 health promoters and eight nurse's auxiliaries and their activities at Levels 1 and 2, attends patients referred
from Levels 1 and 2, performs laboratory analyses, provides health
education for the community, and refers patients to the hospital
when necessary. Previously the Health Center attended all 15,000
inhabitants of the district without the help of Levels 1 and 2.

The Health Center's Head Doctor is responsible for the operation
of the first three levels. Along with his technical and auxiliary
personnel at Levels 1, 2, and 3, the Head Doctor is part of the SMS
of Cali, which administers the health services delivery system.

Level 4. Urban Hospital. The Carlos Carmona Hospital covers
the southeastern area of Cali (approximately 250,000 inhabitants)
including the PRIMOPS area. It has 32 beds and laboratory, x-ray,
and pharmacy services, and it includes physicians, dentists,
registered nurses, and technicians. It provides hospitalization
for a short period (72 hours), surgery with postoperative care at
home, deliveries, and emergency room treatment for patients
referred from other levels, or to those who come on their own
initiative.

Level 5. University Hospital. This hospital has the most
complete resources and concentrates on high obstetric and pediatric
risk pregnancies and illnesses that require specialized methods of
diagnosis and treatment. It treats patients referred from other
levels or who come to the hospital on their own. It serves an area
in which there are about four million people. At present, Level 4
patients are referred only to the University Hospital, but, in the
future, they will also be referred to San Juan de Dios Hospital and
to the Colombian Institute of Social Security.

University Role

The University PRIMOPS participants, at present, act only as
consultants to the health Center. They advise on design,

implementation, and evaluation of the system. Since the program is expected to extend to other urban areas where there may be no university, the University consultants are drawing up guidelines for whatever private or government agencies will run the system. They have in addition become consultants to the Maternal and Child Care Division of the Ministry of Health, which plans to adopt the health services delivery system tested in the program.

Consulting services are provided through three units at the Division of Health of the University of Valle. They are as follows:

Human Resources Unit, which advises the Municipal Health Service on training personnel for the system. The unit is made up of two nurses, a psychological counselor, and a specialist in educational evaluation; its purpose is to design, develop, and validate recruiting instruments and methods of selection, training, and supervision for paraprofessional and auxiliary personnel.

Communication and Motivation Unit. Coordinated by a social worker, this unit seeks to establish and maintain bonds between the program and the community and to obtain whatever cooperation is necessary for the functioning of the service.

Evaluation Unit. This unit, the most recently established, is directed by a public health doctor and includes a systems engineer and four other part-time personnel. Two evaluating approaches, internal and external, are used.

The internal evaluation, financed by the Ministry of Health, is an ongoing process that tests the model health services delivery system for operating effectiveness. This type of evaluation considers the following: (1) observance of established rules and procedures, such as referral of patients from different levels; (2) utilization of services; (3) community participation and acceptance of health promoters and nurse's auxiliaries; and (4) costs of subprograms, activities, and personnel.

The external evaluation tests the model in relation to the health needs of the population of the city of Cali, which the SMS must meet. It includes 12 special investigations of epidemiologic, sociodemographic, and economic factors. By July 1, 1974, data on 2,940 families had been collected through the network of promoters and nurse's auxiliaries in the course of their home visits. Program planners designed 40 questionnaires and a manual of procedures for processing information. These studies add to knowledge about the model but will probably not be duplicated when the model is applied in another area.

Plans for the program were to cover 32,000 people by the end of 1974 and 90,000 people by March 1975. By 1977 the Evaluation

Unit expects to be able to advise the SMS on whether to expand the
PRIMOPS program to the 400,000 people in the city of Cali.

Cooperation with Other Institutions

A number of agencies, besides the University and the SMS,
participate in PRIMOPS, including the Maternal and Child Division
of the Ministry of Health, the Regional Health Service, the Colombian
Institute of Social Security, and Profamilia. (Initial contacts have
been made with the Colombian Institute of Family Well-being.)
These institutions communicate with one another and coordinate
their activities at three levels:

1. At the interinstitutional level. The Inter-Institutional
Committee, composed of representatives of the Ministry of Health,
the Regional Health Service, the SMS, and the dean of the University
of Valle's Division of Health, meets monthly. The committee consults with the administrators of the program, keeps participating
institutions informed, and seeks sources of financial assistance.

2. At the technical level. The Technical Committee, made
up of program directors and the head of the units, also holds a
monthly meeting at which administrative staff of the SMS participate.
This committee is responsible for planning and supervising the units
and for the program's overall development.

3. At the operational level. Ad hoc meetings at both University and Health Center levels are called periodically to plan specific
activities, to report on progress, and to analyze the present state
of service.

Results of the Program

Training

Eleven training manuals have been prepared (approximately
20 pages each) for promoters and nurse's auxiliaries in subjects
such as nutrition and growth, supervision of children up to five
years of age, and supervision of women practicing family planning.
Fourteen programed instruction booklets (20 to 60 pages) have also
been published on activities such as taking vaginal cytology samples
or giving first aid for burns and wounds.

PRIMOPS has so far trained 30 health promoters, 40 midwives,
and 11 nurse's auxiliaries. Various other agencies and institutions
have used these materials to train approximately 500 health promoters

and nurse's auxiliaries throughout Colombia. As a result, the
National Apprenticeship Service (SENA) is planning to revise the
strategy and methodology it follows in training auxiliary personnel,
and the Division of Health is testing the feasibility of using these
materials for training students in primary care. The production
of training manuals for health promoters and nurse's auxiliaries was
financed by the Family Health Foundation of Tulane University.

At present, two manuals are being prepared for supervisors
to help them oversee immunizations and prenatal observation;
manuals for 11 supervisory activities are planned. These manuals
will guide the supervising nurse in controlling the quality of work
done by health promoters and nurse's auxiliaries. The supervising
nurse also receives special training in management and administration.

Changes in Medical Education

As a result of PRIMOPS, the Curriculum Committee at the
University's Division of Health, along with the Medical Education
Office, has structured substantial curricular changes in the first-
and second-year courses for doctors and for nurses, indicating a
positive feedback into classwork.

Programs in Other Parts of the Country

The Ministry of Health is planning to expand PRIMOPS in
1975 in the city of Cali. It also plans to start similar programs
in four other Colombian cities (Bogotá, Medellín, Barranquilla,
and Bucaramanga) and has accordingly organized a seminar for
health professionals from these cities. As seen above, members
of the University group that designed the program have become
consultants to the Ministry of Health.

Programs in Other Countries

To start PRIMOPS-type programs in other countries, the
Pan American Federation of Faculties of Medicine (FEPAFEM)
sponsored and financed courses of information and basic training
for two small groups of Latin American doctors—the first group
from Paraguay, Peru, Mexico, and Colombia, and the second,
five doctors from Brazil, Peru, and Colombia. While no new
projects grew out of the first course, professionals in the second
group, who spent from July to October 1974 seeing the program in
action, are planning similar projects in their own countries. These
projects were described and discussed in a seminar in Cali in
November 1974, attended by representatives from Brazil, Colombia,

Guatemala, Mexico, and Peru and by officials of various agencies
that sponsor such programs.

Resources and Finances

PRIMOPS was financed during 1971, its first year of operation,
with special funds from the University of Valle and from the Family
Health Foundation of Tulane University. During 1972 and 1973, the
program utilized resources from the University, the Family Health
Foundation, SMS, and the Ministry of Health. The program was
financed during 1974 by the University and the Ministry of Health,
and these agencies have also budgeted funds for its operation during
1975 and 1976. The program is thus assured of support for its basic
operations through 1976 but needs financial assistance for both
internal and external evaluations. Support for internal evaluation
has been requested from the Ford Foundation, but no definite proposals for aid have been submitted for external evaluation.

Assessment of the Program

PRIMOPS contributes to social and economic development in
the following ways:

Defining social needs and problems: PRIMOPS has contributed
a means for applying knowledge to the solution of community health
problems. The program has designed and is implementing a new
model that makes it possible for government to meet more efficiently
the health needs of the low-income population group, especially in
urban areas. Government plans for its expansion illustrate the
multiplier effect of a successful program.

Preparing effective contributors to development: The program
has brought curriculum changes to medical education and to nursing
and community health programs in the Division of Health. It has
also trained and designed materials for training promoters, midwives,
and nurse's auxiliaries for the first levels of community health care.

Strengthening education at other levels: SENA has adopted,
in consultation with PRIMOPS's Human Resources Unit, a new
approach for training nurse's auxiliaries throughout Colombia.

Favorable Conditions and Drawbacks

Directors of the program believe the following factors have
contributed to the program's success:

1. The two-year preliminary study (1971-73) in which planners used the University's experience in Candelaria to define needs and design a program for the Cali area.

2. Helpful and enthusiastic support from the dean of the University's Division of Health, from government officials (such as the mayor of Cali), and from the technical coordinator of the Regional Health Service.

3. The opportunity to test aspects of the model in Candelaria.

4. Favorable acceptance by the community.

5. Close and continuing relationships with government agencies. Directors of the program sought such relationships from the beginning, which have been supported and reinforced by agreements as the program has evolved.

6. A willingness to seek new approaches in the structure of health services, resulting from alarm over high mortality figures in a National Mortality survey, published in 1969.

7. The presence in government offices of University medical school graduates, familiar with and sympathetic to innovative approaches to health problems.

The obstacles initially encountered by the directors of the PRIMOPS program are as follows:

1. Skepticism about how well the Candelaria health services delivery system could be reproduced in different circumstances. The Candelaria study had taken a long time, and a large number of professors and university students and other personnel had been used. It seemed unlikely that the model could be adapted easily to a large urban area. Less emphasis has, in fact, been placed on participation of both community residents and University professors and students.

2. Hostility on the part of government agencies. Agencies feared University dominance but were reassured when the University set forth an agreement favorable to the Municipal Health Service.

3. The lack of financial resources at the University for planning and designing a program of this nature. During 1971, Doctors Alfredo Aguirre and Jaime Rodriguez, the program initiators, were able to give only one-fourth of their time to program planning. Financing from Tulane University made more time available.

4. Lack of community materials on health. Few films, for example, were adapted to the needs and interests of viewers.

Lessons Learned

Health programs should seek to satisfy the needs of the community and at the same time take into account the priorities of

government agencies responsible for services. The program should
be relevant not only to the community but also to the agencies.
PRIMOPS's success is due in part to the way it focused its activities
on an area of great need—low-income mothers and children. It used
the experience acquired in Candelaria to design a model that is likely
to fit other health fields, such as odontology, nutrition, psychiatry,
and internal medicine. Health professionals in these fields are
slowly beginning to test the PRIMOPS system.

A thorough study of the community is essential to the effective
operation of a health services delivery system. There is a dearth
of investigators with adequate technical training in fields such as
social psychology, social anthropology, and urban sociology. Starting
new programs will depend on a better knowledge of community conditions and will require more people who can make such studies. The
preliminary study for PRIMOPS was made by a group of university
researchers.

To persuade teaching staff that the program can be used as an
important adjunct to the regular academic program, project directors
must make efforts to overcome indifference and skepticism. Attitudes
change when the relation of the program to academic learning can be
demonstrated.

The roles of the University and government agencies responsible
for the program should be clearly and legally established from the
beginning. The University group that designed and will evaluate
PRIMOPS and SMS, which serves the Cali community, have worked
out a relationship in which work and responsibilities are clearly
assigned. SMS is responsible for delivering health services, for
personnel training, and for preparing the community to accept the
program. The University evaluates and monitors the service.

Special efforts must be made to enlist community support and
participation. Community organizations must be encouraged to take
part in much of the decision making involved in the health services.

A program benefits from multidisciplinary efforts. Even a
limited program requires a great number of academic, technical,
administrative, and financial resources. As the PRIMOPS program
evolved, the University group sought assistance from other disciplines, such as systems engineering, information sciences, psychological counseling, and evaluation of learning. Faculty members
from other departments of the Division of Health are gradually
initiating activities to strengthen the program in other areas of
health such as psychiatry, surgery, and internal medicine.

Results of the program should be publicized. Change does
not take place automatically. If the University and government
agencies are to make use of the program's results, the program
itself must inform them about the experimental process—what it
demonstrates and how it can be duplicated.

Suggestions for the Program

Expansion and structuring: The program can expand in two
directions: first, in the number of inhabitants served, and second,
in other areas of health. The program at present serves 32,000
persons and plans to serve 90,000. Before expanding this experimental model beyond 90,000 people, it would be useful to (1) further
test and evaluate the model (aid is required for developing a better
evaluation system); (2) develop better communication with the
community (population studies and preparing and organizing audiovisual information would be two useful activities); and (3) experiment
with new classroom practices in the Division of Health in which
students actively participate in the program. PRIMOPS has done
more for structuring health services delivery than for producing
curricular changes in the University.

Replication and adaptation: The directors of the project do
not yet consider the model "scientifically evaluated." The Ministry
of Health and FEPAFEM, however, think an attempt should be made
to repeat the program elsewhere. Success depends largely on the
training offered. Personnel must understand the program and should
receive both theoretical and practical information. Running such a
program also involves a knowledge of behavioral sciences, of social
engineering, of organization and administration, as well as of systems
analysis and information sciences.

The success of new programs will depend on the personnel's
ability to adapt elements of the model to new social and political
conditions. It is advisable therefore not only to train program
directors but also to develop interdisciplinary professional groups
who can assume leadership of the program and assist in its adaptation.

Although the purpose of the program was to design a health
services delivery system, improvement of sanitation, housing,
education, and employment is also necessary to the community's
welfare. These fields could transfer and adapt experience already
acquired in health.

Recommendations for Donor Agencies

1. Education for development programs should have long-
range support, based on broad and flexible criteria. PRIMOPS
is the culmination of more than 15 years of varied experience of
the Division of Health, University of Valle, in the field of preventive
family medicine. After ten years in Candelaria and a pre-PRIMOPS
program in 1967, a group of professionals, working with patience
and enthusiasm to identify needs and resources, planned and imple-

mented PRIMOPS as an urban system model. Both programs and institutions take time to develop.

   2. To promote, foster, and stimulate education for development programs, priority should be given to planning and evaluation methodologies. PRIMOPS has produced some guidelines and has been the starting point for CIMDER. Better program assessment, however, is needed to stimulate more programs.

APPENDIX 20.1

Health Changes in Candelaria

1. Decrease in death rates.
   General death rate from 60.2/1,000 in 1962 to 14/1,000 in 1970 to 7/1,000 in 1972
   Infant death rate from 20.3/1,000 in 1970 to 8/1,000 in 1972
   Death rate in preschool population (1 to 4 years of age) from 18/1,000 in 1970 to 6/1,000 in 1972
2. Decrease of malnutrition in preschool children from 40 percent in 1964 to 22 percent in 1971 and eradication of severe forms (kwashiorkor and marasmus)
3. Disappearance of maternal deaths due to neonatal tetanus
4. Increase in the health coverage of:

		Percent
a. Mothers		
(1) Prenatal supervision		80.0
(2) Childbirth care (in the hospital)		50.0
(3) Postpartum supervision		80.0
b. Children		
(1) Growth and nutrition supervision		95.0
(2) Immunizations		70.0
c. Parents		
(1) Education on family planning		50.0
(2) Utilization of family planning methods		27.0
d. Families		
Medical services are offered to the entire population and are given in accordance with the population's demands.		
e. Sanitation		
(1) Potable water supply in the home		95.0*
(2) Sewage disposal system		95.0

*Ten years ago these figures were only 40 percent.

APPENDIX 20.2

Administrative Organization of the
University of Valle

The University of Valle, like all state universities in Colombia,
has an administrative organization made up of the following:

a. A Board of Trustees, including representatives of the
Government and the Church, as well as directors, teaching staff,
and the student body of the institution. Its main activity is to establish
strategies and policies for relations between the University and the
community.

b. A Board of Directors, composed of the rector, vice-rector,
academic dean, dean of students, deans of the divisions, administrator, and a representative of professors and the student body. The
rector of the University presides.

c. The rector is the highest executive authority of the University and its legal representative. Under the direction of the rector
are:

(1) The vice-rector, who collaborates closely with the rector
in the general administration of the institution. The vice-rector is
also in charge of international relations and coordinates technical
assistance and services to the community.

(2) The Planning and Development Office, which prepares the
programs for development of the University academic, financial,
and physical facilities and helps the various University sectors draw
up and present development projects. This office is in charge of
compiling and analyzing statistical data and also coordinates and
integrates regional, national, and international educational development plans.

(3) The Construction Office, which is in charge of coordinating
and carrying out construction on the University campus.

(4) The Promotion Office, whose main objective is to present
information regarding programs and projects for development and
to attract financial support from regional, national, and foreign
individuals, companies, and agencies.

The units of central academic and administrative direction
are as follows:

a. Office of the Academic Dean. This office coordinates
academic activities and University services. It supervises the
Admissions and Registrar's Offices and the Department of General
Studies, as well as the Committees of Curriculum, Research,

Central Services for Instruction and Library and the Credentials
Committee, which controls the academic level of the teaching staff.

   b. The Dean of Students' Office. The main goal of this office
is to promote the physical, cultural, and economic well-being of
both students and community.

   c. The Comptroller's Office. This office is in charge of
developing the financial activities and policies of the University.
It draws up and manages the budget, pays personnel, maintains
general services and accounting, and establishes policies on systems
and procedures.

   d. The Secretary General assists the rector and is in charge
of authorizing all university documents.

   The University has administrative units in charge of direction
and coordination of teaching, research, and academic activities.
These are divisional councils, deans and associate deans, program
directors, department and section heads.

Academic Organization

   Initially, the University's organization was based on a system
of faculties (schools) that each supported a specific academic program.
In 1959-60 the University planned to diversify and strengthen its
academic areas and levels, and in September 1963, the Board of
Trustees modified the University's Rules and Regulations (Article 17)
to give legal support to the reorganization of the University's
academic-administrative structure. As of September 1, 1963, the
University of Valle established the following divisions: Engineering,
Architecture and Arts, Humanities, Health Sciences, Social and
Economic Sciences, and Education.

   Teaching and research activities carried out in the various
fields are based in the Center for Learning and Documentation,
composed of the Library, the Center of Resources for Teaching,
and the Computing Center.

NOTES

1. Mario Carvajal, University Testimony, University of
Valle Library, 1960.

2. Alfonso Ocampo Londoño, Welcome to Students, 1968.

3. Alfonso Ocampo Londoño, Graduation Speech, 1967-68.

4. Ibid.

21

COLOMBIAN STRUCTURE OF HIGHER EDUCATION

A National Education System Study

INTRODUCTION

There are 39 universities in Colombia, 21 of which are public and 18 private (including Catholic). All but nine of these were founded in the twentieth century in response to the increasing demand for higher education and to the desire of individual states for the prestige of their own universities.

The first university of Colombia was the University of Santo Tomás, established in 1580 and followed by Javeriana University in 1622, the Colegio Mayor de Nuestra Senora del Rosario in 1653, and the Colegio Mayor de San Buenaventura in about 1715. The main function of these early institutions was to train clergy and state officials. After independence, some of the early nineteenth-century colegios were converted to universities and later became the universities of Antioquia, Bogotá, Cartegena, and Cauca. The National University in Bogotá was created in 1867.

The private universities are now located in the four most important cities of Colombia: 76 percent of the students registered at private universities are in Bogotá; 17 percent in Medellín; 5.5 percent in Cali; and 1.5 percent in Barranquilla.

The public university system is decentralized, with a public university located in almost every state capital. The regional distribution, however, is illogical. In the city of Bogotá and the state of Cundinamarca, where 17 percent of the total population of Colombia is concentrated, there are 18 universities, which enroll 55 percent of all university students in Colombia. The population of the states of Antioquia and Chocó, also 17 percent of the Colombian total, has access to only 14 percent of the university places.

This introduction is taken largely from Jaime Rodríguez Forero's article "Universidad y Estructura Socio-económica: El Caso de Colombia," presented at the Latin American Seminar on Latin American University Typological Approaches, 1972 CPU (Santiago, 1973), pp. 218 ff.

Each of the other areas of Colombia has about half the student enrollment justified by its proportion of Colombia's population. In the southeastern part of Colombia, for example (the states of Valle, Cauca, and Nariño), which has 15 percent of the total population, there is a student enrollment of only 7 percent of the total places. For the 14 percent of the population living in the states of Caldas, Risaralda, Quindío, and Tolima, only 8 percent of the total places are available. The 16 percent of the population living in the states of North and South Santander and Boyacá have 7 percent of the available places for university students. Only 6 percent of such places are locally available to the 21 percent of the population living in the northern part of the country.

The direction and curricula of the private universities are determined largely by their constituents, while public universities, national, state, or provincial, are under special regulation. Thus, universities offering similar-sounding professional courses may be widely different. They differ sharply in finance, quality of teaching staff, number of students, and other characteristics. There is no single unified system.

RESEARCH

Most Colombian discussions of higher education refer almost entirely to teaching.[1] In 1968 the Colombian Fund for Scientific Research and Special Projects (COLCIENCIAS) was created as a Ministry of National Education dependency to provide services required by national scientific and technological research. It has carried out a number of studies defining the university's role in national research. At the International Seminar on Scientific and Technological Policy, in Madrid, July 1974, COLCIENCIAS presented a diagnostic summary of the institutional structure of research and of the activities and resources of the national science-technology system.[2] The summary is excerpted below.

Institutional Structure of Research in Colombia

The science-technology system is defined as "a wide system of interrelated institutions and a community of scientists and technologists, involved mainly in the generation, transmission, dissemination, and application or utilization of knowledge." The system involves institutions in the following sectors:

1. Government: state or national institutions concerned with generation, spread, importation, or application of knowledge.

2. University or higher education: public and private institutions.

3. Industry: public and private.

4. Private research: profit or nonprofit, including research centers, consultative groups, and design and engineering services.

The national research structure is made up mainly of decentralized institutes annexed to different ministries. Research activity in universities and in industry is very limited. Although government absorbs almost half (47.9 percent) of the funds spent on research in Colombia (see Table 21.1), there is no central mechanism to coordinate the allocation of governmental funds for research and for other science activities. In other words, there is no unified national budget for activities in science and technology, nor an institutional mechanism or formal procedure to analyze, evaluate, approve, or modify this budget.

Activities and Resources of the
Science-Technology System

To assist in planning the development of science and technology, COLCIENCIAS took an inventory of current research projects as well

TABLE 21.1

Financial and Human Resources Dedicated to
Research by Sector, 1971

| Area | Financial Resources | | Human Resources | |
	Thousands of Pesos	Percent	Number	Percent
Government	123,727	47.9	584	51.2
Public education	45,727	17.7	0	0.0
Private education	13,542	5.2	0	0.0
Total education*	0	0.0	285	25.0
Industry	51,348	19.9	239	20.9
Nonprofit	24,025	9.3	32	2.9
Total	258,369	100.0	1,140	100.0

*This figure refers to the public and private education sector.

Source: Inventory of the Science-Technology System in Colombia, COLCIENCIAS, 1971.

TABLE 21.2

Financial and Human Resources for Different Science Activities, 1971

Scientific Activities	Financial Resources		Human Resources	
	Thousands of Pesos	Percent	Number	Percent
Research	258,369	12.9	1,140	10.5
Dissemination and extension	251,471	12.6	417	3.8
Support activities	465,290	23.3	2,015	18.6
Higher and technological education	1,023,772	51.2	7,294	67.1
Total	1,998,902	100.0	10,866	100.0

Source: Inventory of the Science-Technology System in Colombia, COLCIENCIAS, 1971.

as of the financial, human, and institutional resources within the country dedicated to science activities. The inventory included the following categories of activities: research, dissemination and extension, support activities, and higher and technical education. As can be seen in Table 21.2, teaching and support activities absorb most of the financial and human resources; research and dissemination occupy secondary positions.

The research situation in science and technology can be summarized as follows (1971 data): Total expenses for research—$258,369,000; total number of researchers or professionals whose main task is research—1,140; total number of current research projects—991.

These figures indicate that Colombia is investing only 0.2 percent of the GNP in research activities. (See Table 21.3 for comparisons with other countries.) In addition, the 1,140 professionals who carry out research activities in Colombia represent approximately one researcher for each 20,000 inhabitants, a very low figure compared with other countries.

The data in Table 21.1 and an analysis of the condition of many research centers and institutes reveal two handicaps to research efforts in science and technology. First, most activities are limited to pure research, with little emphasis on technology, and seldom lead to new procedures or industrial products. Such research shows a lack of coordination between the science-technology system and industry (see Table 21.3). Second, there are very

TABLE 21.3

Relation between Research Expenses and
Gross National Product in Several Countries

Country	Year	Research Expenses as Percent of GNP
United States	1966	3.0
Union of Soviet Socialist Republics, (USSR)	1967	2.7
Czechoslovakia	1967	2.7
Great Britain	1967	2.3
Netherlands	1967	2.3
France	1967	2.2
West Germany	1967	1.9
Hungary	1967	1.7
Japan	1967	1.5
Canada	1967	1.5
Sweden	1967	1.4
Poland	1967	1.4
Denmark	1967	0.7
Italy	1967	0.7
Argentina	1968	0.28
Trinidad	1970	0.24
Paraguay	1971	0.22
Spain	1971	0.20
Colombia	1971	0.20
Dominican Republic	1972	0.12
Jamaica	1971	0.10

Source: Inventory of the Science-Technology System in Colombia, COLCIENCIAS, 1971.

limited resources available for extension and dissemination of results. Here too there is little coordination between research and its potential users.

According to an analysis of research in Colombia (see Tables 21.3 and 21.4) the government finances 47.9 percent of the research and employs 51.2 percent of the researchers. If all publicly financed universities are included in this figure, government supplies 65.6 percent of all funds for research and technology.

Agriculture and livestock sciences take 32.7 percent of the funds available for research and 30.5 percent of the researchers (see Table 21.4). The field of health sciences occupies second

TABLE 21.4

Financial and Human Resources and Research Projects
by Area of Science, 1971

Area of Science	Financial Resources		Human Resources		Research Projects	
	Thousands of Pesos	Percent	Number	Percent	Number	Percent
Basic sciences	61,233	23.7	188	16.5	180	17.5
Engineering sciences	6,459	2.5	154	13.5	82	8.3
Health sciences	60,200	23.3	127	11.2	284	28.7
Agriculture and livestock sciences	84,487	32.7	348	30.5	209	21.7
Social sciences	45,990	17.8	323	28.3	236	23.8
Total	258,369	100.0	1,140	100.0	991	100.0

Source: Inventory of the Science-Technology System in Colombia, COLCIENCIAS, 1971.

place; engineering has only 13.5 percent of the human resources and 2.5 percent of the funds.

A recent study[3] showed that the research in Colombia often has little relation to the country's problems and development objectives. It is important to determine the science and technology needs of the country in order to establish a national development policy.

In summary, the science-technology system of Colombia seems to be characterized by the following weaknesses: (1) limited financial and human resources assigned to research; (2) a high concentration of research activities in the government or public sector; (3) a lack of coordination between science and technology research and industrial users; (4) too little emphasis on extension and dissemination activities, limiting the use of research results; and (5) a lack of relationship between research activities and the demands and objectives of national development.

Resources and Science Activities in the Educational Sector

Following this general look at the national science-technology system, we shall see how it operates within the university. Table 21.5 indicates human resources assigned to science activities in 1971.

It is clear that most university personnel working in the field of science (94.8 percent) spend their time in teaching. Only 3.8 percent of the science personnel do any research. These figures point up a characteristic of higher education in Colombia: The strong emphasis on teaching to the detriment of research.

The distribution of financial resources also bears out this picture (see Table 21.6). An analysis of both financial and human resources shows how little value the university places on research.

Dissemination and support activities for research, such as statistics and quality control, also have an insignificant place within the university. The figures show that the limited university research remains largely within the institution; the ensuing results are not disclosed. The university appears to confirm its ivory tower image by ignoring national problems and showing little interest in a search for scientific and technical solutions to these problems. It would be unfair, however, to ignore the efforts of individual scientists who take time from their teaching activities to carry out research. Teaching loads, especially for full-time professors, are usually very heavy.

The inventory made by COLCIENCIAS in 1971 revealed a total of 991 financed research projects, distributed as follows:

TABLE 21.5

University Personnel Who Spend Their Time
in Scientific Pursuits, 1971

Activity	Number	Percent
Research	285	3.8
Teaching	7,082	94.8
Dissemination	17	0.2
Support activities	85	1.2
Total	7,469	100.0

Source: Inventory of the Science-Technology System in
Colombia, COLCIENCIAS, 1971.

TABLE 21.6

Financial Resources Available for
Science Activities, 1971
(educational sector)

Scientific Activities	Assigned in U.S. $	Percent
Research	2,834,482	5.5
Teaching	45,224,581	87.4
Diffusion (publication)	2,486,035	4.3
Support activities	1,031,277	1.5
Total	51,576,375	100.0

Source: Inventory of the Science-Technology System in
Colombia, COLCIENCIAS, 1971.

1. Government: 177 projects (22.2 percent) carried out by
16 agencies (38 percent).
2. Education: 586 projects (57.5 percent) carried out by
28 universities (37 percent).
3. Industry: 170 projects (13.7 percent) carried out by 21
organizations (18 percent).
4. Nonprofit organizations: 58 projects (6.6 percent) carried
out by three institutions (7 percent).

At first glance the results appear to contradict earlier data;
more projects were carried out in 1971 within educational institutions
than within government, industry, or nonprofit institutions. These

data reflect a major university effort to increase the number of research projects. Nevertheless, the above university projects represent a lower percentage of the total cost of research (22.9 percent) than do those in the government sector (47.9 percent).

These two indicators show that research activities within the university, with the exception of health, are carried out individually without the decisive institutional support that would permit research to become a basic function of the university. Health, as we shall see, has special community-research bonds. Table 21.7 shows the distribution of projects by areas of science and their cost.

Health sciences account for more than 50 percent of university research, in number of projects as well as their cost, followed by basic sciences (19 percent). There is so little research done in agriculture, livestock, and engineering sciences that it cannot have much effect on national development.

Research in health sciences has flourished, probably because universities have established close ties with the community through university hospitals. This continuous contact makes researchers and health workers aware of community health needs and wishes. The university is thus under pressure to develop major research activities that meet the community's health problems more effectively.

The organization of the medical schools at a national level has also stimulated the development of health research and teaching and their application within the community. The Colombian Association of Medical Faculties (ASCOFAME) encourages good relationships among the different faculties and between the faculties and other

TABLE 21.7

Research Projects and Their Cost by
Area of Science, 1971
(educational sector)

Area of Science	Projects	Percent	Cost	Percent
Basic sciences	100	18.9	19,711	14.7
Engineering	65	12.3	8,484	6.3
Health	213	40.3	66,851	49.8
Agriculture and livestock	32	6.0	16,142	12.0
Social	115	21.7	22,275	16.6
Total	525	100.0	133,463	100.0

Source: Inventory of the Science-Technology System in Colombia, COLCIENCIAS, 1971.

sectors, especially government, through the National Ministry of Public Health and the state and municipal secretaries of public health.

In social sciences, several hypotheses explain the scarcity of relevant research.[4] In the first place, social sciences suffer from the negative attitude of Colombian universities in general toward social science research. Their image as a "subversive force" makes it especially difficult for social sciences to obtain funds from national or international agencies. In addition, there is a shortage of trained personnel, especially in the area of scientific methodology; disciplines such as sociology, anthropology, human geography, and history are relatively new in Colombia* and require comparatively long training. Best supplied is economics, where most research projects are feasibility studies.

Most agricultural and livestock research is being carried out by the government,† principally through the Colombian Agricultural and Livestock Institute (ICA)‡ and through industrial associations such as those of coffee and cotton growers. Here government and private activity has taken the place of university research. In basic sciences, university research is very limited.

Only a university reform in which research becomes considerably more important and more linked to national problems could transform the university into a true agency for development. One step would be strengthening postgraduate programs. In other countries, university research has developed alongside postgraduate studies and appears to have a close connection to postgraduate programs. In the following section we will refer to the present situation of postgraduate studies in Colombia and their influence on institutional research capacity.

TEACHING

In the past few years, the number of institutions of higher education has grown enormously: a university has been established

---

*The National University founded the first department of sociology in 1959.

†Approximately 80 percent of the research carried out by the government is in agriculture and livestock. (Inventory of the Science-Technology System in Colombia, COLCIENCIAS, 1971.)

‡ICA's budget increased from $112,894,000 in 1967 to $774,622,000 in 1974. During 1975, it suffered a considerable decrease (to $506,632,000) because of a reduction in the government budget for that year.

in practically every state. As Rama demonstrated in his analysis
of the Colombian university system,[5] this increase of institutions
is due not only to the pressure of demand but also to each state's
competitive drive to establish its own university.

The proliferation of universities would not be so bad if each
one met the basic requirements for an institution of higher education.
The new universities, however, like most older ones in Colombia,
lack research activity and extension services. They are devoted
almost entirely to teaching, with little research to assure standards
of quality.

Capacity and Expansion of Enrollment in Higher Education

There have been private and governmental efforts to deal with
the increase in enrollment in Colombian higher education (see
Tables 21.8 and 21.9). In our opinion, however, the great demand
for higher education cannot be met within the traditional teaching
framework, no matter what efforts are made. Rather, the number
of students requesting admission to the university will continue to
increase faster than the number admitted.

The reasons for this increase are summarized by Rama as
follows: growth of the school-age population; structural changes
in Colombian society, particularly urbanization; changes in the
areas of study that most attract student interest; and the pressure
of the middle class to achieve social mobility through education.[6]
To the factors listed by Rama, we should add the demand by more
women for higher education as a step to their integration into economic
and social life. Table 21.10 shows the increasing percentage of
women's enrollment. The proportion of women is expected to increase
further in the next few years. These social forces can only be
reconciled with university quality through dynamic and innovative
educational action.

Teaching Staff and Professor-Student Ratio

To solve the problem of academic quality, universities have
made an effort to increase their full-time teaching staff and decrease
the number of part-time professors, although such a move increases
the cost of education. Characteristic of the 1960s, this effort was
more noticeable in the public universities than it was in the private
ones.[7]

TABLE 21.8

Growth of Higher Education Enrollment

Year	1935	1945	1955	1960	1965	1968	1970
Enrollment	4,137	6,512	13,284	23,787	44,817	60,325	85,560
Growth index	100	157.4	321.1	575.0	1,083.3	1,458.2	2,068.2

Source: University Fund: Basic Statistics 1966; DANE: Statistics Year Book (of the respective years); from Germán Rama, "El Sistema Universitaria en Colombia" (Bogota: National University, 1970), p. 29.

TABLE 21.9

Difference between Applications and Available Places in Universities

Years	Applicants	Qualified Applicants	Places Available	Differences Between Number of Applicants and Places Available	
				Number	Percent
1960	14,968	10,691	8,809	1,882	17.6
1961	16,458	11,755	9,702	2,053	17.5
1962	19,361	13,829	11,322	2,507	18.1
1963	23,004	16,431	12,441	3,990	24.2
1964	23,411	16,722	13,061	3,661	21.8
1965	30,729	21,949	16,372	5,577	25.4
1966	36,415	26,010	19,496	6,514	25.0
1967	41,061	29,329	23,758	5,571	18.9
1968	47,605	34,003	24,783	9,220	17.8
1969	53,063	37,902	29,070	8,832	23.3
1970	54,538	38,955	30,491	8,464	21.7

Source: ICFES, Planning Office–Statistics Section, 1960–70.

TABLE 21.10

Distribution of Higher Education Enrollment by Sex

Years	Male	Percent	Female	Percent	Total
1960	18,174	88.3	2,408	11.7	20,582
1961	21,227	87.1	3,140	12.9	24,367
1962	23,463	85.9	3,867	14.1	27,330
1963	25,514	84.8	4,568	15.2	30,082
1964	27,910	83.5	5,511	16.5	33,421
1965	31,754	83.4	6,316	16.6	38,070
1966	36,211	78.6	9,837	21.4	46,048
1967	40,826	78.8	10,836	21.2	51,122
1968	44,822	78.4	12,376	21.6	57,198
1969	49,872	78.2	13,871	21.8	63,743
1970	55,495	78.1	15,563	21.9	71,058

Source: DANE: Statistics Year Books (of the respective years). From: COLCIENCIAS, "Oferta de Egresados de la Educación media, Superior y de Post-grado en Colombia" (Bogotá: Unit of Human Resources, 1972), p. 86.

TABLE 21.11

Teaching Staff by Teaching Category and Type of University
(in percent)

Teaching Category	Public Institutions			Private Institutions			Total		
	1960	1966	1970	1960	1966	1970	1960	1966	1970
Full-time	29.1	50.5	56.7	4.7	13.6	16.6	20.4	36.8	40.9
Half-time	17.3	14.2	15.6	19.7	17.5	17.0	18.2	15.5	16.4
Part-time or hourly	53.5	35.2	27.4	75.5	68.9	66.2	61.4	47.8	42.7
Total percent	100.0	100.0	100.0	100.0	100.0	100.0	100.0	100.0	100.0
Total number	2,523	4,681	5,009	1,418	2,795	3,257	3,941	7,476	8,266

Source: ICFES, Planning Office.

While the total number of professors doubled during the last decade, the number of students has quadrupled. The professor-student ratio, therefore, and probably academic quality, has been gradually deteriorating, especially in private universities. In 1970, slightly more than half the teaching staff in public universities devoted "full time" to the institution while in private universities only about 17 percent did so. Full-time teaching staff in private universities (541 staff members) constituted only 16 percent of the country's full-time staff (3,800 staff members) (see Table 21.11) although private student enrollment was about 40 percent of the total student enrollment of the country.[8] At public universities the student/professor ratio in 1970 was 13 to one; at private universities it was 28 to one.

The terms "full-time" and "part-time" need further explanation. Renner[9] points out that

> full-time (tiempo completo) means that a teacher may lecture in several institutions and also practice his profession. Another term, dedicación exclusive, is used to mean that a teacher works exclusively at a particular university. Of the 1,049 professors listed in major categories at National University in 1967, for example, 42.2 percent were dedicación exclusive, 9.9 percent were tiempo completo, 13.8 percent were half-time, and 32.7 percent were part-time.

Full-time does not mean that the university professor spends all, or even most, of his time in academic activities.

If teaching quality suffers from increased numbers of students, higher education faces a dilemma: increase enrollment and impair teaching quality or improve academic quality and cut down enrollment. A search must be made for ways to meet, with high educational standards, the increasing demand for higher education.

Postgraduate Studies

Postgraduate programs in science, with the exception of the health sciences, were established in Colombia in the 1960s, beginning in 1962 with the creation of the biology "magister" (master) program at the University of the Andes. Thirty science programs, including 18 medical specialties at the National University, were established in 1968, and most of the others began between 1968 and 1970.

In 1970, the distribution of postgraduate science studies in Colombia was as follows:[10]

Area of Science	Number of Programs
Physical and natural sciences	14
Engineering sciences	9
Health sciences	46
Agriculture and livestock sciences	3
Social sciences	14
Total	86

Noteworthy are the large number of health science programs and the small number of agriculture and livestock programs.

The distribution of these programs by cities and universities in 1970 was as follows:

	Medical Programs	Other Programs	Total Programs
Bogotá			
National University	18	9	27
Javeriana University	9	1	10
Los Andes University		7	7
América University		1	1
Caro y Cuervo Institute		2	2
Advanced School of Public Administration		2	2
Subtotal	27	22	49
Cali			
University of Valle	13	16	29
Subtotal	13	16	29
Medellín			
University of Antioquia	5	1	6
National University		2	2
Subtotal	5	3	8
Bucaramanga			
Industrial University of Santander		1	1
Total	45	42	87

It is apparent that 77 of the total 86 postgraduate programs are concentrated in five universities: National University in Bogotá, University of Valle in Cali, Javeriana and Los Andes Universities in Bogotá, and Antioquia University in Medellín.

Table 21.12 shows the distribution of research projects by institutions where they are being carried out and by fields of their application, health, agriculture and livestock, for instance. Only those institutions carrying out at least 20 projects have been included.

TABLE 21.12

Research Projects by Institutions Where They
Are Being Carried out and by Field
of Application

Institutions	Total Number of Projects	Fields of Application		
		Agriculture and Livestock	Health	Other
University of Antioquia	134	2	110	22
University of Valle	116	12	56	48
National Federation of Coffee Growers	86	86	–	–
University of Los Andes	46	–	12	34
National University (Bogotá)	66	19	18	29
International Centre for Tropical Agriculture (CIAT)	46	46	–	–
Colombian Agriculture and Livestock Institute (ICA)	43	43	–	–
National Institute of Cancer	32	–	32	–
Pedagogical and Techno- logical University of Tunja	27	–	2	25
Javeriana University	26	3	19	4
National Federation of Cotton Growers	23	23	–	–
IMPES	20	–	19	1
Total	665	234	268	163

Source: Inventory of the Science-Technology System in Colombia,
COLCIENCIAS, 1971.

From an analysis of the foregoing information, there appears
to be a close correlation between university postgraduate programs
and university research. In the first place, the universities of
Antioquia, Valle, Los Andes, Javeriana, and the National University
in Bogotá, which have the greatest concentration of postgraduate
programs, 77 out of 86 throughout Colombia, show a major capacity
for research (388 projects out of a countrywide total of 665). Only

the Pedagogical and Technological University of Tunja shows a
relatively large number of research programs without a corresponding emphasis on postgraduate study. It would be interesting to find
out why.

In the second place, most of the research activity in Colombia
(74 percent) is in either health or agriculture and livestock. More
than half of all university postgraduate science programs in Colombia
are in health; Colombian universities do 80 percent of all research
in health sciences (217 out of 268 projects). (The remaining 20 percent is carried out by government institutes established for that
purpose.) On the other hand, universities have almost no graduate
programs in agriculture and livestock (there are only three programs
throughout Colombia) and do only 15.3 percent of the applied research
in agriculture and livestock; most such research is done by government and industry.

Perhaps one reason universities concentrate on health—in both
research and graduate programs—rather than on agriculture and
livestock is that university medical schools, associated with government through university hospitals, are encouraged by community
needs to provide good research and teaching, as well as extension
activity, referred to in the next section. There has been no similar
point of contact with agriculture and livestock concerns.

EXTENSION AND/OR SERVICE

University extension permits the university to establish
contact with the society of which it is a part and to confront theory
with practice. Specific extension objectives can be listed as follows:

1. Apply the results of research to the solution of development problems.
2. Use research results as a basis for teaching, especially
in professional (technical) or scientific training programs.*
3. Disseminate knowledge and culture and also draw on the
knowledge and culture of the community.

---

*Innovative teaching techniques and methods, including open
university, university at a distance, and mass education programs,
are presently also considered part of extension. In the future,
when higher education modifies its traditional framework to meet
the demands of the increasing percentage of the population who wish
to receive advanced education, it should be considered part of the
formal teaching of the university.

These three objectives are directly related to the research, teaching, and cultural roles of the university. The first objective involves the explicit organization of the university for research, usually through research institutes or other research units established for this purpose. In some instances, professors and students volunteer technical assistance to the community.

The second objective assumes an intimate relationship among research, teaching, and extension. Students receiving professional or technical training benefit from seeing research in action, learning to apply knowledge and skills in response to needs in situations such as dental and medical clinics. In science training, activities such as theses, honors papers, and research projects help relate practice to theory. Usually these projects are required at a postgraduate level (master's or Ph.D.), but in many universities they are also required for professional (first) degrees.

The third objective refers to cultural dissemination such as concerts organized by a university's department of music, or informal activities such as photography or film clubs. It can also include community workshops and discussion groups in which art, music, or cultural skills and knowledge are shared with university personnel.

Extension Structure

University extension programs take several different forms. Some, such as special research or a university-supported dental clinic, are sponsored solely by the university. Some are carried out in conjunction with other educational institutions (for example two or more universities), and some are carried out in collaboration with government or with industry, jointly or separately. In still other programs, institutions in another country may work with Colombian institutions toward common or regional interests.

In this analysis of the extension activities of the Colombian university system, we did not have available systematically collected data from COLCIENCIAS and ICFES as we did in the cases of research and teaching activities. Brief visits were thus made to some universities to collect information, although limited time and administrative difficulties[11] prevented putting together a truly representative research sample. The results should thus be taken more as an illustration of the problem than as an exact diagnosis of the condition of Colombian higher education. We believe, nevertheless, that the information accurately reflects the national situation.

Application of Research Results

The university applies the results of research—the first objective of extension—largely through agencies established for this purpose. A brief description of the main national research agencies follows:

Center of Research for Development (CID) National University in Bogotá:[12] Established by the National University's (Bogotá) board of trustees by Agreement no. 47 of 1966, the center's main objective is "to promote, coordinate, and apply the work carried out at the university to improve Colombian society." Its functions are to stimulate and carry out research projects related to Colombian development; publish the results of the research; contribute, with the consent of the University faculties, to orienting their professional training toward specific development problems; collaborate with branches of the Colombian government in training public sector personnel in the field of development; prepare teaching materials on aspects of national development; and coordinate the efforts made by national and international organizations interested in Colombian development.

CID's financial resources come from three sources: the University's general funds, income from contracts carried out by CID, and grants. It has been able to carry out its graduate program in education through scholarships awarded by the Institute of International Education (16 person-years at a cost of U.S. $8,000 each, for a total of U.S. $128,000) and through the assistance of Ford Foundation visiting professors.

Although there were initial disagreements regarding the formulation of objectives, CID has carried out and published research in a variety of areas, including urban studies, industrial studies, income distribution, economic theory, foreign trade, political science, agrarian studies, regional studies, and social studies. A CID library, open to the public, distributes its publications.

Division of Research, Industrial University of Santander (UIS):[13] This division was established on June 9, 1958 by Agreement no. 35 of the board of trustees of the University and was restructured in 1974. Its main objectives are to promote and stimulate research incentive within the University in an attempt to achieve a high scientific level and establish a basic structure for technological development; and promote adequate utilization of human resources and technical equipment of the University in order to contribute to the integrated development of the state of Santander and of the country.

The Division of Research is directed by a dean's office and is administered by three departments: Socioeconomic Studies, Design and Engineering, and Industrial Consulting. It also includes four coordinating and consulting units: the Division Council, the Internal Consulting Committee, the External Consulting Group, and the Graduation Projects and Postgraduate Thesis Committee.

The division's projects include food technology, wood technology, petroleum technology, metal technology, paper technology, energy resources, pollution, soil technology, construction technology, technical assistance in mining, and consulting services for small- and medium-sized industry. The division is financed by funds from the University and by those generated by research projects carried out under contract. It seeks principally to secure total financing of its faculty.

University of Los Andes Research Committee: This committee was established by the rector of the University through Resolution no. 8, dated September 26, 1968. Its functions are to formulate suggestions regarding the University's research policy; promote pure and applied research activities; contribute to the coordination of projects and research activities; keep faculty members informed of actual research projects and of existing possibilities in the field of research; and serve as liaison between the universities and the agencies that sponsor and finance research within the country.

The Research Committee is composed of the rector and selected members of the full-time teaching staff. During 1971, it established the General Fund for Research for the purpose of administering financial resources, elaborating research proposals, preparing articles or reports based on unpublished research, and carrying out small projects that lack financial support. Since 1971, the fund has financed more than 55 research projects.

The committee also publishes summaries of student theses and, as an incentive to further student research, offers financial support to students working as research assistants. The committee's close relations with COLCIENCIAS have been of great help in carrying out a number of research projects.

Faculty of Interdisciplinary Studies, Javerian/University:14 This faculty was established at the end of 1973 to interrelate common areas of knowledge, to organize groups of professors and students for integrated professional and personal training, to organize the curricula leading to degrees, and, particularly, to integrate the teaching, research, and service functions of the University. Its main objectives are to carry out research, develop an interdisciplinary work methodology, and promote the effective integration of the sciences; plan and carry out interdisciplinary research programs (many studies, if carried out in only one faculty, suffer departmental

biases; for example, population studies carried out by only the
Faculty of Medicine sometimes lean too heavily to health statistics,
disregarding perhaps problems of migration and job occupation;
the Faculty of Architecture, on the other hand, might emphasize only
migration, or the Faculty of Economics might be concerned only with
occupation); plan and carry out interdisciplinary programs leading
to degrees not otherwise included in any particular faculty; promote
continuing education programs, especially those of an interdisciplinary nature, not included in any one faculty; promote and maintain
relationships with other institutions, public and private, in order
to carry out coordinated research projects and secure the necessary
financial support for them; and collaborate with other faculties of
the University in the promotion, organization, and development of
postgraduate or continuing education research programs.

The Faculty of Interdisciplinary Studies plans the following
academic units: Health, including preventive medicine; Education,
including not primarily pedagogy but rather the problems of general
acculturation; Basic Environmental Sciences, Planning, and Administration; Theology, as a factor in the development of man and society;
Human and Social Sciences, not only as professional subjects but
also as a basis for other university programs; Judicial Sciences;
and Natural and Mathematical Sciences. These units are academic
rather than bureaucratic and will provide the basis for the divisions
of the University. Initial programs of the interdisciplinary faculty
will be political studies, integrated study on population, economics
and human resources, educational research and technology, and
urban studies.

Socioeconomic Research Center, University of Antioquia:[15]
This center was established in 1959 as an annex to the Faculty of
Economics. In 1962, it became a special program of the University.
Its main projects have been: Employment in the state of Antioquia;
Transportation in the state of Antioquia; Property, Industrial, and
Commercial Taxes in the city of Medellín; Formation of Capital
and Increase of Savings, in conjunction with the Bank of the Republic;
Establishment of Rates for Transportation, under a contract with
the National Institute of Transport (INTRA); Regional Accounting;
Enlargement of the Agricultural and Livestock Sample of 1974, in
collaboration with the state of Antioquia (State Planning Office and
Secretary of Agriculture).

Educational Research Center (CIED) of University of
Antioquia:[16] The Educational Research Center, part of the University's faculty of education, is oriented to socioeducational research
and educational technology. The technology grows out of the research
and involves applying knowledge to achieve a more dynamic and
effective educational system. CIED seeks to change teaching into

a continuing research process and to present mechanisms that permit teaching, research, and administrative functions to blend into a teaching-research activity.

CIED focuses its action on the Colombian educational system and encourages innovations meeting the specific needs of society. Its objectives are to carry out continued multidisciplinary research projects that can be utilized as the basis for teaching at all levels of the Colombian educational system and to establish policies for planning and executing these projects; carry out socioeducational research contracted by the University; operate the Center for Documentation and Classification of Information; promote the development of modern theories of education; and evaluate, periodically, faculty programs.

The research units described are those that most frequently carry out research for development. Other universities, however, do additional isolated research, depending mostly on their different faculties or departments. At the University of Valle, for example, most research programs depend on, or are at least closely related to, the Division of Health Sciences.

Most extension research projects are carried out by the institutes described or by technical faculties such as veterinary medicine, animal husbandry, agronomy, or economics. In general, the faculties of medicine or divisions of health have traditionally done applied research through their university hospitals. Universities offering degrees in a specific technical area, moreover, such as the Industrial University of Santander, usually have more extension programs than do those universities that offer degrees mainly in humanities. Finally, although most extension programs are based on research, research does not, therefore, receive priority within the higher education for development structure.

Application of Teaching Results

A great number of extension projects and programs involve teaching. Two types of programs can be mentioned here: traditional programs, which offer teaching only through special courses at the undergraduate or postgraduate levels, and programs that test innovative educational techniques at different levels, such as the project on Flexible Schooling at the University of Antioquia; the Open University Program at the Technological University of Pereira; the Center for Design and Production of Educational Materials at Cauca University; and Education at a Distance at Javeriana University. Although these latter projects are new and experimental, all of them tend to become educational extension programs.

Special emphasis should be placed on the importance of projects that seek innovative techniques to improve university teaching. As mentioned before, the increasing demand for higher education can only be met as the university applies its capabilities to this end. At the same time, the university can gradually focus more attention on research once teaching achieves better results for more students at a lower cost.

Community Recreation Through Cultural Dissemination

There are only a few cultural dissemination programs at Colombian universities. For example, the three cultural programs we found at the National University consisted of presentations of artistic groups that did not belong to the University (Symphonic Orchestra of Colombia, Philharmonic Orchestra of Bogotá, and presentations of the Colombian-German Cultural Institute).

Apparently the Colombian university is not convinced of the importance of art as creative expression and of its influence on society. If Colombian society does not consider artistic activity important enough to be included in university programs, it is proof that it views the university as "imitative" rather than as "creative." University theater groups, musical groups, and arts exhibits are considered extracurricular activities and receive only paternalistic support from the university administration.

In conclusion, it is clear that the university is facing a crucial phase in defining its role in society. University reforms already carried out have, in most instances, been limited to meeting the quantitative demand for higher education, and have ignored the basic problem of quality, which, in essence, defines the university as an educational institution. The university system needs reforms in the quality as well as quantity of its education. Higher education in Colombia continues to revolve around teaching activity, and until this framework is reformed, the university cannot improve its product.

How to meet the needs of both quality and quantity is the great challenge facing higher education for development and those societies which wish to become more independent. Higher education could begin by reforming and reinforcing the creative sector of these societies. The country will begin to develop as educational reforms gradually make it possible to understand and overcome underdevelopment.

NOTES

1. Note in particular: Alberto Alvarado and Eduardo Carras-
quilla, "Análisis de la Educación en Colombia" (Bogotá: CIAS, 1969);
Germán Rama, "El Sistema Universitario en Colombia" (Bogotá:
National University, 1970); COLCIENCIAS, "Oferta de Egresados
de la Educación media, Superior y de Post-grado en Colombia"
(Bogotá: Unit of Human Resources, 1972); ICFES, "Estadisticas
sobre la Educación Superior," 1973.
2. COLCIENCIAS, "Visión del Desarrollo Científico y
Tecnológico de Colombia," Document presented at the Seminar
on Scientific and Technological Policy, Madrid, Spain (Bogotá:
D.E., 1974), pp. 10 ff.
3. Pedro José Amaya, Juan Carlos Gamba, and Milciades
Chaves, "Un Enfoque para el Diagnóstico de la Situación Científico-
Tecnológica a Nivel Nacional: Estudio del Caso Colombiano,"
Bogotá, COLCIENCIAS, Study Series no. 9, 1972.
4. COLCIENCIAS has underway a study of social science
research, but results have not yet been published.
5. Rama, "El Sistema Universitario en Colombia," p. 46.
6. Ibid., p. 30.
7. COLCIENCIAS, "Oferta de Egresados," p. 106.
8. Richard R. Renner, Education for a New Colombia
(Washington, D.C.: U.S. Government Printing Office, 1971), p. 106.
9. Ibid., p. 121.
10. Based on ICFES information.
11. The visits were made in September and October 1974,
at which time changes in administrative personnel at the universities
caused serious difficulties in collecting data.
12. Description taken from Jaime Rodriguez-Forero,
"Universidad y Sistema Cientifico-Tecnologico de Colombia," in
University and Andean Integration, Part Two (Santiago: CPU,
June 1974), p. 163.
13. Information provided by Dr. Jorge Bautista, dean of the
Division of Research of UIS, November 1974.
14. Information provided by Dr. Agustin Lombana, academic
dean of the Faculty of Interdisciplinary Studies, November 1974.
15. Information provided by Dr. Luis Carlos Uribe Correa,
Dean of the Faculty of Economics, Medellín, October 1974.
16. Information taken from the "CEDED Informa" Bulletin,
Educational Documentation Center, Faculty of Education, Antioquia
University, no. 1, August 1974.

22

MONTERREY INSTITUTE OF TECHNOLOGY AND
ADVANCED STUDIES, MONTERREY, MEXICO

Research and Extension Program for Industrial
Development

In 1943, a group of Monterrey industrialists, bankers, and
businessmen agreed that the city's industrial growth required more
technical and professional manpower. After unsuccessful attempts
to enlist the support of the state ministry of higher public education,
they formed a private, nonprofit civic association, which they called
Higher Education and Research, and decided to found and operate a
center for technical education. Their institute was to have high
academic standards and would foster science and technology as well
as national culture and traditional values. Its goal would be to train
professionals with a clear sense of their personal dignity and social
responsibility.

Thus was born the Monterrey Institute of Technology and
Advanced Studies (ITESM), which has a present enrollment of more
than 12,000 students and which has continued to be encouraged and
supported by the business community which established it. It has
remained a private, nonprofit institution for higher education,
largely dependent on tuition (for 65 percent of its funds) and on gifts
from business and industry.

Objectives

Its goals are academic, independent of political, ideological,
or religious affiliation. It is oriented to the training of leaders,
attempting to create a particular attitude toward academic excellence,
self-learning, work, and responsibility for solving national problems.
It seeks to produce professionals, researchers, and university
professors; to provide technical education at the preparatory school
level (following the first three years of high school); to organize
and conduct research; to spread culture and its benefits and thereby
contribute to the country's development; and to carry out any other
activities that improve the training of its students. The Institute
offers 29 professional degrees, 13 master's degrees, and one
Ph.D. degree. About half the student body is registered for technical training at the preparatory school level.

Organization

At present, the Institute has branches in eight cities. In Monterrey, the main site, it has an academic campus with classrooms, workshops, student housing, and recreation and sports facilities, which includes a Division of Administration and Social Sciences (four departments) offering five professional degrees; a Division of Engineering and Architecture (seven departments) awarding nine degrees; a Division of Agricultural, Animal, and Marine Sciences (six departments) offering four professional degrees; a Division of Sciences and Humanities (five departments) offering ten professional degrees; and a preparatory school with three branches: an annex school, three technical preparatory programs, and an open preparatory program.

In Mexicali it runs a preparatory program and an engineering school. In Guaymas there is a preparatory program and a professional school specializing in marine sciences. In Ciudad Obregón it has a preparatory program and a professional school of agriculture. In Querétaro it operates a preparatory program and a professional school of engineering (two years), agronomy, and administration. In Saltillo there is a preparatory program and graduate program in administration. In San Luis Potosí it operates a preparatory program. In Mexico City it runs a graduate program in administration and plans a complete professional teaching unit.

In each region, the Institute encourages the organization of nonprofit civic associations to guide and administer the branch campus in conjunction with the Institute. Such associations have been established in seven of the eight cities. Through them the Institute becomes aware of community wishes; with their cooperation, it carries out studies of special community needs and prepares feasibility studies to determine the most necessary degree program or programs. The associations are autonomous as far as their general policies, functioning, and promotion are concerned; ITESM reserves to itself matters of budget and administration. Such community participation is considered an important contributing factor in development. It motivates Institute members and extends the scope of the Institute to the country as a whole.

The Institute is directed by the Assembly of the Monterrey Civic Association (Higher Education and Research, C.A.), a board of directors appointed by the Assembly, a rector, and five vice-rectors, one each for professional education and graduate programs, finance and development, technical education, student affairs, and administration. (The branches outside Monterrey have their own boards of directors. Some regional leaders are members of ITESM's board of directors.)

Finance and Budget

Student payments, which cover from 60 percent to 65 percent of the total budget, are the main source of funds. The federal government gives limited financial support, between 1.5 percent and 2 percent of the total budget. Other institutional funds, derived largely from lotteries and raffles, cover slightly more than 20 percent of the operating expenses. In six years, the budget has increased by 139.7 percent from M$60,045,477 in 1968 to M$143,951,193 in 1974.*

The deficit, between 10 percent and 20 percent, is covered by donations or contributions from the Civic Association and other friends of the Institute. The vice-rector for Finance and Development is responsible for collecting funds, promoting lotteries and raffles, and raising money from alumni through an alumni association that is both economically valuable to the Institute and of mutual help to the Institute's alumni.

Reliance on foreign resources is small, from 2 percent to 5 percent of the total budget. These resources are generally assigned for staff improvement programs, for research, and for some equipment. Agencies that have contributed include the Ford, Rockefeller, and Tinker Foundations, the U.N. Food and Agricultural Organization (FAO), and USAID (with equipment for technical school workshops). The governments of the United States, France, Germany, and Great Britain have assigned teachers to serve in the Institute, particularly in the area of languages. Local foundations, such as Jenkins, Ferrostaal AG, and Lurgi, also support some of the Institute's programs.

Foreign assistance has been instrumental in improving teaching staff. Some observers feel, however, that this assistance is "inflationary" and, in the long run, becomes a burden since matching funds must be provided initially and subsequently all expenses must be assumed. Because it is strongly felt that Mexico should not have to depend on foreign technology, the Institute has been sending and continues to send members of its staff seeking advanced degrees in technology to countries outside Mexico. Many of these people, with a sophisticated knowledge of technology, return to ITESM.

Students

In 1972-73, there were 12,444 students enrolled in the Institute, of whom 5,798 registered in professional and graduate education and

---

*M$ July 1976 = U.S. $0.08.

the rest in technical and extension education. Approximately 36 percent of the students in the professional and graduate programs come from Monterrey, 34 percent from the northern Mexican states, 21 percent from the other regions of the country, and 9 percent from abroad. Students are selected for admission to the Institute on the basis of College Entrance Examination Board scores (Puerto Rican Spanish version).

Because tuition is relatively high, ITESM attracts mainly the well-to-do, but scholarships and loans are provided to capable students from low-income groups. A total of M$6,324,739 in loans were made in 1974-75, and 160 students received financial assistance through jobs in laboratories and workshops.

Up to 1973, a total of 8,263 students had obtained professional* degrees from the Institute; 823 had received master's degrees, and one student a Ph.D.; 2,868 received technician diplomas (three years training after the traditional preparatory school). ITESM insists on high-quality academic performance and receives it. A study of alumni employment is being carried out, but it is known that many graduates hold important offices in industry, government, banking, and commerce.

Professors

There are 440 professors (as of 1973-74), of whom 209 are full-time, 17 half-time, 20 on leave of absence abroad, and 194 part-time. The average student-professor ratio is 22:1. Twenty percent of the full-time teaching staff have advanced degrees; 53 percent have master of science degrees, and 27 percent have Ph.D.s or the equivalent.

Research and Service

Research is conducted through an agreement between a contracting agency—business, industry, or government—and the respective ITESM division or office. The Institute attempts to provide solutions to problems brought to it. To do so, it develops models, tests materials, makes systems analyses, designs in-service curricula, and provides whatever other research is needed. The four divisions include programs such as demonstration projects for improving seed,

---

*Equivalent to U.S. bachelor's degree, generally after three or four years of undergraduate education.

grazing land, cattle breeding, and water use (Division of Agriculture, Animal Husbandry, and Marine Sciences); testing housing materials (Engineering and Architecture); strengthening community organizations (Administration and Social Science); and research on toxic plants (Sciences and Humanities).

If projects receive administrative approval, they may be financed through a variety of means: course fees, consultant fees, agricultural industry contracts, grants from external agencies, or grants from the federal government through the University. The amount of government money is determined by the number of students involved, the cost per student, and existing facilities. Most government funds come through contracts for individual projects.

While both teaching and research are concerned with practical problems and often with community needs, their primary goals are staff development and student training rather than service. Research or extension projects are viewed as activities that primarily improve teaching and indirectly contribute to development through the formation of sound professionals and well-trained graduates. Professors participate in contracts more often than do students, but students learn from work-study and more formal teaching benefits. In the Division of Agricultural and Marine Sciences, for example, students in their final year learn agricultural field problems and how to solve them by working on an experimental farm for a year under faculty supervision. Each student must design, plan, and carry out his own research project. (In 1974 there were 59 such Research Obligation Projects.) About 25 percent of the students in this division come from Central and South America and, upon completing their course work, return to their respective countries to apply the knowledge gained at ITESM.

Student fees can be used only for teaching expenses, and, because the major portion of the Institute's funds come from tuition, there has been little impetus and few resources, outside the contract projects, for establishing direct community service programs. Laws require, however, that all students must carry out some type of community activity for a period of four months, and the Institute has cooperated with government, particularly in the state of Nuevo León, in farm extension programs. Students also work in primary and adult education programs.

There are no organized efforts, however, to carry out or enforce student service requirements, and, as a result, students generally choose private organizations or work at the Institute itself for their four-month period. The government is organizing an Institute for Community Development, but it is not yet in operation, and faculty attitudes to community service vary. By and large, the ITESM programs have led to a closer relationship with the industrial

community and to the concept that ITESM serves in the study and
solution of industrial problems.

Relations With Government and Private Agencies

Although the Institute has excellent relations with government
at all levels (the minister of education is a former president of
ITESM), it deals mainly with the private sector and its leaders,
who were the founders and remain the principal sponsors of ITESM.
Specific projects and proposals—most in engineering, agriculture,
animal and marine sciences, and administration—are usually received
from business or industry. In each case, however, the Institute
seeks the cooperation of the specialized branches of the government
(Water and Electricity, Sanitary Engineering, and Agricultural
Extension). Government planning officers are frequently invited to
sit in on project meetings, but the region has little overall planning.
Several years ago the Institute drew up a detailed regional plan, but
local government has not given it much notice.

On the other hand, both ITESM and its programs have considerable prestige inside and outside of Mexico. Other regions of the
country look to ITESM for help in organizing new private educational
institutions, and the Institute has frequently been used as a model.
Other universities send students and professors to ITESM to complete
their studies or do postgraduate work. It has acquired leadership
and experience in the fields of educational innovation (educational
technology, microteaching, personalized instruction); engineering
and business administration; and alternate science and engineering
studies through personalized and interdisciplinary instruction. It
is beginning to take on additional leadership in agriculture and marine
biology.

THE RESEARCH AND EXTENSION PROGRAM FOR INDUSTRIAL DEVELOPMENT: DIVISION OF ENGINEERING AND ARCHITECTURE

In its 23 years of operation, the Research and Extension
Program for Industrial Development (formerly the Institute for
Industrial Research, IIR), has carried out almost 600 research
and development projects. It has provided low-cost services to
government and industry through more than 6,000 tests and analyses
of minerals, fuels, paints, and foods and has conducted studies in
chemistry, chemical engineering, economics, agriculture, and
demography.

History

The IIR was created in 1951 as a semiautonomous body engaged in applied research to serve the public, government, industry, manufacturers, and others in matters of agricultural, mining, industrial, and manufacturing development. Although the IIR was created as a nonprofit, scientific institution for public service, it was a private enterprise and supported entirely by industry. It was dependent on ITESM but separate from its academic program.

IIR offered a new service: research applied to specific industrial and government problems. In 1961, for example, wastes in Monterrey City were being dumped in a suburban garbage pickup zone and then sold, creating disposal and sanitation problems but also a source of income for about 400 poor families. The Institute designed a semiautomatic plant to process the wastes, which at the same time offered better working conditions to the families dependent on the income from the sale of wastes. With the support of 50 local industries, the plant was installed and now employs the former waste collectors.

By 1970, although its budget had grown to M$1.5 million, IIR had not become self-sustaining and was subsidized largely by ITESM. It lacked research-trained personnel and had little cooperation or support from ITESM's faculty and department heads—they felt that IIR's researchers interfered with their own consulting activities. With the collaboration of the Southwest Research Institute of San Antonio, Texas, IIR had run a research training program for engineers recently graduated from ITESM, but of the 20 professionals who received training in 15 years, only two continued as members of ITESM. (Most of the rest now have research jobs in big business or government.) In 1970, therefore, in the hope that it could be integrated into the academic program, IIR was merged with ITESM's Division of Engineering and Architecture, which has the largest full-time student enrollment in ITESM. (For descriptions of the Research and Extension Program for Industrial Development's three other divisions—in addition to Engineering and Architecture—see Appendix 22.4.)

Nature of the Program

The Research and Extension Program for Industrial Development (REPID), which resulted from this merger, offers two types of service: services to industry and government in the form of applied research, studies, and consultation; and services to professionals in the form of short courses, seminars, and practice

schools of engineering.* REPID depends entirely on the demand for
services, mostly from Monterrey's industry.† (Requests have also
come from the northern Mexican states, Mexico City, and from
Guatemala and Honduras.) Most of its projects are privately supported, although government has contracted for such projects as
planning the installation of waste-processing and water-purification
plants in Monterrey City. REPID has almost no competitors.
Research is focused on four interrelated areas: systems, materials,
resources, and housing (see Appendix 22.2). While there are approximately 200 research institutions in Mexico, very few conduct applied
and industrial research in these areas.

Objectives

Since becoming a part of the Division of Engineering and
Architecture on ITESM's Monterrey campus, the Research and
Extension Program has acquired a new academic context. Each
department head in the Division both coordinates academic activities
and promotes research and extension, which is viewed as a way to
upgrade academic departments, improve teaching, and, incidentally,
add to faculty salaries.

In addition, REPID attempts to adapt technology so that it
contributes to Monterrey's industrial development and to help solve
local, regional, and national problems. Most projects deal with
applied research or development of products and processes, although
basic or abstract research in electrical engineering has been conducted on a small scale. A third aim is to diffuse knowledge through
extension activities such as refresher and specialized courses,
seminars, lectures, displays, and publications.

Organization

To carry out its research and extension activities, REPID
draws on personnel from three industrial research and extension

---

*ITESM's practice schools of engineering are an adaptation of
the practice schools established and developed at the Massachusetts
Institute of Technology. In these schools, a professor and a group
of 12 engineering students in their last semester work for six weeks
during the summer to define, study, and propose solutions to a
problem of general interest to the group and to the contracting enterprise.

†Research sponsors have been private enterprise, 76 percent;
federal government, 12 percent; decentralized agencies, 6.7 percent;
ITESM, 2.9 percent; other, 2.4 percent.

departments (Special Projects; Tests and Analyses; and Industrial Security) and from seven academic departments (Architecture; Civil Engineering; Electrical Engineering; Industrial Engineering; Mechanical Engineering; Chemical Engineering; and Calorics, Fluids, and Control). REPID also uses personnel from other divisions and, in some cases, specialists not permanently connected with ITESM. It estimates that it can call on sufficient expertise to meet twice the present demand for services.

While almost all the Division's departments participate in some of REPID's activities, heavy teaching loads limit professors' time, and, consequently, only 15 or 20 percent of the professors from the academic departments (about 80 professors) participate in REPID. Some of the investigations also use graduate students, whose work fulfills part of their thesis requirements and thus receives academic credit.

The Research and Extension Program at present has 13 project directors, 15 researchers, 16 graduate students, and 12 research assistants. It is administered by an associate director, assisted by an accounting office and a secretariat. A Consulting Committee, composed of the Division's director, the associate director of research, and the department heads meets every two weeks and discusses the research. The associate director also meets every two weeks with the Department of Special Projects and once a month with each academic department. The director of each study or project meets with its own participants each week. Once a year all members of the Division attend a one-day seminar on the year's activities, and a report on these activities is published annually. Sponsors of the various projects receive monthly progress reports, technical reports at the end of each stage, and a final report upon termination of the project. There is almost no communication with similar programs in Mexico or elsewhere except through national meetings or symposia and through REPID's affiliation to the World Association of Industrial and Technological Research Organizations.

Strengths and Weaknesses

Sources of Strength

Some of the factors that the program director believes account for the success of REPID (originally as the IIR and later integrated into the Division of Engineering and Architecture) are (1) the vision and initiatives of ITESM's founders; (2) the dynamic role played by ITESM's president, divisional directors, and department heads as promoters of research and service; (3) ITESM's rapid growth and development, which made possible the investment in equipment and laboratories; (4) the training program for researchers, financed largely by the Southwest Research Institute; the Rockefeller and Ford Foundations underwrote part of this program with teacher training scholarships; (5) the support of Monterrey's industrialists and of the Board of Trustees that channeled industrial demand to ITESM; (6) economic support since 1966 from the Ford Foundation, which, in 1971-73, for example, donated U.S. $100,000 for research in engineering, an area in which local support was not available; (7) the increasing number of ITESM's professionals (9,000 graduates) who now hold positions in industry; and (8) efforts of REPID's directors to maintain continuing contact with sponsors; about a quarter of the short-term projects lead to new studies that modify or explore further the subject of the original project.

Initial Problems

The most difficult problems, when IIR was first created, were lack of research-trained personnel, laboratories, and equipment; the specialized nature of the research; and the low demand from industry for services, principally because industrialists were not accustomed to investing in research unless they had serious problems and industry was accustomed to securing technology directly from developed countries.

Since 1970, when IIR became the Research and Extension Program, most of these problems have been solved. The academic departments have supplied personnel for interdisciplinary studies, incorporated the research into their programs, and industry has learned what REPID can do.

Recurrent Difficulties

More recently, according to the program director and some department heads, there have been two special difficulties: (1) when the associate director requests faculty assistance, he sometimes runs into competition with department heads jealous of their authority and command over their departments; and (2) because professors have heavy teaching loads (four courses, equivalent to 34 hours a week), they cannot take full responsibility for projects. These difficulties have been largely overcome by clarifying the procedure for requesting personnel from the academic departments and by assigning researchers from the Department of Special Projects to assist professors from other departments.

The Projects

Projects involve housing materials, quality of life, medicine,
and instruction. They include a computer program for the design
of steel frames for tall buildings; studies of housing materials based
upon small concrete models, also fire-resistant paints, and plastic
reinforced with bamboo; mathematical and simulation models to be
used in the construction industry; design of natural ventilation systems
for low-cost housing; drawing up regulations for the control of contaminants in industrial and domestic wastes; measurement of noise
levels in several industries and of contaminants in air and water;
studies on stability analysis in power systems; recycling glass,
paper, and rags; developing industrial uses for arid-zone plants;
a computer program of methods to forecast sales; a simulation
computer program to be used as a teaching tool; perfecting equipment for transmitting heartbeats and for identifying brain waves via
telephone; a feasibility study for the establishment of a Technological
Assessment Center; and planning a civic center for an industrial
suburb of Monterrey.

REPID has also built up a demand for its industrial security
services, which provide factory inspection, courses for supervisors,
lectures for factory employees, noise level studies, and consultation.
The services have reduced accident rates and therefore have saved
money through lower fees charged by the Social Security Service to
factories with security programs. One hundred and twenty industries,
employing about 28,000 workers, have used these services.

Research and extension activities during 1972-73 and 1973-74
are listed in Table 22.1.

While most program activities are determined by requests
from business, industry, and government, some ideas (about 3 percent of the research projects) are generated within the division,
often sparked by international conferences or other projects.

Resources and Financing

REPID charges for its services at cost; that is, the sponsor
pays personnel and administrative costs, but REPID does not make
a profit. (ITESM generally subsidizes some of the administrative
costs.) A detailed account of costs is kept for each activity and
project. (The professor at ITESM is well paid by local standards,
but if he participates in consulting and research projects, he can
add 30 to 50 percent to his income.)

The cost of projects varies substantially. During 1974, the
most expensive project cost M$3,000,000, and the least expensive

TABLE 22.1

Research and Extension Activities

	1972–73	1973–74
Activities		
Research and development projects–		
consulting and advisory services	73	63
Tests and analyses	298	302
Extension courses and seminars	29	23
Practice schools	6	6
Industrial Security		
Factory inspection	10	18
Courses for supervisors	30	32
Lectures in factories	116	105
Phone consultations	900	750
Visits to the plants	60	40
Special prevention inspection	5	10
Noise level studies	3	5
Cost of research and development		
projects, consulting, and advising	M$4,467,500	M$5,822,000
Cost of extension courses		709,110
Cost of tests and analyses		242,360

Source: Monterrey Institute of Technology and Advanced Studies, Research and Extension Program for Industrial Development.

M$5,000. The average project cost fluctuates between M$50,000 and M$100,000. A cost accounting system guarantees the sponsor and the institution efficient management and execution within the time limits set.

The forerunner of the present program, IIR, began in 1951 with an annual budget of M$115,680. Over the next five years its budget went up to M$402,303, and by 1961 it was M$1,180,351. In 1974, REPID's budget was M$7,601,000. (Annual budgets are listed in Appendix 22.3.) The projects represent approximately 75 percent of the program's income; the practice schools 5 percent; and the industrial security activities 10 percent. Extension courses supply the remaining income.

The program has also received financial support from several international agencies. When the IIR began in 1951, the Southwest Research Institute paid the director's salary, provided a car, and financed the scholarship program for training researchers. The Ford Foundation has provided financial support for a comprehensive

program of activities in graduate science and engineering research.
In 1973, after IIR had been integrated into the Division of Engineering
and Architecture, the Mary Street Jenkins Foundation donated
M$20,000. The Rockefeller Foundation has contributed indirectly
by financing the training of professors in agronomy. REPID has
used this trained personnel in special projects.

Assessment

There is no adequate analysis of the project results. A free-
circulation annual report is published, which briefly describes the
year's research and extension activities, but most industrial projects
are confidential, at the request of their sponsors.

Almost all projects, however, have been successfully completed
and implemented. Of the 64 projects initiated during the 1973-74
academic year, only two were abandoned: an applicability range of
inventory models and a computer program for layout design in production systems. (Both project directors left—one to finish his
doctorate at Stanford and the other to work in industry.) Consulting
services have been authorized for preinvestment studies by the
National Financing Agency of the Mexican government and by the
Inter-American Development Bank (IDB). To evaluate research
projects, REPID plans to create a Technological Assessment Center,
to be financed out of fees for project consultation, short courses,
publications, and gifts from industry.

Contributions to Social Well-being

REPID contributes to overall economic and social development
largely through defining industrial and some governmental needs and
problems and by preparing contributors to social development through
its emphasis on improved teaching and on problem-solving skills.
By merging REPID with the Division of Engineering and Architecture,
connections were forged between course work and practical research.
Although few students take part in projects, teaching is benefitted
when faculty learn industrial and government problems firsthand.
The practice schools also provide opportunity for student-faculty
study of actual problems. ITESM claims that, in general, applied
research and extension programs have drawn it closer to practical
problems, but the claim is hard to judge, since ITESM has always
been pragmatic, particularly.with regard to technology and science.

ITESM tries to contribute to well-being through employment.
REPID has created jobs for the unskilled and semiskilled through its

reclamation projects, and it has raised the level of manpower skills by providing in-service training in business and industry. It has successfully reclaimed solid waste as fertilizer, changing previously sterile land into productive soil, and has found industrial use for native plants heretofore considered useless.

ITESM, as an institution, is also contributing with a series of programs using innovative teaching methods and is strengthening education at other levels through projects such as Open Preparatory Schools.

There is no doubt, however, that social development is a secondary and sometimes incidental goal of the Research and Extension Program. While a number of faculty members and department heads within REPID are interested in working on social development projects, such projects lack sponsors and therefore funds. REPID does not have resources for more than a very few projects not paid for under contract, and less than 3 percent of REPID's budget is allocated to ITESM-sponsored projects.

Research projects, moreover, do not always reinforce the quality and content of teaching as they are supposed to do; the ideal relationship between teaching and research has not been achieved at the desired level. Most professors devote almost all their time to teaching and have little time left for the research requested by industry. Such research consumes much time and effort and often returns little benefit to the classroom.

Suggestions

These difficulties lead to the following suggestions for program directors:

1. Prepare proposals for research and extension projects in social development, applying for financial support from agencies interested in broad economic and social problems. For example, ITESM's Division of Engineering and Architecture could carry out projects in rural development, but it has had trouble finding sponsors for this type of study. Program planners should give more thought to defining projects involving community need and seeking donors. Donor agencies should, correspondingly, note opportunities for funding projects directed to social goals.

2. Encourage students to participate in research projects along with professors and grant more course credit for such activities. Classroom work would benefit from student as well as faculty experience in actual problem solving.

    3. Give faculty members who participate in research projects some relief from their teaching loads, perhaps with some equitable pay adjustment.

    4. Conduct follow-up studies to evaluate the impact of development projects on community well-being and to measure changes in employment or standard of living.

    ITESM and the Research and Extension Program have considerable local, regional, national, and international impact; they have become community and national leaders in coping with social, economic, and technological change. ITESM faculty are well-informed scholars in their areas of specialty and often in related ones; many of the faculty are sophisticated technologists and researchers. This excellence is reflected in the caliber of students who graduate from ITESM.

Lessons

    REPID's experience points out a number of lessons that other technological programs, whether more or less oriented to community needs, might bear in mind.

    1. Private institutions or programs, as well as government, can define community needs and induce demand for services in areas of community concern. For example, REPID has acted as consultant to the federal government in drawing up regulations dealing with the control of air and water pollution in cities.

    2. Both program directors and academic department heads must provide active leadership in encouraging faculty members to participate in problem solving, multidisciplinary research projects, and must help relate research studies to curriculum.

    3. Program administration benefits from flexible and decentralized organization (with a manual on policies and procedures), an efficient cost accounting system, and contracts specifying goals and deadlines.

    ITESM's research program is an example of excellent administration and financial management that could be utilized as a basis for specific training for administrators of other research programs. Because ITESM is committed to the management-by-objectives system for reaching its goals, as indicated in its statement of purpose, the degree of competence achieved in all programs is measurable and is measured, resulting in effective operation. It is to be hoped that this efficient research instrument can be used increasingly for solving problems, not only of industrial productivity, but also of community well-being.

APPENDIX 22.1

Number of Studies Conducted at the Institute
of Industrial Research

Area of Study	Number
Civil Engineering Studies (Urban Planning)	15
Bibliographical Studies (Chemical Industry)	71
Product Development or Improvement	43
Development of a Product: Industrial Waste Recovery	27
Market Studies	28
Industrial Waste Recovery	20
Elaboration of Statistical or Economic Indices	7
Water Treatment and Industrial Wastes	34
Chemical Laboratory Studies	41
Technical-Economic Studies: Feasibility of Industries	62
Industrial Appraisal	17
Socioeconomic Studies	9
Verification of Compliance with Quality Control Regulations	4
Industrial Diagnoses	2
Financial and Accounting Studies	4
Studies on Agronomy	10
Technical Assistance: Industrial Engineering Studies	20
Studies on Educational Institutions	3
Electrical Engineering Studies	7
Market Studies of Professional Careers	6
Studies of New Careers	7
Industrial Engineering Studies	19
Water and Mineral Analyses	3
Design, Selection, Construction, Installation, and Operation of Equipment	18
Courses on the Realization and Evaluation of Industrialization Projects	1
Design or Improvement of Products or Industrial Articles	7
Design and Economic Study of Equipment	1
Physical and Chemical Laboratory Tests: Chemical Laboratory Studies	20
Chemical Engineering: Mechanical Engineering	10
Economic Studies	8
Technical Translations	2

(continued)

APPENDIX 22.1 (Continued)

Area of Study	Number
Statistical Data on Production, Resources, Mineral Deposits, and so on	18
Evaluation of Products, Processes, or Equipment	3
Survey of Sources of "Know-How," Prices, Regulations, and so on	4
Study on Image of Enterprises, Products, and so on	3
Elaboration of Booklets and Proposals	2
Surveys Regarding Salaries, Lotteries, and so on	2
Obtention of an Element Having Thermoelectric Characteristics	1
Total	589

Source: Monterrey Institute of Technology and Advanced Studies, Research and Extension Program for Industrial Development.

APPENDIX 22.2

Projects of the Research and Extension
Program for Industrial Development

Research in the Division of Engineering and Architecture has been focused on four interrelated areas:

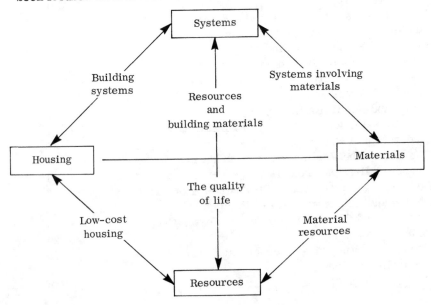

In Systems-Housing, building systems have been considered, leading to the following projects:

1. A computer program for the optimized design of steel frames for tall buildings made with profiles of soldered plates.

2. A study of the properties of the component materials of "microconcrete" to be used in models of structures. Utilization of microconcrete structures for teaching and research purposes.

3. Implementation of a collection of computer programs for the optimized design of reticular structures for teaching and research purposes.

4. Development of administrative models for the construction industry based in inventory systems concepts.

5. Development of mathematical and simulation models to be used in the construction industry.

In Housing-Materials, the theme of "building materials" has been studied in the following projects:

1. A study of the thermal properties of sodium silicate films on building materials exposed to high temperatures, to develop a paint for protection of materials against fire.

2. Development of glass foam as building material (thermal or acoustical insulator) using waste glass.

3. Preparation of light concrete using plastic waste materials as filler.

4. Use of foamed and/or expanded plastic materials reinforced with bamboo for roofing low-cost housing. Determination of thermal, physical, and mechanical properties of these materials.

5. Feasibility study for the establishment of a "Materials Center" determining priority areas for research on materials including the needs of personnel and equipment for selected areas of study.

In the area of Housing-Resources, projects include: analysis of natural ventilation on low-cost housing using a bidimensional air-smoke tunnel and scale models of houses studying the location of walls, windows, doors, the shape of the roof, and the presence of trees or artificial barriers to obtain optimum natural ventilation.

Several projects, sponsored either by government agencies or industries, fall in the area of Resources-Systems. These include the following:

1. Formulation of regulations for the control of contaminants in the discharge of industrial and domestic wastes.

2. Treatment of sewage water for further use in agriculture and industry (in proposal stage).

3. Measurement of noise level and vibration control in several industries.

4. Measurement of contaminants in air and water in several locations.

In the area of Resources-Materials, studies sponsored by government agencies have been made on industrialization of arid-zone plants, especially guayule, gobernadora, and jojoba (the last two in proposal stage).

Also, some work has been done on the industrialization and use of garbage as filler in construction blocks, "compost" preparation as soil-conditioner, and the reuse of components—such as glass, paper, and rags.

Other projects include

1. Development of a collection of computer programs of forecasting methods to be used on demand or sales forecasts for helping in business decisions.

2. Implementation of the simulation computer program PROSIM V to be used as a teaching tool in production systems courses and testing of research models in the area of Production Programing and Control.

3. Development of preliminary text material on Production Systems.

4. Studies on stability analysis in power systems. Developing and evaluation of mathematical models to represent loads and generators.

5. Determination of overvoltages in transmission lines determining critical points during transitories caused by opening and closing of switches or power failures.

6. Feasibility study for the establishment of a "Technological Assessment Center" with the triple purpose of realizing teaching, research, and extension activities in technological forecasting.

APPENDIX 22.3

Annual Budget, Department of
Special Projects*

Period	Budget
1950–51	M$ 115,680.00
1951–52	153,610.00
1952–53	209,725.00
1953–54	311,186.00
1954–55	402,303.00
1955–56	344,563.00
1956–57	600,885.00
1957–58	840,591.00
1958–59	816,389.00
1959–60	796,410.00
1960–61	904,720.00
1961–62	1,180,490.00
1962–63	1,008,095.00
1963–64	1,118,351.00
1964–65	1,024,227.00
1965–66	968,083.00
1966–67	1,247,169.00
1967–68	1,600,451.00
1968–69	1,932,861.00
1969–70	1,637,190.00
1970–71	1,845,200.00
1971–72	2,428,641.00
1972–73	3,138,599.00
1973–74	4,813,736.00

*Designated IIR during 1950-70. From 1971 to date, designated Department of Special Projects.

Source: Monterrey Institute of Technology and Advanced Studies, Department of Special Projects.

APPENDIX 22.4

Divisions of Administration and Social Sciences,
Agricultural and Marine Sciences, and
Sciences and Humanities

Division of Administration and Social Sciences

The Division of Administration and Social Sciences, with more
than 2,000 students, encompasses four academic departments
(administration, accounting, administrative law, and economics),
offers careers in four areas (public accountant, business administration, economics, and administration), and has a large extension
department, the Department of Industrial Relations. During the
1973-74 academic year, the division's faculty was composed of
56 full-time professors, 9 half-time professors, and 103 auxiliary
assistants.

Instruction

The division uses a number of innovative instruction methods:
Students are required to submit a final work-related project in their
field of specialization; personalized instruction (PSI) has been used
in two economics theory courses and is planned for a third; the
division continues to use successfully the seminar method with
audiovisual aids; computerized business games give students experience in making decisions and seeing their results; and workshops
give them a reading knowledge of business English. Marking an
important change in academic policy, the division gives students
credit for participation in approved research projects.

Research Activities

1. The Special Research Unit of the Department of Economics
explored the subject of income and its relationship to expenditures
in the Monterrey metropolitan area. The project is expected to
produce a cost-of-living index that answers such questions as,
Who spends how much on what? One professor and 90 students
have participated in this project.

2. The Unit of Technological Economics (UNET), organized
in February 1974, has been developing a data bank to help public
and private decision makers on regional, national, and international
levels. A professor and 40 students are collaborating on this continuing study. UNET also offers business and industrial models,
conferences and educational services, intermediate studies, models

for property claims and special markets, and policy simulations.
It plans also to offer short-term and long-term predictions regarding
the national economy, an analysis of production costs, consultant
and training services, and time-shared computer use.

3. The Demographic Unit, also organized in 1973-74, is
conducting a study, in collaboration with the University of Missouri,
of the mobile population of Nuevo León, Tamaulipas, and Coahuila.

4. The Unit of International Commerce, just organized, is
expected to deal with external problems affecting Monterrey's
economy.

5. To investigate the need for a master's program in public
administration, two professors have been working on a study,
financed by the Ford Foundation, of employment opportunities and
educational needs in Mexico for persons with advanced training in
public administration.

6. A study to determine U.S. influence on Mexican and U.S.
border cities in terms of history, politics, and demography is
shared with the University of Houston and financed by $100,000 from
the Tinker Foundation.

7. A study will project mortality and life expectancy rates
for the states of Coahuila, Nuevo León, and Tamaulipas.

Both research activities and new course programs are identified chiefly by two means: (1) Business, government, or community
leaders may identify problems and contract for the Division's
services; or (2) Institute administrators, division heads, department
chairmen, and members may initiate steps toward solution of local,
regional, and national problems by gathering data, analyzing it, and
presenting findings to appropriate offices. As a result of both
processes, the division may design new curricula, conduct seminars,
and present conferences.

The Division of Agricultural and
Marine Sciences

The Division of Agricultural and Marine Sciences has 670
students* and contains five academic departments: administration
of agricultural enterprises; agronomy; biology; soils and agricultural
engineering; and animal husbandry. It offers four career curricula
(agronomy administrative engineer, agronomy biological engineer,
agronomy zootechnical engineer, and biochemical engineer) and uses

---

*There are 70 additional students in the School of Marine
Sciences of ITESM in Guaymas, Sonora.

experimental, agricultural campuses for its extension activities.
Ten of its 38 professors hold a doctoral degree; 20 a master's;
and 8 the Licenciatura.

Instruction

The PSI has been applied in microbiology and in the rural sociology course. (Most of the division's professors from the departments of
agronomy and biology participated in the first course of programed
instruction offered outside ITESM; two of the division's professors
assisted in short in-service courses on PSI.) A biology professor
also designed an Integrated Group System, now applied in two courses.
Seven professors of various departments in the division analyzed
instructional materials for teaching cattle raising at the technical
vocational level.

For their entire last year, students work on the experimental
farm under faculty supervision in order to learn actual agricultural
problems and how to solve them. This method of learning by doing
has been used in this division since 1948.

Division Activities

Demonstration courses, conferences, and seminars: From
September 1973 to August 1974, a total of 60 professors participated
in one or more of these activities. Subject areas included cattle
raising, entomology, botany, physiology, hydroculture, microbiology,
soils, use and management of water, management of grazing land,
animal breeding, animal nutrition, cereal research, and agricultural
bookkeeping. Thirty-seven professors participated in one or more
publishing activities, producing four books and 24 articles.

Outreach programs: In El Puerto Coahuila, a demonstration
farm is used to show how to change native vegetation to good grazing
land. Coahuila lends the land, and ITESM builds the program and
shows results twice a year. In a Tropical Livestock Research
Center north of Veracruz, cattlemen provide the land, and ITESM
provides a program designed to improve the breed of cattle, grazing
vegetation, and methods of cattle handling. In the south of Nuevo
León, a program under the sponsorship of the Ministry of Hydraulic
Resources is studying the best use of the existing water resources.
Objectives of the program are to catch and contain water to produce
food and to teach small farmers how to grow crops and increase
production. The program has revitalized the region. At the Experimental Farm Station in Apodaca, improved seed, which produces
a greater yield, is distributed to farmers, who grow the seed and
sell the produce and some of the seed. ITESM has distributed 280

tons of improved wheat, corn, sorghum, oats, forage, and hay seed, which has benefited approximately 400 rural families. ITESM also sends seed to South America. Demonstration projects have made change and innovative methods seem less threatening to farmers.

Consultancies: The division works with 260 other agricultural schools of higher education. It is affiliated with professional organizations in Latin America, Asia, Europe, and the United States, and has received grants for the improvement of corn and wheat from such sources as the Ford and Rockefeller Foundations.

Division activities stem either from the division head and faculty or from farmers' requests to solve their problems. ITESM conducts agricultural courses for farmers both in farm areas and on the ITESM campus. The division also helps farmers make better use of social security, obtain better education and sanitation, and solve family problems.

Division of Sciences and Humanities

The Division of Sciences and Humanities has five academic departments (physics, humanities, mathematics, computer systems, and chemistry) and includes 12 career curricula (licenciados in computer systems, computer systems administration, communications sciences, physical sciences, physical mathematics, community services, chemistry, physics, physical education, English language, Spanish literature, and mathematics.) There are 981 students, of whom approximately a third are women, and there are 168 faculty members, 63 of them full-time.

Communications Sciences, a new four-year program, deals with journalism, television, and radio, and includes public service information programs involving home economics, health, nutrition, and money management.

Division Activities

1. Basic research by the chemistry department on toxic and other plants in northeast Mexico.

2. A computer program in which students earn credits while working in business/industry under the academic supervision of an ITESM professor. On-site supervision is provided by business/industry in terms of measurable objectives decided upon by the professor and the representative from business/industry. There is a need to educate both students and faculty about computer possibilities.

3. In-service courses, which teach English to local company personnel. The humanities and literature departments prepare slide-tape presentations in English for industry. (ITESM also offers courses in French, German, and Russian.)

4. The Community Development Program, under the supervision of a social worker, works with community organizations rather than with individuals and involves students who receive academic credit for their services in the community.

5. The physical sciences departments design curriculum materials for ITESM students.

Social needs and problems addressed by the division are defined largely by the president of the Institute, the division head, department members, and members of the board of directors. Because many of ITESM's professors are consultants to business and industry, community problems and needs are generally well-known.

The division plans to extend adult education and continuing education to the community at large and is also considering designing instructional materials for grade school and high school levels.

23

NATIONAL AGRARIAN UNIVERSITY,
LA MOLINA, PERU

Program for Transferal of Technology

A major objective of the National Agrarian University (NAU) at
La Molina is to use knowledge about the rural environment to serve
the rural community. It trains professionals not only to practice
their profession but also to fulfill their obligations as responsible
and active members of the community. Graduates are expected to
study national problems related to their profession and to participate
in their solution.

In 1972, to help implement the Agrarian Reform Act of 1969,
the University signed an agreement with the Peruvian Ministry of
Agriculture to assist in the transferal of technology as a means of
guaranteeing the success of new forms of land tenancy under the
new law. The University has provided technical cooperation with
various government agencies, largely through the study and solution
of problems relating to agriculture and livestock production. (See
Appendix at end of this case study.)

NATURE OF THE PROGRAM

The Program for Transferal of Technology created by this
agreement got underway in 1973. It seeks to utilize the University's
specialized knowledge and also to acquaint students and professors
with national problems by bringing them into contact with agricultural
work in different parts of the country. The Program includes two
kinds of activities: (1) consulting and assitance services, and (2)
preparation of student theses. Both activities depend on the nature
of requests received from farmers and farm groups, from the
Ministry of Agriculture, and from professors who travel to rural
areas to identify needs.

Consulting and Assistance Services

To participate in consulting and assistance activities, professors or groups of professors from all University departments and

professional areas and students from all levels may volunteer to turn
their attention to immediate problems during their vacations and
weekends. A professor usually devotes from two days to a week to
such efforts; students may work from eight days to three months.
In most cases, mixed groups of professors and students are formed,
according to the type of activity being carried out. When regular
classes are in session, activities must be restricted to areas near
enough to Lima to allow for weekend work. About 10 percent of the
projects take only one or two days while 60 percent last three months
and take place during the summer.

A significant number have participated in these projects. During
the first trimester of 1973-74, a total of 164 students and 58 professors took part. Thirty percent of the students were in their fourth
or fifth year of studies, and 70 percent were less advanced. In each
of the following trimesters, there has been an increase not only in
the number of students participating but also in the proportion of
better-prepared older students. The program can accordingly
select students more in accordance with the demand for service
in each area. As of August 1974, there have been approximately
1,200 student and 80 professor visits. Of the total of 2,800 students
and 250 professors at the University, about one third have participated
in the program in some way.

Students selected to participate in the program's activities
receive an intensive briefing in two basic areas before leaving for
villages and farms. The briefing covers

1. Socioeconomic orientation. Students attend about 30 hours
of lectures given by professors from the University and by specialists
from the National Training and Research Center for Agrarian Reform
(CENCIRA), a branch of the Ministry of Agriculture. Subjects
include the new structure of land tenancy under the Agrarian Reform
Law, the processes of change in agricultural areas, and plans for
tapping resources and credit.

2. Technological training. Students attend 15 days of laboratory sessions, classes, conferences, and group discussions on
general and specific topics that are designed to help them in their
field work.

Heretofore, all requests for services have been answered.
For example, during the first year, 118 groups were served, of
which 30 were associations and 29 branches of the Ministry of
Agriculture. The demand for service has been increasing at such
a rate, however, that priorities have had to be established. The
intent of the program is to serve the poorest and least organized
rural communities.

During the first trimester of 1973-74, consulting and assistance requests from all over the country were answered as follows:

Area Visited	Professors	Students
Piura	1	–
Chiclayo	1	3
Huarás	3	11
Ica	15	40
Chincha, Pisco	1	12
Arequipa	18	44
Tacna, Moquegua	2	–
Cajamarca	1	3
Cerro de Pasco	1	4
Huancayo	2	–
Cusco	10	43
Madre de Dios	–	3
Puno	1	–
Iquitos	3	–
Tingo María, Pucallpa	–	1

During the first trimester of 1974-75, a total of 280 students worked in 12 Agrarian Zones.*

Other universities in the country were also offered a chance to participate. As a result, 154 students in the Academic Program for Veterinary Medicine at the National University of San Marcos took part in the NAU program during the first trimester of 1973-74, and 18 students in their last year of study and three professors from the National University of the Peruvian Amazon joined 290 NAU students and 60 professors in the third trimester.

Student Theses and Feasibility Studies

One of the criticisms of community programs has been lack of feedback into the curriculum. Here students who have a B.S. degree or are pursuing a B.S. in engineering may be assigned a thesis subject under the program director or an adviser. The research may take from six to eight months and may be carried out jointly by two or more students. At the end of each trimester, a group of professors and area coordinators visits the agrarian districts to evaluate student activities and to identify new assistance needs for the following trimester.

---

*The Agrarian Zones are decentralized offices of the ministry in different parts of the country.

Thesis research and feasibility studies complement the consulting and assistance activities. Studies are requested by associations and branches of the Ministry of Agriculture, and some are used as graduation theses. By the end of the first year, 42 research projects were being carried out. At present, 76 research projects are underway, nine theses (technical reports submitted to the beneficiaries as well as to the Ministry of Agriculture) have been completed, and 50 proposals await funding. One of these theses led to the establishment of a cattle food industry.

Short Courses and Extension

Along with the consulting and research work, the program offers a continuing program of short courses in rural areas. Six or seven professors from different fields lecture on specific subjects with groups of 200 to 250 people from farm communities. Higher technical personnel may be referred to the University for special training. In addition, pamphlets, mainly on management techniques, sanitation, and use of technology in relation to crop and animal sciences, have been published and distributed.

Such extension activities are part of the program's efforts to reach out-of-the-way areas and gain acceptance of its services by potential clients. The program is directed mainly to people in rural areas who have little formal education but often have abundant practical knowledge. Through its consulting and thesis activities, the program aids cooperatives, agricultural societies, and rural development plans, which include owners of small and medium-sized plots of land. Although it tries to direct its services especially to communities that have the most limited financial and technical capacity, the largest demand for consulting services and studies tends to come from better-organized cooperatives and associations.

The potential demand is enormous, far more than the NAU can possibly handle alone. As people in the districts become aware of the program's existence, new requests for assistance are made. According to the general coordinator, there have not been enough funds to publicize the program as widely as was hoped, but demand has now increased so much that program directors are distributing information to other universities in the hope that they can form a national technical assistance system coordinated by the NAU. Some coordinated projects have already been carried out; for example the NAU in Tingo María joined in meeting a request from a cooperative, and two theses were completed in cooperation with the National University of the Peruvian Amazon at Iquitos.

ORGANIZATION

A general coordinator was appointed by the Ministry of Agriculture to maintain relations with the eight academic programs and 22 departments that make up the academic structure of the University. Separate coordinators were appointed for agronomy, sciences, forestry, economics and planning, food technology, agricultural engineering, and animal husbandry. These coordinators make up the Coordination Committee, which meets four times a month, receives requests for assistance and analysis, and establishes priorities so that each coordinator may obtain the teaching staff needed for his area's activities. The program is administered by the program director, who sees the program as an important effort to orient university activities toward serving the needs of agricultural and livestock production in Peru.

Professors and students present reports upon termination of the mission in which they participate. These reports are sorted, and their results are noted on a card for each of the participating professors and students. At the end of each period, the reports of professors, students, and area heads are compiled into a general report, which is presented at a meeting attended by the minister, president of the University, and principal ministry and University officials, at which the work of the program is appraised. Written requests for technical assistance are presented through the Ministry of Agriculture or directly to the University.

RESOURCES AND FINANCING

The agreement between the Ministry of Agriculture and the University for the first two years of the program specifies that the Ministry of Agriculture shall finance the project. The University will assign professors and students during vacation periods (January, March, August) for services in rural areas and during the entire year for the development of thesis or feasibility projects. Clients furnish room and board for visiting groups. About 45 percent of the funds are allocated for consulting and assistance services, 45 percent for thesis development, and 10 percent for administration of the program.

The program has functioned through six trimesters under the terms of the present agreement, and negotiations have been initiated to extend the agreement for another two-year period. It is hoped that it will be possible to double the budget for the next two-year period. Funds are being allocated in Agrarian Zones in different

regions of the country to complement the NAU's links with local
universities.

FAVORABLE CONDITIONS, LIMITATIONS, AND DRAWBACKS

Factors favorable to the program include the following:

1. The Agrarian Reform Law made it possible for the University to meet directly the need for technical assistance, normally the
responsibility of the Ministry of Agriculture.
2. Leaders at the highest level in the ministry and the University have made a definite commitment to the program.
3. The program has been accepted by faculty and students.
4. Alumni and former professors of the NAU now in the
Ministry of Agriculture have wanted to break down the barriers
building up between the University and the ministry.
5. A large group of professors with academic and technical
training at the graduate level regard the program as an opportunity
to carry out applied research.
6. Concise terms in the University-ministry agreement
satisfy the ministry's desire to orient the program toward practical
problems determined by service users but maintain University
autonomy and control.

The program's problems, as seen by its coordinators, include:

1. Past deceit on the part of agencies and politicians made
people in rural areas suspect assistance offers. In this sense, the
prestige of the University served as a guarantee of the students'
and professors' helpfulness to community residents. People were
informed about the program's objectives and scope through meetings
and personal contact.
2. The program had to rely on volunteer students in their
second and third years of study because too few fourth- and fifth-year
students were registered. Difficulties arose, since the less advanced
student was not yet prepared to give the rather sophisticated technical assistance that the client needed. This problem was solved by
securing more information about situations which required technical
assistance so that better qualified students could be selected to meet
the demand; and financing the thesis work of fifth-year students,
thus encouraging their participation.
3. Opposition to the program arose on the part of two groups:
students and ministry officials. Initially, most students considered

the program novel and adventurous. Later, they valued this experience as an opportunity to learn about their country and to improve their education. Some activist student groups, however, saw a possibility of combining politics with field work. Since the University barred any propagandizing when it initiated the program, a group of students argued that the present government was using the University to support its policies.

A number of ministry officials also reacted negatively to the program when it was first proposed—because they regarded it as an intrusion on their functions, because of professional jealousies, and because they thought extremist student political views could create problems for the government once students were dispersed in rural areas. Much of this opposition disappeared when professors and students presented reports on the results of their activities.

4. Technical personnel who work in the Agrarian Zones offered a certain amount of passive resistance to the program, viewing participants with suspicion and feeling that the program's temporary assistance might conflict with the more long-range assistance of government. Direct contact with the ministry's technical personnel in the respective agrarian zones, however, has solved most of these difficulties.

5. University professors were initially skeptical about mechanisms that would permit participation of students and professors but would not interfere with University autonomy. They were reassured when the University took direct responsibility for the program.

6. The University cannot respond to all types of requests through this program. The program does not pretend to include feasibility or reinvestment projects which require spending large amounts of money.

APPRAISAL OF THE PROGRAM

The program's contribution to the economic and social development of the country can be classified as follows:

1. Defining Social Needs and Problems: The Peruvian Agrarian Reform Act required that technology be transferred to agricultural production units. Since the Ministry of Agriculture alone could not handle this task, the University, through its professors and students, is helping to fill the gap by identifying problems and needs as well as by explaining new tools and procedures. In the process, a permanent communication link is established with the low-income agrarian population.

2. Preparing Effective Contributors to Social Development:
Theses writers at the NAU formerly used only the resources available at the University (laboratories, production centers, farmhouses,
and so on), and the research was generally irrelevant to national
problems. With the resources made available by the program, however, theses are oriented toward the solution of national problems
and based on requests submitted by beneficiaries of the Agrarian
Reform Act. Thesis research thus becomes a meaningful task for
the student as well as an investigation of urgent development problems.

The program confronts students with the real problems of their
country. As a result of their work in rural areas, both professors
and students are beginning to question the relevance and organization
of the present curriculum and are considering possibilities for its
modification. Limited changes are already noticeable in some
courses.

3. Applying Knowledge to Development Problems: In general,
when underdeveloped rural communities request technical assistance,
they assume that the university professor or students can render
this assistance. On the other hand, professors and students realize
that problems are so complex that they require an integrated approach,
including the help of cooperatives and other community organizations.

The program director plans to evaluate the work carried out
to date in light of the use of such integrated approaches. As a result,
activities may be concentrated in a limited number of pilot centers.
At the moment, pilot programs are being tested at two centers:
Goyllarisquizga and Huasahuasi.* At the first center, a group of
professors is seeking to revitalize a former mining area. At the
second center, a group of professors and students plans to test the
economic and programing techniques to help in the mechanization
of potato growing. In both instances, the program is attempting to
test systematic solutions to problems of food production and distribution, as well as to improve the people's living conditions.

The program's success may be attributed to the following
factors:

1. The way the program was designed to supply both short-
term and long-term answers to requests made in almost any technical
field and in any region of the country. The program, managed with

----

*Goyllarisquizga is a mining town in the central mountain
range, which was constructed for mining a very limited coal deposit.
The enterprise has been abandoned. Huasahuasi is a town in the
central mountain range in the heart of the largest potato-producing
zone in the country.

great flexibility, has created enthusiasm on the part of professors, students, and beneficiaries and has also supplied sufficient information and experience to determine future program plans.

2. Acceptance by the farmers of the services technical assistants offer. The program has achieved not only an increase in production, in some cases relatively dramatic, but also goodwill. Farmers were initially suspicious of university people because of past experience with disruptive agents or with failures in agricultural extension activities. By living with the farmers, students brought about a change of attitude that, in some cases, led to written requests for continuation of services.

LESSONS GAINED THROUGH THE PROGRAM

Although the program has functioned for a relatively short period of time, the following lessons have been learned.

Community Needs and Government Priorities

If the University expects to receive government support, it should consider government priorities in carrying out community activities. Owing to the low level of development in a great number of rural communities, there are obvious needs in areas such as health, education, housing, and communications. Work in these and other areas might be carried out in conjunction with other state agencies and universities, but the complexity of the task and lack of government funds have so far prevented attempts to test this kind of cooperation.

University Interest

Both professor and student participation should be an essential part of a program. Such participation has the following advantages:

1. The University demonstrates its capacity for providing technical assistance through the high quality of its faculty and the desire of professors and students to spread knowledge.
2. It encourages research on practical problems. The University has been preparing many of its faculty at the master and Ph.D. levels, in the hope that they will carry out research. This program offers the possibility of financing applied research within the framework of Peruvian agrarian needs.

3. Work in the rural areas, an essential constituent of the program, creates an informal, close relationship between professors and students and begins to transform the teaching process, since it changes the impressions that professors and students have of each other.

4. Work in the rural areas affords opportunities to create and develop in students and professors leadership qualities that were not demonstrated through the regular academic program.

University, Government, and Community Relationships

The success of the program requires the participation of government officials at the highest level. The community must also play an important role in orientation and implementation. The Transferal of Technology Program has been so successful in achieving community involvement that, although the University, its directors, professors, and students favor renewing the agreement, it is the rural communities who demonstrate the greatest desire for the program's continuation by the increasing number of requests for services (forcing the program coordinators to choose among them).

Management of Resources

A program such as this should fulfill the following administrative requirements:

1. Administrative flexibility and institutional autonomy. The general coordinator of the program and his committee have considerable autonomy regarding the regular administrative channels in the University and ministry. This independence has helped the program achieve its objectives with limited resources and very few administrators.

2. Leadership. The University, through its coordinators, Office of Social Outreach, and its organizational structure has the capacity and power to set up and manage the Program.

3. Decision making and participation. Day-to-day decisions and overall policies are made in the field and are a challenge to the creativity of the professor as well as the student. A continuing record of the program is based on reports that students and professors must present at the end of each mission.

SUGGESTIONS FOR PROGRAM PLANNERS

First, technical assistance services should be continuous as requested by clients in disadvantaged areas rather than dependent on University vacation time. Such an extension of services, however, would require substantial changes in the academic calendar and possibly in the present curriculum. While the calendar and curriculum could be modified, as some of the program participants have proposed, such modification is a slow and difficult process and requires organizational changes in the institution's academic and administrative structures, usually inflexible at a university.

Second, students should receive formal academic recognition for their field work. Students in the upper classes especially are under economic pressure to choose thesis topics that permit them to fulfill the requirements for a professional degree in the shortest time possible. To encourage student participation and to improve the quality of program services, a study of the following incentives is urged: granting academic credit for work carried out in rural areas upon presentation of competent reports and monographs on the work accomplished; and increasing funds for theses, sufficient to cover all students who graduate from the University.

Third, professors should receive additional financial aid to supplement their low salary, already diminished by inflation. Adequate payment for program services is particularly important to faculty members who possess a high level of training and who could obtain work outside the institution. The present modest per diem in the program obliges the professor to accept precarious and at times inadequate housing and transportation.

Fourth, the coordinator of the program should receive more administrative help. Despite the fact that the coordinator is an able and dynamic administrator, he is overloaded with responsibilities and work. He is assisted only by one secretary.

RECOMMENDATIONS FOR DONORS

First, support efforts to coordinate the programs of similar or related institutions. A national technical assistance system would reduce costs for transportation and utilize local personnel who have a special knowledge of local situations. The Ministry of Agriculture is presently considering extending the agreement so that the NAU may work with other universities in the country and with government regional offices. Such coordination, however, requires funds. Organizations and communications facilities capable of carrying out joint activities on a large scale do not exist.

Second, support evaluation of existing programs. If the increasing demand for services is any indicator, the program has wide acceptance. An objective and critical evaluation of the work is needed, however, in order to establish policies and procedures on which to structure future activities. The University possesses the human resources necessary to plan and initiate a systematic evaluation, but such an evaluation would probably require additional financial resources as well as the assistance of specialized personnel.

Third, use flexible criteria for assisting similar development programs, especially at institutions that lack research resources.

Fourth, provide logistical assistance not now covered by the Ministry of Agriculture budget. Special needs include transportation facilities, nonexistent at the moment; means of communication and of distribution of information and results; financial and academic incentives for faculty and students; and technical equipment (such as theodolites and levels) and supplies (tents, flashlights, utensils) for work in rural areas.

APPENDIX

The University

Origin

The National Agrarian University evolved from the National Agricultural and Veterinary School, which was founded in 1902 with the guidance of a mission from the Agricultural Institute in Gembloux, Belgium. The School began on the Santa Beatriz farm in Lima, where the National Agricultural Institute, concerned with agricultural practice, had previously been operating.

In 1933, the School was moved to the La Molina farm, 11 kilometers from Lima, where the necessary buildings had already been constructed, and was incorporated into the newly created Institute for Higher Agricultural Studies in Peru. The Institute included a School for Foremen, the Agricultural Experiment Station of La Molina, the National Institute of Agricultural Microbiology, Serum and Vaccinations, and the National Meterological Service. It thus brought together teaching at different levels, research, and service (soil and plant analysis, plant propagation, seed distribution, manufacture and distribution of serum and vaccinations).

In 1941, the School of Agriculture replaced the Institute of Higher Agricultural Studies. Research and service institutes became a part of the Ministry of Agriculture, and the School, now autonomous, was linked the the Ministry of Education. In 1958, the School was completely reorganized to integrate its teaching, research, and service functions. Academic departments were established, and administrative services were centralized. When the new University Law was passed in 1960, the institution was incorporated into the Peruvian university system and took the name of National Agrarian University. It has gradually broadened its programs to include agronomy, sciences, zoology, agricultural engineering, forestry, graduate studies, fishing, food technology, and economics. The evolution of the NAU, especially during the 1950s, was largely due to the training program for its teaching staff at the graduate level and to the support of national and international agencies.

Teaching

At present (1974), the formal teaching programs have an enrollment of 2,720 students distributed in the following fields: agronomy, sciences, forestry sciences, economics and planning, food technology, agricultural engineering, fishing, animal husbandry, graduate studies, and general studies.

The University requires students to take admission exams. Sixty percent of the students who enter the University have had previous training at preparatory schools, and all students must take full-time programs. Approximately one third of the students come from homes where the parents have had only primary education; one third of the students' parents have had secondary education, and the remaining one third of the students' parents have had a university education. Twenty-five percent of the student body are women.

Students come from all social classes. In 1972, applicants were divided as follows:

(1) By Father's Occupation

Occupation	Applicants		Admitted	
	Number	Percent	Number	Percent
Manual*	262	21.28	29	15.85
Other†	969	78.72	154	84.15
Total	1,231	100	183	100
No data	55		7	

*Laborer, peasant, artisan.
†Office worker, professional, skilled workman.

(2) By Monthly Income

	Applicants		Admitted	
Income*	Number	Percent	Number	Percent
S/.5,000 and under	470	44.76	65	40.36
S/.5,001-20,000	524	49.90	87	54.03
S/.20,001-50,000	52	4.95	9	5.59
Over S/.50,000	4	0.38	0	0.00
Total	1,050	100	161	100
No data	236		29	

On the undergraduate level, the study programs require ten semesters to obtain the bachelor of sciences degree. Upon presentation of a thesis, the corresponding professional degree is awarded. At the graduate level, the master of science degree requires an average of four additional semesters of study.

Research

Research projects are part of the interdisciplinary programs but are carried out in the departments. In 1974 there were 91 research projects in the following interdisciplinary programs: Corn, Native Fruits, Pasture Grass and Forage, Potatoes, Cereals, Genetic Improvement of Cotton, Vegetables, Sheep and Llamas, Swine, Meats, Livestock Improvement, Small Animals, Tropical Agriculture and Livestock, Common Foodstuffs, Milk and Derivatives, Plant and Shrubbery Propagation, and Pre-Colombian Anthropology and Agriculture. During the past two years, students have also been engaged in 158 thesis projects and in 382 projects that were not part of specific programs.

Community Service

The University provides community service through the following activities: (1) short courses for job holders at different levels—professionals, high school teachers, foremen, and community leaders—and for students from other universities (national and foreign); (2) conventions, seminars, symposia, round tables, panels, and conferences; (3) exhibitions, fairs, guided tours through its installation, and field trips; (4) advising and consulting with public agencies, private organizations, universities, and individuals; (5) technical assistance through specific programs and agreements

*Peruvian sol = U.S. $0.015 July 1976.

with universities and public agencies; and (6) publication of research results. The University recently created a center to disseminate the scientific and technical information resulting from research carried out in the different areas.

Besides serving the community through such activities, NAU representatives serve on boards of directors of several public agencies, mainly in the agrarian and fisheries fields. Since the reorganization of the National Agricultural School, NAU has also signed agreements with numerous public and private agencies for specific teaching, research, and community service projects, as an integral part of broader development programs. NAU recently established a Center for Investment and Development Projects and Studies (CEPID) so that it could offer consulting services to public and private agencies. Such services include basic studies, preparation, feasibility studies, consulting and technical assistance, evaluation of ongoing projects, and supervision of projects in the planning stage.

Resources

In addition to administrative and service personnel, there are 336 faculty members at the NAU who are appointed by categories (professor, associate professor, assistant professor, and instructor) in the departments. Their duties and rights are established according to the law that governs the Peruvian university system. About 84 percent of the faculty members are full-time, and 16 percent are part-time. (The 8:1 average student-professor ratio makes it possible for professors to devote a large part of their time to research and community service activities.) In 1973, a total of 42 percent of the teaching staff had advanced degrees: 47 had Ph.D.s or the equivalent, and 94 had master of science degrees.

At La Molina, the University has a farm of 210 hectares and the new 7.5 hectare University campus, which includes a library, a University Center (dining room, kitchen, medical center, conference room), several administrative offices, laboratories, workshops, and service installations. NAU also has various plots of land and buildings in Lima, Callao, and other locations in Peru. On the whole, until the 1974 earthquake, NAU had adequate physical resources to carry out its activities: experimental and demonstration areas, animal farms, laboratories, workshops, processing plants, museums, meteorological observatory, and various centers that support the regular academic activities.

The financial resources of NAU come from the following sources:

Biennial Budget 1973-74
(in millions of sols)

	Operation	Investment	Total
General budget of the republic through Ministry of Education	296.4	4.7	301.1
NAU capital–sale of goods and services	100.3	3.8	104.1
Special agreements with Ministries of Agriculture, Industry, Fishing, and Energy and with other public and private institutions for research, technical assistance, and consulting	50.0	–	50.0
Donations–IBM for the Data Processing Center	0.8	–	0.8
Total	447.5	8.5	456.0

The articles that follow have been included with the case studies because they add new facts or perspectives to the overall study of higher education for development (HED). Four of them—the articles by Frank H. Bowles, A. Babs Fafunwa, Soedjatmoko, and R. Cranford Pratt—were written specifically for the HED project; Frank Bowles's study was originally prepared for a meeting of the project's African Regional Team, held in Dakar, Senegal in September 1974.

David Court's report is a revised version of a study prepared for the Institute for Development Studies. The W. Arthur Lewis article was previously published by ICED as an Occasional Paper. The article by Howard R. Swearer was originally published in a slightly shorter version by Phi Beta Kappa in the Key Reporter (Winter 1974-1975 issue).

24

STAGES OF EDUCATIONAL DEVELOPMENT

Frank H. Bowles

I see in developing nations on all continents an educational growth pattern of five successive stages, each of which represents a level of realization, through programs and institutions, of the political and social needs emerging from the development process. Within each of these stages are certain repeated patterns of action and interaction, and a description of these stages and patterns offers a set of rough standards or criteria by which educational development can be evaluated.

There are, of course, profound differences among developing areas, and many reasons to offer disagreements and/or corrections to sketches as here presented. It is difficult to compare Asia with its long-established intellectual community with Africa, which is building its community, and with South America, which is abandoning elitism before establishing mass education. The sketches are presented despite their flaws because there is need to understand development education's frame of reference to establish valid measures of its achievement and growth.

The five stages are not discrete. One does not build on another in unalterable order, and no one stage develops only in the pattern as presented. In educational growth it is never possible to say that a given stage has been completed or another stage begun during a given year. Rather, the stages must be viewed as forming a continuum from some starting level that represents national ignorance as to the meaning and purpose of education, to some other level that

---

Frank H. Bowles, author of the landmark study <u>Access to Higher Education</u>, was president of the College Entrance Examination Board for 15 years and Planning Officer of Haile Selassie I University in Ethiopia from 1966 to 1972. This study was prepared, at the request of the African Regional Team, for their meeting held at Dakar, Senegal in September 1974. A very brief outline appears as an appendix in Volume 1 of this study.

marks national self-sufficiency in education at all levels. In such a continuum, stages often overlap and run parallel for sometime.

Two general points as to the continuum must be made. First, that the institutions of development and their basic methodologies tend to be the same in all developing nations, including the predictable stage at which innovation is invoked as a method; second, that the patterns and timing in the formation of institutions vary according to the political and social circumstances of the nations involved.

With the above points noted it becomes possible to include and account for some situations that do not always follow the sequential pattern within the development pattern. Broadly speaking, there are three groups:

1. Nations such as Egypt, Iran, Ethiopia, and Thailand, which established their own cultural traditions long before the arrival of Western education and consequently gave strong national flavor to the systems they developed.

2. Nations such as those in the drought-ridden Sahel, which are trying to produce a miracle of development out of a tragic lack of resources.

3. Nations that for essentially political reasons established institutions either before their systems were ready to support them, or long after they were needed, leading to serious confusion as to control, purposes, and standards.

The above—and other exceptions that can be identified—may appear to disprove the concept of the continuum, but, if recognized and analyzed in terms of cause and effect, they tend, in fact, to strengthen it.

STAGE I

Stage I encompasses the formation of a national system of education. Such a system may come into being with an ambitious charter. It may even be created with an instant formal structure reaching to higher education, universities, and research institutes. But it must have a beginning.

In every country, the beginning has consisted of primary schools, followed by postprimary vocational schools, teacher training institutes, and secondary schools. These schools are the foundation institutions on which all others must rest, and from which all others are developed. They are also especially important for the attitude and tone they establish, derived from the concept on which they are based.

An educational system can be founded on either of two basic—and opposed—concepts. It can be established as an elite system, supported by a literate but essentially uneducated working class, or as a mass education system of open access to opportunity. The first was most prominently represented in nineteenth-century Europe and is the concept behind most of the systems established 20 years ago in Africa. The second is the system emerging, with great travail, in South America today. Attitude and tone, of course, establish the characteristics of systems, which, once set, are difficult to change, although, as can be observed both in Europe and South America, change can be accomplished—at a price.

Primary Schools

Primary schools in developing countries are established on paper as either unitary programs of six, seven, or eight years preparing for a final examination which determines further education, or as basic programs preparing for a middle school, which in turn leads to the final school leaving examination. In fact, the appearance of continuity, progression, and a fixed term of years is deceiving. The first year of school is usually a time of devastating failure for half, or more than half the pupils. The failed students come back another, and often a third, year to crowd the classrooms until they are finally passed on. Thus, the first year should be understood as a full cycle in itself and the most powerful selective program in the entire school system.

The problems of failure and selection are partly linguistic, partly instructional, and partly cultural. Linguistically the problem lies in the language of instruction, which is rarely the everyday language of the students. The years of primary school, particularly the first year, are, therefore, the years of elimination of the students who cannot learn the language of instruction. Some countries attempt to solve this problem by using regional dialects in the early grades, and this is sometimes helpful. Even this move, however, does little more than unmask the familiar problem of cultural deprivation in the home.

The instructional problems are complex. Primary teachers are minimally trained and poorly supervised in most developing nations. Classrooms are overcrowded. Textbooks are old, and often nonexistent. Children are hungry and unresponsive. Repeaters drag down the level of performance. Perhaps half the failures are due to instructional failure rather than to lack of student ability.

Finally the cultural problems. Not only the government, the politicians, and the educators, but also the peasants and the schoolteachers know that schools are the only avenue of mobility. The government may mandate high standards, but the peasants and the schoolteachers (who come from the peasantry) know better. If a student can be passed, he will be. If repeaters are prohibited, they nevertheless find their way into the classes. Such matters are too important to the life of the child and the prestige of the family to be left to government directives.

Those who survive the first selection may go straight on past all the other barriers or fail and repeat at each barrier (as two thirds of them will do). The next selection point—that is, the point at which there is a systemwide examination—usually comes at the end of either the fourth or sixth year. Here, because of failures on the examination, there will be another pile-up of repeating students in the grade before the examination, and once again the reduced group of survivors will begin to move toward the next examination barrier.

As a result, it is difficult for the student of average ability to learn at the prescribed rate, and the schools fill up with students who can never pass the leaving examinations. In the last analysis, perhaps one student out of ten who entered the elementary school passes the leaving examination and has an opportunity to enter the next level of schooling.

The next level consists of three very unequal choices: secondary schools, teacher training institutes, and vocational-technical schools.

Secondary Schools

Secondary schools, that is to say schools that prepare for university entrance, are the first choice of all eligibles. Secondary schools in developing nations, like the primary schools, were established on traditional patterns. Their program is a close imitation of the European—a type of general education preparatory to the narrow professionalism of European university faculties—languages, literature, history, mathematics, and science (taught as a theoretical subject). Their purpose was (and is) to select, by elimination of all failing students, a small group of students who, by reason of inherited position, or ability, or both, would be able, as adults, to take the responsibility and authority of national leadership. As part of this process, the schools provided free room, board, tuition, and often clothes and pocket money. To enforce this purpose, the schools have been rigidly controlled by an international examinations standard—usually the French baccalauréat or the British "A levels."

In fact, the secondary schools in developing countries have been even more rigidly controlled than their models in Europe and the United States, which over the last 30 years have broadened their programs and reduced their eliminations. But these program differences between the European models which are now modernizing, and their overseas replications, which have yet to consider change, are not as important as relationships to the rest of their educational systems, to the political systems, and to the power structures.

In the developed nations, secondary schools were, up until the end of the nineteenth century, attached, sometimes informally, sometimes formally and directly, to universities. They were dependent upon universities for their teachers and programs, for the approval implicit in the admission of their students, and for most of their prestige.

In developing nations, by contrast, the secondary schools were almost always established before universities, sometimes as much as 30 years before, and as the highest level of education available, they became, de facto, the higher education in their country. These secondary schools had ample time and opportunity to take on all those university attributes that have to do with the selection and training of their students, and the placement of their graduates in advantageous positions. Under such conditions, they became powerful institutions with strong influence on social mobility, elite formation, and concomitantly, on the development or nondevelopment of other types of education.

With respect to operation, the schools were essentially unitary institutions, modeled on either the French lycée of seven years, the English grammar school of six years, or the U.S. junior-senior high school of six years. (In the few instances where the U.S. system was tried, the idea of the two-or-three-stream comprehensive high school was adopted on paper, but usually without provision of the shop and laboratory facilities and teachers required for genuine implementation of the program.) Faculties, following the European tradition, consisted of university graduates, usually expatriates, and usually qualified and experienced men who had fallen short of their expectations in their own countries.

The most important aspect of these secondary schools has been the provision for selection and elimination of students, operating in three phases. Phase one is selection on the basis of the primary school leaving examination, usually in the ratio of not more than 50 percent of the students who passed the examination. Phase two is a selection after an intermediate examination, which occurs two, three, or four years after entrance—depending on the system. This examination controls entrance to an upper level, and usually eliminates (or forces repetition by) about half of the students. In phase three, students (except in the American system) concentrate on one or two subjects for two years, and then take the secondary school leaving examination, which also becomes the university entrance examination. Elimination through failure on this examination varies widely, from one fourth to more than half of the candidates, and it may be subject to manipulation of the passing grade, depending on openings available for qualified secondary graduates. Failing students are usually allowed at least one year of repetition for a second try.

Because students must go through this long series of elimination, repeating years when they fail, the average age of secondary graduates is ordinarily at least 22, and graduates of 25 or older are not uncommon.

The successful secondary school graduate who has passed all of his examinations is thus a young adult who has acquired linguistic skills, a good social presence, and some cultural knowledge, and is old enough to go directly into government service, unless there is a university available, which he will, of course, enter. Even secondary students who failed along the way, having survived some of the eliminations of the school program, are by national standards highly educated, and, therefore, fit for government employment with its lifetime security.

The influence and importance of secondary schools in developing nations, whether or not they led directly to universities, can be inferred from the above description; both influence and importance were overwhelming. As secondary education has become widespread, their importance may have declined, but they continue to control the rigid primary school curriculum, which prepares for the crucial primary school leaving examination, the only means of admission to secondary school, and therefore to mandate student elimination through a long series of barriers within the educational system. Furthermore, because of secondary school prestige, the other two forms of postprimary institutions have been, in varying degrees, downgraded in the public esteem.

Teacher Training Institutes

Teacher training institutes (or teacher training colleges) in developing countries prepare specifically for primary school teaching. They offer from one to four years of general education, roughly similar to the offering of the higher-status secondary schools. General education is followed by a year of pedagogy. Sometimes, practice teaching and other forms of preparation for classroom work are included, sometimes not. Teacher training schools, like the secondary schools, are usually residential, without cost to the students, and jobs are guaranteed on completion of the course. As first set up within the basic educational scheme, teacher training schools offered

no access to higher education, but arrangements were open to a fa-
vored few permitting study for a higher teaching diploma in foreign
countries. Unlike the secondary schools, teacher training was open
to any student who passed his primary school leaving examination at
the requisite level, and there was no policy of rigid student elimination. As education, the programs were admittedly meager. There
were few textbooks, poor facilities, and in contrast with the university-trained secondary-school teachers, the faculty came from the
ranks of the institute's graduates with occasional specialists added
by donor agencies.

Generally speaking, in the initial formation of the basic system—
Stage I—there were more teacher training institutes than secondary
schools, but as enrollments grew, the number of secondary schools
tended to increase while teacher training remained relatively stable.

Vocational-Technical Schools

Recognition of need for craft skills and technical knowledge
came early in developing nations, dating in most countries far back
into the time of missionaries, but efforts to formalize training have
met repeated frustrations and failure.

Vocational-technical schools have been the last and the forced
choice of primary school leavers. In the face of unlimited need, and
apparent opportunity, the statement is difficult to believe, but the fact
is there and the reasons are cogent. Vocational-technical schools
were rarely residential, students' food and clothes were ordinarily
not subsidized, and, after completing the course, graduates had no
guarantee of jobs. Since technical development, except in a few government agencies, was not sizable enough to support an employed
labor force, there were, indeed, very few jobs. A vicious circle
was thus set up, in which technology could not develop because of
lack of trained manpower, and manpower could not be trained because
there was insufficient development to justify and utilize it. In other
words, no developing nation in its early days of educational development was willing to subsidize either the production or the employment
of skilled workers. The formula for failure of technical education was
completed by the poor caliber of the student body, composed of those
who had failed to be admitted to either secondary school or teacher
training; the constant deficiencies of equipment and supplies; the low
social status of men and women trained to work with their hands; the
poor quality of faculty available; and the absolute block to further
education at the end of the course.

Despite the odds, or perhaps because they were never understood, the training efforts were determined and sometimes, when

under direct donor agency control, of good quality. The result has been a thin trickle of qualified craftsmen and technicians, but, so far, no developing country has built up the critical mass necessary to bring respectability to the schooling.

Postprimary Education as a Social Determinant

Postprimary education is more than a unit or a level in the educational establishment. It is the place where the hopes and taboos of people meet the plans and limitations of government. Thus the people demand whatever amount of education is necessary to attain job security while the government demands only the amount necessary to select elite recruits for the development process. The instinct of the people turns them away from schooling leading to work with hands as not productive for job security, while the government strives to find the needed technicians and craftsmen without being willing to pay for them.

These conflicts and requirements determine the shape of the system through enrollment patterns. But they do more—they determine the shape of things to come. Every postprimary institution has a potential for growth. Secondary schools can and do develop into universities, and, in any event, many of their faculty members, as university graduates, can and will move to university teaching. Teacher training institutes become higher teacher training institutes, then graduate to postsecondary status and become teacher training colleges, and, in time, may move to university status and the granting of degrees. Vocational-technical schools extend their work through the 14th grade, and, may become engineering institutes granting diplomas or even degrees.

In other words, the establishment of a set of postprimary institutions is an irreversible step toward the establishment of postsecondary institutions and a university. University formation is determined not so much by time sequences, methods of planning and organization, sources of support, and manpower requirements as by patterns of development in which industrial and preindustrial cultures meet.

STAGE II

Stage II is the establishment of higher education, which grows out of the basic system described as Stage I. Higher education cannot be established without or before the lower schools, and, if it were (as has been tried in some regions), it would serve a student body so small and ill-prepared as to be unimportant.

In practice, universities are built around needs and problems that are revealed in the operation of lower schools, or in the operation of government and national services. Institutionally, higher education tends to grow out of lower education transformed and renamed to deal with specific problems. The original forms of lower education tend to acquire strength and status until one or several of them form the nucleus of a university, usually being combined with a newly formed theoretical faculty, such as law, humanities, or social sciences, to justify the term university.

There are four distinct sets of reasons for founding universities. First, a developing region may need professional services, particularly in medicine, engineering, and law. It is impossible to afford enough expatriates to supply such services, and, even if they could be afforded, impossible to control their continuity and conditions of service. Second, local training of professionals, which avoids use of expatriates or the expensive overseas training of nationals, is a direct analogue of import substitution in the field of manufacturing, and attracts capital and operational support from international development agencies. Third, both national prestige and ambition on the part of nationals who have been trained in overseas universities contribute to decisions on university formation. Fourth, any society instinctively recognizes the need for a trustworthy repository of knowledge. In the past, such need has been met by priesthood (and some political systems today may still be perpetuating a form of priesthood), but in much of the world this time is past or passing, and the university is the contemporary answer.

The problem as seen within a given country is almost always that of obtaining professional services and building a professional cadre. Supplying the need for higher-level manpower has the incidental advantages of providing outlets for promising young nationals at home instead of having to send them abroad, at great cost and with the danger that they may acquire unsuitable political ideas.

Three points are important to remember. First, universities are rarely born full blown where nothing existed before. Most have been based on one or more existing institutions, programs, colleges, faculties, or schools, and the predecessor institutions influence their successors in many and often intangible ways.

Second, young universities are teaching institutions, often inexperienced, derivative, and very traditional. Attempts to invest them with the missions of research, advanced study, and international exchange are likely to be synthetic and useless to the point of harmfulness. To begin by setting up the ideal conditions for research institutions and advanced study, with time for research figured into teaching loads, sabbatical leaves, research grants, and other pre-requisites is to invite faculty and students to consider themselves privileged to permanent enjoyment of the bounty of the state.

Third, young universities are amateur universities. Any university may be described as two groups of people, one of which is made up of university graduates whose job it is to offer instruction, and the other of which aspires to become university graduates through receiving and responding to the offered instruction. An amateur university may be distinguished from a professional university by the fact that in the latter type, each group understands the rights, priv-ileges, and responsibilities (as well as problems and objections) attached to its position, and is aware that the other group also has rights, privileges, and responsibilities along with problems and ob-jections. Under certain circumstances each group is prepared to join the other to create a single institution. In an amateur university there is no such understanding, either within each group or between the groups. Professional and amateur as labels applied to universities are not affected by institutional wealth, equipment, facilities, or high patronage. They are affected by purpose, experience, leadership, support, national credibility, and social environment. The matura-tion time from amateur to professional status may be estimated at about 20 years, depending on the interaction of numerous variables.

In the actual formation of new universities, a number of salty questions as to student selection and control, program, autonomy, faculty tenure and governance, support, status of administrators, and such other university commonplaces are certain to arise. Much of this discussion is based on an ill-informed idealization of univer-sity organization in developed nations. In fact, observations suggest that at least some of the following conditions prevail in almost every developing university:

Student Selection: There is no doubt in anyone's mind that developing universities must have superior students in order to pro-duce elite graduates, but there is much disagreement as to procedure. Faculty are divided between the merits of rigid selection and open admission, tending to depend on whether they conduct weekly tutorials with small groups of students, or give prescribed lectures to huge assemblies. Students favor open admission and indefinite retention with application of standards postponed until the final examination and then, if possible, waived. Government demands strict selection at admission and instant dismissal of failing students, both for finan-cial reasons and because experience shows that it is the poorer stu-dents who are the most disruptive.

Control and Autonomy: Regardless of guarantees or charter or constitutional provisions, universities are ultimately under direct control of the central government power, exercised by the military and the police. In other words, even though there may be a stated (and to some extent actual) right of freedom of speech, assembly, and political sanctuary on university campuses, the records show that the central government will not hesitate to intervene in university events with force when it, as final judge of necessity, sees the need. In fact mutual distrust is deep-seated. Central governments fear university status and university capability as a focal point of dissent, unrest, and protest, while the university fears government, for its police power, its absolute financial control, and its control of the job market.

Program: The slogans of innovation and relevance relate to the often repeated charge that Western education, inappropriate for developing countries, has been forced on unfortunate nations without regard to their needs. The fact is, however, that in those fields that have the earliest importance in developing nations—health, engineering, and agriculture—no other true choices were available when the universities opened. Theoretically, of course, the present combinations of theoretical study followed by clinical or practical study are not the only methods of training in these fields. But in practice other methods usually turn out to be slight deviations from present programs, or else depart from those programs so radically that graduates have difficulty in receiving recognition.

New ideas and programs are most needed at the postprimary level—technical education, teacher training, or rural development—and at the literacy level—child rearing, basics of tillage and animal husbandry, family health, and basic tool skills. All these areas are open to experimentation and innovation since they do not lend themselves easily to formal treatment. In fact, universities avoid them, primarily because there is no methodology for dealing with them through the standard procedures of university teaching. In most developing countries, students avoid these subjects, if taught at university level, since they consider such studies to offer no career future and to be demeaning by requiring manual labor.

Faculty Recruitment: Faculty recruitment is usually a question of expatriates versus nationals. Most new universities are initially staffed with expatriates, who are replaced, as nationals meet the minimum requirements for appointment. The pattern makes for an unstable and uncommitted faculty, and opens possibilities of gross injustice to expatriates; the expatriate is politically vulnerable whenever his post (or his scholarship) is contested by a national, and young nationals may have less will to achieve when they know the privileges are theirs by right.

Tenure: Nearly every developing university grants instant tenure to all nationals who join the faculty, and nothing short of scandalous public behavior (which includes scandalous political

behavior) will terminate such tenure. To only a slightly lesser degree
this is also true of nonacademic staff. Provable incompetence, dis-
honesty, and arrogance are not considered scandalous public behavior.

Administrators: Administrators' appointments tend to be considered as faculty ranks with higher pay, to be awarded to the most
senior faculty member in the appropriate grade.

University Governance: The faculty insists on autonomy and
self-governance, and tends to ignore the fact that the government can
and does intervene at will. This is a bitter issue in some institutions.

Expansion: Enrollment at developing universities tends to expand slowly depending, of course, on policies of enrollment in the
lower schools. However, unless controlled with care, the universities
may expand rapidly in programs, departments, and public commitments. There are two reasons for this. One is the age-old reason,
which holds in every university in the world, that the surest way to
advancement is to found a new department, faculty, or institute. The
other reason, peculiar to developing nations, is that donor agencies,
when offering program support, tend to seek a distinctive role to
which they may attach their name. In cases of great generosity, this
may mean a new faculty complete with physical plant and staff. In
many other cases, it means research units, fellowships, exchange
professorships, departmental support, and equipment, each of which
requires acknowledgement, and often a specific organization to carry
it on. As a result, developing universities tend to have many func-
tionaries, and often to be physically dispersed. At the same time,
there is no observable relation between the size of the organizational
structure and the size of the student enrollment.

Developing universities in their founding and early formative
period (or redeveloping universities as in South America, where the
ancient foundations are gradually acquiring a new superstructure)
have many weaknesses with little in the way of counterbalancing
strength. They are under strong government control and, in addition,
tend to be internally disrupted by faculty pressures. They sow the
seeds of future difficulties by adopting the external characteristics
of long-established institutions with strong administrations, financial
backing, student bodies, and systems of rewards for effective performance, only to fall into turmoil when their facade fails to protect
them. They are, in brief, amateur universities.

Their problem is that too much is expected too soon in terms
of national benefits of leadership and service from university graduates, and, in turn, universities expect too much too soon in reward
from the nation for their services. University students especially,
are notably overexpectant. Actually, for at least the first ten years,
while they build facilities, programs, and faculties, new universities
can make little contribution to national development in terms of

trained manpower, or expert services, and the period often extends
to 20 years unless there is good institutional management. Manpower
production may, in fact, be cut down during the changeover from postsecondary institutions to university faculties for professional training.
Even after that changeover, there will still be a period of adjustment
to the new standards and the new graduates.

The new universities will in time come to fulfill their purpose,
when they have lived long enough to have produced enough trained
individuals to supply the nation's manpower requirements. When this
has happened, after perhaps 20 or 30 years, the universities will
begin to take their proper place on the national scene.

STAGE III

A third stage of educational development is often unperceived
because it is not conducted within the educational establishment nor,
in general, by professional educators. This stage is characterized
by political action, taken by political and development leaders, seeking
several social and economic benefits. To achieve national development and establish their own political base, political leaders must,
first, slow down the rural out-migration and the uncontrollable growth
of the cities by bettering rural living conditions and increasing rural
purchasing power; second, attract popular support, from the rural
population; and third, develop national unity by establishing a basis
and forum for political education. In addition, economic development
will require, first, extension of the modern sector, through roads,
transport, and communication; second, improvement in agricultural
productivity; third, improved rural purchasing power to support
national industry; and fourth, new development projects to enlarge
the whole modernizing effort.

The basic educational system described in Stage I is not adequate to these tasks because of location, cost, and other limitations.
Schools are largely established in the urban centers, and essentially
serve only the urban population. Although residential teacher training
institutes and secondary schools may sometimes be located outside
of the population centers, their students are, nevertheless, urban
in their origin.

The schools tend to remain urban for several reasons. The
cities grow rapidly and attract families with children as well as
cast-out or runaway children. Hence, much of the annual expansion
of education is merely more city schools. Teachers will not willingly
go to rural schools and sometimes even disappear or resign to avoid
them. Concentrated city populations, moreover, exert more powerful

political pressures for schools than does the more diffused population
of the countryside.

The cost of extending the school system to the countryside is
also a hurdle. Rural education will require building schools, transporting teachers and supplies. It will need adequate supervision of
schools likely to have severe problems of learning, passing examinations, retaining students, and providing economical student-teacher
ratios. The cost arguments are all against establishing rural schools
to support either the development process or the political process.

Finally there are four major limitations of the existing schools,
in terms of political and development goals. First, the pass-fail
options of the school system creates at least as much political dis-
satisfaction among the parents of failing children as it does satisfaction among the parents of children who succeed. Second, a school
does not have any built-in relationship to a local community. While
a hard-working teacher can develop such a relationship, it is not
easy for a school to act as both a teaching institution and a development agency. Third, a school cannot make a direct attack on any
social problem, except at the risk of alienating a part of the community and increasing the very divisiveness it seeks to reduce.
Fourth, a rural school may well be self-defeating in community development since its most successful students will leave for the city
as soon as they finish school in order to share the wealth that is
rumored to be found there.

Because of these problems of the formal system, a nonformal
system of education is growing up, using what are essentially training
techniques, practical lessons supported by demonstrations and presented to small groups of mature and presumably motivated individuals. The purpose of nonformal education is to train a largely illiterate population in such matters as improved animal husbandry,
increased agricultural yields, home improvement, basic sanitation,
family nutrition, or child care, or, if indicated by local circumstances, to offer literacy education to those who may be able to
profit by it.

Basically three forms of nonformal education are utilized in
such programs: radio, supplemented by group sessions and exercises; household demonstrations by community workers; and short
schooling programs to teach such elementary skills as sewing, use
of hand tools, principles of drainage, or home repairs.

The role of the political leadership in the development of
Stage III is to recognize the existence and nature of the problem to
be dealt with and to take the necessary political steps to bring in the
development agencies, to cooperate with these agencies in establishing programs, and to set up the mechanisms whereby the programs introduced by donor agencies will be continued after outside
assistance is withdrawn.

Development agencies have an equal stake in such training.
Their role is to undertake the detailed planning, determine the staffing
and material needs, and introduce the program in a manner politically
and socially acceptable to the receiving country and locality. The
program itself will be largely a training activity in which members
of the community will be selected and trained to carry the actual instructional program, first under the direction and supervision of
imported program leaders, and then, in time, on their own responsibility.

The significance of Stage III lies partly in the fact that nonformal
methods are used, partly in the fact that it is specifically addressed
to rural and largely illiterate groups, and partly in the fact that it is
outside the national educational system. Above all, however, this
stage is addressed directly to development, to improving both production and the daily lives of people without being filtered through
the process of formal education. It is, in the truest sense of the
word, a preinvestment activity, which, if successful, will lead directly
to further investment in that type of project.

In the long run, Stage III carries the concept of development
directly to the basic structure of the economy, serving as a forerunner of broader and more massive efforts to come. Stages I and II
foster elite education at primary, secondary, and higher levels to
achieve a long-range, indirect benefit in terms of services, leadership, and national development; Stage III on the other hand, takes
direct assistance to families and communities, working for their own
immediate and tangible benefit.

It is only fair to note that Stage III is composed of a number of
short-term programs, which must be constantly revitalized and re-
studied if they are to hold the attention of those to whom they are
addressed. In a sense, Stage III opens opportunities for formal education, with its continuing operation and its goals of personal achievement and position.

STAGE IV

The fourth stage of educational development has appeared under
different names in different places. It has been called "educational
effectiveness," "rationalized primary schooling," and "equalization
of educational opportunity."

Whatever it is called, this stage is characterized by the effort
to make the fullest possible use of school capacity; retain as many
students as possible for at least minimal learning; and test new educational strategies to involve more children in formal education. The

purpose of this family of programs is to increase the productivity of educational systems in relation to educational expenditure.

In a sense, this fourth stage responds to demands for permanent educational establishments in rural areas, demands dealt with partially (and often only temporarily) by the rural development programs of Stage III. In another sense, this stage is an attempt to raise the general level of educational opportunity. Its programs indicate maturing professionalism within national educational systems. These systems have by this time had years of experience with the costly problems of early dropout, failure, repetition, overcrowding, inadequate teacher training, and massive failures of learning, and have learned by trial and error how to pick and choose among the suggestions of consultants to find solutions relevant to their own problems.

Fourth-stage programs, in operation or proposed, are not theoretical concepts but administrative reforms planned to improve returns on educational investment. By responding to demands for educational opportunity, they offer tremendous political advantage among large sections of the population that have previously had little access to education. They employ several strategies:

1. Automatic promotion through all grades of elementary school without recording failures or requiring repetition of failed grades. This strategy reduces enrollment in the first and last grades of elementary school by as much as 50 percent, and in overall elementary grades by approximately 30 percent, making possible a corresponding increase in the enrollment of new students who might otherwise have been turned away. One examination—the primary school leaving— becomes the sole criterion of success or failure.

By holding most students through the entire elementary cycle, this strategy also produces more functional literates than the older method, which required repetition of each failed grade. It may—although there are no data available—also produce a higher percentage of passes in the primary leaving examination. In any event, it offers a welcome simplification of programs with a real promise of improved education for more pupils at lower cost per pupil.

2. Automatic promotion to lower secondary school without using a primary school leaving examination as an entrance requirement for secondary school.

This strategy eliminates an important barrier to educational advancement and makes it possible for pupils to go through the first eight or nine years of schooling without facing the yearly possibility of failure followed by either repetition or exclusion.

Administratively more important is the fact that such a strategy produces a large increase in secondary school enrollment and at the same time postpones the selection of students for preuniversity programs (upper secondary), teacher training institutes, or vocational-technical schools.

3. Extended use of radio, television, and other methods of reaching older children and young adults for possible transfer to the formal schools.

Strategies of this type admittedly reach only a determined few students in any area—although the aggregate number may be large—but since these are areas where there is otherwise no educational opportunity, they do respond, at least symbolically, to needs that are otherwise unmet.

There are several significant points that emerge from an analysis of Stage IV.

First, enlarging access to education for social, political, and economic benefits is essentially a developed-nation concept, which accepts mass political participation, mass taxation, and ultimately education for mass consumption. It contrasts sharply with the "chosen elite" concept that underlies Stages I and II and that does not offer either access to education or social, political, or economic benefits to the uneducated mass. It therefore represents a practical change in political philosophy, resulting from 20 years of educational development. It must emerge from Stage III and cannot be imposed earlier, nor can it come from the national and international development agencies.

Second, Stage IV, when entered, is a set of irreversible actions leading to universal public education. In other words, once automatic promotion, free passage to secondary schools, open entrance for older students, use of media, and recognition of nonformal methodologies are brought into a system, they will induce an accelerated rate of educational growth and, by so doing, force the development of yet other strategies to deal with further increments of demand, until, in a surprisingly short time, a majority of children of school age are within full reach of educational opportunity.

STAGE V

The fifth stage of educational development is, in the terms referred to in the discussion of Stage II, the achievement of university maturity. It is the time when the university passes from a limited role as a teaching institution preparing for professional life or government service to a larger role as the institution central to the support of national development. It takes and holds this larger role not only through its manpower selection and training, but through research, planning, program development, and project management and evaluation. In other words, only when a university moves from a service role to an operational role in development, may a nation be considered to have entered the fifth stage of educational development.

University expansion during Stage V cannot be limited to the addition of new professional faculties but must include new approaches to delivery of education and the formation of research programs and activities directed to specific development goals. Three forms of expansion cover most of the present patterns.

1. University Extension. This means the extension of university activity into additional hours—evenings and weekends; into additional sites—other communities, public school buildings, government offices, community halls, or military barracks, wherever, in fact, the demand lies; into new programs—such as the training of development workers, nonformal group leaders, census enumerators, or any of myriad other types of specialists who need training that is otherwise unavailable. In brief, university extension is the expansion of university activities into new hours, new places, and new programs as the most direct route to development. Universities that are not prepared to enter extension work because they do not understand this do not understand the true role of the university in development.

2. The Open University. In England, where the term originated, an open university is one that offers university programs leading to degrees at full university standard, using radio, television, and correspondence courses as instructional media, but with provision, when possible, for direct contact between student and tutor. It offers university programs with broadened methods of communication between teacher and student.

The concept need not be limited to university programs and has been under study and discussion in developing nations that are interested in applying it more broadly. Actual use of the concept, however, has been slow in developing, perhaps because the commitment of university personnel and resources to a multimedia type of instructional program is, like commitment to a university extension program, a serious, and, even more important, an irreversible action.

3. University Task Forces and Research Institutes. As suggested earlier, universities in developing nations are the principle repositories of knowledge and the principle concentrations of intellectual competence. One of the most important—and most difficult—university tasks is the organization of interdisciplinary groups into task forces and research institutes to identify, define, analyze, and attack development problems. The question of how such activities are

organized and operated may be largely a matter of local style and
resources. Some countries may need to emphasize research and
training in support of nonformal education; others to expand their
field programs in public health; others to devise new approaches to
agricultural productivity. The point is that each effort is both a research and a training program, each is interdisciplinary, and each
demands a level of intrauniversity cooperation and support that no
amateur university can conceive or deliver.

The pressure produced by the programs and reforms of Stages
III and IV will inevitably bring new thousands of candidates to the
schools, and eventually to the doors of the university. It is a measure
and test of university leadership and of the mature, professional
university, to take responsibility for expanding other forms of higher
education, such as teacher training and technical training, particularly when the results of such expansion are sure to lead toward mass
education, which most universities and certainly all amateur universities oppose.

THE FUTURE

Educational self-sufficiency, in today's world, can be achieved
in two generations—50 years at most. But self-sufficiency will mean
only that a nation can supply its own teachers, research, and development programs, can train its own leaders, and build its own institutions.

Beyond such self-sufficiency lie two tremendous movements in
education: universal education and mass education. Universal education, which signifies universal access to education, does not mean
that all youth will actually go to school; in fact, relatively small per-
centages may go to the higher schools. Mass education, which is the
next phase, means literally mass pursuit of education, such as is
presently seen in the United States.

It is predictable that education in developing nations will move
beyond self-sufficiency with surprising speed to establish the conditions of universal education. Despite the problems of national poverty,
ways will be found of developing universal programs without damage
to national economies.

This prediction may seem statistically impossible, but whatever
the statistics, whenever the mass of people decide upon and demand
the goal of increased education, they will reach it.

It is in this context that long-term evaluations of educational
experience must take place. The fundamental question for every
nation remains the same. "Has the country's total experience with

formal education justified continued educational expansion and development?" If the answer to the question is yes, there can be no doubt that ways will be found to make it happen.

25

HIGHER EDUCATION IN EAST AFRICA

David Court

THE PROBLEM: CONDITIONS FOR
UNIVERSITY CHANGE

There is a growing worldwide disquiet about the performance of higher education in relation to a view of development that emphasizes the redistribution of resources and improvements in mass welfare rather than undifferentiated economic growth.[1] The essence of the critique of higher education in the Third World is the suspicion that the version that has emerged here may be in danger of losing touch with the realistic needs and aspirations of the societies in which it is located. Applying the criterion of willingness to serve, development critics have found limited nourishment in the quality of response of most universities to accumulating national problems of unemployment, malnutrition, income inequality, and so forth.[2]

The purpose of this essay is to identify some of the influences that seem to determine the ability and willingness of East African universities to make the understanding and alleviation of underdevelopment a central and organizing concern.[3] In doing this we look particularly closely at the University of Dar es Salaam because it has been the most self-conscious of the three East African universities in trying to reorder itself for a new developmental role. Its recent experience is, therefore, particularly instructive in revealing some of the issues and possible directions that may be involved in the general task.

David Court is on the staff of the Institute for Development Studies, University of Nairobi, Kenya and is also the Rockefeller Foundation representative in East Africa. This report is a revised version of a study prepared for the Institute. The views expressed are those of the author. They should not be interpreted as reflecting views of the Institute for Development Studies or the University of Nairobi.

BACKGROUND

The three East African universities, Nairobi (Kenya), Makerere (Uganda), and Dar es Salaam (Tanzania) became autonomous national institutions in 1970, but their emergence was preceded by seven years as constituent colleges of the federal University of East Africa. The main characteristic of that period was one of rapid growth. In 1961 there were 99 locally trained university graduates for the whole of East Africa, with its population of 23 million people. The growth of facilities for university education alone since then has been rapid (see Table 25.1). Student enrollment in the three institutions rose from 2,193 in 1964 to 9,818 in 1973; the number of established teaching posts from 279 to 1,440 over the same period; and the number of East Africans occupying such posts from 48 to 487. The University of Dar es Salaam, which in 1961 had but one faculty operating in a borrowed building now has six, and each of the original colleges of the University of East Africa is a full-fledged autonomous university, either possessing or anticipating a full panoply of professional faculties.

This growth has occurred in a social context characterized by a rapid and dramatic transition from colonial status to independence, and the quest for distinctive national identities. The end of colonial rule in the early 1960s has been followed by a continuing search for forms and structures that would provide for expanded popular participation, allocate resources so as to reduce regional inequalities and minimize fissiparous tendencies, and give authentic expression to national, regional, and continental conditions and requirements. The economic challenge has been to accelerate growth, generate employment, and improve living conditions within the framework of a large agricultural economy, a limited resource base, and a rapidly increasing population. The major task of social policy has been to cope with the problems of urbanization and the consequences of improved communications and, while dismantling racial barriers in commercial and social life, to prevent the growth of equally invidious forms of stratification based on accumulated wealth. Within the education system, the overriding feature of the period has been expansion, particularly at the secondary level, in response to massive popular demand.

Although there are commonalities of regional history, background, and interest within East Africa, Kenya, Tanzania, and Uganda display important differences, particularly in the area of social policy, which have had significant effects on the development of their universities. Tanzania has given increasing emphasis to manpower planning, while Kenya has preferred to rely more on market mechanisms for

TABLE 25.1

Selected Indices of Expansion of the Universities of Nairobi, Dar es Salaam, and Makerere

University	1964-65	1967-68	1970-71	1973-74
Nairobi				
Recurrent expenditure (£)	676,631	1,348,970	2,597,483	5,076,650[a]
Undergraduate enrollment	635	1,539	2,582	3,437
Established academic posts	101	185	373	544 (388)[b]
East Africans in established posts	20	56	115	174
East Africans as percent of academic establishment	19	30	31	32 (45)[c]
Dar es Salaam				
Recurrent expenditure (£)	206,622	799,033	1,500,000	2,547,322
Undergraduate enrollment	227	987	1,814	2,176
Established academic posts	31	112	266	402 (302)[b]
East Africans in established posts	5	18	86	102
East Africans as percent of academic establishment	16	17	32	25 (30)[c]
Makerere				
Recurrent Expenditure (£)	938,480	1,433,999	1,929,489	3,696,550
Undergraduate enrollment	1,331	1,805	2,602	4,205
Established academic posts	147	175	353	495 (291)[b]
East Africans in established posts	24	45	92	211
East Africans as percent of academic establishment	17	20	27	43 (73)[c]
Combined Universities				
Recurrent expenditure (£)	1,821,733	3,582,002	6,026,972	11,320,522
Undergraduate enrollment	2,193	4,331	6,998	9,818
Established academic posts	279	472	992	1,440 (981)[b]
East Africans in established posts	49	119	293	487
East Africans as percent of academic establishment	17	25	30	35 (50)[c]

[a]Estimates.

[b]Positions filled.

[c]Proportion of "positions filled" (footnote b) held by East Africans.

Source: University records.

the allocation of trained individuals. Likewise, the effect on Makerere University of recent political events in Uganda simply underscores the point that one cannot assess the role of universities in development without reference to the political context in which they are operating.

THE UNIVERSITY OF EAST AFRICA, 1963-70: ITS DEVELOPMENTAL ROLE

The foundation of the University of East Africa in 1963 was accompanied by strong proclamations of commitment to the idea that the University and its constituent colleges must serve the goals of development by meeting the needs of the surrounding society. Since then, the commitment and rededication of university education to serving the needs of development have become a recurrent pledge of University leaders and a stated objective of policy at all three University centers. There has also been extensive agreement on the ways in which this role might best be accomplished. The components of a developmental role for the University were seen to be the training of skilled manpower; the provision through research of knowledge relevant to the solution of developmental problems; and the East Africanization of the staff, the curriculum, and the ethos of the University itself.

Providing Skilled Manpower

Throughout the first decade of independence the preeminent and imperative task of higher education was perceived to be that of providing high-level manpower. It stood to reason that the University should devote most of its resources to training those who could proceed to staff and lead the burgeoning institutions of the newly independent states.

The pervasive manpower objective was present in both Kenya and Tanzania but has been made relatively more explicit in Tanzania with its stated goal of achieving self-sufficiency in skilled categories by 1980. The University, formerly University College Dar es Salaam, has attempted to meet this goal by the strict regulation of intake, the tailoring of offerings to perceived manpower requirements, the increasing vocationalization of courses, the use of tied bursaries, and the subsequent direction of labor. The University of Nairobi has displayed a less regimented approach to manpower provision in line with Kenya's policy of a relatively free labor market, but there is no doubt that providing manpower has remained its guiding objective.

There are two reasons why the University centers saw manpower provision as their main task. In the first place, if independence was to have visible meaning, dependence upon expatriates had to be removed as rapidly as possible by producing more formally educated East Africans. This political imperative was reinforced by the intellectual climate of the 1960s in which manpower planning, under the presiding influence of Fredrick Harbison, was in its heyday. East Africa was the subject of a series of commissions and conferences, all of which created elaborate projections of the need for well-trained individuals in the various conventional categories of upper-level employment.[4] In view of the large measure of consensus between government and international economists on what the University ought to be achieving, it is not surprising that the University itself did not engage in much serious introspection about its role.

Judged by the number of East Africans who have taken over categories of jobs held previously by expatriates, the objective of achieving self-sufficiency in high-level manpower has been virtually achieved in the first decade of independence. (Some relevant data from Tanzania are provided in Table 25.2.)

However, the provision of trained manpower has been an inherently conservative activity. Because initially and perhaps inevitably it was synonymous with the replacement of expatriates, the aim was to create the qualifications held by the expatriates. This definition of the University's role in turn tended to nurture a desire to preserve inherited "international" academic standards and qualifications along with the recognized means to their attainment. In the psychological climate of the postindependence period, the University was reluctant to redefine its offerings and objectives, risking the charge that different was inferior. At the same time the bulk of staff of the constituent colleges were from European universities and were inclined to reinforce practices with which they were familiar. The fact that manpower training programs were undertaken with imported standards has had a number of inhibiting consequences for the universities' contribution to development.

In the first place, the programs assumed that the pattern of available jobs would remain relatively static. University programs, consequently, overtrained and often provided skills and knowledge bearing little relationship to those required for a given job. The corollary of this was an expansion of university-level education with relative indifference to its inordinate expense.

The emphasis on expansion was accompanied by the apparent disinclination of the University of East Africa to bring to bear its intellectual resources upon the problems of subuniversity training and the wider educational system. There seems to have been little

TABLE 25.2

Localization in Senior Echelons of Tanzanian Civil Service Since Independence

Date	Officers Serving in Senior and Middle-Grade Posts on Permanent Terms			
	Citizens	Others	Total	Percent Citizens
December 1961	1,170	3,282	3,352	26.1
December 1962	1,821	2,902	4,723	38.5
December 1963	2,469	2,580	5,049	48.9
December 1964	3,083	2,306	5,389	57.2
December 1965	3,951	2,011	5,962	66.3
December 1966	4,364	1,898	6,262	69.7
December 1967	4,937	1,817	6,754	73.1
December 1968	6,208	1,619	7,827	79.3
December 1969	6,123	1,351	7,474	81.9
December 1970	8,042	1,377	9,419	85.6
December 1971	9,708	1,015	10,723	90.5
December 1972	11,988	745	12,733	94.1

Source: Compiled by the author.

pressure on the University administration to "prepare a systematic assessment of how it can contribute to development apart from the tacit drive for more and more graduates. "5

The manpower and vocational emphasis also implied that the self-interest of the students and the welfare of the nation were synonymous. There seems to have been consensus among students and staff in the early days of the University of East Africa that students could make their contribution to development simply by doing their chosen job well. During the initial replacement of expatriates this was perhaps the case, but, fairly early in the life of the University colleges, this self-interest ceased to be an automatic road to national development. The problem was dramatized by the student demonstrations in 1966 in Tanzania against the introduction of national service there, and a continuing divergence between development plans and student interests has been caused by the reluctance of trained graduates to work in the relatively poorer and more remote areas of East Africa.

The vocational emphasis has tended also to have an inhibiting effect upon the development of critical thought. The question of the dual allegiance of universities to the unfettered pursuit of knowledge and to training for jobs is an eternal one. Peter Marris, presenting the Oxbridge ideology, has argued that the main goal of university education in East Africa, as elsewhere, should be to develop the ability of students to think imaginatively and with intellectual integrity. He views this as the precondition for genuine self-reliance and the ultimate ability of a society to command its own destiny. Because societies and jobs are in constant transition and all knowledge is provisional, the development of such an ability amounts to real vocational training. Any more rigid emphasis on training for specific tasks is likely to impinge upon the development of creative thought and to turn the universities into little more than staff-training colleges for the technical and administrative elite. [6] We can concede the importance of this dimension without necessarily viewing it as excluding more specific service, as Tanzania's president, Julius Nyerere, has made clear:

> What we expect from our university is both a complete objectivity in the search for truth, and also commitment to our society—a desire to serve it. We expect the two things equally. And I do not believe this dual responsibility—to objectivity and to service—is impossible of fulfillment. [7]

East Africanization: Producing East African
Staff Members

A second developmental task that was self-defined for the University of East Africa by its own manpower situation was that of producing East African staff members. This task had a quantitative dimension—reducing the overall dependence upon expatriates—and a qualitative dimension—providing a type of training appropriate for future staff members.

At the time of the creation of the University of East Africa, less than 10 percent of the members of the academic staff of the three university colleges were East Africans, and, with a few exceptions, those in this small minority held positions at the most junior level. Heads of departments, deans of faculties, all senior administrators, and all but a few members of the governing bodies of the University were foreigners. Since that time there has been a tenfold increase in the overall number of East Africans occupying permanent university positions (see Table 25.1). At present, moreover, virtually all administrators, deans, and heads of departments are East Africans. In overall terms, East Africans now occupy 45 percent of positions filled at Nairobi, 30 percent at Dar es Salaam, and 73 percent at Makerere. This level of localization may seem a relatively low one for ten years of effort, but it has been difficult, over the past ten years, to retain staff members in the face of competing inducements for which their training has made them eligible, or, in the case of Tanzania, of competing demands for their expertise in parastatal organizations. Indeed Tanzania, like Zambia, has implicitly decided that the University should have relatively low priority in localization and so has often deprived it of some of its outstanding staff members.

During the life of the University of East Africa, there was little debate about the type of training needed for future members of the University staff. It was accepted that the only relevant qualification was a Ph.D. at an overseas university and preferably at one of the best-known universities. One of the most important staff development programs for higher education has been that financed by the Rockefeller Foundation, which since 1963 has provided 163 full scholarships for East Africans to complete postgraduate degrees, [8] as well as extensive additional support for the specific study programs of prospective university staff members.

Many of the assumptions and expectations that a scholar picks up in the course of a protracted overseas training are not helpful in a Third World university. Much of the training is not specifically geared to the conditions in which the scholar will find himself. The requirements of the overseas Ph.D. program often make abstruse theory the core of the program, and the applicability of such theory to

East African conditions is not always evident. At the same time, because the thesis has to be conceived within the framework of an overseas Ph.D. program, it often calls for the application of tools of analysis that are more sophisticated than the data available in the home country. The problem with irrelevant theory or the overly quantitative orientation of some of the Ph.D. courses is that (1) either the student is overwhelmed and loses motivation or changes his program (particularly true in economics), or (2) he triumphs over it, becomes seduced by it, and returns to perpetuate it in his own country.

Yet despite some of the now visible problems of overseas training, it is hard to see how it could have been dispensed with in the early days of the growth of higher education. One beneficial effect was that many East Africans went to universities other than those of the colonial power in whose tradition they had received their earlier education. They were thus exposed to new subjects, teaching styles, degree structure, and content emphasis. If with the benefit of hindsight, it is clear that some of the training received has been at least partially inappropriate to East African conditions and problems—rooted as it has often been in specialization, a traditional academic style, and culturally specific assumptions—it has, at the same time, provided exposure to and mastery of principles and techniques of excellence. It is at least arguable that in the long run these techniques may be more important than the specific content they conveyed.

Running through statements of the East Africanization goals of the University of East Africa was the implication that it is not until the University is led and dominated by local citizens that there will be momentum for internal reform in the direction of a more locally relevant University. It is clear that expatriate-dominated university are almost always incapable of leading lasting innovation. At the same time, some of the most ardent defenders of inherited practice can be found among the first generation of East African academics. The objective of East Africanization of the University of East Africa was largely one of continuity involving the takeover of the existing institutional framework. This was a necessary initial stage, but while the longer-term goal was to move quickly into substantive change, the imperatives of change seem to have become less compelling once the existing framework has been taken over. Where an individual's overseas training has not inspired him to think about the nature of a university and its connection with development in his home country, he is likely simply to defend the standards and practices through which he gained his own academic legitimacy and to reproduce and reinforce a pattern of education that derives from an alien context and a past time.

Now that they are approaching 50 percent East African staff, and leadership is entirely in East African hands, a crucial numerical threshold has been reached. The institutions are less fragile than before and better able to generate that degree of self-criticism that is a necessary prelude to reform. In face of the pressing visibility of the problems of development, the crucial question is whether those East Africans who are now concentrated in the universities will use the yardstick of contribution to development or rely on the precedents of older universities in redefining the structure and aspirations of their institutions. The future is uncertain, but, as we will attempt to show, changes at the University of Dar es Salaam in particular provide some prospect for optimism about future possibilities.

Applying Social Science Research

The third major strand in the University of East Africa's view of its developmental task was that of contributing to national policy by means of applied research. The need for a distinctive and legitimate identity as a valued institutional part of East African society led the University to seek ways of demonstrating its relevance to that society through a capacity for helping to solve its most pressing problems. Research was a traditional function of universities, and its application to local problems enabled the University to follow a universal role while also responding to then current notions of development, which called for the generation of new knowledge to overcome obstacles impeding progress. Perhaps the most interesting illustration of this attempt to develop an applied research capacity occurred in the social sciences. At all three University colleges, social science research units were developed to organize policy-oriented research and provide data useful to the solution of urgent economic and social problems, hence linking University facilities to expressed needs of government and the wider society.

The applied social science research units made and continue to make a significant contribution to economic and social planning in East Africa. In the first place they have collected and presented information that has contributed to an increased understanding of some of the critical economic and social problems confronting East Africa. For example, the government of Tanzania placed heavy reliance on the Economic Research Bureau at the University to provide the factual basis for much of its economic decision making and upon the Bureau of Resource Assessment and Land Use Planning for analysis of population and environmental issues. Second, each of the research centers has performed, at the request of government, a variety of specific research and evalution tasks. Thus, the Institute for

Development Studies at the University of Nairobi undertook a comprehensive evaluation of the Kenya government's Special Rural Development Program, while its work in the field of education has led to
major improvements in selection and career guidance procedures at
the secondary level and the reduction in inequities in the primary
school-leaving examination. [9] Third, members of staff at the research
units served on a variety of government committees and working
parties. Perhaps an even more important contribution than the formal preparation of research reports and background data has been
the extensive informal interaction through memos, personal communication, and joint participation that has characterized the relationship
between the staff of the research centers and those of ministries during
the first decade of national independence. The overall contribution of
the research centers has been to reinforce a research climate at the
University that emphasizes applied research objectives.

The accomplishments of these social science research centers
in East Africa have been impressive. Yet despite their achievements
their potential impact has been diminished by a number of factors.
Some of their difficulties derived from localized problems such as
the absence of tenured positions at the Institute for Development
Studies, Nairobi, or from ambiguities arising out of their dual loyalty
to both government ministries and academic departments; these have
been well documented elsewhere. [10] Other difficulties, however, are
a consequence of a disjunction between the particular concept of development that the University of East Africa accepted during its formative period and the research tradition in which it tried to respond to
developmental problems.

The view of development that emphasized missing knowledge
placed a premium on the speedy production of results and recommendations for policy makers. The immediate impact of the new
emphasis was a shift in the type of problems studied from scholastic
investigations of institutions and practices of very small social units
and to the study of broader issues of economic and social organization
on a national scale. Accompanying this change in the type of problem
studied came a change in the type of methods and disciplinary approaches used. The dominance of history, anthropology, and philosophy was replaced by the "new" social science with its distinctive
emphasis upon theory building as the goal, individual behavior as the
unit of analysis, and quantitative formulations as the style of measurement.

Looking back at this period, we can see that there was perhaps
an overly uncritical acceptance of those approaches and insufficient
recognition of the fact that the social science that flowered most
dramatically in the new research units was a new type of intellectual
technology derived from an industrial context and particular model of

development. Insufficient consideration was given to how it needed to be modified and developed and under what conditions it could best contribute to understanding East African needs and problems. Most important, insufficient thought was given to what kinds of training could help to meet the goal of applied research. In part of course the limitations could not become apparent until the technology had been tried. But there can be little doubt that the unqualified claims that accompanied the introduction of a science, which was at best embryonic, have led to a measure of disillusionment when the product failed to live up to expectations. This disillusionment, in turn, has impeded its application to the new conditions facing the universities.

Furthermore, the desire of the University to produce research-based policy recommendations and its faith in a value-free social science technology led to a willingness to rely on large numbers of expatriates as the best available practitioners. The resulting situation at the research centers has been summarized in this way:

Social science research institutions which are nominally national, have to a great extent been dominated by foreign scholars. The quality of their work has often been high and certainly much research has been done which would otherwise not have been done. This pattern nevertheless suffers from severe disadvantages. Research or teaching conducted in such circumstances by expatriates may have only nominal reference to local needs and priorities, despite the urgent demands for policy oriented research.[11]

It is certainly correct that, throughout the life of the University of East Africa, social science research was dominated by foreign scholars. But if the work of foreign scholars had only nominal reference to local needs and priorities, it was not usually out of malevolent self-interest. More important was the fact that many foreign scholars were ill-equipped by virtue of their academic training to do policy-oriented research. The intellectual concerns and normative principles provided by professional academic training in major universities in the United States and Europe did not always fit the scholar for responding easily to this demand. Rather, such training aimed to foster understanding of the scientific basis of a defined discipline and research that advanced knowledge within it. At the same time it encouraged a belief in academic autonomy, which made scholars uncomfortable with demands for results in a specified time period, particularly if those demands emanated from government.

However, even where the foreign scholar was attuned to the need for policy-oriented research, many of the policy makers in a position to make demands for research and information were not sufficiently familiar with the nature of research activity to know what kinds of requests they could justifiably make on the University, as they had had little training in research methodology and appreciation. Although expertise in social science research was concentrated in the research units, none of the units played much part in running training courses in research methodology for undergraduates or indeed anyone else. The assumption seems to have been made that the benefits of social science would be compellingly self-evident and that there was therefore no necessity to make the case for it through education and carefully demonstrated utility. The experience of the research centers during the period of the University of East Africa made it clear that there was a need for broad education in research, especially in how to read tables, in distinguishing valid from invalid assertions, and in knowing the limits as well as the possibilities of social science research, so that policy makers could know what the University was capable of providing and make intelligent demands for it. As Arnold Anderson has recently pointed out:

> It must become widely believed that research techniques
> are truly supra cultural and that only by such techniques
> can an LDC attack its own problems with hope of success. But only if such techniques are used in the open
> to train competent analysts of social change will investigation of local problems yield knowledge of general
> value.[12]

Despite the emphasis on policy-oriented research and some impressive achievements, the research enterprise and the research constituency remain fragile for some of the reasons mentioned. There has been a disjunction between the applied function adopted by the University of East Africa as part of its contribution to relevance and the academic preparation and normative outlook of those expected to carry this out.

The experience under the University of East Africa has not denied the relevance of the technology but has rather pointed to the need for the autonomous universities to give more deliberate consideration to what kinds of social science research make most sense now. Such consideration could then be the basis for more effective education to expand the community of those able to understand and use social science research and for the recruitment of foreign scholars able to contend with local developmental research. In short, the experience of the 1960s brought home the realization that universities needed more deliberate consideration of the individual and institutional attributes that prepare them to perform a role in developmental research.

The foregoing section has considered three main features of the development role exemplified by the University of East Africa. In concentrating upon some of the problems and limitations I have not taken space to detail some of the major achievements that accompanied the growth of higher education. The intention has not been to diminish these achievements by ignoring them, but rather to emphasize the urgency of the problems that now confront the universities. It is to this challenge and the prospects for a constructive university response that we now turn.

THE NEW CHALLENGE OF DEVELOPMENT

During the 1960s a vastly expanded system of higher education was created in East Africa, culminating in the emergence of three major national universities. From their foundation, the University colleges had aspired to contribute to national development. The institutions that emerged—conceived and built as they were under a strong outside influence—remained, in ethos and organization, reminiscent of established universities in the industrialized world. There were some important modifications, but, on the whole, the new institutions have striven to acquire, through the recruitment of visiting staff and the export of its own citizens for overseas training, the types of expertise that characterize a university in an industrial nation. Running through statements of University objectives was the view that the nature of development was known and the task for the University of East Africa was to increase the East African arsenal of skills and knowledge by importing and adapting a definite university structure. The nature of the developmental process and how the University might relate to it were not questions of major continuing investigation.

With the benefit of hindsight, it is relatively easy to document some of the limitations of the concept of development exemplified by the University of East Africa. Given the legacy of colonialism, the practical and psychological need to run institutions inherited at independence, the apparent dependence upon foreigners, and preconceptions about the nature of development, it is doubtful whether the University colleges could have grown in a pattern much different from that followed. The question now is whether the type of institution that has enabled the countries to meet specific employment and research needs can adapt itself to the larger and more complex challenge of development in the last quarter of the twentieth century.

Several conditions are becoming apparent to these institutions. In the first place, they see they cannot emulate the rich industrial nations. Secondly, there are limits to the size of the world resource cake, and if the Third World is to get a share, it will have to come from a major worldwide redistribution of wealth. In the absence of such redistribution, or in conditions specifically preventing it, poorer nations need to adopt new development goals and the educational means to attain them. The so-called energy crisis and environmental problems have dramatized this situation but have not really caused it.

What for example is the role of a university in a country such as Tanzania? Although primarily agricultural this country had in 1974 to import £30 million of food to fend off starvation for its people. How can the University of Nairobi justify its existence when the cost per student is 35 times the annual per capita income?* The only possible answer to these and similar questions is that the peculiarly relevant role of the universities must be to contribute to understanding the nature of the challenge of development and to lead in helping define the national, regional, and continental response.

The ability of the universities to respond to the new challenge depends upon two sets of factors—those internal to the universities over which they have substantial control and those external to the universities that place them in a social and economic context over which they have much less control.

The very speed of their growth has made it difficult for the universities to be concerned with much more than institutional maintenance. The biggest obstacle to university self-reform is the durability of the inherited structure and values. Most staff members were familiar only with a traditional institution and necessarily conceived the East African universities in a recognizable image. This tendency to perpetuate a Western model was further reinforced by the practice of training future staff members on conventional lines in the same kind of university. The first generation of academics, in particular, having been trained mostly in British universities, have had a strong interest in creating a type of institution that helped to protect their own type of training.

Finally, until recently, there has been no dramatic alternative model of what a different kind of university might look like. Interesting non-Western experiments have been shrouded in the mists of ideological untouchability, and there have been few systematic attempts to think through the nature of a different development-oriented university. Now, however, these conditions are changing, and there are grounds for feeling that radical change is possible within the

---

*See Asian Regional Report for Asian cost-per-student comparison.

university. These possibilities must be considered, of course, in
terms of the wider social and political culture in which the universities are located.

Perhaps the most important fact about the political context to
which the universities relate is its small scale. In each of the East
African countries, we have a single university located very close to
the main center of events. As a result, the universities are political
institutions. University strikes are discussed at cabinet meetings
and in the National Assembly. Furthermore, because these single
universities are the pinnacles of hierarchical national education systems, they tend to concentrate the intelligentsia of the nation. In this
context, students inevitably see themselves as an incipient elite. By
the same token, they constitute a threat to the established elite should
they attempt to change the rules or structure, including that of Western
education, through which that elite derives much of its legitimacy.
Because students expect, realistically, to enter the elite in East Africa
they have not been sources of radical innovation within the universities.
The temptation to think of little more than satisfying the academic
requirements necessary for cooption into the national elite is overwhelming, while the coercive power of government is immediately
available to deal with any individuals who might wish to change the
rules of the game.

Perhaps even more important is the fact that the kind of development role that the universities are able to play depends in large
measure on the interest of government in solving developmental problems. In countries such as those of East Africa, government must
articulate national interest. If it is not clearly defined, the university
has a problem relating to it. More seriously, if the governing elite
is actually repressive, the university may have difficulty avoiding a
situation where it is contributing to repression. Assisting governments to staff their public sector is only a contribution to development
if that government is interested in development.

Similarly, applied research does not contribute to development
in a government disinterested in development. This dilemma in relation to research institutes has been stated thus:

> all too often technical advice, narrowly defined, is
> being made available to elites who are not prepared to
> make the structural transformations necessary to de-
> velopment; at best, therefore, the institute may rein-
> force and legitimise a mood conducive to mere tinkering
> with the system, at worst it may provide active assist-
> ance to classes concerned only with buying time for the
> system (and their own stake in it) by efficient management
> and marginal re-adjustment.[13]

There is another political constraint on university change. The university is at the pinnacle of a wider educational incentive and employment structure. To initiate change in university goals and procedures may involve challenging that structure and perhaps threatening the whole edifice of credentials on which most people's jobs depend.

THE NEW MODEL UNIVERSITY: DAR ES SALAAM AS PROTOTYPE

Most of the factors just mentioned remain influences upon the development of the East African universities. The important question is how the universities can respond to changed conditions and take the lead in promoting a new understanding of underdevelopment and action for development. Among the East African universities, the University of Dar es Salaam has been most concerned with trying to fashion a new response to new conditions, partly because Tanzania is poorer than Kenya and Uganda, and the challenge of the new conditions is most immediately visible there. The University of Dar es Salaam has set the pace in East Africa in striving to achieve a new model of relevant university education. It is important to emphasize that the model still consists as much of tendencies as of tangible achievements, but the direction is clear, and its recent experience does provide some guide to the likely dimensions on which change can occur and some of the conditions that influence such change.

In general terms, the explicit aim of the University has been to make each of its aspects reflect a concern for understanding the fact of underdevelopment, as a basis for fashioning a response to it. This has led to some intense consideration of the philosophy of university education itself and to the beginning of change in a number of aspects of the University's life. These aspects have included the teaching program and degree structure, the organization of the University, its research priorities, and its relationships to government, to the wider national community, and to the international university community.

Educational Philosophy and Intellectual Climate

Higher education in Tanzania gains strength from the fact that it is developing within a clear educational philosophy that assigns the University a central role in the task of serving and generating national development. In the words of Tanzania's President Nyerere:

> The University in a developing society must put the
> emphasis of its work on subjects of immediate moment
> to the nation in which it exists, and it must be commit-
> ted to the people of that nation and their humanistic
> goals. . . . We in poor societies can only justify ex-
> penditure on a University—of any type—if it promotes
> real development of our people. . . . The role of a
> University in a developing nation is to contribute: to
> give ideas, manpower, and service for the furtherance
> of human equality, human dignity and human develop-
> ment.[14]

A context in which an educator president has initiated a national debate about the meaning and purposes of education in Tanzania has been a most productive one and has stimulated University members into lively and self-conscious consideration of what they ought to be doing and how they can help their University better to serve the purposes of "Education for Self-Reliance." At times this debate has reached a pitch of ideological fervor that has threatened the integrity of intellectual life, but at a more fundamental level it has reflected the lively commitment of the University community to keeping the University attuned to development issues. The recent experience of the University of Dar es Salaam is evidence that a favorable ideological or philosophical climate is critical to a university's ability to conceive and practice a new developmental role. Because those outside the University constantly and publicly attribute importance to the University of Dar es Salaam in the struggle against underdevelopment, those inside it are encouraged to respond to that trust.

The Teaching Program

Under an ideal of development that emphasized the goal of economic growth and development on the pattern of the industrial nations, it was sufficient for the universities to train students for identified slots in an existing economic structure. However, it is now clear that if technical training is to be applied on behalf of mass welfare it has to be part of a wider understanding of development. John Saul has summarized this need:

> Obviously technical skills of a very high order are in
> short supply and a major chore of the university must
> be to provide them. But it would be a "false economy"
> to think that this can be done at the expense of the

broad insight that alone makes their use wholly relevant
to contemporary Tanzania.[15]

In the past, two factors have inhibited the creation of this broad
insight: the elitist mentality, which was a product of the hierarchical
education system, and the fragmented vision of highly specialized
training, which derived from the intellectual organization of the inherited model of a university:

> In particular it is the fragmentation of perspective
> entailed by separate academic "disciplines" which
> provides the main obstacle to the development of an
> integral and coherent vision of man in history and
> society.[16]

The University of Dar es Salaam has attempted to tackle both
of these inhibiting factors. While it has continued to place great emphasis upon manpower planning and skill training, it has also been
concerned with ensuring that those who receive skill training feel
morally committed to using it to the best advantage of the nation.
This commitment has been encouraged by exhortation, inculcation
in courses, and the use of a two-tier system of national service in
which students, before going to the University, have a period of intensive work in Spartan conditions with nonelite citizens and then,
after graduation, work for two years in a job to which they are assigned at a reduced salary. The intention is not to deemphasize manpower training but to ensure that it becomes part of a wider pattern
of training in which the ability to think clearly and solve problems
develops along with a commitment to understanding and doing something about the conditions of underdevelopment.

It is hard to judge whether these efforts have paid off in fostering a sense of altruism and self-sacrifice or whether such moral
incentives are more effective than the material ones that prevail in
Kenya. Certainly Tanzania has been able to allocate its limited expertise throughout the country, and the educated elite has accepted
perquisites less than those of its Kenyan counterpart. The proportion of implicit coercion to volunteerism involved in this achievement,
however, is impossible to gauge.

The problem of a highly specialized and discipline-based degree
structure that was part of the inherited colonial pattern has proved
difficult to resolve, particularly because of the nationally hetero-
geneous composition of the University staff. The Faculty of Arts and
Social Sciences has taken the lead in experimenting with degree structure and course content. In 1971, the faculty was reorganized to establish a problem-solving and career orientation, rather than a

certificate-seeking and discipline-based one. The traditional subject divisions of the degree structure have been replaced by multisubject "streams," and numerous common courses introduced under the rubrics "Developmental Studies" and "East African Societies and Environment" have the object of ensuring that all students gain some systematic exposure to the cultural, physical, and social conditions of their own society. The rationale for this reorganization was stated thus by the dean of the faculty:

> The basis of the University should be responsiveness
> to the needs of Tanzania by providing our students
> with the ability to understand Tanzania's problems
> and to contribute towards their solution. It should be
> established with the expectation of preparing students
> to think for themselves, addressing themselves to
> local problems first and using this local experience
> to contribute to universal knowledge.[17]

Perhaps the best illustration of this new approach is provided by the "East African Societies and Environment" course for students in the Faculty of Arts and Social Sciences. The course is divided into three sections corresponding to the three years of a student's stay at the University. It aims to stimulate understanding of the nature of underdevelopment in Tanzania and the role of science and technology in this context, and to consider socialist strategies for surmounting underdevelopment. More generally, by means of group teaching methods, the course aims to develop modes of analysis for proposing solutions to the problems with which the course deals. With such ambitious objectives it is perhaps not surprising that the annual re-ports on the different sections of the course amount, with refreshing self-criticism, to a catalogue of problems encountered and caveats to achievement. But, despite these qualifications, there is no reason to dispute the contention of one of the coordinators of the course that

> Whatever its present weaknesses, inherently or as
> reflections of the wider society, EASE is one of the
> very few instances of successful (or relatively success-
> ful) experiments in African universities to create areas
> of knowledge, and methods of acquiring knowledge,
> that are both indigenously relevant and interdiscipli-
> nary.[18]

Part of the broader problem involved in experimenting with degree structure is to know what is the minimum basis of specialization relevant to any type of training and hence to what kinds of standards one wants training to relate. During the period of the University of East Africa, the quality of work was dependent upon standards safeguarded by a system of external examinations derived from the earlier "special relationship" between the University and the University of London. The University of Dar es Salaam has displayed a willingness to follow the advice of the Tanzanian minister of national education: "Nor should we be too influenced by a desire for the maintenance of so-called international standards. We must be our own arbiter of what is best for us."[19] It has, however, proved easier to make this broad claim than to find new and innovative criteria of educational quality relevant to the new developmental role to which the University aspires.

There are some in the University who argue that the potential dangers of a self-defeating parochialism are already evident. It is claimed, for example, that some students in economics, while sensitive to global issues of underdevelopment, are not correspondingly equipped with the specific skills necessary to analyze local problems.

Staff Development

The development of a teaching program that can inspire students to a lasting concern with problems of development is dependent upon a correspondingly relevant type of training for the members of the staff who will be responsible for that program. In looking at the experience of the University of East Africa in an earlier section, we noted a growing sentiment among East African academics that professional irrelevance and cultural disorientation were too frequently the consequence of protracted overseas training. At the same time, there is almost equal recognition of the dangers of a narrow intellectual incestuousness, which can occur if an individual does all his academic training in the same university. The University of Dar es Salaam has made some moves to counteract the harmful consequences of extended overseas training while at the same time recognizing the need, particularly in technical and professional fields, for continued access to overseas facilities and expertise. The new pattern toward which the University is moving discourages a conventional overseas Ph.D. program and instead encourages prospective staff members to undertake a shorter intensive period of work in an overseas university in a program designed to provide specialized and individualized experience. This intensive program may then be combined with more extensive work in the home university and perhaps be part of a home university Ph.D.

At the University of Dar es Salaam, as part of its approach to staff development, promising graduates identified as prospective staff members are, from the moment of their identification, listed and considered staff members and, during the period of their overseas work, are paid a part of their staff salary. This practice has the virtue of providing security, encouraging commitment, and minimizing subsequent loss of the scholar. It contrasts with the practice at the University of Nairobi, which prefers not to consider any Kenyan for appointment until he has his Ph.D. in hand. The Dar es Salaam practice can be viewed as a small step in the direction of reducing the emphasis on paper credentials, which is the hallmark of academic recruitment according to the colonial model.

The University of Dar es Salaam, however, has not gone far in thinking through precisely what might be the ingredients of an appropriate training for a university committed to the service and understanding of development. The need and some possible implications have been summarized by Aklilu Habte, the former vice-chancellor of the national university in Ethiopia:

> It is crucial that we re-think the role of university
> teachers . . . for we cannot borrow indiscrim-
> inately from a model which perceives a teacher
> simply as a detached tenured scholarly critic of
> society. [20]

Changes implicit in this approach might include a redefinition of policies governing recruitment, promotion, and required credentials. The University might emphasize such things as prior experience in rural areas or the public sector, or commitment to a problem-centered and multidisciplinary perspective in teaching and research. It might also provide flexible career tracks, permitting easy interchange between university teaching and other roles.

It is much easier, however, to propose desirable qualities and practices than to discover how they are inculcated in individuals or implemented in institutions. The University of Dar es Salaam has made some tentative moves in some of these directions. As part of an attempt to encourage broader awareness, staff members are encouraged to participate in the activities of the Tanganyika African National Union (TANU, the national political party of Tanzania) Youth League and the public militia. At the same time, most University of Dar es Salaam staff members participate in aspects of policy planning through service on various government and semi-governmental committees. Ideally, a two-way flow between University and government positions would minimize the danger that university positions can become a basis for a divisive social status. In practice, the flow has been largely one-way, from university department to civil service position and seems to have been mainly determined by

shortages in key positions outside the University. For example, in
the Ministry of Economic Affairs and Development Planning, the minister is the former vice-chancellor of the University, the principal
secretary the former chairman of the department of economics, and
the coordinator of development planning the former director of the
Economic Research Bureau. There has been some movement in the
opposite direction; for example, the head of the Institute for Development Studies at the University is the former principal secretary in
the treasury. The reasons for this kind of interchange are understandable in terms of a desire to make maximum use of scarce expertise and to prevent the growth of undesirable status differentation
between the University and other institutions. The price, however,
in disruption and discontinuity of teaching and academic leadership
at times appears to outweigh the dangers of less frequent transfers.

Research

Accompanying changes in the degree structure of the University
of Dar es Salaam have been efforts, first, to incorporate research
materials into the curriculum wherever possible and, second, to
develop a common course for social scientists in research methodology and appreciation. One of the most important development-
related activities of the University has been the so-called teaching-
through-research program for second-year students, pioneered at
the University of Dar es Salaam and taken up at the other two universities. These programs provide opportunities for the student to engage
in research on his own environment and help not only to deepen his
knowledge of his society and its problems but also to enlarge the body
of empirical information available for teaching use.

The broader importance of the programs is that successive
generations of students who will not go on to graduate research or an
academic career have gained familiarity with basic processes of data
collection, collation, and analysis. As the majority of these students
will be involved in planning roles of some sort, their ability to read
tables and evaluate data will be a great aid in their day-to-day work.
Moreover, the programs will equip them to make demands on the
University for research, thereby enlarging the University's research-
literate constituency. Within the University, a feeling is growing that
development may be best served by an integrated social science
methodology that draws on common elements from the main disciplines rather than on separate disciplinary approaches. One can look
toward the emergence of an M.A. program in development or rural
development as one possible future vehicle for this integrated approach.

The particular strength of these programs is that they are concerned with the basic common essentials of a social science approach. Social science is treated not as a narrow discipline-based technology but as a way of approaching problems—propositional thinking—and a way of organizing data. When social science is seen in this way, as one of a number of possible routes to increased understanding of social reality, it would seem to be a very important means by which the University can contribute to development, however defined.

University-Government Cooperation

The University of Dar es Salaam itself has a very close relationship with government. The relationship takes a number of different forms. At Dar es Salaam, as at Nairobi, postgraduate degrees in the departments of economics, political science, and education have been designed to serve a civil service clientele. The department of political science emphasizes the training of students in management with a broadly developmental approach while the department of education offers a new M.A. program for education administrators. These efforts are mirrored at Nairobi in the B.Phil. degree in the Department of Economics, which aims to provide upgrading for government economists, and in the diplomacy course, for foreign service officers.

The two applied social science research bureaus provide advice, research information, and personnel to planning units, and there is the two-way flow of staff between the University and government. At the same time, TANU is represented on the various University committees, and the president of the republic himself displays a particular interest in the University in his capacity as chancellor. In short, there are channels for a constant interchange of ideas between the University and government, and there can be little doubt that the explicit interest of government in development and the relative identity of interest between the University and government have provided a climate that has encouraged the University to try to reorder itself so that development can become an organizing concern of its every activity.

The danger for the University is perhaps less that of a gulf between government aspiration and University response than that the very similarity of outlook may lead to an unthinking conformity on the part of the University that will not serve the goals of development. However, the danger has been greatly diminished in the past five years by the development within the University of a comprehensive critique of Tanzanian socialism from the left. Whatever the government attitude toward development, a degree of distance seems essential if a university is to retain the flexibility it needs, not simply to

serve already defined and agreed-on developmental tasks but to contribute what it is in a unique position to supply, namely the constant
reexamination and redefinition of the nature of underdevelopment and
the task of development. Without a degree of distance from policy
making, the university simply becomes another ministry of government, and, in the face of day-to-day tasks, the pressure to conform
rather than think about and improve policy assumptions becomes ir-
resistible. As one analyst has stated,

> The greatest service the few can give is to question
> continually the validity of every policy and belief—to
> re-examine as boldly as Nyerere himself, the nature
> of society and explore original interpretations of its
> needs.[21]

Community Service Activities

Central in the University of Dar es Salaam's emerging view of
its developmental role is the idea that it should serve not only government but also the mass of people directly. One form that this idea
has taken has been the expansion of University courses to include vocational activities beyond the conventional and professional disciplines—
such as medicine, law, agriculture, engineering, and education. The
University has also tried to design ways in which students and faculty
can identify with the problems of the masses by involving themselves
in practical tasks. The main intention here is political, to let students
appreciate some of the problems of peasants and workers and imbibe
some of their outlook by sharing in the tasks. Until recently this
aspiration has taken the form of occasional work on a self-help project,
such as building a primary school or digging a water furrow or contributing to adult education. However, the recent decision to end
direct entry to the University from secondary school and to admit
only those with previous work experience, testifies to the serious-
ness of the government's intention to restructure national education
and to integrate it more fully with the realities of Tanzania's condition
of poverty. The new procedure will take effect starting in the 1975-76
academic year. Admission to the University will henceforth require
not only relevant academic qualifications but also several years of
work experience and recommendations from the student's employers
and TANU branch regarding suitability (in terms of character, general work performance, and commitment) for University-level training. The general expectation is that a student coming from a job, and
sponsored by his village and employers, will have a basis of understanding, commitment, and knowledge that will enable him to make

use of University resources in a way that maximizes his future contribution to his society. In the first place, it is hoped that the work
break after 13 years of continuous school experience will help the
student acquire a sense of common cause with the mass of the population and reduce the spirit of antisocial elitism that university students have been accused of exemplifying in the past. Second, it is
hoped that the period of work will give the student a sense of why he
needs a particular type of University training and how much theory
he requires. One interesting aspect of this experiment is likely to
be the impact of the demands made by the new type of student upon
the content and methods of teaching at the University. [22]

The University is also beginning to provide leadership to the
rest of the educational system. The initial contribution of the University in this area was its crash program to provide teachers for the
secondary-school system, so that at one time almost half the total
number of students at the University were taking courses that prepared them for the teaching profession. Now the emphasis is more
upon the preparation of good teaching texts, and the preparation and
marking of national examinations. The University is also beginning
to evaluate educational practices after a long period of inactivity in
this critical sphere, following the publication of Education for Self-
Reliance. [23]

The outstanding example of direct University involvement in a
service program has been the literacy and educational campaigns of
the Institute of Adult Education at the University of Dar es Salaam.
The mass health campaign initiated and orchestrated by the Institute,
for example, aimed to reach two million people. It involved distributing over two million booklets, training 75,000 discussion leaders
to lead local discussion groups after radio broadcasts, and creating
supplementary materials in a variety of media including local cloth
designs keyed to messages of the project. The Institute is part of
the University and draws heavily on a range of University departments
for assistance in the production and radio presentation of materials.

At Nairobi, there has been rather less enthusiasm for involvement of a community development type. The diplomacy course referred to encountered strenuous opposition from those quick to mount
the barricades of "academic freedom," and the B. Phil. program in
economics is in danger of succumbing to the same kind of purist opposition. At Dar es Salaam, too, there remains ambiguity about
community involvement, illustrating the University's dilemma of
where to draw the lines of "higher education," as it tries to decide
its developmental role. Notwithstanding the exceptions mentioned,
the University remains uncertain about how far it should go in expanding occasions for involvement in outside service tasks and reorganizing itself for this purpose. Clearly, advanced research and

teaching are a fundamental function, however the University defines
its developmental role. This function, however, is not necessarily
compromised, and may well be strengthened, by contact with lower
levels of training. It is difficult for University members to think constructively about development if they do not know underdevelopment
first hand.

Cooperation With the International Educational
Community

While Tanzania's concept of development stresses self-reliance,
the paradoxical fact about the University is its continuing dependence
upon external sources for research funds, staff, and postgraduate
training. For example, the majority of the faculty are expatriates,
most postgraduate training is still done in Britain and North America,
and the bulk of research money comes from outside the country.
Moreover, in Tanzania as elsewhere in East Africa, these conditions
seem unlikely to change in the near future. Although the capacity of
the University to provide postgraduate, and particularly M.A. training
will continue to expand, much training seems likely to remain an
overseas activity, at least for the immediate future, and the dependence upon the outside for staff and research funds will not quickly be
removed. At Dar es Salaam as at Nairobi, the proportion of East
Africans on the staff has fallen over the past two years, and, as the
political pressure to take in more students leads to an increasing
emphasis upon classroom teaching, funds available for research are
likely to decrease. While there may be changes in the sources of
assistance—as the latest standard bearers of this enterprise, the
Swedes, the Dutch, the Germans, and the Japanese, increase their
activity—the basic condition of dependence seems unlikely to change
over the next five years. If this estimate is correct, the University
must continue to devise its new developmental role within a framework of technical assistance.

One of the most striking aspects of technical assistance to the
University of Dar es Salaam is the supply of foreign teachers. Where
the University is committed to understanding the problems of underdevelopment and improving the condition of the common man, foreign
academics are more than ever handicapped; teaching and research
must be based on a knowledge of the social environment and the ability
to interpret local conditions. In the past, the University relied upon
external recruiting agencies such as the Inter-University Council to
supply staff. The University of Dar es Salaam seems to have been
more assiduous than either of the other universities in developing the
network of relationships that permits personal recruiting by a

department head. There has been an emphasis on recruiting those whose intellectual interests revolve around problems of development, who are willing to make a commitment for at least two years, and who preferably have prior experience in the Third World. The University is increasingly realizing that, although prior identification of cultural sensitivity is difficult, it is possible to predict the likelihood of insensitivity, and the University need no longer recruit foreign academics who have no previous experience of underdevelopment or long-term commitment to its understanding and alleviation. One of the distinctive features at the University of Dar es Salaam has been its willingness, contrasted with Nairobi and Makerere, to recruit staff members from outside traditional channels in the United States and Britain. While the resulting heterogeneity in staff composition has occasionally caused problems in consistency of offerings, such problems have been more than compensated for by the educational benefits to students from being exposed to a range of perspectives.

There has been an element of self selection in the composition of foreign staff at the University of Dar es Salaam, with individuals choosing to apply or not to apply because of the University's socialist aspirations. This too has led to problems where ideologues of various stripes have treated Tanzania as a field station for their own imported notions and have aroused some antipathy where the ideology was not congruent with that of the mainstream or not tempered with cultural sensitivity. The proposal made recently that technical assistance personnel should submit to a formal affirmation of faith in the Arusha Declaration* has overtones inimical to the kind of individual integrity that is the ultimate meaning of a university community.[24] But it does illustrate the important point that faculty recruitment, like other aspects of the University life, can be subject to the criterion of relevance.

University Organization

Clearly some modes of academic organization are more conducive than others to the search for a new developmental role. However, beyond this question-begging proposition it is not easy to identify what these styles might be. The East African universities have inherited the British pattern of university administration and teaching styles. The vice-chancellor is the chief executive; he reports to an external council and is served by an internal senate and

---

*Tanzanian Declaration on Socialism and Self Reliance, 1967.

a registrar. On the teaching side, the familiar two-pronged device has been the mass lecture and the small tutorial.

It is clear that both patterns have been subjected to severe strain resulting from rapid university expansion. Symptoms of this strain, for both administration and teaching, have been characterized by a predominantly authoritarian and hierarchical style and relationships. It seems safe to conclude that these patterns are not very conducive to an intellectual climate that encourages a free-ranging approach to issues of underdevelopment.

To break down hierarchical relationships, the University of Dar es Salaam has instituted a comprehensive system of student election and representation; students participate in University governance more fully at Dar es Salaam than at most other universities in the world. Six students, two for each year, are represented in each department, and five for each faculty board, with similar levels of institutionalized representation on all University committees. Since students often make up half the committee complements, administrative authoritarianism is diminished. At the same time, student organizations and forums are encouraged as channels of communication and expression. The vice-chancellor, who was himself an M.A. student last year, was a member of the main student organization, the Dar es Salaam University Students Organization (DUSO). The fact that student studies—such as those contained in the Report of the University Reform Committee, and another on staffing problems—are made public and discussed in the senate and council is indicative of the way in which all members of the community are enabled to participate in decision making that affects them.

In teaching, the use of the long vacation for research programs and community work programs also helps to break down hierarchical relationships. The physical location of the University, on a hill ten miles outside the present capital, has been a source of concern on the grounds that it isolates the University from the real life outside, and attempts have been made to open up University housing to the wider community as a way of breaking down academic isolation. Yet the "nine-to-five" atmosphere that pervades the University of Nairobi, where staff live off campus, suggests that the proximity of staff and students and resulting mutual accessibility at Dar es Salaam may have advantages in terms of the intellectual vitality of the University community, which outweigh any disadvantages of social isolation.

Part of the problem of University organization is the issue of access to higher education. It is now clear that the rigorous competition for entry to the University has resulted in disproportionate representation of students from areas with the most developed primary and secondary schools. Tanzania is attempting to correct the imbalance by concentrating new educational resources in the relatively poorer regions, but such such patterns of inequity are difficult to reverse at that level. The University has not yet resorted to a regional quota system of recruitment, but it does make provision under the "mature age entry scheme" for a substantial intake of older students whose educational careers may not have followed conventional channels. In some measure this scheme tends to give a second chance to those from areas less well endowed with education facilities at the primary and secondary levels.

It is important to recognize that the choice of the University of Dar es Salaam to illustrate certain tendencies should not suggest that Dar es Salaam is a definitive model of a development-oriented university. University initiatives may be dwarfed by the sheer size of its own and its country's problems. For example, it is a matter of some irony that a university that places such emphasis upon the development of management and planning skills was forced during much of 1974 to spend Shs 240,000 per week on keeping staff members and their families in hotels because it had not been able to plan accommodation for them. The DUSO Report of its University Reform Committee provides a long list of problems with the University, which are the subject of proposals for administrative reform.[25] Despite the impressive system of student representation referred to earlier, problems of internal communication remain. The isolation of the administration, problems of "bureaucratic centralism," and the tendency of the University to resort to and submit to "directives from above" are all singled out as continuing weaknesses of the institution. Among other problems identified are the slow pace of localization, the absence of an academic staff organization, the adverse effect on the University of some national policies such as income tax and decentralization, deteriorating academic standards, and the use of nonmerit criteria in academic promotions. The discrepancy between intent and practice is evident in the University as well as at the national policy-making level. Every promising move risks foundering on the rock of bureaucratic inflexibility, and the capacity of the University to initiate developmental change is compromised by its own as well as by government bureaucracy.

In the country at large, the problems in a number of areas similarly combine to suggest that all is not yet for the best in the best of all possible worlds. Illustrative of such problems are inefficiency in public transportation and commodity distribution, port handling delays, cooperative-society corruption, the increasing use of coercion in moving people to ujamaa villages, and a pervasive bureaucracy whose demands on individuals at times defy credence. Beyond inefficiency is the ultimate specter of mass starvation. However, the significant feature that distinguishes Tanzania from some of her more immediate neighbors is the fact that these problems are acknowledged and, more important for present discussion, the University is looked upon as a vital part of the campaign to alleviate them.

CONCLUSION

This essay has attempted to identify some of the obstacles and deterrents on the one hand and incentives and positive pressures on the other that determine the ability and willingness of the universities in East Africa to confront the issue of development.

It has been argued that new understanding of the nature of underdevelopment and new problems of development have exposed the limitations of the model exemplified by the University of East Africa. The need now is for the universities to take stock of the limits and opportunities of their situation and to work out a meaningful developmental role that corresponds to the magnitude of the challenge.

Despite the scope of the problems and the continuing influences that sustain the old pattern of higher education, there are important prospects for change. Implicit in much of what has been said is the view that the unique role of the university is its ability to provide intellectual leadership but that thinking about development can only make sense where society as a whole is committed to understanding and solving problems of underdevelopment. The University of Dar es Salaam should thus be viewed within an emerging framework of thought and action, struggling with the untidy process of thinking about development. Any more comprehensive approach, such as is implied in the much heard rhetoric about "applying University capacity to solving problems of development," risks disregarding the individuality of students. Teaching students to think more imaginatively and critically about development must remain a preeminent goal. Thus, for example, the best way in which a university can reduce inequality, one of the paramount goals of development, is to train students in the analytical capacity to describe and expose its different manifestations.

Two features of the universities of East Africa provide particular grounds for optimism about a constructive response to the challenge of development. In the first place, a number of young, able, and well-trained scholars—exposed perhaps to the ideas of Pavlo Freire and the literature on Latin American development—are taking positions in the universities here and beginning to question conventional practices and assumptions. Perhaps the main hope for reform lies in the intellectual interaction between two university generations: the second generation of able and critical scholars and the first generation of more cautious academics, products of different training in the earlier days of institution building, [26] who now occupy leadership positions in the universities. The hope for reform, however, lies also in the capacity of the universities to rise above the wider educational and social structure of which they are a part. Because this structure is cemented by vested interests in the status quo, it has been an inhibiting influence on developmental change within the universities. But precisely because the university is at the pinnacle of the education-incentive structure, it need be less subject to the demands of a higher level. Furthermore, by its practices and requirements, the university can have a dominating influence upon what happens at the lower levels. It is hence in a potentially strategic position for initiating widespread change.

From these points of hope, the task remains, as it always has been, that of deciding what is the fundamental basis of a university in East Africa and of assessing which imported ideas and values have universal reference or specific applicability to the needs of the last quarter of the twentieth century.

NOTES

1. I am grateful to David Leonard and Goran Hyden for helpful comments on an earlier draft.

2. See, for example, the collected papers in ed., T.M. Yesufu, Creating the African University (Ibadan: Oxford University Press, 1973). See also the "Task Force Report on Higher Education for Development in Education and Development: Agenda Papers," prepared for a conference at Bellagio, Italy, November 7-9, 1973, subsequently published as Education and Development Reconsidered: The Bellagio Conference Papers, ed., F. Champion Ward (New York: Praeger Publishers, 1974).

3. This formulation of the problem owes much to the analysis presented by Colin Leys in "The Role of the University in an Underdeveloped Country," Journal of Eastern African Research and Development 1, no. 1 (1971).

4. These are usefully summarized and discussed in Chapter IV of Rastad, "Issues of University Development in East Africa."

5. C. Arnold Anderson, "Commentary on the University of East Africa Plan 1967-70," Minerva 8, nos. 1-2 (Autumn-Winter 1968-69).

6. Peter Marris, "What Are Universities for?" Mawazo 1, no. 1 (1967).

7. Julius K. Nyerere, "The Role of Universities," in Nyerere, Freedom and Socialism (Nairobi: Oxford University Press, 1968), p. 182.

8. The Rockefeller Foundation Directory of Fellowships and Scholarships 1917-1970 (New York: Rockefeller Foundation, 1972).

9. See for example the articles by H. C. A. Somerset in eds., David Court and Dharam Ghai, Education, Society and Development: New Perspectives from Kenya (Nairobi: Oxford University Press, 1974).

10. James S. Coleman, "Some Thoughts on Applied Social Research and Training in African Universities," Taamuli (Dar es Salaam), 1973; and Dharam P. Ghai, "Social Science Research on Development and Research Institutes in Africa," The Social Sciences and Development (Washington, D. C.: International Bank for Reconstruction and Development, 1974).

11. Gerald K. Helleiner and R. Cranford Pratt, "Untied Aid for Third World Universities," International and Development Review 15, no. 3 (1973): 5.

12. C. Arnold Anderson, "Fostering Educational Research in the Third World," in Education and Development Reconsidered.

13. John Saul, "The Political Aspects of Economic Independence," in Economic Independence in Africa, ed. Dharam P. Ghai (Nairobi: East Africa Literature Bureau, 1973).

14. Nyerere, "The Role of Universities," p. 183.

15. John Saul, "High Level Manpower for Socialism," eds., Lionel Cliffe and John Saul, Socialism in Tanzania, vol. 2 (Nairobi: East African Publishing House, 1973), p. 281.

16. Ibid., p. 279.

17. Justinian Rweyemamu, "Reorganization of the Arts and Social Sciences," Taamuli 2, no. 1 (1971).

18. Yash Tandon, "1973/74 Status Report on Third Year Faculty Course, East African Society and Environment," University of Dar es Salaam, Faculty of Arts and Social Science, mimeo, 1974.

19. "Revolution in Education," report by the Minister of National Education in Republic Day Supplement of Tanzania Standard, December 7, 1968.

20. Aklilu Habte, "Higher Education in Ethiopia in the 70s and Beyond," mimeo, 1974.

21. Marris, "What Are Universities For?" p. 9.

22. The origin and details of this decision are described in an article entitled "Admission into University" in the Tanzanian Daily News of January 8, 1975.

23. Julius K. Nyerere, Education for Self-Reliance (Dar es Salaam: Government Printer, 1967).

24. Peter Temu, "The Employment of Foreign Consultants in Tanzania: Its Value and Limitations," African Review 3, no. 1 (1973).

25. Dar es Salaam University Students Organization, "Report of the University Reform Committee Set up to Probe into the

Inadequacies of the University Structure as Set up by the University of
Dar es Salaam Act 1970 and Other Matters Pertaining to or Incidental
Thereto," University of Dar es Salaam, mimeo, 1974.

26. For advocacy of generational pressure as a tactic and
precondition of university reform, see G. C. M. Mutiso, "The Future
University: Towards a Multi-Disciplinary Research and Teaching
Approach," ed., T. M. Yesufu, Creating the African University
(Ibadan: Oxford University Press, 1973).

THE ROLE OF AFRICAN UNIVERSITIES IN
OVERALL EDUCATIONAL DEVELOPMENT

A. Babs Fafunwa

The modern African universities, unlike the European universities founded in the Middle Ages, were established by their various
governments to meet specific societal needs while at the same time
sharing the common tradition of universities the world over—that is,
to seek the truth, to preserve the truth, and to teach the truth.

Except for the University of Liberia and the Fourah Bay College,
Sierra Leone, which were founded in the nineteenth century, all other
African universities south of the Sahara and north of the Limpopo
were established during the second half of this century. There are
two principal types of universities in this region, the Anglophone and
the Francophone. The former group consists of those universities
or colleges established by British colonial governments in West and
East Africa, while the latter is made up of institutions established
by the French colonial regime, principally in West Africa. Each
group was fashioned after the metropolitan country's own university
system, and the universities in each group were affiliated to the
parent universities in Britain and France; their degrees were awarded
or guaranteed by the "home" universities. Haile Selassie I University (now Addis Ababa University) was opened in 1961 by the Ethiopian
government as an independent university, while the University of
Nigeria in Nsukka, the University of Lagos, Ahmadu Bello University
in Zaria, and the University of Ife in Ile-Ife were established after
Nigeria's independence as autonomous universities and granted their
own degrees. The University of Lovanium (now Université Nationale
du Zaïre) in the former Belgium Congo (now Zaïre) was opened in
1954 while Zaïre was still a colony of Belgium.

Today most of the universities in Africa are autonomous, with
the exception of those in Francophone Africa, which still maintain a
very close liaison with French universities and are staffed

A. Babs Fafunwa is Dean of the Faculty of Education at the
University of Ife in Nigeria.

substantially by French academics. Although autonomous, many Anglophone universities too still cling to the British pattern of higher education and use British standards as a measuring rod for academic excellence.

Between 1950 and 1970, the newly independent countries of Africa and their citizens were under the illusion that their newly established institutions of higher learning would help transform the economy and improve the lot of the people. Consequently, the various African governments gave generous support to education in general and higher education in particular. But by the late 1960s and early 1970s the taxpayers and the governments of most developing countries began to question the role of the universities and felt that their universities were failing them in many ways. The universities had not helped to transform the economy of their nations; instead they were becoming too expensive for poor countries to finance. There was also a growing feeling that the university community had constituted itself an "elitist group"—an island of privilege in a sea of poverty.

Tanzanian President Julius Nyerere expressed the yearnings of most African governments when he said:

> For let us be quite clear; the University [of East Africa] has not been established purely for prestige purposes. It has a very definite role to play in development in this area, and to do this effectively it must be in, and of, the community it has been established to serve . . . And it must direct its energies particularly towards meeting the needs of East Africa.
>
> . . . this University cannot be islands, filled with people who live in a world of their own, looking on with . . . objectivity or indifference at the activities of those outside. East Africa cannot spend millions of pounds, cannot beg and borrow for the University, unless it plays a full and active part in the urgent task of East Africa. Even if it were desirable, we are too poor in money and educated manpower to support an ivory tower existence for an intellectual elite.
>
> It is true that the University must be concerned with the year 2000 and beyond; but there is also the year 1963. It is NOW that we have to engage the three enemies (poverty, ignorance and disease). . . . Our problem will not wait. We must, and do, demand that this University takes an active part in the social revolution we are engineering. . . . Most of all, the University, its members and its students, must join with the people of East Africa in the struggle to build a nation worthy of the opportunity we have won . . . [1]

Despite their intellectual dependence, the universities have been, at least in recent years, the major suppliers of high-level manpower. They trained teachers for schools, and technical and administrative officers for governments, commercial houses, and industrial concerns in their respective countries. Many of their graduates are now serving in the universities, the army, the navy, and the air force, while a few are commercial entrepreneurs.

They have also contributed to the improvement of education at other levels. Below are selected examples of such contributions.

ADULT EDUCATION AND EXTENSION

Many of the Anglophone universities have departments of adult education or continuing education, and extension services. The adult education department, sometimes called the extramural, or continuing education department, is designed to meet the needs of youth and adults by providing evening classes for those men and women who wish to complete their secondary education, study for university entrance examinations, or acquire industrial or commercial skills to enable them to procure better employment. Courses offered by these departments include academic and practical courses: history, economics, shorthand and typing, accountancy, bookkeeping, mathematics, and English. Some departments organize seminars and workshops for farmers, small-businessmen, lawyers, engineers, and others who wish to update their knowledge in their respective fields. At the University of Nigeria, Nsukka, illiterate farmers are encouraged to attend a week's conference on maize or yams where they are acquainted with the latest developments in this area. At the University of Ibadan, the extramural department, in collaboration with Unesco, ran a functional literacy program for tobacco farmers in Oyo, a town in Western Nigeria. The program was based on tobacco growing, and the text materials were intimately related to tobacco farmers' experience.

At the University of Ife, the Department of Extension Education runs the Isoya Rural Development Project. The objectives of the project are to develop a model for approaching rural development in selected villages in Ife Division, to be applied later on a wider ecological scale; to serve as a laboratory for the training of potential rural development and agricultural extension workers; to serve as research center for testing social science concepts related to community development and extension methodology; and to assist the inhabitants of the area to improve their standard of living.

Ten villages, situated between 10 and 15 miles from the University, with 2,000 people, are involved in the experiment, and some 400 households are participating. The Department of Extension Education introduced new crops—such as high-yielding maize, cowpeas, tomatoes, cassava, yams, and oil palms—to the farmers and helped to build storage facilities. It also assists in collective marketing of the farmers' products. The department also runs health and nutrition programs in cooperation with University of Ife Faculty of Health Sciences and Home Economics. Recently the Department of Adult Education of the same University, in collaboration with the Department of Extension Education, introduced a functional literacy program in the local language and developed textbooks based on maize, beans, and cocoa. About 30 farmers and their wives learned to read and write within three months in one village. The literacy campaign is being planned for four other villages. Newsletters are produced regularly to maintain the level of literacy among the new literates.

UNIVERSITY EFFORTS TO STRENGTHEN PRIMARY, SECONDARY, AND ADULT EDUCATION

In most Anglophone universities, the faculties, institutes, and departments of education are involved, directly or indirectly, with activities at the preschool, primary, and secondary education levels. Staff members of faculties of education participate in conferences, seminars, task forces, and committees on curriculum development at the lower levels, organized by the government or the ministries of education. Staff members and students in education faculties conduct research and surveys on primary, secondary, or teacher education problems with the assistance of various Ministry of Education personnel. Such research projects are often funded by the university but occasionally by the ministry or a foreign foundation. Institutes of education assist ministries of education and teachers in organizing preservice and in-service courses for teachers at the primary, secondary, and teacher education levels. Many of these in-service courses are run during the long vacation when the university facilities are not in regular use; there are also other courses that run throughout the academic sessions, especially in institutes with full-time staff and full-time students.

While the idea of institutes of education was copied from the British system, the universities in the English-speaking countries of Africa have transformed the objective, function, and programs of their institutes to meet the demands of each country's needs and aspirations. Some of the activities of the various universities and their appropriate departments will illustrate their scope.

Haile Selassie I University: Alemaya Accelerated
Science Teacher Training Program

During the 1971-72 academic year a special committee representing the Faculty of Education, the Faculty of Sciences, and the
College of Agriculture was charged with the responsibility of developing an accelerated science teacher training program to help solve
Ethiopia's chronic shortage of secondary-school science teachers.
The program drawn up by the committee sought to give strong emphasis to Ethiopian problems especially in the area of agriculture.
In Phase I of the program, students selected from special preparatory
schools were to take 95 to 100 credit hours of work, arranged over a
27-month period to include four semesters and three summers. Each
student was to be prepared equally in two subjects—for example,
biology-chemistry, chemistry-mathematics, chemistry-physics, or
physics-mathematics. At the end of Phase I, students were to teach
full-time in Ethiopian schools and then to be given the option of re-
turning to the University for one academic year to complete the requirements for the B.Sc. degree in Phase II.

University of Botswana, Lesotho and Swaziland:*
Primary School Headmasters Program

To assist the ministries of education in Lesotho, Botswana,
and Swaziland to improve the quality of instruction, improve administration practices, and encourage curriculum development in the
primary schools, the former University of Botswana, Lesotho and
Swaziland, in cooperation with the USAID and California State Polytechnic College, established a four weeks residential program for
primary school headmasters, in 1970 in Gaborone, later moved to
the Teacher Training College in Francistown, Botswana.
As part of the follow-up phase of the program from 1970 to
1972, the workshop staff visited 188 schools.
The Botswana Ministry of Education provided two education
officers as counterparts for the program, who participated in a
seven-month program of study at an American university in 1973;
the ministry expected primary school improvement to continue as an
ongoing activity of the Ministry of Education in conjunction with the
University of Botswana, Lesotho and Swaziland. An identical plan
was to be implemented in Swaziland and Lesotho. It is not clear, as

_____

*The University of Botswana, Lesotho and Swaziland was dis-
solved in 1975.

this goes to print, how the dissolution of the University will affect these plans.

Makerere University: Faculty of Education

Innovative programs at Makerere University include training of Uganda national-language teachers and primary-school teachers, the setting up of a rural education project, audiovisual center projects, internship programs, postgraduate education programs, and social science programs. The operation of these programs, established in 1967 under Unesco sponsorship, has been taken over by the Ugandans.

A primary school program has made efforts to bring together children and parents, the school and the community, in a new learning situation. Instead of confining learning to the classroom, this new program has moved the child from the classroom into outdoor activities, where he learns about his environment, directly rather than from books only.

Ahmadu Bello University: Institute of Education*

The Institute, in cooperation with the six northern states, provides the following services:

1. Regular courses of instruction for teachers.

2. Vacation courses for teachers, for example, courses for primary school inspectors and secondary school mathematics and science teachers.

3. Advisory and consultancy services to the governments of the six northern states.

4. Professional meetings with teachers to improve curriculum and instruction.

5. Experimental schemes on the improvement of curriculum in primary schools and teachers colleges.

6. Village vocational centers for primary school leavers and school dropouts.

Primary Education Experiment

A Unesco-UNICEF experiment now going on at the Institute reorients primary school curricula so that they reflect more accurately

*See also Case Study 8 in this volume.

the student's environment. Sixty-six pilot schools have been selected for the program, and it is hoped that by 1976 about 600 additional schools will be using some parts of the curriculum. Teachers at the pilot schools attend courses at the Institute on the new
curricula and how to use it. After their return to their schools, mobile
teacher trainers visit periodically to observe the use of the curricula
and to follow up on the retraining the teachers received at the Institute.
The experiment has enabled the Institute to produce innovative materials for primary schools in the areas of reading (Engligh and
Hausa), science, mathematics, social studies, physical and health
education, and creative activities.

Village Vocational Centers

The problems of dropouts from primary schools and of those
who cannot go beyond primary schools are multiplying daily. This is
aggravated by the many school-age children who are not in schools
at all. To assist in this area, the Institute has submitted a proposal
to the World Bank for establishing village vocational centers, to be
attached to the experimental schools, where the dropouts, unemployed
primary school leavers, and older children who have never been to
school can be taught useful crafts.

University of Liberia: Accelerated
Curriculum Experiment

The William V.S. Tubman Teachers College at the University
of Liberia, in cooperation with the Ministry of Education and the
United States Peace Corps, launched a pilot project known as the
Accelerated Curriculum Experiment (ACE) in August of 1971, which
involves over-aged elementary-school pupils. The project is designed
to discover what happens when over-aged pupils are given the opportunity to leave the lock-step organization of the graded school and
proceed through the elementary grades at their own rate. It is hoped
that the project will contribute to correcting one of the basic problems
in Liberian schools—the age/grade structure.

In 1972 actual work at the schools began. One class for over-
aged students was established in each of ten selected elementary
schools in five counties in rural and urban areas of Liberia. Teachers
and students participating in the project meet four to five hours in
the afternoon, four days a week, after the regular school day. The
teachers participating in the project have regular teaching assignments during morning hours as well, but it is hoped that in the near
future ACE teachers can teach only in the ACE program and class
schedules can be shifted to the morning.

In order to facilitate rapid progress of ACE students through
the elementary grades, priority is given to mathematics, science,
and language arts built on a social studies core. Teachers group
students and conduct classes by the use of individualized and group
instructional methods. To improve teaching methods, instructional
aids, and evaluation techniques, three workshops were held for the
ACE teachers on the University of Liberia campus and one tour of
the schools was made by two of the Teachers College faculty members who serve as field officers in the program.

University of Cape Coast: New Trends in Teacher Education

Ghana, like other English-speaking countries of tropical Africa,
has inherited a system of education best described as "gentleman's
education," which was introduced during the second half of the nineteenth century when Europe embarked upon a crusading mission to
"civilize" and "Christianize" Africa. This system of education had
not been significantly restructured since independence and was unable
to meet Ghana's manpower requirements or avoid swelling the ranks
of the unemployed school leavers. In May 1972, therefore, the Ministry of Education decided to reform the whole preuniversity education
system of Ghana to meet the present and future economic and social
needs of Ghanaian society. The new system was based on the belief
that Ghana must combine liberal and vocational/professional education
in one program of study and diversify the content of elementary and
secondary school education so as to provide the appropriate mix of
academic and practical courses.

With the help of an education advisory committee headed by the
dean of the Faculty of Education, a new system of preuniversity education has been worked out for Ghana. In the future, elementary education will last six years instead of ten and will be followed by seven
years of secondary education. The length of preuniversity education
is thus cut down from 17 to 13 years. The first nine years will be
compulsory and free.

The first six years will be devoted to general education and the
seven years of secondary education will be given equally to general
(liberal) education and specific (vocational, pretechnical, commercial,
agricultural) studies.

In addition, the new plan proposes to set aside the ninth and
tenth grades as "continuation schools" to provide vocational and elementary technical skills so that, at 15, the school leaver may be able
to go into gainful employment or qualify for further vocational training.
The continuation schools are a response to the overproduction of

middle-form-four leavers in relation to the type of job openings available to them. Middle-form-four leavers are pupils from the last classes of the elementary school, most of them in the rural areas, who do not go on to secondary education. In 1961-62 there were 35,626 middle-form-four leavers. Ten years later, the number rose to 91,551; and in 1974 it was over 100,000 more than twice the number of pupils enrolled in the secondary schools. Continuation schools will prepare these pupils in practical skills, which will predispose them to further vocational training.

The aim of the continuation schools is to correct the notion, derived from an earlier understanding of Western education, that general academic education is superior to technical and vocational education. The continuation schools seek, therefore, to provide education appropriate to the future calling of those who do not continue formal academic education. The courses are patterned on the farming and industrial needs of the local community of the continuation school, which may be agricultural, technical, domestic, or commercial subjects. At the moment, continuation schools offer over 40 different courses, ranging from charcoal burning to kente weaving, rabbitry, hairdressing, farming and fishing, masonry, motor repairs, pottery, dressmaking, and metal work. This is the first serious attempt in the history of education in Ghana to orient middle-school pupils on such a large scale toward technical and vocational training.

Another important innovation in preuniversity education is the introduction of Ghanaian languages into the schools and their use as the media of instruction in the first three years of school and also as subjects of study later on. The introduction of practical courses into all secondary schools as an integral part of the secondary-school curriculum and the new language policy have made the training of specialist and Ghanaian language teachers a top-priority need.

University of Nigeria: Institute of Education

The Institute of Education runs in-service courses, acts as the research wing of the faculty, and maintains cordial relationships with teachers colleges, ministries of education, the Educational Material Units, and the Consultative Council on Education. All members of the Department of Education are closely associated with the work of the Institute, both in running vacation courses for serving teachers, and in conducting the research projects. The Institute has planned a child development and research center and launched a Curriculum Development and Instructional Material Resource Centre (CUDIMAC) designed to help revitalize curricula in schools and produce teaching materials.

University of Lagos: Associateship Course For
Primary-School Teachers

This course, at the University's College of Education introduces primary-school teachers to mathematics and science and gives them a deeper understanding of these two subjects. After completing the course, the teachers are expected to introduce these subjects in their schools.

University of Ibadan: Institute of Education

The Institute's major emphases are on the teaching of science and on the operation of an International Evaluation Centre, which trains evaluators, conducts research in evaluation techniques, and supplies manpower resources. The Centre runs three-, six-, and 12-month courses for participants from various ministries of education in Anglophone Africa.

University of Sierra Leone: Institute of Education

The new Institute of Education in the University of Sierra Leone runs a series of in-service training programs throughout Sierra Leone. There is a curriculum development unit, started by the ministry and then passed on to the Institute, whose main purpose is to develop material in the teaching of English, mathematics, science, and social studies at the secondary level. Attention is also paid to primary work. The center has received support from bodies such as Unesco, UNICEF, and the World Bank.

Kenya Institute of Education

A majority of Kenya's districts have teacher-advisory centers, organized by the ministry, the Institute, and UNICEF. These centers seek to raise the standard of teaching in the primary schools in the district and thereby to strengthen the dual role of the schools: to prepare most primary school leavers for a productive life and to provide basic schooling for the small proportion of primary school leavers who go on to further education. The centers also assist in developing curriculum, placing emphasis on knowledge and employment skills, independent, logical, and imaginative thinking as a preparation for useful citizenship, and integration of school and community activities, by making features of daily life the focus of the primary education course.

These UNICEF-supported centers are also operational points for the newly established primary school inspectors whose work includes assisting and guiding the headmasters of primary schools; improving the classroom performance of teachers by observing their teaching methods, noting and improving their weaknesses, and demonstrating improved methodology; assessing the performance of experienced and recently trained teachers with a view to identifying difficulties and shortcomings requiring improvement and adjustment of the current teacher education programs and/or the primary education curriculum; and developing and introducing new teaching techniques and related simple and self-made teaching aids.

University of Ife Institute of Education: Six-Year Primary Project in the Mother Tongue

Of all the institutes' activities described so far, perhaps the most innovative is the Six-Year Primary Project with Yoruba as medium of instruction. It is universally accepted (except in most African countries) that a child learns best in his mother tongue. No other nations in the world, except most of the ex-colonies and those still under colonial rule, prepare their children for citizenship in languages foreign to them. The first 12 years are the most formative period in a child's life, for it is during this period that the child requires intelligent care of his physical needs and trained guidance in his mental, emotional, and social potentialities. If, therefore, the Nigerian child is to be encouraged from the start to develop curiosity, manipulative ability, spontaneous flexibility, initiative, industry, manual dexterity, mechanical comprehension, and the coordination of hand and eye, he should acquire these skills and attitudes through the mother tongue as the medium of education, which after all is the most natural way of learning. The average European or English child has a decided advantage over his African counterpart, for while the former is acquiring new skills during the first six years in his mother tongue, the latter is busy struggling with a foreign language during the greater part of his primary education.

The Institute of Education at the University of Ife contended that a child benefits culturally, socially, linguistically, and cognitively through the use of his mother tongue as the medium of instruction throughout the six years of primary school and that his command of English will be improved considerably if he is taught English as an entirely separate subject by a specially trained teacher throughout the six years. Accordingly, in 1970 the Institute, with a Ford Foundation grant, launched the Six-Year Primary School Project with Yoruba as the medium of instruction and English as a second language. (See Tables 26.1 and 26.2.)

TABLE 26.1

Number of Children in Experimental Classes of
Project by Classes and Years at St. Stephen's
"A" Primary School in Ile-Ife Town

Grade	1970	1971	1972	1973	1974	1975
I	80	80	80	80	80	80
II	—	80	80	80	80	80
III	—	—	80	80	80	80
IV	—	—	—	80	80	80
V	—	—	—	—	80	80
VI	—	—	—	—	—	80
Total	80	160	240	320	400	480

These are approximate figures as a few children have dropped
out and a few repeated the same class as decided by educational
authorities.

Source: Compiled by the author.

TABLE 26.2

Number of Children in Control Classes of Project by
Classes and Years at St. Stephen's "A"
Primary School in Ile-Ife Town

Grade	1970	1971	1972	1973	1974	1975
I	40	40	40	40	40	40
II	—	40	40	40	40	40
III	—	—	40	40	40	40
IV	—	—	—	40	40	40
V	—	—	—	—	40	40
VI	—	—	—	—	—	40
Total	40	80	120	160	200	240

Source: Compiled by the author.

The main objective of the project is to develop a primary school curriculum that is relevant and functional both to the children whose formal education may terminate at the end of primary school and to those whose education continues thereafter; to design appropriate teaching materials for the proposed curriculum; and to employ the Yoruba language as the medium of instruction. The project also seeks to teach the English language effectively as a foreign language using specially trained teachers throughout the six years and to evaluate the project continually with a view to determining the presence or absence of certain significant differences between the project children and those of primary schools not connected with the project. The total number of children in both the experimental and control classes was approximately 480 in 1973 and will rise to 720 in 1975.

Initial Difficulties

The Western State Ministry of Education officials charged with the administration, control, and supervision of primary and secondary education in the state had grave reservations about the use of Yoruba, or any other African language, as a medium of instruction in primary or secondary schools. Because of this initial official position, it took almost a year of protracted negotiation between the officials and the representatives of the University's Institute of Education to obtain the Ministry's permission to use one of its primary schools in Ile-Ife for the experiment.

The ministry was not alone in its opposition. Some Nigerian scholars and administrators objected that as a language Yoruba was not fully enough developed to cope with science, mathematics, social studies, and other school subjects. A major reservation was that the children would be so immersed in Yoruba language and culture that national unity would be undermined. Still another objection was that the children would be at a disadvantage linguistically and cognitively when they entered a secondary school at the end of their primary education.

One answer to these and other objections is that the experiment is launched to find out whether all these reservations would be confirmed or rejected at the end of the project. Critics were answered, however, on each point raised. Yoruba, like English, German, or any other language, does not have an adequate vocabulary to cover all situations and new discoveries, but like other dynamic languages it has tremendous capacity to accommodate new situations by coining words, changing meaning, and borrowing. All actively spoken languages respond to new situations in this fashion. On the question of disunity, project proponents maintained that while a commonly spoken language is helpful in promoting unity among people of diverse tongues,

it is not sufficient. Nations that speak the same language have gone
to war with one another; even countries with the same cultural background have done so. The present approach to the teaching of English
in Nigeria today is not likely to Anglicize Nigerians in 100 years.
What is more, fewer than 10 million out of 60 million Nigerians speak
anything akin to English whereas 10 million speak Ibo, 10 million
speak Yoruba, and 25 million speak Hausa. A good education in any
language can inculcate the spirit of unity, freedom, mutual respect
for others, and promote appreciation of cultures different from those
in which the children grew up. If a Yoruba, Ibo, Ijaw, or Bini boy
swears allegiance to his country in his own language it will mean
more to him than if he does it in a language less familiar to him. As
to the question of admission to the secondary level where English is
still the medium of instruction, project educators believe that the
experiment children will not be worse off than other children since
they are exposed to English as a foreign language from year one to
six. Finally, since primary education is terminal for the majority
of the children, proponents believe they should have a good six-year
education that is functional and has some surrender value.

The Project School

     The school selected as the experimental site is an average
primary school in the town of Ile-Ife. The homes of the children and
neighborhood of the school are typical of any Yoruba town, though
Ile-Ife is considered generally to be conservative and traditional because of its significance as the cradle of traditional Yoruba culture.
All the children come from Yoruba-speaking homes, and only two are
children of staff members of the nearby University of Ife. Two first-
year classes were designated as experimental classes and the third
as a control. These designations have been maintained through the
ensuing six years, and each year three such classes have been added
at Year I. No new intake has been permitted in Years II, III, and IV
of the experimental classes.
     All the classroom teachers involved have the Grade II Teachers
Certificate required for teaching in primary schools all over the
Federation of Nigeria. The specialist English teachers have been
Grade II Teachers with a one-year associateship (diploma) available
to experienced primary teachers. All of the specialist and classroom
teachers have received in-service training, provided by the project
staff, in the use of the new materials and methods. The specialist
teachers have now become members of the curriculum writing teams.
     The differences between the experimental classes and the
control classes have been confined to those that relate to language
policy. The control classes are provided with new curriculum

materials, teaching aids, and consumable supplies, and the control
teachers are given in-service training. However, they teach English
themselves according to the state syllabus and without the aid of a
specialist teacher, and they are allowed to mix the two languages in
the course of their instruction, according to the general practice in
the primary schools.

Writing Workshops

An essential part of the project is the annual Summer Writing
Workshop, made up of 30 persons drawn from the ranks of university
teachers, primary- and secondary-school teachers, and some principals of teacher training colleges. The group meets every long
vacation for three to four weeks to examine the existing curriculum,
design a more appropriate one, and produce the necessary materials
for teachers and pupils in the five key selected areas: Yoruba, social
and cultural studies, science, mathematics, and English. Five such
workshops were conducted between 1970 and 1974.

The existing Yoruba syllabus was found to be inadequate, since
it was aimed at producing only limited competence in Yoruba. This
was the first time that indigenous materials had been considered
seriously for teaching and instruction, and local people—ranging from
drummers, diviners, farmers, and craftsmen to medicine men and
women traders—were delighted to be consulted and gave their assistance freely and generously. The social and cultural group produced
28 new books between 1970 and 1974.

Until the project started, the little science that was taught in
most Nigerian primary schools was taught in English, while mathematics was done mostly in English buttressed by Yoruba or Ibo whenever the teacher ran into linguistic difficulties. The science panel
adapted the Science Education Programme for Africa (SEPA) and the
Nigeria Primary Science Programme (NPSP), which were developed
specifically for African children between 1964 and 1970. Interesting
and challenging problems were met and mostly resolved. A number
of scientific words and phrases had no Yoruba equivalents, but words
were coined, borrowed from other languages, changed, and translated.

Similar adaptation was made of the African Primary Mathematics. One delightful "discovery" was made in counting in Yoruba. One
can count to billions in Yoruba, but the language has no numerals.
Mathematical computation was therefore difficult, if not impossible.
Curriculum designers then realized that English, French, German,
and other European languages all use Arabic and Roman numerals.
If the English, the French, and the German can borrow freely and
shamelessly from the Arabs, so could the Yoruba, who is perhaps
closer to the Arabs than the English or the French. The children

from then on learned mathematics in Yoruba and Arabic just as German or English children do in German or English, using Arabic numerals.

The project has proved that any dynamic language has a means of adjusting to new situations and new challenges. Yoruba as a medium of primary education has coped with the teaching of science and mathematics, earlier bones of contention.

Extension of the Project to Other Schools

The original design of the project provided for experimentation, in a single primary school, with the innovative language policy in the hope that the experimental model would help determine state and national language policy. It was understood from the outset that new curriculum materials would have to be produced in each instructional area, since educators were generally dissatisfied with the progress attained in both English and the mother tongue in primary schools and since there were no adequate instructional materials in Yoruba. New curriculum materials necessitated the training of teachers in their use and in new teaching approaches and techniques. Very quickly, then, the project was seen as one that would influence the quality of primary education as a whole, with language being central to the process of change.

An extension of the project was needed in order (1) to test reliably the hypotheses upon which the project is based and (2) to assure a multiplying effect for all the effort and expenditure which has gone into the project. Extension of the project would also strengthen the creation of a new breed of professionals in the field of education in Nigeria. This is the only extensive, truly Nigerian curriculum development project at the primary level in Nigeria. In the course of their work, many already established professionals (such as the university lecturers) have acquired new insights into primary education and new skills in the curriculum development process which will inevitably carry over into other areas of their work in the future.

In 1973-74, ten schools representing urban, semiurban, and rural areas in the Western State were brought into the experiment, adding 18 classes with 720 children and 18 new teachers. Expanding the program involved recruitment of supervisory staff, induction of the Primary One teachers of the ten schools, and the production of sufficient materials for them and their pupils. The extension has increased the number of children in the experiment to 1,440.

Some Observations So Far

At the end of the fourth year of the experiment, the following observations can be made:

1. Generally, the children in the experimental classes show more evidence of self-reliance and resourcefulness, and are relatively happier as a group as compared with those in the control group.

2. Parents assist the classes through their children by supplying information on local mores, folklore, and festivities whenever requested by the teachers, and both parents and children now communicate in a common language in regard to school education. This situation is unique in almost 150 years of formal education particularly in the Western State and perhaps in Nigeria as a whole.

3. The children in the experimental classes seem to express themselves more fluently in both Yoruba and English, compared with those in the control classes.

4. It is becoming more obvious that the so-called control classes at the project school cannot be truly called control classes, and maybe only the classes outside the project school can truly be called control.

5. The experiment has enabled the project to incorporate many social and cultural items into the curriculum.

6. The experiment has opened the way for extensive use of science materials for adult and literacy education.

7. Two of the six northern states of Nigeria have decided to use Hausa as medium of instruction at primary education level.

Finally the project may have a lasting effect upon Nigerian education in four ways: in influencing the quality and focus of primary education, in introducing changes in the system of primary teacher training, in creating new kinds of professionals with new skills and insights, and—most prominently—in providing a demonstration of one way of dealing with the chronically disturbing and destructive language problem in the Nigerian schools.

SECTOR REVIEWS

In addition to the various activities of institutes and departments of education in Anglophone Africa three countries have engaged in a global review of the education sector. The first major review of education took place in Nigeria in 1969. It was the first review of the curriculum after Nigerian independence and the purpose was to

devise a curriculum that would respond to the needs of an independent
Nigeria. The idea was spearheaded by university institutes of education and adopted by the federal Ministry of Education. A cross section
of the Nigerian public was represented: farmers, workers, teachers,
parents, government officials, professional organizations, employers,
and youth workers.

Ethiopia conducted a sector review in 1972 and Sierra Leone in
1974. The staff of the Haile Selassie I University* and the University
of Sierra Leone played leading roles in these exercises. In both cases
the reviewers attempted to harmonize the various sectors of the educational enterprise, incorporate nonformal education into the overall
system, and to project education development on a long-term basis.

THE CHALLENGE OF THE FUTURE

We reviewed the various activities of a number of African universities and their numerous efforts to strengthen primary, secondary,
teacher training, and adult education and extension services. These
universities have been involved in research activities, teaching and
consulting, curriculum development, writing of text materials for
primary, secondary, and adult education classes, and setting,
marking, and moderating national examinations for secondary and
teacher-training levels.

As indicated earlier, the African universities in the 1970s need
to redefine their roles within the African context. There are many
emerging issues, but we shall concern ourselves with those relating
to what universities might or ought to do for other levels of education
in their countries.

African universities, unlike Western universities, ought to be
totally committed to the service of their nation, at least for the
remainder of this century. To achieve this commitment, there must
be a marked departure from their present outlook, policies, and
functions. For instance, their work in extramural and extension
services should cease to be "extra" and become a "normal" function
of the university, and those engaged in this work should not be regarded as second-class citizens within the university community. The
principle of total commitment to nation building implies that a university should be ready and willing to assist the nation in whatever capacity and at whatever level it is called upon to assist. Faculty

*See Case Study 4, p. 56.

members who are engaged in writing text materials for primary and
secondary levels are often denied adequate recognition for their work
because such exercises are not "academic pursuits." Yet in African
countries where most primary and secondary school materials are
few and far between and where limited high-level manpower is mostly
concentrated within universities, it is only reasonable that university
staff should assist in developing materials for primary and secondary
schools. We believe that such involvement is more valuable than the
production of scholarly papers on esoteric topics, particularly at this
stage of African development.

We believe that all African universities should commit at least
60 percent of their resources to teacher education in arts and sciences,
at least for the next 25 years; that is, 60 percent of their manpower,
physical plant, and curriculum should be concentrated on the improvement of primary, secondary, and adult education. To this end we
recommend the following strategies for implementation as cited in
one of our recent works.[2]

We need to reorient the staff or, as we say in Africa, decolonize
the African's colonial mentality and de-Anglicize him if he is to be
sensitized to the needs of his people. Africanization of the university
faculty is helpful, but it does not guarantee awareness and relevance.
The local staff member differs only in color, not in attitude, from
his expatriate counterpart. Both were probably trained in the same
overseas institution, and both have imbibed the same idea of what a
university is in an affluent society. Their research orientation and
their attitude to teaching and curriculum are those of a developed
economy. In other words, we should change our attitude as university
men and women and rethink our role. We need to make ourselves
relevant to our society before we can produce relevant curriculum
and relevant students.

The next priority is to change the present university structure,
which in many places is inflexible if not impervious to change. As one
African educator rightly observed:[3] "If you want to change the speed
of the train, you need to change the rail first." The Western model
is proving not only inadequate, but also expensive and largely irrelevant. As we see it, what should be international or universal is the
common search for knowledge and truth—not particular knowledge or
truth, not models or structures or traditions per se but the tradition
of seeking truth and knowledge. Beyond these, the newer universities
need not conform to anything else. They should be propelled by their
own societal momentum and not the dictates of a foreign institution,
ideology, or idiosyncrasy. To this end we propose a less structured
university system based on the idea of a university without walls.

In this new, more open university, training—at the master's,
doctoral, and postdoctoral degree levels, or at postgraduate certificate

or diploma levels in the academic disciplines and the professional courses—should be directed at five types of personnel:

1. Those who will be pure researchers in national institutes;
2. Those with academic orientation for university and post-secondary teaching;
3. The intermediate cadre in arts, science, technology, education, medicine, agriculture, and so on;
4. Professionals in different walks of life who require additional competency to be more efficient and productive on the job; and
5. Literate and nonliterate adults reached through extension and adult education.

At the undergraduate level, the university's role is training the bulk of the high-level manpower needed in different fields including teachers for the nation's schools, engineers, architects, doctors, and other professionals for the maintenance of essential national services, and a core of future academicians and researchers. Thus, training at this level will seek to produce (1) general degree holders in a variety of fields, people who will ultimately become practitioners within the country, and (2) a few specialized graduates, selected because of their talents, who intend to go into academic and research life.

The intermediate sector is concerned with preparing sub-degree-level candidates for the professions and skilled labor in the intermediate sector of the national economy. These students will be diplomats of the university, who go through short and long nondegree courses in specific professional and subprofessional areas, such as engineering, technical, commercial, agricultural, nursing, teaching; hundreds of thousands of these skilled workers are needed for development of the country.

Informal, continuing, life-long education schemes are in the nature of adult evening classes to improve proficiency and skills or inform, entertain, or enrich the cultural background of adults. This level also includes programs aimed at elementary and high school dropouts, primary and secondary school leavers, adults, and adolescent workers who want to improve their competencies in any way through programs like the "University of the Air," refresher courses, correspondence courses, in-service and on-the-job orientation classes, seminars, symposia, lectures, and others. These groups represent millions of people who must feel the impact of the university one way or another.

Each of the major functions of the university—instruction, research, and dissemination of knowledge—will take place at all levels—postgraduate, undergraduate, intermediate (subdegree) and informal,

continuing, life-long education levels—in each division—arts and
humanities, the basic sciences, education, the health sciences,
agriculture, and technology.

It is our contention that if we are to develop a multipurpose,
comprehensive, or innovative university that is development oriented,
our distribution of students and staff within this structure and in terms
of overall commitment to nation building should be as follows:

		Staff (percent)	Students or Participants
1.	Teaching, research, and information center	1	in ones
2.	Postgraduate	4	in tens
3.	Undergraduate	10	in hundreds
4.	Intermediate	35	in thousands
5.	Continuing education	50	in tens of thousands

The new university must cease to regard itself as the final
authority on teaching, research, and dissemination of knowledge. It
must open its doors wide to receive new ideas and new knowledge
from the populace as a whole—lettered and unlettered farmers, artists,
poets, historians, medicine men, musicians, as well as students,
graduates, industrialists, government officials, and private citizens.
The doors of the university are wide open not only to hand out knowledge but also to receive as much if not much more than it gives. In
the Africa of today some of the best professors of agriculture, music,
art, poetry, drama, and so on are Africans who never saw the inside
of a formal school.

African universities cannot continue indefinitely as an oasis of
privilege in a sea of poverty; nor can they afford to ignore the pressing
needs and aspirations of their people. They can only do so at their
own peril. These institutions were creations of their respective governments in response to the needs of the people. The university
teachers and administrators in Africa, if they are to survive the
present century, must move ahead of government in planning the
social and economic order. They must strive relentlessly to help
solve social and economic problems.

The African university of our dream is a community essentially
of African scholars, men and women, old and young, lettered and
unlettered, dedicated to serving knowledge to its society and the
world and committed to the total development of the African society
with the express goal of totally liberating the common man from all
that obstructs his physical, material, and intellectual well-being.
The staff of African universities should be physically and intellectually committed to service education at the lower levels, not as a
concession but as a normal practice.

NOTES

1. A.B. Fafunwa, New Perspectives in African Education
(Lagos: Macmillan and Co., 1967), pp. 122-24.

2. In T.M. Yesufu, ed., Creating the African University:
Emerging Issues in the 1970's, published for the Association of
African Universities (Ibadan: Oxford University Press, 1973),
pp. 116-30.

3. Joseph Ki-Zerbo, in a paper delivered at the AAU Seminar
in Accra in July 1972.

27

THE UNIVERSITY IN DEVELOPING COUNTRIES:
MODERNIZATION AND TRADITION

W. Arthur Lewis

Let me start by telling you how I have divided the subject.
More precisely let me give you the four headings under which have
been marshalled the various topics which will pop up as I try to assess the special problems of the university in a less developed country (LDC). These headings are The University as the Bearer of the
Culture; The University as the Trainer of Skills; The University on
the Frontiers of Knowledge; and The University as a Service Agency.

THE UNIVERSITY AS THE BEARER OF THE CULTURE

The relative stress on the role of the university as the bearer
of the culture and its role as the trainer of skills is not everywhere
the same. The British, it used to be said, designed their public
schools and universities in the nineteenth century in the belief that
they were the inheritors of Periclean Athens; their role was to make
the cultured gentleman, knowing something about every aspect of
human knowledge, well mannered, and an active participant in public
discussion. This inheritance has now passed to the American educators, who are forthright in articulating it.
The situation in LDCs is complicated. For there are senses in
which the university, far from transmitting the culture, is rather

---

W. Arthur Lewis, born in the British West Indies and educated
at the University of London, served as vice-chancellor of the University of the West Indies in Jamaica and is now James Madison
Professor of Political Economy at Princeton. This paper was given
at the Vice-Chancellor's Conference in January 1974, at the University of Ibadan, Nigeria. It was previously published as one of
ICED's Occasional Papers.

part of the forces that are eroding traditional society. Much that the traditionalists weep over and think so special to their own geography is really no more than the universal culture of poverty, which could not possibly survive development. The university, however, is one of the destructive agents so, despite the small ratio of the population that it educates, it has inescapably to define its creative cultural role, and to make its contribution to the evolving patterns.

Let us treat separately two different aspects of "culture"— namely, social relations and aesthetics.

Traditional social systems are breaking down fast in LDCs. Extended kinship is giving way to the nuclear family. Religion is losing its authority. Tribal, princely, and other political allegiances have been overthrown. The youngster has to find a new code defining his rights and obligations and modes of behavior in relation to other categories of persons. He needs a new code of social ethics.

The students who pass through our hands are particularly bereft of signals because they are joining a new class, which has not previously existed in LDCs, and for which no traditional code exists within their own cultures. These students are creating a new middle class of professionals, managers, scientists, and artists. When this class emerged in Western Europe, slowly from the fifteenth century onwards, it inherited the code of the medieval guilds: pride in the craft, honest workmanship, honest dealings with the client, the goal of "zero defect." This same code exists in all countries that have a tradition of fine handicrafts, especially in Asia, where sometimes the handicraft workers have been as much as 15 percent of the labor force. Latin America and Africa also have their handicraftsmen, but, except in Sudanese West Africa, these are a small part of the labor force. The new middle class has therefore to grow into an ethical code that is not a part of its tradition. It is the old ethical code common to all those religions and philosophies that are society-oriented, rather than spirit-oriented, but it has to be articulated in new circumstances.

LDC universities have done this part of their job poorly, mainly because we have not recognized its urgency, and have not set up our programs to deal with it. Our graduates, however much admired for their technical proficiency, tend to be scorned in their own countries for their lack of social conscience, their desire to get rich quick, and their lack of responsibility in dealing with their clients. Some of this scorn derives from expecting too much from ordinary human material, but there is a hard core of truth in the complaint.

Our governments are much concerned with this problem of an ethical code and are adducing their own remedies. The current favorite is to impose some form of national service on all university graduates. Some think, like the Chinese, that it should be done before

university entrance, and that it must be manual work, with preference
for farming. This is hard on those disciplines, like music or mathematics, where an interruption of intellectual excitement may hamper
intellectual growth. Other governments prefer service after graduation, content that the graduate then practice his profession, whatever
it may be. Some form of national service may indeed be the only way
of getting teachers and professionals to work in the isolation of rural
areas. Whether it also gives the graduate a greater social conscience
I do not know.

The traditional approach of the university to its role in developing the social conscience is to emphasize the value of teaching the
humanities and the social sciences to all students, because these are
the subjects where the great problems of man's relationship to man
have been intensively debated over 3,000 years. Americans, recognizing that most of their university students do not have a middle-
class or professional family background, generally make these subjects compulsory. Should an LDC university similarly require all its
undergraduates to take courses in the humanities and social science?
How would this indoctrination, which normally emphasizes the democratic values and independence of mind, fit into the political framework that LDCs seem to be adopting? And is it really possible to
teach 20-year-olds in college basic ethics, which they should have
learned in secondary school at 15 or at home at 12?

Arts and the University

In aesthetics, our universities tend to be particularly barren.
The arts are the special interest mainly of the middle and upper
classes, and most of our students do not have such backgrounds. By
contrast, today there are relatively few working class students in the
English universities. English students arrive from homes where they
have been introduced to the arts at an early age, and from secondary
schools, which have made some effort in these directions. Most LDC
students, on the other hand, come from homes that do not have a book,
and the parents of a large proportion are illiterate. We know, however, what our universities have to do; our chief problem is how to
persuade our senates and councils to allocate more money for aesthetic activities, at the expense of departmental budgets.

LDCs have, however, a problem that most developed countries
escape, namely disagreement as to what culture is to be transmitted.
Western universities at home have no doubt that their task is to promote Western music, Western painting, and Western literature. As
the Western university spread into India, 115 years ago, it also assumed that it should promote Western culture in India, although India

has its own superb traditions of music, painting, sculpture, and architecture. A similar assumption in other continents has produced a violent reaction, and now everywhere LDCs emphasize the desirability of teaching and developing their own artistic traditions.

This is easier in some places than in others. My own West Indies, for instance, has no aesthetic traditions of its own, the original inhabitants, the Arawaks, having died out 300 years ago. We have, of course, since then developed a popular music of our own, but when it comes to classical styles, whether in dancing, music, painting, or theater, our aesthetic background includes large elements from Western Europe and India, with trace elements from China and various parts of Africa. Our most aggressive spokesmen demand that we should reject everything except what comes from Africa, and students have, for example, gone so far as to disrupt a performance of Mozart on our university campus, claiming that "Mozart is not a part of our culture." What line is the university to take in such circumstances? My own prejudice is simple: I think that the whole human achievement, whatever its geography, is part of the heritage of each one of us, wherever he may be, and that the "cultured gentleman" who neglects the opportunity of benefitting from the aesthetic experience of all nations is the poorer for doing so.

Dilemmas of Plural Societies

Now, when one is talking about culture, whether aesthetics or social relations, LDCs have an additional complication; namely the fact that, especially in Africa and Asia, our countries are not homogeneous but are deeply divided by race, religion, language, or tribe. Our political scientists used to think that the basic political division in all societies is between the haves and the have-nots. Bitter experience has shown that in our countries this "vertical" division has trivial political significance when compared with the "horizontal" rifts.

(It is true that even in European societies some demand is made to preserve and dignify a separate working class culture, or various regional, folk, or immigrant cultures; but most Anglo-American universities do not take this seriously; even separate dormitories for women are disappearing, let alone the cultivation of "feminine interests.")

In nineteenth-century England the University of London led the way in creating the tradition that the horizontal differences do not matter within the university walls and, in this, was ultimately followed by Oxford and Cambridge and the others. This is a recent and insecure tradition, which has not easily taken root in LDCs. Instead, our universities are subjected to one of two pressures. The first is to have separate universities for different racial, tribal, or religious groups. Our university spokesmen have always resisted this, asserting that the communities will quarrel less if their young people are educated together. But even when this point is conceded, we are faced with the tendency of the students to segregate themselves within the university, just as black students in the United States, having clamored for admission into white universities, are now demanding separate curricula, teachers, halls of residence, and recreation facilities.

The other pressure on us, where there is only one university, is to impose quotas, for each race or what you will. This we have resisted even more vigorously, on the ground that it is wrong to exclude a well-qualified applicant of race A in order to admit a less qualified applicant of race B; our attitude is rather that there should be enough places for all who qualify. This is not, however, so simple, even leaving aside the fact that one may not be able to afford enough places for all who qualify. It is simple enough if all students have equal opportunities to prepare for admission; then quotas are needed only where it is necessary to combat prejudice, such as that against admitting women to medical schools or tribal favoritism of various kinds. But it is also a fact that our basic principle—that the prizes should go to those who win in competitive tests—is not always applicable in plural societies. One's ability to pass the competitive tests depends not only on innate intelligence, but also on family and social background. If members of only one group have the appropriate background, the competitive test serves only to solidify an existing social structure, in which racial or other inequality is embedded. One cannot break this vicious circle except by insisting on quotas reserved to the underprivileged.

I have said that it is part of our tradition to resist pressures for separate treatment, but where these matters are felt keenly, we are not likely to succeed.

One's attitude to these matters depends on what one thinks to be the future of plural societies. Pessimists, reading largely from history, assert that they have no future. Sooner or later one group will become dominant economically and politically, and will suppress the religion, language, and culture of all the others, thus enforcing homogeneity, within the borders of the nation state. Others think that the bitterness of these divisions is a passing historical phase, and that just as Protestants and Catholics have learned to tolerate each other in most of Europe (except the Netherlands, Belgium, and the United Kingdom of Great Britain and Northern Ireland), so also in due course men will wonder that their ancestors used to fight each other over questions of language or skin color. If you hold to this

latter view, then, however great the pressures, you will keep your
university as open as you can, and will make every effort to cooperate
closely with other universities of different complexion.

Personally I incline to the view that this is a passing historical
phase, for two reasons. First, the spread of a universal youth culture. For example, Japan used to be held up as an example of a country that had absorbed Western science and technology without affecting
the rest of its traditions. But Japan is now rapidly Westernizing itself; its rich buy and grossly inflate the prices of French wine, European painting, sculpture, and other treasures, and its young model
themselves upon the young people of California, whose dress, drugs,
music, dances, religions, and attitudes to parents and teachers now
set the fashion for young people throughout the rest of the world. If
the young of all tribes make themselves a common culture, then all
other cultures will die out.

Even more important is an element that derives from what the
universities themselves are doing. The graduates we all turn out are
quite different from their parents; more logical, scientific, open-
minded, with fewer allegiances and a different set of superstitions;
essentially, all children of the French Enlightment. Our product is
managing the world, whether in the public or the private sectors. A
Russian physicist, an American physicist, an Indian or a Nigerian
physicist, have more in common with each other, whether in outlook
or in life style, than any of these has with a bus conductor from his
own country. The university is educating a middle class that is homogeneous throughout the world and that, within any country, must
ultimately scoff at the barriers which are now so divisive. Is this
not why our various brands of separatists are so vociferous in de-
nouncing "middle-class values"? I may be wrong; there is no lack of
highly educated racists. But if I am right, then nothing is more important than for us to keep our universities as free from sectional
division as our political bosses permit.

THE UNIVERSITY AS THE TRAINER OF SKILLS

One has to begin by recognizing the revolt, in some student
quarters, against the university as a place for "training fodder for
capitalist employers." This is largely an American phenomenon.
When 40 percent of the age cohort is in college, it is inevitable that
what most of them do there will have little bearing on the jobs they
ultimately get. Hence the university is not for them a place for
training. It is a place for spending four years as enjoyable as one
can; choosing only such subjects as interest one, and abandoning them

as soon as one reaches into fundamental theories or models that demand too much intellectual exercise; skipping exams, or at least
examination grades. The college is seen as a young people's Eden,
which they may regulate as they please without interference from
adults, whose only duty is to pay the bills. The advantage to the
adults is that the young are shut away in institutions while they grow
up, especially as their preference for inelegance offends our sense
that form ranks equally with substance. It is also thought (but incor-
rectly) that to keep them off the labor market reduces unemployment.
I need hardly add that the number of serious American students is
greater than it ever was; all that has happened is that the nonserious
have multiplied even faster, and have become shamelessly strident.

Echoes of this disturbance are heard in our LDC universities,
since, as I have remarked, everything that starts in California ultimately comes to all of us. It has some relevance to overpopulated
LDC universities, such as those of India, where the struggle between
the students and their universities has already had such devastating
effects on higher education. But in Africa and the Caribbean, where
the demand for trained graduates still exceeds the supply, hardly any
serious person doubts that one of the principal functions of the university is to train the middle class for the jobs it has to do. This
attitude is fortified by the fact that the cost per student is such a large
multiple of national income per head; though the cost would not matter
so much if students were paying for their education out of loans, as
they should be, since one could then provide all the places for which
there was demand.

To the perennial question of which skills are fit to be taught in
a university and which are not, the traditional answer is that the university skills are only those that have a major intellectual content.
In practice, however, our universities are asked to teach (or to
supervise other schools that teach) many skills that do not pass this
traditional test for two reasons.

The first reason is administrative capacity. LDCs are short
of administrative talent. We have reached a stage of modernization
where we have learned the tricks of managing things and ideas
(science, power stations, open heart surgery, pianos) but not the
tricks of managing people. So when you get a university with a good
vice-chancellor, a good registrar, and a good bursar, you ask them
to take responsibility for as much postsecondary education as they
will swallow (medical technologists, agricultural assistants, primary-
school teachers, and technical institutes). This inclusiveness makes
sense if the university does indeed have a first-class administration,
but when it has not (as is more often the case in LDCs), it is easily
overburdened.

The second reason for trying to bring as much postsecondary education as possible under the wing of the university is to give this kind of training social status and intellectual prestige. Any ambitious student who gets good "O" Levels wants to take a university degree, since people with degrees get higher salaries than people without. Hence, all the nonuniversity institutions are deprived of good talent, and in many LDCs the crucial shortage is not of university graduates but of intermediate personnel. In a free market the salaries of technicians would rise relatively to those of skilless and mediocre graduates in arts, but since the government, the principal buyer, bases relative salaries on tradition rather than on scarcity, the market situation cannot right itself.

Faced with these problems, I have never been able to get hot under the collar about what is properly or not properly a university subject. I am even willing to accept mortuary science, which you can study in such highly respectable U.S. institutions as the University of Minnesota, Wayne State University, and Temple University. Each community should settle such issues in accordance with its circumstances.

A much more serious problem is that of the number to be trained. This depends first on the structure of the economy. The biggest user of graduates is the services sector, followed by industry and mining, and lastly by agriculture. Since services employ more than 50 percent of the labor force in the United States, and agriculture only about 5 percent, the demand for graduates is enormous, and anything less than 20 percent of the age cohort would produce a serious shortage. In LDCs, on the other hand, agriculture employs half the labor force or more, and even 1 or 2 percent of the cohort can produce a glut of graduates.

The economy's capacity to absorb graduates depends also on their salaries, relative to per capita national income. In LDCs this ratio is very much higher than in developed countries, making the cost of services too high for the economy to afford as much as it needs. As educated numbers increase, salaries fall and absorptive capacity automatically increases, so the way to create demand is to flood the market; but this is a painful and politically dangerous process.

Most LDC universities admit too many undergraduates, and then have high dropout rates (not to speak of those that have too many students but are prevented by their governments from failing more than x percent). This situation could be improved by giving other postsecondary schools a higher status and deflecting more students there. Another solution would be establishing comprehensive community colleges that offer two- or three-year courses from

"O" levels in both technical and academic subjects. The university could then raise its admission level and take fewer students.

Universities try to insist on determining for themselves what their entrance level should be, but this position is hardly tenable. The university has to relate to other educational institutions. For example, rural secondary schools have difficulty in attracting and holding sixth-form teachers. If, in the absence of community colleges, the university insists on entrance only at "A" level, it will produce fewer sixth-form teachers, discriminating, therefore, against half the secondary school population. Since university senates tend to insist on high entrance levels, the government, which pays the bill, will want to have a say in determining such levels, which in turn affects the demand for student places.

Besides the total number of students, there is the question of the relative numbers in different subjects. Usually there are not enough in mathematics or sciences, while there are too many in social sciences (especially the "soft" social sciences) and in law. Humanities also tend to be starved, relative to the need for secondary-school teachers.

Here again the government may be expected to take a hand, by fixing maximum quotas for social science and for law. It is true that the basic solutions are rather to teach more and better science and mathematics in the secondary schools and for the government to pay higher salaries for graduates in the subjects that are in short supply. A quota probably does not help much in deflecting students toward scientific subjects, but at least it cuts down on the cost of producing a lot of low-grade social "scientists" and may also push some students toward the more practical kinds of training, which they now avoid.

Universities claim autonomy in determining what subjects they will teach, but senates are reactionary and slow to admit new subjects even of a highly scientific nature. It is thus inevitable that almost all LDC governments are involved in deciding what subjects shall be taught at their expense.

THE UNIVERSITY ON THE FRONTIERS OF KNOWLEDGE

To advance the frontiers of knowledge is rather a recent function of universities; knowledge used to be advanced rather by gentlemen scholars outside the universities. Nowadays, however, all the best universities claim that the advancement of knowledge is their pride and joy, and that they must thus hire only staff with first-class creative minds, use them in teaching only for eight to ten hours a week, and enforce the "publish or perish" rule. However, the number

of scholars with first-class creative minds is small; they get more
job satisfaction (not to speak of better pay) working in the well-
equipped laboratories and libraries of U.S. institutions and frequently
don't much care for teaching undergraduates. So, many of our LDC
universities, clinging to the research ideal and its corollaries, get
the worst of both worlds; they have to pay salaries competitive with
Oxford and Cambridge, and to limit teaching hours, without getting
much creativity for the money.

This is a British trap; the United States is not caught in it. The
United States has 1,500 degree-granting institutions, of which less
than 100 expect to advance the frontiers of knowledge. The rest hire
teachers at lower salaries and work them 20 to 25 hours a week. The
100 or so are supplemented by a great many research institutions,
public and private, which have no students, or have only graduate
students. India is travelling the same way. The money now goes increasingly into wholly postgraduate institutions, like the new Jahawaral
Nehru University, or into research institutes that have no teaching
function.

At the University of the West Indies, I became convinced that
we had started on the wrong track in adopting the English pattern. We
would have done better to have had two separate institutions—one
offering undergraduate degrees, and the other concentrating on graduate and professional studies—with two entirely different staffs, different pay, different teaching loads, and different objectives. The
cost per undergraduate place in our university is much too high in
relation to per capita national income, and would be smaller if we
had started from more appropriate staff/student ratios and from
salary scales more closely akin to those of civil servants.

The current situation in most of our countries is not tenable.
Our governments are beginning to see through the pretense that we
are advancing the frontiers of knowledge (some staff do, of course,
but not enough of them for the money), and the unruly behavior of our
undergraduate students has not increased our popularity with the public. I expect a shift of government emphasis away from university
research toward the establishment of separate research institutes.
I would hope these latter would provide for graduate students, since
I agree that the skepticism of the good student spurs the teacher
toward a clearer understanding of his own thesis.

I am not arguing that universities should not do research, or
that research institutes should not be under the sponsorship of universities. My sole point is that as the number of students increases,
we should restrict the number of research-dominated universities
and increase the proportion of essentially teaching institutions, on
the American rather than the British pattern, which is simply too
expensive for us.

THE UNIVERSITY AS A SERVICE AGENCY

When once a university has started in a new community, its collection of relatively high-powered people can make an enormous contribution outside its walls, and they are normally expected to do so. They create scientific societies, embracing practicing professionals; they serve on public committees; they accept offices of various kinds; and they serve as consultants to the private sector as well as to governments. More formally, the university organizes extramural teaching and perhaps school examinations. It sponsors concerts, lectures, exhibitions, and sporting spectacles, which it opens to the public. Well-endowed private universities in the United States are now expected to spend funds on improving their neighborhoods, even to the point of slum clearance; but universities on the public payroll escape this imposition.

Performance of functions for the whole community, financed from the public treasury, involves some element of political neutrality. It is inappropriate for your one and only heart surgeon to be a prominent member of some political party, since members of other parties may fear that his knife may inadvertently slip when he performs for them. It is equally inappropriate for your one and only professor of economics, whose salary is paid by all, so to conduct himself that he has the confidence of and is consulted by only the Chamber of Commerce, or the trade unions, or the government, or the opposition. Such conduct does not matter in a developed country, where professors are two a penny and available in every hue. But in our countries with one university only, or only one per province, the political professor fails in his duty as a public servant.

Some of our professors have gone to the limit of the obnoxious. We have professors who are leaders of political parties (even the official leader of the opposition in Parliament) and who publish political tracts that are way below normal intellectual standards. Some see their salaries and their eight-hour week merely as a means of financial support for their political activities, doing no research to justify their pay. Some LDC universities are sanctuaries for subversive movements pledged to overthrow society by violence. All of which is defended in the name of academic freedom.

Of course our governments retaliate. If public funds are going to be used to support political activity, they wish to choose the politicians. So the right of the university to choose its own teachers is challenged, and the government seeks a hand. Actually this right, which Anglo-American universities see as fundamental to their autonomy, is by no means universal; it is quite common for those who put up the money, whether it be the state or the church or the private benefactor, to insist on the right to veto teaching appointments. In France, university teachers are appointed by the minister. Universities on the public payroll may be permitted to exercise autonomy of appointment if they keep out of politics; if they become havens for political activity, they must not be surprised if the politicians take over the appointment of their staffs.

This is not a simple matter. I would like to see our professors practice both less party politics and also more participation in political life. In an LDC with only one university per province, professors in publicly financed universities should not identify themselves with political parties, and should even try to make it clear that their advice is available to clients of all religions, languages, or tribes. I recognize that this is a limitation on academic freedom, as traditionally understood in British and American private universities. Academic freedom, however, has two parts. The more important part, which I fully accept, is the right or rather the duty, of the academic to publish the considered results of research, study, or reflection without regard to their effect on existing interests or opinions. On this we cannot compromise without embedding hypocrisy at our core. The lesser part of academic freedom, which I would limit in the aforementioned circumstances, is the right to participate in party politics. This limitation would put professors into the same category as civil servants, which is what they essentially are in these circumstances. Academic freedom in this latter sense is of recent vintage and narrow geographical extent.

At the same time I should like to see professors participating more freely in debates on public issues than they now do in most of the Third World. Good government depends on the existence of a well-informed and articulate public opinion; the teachers in the university, with their free time for study and research, are better placed than almost any other group to raise the level of public discussion by communicating information and criticism, from a non-political-party standpoint. We do not get as much of this discussion in LDCs as we need, because most of our politicians do not want an independent public opinion; their motto is "He who is not with me is against me." Universities should insist on this right (nay, duty) of free comment but will win and hold it only in so far as they scrupulously steer clear of party entanglements.

I should emphasize that my image of the LDC professor as voluntarily nonpartisan, yet active in public affairs, applies only to countries that are trying to maintain a democratic framework, including political opposition. The professor is not needed in party politics when there are plenty of other people for that role. My prescription could not work in a society where opposition is suppressed. In such a society some professors who feel very strongly about government wrongdoing will inevitably become involved in organized antigovernment activity, as will some of their students. The freedom and neutrality of a university can be maintained only in societies with a democratic atmosphere; in oppressive societies the freedom of the university almost always disappears in conflict between its members and the government. The essence of my point is that even in democratic developing societies, the freedom of the government-financed university depends on its trying to maintain political neutrality.

CODA

So far, I have spoken only of the obligations of the university to society, and not about the obligations of society to the university. Let me just sketch three aspects of this side.

First, recognizing as we do the right of the government to infringe on university autonomy in so many ways, we are entitled to demand that what it does be done with due care, after proper consultation and advice. The government will nominate to many committees and institutions affecting the university its council; some form of university grants committee; appointments committees; the scientific research council, and so on. Let its nominees be persons of intellectual substance, accustomed to disciplined thought and behavior. Several confrontations have occurred not between the university and the government, but within the university itself, between the academic senate and the government appointees to the council.

Second, the university is entitled to financial support adequate for agreed-upon programs. The university is not entitled to determine by itself either the program or its cost, but, once the appropriate parties have agreed on these matters, its decisions should be carried out. This has to be because, alas, some of us have to deal with governments that agree and promise, but do not eventually pay up.

Third, we need the support of government and society in our efforts to lead students along disciplined paths. The students of these days are confused as to why they are in the university; where supply exceeds demand, they are terribly frustrated and worried about jobs. They also live in an era where respect for law, authority, and nonviolent persuasion is no longer fashionable. So they do things that horrify their elders—from burning down property to preventing freedom of speech. University authorities cannot cope unless their attempts to enforce discipline are supported by the government and other responsible opinion, including that of the great majority of the student body itself. If they do not have such support, a minority of students can reduce the university to a shambles, as has already happened in many parts of the world.

The university cannot fulfill its obligations to a society that does not, in its turn, fulfill its obligations to the university. But to explore this further would outrun my mandate.

28

UNIVERSITIES AND SOCIAL VALUES IN DEVELOPING AREAS

R. Cranford Pratt

The relationship between the social values of a country and the life and work of its universities is complex. Very often universities merely reflect the dominant values of their society (or, more precisely, the values of the dominant strata of their societies) and play an important role in the overall socialization process within that society. There are also, however, situations in which real tension exists between the dominant values in the society and those that predominate in the universities. For example, those who control the machinery of government may differ ideologically or ethnically from those who are most prominent in the universities, or they may be from different and rival social classes. The university may be part of a modern bourgeois sector of the society that has not established its control over the government. In another situation a university may succeed in standing apart from irrational currents of mass opinion that have seized hold upon a majority of the people. In situations such as these, tensions between the society and its universities are inevitable.

There is further interrelationship. Universities are used as instruments of social planning. This is most obviously true of those faculties that provide training in subjects of high priority to their society. However, the significance of a university in this regard goes far beyond the straightforward training of higher-level manpower. Which students are admitted to the university, what they are taught, how their life is organized, and who teaches them, all of this influences the attitudes and values of a particularly important stratum of society. Governments, therefore, often seek to direct this influence in ways that will support the basic social and political values of this society.

R. Cranford Pratt, a distinguished political economist at the University of Toronto, served as principal of the University College, Dar es Salaam from 1961 to 1965 and as Research Assistant to President Julius Nyerere of Tanzania in 1965.

Universities in many Third World countries have an even more complex relationship with their society. Many of these universities are transplanted institutions, established by a colonial ruler. They are not in origin entirely a product of indigenous effort or aspiration, nor are they, in their initial years at least, an integral part of their societies. Their influence upon the values of their societies has nevertheless been great. This was clearly understood by the colonial powers. The university colleges founded by the British provided an alternative to studying abroad, an experience that often had a far greater radicalizing impact upon the student than studying at a colonial university.* Close copies of British residential colleges, the university colleges were modeled on the university institution that the British understood best. There was also a basic congruence between the value system implicit in these colleges and the values of the colonial power. The colonial university colleges were elitist in every aspect of their life, fitting the objectives of the colonial power. They sought to produce an indigenous elite, culturally and intellectually similar to the colonial administrators and able and willing to work in harmony with them. To that end, the British authorities controlled the colleges in order to limit the intrusion into these colleges of undesirable social values and attitudes. Law faculties, for example, were not begun until just before independence; political science, to the extent that it was taught at all, was "slipped in" as public administration and government, and expatriate appointments were quietly reviewed by British intelligence, with visas being withheld from "undesirables."

The result was the production of an elite separated in many ways from its fellow Africans. The members of this elite were educated to see themselves members of a Platonic elite. They demonstrated the positive aspects of that training and of the inculcation of these values by their capacity after independence to accept substantial and rapid increases in the responsibilities that they carried in the civil service. Nevertheless there were negative aspects as well. Their confidence in and understanding of their indigenous culture was often thoroughly undermined. Their social and cultural interests were divorced from their African roots, and their economic aspirations were out of harmony with the poverty of their country. West Indians and West Africans sometimes use the term "Afro-Saxon" to describe the typical product of these colonial institutions.

With political independence, the African universities had to find ways to become <u>African</u> universities. There were, in fact, two

---

*The validity of this insight was later borne out in Africa when the leadership of the independence movements was in almost every case taken by men who had studied <u>overseas</u> rather than locally.

different ways to accomplish this. One alternative for such a university is to stay within the intellectual tradition it has inherited from Britain, modifying it and adapting it but never totally abandoning it. Where this can be done, as for example at Ibadan, Makerere, and Legon, the university stays an intellectually harmonious institution, still very much reflecting the academic and social values that predominate within the English-language universities of the Commonwealth. This pattern need not mean that the university is out of harmony with its own society. Rather it means that this tradition is itself being "nationalized," being made into a Nigerian or Jamaican tradition just as in the latter half of the nineteenth century it had been transformed into separate Canadian and Australian traditions.

This process is only possible—or at least is much more easily accomplished—when there is a fundamental compatibility between many of the values implicit in this type of university and the values of the dominant social classes in the society concerned. Thus societies that are dominated by well-entrenched modern ruling oligarchies are likely to accommodate readily universities that perpetuate the social elitism of their colonial predecessors. In contrast, in societies that are dominated by traditional oligarchies, these oligarchies, though accepting the elitist features of these universities, will be suspicious of its antitraditional biases. Similarly, the leadership in a society that is seeking to transform itself into a socialist society will be likely to see the elitism of its inherited universities as an important obstacle to the development of socialist values.

Where incompatibilities of this sort become too great, or where history and political choice require that transplanted tradition be abandoned, the university has no alternative but to draw in an eclectic fashion from a wide variety of traditions, particularly from those that share its basic social and political values. The selection of this option is not really made by the university itself. It is rather a consequence of major sociopolitical developments in the society itself. This effort by a university to reshape its character to reflect profound shifts in the dominant social and political values of its society is no easy matter. It is hard to accomplish and hard for outsiders to assist. It is, however, easy for outsiders to misunderstand this effort and to regard it as the intrusion of politics into the life of an institution previously free of such intrusions. Such an interpretation is oversimple—the maintenance of an elitist institution on the old colonial model in a society that is dominated by a modern oligarchy is no less "political" an undertaking than the effort to adapt a colonial-type institution to more egalitarian ways in a society that is seeking to achieve a socialist transformation.

Perhaps the hardest aspect of this whole question for outsiders to understand is the frequent use of the university for what might best be called social engineering purposes. Many universities in the Third World attempt to promote social values and political attitudes that are not yet widely accepted in their societies. They often do this under prompting from their governments. Whatever may be the risks of such efforts, they cannot in toto be dismissed as unacceptable. When the University of Malaya insists upon intermixing Chinese and Malaysian students in its residences, when Addis Ababa University organizes summer projects for its students that send them into the villages, when the students of the University of Dar es Salaam are required to join the National Service, these are important efforts to influence the values of the students and through them, the social values within the society.

There is a final form of social engineering through the universities that occurs when a university seeks to influence the values and attitudes of its students by changes in the curricula. Even this cannot be dismissed as wrong in principle, as some examples quickly demonstrate. The new courses on indigenous languages and culture, on national history, and on rural development problems that were introduced in university after university after independence have as one of their central purposes the generation of an attachment to the society into which the student was born and a concern for its welfare. Similarly, courses on underdevelopment and on imperialism in some countries seek the generation of an awareness of the international dimensions of the continued poverty in much of the Third World. It is extraordinarily difficult to define criteria with which one can assess the value and legitimacy of these efforts to influence student values through changes in their courses of study. However, if the effort is not made, we are likely merely to accept as legitimate those new courses of which we approve and to deplore those we do not like.

The argument must now be further complicated. There will be many situations in which universities must be ready to stand out against the currently dominant values of its society. In some situations, the university expresses, at least in part, a liberal and humanistic tradition that is a challenge to the dominant values of its society. (One thinks for example of the Universities of Witwatersrand and Capetown in South Africa and Makerere University in Uganda.) In other cases, the university represents the modernizing force of rationality in a society still dominated by tradition. In still other societies, an all-pervasive materialism within the ruling elite constantly threatens to erode the commitment to scholarship and teaching at a university, drawing its staff members increasingly into nonacademic money-making "sidelines." In all of these cases the university is, in part at least, an oasis, seeking to maintain the special character of its life in an uncongenial environment.

History sometimes calls the university to a more heroic role, in which the university becomes a beleaguered champion of values and rights that are being suppressed by those in authority. In a society that is ruled unjustly and oppressively, a university must decide how it can best remain an oasis where other values can still be acclaimed, and to what extent it dare aspire to be a center of critical social comment and an active proponent of alternative values. These universities in particular merit active support and imaginative assistance from the international university community.

The position being argued here has what some may regard as a certain moral arrogance. I have suggested that there will be some situations in which universities in the Third World ought to seek actively to assist the processes of social change being promoted by their governments, and there will be others where they should strive to stand aside from these efforts, bearing witness to alternative values and providing a base for informed and critical analysis of these efforts. I am thus saying that value judgments must be made. Let me be more concrete. The obligations of the University of Dar es Salaam, the University of Santiago under Edoardo Frei and Salvador Allende, and the University of Havana to their societies require a degree of cooperation with their political regimes that would be totally inappropriate for, say, Makerere University or for the University of Havana before Fidel Castro came to power. To say this, of course, is to say that universities must make political and ethical decisions. There are other cases where the value judgment to be made is not as easy as it is in the examples I have given. But universities cannot avoid such decisions. Universities are major actors in most developing countries. Their style of life, their courses of study, and their policies unavoidably have important social and political consequences. Their choice is not between being an ethically neutral institution and being an ethically committed institution. The first option, ethical neutrality, is not in fact available to them. Their only choice is between a thoughtless ethical position, usually in the form of a quiet serving of the interests of those in power in the society, and a consciously identified and deliberately chosen ethical position. This essay recommends the latter and has sought to identify some of the complexities involved in the effort to think through the relationship between a university in the Third World and the social and political values of the people it seeks to serve.

29

HIGHER EDUCATION AND DEVELOPMENT: AN
OVERVIEW

Soedjatmoko

Let me state my sympathy and support for the need to relate,
much more effectively, the role of the universities in most developing
countries to the needs and problems of development, especially to the
needs of rural and social development. This new relationship between
the universities and social needs may require fundamental structural
university reform—possibly including a shift from a discipline-oriented
to a problem-oriented structure—and student and staff participation in
development activities and in the planning and evaluation process.
This development role, however, should not close our eyes to other
equally important roles the universities are called upon to play, which
it would be unwise to overlook in any study of institutes of higher
learning.

If the rural and social development orientation could be considered one end of the spectrum of roles these institutes of higher
learning should play, at the other end there is another set of problems
to which universities must be capable of responding.

In the first place every new nation feels compelled, over and
above the general development effort, to develop certain minimum
capabilities in the area of science and technology, industry, and
security, and certain basic commodities that are needed to maximize
its independence and freedom of choice, even in this interdependent
world. The effort to reduce dependency in food, fertilizer, cement,
and energy and to retain adequate control of national resources are
examples of this desire.

Second, an inherent element in the nationalism that brought
many developing nations to independence is their desire to change as
rapidly as possible their subordinate place in the international division

Soedjatmoko is a leading Southeast Asian philosopher and
thinker. Former ambassador to the United States from Indonesia,
he is presently an adviser to the National Planning Agency in Jakarta.
He served as a consultant to the Asian Regional Team.

of labor as mere producers of raw materials and markets for other
people's finished products. This desire means rapid industrialization,
whatever other development goals are to be pursued at the same time.

Third, it has also become clear that no viable new international
economic and monetary system, capable of reducing the built-in inequities of the past, can be worked out without the consent and participation of the developing nations. These nations need to develop
their capabilities to deal with new and complex international questions
on an equal footing with other countries in terms of general principles
and at the technical and operational levels. A whole range of functional
transnational organizations may be required to deal with the many new
problems of a global nature.

The access to the most recent advances in the sciences and in
technology the world over that this capability implies is also of importance in another area. Development of the so-called intermediate
technology needed for a broadly based, employment-oriented development strategy also requires familiarity with sophisticated scientific
advances and high technology. Without such familiarity, no break-
throughs in this area could be expected.

All this, then, will require national capabilities that the universities must be capable of providing. In short, the universities must
not only be capable of responding to internal developmental problems
of poverty and inequality, they must also be capable of responding to
problems of dependency. Granted, the need to respond more effectively to the internal problems of development is very urgent, and a
great deal more should be done in this direction, both conceptually
and operationally; however, a study that concentrated on this aspect
alone would inevitably leave itself open to the accusation, however
unjust, of wanting to downgrade LDC universities and to close their
access to the real sources of wealth and power of industrial countries,
thus keep the developing countries as pastoral societies. The great
problem the developing countries face is how to adjust their universities to these two goals—internal well-being and external independence—that lie in opposite directions, and how to do so within a single
university system.

There are two more points that have to be made briefly. The
teaching roles universities have to play are not limited to their own
students. Increasingly the need is being felt for a continuous effort
to strengthen what might be called "the learning capacity of the nation," the ability of a range of institutions at all levels of society to
absorb and utilize creatively new information and skills. Institutions
that must develop such ability include the government bureaucracy,
the press and communications media in general, the formal and
nonformal educational systems, the business world, and the voluntary
associations of various kinds. They need information about their own

rapidly changing societies as well as about the great changes in the international environment and in the state of science and technology directly affecting their societies and their development efforts. The universities must be able to help them acquire the information and the learning capacity they need.

In addition, it should be realized that as the median age of the population in many developing countries goes down, the social pressures exerted by an increasingly large youth cohort on jobs and careers will make early retirement policies in a number of areas inevitable. Preparing for a two-career life, for government civil servants especially, will require adding university facilities for retraining and reeducating people.

Finally, development is not merely an economic process. The improvement of living conditions as a goal is not enough; it has to make sense in terms of the broader purposes of society if motivations for development are to be maintained. A sense of moral direction, cultural continuity, self-image, and identity as a nation, as well as the capacity to relate economic and social goals to moral purpose, are crucial elements in any sustained development effort.

Almost all developmental decisions have ethical implications that in the long run may be of great importance. The universities in developing countries should relate, more effectively than they have done so far, the study of the humanities to both the "little" and the "great" moral questions regarding social purpose and national goals, in a national, regional, and global context. These questions must include the search for a more humane society in an increasingly technology-dominated environment. The universities must thus strengthen the national capacity for moral reasoning in relation to the development effort.

In addition, the viability of many developing nations on the road of development, as well as their capacity for increased self-reliance, will to a large extent depend on the nation's capacity to provide for a meaningful and culturally satisfactory life at what, for a long period, will inevitably have to be low levels of per capita income. Similarly, the social cohesion of these nations will depend on the gradual transformation of traditional social structures into modern communities, capable of cultural self-entertainment and enjoyment. Developing-nation universities must stimulate and experiment with creative participation in the arts, traditional as well as modern, and use the communications media toward these ends.

30

HIGHER EDUCATION IN CONTEMPORARY CHINA

Howard R. Swearer

Higher education in China is gradually emerging from the holocaust of the Cultural Revolution (1966-69), which closed most universities for several years and interrupted the flow of college graduates for seven years. Recovery began in 1971, when most universities timidly reopened with minimal enrollments of first-year students; but movement has been slow and cautious, with academicians keeping a watchful weather eye on the political barometer as manifested in such politicocultural phenomena as the anti-Confucian/anti-Lin Piao campaign. Higher education was the locus of much of the action of the Cultural Revolution and felt some of its heaviest blows. Universities emerged from this national frenzy fundamentally changed and uncertain in precise policies and activities. By late 1974, some post-Cultural Revolution lines of development were beginning to emerge more clearly; but it will be some time before the lasting permanence of the Cultural Revolution on higher education can be gauged.

Given the high level of politicization of Chinese society and the heavy—to an American's eyes, heavy-handed—use of propaganda to govern the citizenry and shape attitudes, it should be no surprise that universities are extremely sensitive and vulnerable to political currents and cross-currents. In a country where every institution and social process is supposed to further directly the purposes of the revolution and societal development, considerations of institutional

---

Howard Swearer, president of Carleton College, visited the People's Republic of China for three weeks in November 1974, as a member of a delegation of U.S. university presidents under the sponsorship of the National Committee on U.S.-China Relations. The delegation visited six universities, primary and middle schools, research institutes, communes, factories, and other institutions. A version of this report was published by Phi Beta Kappa in the Key Reporter, Winter 1974-75 issue.

autonomy and the "marketplace of ideas" are simply beside the point.
Moreover, the sensitive position of institutions of higher education is
heightened by their limited number, only some 370 in all. The major
task of the social sciences and humanities is to reject and eradicate
those remnants of the Chinese past judged counterproductive for the
new society, such as Confucian ideas of harmony and stability and
the Mandarin tradition of rule by scholar/bureaucrats, while high-
lighting the plight of the masses under the old regime. Students,
teachers, workers, peasants, and members of the People's Liberation Army (PLA) are organized in thousands of study groups to criti-
cize and rewrite historical texts and to spread the new history to the
masses. We observed several of these study groups at the universities, all working on narrow variations of similar themes, refash-
ioning history to support current ideological positions. As one
spokesman at Peking University put it, "Education must serve pro-
letarian politics" and "The past must serve the present."

An intertwining, concurrent theme is the need to prevent not
only the reemergence of the old China through stabilization of the
revolution, but the creation of a society on the Soviet model (as interpreted by the Chinese) embodying new social stratifications, and relying substantially on individual incentives and heavily bureaucratized
structures. These tandem enemies—old China and Soviet revisionism—
explain the curious linking of the criticism of Confucius and Lin-Piao,
for the latter, as has been Liu Shao-ch'i, was condemned for an
alleged attempt to subvert Maoist thought by a revisionist infection
from the Soviet Union.

Three major themes of the Cultural Revolution have been (1) to
prevent the establishment of a new educated elite divorced from the
mass of the population and, ultimately, subversive of Marxism-
Leninism as interpreted by Mao; (2) to link physical and mental labor
and theory and practice; and (3) to harness directly universities to
the strategy of "boot-strap" economic development characterized by
the ubiquitous Maoist trinity: "Frugality, self-reliance, and independence." Stress has been placed on the recruitment of students
from peasant, working class, and PLA backgrounds. At Nanking
University we were told that before the Cultural Revolution less than
30 percent of the students there had been workers, peasants, or
military personnel but that now they comprised 80 percent of the
student body, while only 20 percent came from cadre backgrounds.
While such figures should be treated cautiously, since it may be possible to expunge an undesirable background through labor, still there
is no doubt that great efforts are made to recruit intensively from
the communes and the factories.

Before being considered for admission to higher education, a
student is supposed to have worked for at least two years in a factory

or commune—a stipulation that appears to be universally enforced
and, for now, publicly unquestioned. If a person has had over five
years' working experience he will receive full pay during his university studies rather than the standard student stipend. Students and
faculty are required to engage in productive labor a certain portion
of each year in the countryside, special May 7 cadre schools, factories, or shops run by the university. There is considerable variety
from university to university in the ways in which this work requirement is fulfilled and the amount of time spent; but exemptions are
only for physical disability and even students newly arrived from the
countryside or factories must participate.

The recommendation of a candidate's work unit is an important
consideration in the admissions process. Local party authorities
surely have a strong voice in selecting and recommending candidates,
and there may exist the possibility of manipulation and favoritism;
but soundness of political views, demonstrated positive attitudes
toward physical work, and general approval by one's fellow workers
are given heavy weight.

In pursuance of the "open door" policy, universities—more
typically, departments—are required to establish relationships with
communes, factories, and army units through which teachers and
students assist production units with technical and political work,
and workers and peasants consult on the policies and curriculum of
the university. At several universities the standard briefing provided
figures on the number of such relationships. Universities are providing a variety of short and correspondence courses, both on and
off campus, and teaching and research is supposed to be related as
directly as possible to the practical requirements of agricultural and
industrial production.

The length of time required to complete a university course of
study (degrees have been abolished) has been reduced from five-six
years to three-four years. In addition, time spent on formal academic
studies is further reduced by the physical labor requirement. The
number of courses required of a student has been cut nearly in half.
It was asserted that these reductions were compensated for by the
higher motivation of the new students and by the elimination of irrelevant theoretical material through the combination of theory and practice in courses stressing practical application and problem solving.
Furthermore, students specialize from the outset, and there is little
"general education" beyond the omnipresent study of ideology and
politics. There has been no graduate program since 1966. Without
a longer, in-depth exposure, firm judgments are difficult to make;
but, at least in science and mathematics, the curriculum appeared
closer to vocational-technical training than to a normal baccalaureate
program.

We heard repeatedly about changes wrought in the internal management of the university: that the students are masters of the university; they are "remolding the university with modern thought"; and a major problem is the reorientation of older faculty members. This rhetoric stems from the Cultural Revolution and did not seem to accord with the reality observed. Students do sit on the revolutionary committee, the university governing authority, but, as a rule, are not members of the real management committee, which is the standing committee, educational bureau, or some similar body. No doubt students have more influence than before 1966, but certainly much less than during the Cultural Revolution and probably less than in most American universities. The new students appeared primarily occupied with their immediate tasks at the university. On the other hand, with the memory of Cultural Revolution still fresh, university authorities are awake to student opinion and student criticism, still sometimes expressed through wall posters and student appeals to higher authorities.

The composition and size of university revolutionary committees vary but they normally have from 20 to 30 members representing teachers, students, cadres, workers (from within the university and from associated enterprises), and the PLA who are chosen by "democratic consultation" and most of whom are party members. In the late 1960s, army personnel, in many instances, were put in top positions to restore order from the havoc wrought by the Red Guards. Several of these military men are still in place, but there are signs that army direction is being withdrawn (at one university we were told the PLA propaganda team had been removed) and the party is reasserting control. At several institutions older faculty members, some of whom had been severely criticized only a few years ago, appeared to be exercising considerable influence. However, the governance of universities is fluid and variable and makes impossible easy generalizations about the balance of power among constituencies. Open differences of opinion, as would be expected, were not voiced; but one does detect differing emphases and nuances about current and prospective policies. A number of policy decisions in higher education are hanging fire awaiting signals from above. While some minor experiments are being tried at different universities, local authorities are understandably cautious in taking initiatives.

Much is made of the new teaching techniques and the closer relationships between faculty and students. Translating these new practices from ideological language into terms familiar to American ears, they include field study and observation; more class participation and group discussion and less formal lecturing; "self-study" with faculty coaching; class projects; evaluation of performance by take-home examinations and problem-solving projects. These practices do not sound very revolutionary to American educators, but they are a distinct change from past university procedures in China, and faculty members are still groping, with some false starts, to apply them effectively. Still, as compared to higher education in the United States (a comparison that may have little meaning aside from orienting an American audience), Chinese university students pursue their studies within a highly structured curriculum permitting few options. Student life is also austere and well-organized: lights out at 10:00 p.m., arise at 6:00 a.m., exercises, classes commence at 7:30 a.m., and so forth. Students appear poised, grateful for the opportunity for higher education, and rather unsophisticated.

China, at least for the present, has opted to pursue a policy of very limited access to higher education. There are only 400,000 university students, some 250,000 fewer than in 1966; and all indications suggest a quite gradual and moderate growth in enrollments in the next few years, even though student/faculty ratios run from 2/1 to 3/1, indicating the faculty is available for rapid expansion of student enrollment. When pressed about these enviable ratios, the answer was typical of the world over: There are too few teachers, rather than too many, in view of the need to write new teaching materials and give instruction to workers and peasants in new forms. As would be expected, with the size of the population and the stage of economic development, there is considerable underemployment, and higher education is no exception.

The policy of putting stringent limits on the allocation of scarce resources to higher education makes considerable socioeconomic sense at this stage of national development. First priority is being given to primary and middle schools in which there are now 130 million and 34 million students, respectively. These numbers have rapidly increased in recent years, and there is a shortage of schools and a pressing demand for qualified teachers, especially in the rural areas and at the middle school level.

This allocation of priorities is also in line with the development strategy China is currently following, namely: fairly balanced growth, with considerable attention to agriculture, at a reasonably rapid but not breakneck pace; continued use of labor-intensive methods while gradually introducing mechanization and modern technology, often of a fairly low-level nature; improvement of basic living conditions and medical and social services without frills in a markedly egalitarian manner. Technology is being developed domestically and imported from abroad but judiciously introduced in a way to prevent major dislocations in the economy. Although the policy of linking higher education as directly as possible to economic development and social mobilization raises grave questions about the impact on the quality, standards, and very nature of education, it does fit the concept, held

by the Chinese leadership, of national development. In addition, the
Chinese may avoid the pitfall encountered by some developing countries: an excess of college graduates unemployable or underemployed
at home.

University education is being complemented by a considerable
amount of worker education running the gamut from short courses in
basic vocational skills to elaborate three-year programs in "factory
universities"—such as that pioneered in 1968 by the Shanghai Machine
Tools Plant and since emulated throughout the country with Mao's
blessing—which give instruction in English, basic mathematics, principles of electricity and hydraulics, and so forth. These factory universities, a kind of advanced and enriched vocational-technical school,
have been widely publicized, but it is difficult to know whether their
numbers continue to grow or whether the movement has reached a
plateau.

Several issues in higher education are unresolved and were
treated gingerly by our Chinese hosts. The subject of teachers' ranks
and pay scales is especially tender. Some 80 to 90 percent of teachers
are assistants or lecturers; there have been no promotions since 1966.
Professors and associate professors retain their pre-1966 titles and
salaries, which may be as much as three to five times those of assistants and lecturers. Repeatedly, we were told that the whole issue
of ranks was "under discussion" with apparently some people arguing
for abolition of titles and a leveling of salaries.

Evaluation of individual performance and potential—whether
university applicant, student, or teacher—causes difficulty because
of ideological emphasis on the collective over the individual; the
ability of people to overcome obstacles and advance through proper
political understanding, self-reliance, and will; and the need to give
priority in recruitment of students to workers and peasants (who may
be less well-qualified than those from cadre background). Questions
about how truly understanding talent can be identified by the current
university selection process and the role of testing tended to be
glossed over. One did get the impression, however, that academic
preparation and ability are gradually becoming more significant in
the selection of university students; and, apparently, universities
are beginning to have some say in selection. Queries about student
failure and the dismissal of teachers for poor performance elicited
responses to the effect that such occurrences were almost nonexistent
because of helpful assistance by friends and colleagues. At Nanking
University, it was said that 99 percent of the students successfully
complete their studies. After a while, simply asking the question
made one feel like a social Darwinian.

Chinese higher education is heavily influenced by Mao's early
formative experiences during the Long March and the Yenan period

when he developed his ideas on egalitarianism, self-reliance, and close contact with the masses, on the one hand, and his suspicions of the formally educated elite and narrow professionalism on the other. As Vice Premier Teng Hsiao-p'ing said in an interview with the U.S. delegation, "I never attended a university but have always been in one, the name of which is society."

When one cuts through the ideological phraseology, many of the motivations behind the changes in higher education are both sensible and laudable—for example, skepticism about an overly "credentialed" society; the need for a higher educational system more closely attuned to the needs of the country; and the introduction of more effective teaching methodologies. Some of these ideas have a very familiar ring to an American educator. Moreover, the Western observer must remind himself that the alternatives to the present system may not be those of the more advanced industrial societies but a reassertion of older Chinese traditions.

However, a number of these concepts have been pushed beyond reasonable limits. There is much that is deeply disturbing about the current condition of Chinese higher education, especially the manipulative and blatantly tendentious nature of the social sciences and the humanities and the tiny, almost meaningless, spectrum within which ideas may be debated. Mass propaganda and higher education have been melded together producing students who are misinformed about many subjects.

Mao's vision of higher education may also prove to be anachronistically romantic and inhibiting to the creation of strong universities and institutes productive of the skills, knowledge, and professionalism required for higher levels of national development.

Either by design or consequence, Chinese educational policies are not leading to the advancement of knowledge or sophisticated science or technology in most fields. This may be a rational strategy, given very limited resources and other pressing national tasks, so long as China may borrow on the world intellectual capital. However, scientists must be well-trained to take advantage of these foreign resources; and training and research cannot be separated. It was clearly discernible in several visits that scientific research in many fields has been severely set back, and older scientists are worried about who will man their laboratories and, eventually, replace them. A straw in the wind is the possibility mentioned at one university that graduate programs may be reinstituted in a couple of fields next year. Another is the already mentioned sign that academic preparation and intellectual potential appear to be gaining some weight in consideration for university entrance, along with correct attitudes toward work and politics.

As the middle schools turn out greatly increased numbers, will the severely restricted entry to higher education cause difficulty? Very powerful psychological and economic levers are now being applied to hold down individual aspirations for higher education. The incessant incantations honoring physical labor and service to the masses while condemning individual ambition, plus the leveling of pay between college graduates and other workers, certainly have a strong effect, but for how long can it be effectively maintained?

Mao likes to present himself, above all else, as a teacher, and higher education in China today reflects closely his teachings. How lasting his impact on the universities will be once he no longer dominates the scene is at least open to question.

PROJECT STAFF,
TASK FORCE MEMBERS,
AND CORRESPONDING MEMBERS

NEW YORK STAFF

Director — Kenneth W. Thompson

Assistant Director — Barbara R. Fogel

Editorial and Research
Associate — Helen E. Danner

TASK FORCE MEMBERS

Duncan Ballantine — Director, Education Department, International Bank for Reconstruction and Development

Jacques Grunewald — Conseiller des Affaires Etrangères, Section des Etudes Générales, Ministère des Affaires Etrangères, France

A.R. MacKinnon — Special Adviser, Policy Branch, Canadian International Development Agency

William T. Mashler — Director, Division for Global and Interregional Projects, United Nations Development Programme

D. Najman — Director, Department of Higher Education and the Training of Educational Personnel, Unesco

Names of Regional Team Members appear at the beginning of the African, Asian, and Latin American parts of this volume.

Robert Schmeding	Deputy Director, Office of Education and Human Resources, Bureau for Technical Assistance, U.S. Agency for International Development later replaced by:
James B. Chandler	Director, Office of Education and Human Resources, Bureau for Technical Assistance, U.S. Agency for International Development
Tarlok Singh	Deputy Executive Director, United Nations Children's Fund later replaced by:
Newton Bowles	Deputy Director, Programme Division, United Nations Children's Fund
J E C Thornton	Chief Education Adviser, Ministry of Overseas Development, United Kingdom
Michael P. Todaro	Associate Director, Social Sciences, The Rockefeller Foundation later replaced by:
R. Kirby Davidson	Deputy Director, Social Sciences, The Rockefeller Foundation
F. Champion Ward	Program Advisor in Education, International Division, The Ford Foundation
Alfred C. Wolf	Program Advisor to the President, Inter-American Development Bank
Ruth K. Zagorin	Director, Social Sciences and Human Resources, International Development Research Centre, Canada

CORRESPONDING MEMBERS

Robert L. Clodius	Project Administrator, MUCIA, University of Wisconsin, Madison, Wisconsin, United States
Carl K. Eicher	Department of Agricultural Economics, Michigan State University, East Lansing, Michigan, United States
Robert F. Goheen	President, The Council on Foundations, New York, United States
John Hannah	Executive Director, World Food Council, United Nations, New York, United States
J. George Harrar	Former President, The Rockefeller Foundation, New York, United States
The Rev. Theodore M. Hesburgh	President, The University of Notre Dame, Notre Dame, Indiana, United States
John F. Hilliard	Consultant, USAID, Bethesda, Maryland, United States
Choh-Ming Li	Vice-Chancellor, The Chinese University of Hong Kong, Shatin, New Territories, Hong Kong
Helen M. Muller	New York, United States and Geneva, Switzerland
Harry K. Newburn*	Arizona State University, Tempe, Arizona, United States
Arthur T. Porter	Vice-Chancellor, University of Sierra Leone, Freetown, Sierra Leone

---

*Died August 1974.

R. Cranford Pratt

Professor of Political Science,
University of Toronto, Toronto,
Canada

The Hon. Carlos P. Romulo

Secretary of Foreign Affairs,
Government of the Philippines,
Manila, Philippines

Vernon Ruttan

President, Agricultural Development
Council, Singapore

Sir Philip Sherlock

Secretary General, Association of
Caribbean Universities and Research
Institutes, Kingston, Jamaica

Soedjatmoko

National Development Planning
Agency, Indonesia

Clifton R. Wharton, Jr.

President, Michigan State University, East Lansing, Michigan,
United States

Gilbert F. White

University of Colorado, Boulder,
Colorado, United States

Herman B Wells

Chancellor, Indiana University,
Bloomington, Indiana, United States

ABOUT THE EDITORS

KENNETH W. THOMPSON, Director of the Higher Education for Development project at the International Council for Educational Development, is now Commonwealth Professor of Government and Foreign Affairs at the University of Virginia. Previously he served as vice president of the Rockefeller Foundation. He has written several books about international affairs, including Understanding World Politics, and has published articles in numerous magazines and scholarly journals. Dr. Thompson holds a Ph.D. in political science and international relations from the University of Chicago.

BARBARA R. FOGEL, Assistant Director of the Higher Education for Development project is now Acting Director of the continuing HED program at the International Council for Educational Development. She is the author of What's the Biggest? and has written articles for a number of journals. She has served in an editorial capacity on the staffs of several periodicals, including Public Opinion Quarterly. Ms. Fogel is a graduate of Smith College.

HELEN E. DANNER was Research and Editorial Associate, International Council for Educational Development. She has worked as an editorial associate with Kenneth W. Thompson at the Rockefeller Foundation, and has traveled widely around the world. Ms. Danner holds a master's degree from New York University.

HIGHER EDUCATION AND SOCIAL CHANGE:
Promising Experiments in Developing Countries/
Volume 1: Reports

> Kenneth W. Thompson
> and Barbara R. Fogel

EDUCATION AND DEVELOPMENT RECONSIDERED:
The Bellagio Conference Papers

> Ford Foundation/Rockefeller
> Foundation
> edited by F. Champion Ward

EDUCATIONAL PLANNING AND EXPENDITURE
DECISIONS IN DEVELOPING COUNTRIES: With a
Malaysian Case Study

> Robert W. McMeekin, Jr.

COMPARATIVE HIGHER EDUCATION ABROAD:
Bibliography and Analysis

> edited by Philip G. Altbach

EDUCATIONAL COOPERATION BETWEEN DEVELOPED
AND DEVELOPING COUNTRIES

> H. M. Phillips

EDUCATION FOR RURAL DEVELOPMENT: Case Studies
for Planners

> edited by Manzoor Ahmed
> and Philip H. Coombs

THE ECONOMICS OF NONFORMAL EDUCATION:
Resources, Costs, and Benefits

> Manzoor Ahmed

HIGHER EDUCATION IN DEVELOPING NATIONS:
A Selected Bibliography, 1969-1974

> Philip G. Altbach
> and David H. Kelly